The World War Two Reader

World War Two changed the face of the world forever. Historians' work on the war, its aftermath, and its legacy has advanced over the past few decades to include a variety of new perspectives, and to take account of new aspects of wartime history.

This comprehensive reader provides a unique overview of recent directions in research on World War Two and includes chapters by some of the best-known and most innovative scholars in the field. It gives attention to the fighting of the war throughout the world, and to its political and strategic backdrop. This volume provides coverage of the experiences of women during the war, the home front, and the dropping of the atomic bomb. Issues of gender and ideology are recurrent themes of the collection and the representation and memory of war also feature prominently.

The World War Two Reader includes a comprehensive introduction, chronology, guides to key terms and key figures, and introductions to each chapter which provide context and historiography. It is wide ranging and innovative, and provides essential reading for all students of the history of the modern world.

Contributors: Martin S. Alexander, Benjamin L. Alpers, John Bodnar, D'Ann Campbell, Saki Dockrill, John Dower, Lawrence Freedman, David French, Jose Harris, Pieter Lagrou, Marilyn Lake, Mark H. Leff, Lucy Noakes, Richard Overy, Geoffrey Roberts, Paula Schwartz, Jonathan Steinberg, Jill Stephenson, Edward B. Westermann, and Lisa Yoneyama.

Gordon Martel is Professor and Chair of History at the University of North British Columbia. His books for Routledge include *Origins of the Second World War Reconsidered* (1999), *American Foreign Relations Reconsidered: 1890–1993* (1994), and *Modern Germany Reconsidered, 1870–1945* (1992).

The
World War Two
Reader

Edited by

Gordon Martel

Routledge
Taylor & Francis Group

NEW YORK AND LONDON

First published 2004
by Routledge
29 West 35th Street, New York, NY 10001

Simultaneously published in the UK
by Routledge
11 New Fetter Lane, London EC4P 4EE

Routledge is an imprint of the Taylor & Francis Group

Typeset in Perpetua and Bell Gothic by
Florence Production Ltd, Stoodleigh, Devon

Printed and bound in Great Britain by
TJ International Ltd, Padstow, Cornwall

Library of Congress Cataloging in Publication Data
The World War Two reader/edited by Gordon Martel.
   p. cm.
   Includes bibliographical references and index.
   1. World War, 1939–1945.   2. World War, 1939–1945—Historiography.
   I. Martel, Gordon.
   D743.W674 2004
   940.53—dc22   2003023343

British Library Cataloguing in Publication Data
A catalogue record for this book is available from the British Library

ISBN 0–415–22402–0 (hbk)
ISBN 0–415–22403–9 (pbk)

For my students at the University of Northern British Columbia, particularly the "veterans" of my seminar on the Second World War

Contents

PART FOUR
Memories: Victims, Heroes, and Controversies   **383**

Illustrations

Figures

Tables

Contributors

Martin S. Alexander is Professor of International Relations at the University of Wales, Aberystwyth. He has published widely on the subject of the military history of modern France and is currently engaged in writing a book entitled *The Republic at War: French politics, allied strategy and defeat by Hitler, 1938–40*. Among his many essays and articles on the subject is "No Taste for the Fight? French combat performance in 1940," in Paul Addison and Angus Calder (eds), *Time to Kill: the soldier's experience of war in the west, 1939–45* (Pimlico, 1997).

Benjamin L. Alpers is Associate Professor of Honors at the University of Oklahoma. He is particularly interested in the subject of war, memory, and film in American culture. His publications include *Dictators, Democracy, and American Public Culture* (University of North Carolina Press, 2003). He is currently writing a book on *The United States and the Second World War* in the "Seminar Studies in History" series published by Longman/Pearson.

John Bodnar is Chancellor's Professor and Chair of the Department of History at Indiana University, as well as the Co-Director of the Center for the Study of History and Memory. His current research involves American memory of the Second World War, which follows from his earlier work, including *Remaking America: public memory, commemoration and patriotism in the twentieth century* (Princeton University Press, 1992), and the collection of essays: *Bonds of Affection: Americans define their patriotism* (Princeton, 1996). His most recent book is: *Blue-Collar Hollywood: liberalism, democracy and working people in American film*.

D'Ann Campbell is currently Education and Research Consultant at the Mary Baker Eddy Library in Boston and Professor at Colby-Sawyer College. She has written over thirty articles and essays on the inter-connected subjects of women's history, social and military history. Her interest in women in combat began when she taught at the United States Military Academy at West Point, 1989–91. Her book *Women at War with America: private lives in a patriotic era* was published by Harvard University Press in 1984.

Saki Dockrill is Professor of Contemporary History and International Security in the Department of War Studies at King's College, University of London. She is the general editor of the Macmillan/Palgrave "Cold War History" series, as well as co-editor of *The Cold War History Journal* published by Frank Cass. Among her numerous publications on twentieth-century international history is an article focussing on World War Two, "Hirohito, the Emperor's Army and Pearl Harbor," *Review of International Studies* 18 (1992). Her most recent book is *Britain's Retreat from East of Suez: The choice between Europe and the world* (Palgrave Macmillan, 2002).

John Dower is the Ford International Professor of History at the Massachusetts Institute of Technology in Boston. His books, *War Without Mercy: race and power in the Pacific War* (Pantheon, 1986) and *Embracing Defeat: Japan in the wake of World War II* (W. W. Norton, 1999) have won numerous awards. Especially note-worthy is his usage of visual materials in exploring US–Japanese relations.

Lawrence Freedman is Professor of War Studies and Head of the School of Social Sciences and Public Policy at King's College, University of London. His principal publications are in the field of nuclear strategy and international diplomacy during the Cold War era, with the most recent monograph being *The Revolution in Strategic Affairs* (Oxford University Press, 1998).

David French is Professor of History at University College London. His latest work, of which the article reproduced here is a by-product, is *Raising Churchill's Army: the British army and the war against Germany* (Oxford University Press, 2000). His articles on the British military during World War Two include "Colonel Blimp and the British Army: British divisional commanders in the war against Germany, 1939–1945," *English Historical Review* 111 (1996) and "'Tommy is no soldier': the morale of the second British Army in Normandy, June–August 1944" in Brian Holden Reid (ed.), *Military Power: land warfare in theory and practice* (Frank Cass, 1997).

Jose Harris is Professor of Modern History in the University of Oxford and a fellow of St Catherine's College. She specializes in modern social and intellectual history, which includes an interest in the non-military history of the Second World War. Her numerous works include a biography of William Beveridge and *Private Lives: public spirit 1870–1914*. She is currently working on a study of intellectuals in Britain and elsewhere during the Second World War.

Pieter Lagrou is Professor of History at the Institut d'Histoire du Temps Présent in Paris. He has published widely on the subject of war and memory, most notably in his monograph, *The Legacy of Nazi Occupation. Patriotic Memory and National Recovery in Western Europe, 1945–1965* (Cambridge University Press, 2000). Another essay on the subject is "European Integration and the Legacy of the Second World War: the invention of a European tradition as a means of overcoming the German problem, 1945–1965," in Barrie Axford, Daniela Berghahn, and Nick Hewlett (eds), *Unity and Diversity in the New Europe* (Peter Lang, 2000), 79–95.

Marilyn Lake is Professor of History at La Trobe University in Melbourne. Between 2001 and 2002 she held the Chair in Australian Studies at Harvard University. She has written widely on gender, sexuality and war, publishing "The Desire for a Yank: Sexual Relations Between Australian Women and American Servicemen during World War II" in the *Journal of the History of Sexuality* 2/4 (1992) and co-editing, with Joy Damousi, the collection *Gender and War: Australians at war in the twentieth century* (Cambridge University Press, 1995). Her interest in this subject is located within a broader political context in her *Getting Equal: the history of Australian feminism* (Allen & Unwin, 1999).

Mark H. Leff is Associate Professor of History at the University of Illinois at Urbana-Champaign. His major research interest is in the area of American social policy before and during the Second World War. His first book, *The Limits of Symbolic Reform: the new deal and taxation 1933–1939* was published by Cambridge University Press in 1984.

Lucy Noakes is Senior Lecturer in Media Studies at the University of Portsmouth. Her monograph *War and the British: gender, memory and national identity* was published by I. B. Tauris in 1998. She is currently working on a history of the role and representation of women in the British army.

Richard Overy is Professor of Modern History at King's College, in the University of London. He has written widely on World War Two, particularly from the perspectives of Nazi Germany and Stalinist Russia: *War and Economy in the Third Reich* (Clarendon Press, 1994) and *Russia's War* (Allen Lane, 1998). His latest book, *Interrogations: the Nazi elite in allied hands* was published by Allen Lane in 2001. He is now completing a comparative study of the Hitler and Stalin dictatorships.

Geoffrey Roberts is Statutory Lecturer in Modern History at University College Cork, Ireland. He is a specialist in Stalin, Soviet foreign policy, and World War Two. His books include: *The Soviet Union and the Origins of the Second World War* (Macmillan, 1995), *The Soviet Union in World Politics: coexistence, revolution and Cold War, 1945–1991* (Routledge, 1999), and *Victory at Stalingrad: the battle that changed history* (Longman, 2002).

Paula Schwartz is Associate Professor of French at Middlebury College in Vermont. She has published numerous articles and essays on the subject of gender and resistance in France; those in English include: "The Politics of Food and Gender in Occupied Paris," *Modern and Contemporary France*, 7/1 (1999), and "Redefining Resistance: the activism of women in wartime France," *Behind the Lines: Gender and the Two World Wars*, edited by Margaret Randolph Higonnet *et al.* (Yale University Press, 1987). She is currently engaged in a project on "Gender, Food, and Memory: political protest in occupied France" — an in-depth study of the demonstration of the rue de Buci on May 31, 1942, which took place at a prominent marketplace in central Paris.

Jonathan Steinberg is Walter H. Annenberg Professor of Modern European History at the University of Pennsylvania. He has specialized in the naval, political, and military history of modern Germany, in which field his works include: *Yesterday's Deterrent: Tirpitz and the birth of the German battle fleet* (Macdonald, 1965); *All or Nothing: the axis and the holocaust, 1941–1943* (Routledge, 1990); and, most recently, *Deutsche Bank and its Gold Transactions during the Second World War* (Beck, 1999).

Jill Stephenson is Reader in History at the University of Edinburgh. She has published widely on modern Germany, particularly with reference to women and Nazism. Her books include *Women in Nazi Society* (Croom Helm, 1975), *The Nazi Organization of Women* (Croom Helm, 1981), *Women in Nazi Germany* (Longman, 2001), and *The Third Reich in Colour* (Caxton, 2002). Her next book is entitled *Hitler's Home Front: rural society in Württemberg in the era of the Second World War*.

Edward B. Westermann teaches at the School of Advanced Air and Space Studies, the United States Air Force's graduate school for airpower and spacepower strategists. He has published a number of works on airpower, including *Flak: German anti-aircraft defences, 1914–1945* (University Press of Kansas, 2001). His work on "ideological soldiers" is continued in his essay "Shaping the Police Soldier as an Instrument for Annihilation," in Alan Steinweis and Daniel Rogers (eds), *The Impact of Nazism: new perspectives on the Third Reich and its legacy* (University of Nebraska Press, 2003), and a fuller work, *Himmler's Political Soldiers: the uniformed police and the conduct of racial war, 1933–1945* is to be published by University of Kansas Press.

Lisa Yoneyama is Associate Professor of Literature at the University of California, San Diego. Her research interests focus on the cultural dimensions of transnationalism, colonialism and neo-colonialism and Cold War and post-Cold War US relations with Asia. Her first book was *Hiroshima Traces: Time, space and the dialectics of memory* (University of California, 1999); she co-edited *Perilous Memories: politics of remembering the Asia-Pacific war(s)* (Duke University Press, 2001) and is currently engaged in a project entitled 'Transnationalism and Its Justice' which will examine sites of redress and reparations concerning twentieth-century wars.

Preface

My purpose in making the selections for this book was quite straightforward: to introduce readers to both the complexities involved in making sense of World War Two and the richness of the research that has gone into understanding what it meant to those who participated in it and to those who lived with its legacies. The purpose may have been simple, but making the selections was not. The periodical literature (articles in journals, essays in books) on the war is as vast as the war itself. There are, quite literally, thousands of such writings from which to choose – and certainly hundreds that merit inclusion in an anthology of this kind. As far as quality of writing and research is concerned, I could certainly have put together three volumes without lowering the level of contributions. But selections had to be made, and I made them with several criteria in mind: contributors had to have made what I believe to be a singular contribution to our understanding, either through their mastery of the historiography involved, through an innovative research project, through a new perspective on events, or through a provocative interpretation. I believe that all of the selections in this book fulfill one or more of these criteria.

Of course it was necessary to leave many things out, and there are entire theaters of war, campaigns, events, and experiences that are barely mentioned. Primary among these is what has come to be most widely known as the Holocaust. This is a subject that is itself so vast, with such a rich and controversial literature, that to choose a single essay or article would have been deeply problematic. There are several "Readers" on this subject already, and undoubtedly more are in preparation. Some of the essays herein certainly refer to important aspects of the Holocaust (most notably those by Jonathan Steinberg and Edward Westermann) but these were chosen because they seemed to me to refer particularly to the experience of "war" in terms of the policies adopted by a victorious, occupying power and the men who were responsible for carrying out these policies.

I have tried to remedy the gaps through the sections on "further reading" that follows each of the four parts of the book. Here again selections are difficult – there are bibliographies on the Second World War that are longer than this book – but what I have tried to do in making choices is to direct readers to the most recent literature in English, and to try to indicate where to go for areas and themes that receive only slight treatment in the essays and articles chosen for the Reader. In the "Who's Who" section readers will find suggestions for reading about particular individuals mentioned in the essays.

Because of the selection criteria that I adopted at the outset of this project, I decided against "editing down" any of the contributions. Believing that each of the essays or articles reproduced here makes an important argument, it seemed to me that it would be doing a disservice to the authors to pare down the evidence that they have used to make their case. Thus, the contributions appear exactly as they did originally (with a few minor corrections of typographical errors, etc.) – with the result that the style, spelling, and reference system varies from essay to essay.

Finally, I wish to thank my students at UNBC whose opinions of the readings that I assigned them on this subject played a vital role in my decisions on what should be included here, and Victoria Peters of Taylor & Francis for her infinite patience in waiting for a long-overdue manuscript.

Acknowledgments

The authors and publishers wish to thank the following for their permission to reproduce copyright material:

M. S. Alexander, "The Fall of France, 1940," in *Journal of Strategic Studies* 13, 1990. Reproduced by permission of Frank Cass Publishers.

R. Overy, "Mobilization for Total War in Germany, 1939–41," in *English Historical Review* 103, 1988. Reproduced by permission of Oxford University Press and Richard Overy.

L. Freedman and S. Dockrill, "Hiroshima: A Strategy of Shock," in S. Dockrill (ed.) *From Pearl Harbor to Hiroshima: The Second World War in Asia and the Pacific, 1941–1945*, Macmillan, 1994. Reproduced by permission of Palgrave Macmillan Publishers.

G. Roberts, "Ideology, Calculation, and Improvisation: Spheres of influence and Soviet foreign policy, 1939–1945," in *Review of International Studies* 25/4, 1999, Cambridge University Press © British International Studies Association.

J. Steinberg, "The Third Reich Reflected: German Civil Administration in the Occupied Soviet Union 1941–4," in *English Historical Review* 110, 1995. Reproduced by permission of Oxford University Press and Jonathan Steinberg.

B. L. Alpers, "This is the Army: imagining a democratic military in World War II," in *Journal of American History*, 1998. Reproduced by permission of the Organization of American Historians.

D. French, "'You Cannot Hate the Bastard Who is Trying to Kill You . . .': combat and ideology in the British Army in the war against Germany, 1939–45," in *Twentieth Century British History* 11/1, 2000. Reproduced by permission of Oxford University Press and David French.

E. B. Westermann, "'Ordinary Men' or 'Ideological Soldiers'? Police Battalion 310 in Russia, 1942," originally published in *German Studies Review* XXI/1, 1998. Reproduced by permission of German Studies Review.

J. Dower, "Race, Language, and War in Two Cultures: World War II in Asia," in J. Dower, *Japan in War and Peace: selected essays* © 1995. Reprinted by permission of The New Press.

D. Campbell, "Women in Combat: The World War II experience in the United States, Great Britain, Germany, and the Soviet Union," in *Journal of Military History* 57, 1993. Reproduced by permission of *The Journal of Military History*.

J. Stephenson, "Nazism, Modern War and Rural Society in Württemburg, 1939–45," in *Journal of Contemporary History* 32/3, 1997. Reprinted by permission of Sage Publications Ltd.

P. Schwartz, "*Partisanes* and Gender Politics in Vichy France," in *French Historical Studies* 16, 1989. © 1989, Social Science History Association. All rights reserved. Used by permission of the publisher.

J. Harris, "War and Social History: Britain and the home front during the Second World War," in *Contemporary European History* 1, 1992 © Cambridge University Press.

M. H. Leff, "The Politics of Sacrifice on the American Home Front in World War II," in *Journal of American History* 77, 1991. Reproduced by permission of the Organization of American Historians.

M. Lake, "Female Desires: the Meaning of World War II," in *Australian Historical Studies* 24, 1990. Used by permission of Marilyn Lake.

P. Lagrou, "Victims of Genocide and National Memory: Belgium, France and the Netherlands 1945–1965," in *Past & Present*, 154, 1997. Reproduced by permission of Oxford University Press and Pieter Lagrou.

L. Noakes, "Making Histories: experiencing the blitz in London's Museums in the 1990s," in *War and Memory in the Twentieth Century*, Berg Publishers, 1997. Reprinted with permission.

J. Bodnar, "*Saving Private Ryan* and Postwar Memory in America", in *American Historical Review* 106/3, 2001. Reproduced by permission of the American Historical Association and John Bodnar.

L. Yoneyama, "For Transformative Knowledge and Postnationalist Public Spheres: the Smithsonian *Enola Gay* controversy," in *Perilous Memories: The Asia-Pacific wars*, Duke University Press, 2001. Copyright © Duke University Press. All rights reserved. Reprinted with permission.

Every effort has been made to obtain permission to reproduce copyright material. If any proper acknowledgement has not been made, we would invite copyright holders to inform us of the oversight.

Abbreviations

AA	Anti-Aircraft
ABCA	Army Bureau Current Affairs (UK)
AFAT	*Auxiliaire féminin de l'armée de terre* [Women's Auxiliary of the Army] (France)
ATS	Women's Auxiliary Territorial Service (UK)
CIO	Congress of Industrial Organizations (US)
CNPPA	*Confédération Nationale des Prisonniers Politiques et leurs Ayant-Droits* [National Confederation of Political Prisoners Having the Rights of Belgium]
ExPoGe	*Nederlandse Vereniging van Ex-Politieke Gevangenen uit de bezettingstijd* [Netherlands Association of ex-political prisoners of the period of occupation]
FFI	*Forces Françaises de l'intérieur* [French Forces of the Interior]
FNDIR	*Fédération Nationale des Déportés et Internés de la Résistance* [National Federation of Deportees and Internees of the Resistance] (France)
FNDIRP	*Fédération Nationale des Déportés et Internés Résistants et Patriotes* [National Federation of Deportees, Internees, Resisters and Patriots] (France)
FTP	*Francs-tireurs et partisans* [Guerrillas ("independent gunmen") and partisans] (France)
IWM	Imperial War Museum (UK)
MIA	Missing-in-action
MOI	*Main d'oeuvre immigrée* [Immigrant laborers] (France)
NASM	(Smithsonian) National Air and Space Museum (US)

NSDAP	*Nationalsocialistiche Deutsche Arbeiterpartei* [National Socialist German Workers' Party] (Germany)
OKH	*Oberkommando des Heeres* [High Command of the Army] (Germany)
OKW	*Oberkommando der Wehrmacht* [High Command of the Armed Forces] (Germany)
Omi	*Ostministerium* – shorthand for "Reichministerium für die Besetzten Ostgebiete" [Reich Ministry for the Occupied Eastern Territories] (Germany)
OWI	Office of War Information (US)
PCI	*Partito Comunista Italiano* [Communist Party of Italy]
PCF	*Parti Communiste Français* [Communist Party of France]
RM	*ReichMarks* (Germany)
SA	*Sturmabteilung* [Storm troopers or "Assault division"] (Germany)
SD	*Sicherheitsdienst* [Security Service] (Germany)
SHAEF	Supreme Headquarters Allied Expeditionary Force
SPD	*Socialdemokratische Partei Deutschlands* [Social Democratic Party of Germany]
SS	*Schutz-Staffel* [Protection-squad, commonly: "blackshirts"] (Germany)
STO	*Service du travail obligatoire* [Forced Labour Service] (France)
UAW	United Associations of Women (Australia)
UNADIF	*Union Nationale des Associations de Déportés et Internés et Familles des Disparus* [National Union of Associations of Deportees, Internees and Families of the Missing] (France)
WAAC	Women's Auxiliary Army Corps
WAVES	Women Accepted for Volunteer Emergency Service [Women's Naval Reserve] (US)
WEB	Women's Employment Board (Australia)
WVS	Women's Voluntary Service for Civil Defence (UK)

In notes

ibid.	abbreviation of *ibidem* ("in the same place") – used to repeat the preceding reference; if page references are different, these are added
idem	("the same") – the same author, title as mentioned previously, used in order to avoid repetition
loc. cit.	abbreviation of *loco citato* ("in the place cited") – used to indicate the reference is identical to the preceding one, including the page number
op. cit.	abbreviation of *opus citatum* ("the work quoted") – used to refer to a work which has been cited previously in full form
passim	"scatterdly" – used to indicate occurrence throughout a book, rather than citing specific page numbers

Chronology

1939

August 23:	German–Soviet non-aggression treaty ("Nazi–Soviet Pact") divides Poland into spheres of influence; places Finland, Estonia, and Latvia in Soviet sphere
September 1:	Germany invades Poland
September 3:	France, Britain, Australia, and New Zealand declare war on Germany
September 4:	War Economy Decree was published in Germany, enjoining "every citizen to impose upon himself the necessary restrictions in living standards"
September 10:	Canada declares war on Germany
September 17:	Soviet Union invades Poland
September 27:	Warsaw surrenders to German forces
September 28:	German–Soviet Boundary and Friendship Treaty adjusts Polish boundaries and adds Lithuania to Soviet sphere of influence
November 30:	Soviet Union attacks Finland

1940

March 12:	Soviet Union and Finland sign peace treaty
April 9:	Germany invades Denmark and Norway
May 10:	Germany invades France, Netherlands, Belgium, and Luxembourg
May 15:	German troops cross the Meuse river in the attack on France

May 20:	Netherlands defeated by Germany
May 26–3 June:	Evacuation of Allied forces at Dunkirk
May 28:	Belgium defeated by Germany
June 10:	Italy declares war on Britain and France
June 12:	German troops enter Paris
June 16:	France signs armistice with Germany
June 29:	Japanese declare objective of "Greater East Asia Co-Prosperity Sphere"
July 10:	"Vichy" France established; "Battle of Britain" begins
August 31:	The "Vienna Award" – Italian–German arbitration of territorial disputes between Rumania, Hungary, and Bulgaria
September 13:	Italy invades Egypt
September 27:	"Axis" pact signed by Germany, Italy, and Japan
October 28:	Italy invades Greece
December 18:	Hitler signs directive authorizing 'Operation Barbarossa'

1941

January 6:	Roosevelt makes "Four Freedoms" speech to Houses of Congress
March 11:	Roosevelt signs Lend-Lease Act
April 6:	Germany invades Greece and Yugoslavia
April 17:	Yugoslavia surrenders to Germany
April 27:	Greece surrenders to Germany
June 6:	"Commissar Order" directs German police and army to execute without trial any political commissars of the Soviet Communist party found in uniform among Soviet prisoners of war
June 22:	Germany invades Soviet Union
August 14:	Roosevelt and Churchill announce "Atlantic Charter"
December 7:	Japanese attack Pearl Harbor
December 8:	United States and Britain declare war on Japan
December 18:	National Service Act passed in Britain (allows for drafting of women)

1942

January 20:	Wannsee Conference held in Berlin suburb to determine strategy of the "Final Solution"
February 15:	Singapore naval base captured by Japanese forces
April 9:	Filipino and American forces surrender to Japanese at Bataan (Philippines). Those captured were forced to walk 55 miles through rugged terrain on the "Death March" in which thousands of prisoners, deprived of food and water, died
April:	Japanese-Americans sent to "relocation centres"
July 3:	Germans capture Sevastopol, in Crimea
July:	General Service Corps formed in UK

August 12:   Stalin and Churchill meet in Moscow
August 18:   Hitler orders the extermination ("Ausrottung") of all partisan
                  forces on the eastern front
September 13:   Battle of Stalingrad begins
October 23:   Germans defeated by British forces in Egypt at Battle of El
                  Alamein

1943

January 4–14:   Churchill and Roosevelt meet in Casablanca
February 2:   Germans surrender at Stalingrad
May 13:   Germans and Italians surrender to Allied forces in North Africa
June 23:   Legislation creating the Women's Army Corps passed by US
                  Congress
July 9/10:   Allied forces invade Sicily
July 25/26:   Fascist government in Italy falls; Mussolini arrested
September 8:   Italy surrenders to Allies
October 13:   Italy declares war on Germany
October: Conference of Foreign Ministers held in Moscow to prepare for
                  "Big Three" meeting in Teheran
November 28:   Stalin, Churchill, and Roosevelt meet at Teheran

1944

March: The "Salerno Turn" of the Italian Communist Party – in which
                  they agreed to participate in the post-fascist Badoglio
                  government, to refrain from calling for the abolition of the
                  Italian monarchy, and to work for anti-fascist national unity
May 9:   Soviet forces recapture Sevastopol
June 6:   D-Day invasion launched by Allied forces in Normandy, France
June 13:   Germany launches first V-1 rocket attack on Britain
August 25:   Paris liberated by Allied forces
October 9:   Churchill and Stalin arrange so-called "percentages agreement"
                  on future spheres of influence in eastern Europe
December 4:   Civil war begins in Greece

1945

January 17:   Soviet forces liberate Warsaw
February 4–11:   Stalin, Churchill, and Roosevelt meet for last time at Yalta
March: Air bombardment of Tokyo kills 80,000 and destroys 300,000
                  buildings
April: Soviet Union announces that it will not renew neutrality pact
                  with Japan

April 21:   Soviet forces reach Berlin
April 30:   Hitler commits suicide
May 2:   German forces in Italy surrender
May 7:   Germany surrenders "unconditionally"
June 26:   United Nations charter signed in San Francisco
July 16:   Atomic bomb tested in New Mexico
July/August: Allied leaders meet at Potsdam (an unbombed suburb of Berlin)
August 6:   Atomic bomb dropped on Hiroshima
August 9:   Atomic bomb dropped on Nagasaki
August 14:   Attempted *coup d'état* by younger Japanese officers opposed to
                surrender fails
August 15:   Japan accepts terms of Potsdam declaration and surrenders
                "unconditionally"

PART ONE

Strategy

Failures, Shocks, and Mythologies

WAR SURPRISES. Strategists, who have devoted themselves beforehand to the task of preparing for the war they believe most likely to occur discover that their expectations were faulty – that the war is longer or shorter, slower or faster, than the one for which they were prepared. Politicians, who tend to leave the strategizing to the strategists during times of peace, discover that they cannot afford this luxury once war breaks out, that the way they choose to fight (or not) will determine more than success on the field of battle, that it may determine the fate of the regime and the shape of the future. An uneasy peacetime relationship between soldiers and statesmen becomes tense and combative during war: soldiers are told not to meddle in politics; politicians are told to leave the fighting to the experts. Neither can afford to do as they are told: the strategist who neglects the political dimension will find that he lacks the support to sustain the strategy; the politician who ignores the strategic dimension will find that he is committed to a political direction which it is impossible to reverse. One of the first results of war is to transform soldiers into politicians, politicians into soldiers. Thus did Winston Churchill design his own quasi-military uniform; thus did Joseph Stalin declare himself "generalissimo"; thus did Generals Eisenhower and De Gaulle find themselves at the head of state after the war.

The essays chosen for this section demonstrate some of the surprises that lay in wait for those engaged in grand strategy or politics at the highest level. The first surprise of the war was not the defeat of Poland by Germany within a month of launching the invasion of September 1, 1939, but the "phoney war" which followed that victory – when, for more than half a year, not much happened and people everywhere wondered why. Would this war be limited to a month-long campaign in eastern

Europe? Was a negotiated peace possible? Britain (including most of the empire) and France had immediately declared war on Germany following the invasion of Poland, but there was so little fighting between the Great Powers in the months that followed that it could hardly be described as "war." Most adults could remember that World War One – which was supposed to end before the first Christmas – had immediately turned into a titanic struggle between the largest armies that Europe had ever seen. So the absence of action in the months that followed October 1939 was surprising. But when in June 1940 France collapsed in about the same time that it had taken in Poland, it was shocking. No trenches this time, no gas, no war of attrition, no heroic "miracle of the Marne," just a humiliating French submission and a hasty evacuation of Allied forces at Dunkirk.

But shocks create "history." One of the first questions asked of World War Two was "why did France fall?" Blame was variously attributed, and mud was thrown everywhere: on the generals, on the politicians; or on the socialists or the conservatives. The shocking failure of France to defend itself from a German invasion for which it had been preparing more than a decade (or even since the Treaty of Versailles) created history in the sense that the "historical record" was exhumed and examined in order to account for this failure. Martin Alexander surveys this literature from the 1950s to the 1980s and shows how both the questions and the answers have changed over time. Gone today are the legends that the failures may be attributed to individual generals or politicians, gone are the myths that the French were unprepared, that the Allies were outmanned and outgunned by superior German forces. In their place is a more sophisticated and complicated set of explanations that attribute the failures to the political culture of the interwar years, to the lingering emotional consequences of World War One and to the absence of a coherent Anglo-French strategy supported by the politicians in both countries.

It may be argued that if there is any such thing as "progress" in historical understanding, it consists of complicating the early, simplistic answers offered by those who have participated in the events themselves. Blame for the failures of strategy and diplomacy is easily attributed to the stupidity or weakness of individual soldiers or statesmen – and this "interpretation" of events is fuelled by the sticks that the participants hurl at one another in the memoirs, or *souvenirs*, or *Errinerungen* that pour from the presses after the event. Apart from their understandable desire to exculpate themselves, such writers are addicted to two contrary ideas that account for failures: other individuals – either incompetent or wicked – opposed sensible policies that would have averted disaster; or, alternatively, great historical "forces" were at work which were too powerful for mere mortals to withstand – and thus the "tide of history" swept them along the path to destruction. After World War One in Germany there emerged the alluring explanation that the war had not really been "lost" – and certainly not by the heroic soldiers or the brilliant officers that commanded them – but that the army had been stabbed in the back ("*dolchstöss*") by socialists and Jews at home. And thus there grew the sense that a new regime firmly grounded in nationalist ideals and military values could avert a second tragedy. Ironically, after the second tragedy, there emerged a convoluted interpretation of the German failures: these – western, liberal observers argued

– could be found within the ideology itself. Nazism, committed as it was to a backward, atavistic view of life, could not, ultimately, compete with modern, open societies. The machinery of the police state, its denigration of all who might oppose it, its refusal to mobilize fully its resources, was the fatal flaw in the system.

Richard Overy summarizes the argument that the Nazi regime failed to commit itself to "total war" until it was too late, until after the tide had turned against it in the Soviet Union in 1943. He argues, convincingly, that this was not the case, and that the legend of this failure is attributable largely to the unsophisticated use of statistics. In fact, he argues, the experience of World War One convinced the Germans that the next war would be another long one of attrition, and thus that "armament in depth" must be an essential part of her preparations for it. And the Nazis began in earnest in 1939 to prepare for total war: creating the machinery, organizing the factory capacity, stockpiling the raw materials, and mobilizing the labor necessary to produce the military equipment that would be required when war came c.1943. Most of the shortcomings of German production are attributable to the fact that the war broke out sooner than expected. Two areas in particular have usually been cited as indicating the Nazi aversion to total war: the absence of rigorous rationing and cutbacks on consumer goods and spending until late in the war, and the failure to mobilize women – largely because of their ideological commitment to keeping women locked into their historical roles as housewives and mothers. Overy shows that both these interpretations are grounded in misleading statistics. Observers have focussed attention on the rates involved during the war itself. But, if Germany was already close to total mobilization by 1941, it was practically impossible for her to increase rates according to the same pace as Britain and the United States, which had not mobilized on anything like the same scale until after they were at war. Thus, it is a statistical illusion that Nazi Germany failed to mobilize its women to the same degree as the Allies: simply put, there was much greater employment of women in Germany before the war, and thus the rate of increase was lower; throughout the war, there was a significantly higher proportion of German women employed in the workforce than there was in Britain. Overy acknowledges that there were increases in German productivity in the latter years of the war, but these are attributable to better, more streamlined organization which ended unnecessary duplication and improved coordination.

The war ended not in Europe, but in Asia, and it ended with a shock of a different kind. Here a new "weapon of mass destruction" was utilized for the first (and, thus far, the only) time in history – and pictures of the mushroom cloud over Hiroshima or Nagasaki are now firmly fixed in the memory of all who lived after these events – even if they had not been alive at the time to experience the horrors themselves. Here, the shock that human beings could resort to the use of such a devastating device as the atomic bomb, has engendered a fierce debate: was it really necessary to resort to it in order to end the war? Why did they not demonstrate the power at their disposal by dropping it on a deserted, or relatively uninhabited spot? (Or, at the very least, why did they not warn the Japanese beforehand?) Was it really utilized in order to end the war with the minimum loss of Allied lives or was it the first shot in a Cold War between the West and the USSR? Lawrence Freedman and Saki Dockrill survey the arguments that ensued and offer their own conclusions, that there was great uncertainty concerning the destructiveness of the bomb – and thus there was little hesitation in utilizing it; that the strategy was to shock the Japanese people – and thus the choice of cities as targets; that the bombs were decisive in bringing about an early armistice on Allied terms; and, finally, that the USSR was a factor that loomed more largely in the minds of the Japanese than Allied leadership – that some had hoped that the Soviets would act as a moderating factor in the terms of peace, but that the use of the bomb dispelled this hope.

It might be argued that the outcome of the war was also shocking to those who had participated in it. The experience of Paris in 1919 was not to be repeated: in spite of the fact that the Second was much more legitimately called a World War than the First, this time there was no grand gathering of all participants coming together to create a new world order. Instead, almost before people noticed what had happened, the world was divided into two camps and, in the eyes of the west, the Soviets had cunningly installed "puppet regimes" throughout eastern Europe. Perhaps the war had not been as it appeared, perhaps it was not so much a struggle against Hitlerism and Nazism as it was an ideological confrontation between socialism and capitalism. Thus, the question of what Stalin and the Soviets were after became one of the most hotly-debated issues in the postwar era. Many suggested that the Nazi–Soviet pact, the Soviet invasion of Poland and Finland had shown the regime's true colors, that it was inherently expansionist and authoritarian; others argued that the west had attempted to use the Nazis to destroy the Soviet regime, happily permitting the peoples of the USSR to bear the brunt of the fighting. Geoffrey Roberts, using many sources that became available either during the *glasnost* period in the USSR or following its demise in 1989, argues that there was no preconceived initiative on the part of Soviet leaders to expand territorially or to define the west as their enemy in the postwar world. Analyzing the evolution of Soviet strategy over the course of the war leads him to conclude that they sought to establish "spheres of influence" in those territories that they perceived to render them strategically vulnerable: in Poland and Turkey, that they were entirely prepared to recognize the validity of similar western spheres elsewhere in Europe, and that they did not assume that the creation of such spheres would rupture the wartime grand alliance or that it was incompatible with Roosevelt's vision of a new international organization dominated by four "policemen."

In the case of the Soviet Union, Roberts argues persuasively that the practical requirement of defending territory against future invaders vastly outweighed any ideological factors. Different policies were adopted at different times in different areas because the regime was pragmatic, seeking to preserve itself and the political system it had created within its own frontiers. But in the case of Nazi activities within the Soviet Union during the war, Jonathan Steinberg offers a very different perspective. After the initial victories of the first year of war against the Soviets, the German authorities were divided on how to proceed – between the "exploiters" who wished to utilize the resources suddenly available to them, and the "colonizers" who wished to make the space available for the *lebensraum* of the German *Volk*. The contrast between these two views was stark and mutually exclusive: the resources of the newly-captured territories could not be utilized without the assistance of the inhabitants; the territories could not be made available to racially-pure stock unless cleared of the inhabitants. Steinberg shows how the murderous, ideologically-driven exterminationist policies of the SS triumphed over what might otherwise have been regarded as the "real" interests of the Nazi regime in working with native elites in order to better exploit the opportunities that lay before them. But *Untermenschen* were deemed unsuitable as partners, and thus millions of people who may have been disenchanted with the Soviet regime and prepared to cooperate with their "liberators" were turned into enemies when the Nazis proved unwilling to do anything other than enslave or murder them. In this case, as Steinberg says, the very essence of the regime, "the heart of Nazi darkness" was revealed: they took their racist ideology so seriously that they acted upon it even when it was contrary to the practical needs of Germany fighting a war on several fronts.

Chapter 1

Martin S. Alexander

THE FALL OF FRANCE, 1940

THE FALL OF FRANCE – a shorthand for the political and military crisis for the Allies of May–June 1940 – was the first real upset of the Second World War. It was the first occasion on which the 'form book' of the conflict was over-turned. It set the world reeling. Contemporaries struggled to conceive that the collapse was possible, even as it gathered pace around them. They were reluctant to believe the unbelievable, loath to mention the unmentionable – to utter the words 'evacuation', 'defeat', 'armistice', 'surrender'. As the first rumours of the German breakthrough on the Meuse reached Paris on 15 May 1940, the veteran corres-pondent of the *Manchester Guardian*, Alexander Werth, articulated the general perplexity when he mused: 'what if the French Army turns out to be like the Polish cavalry and the Dutch flooding, and the Albert Canal – just another legend? [But] I can't quite believe it'.[1] The reality became all too horribly apparent just a month later, on 12 June, when the Champs Elysées itself echoed to the tramp of the first of the invader's jackbooted columns.

1940 witnessed the undoing of an entire alliance of the western democracies of Europe, not simply the fall of France. The Netherlands was knocked out of the battle within five days; Belgium followed after a further 13 days, on 28 May. The British were driven from the continent. But it was France's downfall that stunned the watching world. The shock was all the greater because the trauma was not limited to a catastrophic and deeply embarrassing defeat of her military forces – it also involved the unleashing of a conservative political revolution that, on 10 July 1940, interred the Third Republic and replaced it with the authoritarian, collabo-rationist *Etat Français* of Vichy.

All this was so deeply disorienting because France had been regarded as a great power, certainly a mainstay of the alliance which had resolved to see that the attack on Poland in September 1939 would be the last of Hitler's easy conquests. When the débâcle overtook the western nations in their turn in May 1940, observers could, perhaps, take Belgian and Dutch defeat in their stride. These were lesser powers by any yardstick. The collapse of France, however, was a different case (a 'strange defeat' as it was dubbed in the haunting phrase of the Sorbonne's great medieval historian and Resistance martyr, Marc Bloch).[2] Perhaps some who had monitored her appeasement of Germany in the 1930s may have had nagging doubts about her long-term prospects as a truly front-rank power. But few, even in Germany, had questioned that she remained a first-line military nation and would prove to be a redoubtable and resilient obstacle to Hitler's ambitions. Had not France spent over seven billion francs constructing the Maginot Line to shield the strategic industries of Lorraine between 1930 and 1937? Had not France committed twice that sum in September 1936 for a four-year programme to rearm her land forces? Was it not France that deployed 115 divisions – 91 of them in the North-Eastern theatre facing Germany – on 10 May 1940? Evidently for military might on these dimensions to be simply swept away by the Wehrmacht was bemusing, bewildering, befuddling. Contemporaries, along with those who came later, wanted to know how it could possibly have happened. And so began the inquests, the inquiries, the investigations, from the 1940s to the present time.[3] This essay will seek to identify what has been learned; more specifically, it will seek to give focus to the light that has been shed by modern scholarship on that twilight war and blitzkrieg as the events themselves now slip murkily into the twilight of modern memory.

In 1974, in the *Journal of Modern History*, the Canadian historian John Cairns critically reviewed the literature on the fall of France and concluded that 'the phantom of that defeat eludes us yet. The only certainty is that the problem will continue to have some interest and that a mass of studies of various aspects of the affair will one day come into being'.[4] The succeeding decade-and-a-half more than bore out the prediction. During the 1970s and 1980s books and articles on France's approach to war have continued to make a steady appearance. Nor has the flow of memoirs and the publication of diaries abated (even if it is no longer the torrent of the 1950s).[5] Here, then, all that can be attempted is a mapping of the principal contours of the writings since the mid-1970s, to draw attention to those features on the historiographical landscape that have become most salient in the last 15 years.

Cairns voiced a good deal of disappointment with what had been done down to 1974. He was discouraged not just by the analyses of the fall of France under-taken by French authors but also by the inadequacies of the treatments offered by the British and Americans. In the case of the former, he complained that few pro-fessional historians in France had 'seriously taken up the overall challenge of the episode'. There was much justification in the charge: French academics had, Cairns continued, 'to an unusual degree surrendered contemporary history to journalists and politicians'. He opined that the relative neglect by French scholars of the 1940 problem had to be explained, in part, by the uneasy consciences still liable to be stirred in the early 1970s by any evocation of the defeat and the ambiguities of collaboration and resistance that followed. In part, however, Cairns felt that the comparative inattention to the fall of France down to the early 1970s resulted from the politics of French academe itself and above all from the ascendancy in the 1950s and 1960s of the social history of the *Annales* school over university historians and their research agendas.[6]

Cairns was also critical of the Anglo-Americans who, during the 1960s, addressed the problem of the collapse of France. The books of John Williams, Alistair Horne, William Shirer and Guy Chapman (all published in 1968–69) were extensively reviewed.[7] All were judged wanting on three general counts. These were, 'failure to read the evidence at hand; (2) failure to sort out seriously the political, social, economic and military parts of the problem and to relate them to each other; and (3) failure to think outside the stereotypes and even caricatures of the time itself'. Quite properly, these criticisms were tempered by mention of the fact that none of these writers had access to the unpublished British official documents (Britain's 50-year rule on government archives being liberalised to a 30-year rule only in 1968), or to the corresponding French records (for which a 50-year closure on papers down to the end of the Second World War was lifted in theory by legislation passed in 1969, but implemented in fact only after May 1975).[8]

Despite the many shortcomings that he identified in the historiography that he surveyed, Cairns nevertheless expressed guarded optimism about the future of serious study of the fall of France. The 'inaccessibility of materials', he shrewdly suggested, was probably 'less of a problem than the burden of the past itself'. He voiced a cautious confidence that both these obstacles would be flattened down by the further passage of time.[9]

So, indeed, have things transpired. At a distance of 50 years it does seem possible to say that even for the French, the events of 1939–40 (and, perhaps, the more conscience-troubling experiences of Vichy and the Resistance) have at last become history, rather than burning issues of present political concern. Time has brought dispassionate appraisals on even the controversies which were once most bitter. One example would be the insistence of a director of the French air force historical service for putting it on the published record in 1983 that the British had been completely correct to husband their remaining fighter aircraft in the UK by mid-June 1940 and justified in rejecting entreaties to expend even more Hurricanes and Spitfires than had already been lost in the forlorn fight on the continent.[10]

It has been refreshing, then, to note how the debates that formerly were most impassioned have lost their emotional edge. Equally encouraging has been the correctness of Cairns's prediction that the French sources would become available. The 'signs of greater flexibility regarding access', that were noticeable by 1973 turned out to be the first breaths of a liberal wind that blew through the hitherto stuffy corridors of the record repositories.[11] This new openness was more than welcome. It heralded a conversion to an altogether more relaxed and hospitable attitude towards contemporary diplomatic, political and military historians on the part of the archival custodians and *conservateurs*. In the bracing new climate, French and foreign scholars alike suddenly found help rather than hindrance when they sought out the documentary milestones marking what Cairns, at another time, hauntingly referred to as 'the road back to France, 1940'.[12] Moreover, going hand in hand with liberalised access, appointments were made to directorships of the official French military historical services of officers with well-founded reputations as academic scholars and authors in their own right.[13] From the mid-1970s onwards these in-house research teams increasingly came together with university historians, centres such as the Institut d'Histoire du Temps Présent, and historical commissions (such as the Comité d'Histoire de la Deuxième Guerre Mondiale and the Commission Française d'Histoire Militaire), to co-operate in exploring the great issues of France's recent past.[14]

As far as the study of the 1940 problem is concerned, the 'new' historiography appears to have uncovered four particularly marked features. The first of these is the characteristics of 1940 as an *Allied* defeat rather than as something singularly *French*. The second is a new emphasis on continuities between the Franco-British experiences in the phoney war of 1939–40 and the crisis of the following Summer. The third is a recognition that – notwithstanding the military defeat on the continent in 1940 – Franco-British organisation for war displayed an impressive degree of foresight and coherence. Fourthly, there has been a still-unresolved swing back and forth, in regard to the fall of France as a narrower military experience, between interpretations focused on the Allied order-of-battle's intrinsic or 'structural' makeup and those that seek to explain the collapse in terms of the under-performance of Allied generalship.

Taking the first of these features in recent writing, it has become virtually the modern historiographical orthodoxy to argue that the downfall of France can only be satisfyingly explained in the context of the destruction of an entire west European alliance. This case was advanced with verve by the American-Israeli historian Jeffery Gunsburg, writing in the late 1970s.[15] Cairns, however (demonstrating the kind of insight that has made him, since the 1950s, one of the most sensitive and perceptive commentators on recent French history), had already cautioned in his 1974 survey that it 'was unwise to write of this war' without taking advantage of the vast array of available British primary sources, since it 'was very much a Franco-British war on the one side'.[16] The fall of France, continued Cairns, 'was, after all, only the collapse of the most exposed member of the wealthy Atlantic powers, not one of which had provided adequately for its defense after 1918'.[17] And he added (explicitly criticising Chapman's *Why France Collapsed*), this was a point that Chapman discerned but did not always remember as he shaped his book:

> Thus [noted Cairns] the first words in his preface: 'The following pages are concerned with the defeat of the French Army in 1940. They are not concerned with the armies of the Netherlands, Belgium or the British Commonwealth. Those of course appear, but only in relation to the French forces.' This seems very much like acknowledging, on the one hand, the integral nature of the 'allied defeat', while saying, on the other, that it will not be treated. As an approach to the study of the opening phase of a world war it is certainly open to question.[18]

Gunsburg took up the gauntlet that, at least figuratively, had been thrown down by Cairns's strictures before scholars coming after the early 1970s, to the problem of the débâcle.

Profiting from access to Belgian and Dutch unpublished sources, as well as British and French, Gunsburg sharply revised older portrayals of France as a tired, lacklustre and ineffectual coalition leader. In a bold, and no doubt sometimes exaggerated, inversion of what had become a historical commonplace, he took the argument that France had disappointed a retinue of faithful followers and stood it on its head. Gunsburg contended, instead, that it was the French political and military chiefs – men such as Edouard Daladier, minister for national defence and war from June 1936 to May 1940, whilst also prime minister from April 1938 till March 1940, and General Maurice Gamelin, head of the French general staff from 1935 to 19 May 1940 – who conscientiously and carefully addressed the problems of defending western Europe. These leaders, affirmed Gunsburg, worked hard and achieved a great deal, especially in refurbishing the French land forces with modern equipment, munitions, mechanised fighting vehicles and motor transport. 'There is', he wrote, 'much to admire in the way Gamelin built a smaller and industrially weaker France into a powerful military machine to oppose Germany'.[19] That this proved insufficient to contain the Germans was in large measure, he argued, because the other western European powers were too reluctant to assist France in preparing a concerted defence and too reticent about making a sufficient commitment of their own money, manpower and material to achieve a common security.[20]

Gunsburg demanded – as did Robert Young in regard to France's broader external policy-making in the 1930s – that historians look anew at the Third Republic's final years. The accomplishment of these writers and others of their stamp has been substantial. They have given credibility to the view that in much of what was attempted by the last governments of the *Troisième* there was competence and conviction, where earlier interpretations had emphasised only irresolution, incoherence and inefficiency – if not corruption, scandal and farce. As a result the portrait of France as the 'sick man of Europe' of the 1930s has been adjusted, changed to one of France as a major power wrestling with age-old dilemmas brought on by relative decline.[21] In the retouched picture it can now be seen that French ministers, and particularly Daladier at the ministry for national defence and war after June 1936, strove determinedly to put France in a position where Hitler would not reckon war to be a game worth the candle. 'The urgency with which an often maligned Daladier expanded the armed forces, developed new weapons and prepared for a war that he . . . looked upon with loathing . . . has seldom been recognised', chided Vivian Rowe, writing 30 years ago.[22] Now, however, these achievements have gained acknowledgement.[23]

Admission by some scholars that France stood up in 1939 not just for herself but also for neighbors who gave little practical help and even less gratitude has come out of the renewed focus on the other western powers in 1940. The so-called minor Allies have been brought back to the centre, rather than the periphery, of explanations of what went wrong. As a consequence, the literature has assumed a greater balance, a greater fairness. Increasingly, research has been devoted to the problems in the later 1930s of the British, the Belgians and the Dutch. Attention has been paid to their efforts at rearmament, their intelligence operations towards Germany, their diplomatic postures, their degrees of political and economic mobilisation. Historians such as Jean Vanwelkenhuyzen, Jean Stengers and Jonathan Helmreich have advanced our understanding of Belgium's reasons for reluctance to join any alliance at all between 1937 and 1940. These writers have demonstrated how far Belgian desires to be independent of France resulted from domestic constraints on the governments in Brussels (socio-economic pressures as well as linguistic-cultural ones) as much as from Belgian foreign office illusions that their country might be left in peace provided it renounced any partnership with Paris.[24]

Likewise, the Netherlands and its policy has been illuminated by the spotlight of modern historical inquiry. No longer is attention confined to the Dutch experience of occupation from 1940–45 (so capably dissected by Dr Louis de Jong and his associates).[25] For, above and beyond that research, there has been attention to Holland's relations in 1939–40 with the Belgians, the British, the French and the Germans. This has revealed more about the immense value to the west of the Dutch connections to anti-Nazi Germans – notably the link between the Netherlands military attaché in Berlin, Major Sas, and the Abwehr deputy chief, Colonel Hans Oster, that gave early warning about German plans for a western offensive during the phoney war.[26] Beyond this even, the work of André Ausems has begun a positive revisionism regarding the Dutch endeavour to improve their army and strengthen their fixed defences before they were invaded.[27]

In respect of Franco-British relations, too, modern authors have shown themselves ready to renounce the older polemical style. In this regard it seems worthwhile to restate that shifts in attitude – not least among historians themselves – have been as crucial an agent for positive change as has the opening since 1975 of most of the archives. (Among those that have become accessible are the papers of the parliamentary commissions, the Quai d'Orsay, the ministries of finance, labour, commerce and industry, and colonies, as well as the documents of arms-manufacturing companies such as Renault and Panhard and the archives of individuals such as Daladier, Gamelin, Paul Reynaud, Léon Blum, Vincent Auriol, Pierre Cot and Raoul Dautry.) The outcome, by and large, has been a more widely-accepted appreciation of how greatly the French authorities in the late 1930s stretched their minds, their muscles and their money to confront Hitler and the dark, dimly-understood horrors that he represented. Furthermore, it has become increasingly appreciated that the exertions of the French did not occur in some eleventh-hour awakening in 1939–40 but were made from at least as far back as 1936. Here, then, is an additional instance where the historians of the last 15 years have successfully taken up another of Cairns's challenges – to show 'awareness of the importance of getting the 1940 events properly situated'.[28]

Admittedly it is the case that even in the late 1970s and 1980s books peddling a more old-fashioned view of pre-war France have still come off the presses. In France, for example, two volumes were authored by Jean-Baptiste Duroselle, one of that country's most eminent and highly-respected modern international historians and successor to Pierre Renouvin, the founder of the Sorbonne's Institut d'Histoire des Relations Internationales Contemporaines.[29] Duroselle's studies appeared under provocative – not to say evocative – titles: *La Décadence* (1979) and *L'Abîme* (1983). The works expounded an unforgiving critique of the makers of French foreign and defence policy in most of the period from 1932 to 1945. They censured a generation of statesmen, soldiers and civil servants for lacking a sense of international morality, a vision for the place of France in the wider fate of Europe, a determination to obtain, by hook or by crook, the means for a stalwart, reputable national policy (and, one instinctively feels, one on which Duroselle himself, in quite a personal sense, would be able to reflect with pride).[30]

Some of this interpretative recidivism has also found its way into modern English-language writings. One prominent example would be the often counterfactual but inventive and interesting *Change in the European Balance of Power*, by Williamson Murray (1984).[31] This book argued that the nations threatened by Hitler's aggressiveness had more interest – if only they had understood – in standing up to Germany in 1938 over the Sudetenland than in 1939 over Poland. Curiously, however, the volume devoted relatively little space to comparing the condition of France in 1938 to that a year later. It did not pay a great deal of attention to exploring the state of French politics, economic and social financial health or armed readiness at the two moments in question. This was an odd oversight, because France, much more than Britain, would have had to stand in the front line to fight Germany in support of the Czechs – just as she had to in 1939–40 for the sake of the Poles. The result was an interpretation that inclined to lay blame rather than understanding; one, too, that does not convincingly square with the evidence available in the French archives, demonstrating the steadily more intensive French efforts towards military preparedness and the step by step rise in the effectiveness of French forces as each year went by, from 1935 to 1940.[32]

Yet it was precisely this total context of French political, economic and strategic conditions that made Daladier certain that he had to go – however shamefacedly – to Munich. The French prime minister's parallel responsibilities for national defence and war made him all too familiar with what had been achieved in rearmament at that juncture – and with how much still remained to be done. His journey to meet Hitler was made in the full realisation that he was not negotiating a peace with honour but was simply engaging in a sordid barter for time. All the information available to him in 1938 indicated that French material and moral deficiencies argued decisively for deferring hostilities with the Third Reich. Cheered to the echo at Le Bourget airport by the delirious crowds that greeted him as a peacemaker on his return from Germany, Daladier was impressed by nothing so much as France's psychological unpreparedness for war at that moment. His compatriots, he remarked to an aide, required educating as to the national humiliation to which France's weaknesses had obliged him to submit – and to the tough demands that he would from then on be making of them.[33]

If French leaders such as Daladier and Gamelin appeared ready to postpone the looming trial by arms, this was not least because of their sense of the size of the stakes. As the general put it, when visited at his Vincennes headquarters by Reynaud (then minister of finance), five weeks after the start of the war: 'just at the moment, as at the time of Verdun, what we are witnessing is the world gazing, petrified, on the salute of the gladiators. Once again, it is the duel between France and Germany that is going to decide the fate of the world'. Reynaud responded by invoking other historical images of the glory won against the odds by French arms. 'Never before', he said,

> had France's situation been this serious. In the days of the 'Patrie en danger' [an allusion to the cannonade of Valmy in 1792 that saved the infant Republic from the Prussian-backed counterrevolution] France was a 'mammoth' opposed to tiny little unorganized nations. Today, it's the 'struggle of the petits bourgeois against the gangsters' . . . And the

French army is the world's final barrier against the predators out there.
Will it be up to the task of resisting them?[34]

No doubt some scholars who seek to interpret exchanges such as this one, and
relate it to the French collapse the following spring, will still insist that France took
excessive counsel of her fears. They may still wish to argue that too little heed
was paid to the information being gleaned by the 2e Bureau and the Service de
Renseignements (the French intelligence agencies), about the difficulties confronting
the Germans in the phoney war. Gamelin admitted in his memoirs that he was
told how a 'large number of panzers had been destroyed or damaged in Poland',
and that the German tank divisions in late 1939 were back behind the Rhine and
'apparently undergoing reorganization and reinforcement'. The French awareness
that the German army had its problems is confirmed in a dispatch from Belgium's
military attaché in Paris, of 21 October, in which it was reported that the '2e Bureau
has reliable intelligence telling it that the German armoured vehicles have suffered
severely in Poland, some having been destroyed in combat but many requiring
serious and time-consuming repairs.'[35]

Against this knowledge, however, French commanders had to set their own
deficiencies in training and continuing bottlenecks in munitions manufacture. In
November 1939 Gamelin instigated an emergency programme (the 'Five Month
Plan') to scrape together seventeen new divisions (of which one was mechanized).[36]
In December he ordered the upgrading of the two heavy tank brigades, formed
with the formidable but scarce Chars B in September, to divisions.[37] These steps,
however, could not improve the Allied armies overnight. Meanwhile, French
generals showed the Wehrmacht the respect that it seemed due after its triumph in
the east. As the French historian François Bédarida has noted in his study of the
Franco-British Supreme War Council (SWC), 'Those responsible for national
defence never ceased to be haunted by their knowledge of their inferiority in armaments, especially in aviation.'[38]

There is now a literature, therefore, which credits the governments and military
strategists during what we now see as the twilight of the *Troisième* with purpose-
fulness as well as patriotism, with coherent policies as well as rationally-framed
objectives. This interpretation relates to the awareness that has grown up of the
historical continuities between the phoney war and the events of 1940.[39]

Whether it be the development of the Allied mobilisation and military build-
up that is investigated, or French civil-military relations, or the framing of strategic
plans, it makes increasingly good sense to view September 1939 to June 1940 (and
perhaps September 1938 to June 1940) as a whole. The problems as well as the
progress evident in the alliance by 1940 appear, more than ever, to have been
expressions, exacerbations, extensions of a series of knotty questions tabled on the
Allied agenda in the preceding months or years. We have already tried to suggest
how this was true in regard to inter-Allied affairs. Surely the flaws that opened into
gaping chasms of misunderstanding and recrimination, splitting asunder the Allied
camp in 1940, resulted from fissures that already ran deeply beneath Anglo-French,
Anglo-Belgian and Franco-Belgian relationships in September 1939.[40]

The connections that are evident between trends seen in the phoney war and
the events of 1940 themselves are not straightforward, however. This is, in part,

because of the two-edged effect of the respite in 1939–40 on Allied morale and military readiness. In the main, historians to date have tended to treat it as axiomatic that Franco-British passivity in the phoney war caused an insidious and eventually-decisive undermining of military as well as civilian belligerence and fortitude. According to this view, the quiet on the western front for seven months after the fall of Poland induced a false sense of security among the Allies; allegedly, it sapped the staunchness of their fighting spirit. It was argued, in this interpretation, that the Franco-British commanders became deluded that their armies could safely entrench behind the Maginot Line and then simply wait till they overcame Hitler by 'blood-less victories' – squeezing the life out of the German economy by blockading her supplies of essential industrial materials, fuels and foodstuffs.[41]

As a satisfying 'structural' or non-operational explanation for the fall of France, this needs to be treated with extreme caution. Undoubtedly there was something that seemed unreal about the lull in the west at the end of 1939, as disputes between Hitler and his generals, along with deteriorating weather, forced repeated post-ponements of the projected German offensive.[42] The Winter *was* an exceptionally harsh one and Allied commanders did not lightly use it as an excuse for abandoning military preparations and training. But it had the unavoidable effect of inclining the rank-and-file who were huddled along the frontiers to think rather less about war and rather more about their creature comforts. As an officer of Gamelin's staff recol-lected, the 'overriding preoccupation of our troops was to ensure their immediate security and shelter themselves from the inclement weather.'[43] These problems naturally affected the Germans too, though to a lesser degree because they were not so fearful of being attacked and were thus able to hold many divisions in purpose-built camps behind their lines rather than in rudimentary billets at the front.

For all the phoney-ness of the phoney war however, the French high command never lost sight of the fact that the Winter represented a temporary respite, not a permanent reprieve. This much is apparent from the recently-released evidence in the war diary of Gamelin's headquarters. This document, a detailed day-by-day record of Gamelin's meetings and conversations, demonstrates that nobody was more alive than France's leading soldier to the risks of lowered Allied vigilance. 'Once the real war begins over here', he warned his staff as early as 18 September 1939, 'it will come as a very rude awakening'.[44] During that month and the next he reiterated the importance of watchfulness as well as intensified training for the French and British armies. To oversee this he charged his most experienced sub-ordinates – Generals Georges (responsible for the North-Eastern theatre, facing Germany), Billotte and Prételat (commanding that theatre's army groups), Dufieux (inspector-general of infantry) and Bineau (the *major-général*, or chief of staff, for the North-East). Nor did Gamelin leave everything to these officers and skulk away himself, like some troglodyte, in his Vincennes command post. Three times in the first two months of the war, on 27 September, 7 October and 15–16 October, he personally toured his own armies and the BEF along the fron-tier. He paid further visits to the front-line formations in March 1940.[45] In the end the campaign in France and Belgium made it plain that his bidding was too often not done well – and, in some instances, apparently not done at all. One of his personal staff officers reflected later that 'At no level of the echelon [of command] were General Gamelin's sage suggestions followed by action. The [subordinate] commanders, who were generally too old, lived on memories of the victory of 1918 and failed to show evidence of the activity that was desired.'[46] Part of the problem was that Gamelin had little concrete evidence on which to base a *limogeage* or clear-out of his generals until the blitzkrieg began – and when he resolved to undertake one in mid-May 1940 he found himself dismissed before he could effect the changes. He was left only to ponder ruefully what would have happened in 1914 if his own mentor, Joffre, had been sacked after the débâcle of the Battle of the Frontiers and not given time to redeploy, appoint new subordinates and win the Battle of the Marne.[47]

During the phoney war Gamelin was up against the fact that (as he had himself remarked to a contemporary biographer) 'At certain levels of responsibility, it is no longer a matter of giving orders but of persuading'.[48] Nevertheless, it is now apparent that what Cairns called the 'thirty years of open season' for Gamelin hunters is closed. Henceforth 'history will have to try to consider Gamelin as fairly as it considers every commander on whom finally the sun did not shine'.[49] It would appear that a start is at last being made, one historian acknowledging recently that, after all the years of making Gamelin the convenient scapegoat, 'he does not appear to be the weak and characterless man of legend'.[50]

Time and again before May 1940, Gamelin emphasised in conferences with his senior commanders and staff that the Allies would be in perilous danger if they made the mistake of underestimating the Wehrmacht, buoyed as it was by its success in Poland.[51] Admittedly, Gamelin did not question the prevailing belief in Paris and London that time's passage would help the Allies to increase their strength more than the Germans. Nevertheless, he remained much more sensitive than most Allied leaders to the delicate balance that needed preserving between the point at which prolonged inactivity assisted the Franco-British build-up and the point where it started to sap their will to fight. As regards this psychological dimension to the struggle, the general showed himself to be more perceptive than many inside the French and British governments who reacted to the war's stagnation as if it were a Godsend.

One with this attitude, at any rate during the closing months of 1939, was Reynaud, whose calculations in the Autumn and Winter appear not to have gone any deeper than 'bean counting'. Whilst his responsibilities, as finance minister, were for the state of the treasury, economic mobilisation and output, Reynaud assessed the costs and benefits of the phoney war in purely material and measurable terms. What was in his sights at this time was the number of men and the amount of munitions that the Allies were accumulating. 'Why risk seeing Hitler under the Arc de Triomphe', Reynaud asked Gamelin when he visited the latter's headquarters in mid-October 1939 'especially if a few weeks or a few months of respite can lessen the imbalance between France's potential and that of Germany?' Gamelin rejoined that 'It would certainly be good to gain time to continue the material preparation of the country and the units [of the army]' but added, with a note of circumspection, that 'there is the home front to be held too, and that demands high and undivided morale'.[52] Nor was Reynaud alone among the civilians in having boundless confidence in the strength of the Allied strategic position. Fernand Gentin, the minister of commerce and industry, was at this time tenaciously resisting any further encroachment of armaments programmes on the labour and productive capacity still engaged in making civil export goods. 'We need to continue to manu-facture for the export market', he insisted, 'in order to hang onto our customers for when the war is over'.[53] French political leaders, in sum, were not so much exercised by what needed to be done to prevent a short-term military defeat as they were preoccupied with safeguarding France's position among the victorious Allies.

The manner in which the 1914–18 conflict had drained French national finances and caused the indebtedness and economic instability of the 1920s haunted govern-ment leaders in Paris in 1939–40. Hanging over them was a pervasive belief that, after the earlier war, France had been cheated out of the rewards that ought right-fully to have been hers in return for the disproportionately heavy sacrifices she had borne for the Allies. Hence, in the opening months of the Second World War, French ministers opposed an unrestricted conversion to a war economy; they were too concerned not to be held responsible for 'losing the peace' a second time to countenance anything so drastic. After flying over the Aisne and Somme to Abbeville for the first SWC meeting with Chamberlain, on 12 September 1939, Daladier expressed his shock at seeing the fields still full of unharvested crops and caused a bitter quarrel with Gamelin by pressing for a wholesale demobilisation of farm workers who had been called up at the outbreak of the war.[54] Daladier reflected the view of the politicians that France needed to conserve a sound economy which would enable her to survive the long haul without mortgaging her future standing as a trading nation and international power. As an objective this may, in retrospect, appear to have been extraordinarily naive in view of the colossal costs of the 1939–45 war to all the belligerents and in relation to the huge changes in the world order that it brought about. But the French ministers were seeking to make the most sensible preparations they could in terms of the grim challenge they faced. The goal was, as Daladier defined it in a directive of February 1940:

> on the one hand to establish a balance between our military effort and our means to meet it . . . on the other, to apportion the effort of France and England judiciously . . . our entire policy must be directed at enabling us to hold on in the long term as much from the viewpoint of our financial resources as from that of our military effort [and] must be framed as though England and France have to win the war by themselves without the aid – even financial – of the United States. A balance . . . will be the best guarantee that we shall be able to keep up our effort until total victory.[55]

When, the next month, Gamelin found Daladier expressing the view that he 'no longer thought there'd be a battle [in 1940] and that men could be sent back to the interior for other duties', the general realised how complacent the politicians had grown about the possibility of a military crisis.[56]

It was Allied soldiers (not just Gamelin but also Lord Gort and Henry Pownall, the BEF commander and chief-of-staff, who kept clear heads about the problems on the French home front and the short-to-medium-term deficiencies of the French and British forces.[57] This in turn served to strengthen their cautious strategic instincts. It also hardened their preference for husbanding resources in the first two or three years of the war, for the military build-up in France.[58] Since he had been one of Joffre's key operations' staff in 1914–16, Gamelin had the temperament, training and experience of a 'westerner'.[59] To him France and Belgium in 1939–40 was – just as it had been 25 years earlier – the principal theatre of war. Not surprisingly, therefore, he strenuously opposed the pressures from British and French political and military quarters to divert some of the accumulating Allied military forces into opening secondary campaigns on the rimlands of Europe, far from the western front. The task of resistance required considerable energy, for there was no shortage of outlandish proposals that Winter to widen the war and extend Allied commitments. General Maxime Weygand (Gamelin's predecessor, brought out of retirement in August 1939 to head French forces in Syria and Lebanon), envisioned launching bomber aircraft from Beirut to raid Soviet oilfields in the Caucasus, even though this would have shifted Russia from non-aggression to an active military partner of Hitler against the Allies. He also proposed landing a corps at Salonika in Greece, in a puzzling wish to repeat the indecisive Allied expedition there in 1915. Winston Churchill on the other hand (whom Neville Chamberlain brought back into government in September 1939 with charge of the Admiralty), canvassed the deployment of obsolete battleships into the Baltic to harass Germany's ore trade with Scandinavia. And many Allied politicians were quite serious when they assembled, and almost dispatched, an Anglo-French expedition to assist the Finns after the latter's attack by the Soviet Union in November 1939.[60]

Gamelin was to the fore in dampening enthusiasm for these assorted adventures that captured the imagination of Allied committees in the Winter afternoons of 1939–40 when it seemed 'that eventually the war would die of dry rot' (as one Paris-based journalist put it).[61] But if these calls for a more aggressive and risky strategy alarmed Gamelin, so did the siren voices of the unrepentant appeasers. In France enough of these were active, and of sufficient political standing, to have Gamelin and Daladier looking over their shoulders – and to raise some doubts about French steadfastness among British observers. A number of French ministers and ex-ministers were suspected of supporting the idea of a negotiated settlement with Berlin after the defeat of Poland. Admittedly Daladier broadcast an uncompromising rebuff to the overtures that Hitler indeed made in October 1939.[62] But, in the very first month of the war, Gamelin found him privately afraid of being ousted by a cabal of politicians who had laboured on behalf of a *modus vivendi* with Hitler before the war. (Those named were three former prime ministers, Pierre Laval, Pierre-Etienne Flandin and Camille Chautemps, and Georges Bonnet, Daladier's foreign minister in 1938–39, who had been moved to the justice ministry in a cabinet reshuffle ten days after France went to war.)[63] From this point on, Gamelin increasingly doubted the robustness of Daladier's morale and his toughness as a *chef de guerre*.[64] It was an ominous precursor of the breakdown of confidence and consensus between the civilian and military leaderships that would plunge France to such a nadir of division and despair in May–June 1940.

So long as Daladier remained head of the government, the discontents that were seething beneath the surface could be contained. This ceased to be possible once Daladier's position as prime minister became untenable in the second half of March (when parliament, meeting behind closed doors in secret session, used the Finnish–Soviet armistice as a pretext to instigate a critique of Daladier's allegedly over-cautious conduct of the entire war). Heading the long line of inquisitors was the thrusting and ambitious firebrand, Reynaud. He demonstrated how the time-honoured ploy of seeking to disarm rivals by keeping them inside the government might disastrously backfire on a prime minister in a poorly-disciplined system such as the French, which had little attachment to the doctrine of collective cabinet responsibility. On 19 March the battle in parliament reached a climax as Daladier moved a motion of confidence in his administration in the Chamber. 239 deputies expressed their support, against just two openly hostile votes. But 300 abstained. Daladier concluded that after the acerbic debates of the preceding days, those who were not explicitly for him had to be counted against him. The next day he visited the Elysée and tendered his government's resignation to President Albert Lebrun. Reynaud was immediately summoned and invited to form a ministry of his own. Presented for the Chamber's approbation on 21 March, the new government was invested by the narrowest possible majority of just one vote.[65]

Reynaud's margin of authority could not have been more wafer-thin. Yet, after accusing Daladier of pusillanimity and procrastination, the new prime minister perceived a need to cloak some substance round his self-styled image as a man of action. It was not possible for him to begin by another attack on Daladier. For the latter's participation in the new government (where he stayed on as minister for national defence and war), had proven to be essential to the parliamentary arithmetic of the slender majority cobbled together on 21 March.[66] Instead, Reynaud seized on a strategy of indirect approach, turning his fire against the performance of 'the high command' (a euphemism or code which, everyone understood, really meant Gamelin). If he were to succeed in ousting Gamelin, Reynaud knew that he would achieve two objectives in one. For not only would he be able to install a soldier more attuned to his own impetuous personality and beholden to him for his appointment, he would also neutralise Daladier's influence in the direction of the war effort by eliminating his protégé and strategic *alter ego*. Reynaud's understanding was that (as one commentator has put it), 'Gamelin was, and remained, Daladier's "man"' and to try to differentiate between their military outlooks was as purpose-less as 'trying to distinguish between Tweedledee and Tweedledum'.[67]

As a result of Reynaud's determination to force the issue with Gamelin a civil-military relationship that had already become unsteady degenerated precipitately into an unrestrained brawl. Reynaud's intentions were first intimated on 3 April when he revealed that – without so much as notifying Daladier and Gamelin – he had recalled Weygand from Beirut to Paris, to give a special briefing to the war cabinet convened that evening at the Quai d'Orsay. Gamelin was 'surprised' and Daladier 'furious' at a decision which so provocatively bypassed their authority. The critical reaction of most military figures the next day showed they regarded Weygand as an unwelcome interloper. The 'meeting yesterday was heartbreaking', thought Gamelin; 'General Weygand's behaviour was maladroit. His entire briefing was a critique of our action and our foreign policy'. Even Darlan (whose conserv-ative politics might have been expected to put him on Weygand's side) complained sarcastically at having 'been required to make a 180 kilometre round trip just to listen to Weygand deliver a lecture like they get at the College des Hautes Etudes de Défense Nationale'.[68]

On 8–9 April the French leaders were suddenly given a whole new cause over which to wage their private wars. For Hitler had ended the phoney war game of cat and mouse by launching Operation *Weserübung* – the invasion of Denmark and Norway to head off Allied plans to mine the northern waters and cut Germany's sea-borne Scandinavian ore supplies. The extension of the conflict gave Reynaud a new pretext for stepping up his pressure on Gamelin. For whereas he enthusiastically supported Allied contingency plans to intervene by major landings at Norwegian ports, the general preferred that the Allies restrict themselves to a smaller and mostly British expedition and naval riposte. The two Frenchmen's positions were not in practice as far apart as they were made to appear. Gamelin did not disagree that a military operation should be mounted to attempt to deny the Germans a clean sweep in Norway. What was at issue was not the principle of an intervention but its nature and especially its scale. Long and rancorous meetings occurred throughout 9 and 10 April as the French political, military and naval leaders discussed the timetable and the availability of forces to support the troop convoys that the British had already dispatched for Norway on the 8th.[69]

The concern uppermost in Gamelin's mind was to prevent an over-reaction to *Weserübung*. His wish was to limit what he feared would be the diversion of Allied military resources away from the main front to a secondary theatre – one he suspected might become a hopeless cause anyway. The tension between Gamelin's and Reynaud's views was given particular point since, during the first week of April 1940, French intelligence had received a series of warnings from reliable sources that the German attack in the west was imminent, with Holland and Belgium the most likely invasion route.[70] Gamelin suspected that *Weserübung* was, at least in part, a stratagem to distract the Allies. As one of his personal staff explained later, Gamelin felt duty-bound to demand that the intervention in Norway not cause any weakening of the Franco-British situation on the western front. The 'drama of our participation in the Scandinavian operations', wrote this officer, lay in the fact 'that at the moment when the support of our forces was sollicited, these forces were still hardly adequate to guarantee our own frontiers. . . . The dispatch of an expeditionary corps to so distant a locale entrained, *ipso facto*, a weakening of the principal theatre of operations.'[71] The deliberations among the French leaders over how far to assist the British in Norway were agitated and acrimonious. After more meetings on 10 April, Gamelin rejoined his staff at Vincennes late in the evening and exclaimed, 'We're swinging from one extreme to the other. After Daladier, who couldn't manage to make a decision at all, here we are with Reynaud who makes one every five minutes.'[72]

The Norwegian affair, without question, held a strategic significance in its own right for the later course of the war. But its importance for the Allies in immediate terms was in the way it plunged French civil-military relations to a new low. The Reynaud–Gamelin feud assumed its most naked guise in the context of the dispute as to appropriate responses to *Weserübung*. But the underlying issue concerned the relative powers of politicians and professional military chiefs over the conduct of the war effort. It was, reflected Gamelin's staff officer quoted previously, 'to be noted how far the war in Norway was detrimental to the harmony and understanding that ought to have existed among those in France responsible for the direction of the country'.[73] The quarrelling in the Spring of 1940 was a prolongation – as well as a personalisation − of the unresolved questions about the extent of civilian competence and supremacy in military policy that had bedevilled the French state at least since the 1870s. Around this central concern, furthermore, there revolved the ongoing and immediate political trial of strength between Reynaud and Daladier (the latter being the real target of the former's guerrilla campaign against Gamelin).[74]

By 12 April the general had no doubt left what was in the offing. 'We're no longer waging war', he told his adjutant, Major Christian de l'Hermite, that day; 'we're seeing pure cinema. *Ce Reynaud, c'est un fantôche*'. Leaving a further meeting of the war cabinet held at the Quai d'Orsay that evening, Gamelin offered a terse summary of the situation as he perceived it, to Captain Lorenchet de Montjamont (his ordnance officer). The crisis, he thought, was fast coming to a head. 'I truly believe that president Daladier is going to resign', he said. 'He'd have done better for himself if he hadn't remained part of this [ministerial] combination', ventured the aide. 'On his own account', rejoined the general, 'that's right, but he has covered the high command'.[75] Reynaud, he realised, wished to lever him out.

Gamelin bridled, not surprisingly. He gathered that what was afoot was a calculated manoeuvre to sacrifice his career and reputation to the ego and ambition of an untried prime minister. The fact that he was being made a stalking horse in *Reynaud's* grander design to discredit and be done once-and-for-all with Daladier put in better perspective his disillusionment with the latter's conduct as a war leader in the closing months of 1939. This, he now appreciated, had been caused by the inevitable frictions of war, not by conflict over fundamentals. With the new prime minister at both their throats, Gamelin recalled the common cause he and Daladier had made on the army's behalf since 1933. In particular, he remembered the minister's key role in bringing about re-equipment and rearmament after June 1936.[76] And, since Reynaud appeared bent on menacing his professional survival, Gamelin found it expedient to see how Daladier and his bloc of Radical deputies in the Chamber might serve to protect his own position.

For Gamelin had long since learnt the crucial part that lay in mastering the art of Republican politics in order to advance − and afterwards defend a career in the army. He had learnt in 1916, seeing his own mentor, Joffre, become a scapegoat for ministers disgruntled at the failure of the Allies to break the German lines on the western front. He had learnt in the Levant in 1925–26, watching the government in Paris sacrifice the high commissioner, General Sarrail, because the depleted local forces proved unable at the first attempt to quash the revolt of the Druzes. He had learnt by observing the favour shown him because of his own consensual style by politicians of such contrasting hues as the conservatives André Tardieu and Jean Fabry, the independent socialist Joseph Paul-Boncour, and Radicals such as Maurice Sarraut, his brother Albert, and Daladier himself. Gamelin was a 'political' general in this sense that he understood how it was the skills of the military manager, rather than the bravery of the boots-and-spurs commander, that had become essential in the complex world of twentieth-century military leadership. He was, perhaps, the first of a line of the most senior generals, admirals and air marshals who found in 1939–45 that, for men in uniform at the very top, the conduct of war now lay in a grey, blurred world where grand strategy overlapped with politics. This was noticed by the more astute observers even at the time. (The novelist Jules Romains, for example, after interviewing Gamelin at Vincennes in December 1939, wrote that 'those who tell you that Gamelin has made his successful career thanks to the politicians . . . forget that high-ranking military men always have to reckon with politicians. Recognizing that this is so is neither to pronounce for nor against the military worth of these officers.')[77] Some modern historians have begun taking a not-dissimilar view, Douglas Porch recently arguing that 'Gamelin had . . . great finesse. . . . Simply because he was a "political" general and declined to pound the table and shout as had his irascible predecessor, General Weygand, this did not mean that he lacked character'.[78]

As the crisis in Paris in April 1940 intensified, Gamelin resolved to fight for his professional life. He did so with no holds barred, displaying his considerable accomplishments as a past-master in the arts of French military politics. Unlike Reynaud, he had built himself a handsome bank of parliamentary patronage down the years. The moment had arrived, he realised, to draw deeply on its reserves; for all that it was Reynaud who was the professional politician, the new prime minister had chosen to play in a game for which his own skills were not nearly as finely-honed as those of the general. After the war cabinet in the evening of 12 April, Gamelin unveiled his strategy to his ordnance officer:

> As long as Daladier remains part of the ministry, I shall stay on. If he resigns without the Reynaud Cabinet failing, I shall resign too. I cannot tolerate for a moment longer being treated as I have been by Reynaud. This is not a question of personal pride, it's the general interest that's at stake. The commander-in-chief cannot have his prerogatives trampled on in this fashion.[79]

Furthermore, through an anonymous interlocutor's 'indiscretion', Gamelin had been told that Reynaud had for some time been toying with 'a Weygand–Georges replacement team'. Since it seemed that the climax of the struggle was approaching, Gamelin sensed that it was time to mobilise some heavy political firepower on his own account. Accordingly, late that evening, he had one of the section heads of his personal staff, Lieutenant-Colonel François Guillaut, telephone Maurice Sarraut, one of the general's oldest and most trusted friends and political allies, 'to bring him abreast of the situation'. Sarraut, among the most senior Radicals in the Senate, was also owner of the major provincial paper, *La Dépêche de Toulouse*. His power in south-western France was so great that it gave him an almost baronial domination over the parliamentarians elected in that region. He did not disappoint Gamelin's call for support, replying 'that he was going to throw himself into action immediately and consult his brother' Albert, who had been Daladier's minister of the interior till 20 March (and had twice been prime minister in his own right earlier in the 1930s).[80]

During the next day, 13 April, Gamelin took further measures to bluff or apply pressure to those whose political backing he needed for survival. Early in the morning he sent a message to tell Daladier of the decision he had reached to resign if Daladier himself quit the government. Also in the course of the day Guillaut (who had telephoned Maurice Sarraut) arranged to see Albert Sarraut to present Gamelin's viewpoint on his running battle with the prime minister. By now, as the general's war diary noted, the dissensions between himself and the head of the government had boiled over into the 'acute phase of the Daladier-Reynaud conflict'. Following a meeting of the French *comité de guerre* at the Elysée in the afternoon, Gamelin was visited by another long-standing political ally, Jean Fabry. Once the general's superior (when war minister, in 1935–36), Fabry was a leading figure in the Democratic Alliance (one of the two main French conservative parties). Although sitting in the Senate since late 1936, Fabry retained extensive influence throughout parliament for he had chaired the Chamber's army commission between 1928 and 1935 and was widely regarded as an authority on defence issues. Though it was hardly a warning that Gamelin needed to be given by this stage, the purpose of Fabry's visit was to tip off his old friend, and 'he did not hide the fact from him that Reynaud looked on him with disfavour'.[81]

As April went on the Allied operations in Norway had some success at sea but were in deepening trouble ashore. In both cases German air superiority gave Hitler's forces an edge. From varied quarters in London and Paris it was proposed to cut Allied losses and withdraw. Reynaud, however, vehemently opposed all talk of evacuation. It would, he claimed, paint Franco-British determination and military competence in a very bad light in the eyes of the neutrals. In reality, Reynaud was afraid of the personal consequences of a pull-out. On the French side, the intervention was largely undertaken at Reynaud's insistence. The commitment of French troops alongside the British was an expression of the new French government's more pugnacious approach to the war. On the campaign's outcome rested a good deal of Reynaud's prestige and, perhaps, the future of his ministry.[82] But, as far as Gamelin was concerned, Reynaud was guilty of his individual fortunes above French strategic interests. En route to another *comité de guerre* on 16 April, the general turned to his adjutant and exclaimed, in alarm as well as exasperation: 'This M. Reynaud is deranged. If he goes on, he'll lead France to her ruin . . . he must not be left where he is.'[83]

In the closing days of April and first days of May the situation of the Allied bridgeheads in Norway deteriorated so much that withdrawal became not an option but an urgent necessity. The evacuation was completed – except for the force at Narvik – by 3 May. But if the military disengagement was accomplished without disaster, the political after-effects in both London and Paris were considerable. In France both the Senate and the Chamber reconvened in secret session. Daladier as well as Reynaud was interpellated about the course of the campaign and about the reasons for the Allied reverses. Reynaud learnt – as had Daladier before him – that the opposition was having no truck in this war with any 1914-style *union sacrée*, or parliamentary truce. The inactivity of the phoney war had not eradicated the partisanship of French politics. It had merely put it under a temporary anaesthetic. Coming on the heels of the Finnish embarrassment, the failure to thwart the Germans over Norway was quite enough to re-infuse French politics with their accustomed bile. Moreover, not only were the French inveighing against one another, the Allies were now trading recriminations between themselves with an unhealthy zest.[84]

Under these circumstances, the SWC meetings that took place on 22–3 and 26–7 April 1940 were uncomfortable affairs. Chamberlain's continuation as prime minister was increasingly under pressure in London. Reynaud, likewise, appeared to be tottering on the brink. As a British diplomat in the Paris embassy noted in his diary on 1 May: 'P.R. will almost certainly fall. . . . But the rot may go further. Laval is active in the background. P.R. is in a nervous state and inclined to blame us and Gamelin and the two General Staffs for what has happened.'[85]

Over the first week of May French intelligence (partly exploiting its decrypts of intercepted German air force ENIGMA signals) again reported firm indications that Hitler's attack on the west was imminent. So far as Gamelin was concerned, the Norwegian expedition had succeeded only in diverting Allied forces – and distracting Allied leaders' attentions – from the much more critical German threat close to home. On 3 May he offered a forecast to his adjutant that, with hindsight, appears to have had a grim clairvoyance: 'France (he prophesied) is going to experience one of the hardest summers of her history.'[86]

The scene was thus set for the climactic final act of the tragicomedy between Reynaud and Gamelin, on the very eve of the blitzkrieg. The setting was the notorious meeting of the full cabinet which the French prime minister, with the theatrical touch of a political showman, called without warning for the morning of 9 May. Since this was a meeting of the government, rather than of the *comité de guerre*, neither Gamelin nor the other professional military chiefs was present. The proceedings have been vividly captured in the diary-style memoir of one eyewitness who was a little away from the eye of the storm, the minister of public works, Anatole de Monzie. Convened in an elegant salon at the Quai d'Orsay, the meeting opened in an atmosphere of unusual solemnity and tension. The arriving ministers found Reynaud sitting before a number of bulky dossiers spread out on the conference table. 'Gentlemen', he began, 'I have to talk to you about the state of the command'. He proceeded to launch into a detailed and minutely-documented history of his relations with Gamelin. It was, noted de Monzie in astonishment, an 'indictment rather than a chronicle'. Reynaud spoke for over an hour, the monologue punctuated only when he paused from time to time to extract another paper from the files of letters, directives and instructions that he had exchanged with the general over the previous seven weeks. Nobody else spoke; nobody moved. Presented so one-sidedly, without contradiction, the case made against Gamelin appeared devastating. 'This is an execution' whispered the minister of finance, Lucien Lamoureux, in de Monzie's ear. Finally, Reynaud shut his dossier and concluded. 'I do not agree', replied Daladier weakly. The room fell silent. Morally speaking, thought de Monzie, at that moment the French army no longer had a leader. 'So long as the enemy doesn't benefit from . . . this disavowal of the commander . . .', he ventured to the minister for the merchant marine as they departed.[87]

It did not take Gamelin long to learn that at the meeting he had been the object of a 'violent attack' by the prime minister, but that Daladier had stood by him, having remarked that 'the matter appeared to be his concern, since he was still the minister for national defence'. Reynaud was reported to have rejoined that, feeling unable to collaborate with Gamelin any longer – and in view of the general's support from Daladier – he felt obliged to tender his resignation (a decision that was not made public at the time, however). Daladier had actually argued that Norway was primarily a British responsibility, a matter for the Admiralty in London. Gamelin, he had insisted, was not to be blamed for the Allied misadventures in Scandinavia.[88] More than a quarter of a century later, Daladier's view remained unchanged. As he reflected from that distance on his fidelity towards Gamelin during the Spring crisis, he wrote that 'If I disapproved of the general being relieved of his command, in the meeting on the morning of 9 May 1940, it was because he had my confidence. And I thought that, with the German attack [in the West] imminent, General Gamelin had taken what military measures were necessary'.[89] Before dawn the next day, the German blitzkrieg began. Gamelin had warded off the stigma of being relieved of command as a result of losing the prime minister's confidence, only to suffer the humiliation of being dismissed ten days later as the price for disintegration of the Allied front.

Gamelin received the news of his replacement late in the evening of 19 May, in a short note delivered to Vincennes by an officer from Reynaud's *cabinet*. Accompanying the 'thanks of the government for the services that you have rendered the country in the course of a long and brilliant career' were copies of decrees naming Weygand commander-in-chief of all theatres of operations.[90] The succession, however, had an importance that went far beyond closing Gamelin's career. For, in seizing the moment to score this final and singularly vindictive triumph over Gamelin, Reynaud opened the way for his own political defeat over the armistice question at Bordeaux on 16 June and for the Republic's demise at Vichy on 10 July. In replacing Gamelin with Weygand, a general who kept faith in ultimate Allied victory was substituted by a man totally without a vision of the war's global context – and a grave-digger of the regime to boot. In the terse exchange that marked the handover of command at Vincennes on the morning of 20 May, Gamelin caught an unnerving glimpse of what was coming to France. 'All this politics', suddenly exclaimed Weygand, 'that's got to change. We've got to be done with all these politicians. There's not one of them worth any more than the others'.[91] Five days later, when ministers assembled for a *comité de guerre* on 25 May, Weygand said, to general consternation, that if his improvised defensive line along the Somme failed to hold the next phase of the German offensive, he could see no further way for France to continue in the war at all.[92]

Weygand was not, after all, the never-say-die spirit that Reynaud had believed. But Reynaud made this discovery when it was too late: the alternatives had been eliminated. Gamelin was disgraced; Georges had collapsed under the strain on 14 May; Billotte died on 22 May after his staff car had crashed; Giraud was surprised and taken prisoner by a German patrol; Huntziger, although briefly considered, was too discredited by his Second Army's defeat at Sedan. In reality, Weygand had been placed in an unassailable position. Reynaud's misjudgement in recalling him (and in appointing Pétain deputy prime minister on 18 May), ensured that the failure of the Allied armies was not just a military setback but the prelude to the overthrow of the French Republic, to the 'fall of France'.[93] As de Monzie noted sceptically on the day Pétain was brought into the government, a strategic crisis was being met by symbolic gestures to try to jolt France back onto her feet. 'The search after psychological shocks', mused the minister, 'occupies Paul Reynaud's mind whether he's at the finance ministry or the *présidence du conseil*. He mistakes himself for a psychiatrist.' France's tragedy was that in this case the Reynaud therapy killed off the patient.[94]

The foregoing discussion provides only one of the numerous instances where the fall of France cannot be understood without relating the continuities of the phoney war to the politico-military crisis of 1940 itself. Such an integrated analysis is required in order to respond to Cairns's point that 'it is hard to discuss sensibly the war of 1939–40 and the *French* conduct of that war, in particular, without evaluating the regime'.[95]

Nor can military history be presented in a vacuum when consideration is given to the third focal point in recent historiography: the Franco-British organisation for war in 1939–40. This, it is apparent, was characterised by far-sighted anticipation of what the Allies would require, logistically and institutionally, to win the Second World War. It was 'no good thinking this is going to end soon with the internal collapse of Germany', Britain's military attaché in Paris accurately predicted in September 1939; 'It's going to be a long, hard business and one must plan as well as one can on that basis'.[96] This planning was, as modern scholarship has demonstrated, remarkably sophisticated and systematic by 1939–40. It ranged from the establishment of permanent committees and reciprocal liaison missions to co-ordinate the Anglo-French military efforts, to the initiatives taken since as early as 1937 to rationalise the application of the economic resources of the two powers in accordance with each's economic requirements.[97]

In much of what was accomplished, the blueprint that was followed was the organisation for managing an industrialised war that the French and British had laboriously learned to fabricate twenty years earlier. The French and British had retained the lessons learnt by 1917–18 about the part that a genuinely joint conduct of the conflict could play in securing victory. In the approach to war with Hitler's Germany, therefore, they did not wait till 1939 before setting teams of officials to work to plan the pooling of the two nations' resources, or the fashioning of the administrative apparatus to balance each's financial and military burdens. As far as they could, the leaders of France and Britain prepared in 1939–40 to wage the war against Hitler in unison, meshing their two empires into one grand alliance. Notwithstanding the blow that the fall of France administered in the short term to these designs, the governments of Chamberlain and Daladier, their officials and military staffs, had correctly divined the shape of the Second World War.[98]

When one turns, finally, to the narrower military side to the events of 1940, the recent historiography is rather less sure of its interpretative direction. One trend has been the shift away from the detailed attention given in the past to the battles themselves – away from the exploits of commanders and combatants. In its stead a greater interest has arisen in the part ascribable in victory and defeat to the different doctrine and training of the German forces on the one side, the French, British and Belgians on the other.[99] There have been, also, some illuminating investigations of the planning processes, the military reasoning and the political influences that produced the opposing strategies of *Fall Gelb* and the Dyle-Breda manoeuvre.[100] Nor has concern with the operations themselves, with chronicling particular portions of the fighting, by any means entirely disappeared. The gallantry of individual formations, the performance of commanders (especially subordinate generals destined for greater heights, such as Alan Brooke, Alexander and Montgomery with the BEF), these have still found their historians in the 1980s – and perhaps always will.[101]

At least one old legend, that the Germans simply swept through France in 1940 because of their material superiority, has been conclusively interred. As far back as

1947, in the *Revue de Défense Nationale*, the notion that the Allies suffered from a quantitative inferiority in armoured vehicles was exposed as a myth by Charles de Cossé-Brissac. A seminal article in 1970 by an American, R.H.S. Stolfi entitled 'Equipment for Victory in France in 1940', in the British journal *History*, went a stage further by persuasively attacking the shibboleth that the western powers were even qualitatively outclassed in the tank balance.[102] Modern scholarship has also demonstrated that by April, May and June 1940 the Franco-British war industries were manufacturing greater amounts of munitions each month than were the Germans. Thus the French air force, greatly outnumbered though it was by the Luftwaffe at the outset of the campaign, actually had more serviceable aircraft (though fewer trained aircrew) when the armistice was signed on 22 June than it had put into line on 10 May.[103] In sum, a consensus has emerged that the Allies were, on a material calculation alone, sufficiently equipped to have avoided defeat – if not yet sufficiently to have tried to win the war. As Gary Sheffield, writing in 1988, put it: 'Superior doctrine and tactics, not superior technology, decided the battle for France'.[104]

In conclusion, it may be worth attempting to signpost some of the paths that study of 1940 seems likely to travel in the future. In the first place, it appears that the drawing up of the more favourable *bilan* or ledger-sheet in respect of Franco-British provision with armaments will redirect attention to more contingent factors, to the strategic planning and the operational decisions of each side. In other words, it can be expected that the human rather than the material shortcomings of the Allies will receive further reappraisal. There will probably be more of a focus, too, on the reasons for the ineffectiveness of Allied methods of combat at the level of the division and below. There may be renewed emphasis on Franco-British deficiencies in air-ground support and in combined-arms tactics, together with a more systematic investigation of the long-term modes of thought and methods of instruction that produced such unimpressive Allied middle and junior leader cadres. In a central place in the historians' spotlight, then, will be the decisiveness of the initial deployment and missions of the Allied order-of-battle on 10 May; the poor training of so many Allied formations (especially French B-series reserve divisions); the calamitous consequences of having Allied generals who were aware of new military technologies but had not understood that these made possible a three or fourfold increase – a revolution – in the pace of warfare.[105]

Bound up with the question of changes that had transformed the speed at which battles could be fought were the crucial issues of command, control, communications and intelligence. These – C^3I as they are termed in strategic studies – constitute the second area to which future historians of the 1940 campaign must give more attention than did those of the past. As it is, the research so far done by John Ferris into the shortcomings of the BEF's signals apparatus and security, together with that of Robert Doughty into the similar deficiencies of the French, indicates the promising avenues for inquiry that may be followed through this terrain. A deeper understanding of the nature and impact of the Allied C^3I limitations bids fair to provide some major new insight into what brought about their undoing on the battlefield in 1940.[106] The Allied communications' systems were defective at virtually every level. 'Gamelin's command post', recalled an officer of his *cabinet*, 'had neither a wireless telegraph office nor even carrier pigeons'. It was completely dependent on telephone landlines. 'It was [therefore] impossible for it to receive information direct from the front, or intercept radio messages broadcast by the armies and air force formations. As a result, from the first hours of the battle, the *cabinet* of our most senior general found itself relegated to the fringe of an insufficiently centralized communications network'.[107] As another commentator added, this 'outmoded equipment contributes partially to explaining the slow reactions of Billotte, of Georges, of the staff, of Gamelin'.[108] The position lower down the chain of command proved to be every bit as flawed. 'At divisional level, taken as a whole, communications by wireless telegraph failed to give the results for which we were looking. The apparatus in the hands of our small units proved defective, the encoding complicated; the communication posts and their equipment had no protection against low-flying aircraft'. Some French it is true, were fitted with radio sets; but too many were not, or had either a transmitter or receiver but not both.[109] Throughout the Allied forces there was a disastrous mismatch between the types of communications systems commonly available and the fast, flexible type of war which the Germans made them fight.

These are matters which historians have only recently begun to tackle in earnest. Yet they have already yielded sufficiently significant findings to mark them out for additional work. Might the overwhelming of the Allied forces – as distinct from France's political collapse and withdrawal from the war – have remained a 'strange defeat' for so long if scholars in former times had taken half the pains with the unglamorous subject of military communications that they lavished on studying the generalship of Rommel and Guderian?

Thirdly, the politics of both the Franco-British alliance and the closing months of the Third Republic require further attention. In this respect there are encouraging signs in, for example, the renaissance in France of the scholarly political biography – so long a Cinderella of the French historical genre – and the production of specialist monographs on the French political parties.[110] Despite progress in these directions, however, the gaps that remain are important. There is still no biography of Chautemps, thrice prime minister in the 1930s and a key figure in resolving the French to explore armistice terms in 1940, nor of Pierre Cot and Guy La Chambre, the air ministers between 1936 and 1940; still no book on one of France's two main conservative parties, the Democratic Alliance.

Finally, it may be asked whether the fall of France merits inclusion as a 'decisive campaign' of the Second World War? An answer can be provided at several levels. Militarily, despite a good measure of recovery under the Fifth Republic, France has never been able fully to regain the status or strength that were swept away in 1940. In this sense, de Gaulle was only partially correct when he courageously prophesied that France had lost the battle but had not lost the war. Militarily, too, the 1940 campaign sounded the death knell of British as well as French hopes that the overthrow of Germany could be accomplished without resort to the giants waiting in the wings – the USA and the Soviet Union.[111] For Hitler, also, the fall of France had decisive repercussions, since it deluded him and most of his senior commanders into the disastrous overestimation of Wehrmacht power that encouraged them to turn against Russia the following Summer. Hitler, it would appear, became ensnared in an illusion of his own invincibility after 1940, so surprised and delighted was he at the speed of the Allied collapse. But he, just like the French leaders gathered around Gamelin's lunch table in October 1939, had overestimated the significance of the 'Franco-German duel' in this war. No longer did the familiar contest between these two gladiatorial adversaries hold the world's destiny in its grip: the world outside their arena had changed in ways that neither had sufficiently noticed. 1940 was not so much the final act of a change in a *European* balance of power as it was the prelude to a bigger change in the whole world order.[112]

Acknowledgements

The author is indebted to the University of Southampton for special leave and to Yale University for electing him to a John M. Olin postdoctoral fellowship for 1988–89, which facilitated the work for this article. He is likewise grateful to Generals Delmas and Bassac along with their staff at the Service Historique de l'Armée de Terre (SHAT), and to General Robineau and his colleagues at the Service Historique de l'Armée de l'Air (SHAA), Vincennes, France. Thanks are owing also to Jean Vanwelkenhuyzen, Jean Stengers and Jacques Willequet for helping locate Belgian sources bearing on 1940, and to Mlle. F. Peemans, archivist at the Ministère des Affaires Etrangères et du Commerce Extérieure, Brussels.

Notes

1   Alexander Werth, *The Last Days of Paris: A Journalist's Diary* (London: Hamish Hamilton, 1940), p. 40.

2   Marc Bloch, *L'Etrange Défaite: Témoignage écrit en 1940* (Paris: Edns. Francs-Tireur, 1946); *Strange Defeat: A Statement of Evidence Written in 1940* (English-language ed. trans. Gerald Hopkins, New York: W.W. Norton, 1968).

3   Pétain's Vichy regime conducted its own show trial of six former leaders of the Third Republic at the town of Riom between late 1940 and Spring 1942. See Henri Michel, *Le Procès de Riom* (Paris: Albin Michel, 1979). After the war the Fourth Republic conducted an inquiry: see *Commission d'Enquête parlementaire sur les évènements survenus en France de 1933 à 1945* (Paris: Presses Universitaires de France, 1951–52, 2 vols. of report; 9 vols. of testimony and annexed documentation).

4   John C. Cairns, 'Some Recent Historians and the "Strange Defeat" of 1940', *Journal of Modern History* 46 (March 1974), 60–85 (quote from p. 84).

5   For example, Col. Paul de Villelume, *Journal d'une Défaite. Août 1939–juillet 1940* (Paris: Fayard, 1976); Sir John R. Colville, *The Fringes of Power: Downing Street Diaries, 1939–1955* (London: Hodder & Stoughton, 1985); Charles de Gaulle, *Lettres, Notes et Carnets. Tome II: 1919–juin 1940* (Paris: Plon, 1980); Jacques Rueff, *De l'Aube au Crépuscule* (Paris: Plon, 1977); Jean Daridan, *Le Chemin de la Défaite, 1938–1940* (Paris: Plon, 1980); Charles Rist, *Une Saison Gâtée* (Paris: Fayard, 1984); Hervé Alphand, *L'Etonnement d'être: Journal, 1939–1973* (Paris: Fayard, 1977); Michel Debré, *Mémoires. Tome I: Trois Républiques pour une France* (Paris: Plon, 1985); Charles Ritchie, *The Siren Years: A Canadian Diplomat Abroad, 1937–1945* (Toronto: Macmillan of Canada, 1974 and Laurentian Library, 1977); Orville H. Bullitt, *For the President: Personal and Secret: Correspondence between Franklin D. Roosevelt and William C. Bullitt* [US ambassador to France, 1936–40] (London: André Deutsch, 1973); Miles Reid, *Last on the List* (London: Leo Cooper, 1974).

6   Cairns, 'Some Recent Historians', 67–71. French journalists, however, still remain encamped in force in the field of recent French history. See, for example, Claude Paillat, *Dossiers Secrets de la France Contemporaine* (Paris: Laffont, 7 vols., 1979–86); Henri Amouroux, *La Grande Histoire des Français sous l'Occupation, 1939–1945* (Paris: Fayard, 6 vols., 1977–83); see Rémy (pseud. of Gilbert Renault-Roulier), *Chronique d'une Guerre Perdue* (Paris: France-Empire, 5 vols., 1979–82) [Rémy was an important wartime France Libre agent and Resistance leader].

7   The works were John Williams, *The Ides of May: The Defeat of France, May–June 1940* (London: Constable, 1968); Alistair A. Horne, *To Lose a Battle: France 1940* (London: Macmillan, 1969); Guy Chapman, *Why France Collapsed* (London: Collins, 1968); William L. Shirer, *The Collapse of the Third Republic: An Inquiry into the Fall of France in 1940* (New York: Simon & Schuster, 1969).

8   Cairns, 'Some Recent Historians', 63; for a comparison between British and French record-conservation and record-access policies and practices see Julia G.A. Sheppard, '"Vive la différence!": An Outsider's View of French Archives', *Archives: The Journal of the British Records Association* 14, No. 63 (Spring 1980).

9   Cairns, 'Some Recent Historians', 73.

10 Gen. Charles Christienne, 'La R.A.F. dans la bataille de France au travers des rapports Vuillemin de juillet 1940' in *Recueil d'articles et études (1981–1983)* (Vincennes: Service Historique de l'Armée de l'Air, 1987), pp. 313–32. (The article began as a paper under the same title, delivered to the Franco-British historians' colloquium on 'Relations between France and Great Britain from 1935 to 1940', fifth meeting: 'La rupture franco-britannique, mai–juillet 1940', London, 14–16 Dec. 1983.) 'It is said', wrote Christienne,

> that Air Chief Marshal Barratt [commander of Britain's Advanced Air Striking Force in France in 1940], an outspoken defender of French standpoints moreover, observed one day 'that the R.A.F. could not win the war if the French infantry had lost it'. I have not been able to prove the veracity of the remark but I find myself compelled to admit its force. . . . Today, with the passage of time, problems take on a different light and one cannot but offer thanks that Fighter Command managed to convince the politicians not to make it a useless sacrifice in a hopeless cause.
>
> (ibid., pp. 328, 330)

11 Cairns, 'Some Recent Historians', 69 (n.33).

12 See idem, 'Along the Road back to France, 1940', *American Historical Review* 64 (April 1959), 583–603.

13 These included Gen. Jean Delmas, head of the SHAT, 1978–86; General Christienne (SHAA head, 1974–85) and his successor, Gen. Lucien Robineau, as well as the chiefs of the SHAT *section d'études* from the late 1970s to the mid-1980s, Cols. Michel Turlotte and Henry Dutailly – to all of whom I am grateful for co-operation and scholarly comradeship over many years.

14 See Henri Dubief, *Le Déclin de la Troisième, 1929–1938* and Jean-Pierre Azéma, *De Munich à la Libération, 1938–1944* (Paris: Seuil, 1979, 1980) now in English translation as volumes in the *Cambridge History of Modern France* (Cambridge: Cambridge University Press, 1984–86); René Rémond, *Histoire de France. Tome 6: Notre Siècle, 1918–1988* (Paris: Fayard, 1988); Jean Doise and Maurice Vaisse, *Politique Etrangère de la France, 1871–1969: Diplomatie et Outil Militaire* (Paris: Imprimerie Nationale, 1987); *Pour Une Histoire Politique* sous la dir. de René Rémond (Paris: Seuil, 1988).

The IHTP, directed by Professor François Bédarida, is located at 44 rue de l'amiral Mouchez, 75014 Paris, and produces the quarterly journal *Vingtième Siècle* (launched 1985). The CHDGM has been reorganised as the Institut d'Histoire des Conflits Contemporains, under Professor Guy Pédroncini of the Sorbonne. Its periodical, the *Revue d'Histoire de la 2e Guerre Mondiale* was founded in 1951 and renamed, in 1983, the *Revue d'Histoire de la 2e Guerre Mondiale et des Conflits Contemporains*.

15 Jeffery A. Gunsburg, *Divided and Conquered: The French High Command and the Defeat of the West, 1940* (Westport, CT: Greenwood Press, 1979).

16 Cairns, 'Some Recent Historians', 64, n.18. Cairns's other relevant publications include 'International Politics and the Military Mind: The Case of the French Republic, 1911–1914' *Journal of Modern History* 25 (Sept. 1953), 272–85; 'Great Britain and the Fall of France: A Study in Allied Disunity', *Journal of Modern History* 27 (Dec. 1955), 365–409; 'A Nation of Shopkeepers in Search of a Suitable France', *American Historical Review* 79 (1974), 710–43.

17 Cairns, 'Some Recent Historians', 75. See the remark by Richard D. Challener ('The Third Republic and the Generals: The Gravediggers Revisited', in Harry Coles [ed.], *Total War and Cold War. Problems in civilian control of the military* [Columbus, OH: Ohio State University Press, 1962] pp. 91–107) that: 'In the memoirs of General Weygand . . . France emerges as the advance guard of a world coalition which had not as yet fully mobilized' (p. 92). The same line was argued earlier in respect of Germany's initial conquest of Poland, by the head of France's air liaison mission in Warsaw in 1939, General Jules Armengaud, who tried to comfort the defeated Poles, saying: 'The battle of Poland was only the first battle of the war. . . . The Polish army was only the advance guard of the armies of the coalition' (*Batailles Politiques et Militaires sur L'Europe: Témoignages, 1932–1940* (Paris: Editions du Myrte, 1948) pp. 133, 138).

18 Cairns, 'Some Recent Historians', 75–6.

19 Jeffery A. Gunsburg, 'General Maurice-Gustave Gamelin, 1872–1958' in Patrick Hutton (ed.), *Historical Dictionary of the Third Republic* (Westport, CT: Greenwood Press, 2 vols., 1986), I, pp. 412–13.

20 Idem, *Divided and Conquered, passim*.

21 See Robert J. Young, *In Command of France: French Foreign Policy and Military Planning, 1933–1940* (Cambridge, MA: Harvard University Press, 1978). The influence of the 'revisionist' case for 1930s France is generally visible in such modern syntheses as Philip M.H. Bell, *The Origins of the Second World War in Europe* (London: Longman, 1986), pp. 90–100, 135–8, 166–74, 208–12, 233–4; Paul M. Kennedy, *The Rise and Fall of the Great Powers: Economic Change and Military Conflict from 1500 to 2000* (London: Unwin Hyman, 1988), pp. 310–15, 335–9. See also Robert J. Young, 'A.J.P. Taylor and the Problem with France' in Gordon Martel (ed.), *The Origins of the Second World War Reconsidered: The A.J.P. Taylor Debate after Twenty-five Years* (London: Allen & Unwin, 1986), pp. 97–118.

22 Vivian Rowe, *The Great Wall of France: The Triumph of the Maginot Line* (London: Putnam, 1959), p. 94.

23 See Susan Bindoff Butterworth, 'Daladier and the Munich Crisis: A Reappraisal' *Journal of Contemporary History* 9 (July 1974), 191–216; René Rémond, Janine Bourdin (eds.), *Edouard Daladier: chef de gouvernement* and *La France et les Français en 1938–39* (Paris: Fondation Nationale des Sciences Politiques, respectively 1977, 1979); J. Kim Munholland, 'The Daladier Government and the "Red Scare" of 1938–1940', in John F. Sweets (ed.), *Proceeding of the Tenth Annual Meeting of the Western Society for French History*, 14–16 Oct. 1982 (Lawrence, KA: The Regents' Press of the University of Kansas 1984), pp. 495–506; idem, 'Between Popular Front and Vichy: the Decree

Laws of the Daladier ministry, 1938–40', unpublished paper read at the Fourteenth annual meeting of the Western Society for French History, Baltimore, MD, 19–22 Nov. 1986. A full reassessment of Daladier awaits the forthcoming book, *Edouard Daladier et la sécurité de la France*, by Elizabeth du Réau of the Université du Maine, Le Mans.

24   See Jean Vanwelkenhuyzen, *Neutralité armée: la politique militaire de la Belgique pendant la drôle de guerre* (Brussels: La Renaissance du Livre, 1979); idem, *Les Avertissements qui venaient de Berlin, 1939–1940* (Paris and Gembloux: Duculot, 1983); idem., 'L'Alerte du 10 janvier 1940. Les documents de Mechelen-sur-Meuse', *Revue d'Histoire de la 2e Guerre Mondiale* 3, 12 (Sept. 1953), 33–54; Jean Stengers, *Léopold III et le Gouvernement: aux origines de la Question Royale belge* (Paris and Gembloux: Duculot, 1980); Jonathan E. Helmreich, *Belgium and Europe: A Study in Small Power Diplomacy* (The Hague: Mouton, 1976). Cf. Daniel H. Thomas, *The Guarantee of Belgian Independence and Neutrality in European Diplomacy, 1830s-1930s* (Kingston, RI: D.H. Thomas Publishing, 1986), pp. 553–98.

25   Louis de Jong, *Het Koninkrijk der Nederlanden in de tweede wereldoorlog* ('s-Gravenhage: Martinus Nijhoff for the Rijksinstituut voor Oorlogsdocumentatie, 1969–86, vols. 1–11 c).

26   See Vanwelkenhuyzen, *Les Avertissements, passim.*

27   André Ausems, 'The Netherlands Military Intelligence Summaries 1939–40 and the Defeat in the Blitzkrieg of May 1940', *Military Affairs* 50, 4 (Oct. 1986), 190–99; idem., 'Ten Days in May: The Netherlands and Fall Gelb', unpublished Master's dissertation, San Diego State University, 1983.

28   Cairns, 'Some Recent Historians', 67.

29   This convened major international history colloquia, holds research seminars at the Université de Paris I (Panthéon-Sorbonne) and sponsors the important periodical, *Relations Internationales*, founded in 1972.

30   Jean-Baptiste Duroselle, *Politique Etrangère de la France, 1871–1969: La Décadence, 1932–1939* (Paris: Imprimerie Nationale, 1979); idem, *L'Abîme, 1939–1945* (Paris: Imprimerie Nationale, 1983).

31   Williamson Murray, *The Change in the European Balance of Power, 1938–1939: The Path to Ruin* (Princeton, NJ: Princeton University Press, 1984). See its critical appraisal by Wesley K. Wark, 'Williamson Murray's Wars, A Review Essay', *Intelligence and National Security* 1, No.3 (Sept. 1986), 472–81.

32   Murray has entire chapters on German strategic problems (pp. 3–49) and British (50–92), analysing political structures, economic constraints and rearmament. France, however, is relegated to a survey section on 'The Rest of Europe' and allotted barely 18 pages (93–110). Further, though still limited, attention to French perspectives occurs at pp. 162–9, 190–3, 197–8, 211–12, 241–3, 262–3, 274–8, 348–51, 364–5. A weakness throughout is the tendency to evaluate French policy according to British sources from the 1930s. More satisfying are the essays in *La Puissance en Europe, 1938–1940*, sous la dir. de René Girault et Robert Frank (Paris: Publications de la Sorbonne, 1984).

33   See Anthony P. Adamthwaite, *France and the Coming of the Second World War* (London: Frank Cass, 1977), pp. 224–5; also the special issue of the *Revue des Etudes Slaves* (1979), devoted to a fortieth anniversary assessment of 'La France et la crise de Munich'.

34   Cabinet Gamelin – Journal de Marche, 9 Oct. 1939, Fonds Gamelin 1K 224 Carton 9, SHAT. I am indebted to M. Pierre Uhrich, Lt. Col. Jacques Uhrich and the late M. Paul Gamelin for permission to use the Gamelin archives.

35 General Maurice Gamelin, *Servir* (Paris: Plon, 3 vols., 1946–7), III: *La guerre: Septembre 1939–19 Mai 1940*, p. 115; L'Ambassade de Belgique en France. L'Attaché militaire et de l'Air, No. 1 O.D./5836/210 c: le Colonel Maurice Delvoie au Lieutenant-Général . . . chef d'état-major général de l'armée, 2e section: 21 Oct. 1939 (Archives du Ministère des Affaires Etrangères et du Commerce Extérieure, Brussels: microfilmed copy of the dispatches of Belgian military attaché in France, 1937–39).

36 See Fonds Gamelin 1K 224, Carton 7, Dossier labelled 'Le Problème des Effectifs, 1939–40' sub-dossier III, 'Le Plan de Cinq Mois', SHAT; Minart, II, pp. 51–78; Gamelin, *Servir*, III, pp. 228–44.

37 General Gaston Billotte, 'Etude sur l'emploi des chars', No.3748 S/3, 6 Dec. 1939 [sent to Gamelin and Georges], Archives Daladier 4 DA 7, Dossier 1, sub-dossier a, FNSP; see Gamelin, *Servir*, III, pp. 275–81.

38 François Bédarida, *La Stratégie secrète de la drôle de guerre. La Conseil Suprême interallié, septembre 1939—avril 1940* (Paris: Centre Nationale de la Recherche Scientifique, 1979), p. 553.

39 See Brian Bond and Martin S. Alexander, 'Liddell Hart and De Gaulle: The Doctrines of Limited Liability and Mobile Defense', in Peter Paret (ed.), *Makers of Modern Strategy: From Machiavelli to the Nuclear Age* (Princeton, NJ: Princeton University Press, 1986), pp. 598–623. Cf. Bradford A. Lee, 'Strategy, Arms and the Collapse of France, 1930–40', in R.T.B. Langhorne (ed.), *Diplomacy and Intelligence during the Second World War: Essays in Honour of F.H. Hinsley* (Cambridge: Cambridge University Press, 1985), pp. 43–67.

40 For Anglo-French relations see Eleanor Gates, *End of the Affair: The Collapse of the Anglo-French Alliance, 1939–40* (London: Allen & Unwin, 1981); Nicholas Rostow, *Anglo-French Relations, 1934–36* (London: Macmillan, 1984); Philip M.H. Bell, *A Certain Eventuality: Britain and the Fall of France* (Farnborough: Saxon House, 1974); on Belgian diplomacy, Fernand Vanlangenhove, *L'élaboration de la politique étrangère de la Belgique entre les deux guerres mondiales* (Gembloux: Duculot, 1980).

41 See recent variations on this theme in Murray, pp. 347–53, 361, 369.

42 See Harold C. Deutsch, *The Conspiracy against Hitler in the Twilight War* (Minneapolis, MN: University of Minnesota Press, 1968).

43 Col. Jacques Minart, *P.C. Vincennes: Secteur 4* (Paris: Berger-Levrault, 2 vols., 1945), I, p. 48. See Brian J. Bond (ed.), *Chief of Staff: The Diaries of Lieutenant-General Sir Henry Pownall* (London: Leo Cooper, 1972; Hamden, CT: Archon Books, 1973, 2 vols.), I, pp. 249, 279, 283. The *poilu's* experience emerges in Robert Felsenhardt, *1939–40 avec le 18e corps d'armée* (Paris: Editions La Tête de Feuilles, 1973); Georges Sadoul, *Journal de Guerre, 2 septembre 1939–20 juillet 1940* (Paris: Les Editeurs français réunis, 1977); Jean-Paul Sartre, *Carnets de la drôle de guerre: novembre 1939 – mars 1940* (Paris: Gallimard, 1983), English edn., *The War Diaries of Jean-Paul Sartre: November 1939 – March 1940* (London: Verso, 1984), trans. Quintin Hoare.

44 Gamelin – Journal, 18 Sept. 1939, 1 K 224/9, SHAT.

45 The formations visited and subordinate commanders briefed are listed in ibid., 27 Sept., 7 Oct., 15–16 Oct. 1939. The later missions were to the French 7th, 1st and 9th armies and the BEF (8–9 March 1940), and to the French 2nd and 3rd armies (22 March 1940). See Colonel Roderick Macleod, Denis Kelly (eds.), *The Ironside Diaries, 1937–1940* (London: Constable, 1962), pp. 231–3; Gamelin, *Servir*, III, pp. 116–17, 292.

46 Minart, I, p. 77.

47   Gamelin, *Servir*, I: *Les Armée Françaises de 1940*, pp. 15–16; III, pp. 405, 414–19, 427–33; Minart, II, pp. 176–7, 189–92.

48   Quoted in Maurice Percheron, *Gamelin* (Paris: Editions Documentales Françaises, 1939), p. 27.

49   Cairns, 'Some Recent Historians', 81.

50   Douglas Porch, 'French Intelligence and the Fall of France, 1931–1940', *Intelligence and National Security*, 4, 1 (Jan. 1989), 28–58 (quote from p. 45). See also Jeffery A. Gunsburg, 'Coupable ou non? Le rôle du général Gamelin dans la défaite de 1940', *Revue Historique des Armées*, 4 (1979), 145–63; Martin S. Alexander, 'Soldiers and Socialists: The French Officer Corps and Leftist Government, 1935–7' in Martin S. Alexander and Helen Graham (eds.), *The French and Spanish Popular Fronts: Comparative Perspectives* (Cambridge: Cambridge University Press, 1989), pp. 62–78. A full appraisal of Gamelin will occur in Martin S. Alexander, *The Republic in Danger: Maurice Gamelin, The Defence of France and the Politics of French Rearmament. 1933–1940* (Cambridge: Cambridge University Press, forthcoming).

51   See Gamelin – Journal, 9, 10, 14, 21 Sept. 1939, 7 Oct. 1939; *Servir*, I, pp. 294–6; III, pp. 61–4, 88–91, 94–7, 101–5; Pierre Le Goyet, *Le Mystère Gamelin* (Paris: Presses de la Cité, 1976), pp. 235–9.

52   Gamelin – Journal, 9 Oct. 1939.

53   Commission du Commerce et de l'Industrie: Chambre des Députés. Audience de M.F. Gentin, ministre, le 18 Octobre 1939: procès-verbal, pp. 13–14 (Archives de l'Assemblée Nationale, Palais Bourbon, Paris).

54   Gamelin – Journal, 12 Sept., 18 Sept. 1939. Cf. Gamelin, *Servir*, I, pp. 215–20; III, pp. 65–8, 224–8; Minart, II, pp. 41–9.

55   Présidence du Conseil: 'Directives de la politique économique française: Programmes de production et d'achat pour 1940', 24 Feb. 1940, pp. 2–4, Archives Edouard Daladier, Fondation Nationale des Sciences Politiques, Paris: 3 DA 5, Dossier 2, sub-dossier c.

56   Gamelin – Journal, 11 March 1940; cf. *Servir*, III, p. 125.

57   See Bond, *Chief of Staff*, I, p. 292 (Pownall diary, 21 March 1940); Sir John R. Colville, *Man of Valour: The Life of Field-Marshal the Viscount Gort* (London: Collins, 1972), pp. 170–80.

58   See Robert J. Young, 'La guerre de longue durée: some reflections on French strategy and diplomacy in the 1930s', in Adrian Preston (ed.), *General Staffs and Diplomacy before the Second World War*, (Totowa, NJ and London: Croom Helm, 1978), pp. 41–64.

59   Le Goyet, pp. 18–38; General Maurice Gamelin, *Manoeuvre et Victoire de la Marne* (Paris: Grasset, 1954); René Gustave Nobécourt, 'Gamelin et la bataille de la Marne (septembre 1914)', *Bulletin de la Société d'Histoire de Rouen*, 10 Nov. 1973, 181–7; idem, 'Gamelin, 1914–1918' (unpublished typescript consulted through the generosity of M. Nobécourt).

60   Especially illuminating for French perspectives on these projects are, Charles O. Richardson, 'French Plans for Allied Attacks on the Caucasus Oil Fields, January–April 1940', *French Historical Studies* 8, No.1 (Spring 1973), 130–56; R.A.C. Parker, 'Britain, France and Scandinavia, 1939–40', *History* 61 (1976), 369–87; Jukka Nevakivi, *The Appeal that was Never Made: The Allies, Scandinavia and the Finnish Winter War, 1939–1940* (London: Hurst, 1976); Patrice Buffotot, 'Le projet de bombardement des pétroles soviétiques du Caucase en 1940', *Revue Historique des Armées* No.4 (1979); François Kersaudy, *Stratèges et Norvège, 1940: Les Jeux de la guerre et du hasard*

(Paris: Hachette, 1977); Duroselle, *L'Abîme*, pp. 87–94, 108–16; Villelume, pp. 90–104, 114 ff., 262–327; Martin Gilbert, *Winston S. Churchill: Finest Hour, 1939-1941* (London: Heinemann, 1984); Ronald Wheatley, 'La guerre russo-finlandaise, les plans d'intervention alliés et les relations britanniques avec la Russie'; René Girault, 'Les relations franco-soviétiques après septembre 1939'; François Bédarida, 'Convergences et divergences stratégiques franco-britanniques'; Philippe Masson, 'La préparation de la campagne de Finlande', all in *Français et Britanniques dans la drôle de guerre: Actes du colloque franco-britannique tenu à Paris du 8 au 12 décembre 1975* (Paris: Centre National de la Recherche Scientifique, 1979), pp. 245–61, 263–79, 359–77, 583–7.

61 A.J. Liebling (Paris correspondent for *The New Yorker, 1939–40*), 'Paris Postscript', *The New Yorker Book of War Pieces: London 1939 to Hiroshima 1945* (New York: Schocken, 1988 [reprint of 1947 original]), pp. 39–53 (quote from p. 49). See Gamelin – Journal, 15 Sep., 20 Sep., 22 Sep. 1939; Armengaud p. 201; Bond, *Chief of Staff* I, pp. 268–72, 293.

62 Bell, *Origins*, pp. 269, 271–2.

63 Gamelin – Journal, 19 Sep. 1939, 3 Oct. 1939. Cf. Bullitt, p. 373; Jean-Louis Crémieux-Brilhac, 'L'opinion publique française, l'Angleterre et la guerre (septembre 1939–juin 1940)'; Philip M.H. Bell, 'L'évolution de l'opinion publique anglaise à propos de la guerre et de l'alliance avec la France (septembre 1939–mai 1940)'; Guy Rossi-Landi, 'Le pacifisme en France (1939–1940)'; Philippe Masson, 'Moral et propagande', all in *Français et Britanniques dans la drôle de guerre*, pp. 1–79, 123–51, 163–71; Guy Rossi-Landi, *La Drôle de Guerre: la vie politique en France, 2 septembre 1939–10 mai 1940* (Paris: Pedone, 1971).

64 See Gamelin – Journal, 14 Sept. 1939, 18 Oct. 1939, 11 March 1940.

65 See John Harvey (ed.), *The Diplomatic Diaries of Oliver Harvey, 1937–1940* (New York: St. Martin's Press, 1971), pp. 339–40; Paillat, *Dossiers Secrets: La Guerre Immobile*, pp. 411–43.

66 See Anatole de Monzie, *Ci-devant* (Paris: Flammarion, 1941), pp. 173, 176–7, 182–3, 188–9, 190–92, 194–5, 198, 200–201, 203–7; Gamelin, *Servir* III, pp. 187–205, 287–90.

67 Challener, p. 96; cf. Harvey, pp. 341–2; Minart, I, pp. 167–89.

68 Gamelin – Journal, 3–4 April 1940; *Servir*, III, pp. 292–311. On the CHEDN, established as an inter-service college for senior officers and civil servants by Daladier in 1936, see Eugenia C. Kiesling, 'A Staff College for the Nation-in-Arms: The Collège des Hautes Etudes de Défense Nationale, 1936–1939' (unpublished Ph.D. dissertation, Stanford University, 1988).

69 Gamelin – Journal, 8, 9, 10 April 1940; *Servir*, III, pp. 312–18; Minart, I, pp. 189–99; Le Goyet, pp. 257–8; Harvey, pp. 346–8.

70 Gamelin, *Servir*, III, pp. 312–14; Gamelin – Journal, 31 March 1940; Paul Paillole, *Notre Espion chez Hitler* (Paris: Laffont, 1985), pp. 173–81; Minart, I, pp. 139–49; Porch, 48–9.

71 Minart, I, p. 225. Cf. Armengaud, p. 205.

72 Gamelin – Journal, 10 April 1940; see Monzie, p. 209; Gamelin, *Servir*, III, pp. 315–30; Le Goyet, pp. 271–4, 292–7; Bédarida, *Stratégie Secrète, passim*.

73 Minart, I, p. 229.

74 See Harvey, pp. 348–9; Pertinax (pseud. Of André Géraud), *Les Fossoyeurs: Défaite militaire de la France. Armistice. Contre-révolution* (New York: Editions de la Maison Française, 1943: 2 vols.), I, pp. 192–233.

75 Gamelin – Journal, 12 April 1940.

76   See Philip C.F. Bankwitz, *Maxime Weygand and Civil-Military Relations in Modern France* (Cambridge, MA: Harvard University Press, 1967), pp. 95–105, 165–7.

77   Jules Romains, *Sept Mystères du Destin de L'Europe* (New York: Editions de la Maison Française, 1940), pp. 99–100. Cf. A.J. Liebling, *The Road back to Paris* (New York: Paragon House, 1988), pp. 25–33.

78   Porch, 52.

79   Gamelin – Journal, 12 April 1940; *Servir*, III, pp. 336–9.

80   Ibid.; on the origins of Gamelin's political friendships and alliances see *Servir*, III (*Le Prologue du Drame, 1930 – Août 1939*), pp. xxvii–xxx.

81   Gamelin – Journal, 13 April 1940; *Servir*, II, pp. 3–4; III, pp. 338–52; Paul Baudouin, *Neuf Mois au gouvernement, avril–décembre 1940* (Paris: La Table Ronde, 1948), pp. 22–34; translated as *The Private Diaries of Paul Baudouin, March 1940–January 1941* (London: 1948).

82   Harvey, pp. 349–50.

83   Gamelin – Journal, 16 April 1940; *Servir*, III, pp. 352–5. Cf. Minart, I, pp. 191–210; Pertinax, I, pp. 212–17, 229–38; Le Goyet, pp. 258–9.

84   See de Monzie, p. 216; Bond, *Chief of Staff*, I, pp. 296–303; Colville, *Fringes*, pp. 96–104.

85   Harvey, p. 354; Colville, *Fringes*, pp. 105–15; Bond, *Chief of Staff*, I, pp. 304–5; Gamelin, *Servir*, III, pp. 356–79.

86   Gamelin – Journal, 3 May; cf. ibid., 30 April 1940: 'Au cours de la nuit, plusieurs coups de téléphone annoncent de trés bonne source l'attaque allemande à l'ouest pour le 1er ou le 2 mai'. See *Servir*, III, pp. 380–82; Paillole, p. 183 (which describes Allied consternation when ULTRA fell silent on 2 May, the Germans having abruptly changed their ENIGMA settings; Bletchley broke back into the new codes on 22 May but by then the débâcle in France was well under way). See also General Louis Rivet [chief of French secret intelligence, 1934–40] 'Le camp allemand dans la fièvre des alertes (1939–1940)', *Revue de Défense Nationale RDN*, 5e année, IX (juillet 1949), 33–48; idem, 'Etions-nous renseignés en mai 1940?', Part 1, *RDN* 6e année, X (juin 1950), 636–48, Part II, *RDN*, 6e année, XI (juillet 1950), 24–39; Gerd Brausch, 'Sedan 1940: Deuxième Bureau und strategische Überraschung', *Militärgeschichtliche Mitteilungen* 2 (1967), 15–92; General Maurice-Henri Gauché, *Le Deuxième Bureau au Travail* (Paris: Amiot-Dumont, 1953), pp. 206–13.

87   De Monzie, pp. 218–19; Harvey, p. 355.

88   Gamelin – Journal, 9 May 1940; cf. *Servir*, III, pp. 382–3; Pertinax, I, pp. 238–9; Paul Reynaud, *La France a sauvé L'Europe* (Paris: Flammarion, 1947, 2 vols.), II, pp. 22–43, 51–4; Le Goyet, pp. 300–301.

89   Daladier, letter dated 20 May 1966 in response to Colonel Adolphe Goutard's article, 'La surprise du 10 mai', *Revue de Paris*, 10 May 1966, in Archives Daladier, 4 DA 7 Dossier I, sub-dossier a, FNSP.

90   Gamelin, *Servir*, I, pp. 6–8; III, pp. 427–34; Gamelin – Journal, 19 May 1940; Minart, II, pp. 183–98; Pertinax, I, pp. 95–6. On the question of the extent of Weygand's powers and whether they extended (as Gamelin's had not) to command of all French naval and air forces as well as the armies, see Colonel Robert Villatte, 'Le changement de commandement de mai 1940', *Revue d'Histoire de la 2e Guerre Mondiale* II, 5 (Jan. 1952), 27–36; André Reussner, 'La réorganisation du Haut Commandement au mois de mai 1940', ibid. III, 10–11 (June 1953), 49–59.

91   Gamelin, *Servir*, III, p. 436. See Bankwitz, *Weygand and Civil-Military Relations*, pp. 290–96, 328–37; idem, 'Maxime Weygand and the Fall of France: A Study in Civil-Military Relations', *Journal of Modern History* 31 (Sept. 1959), 225–42.

92   Bankwitz, *Weygand and Civil-Military Relations*, pp. 296–305; Pertinax, I, pp. 258–70.

93   Minart, II, pp. 196–7; Bankwitz, *Weygand and Civil-Military* Relations, pp. 299–300, 312.

94   De Monzie, p. 231; cf. Harvey, pp. 360–68, 372–3; Colville, *Fringes*, pp. 132–44, 151–68; Henri Michel, *La Défaite de la France. Septembre 1939–Juin 1940* (Paris: Presses Universitaires de France, 1980), pp. 96–101, 106–17.

95   Cairns, 'Some Recent Historians', 76.

96   Colonel William Fraser, letter to his wife, 17 Sept. 1939. I am indebted to Colonel Fraser's son, General Sir David Fraser, for permission to consult this correspondence.

97   See, for example, the arrangements made from 1938 onwards to replace French imports of high-grade coal from Germany with British supplies in the event of war: de Monzie, pp. 67–8, 93, 124–5, 139, 178–9, 196–8, 200, 208. Also Robert Frankenstein, 'Le financement français de la guerre et les accords avec les Britanniques, 1939–40' and L.S. Pressnell, 'Les finances de guerre britanniques et la coopération économique franco-britannique en 1939 et 1940', in *Français et Britanniques*, pp. 461–87, 489–510.

98   See Alphand, pp. 25–39; Jean Monnet, *Mémoires* (Paris: Fayard, 19–76), pp. 13–36, 59–89, 137–78 (English edn., trans. Richard Mayne, *Memoirs* [London: Collins, 1978]); Lord [Arthur] Salter, *Memoirs of a Public Servant* (London: Faber & Faber, n.d.), pp. 254–67; John McVickar Haight, *American Aid to France, 1938–1940* (New York: Athenaeum, 1970); idem, 'Jean Monnet and the American Arsenal after the Beginning of the War', in Evelyn M. Acomb, Marvin L. Brown (eds.), *French Society and Culture since the Old Regime* (New York: Holt, Rinehart & Winston, 1966), pp. 269–83. A key part was played by Méric de Bellefon, commercial counsellor at the French embassy in London, in arranging the coal supplies mentioned above, as well as requisitioning and pooling of Franco-British merchant shipping. (See *Documents Diplomatiques Français, 1932–1939* [Paris: Imprimerie Nationale, 1963–85, two series], 2nd ser., XV, Docs. nos. 19, 39, 284, 399, 517.) For embryonic coordination of arms procurement see the documentation in the files of the French military attaché in London. EMA/2 Grande-Bretagne, cartons 7N 2815–19 (Sept. 1938 to Feb. 1940), SHAT; in Fonds Gamelin 1K 224 carton 7, Dossiers labelled 'Correspondance avec les Britanniques' and 'Problème des effectifs, 1939–40', SHAT; and in Archives Daladier, 3 DA 2 Dossier 3, sub-dossier c; 3 DA 5 Dossier 2, sub-dossier c; 4 DA 23 Dossier 1, sub-dossier b, FNSP.

99   See Williamson Murray, 'The German response to victory in Poland: a case study in professionalism', *Armed Forces and Society* 7, No.2 (Winter 1981), 285–98; idem, *Change*, pp. 338–40; Charles W. Sydnor, Jr., *Soldiers of Destruction. The SS Death's Head Division, 1933–1945* (Princeton, NJ: Princeton University Press, 1977), pp. 37–119; Colonel Henry Dutailly, *Les Problèmes de L'Armée de Terre Française, 1935–1939* (Paris: Imprimerie Nationale, 1980), pp. 175–204; Robert A. Doughty, *The Seeds of Disaster: The Development of French Army Doctrine, 1919–1939* (Hamden, CT: Archon Books, 1985); idem, 'De Gaulle's Concept of a Mobile, Professional Army: Genesis of French Defeat?', in Lloyd J. Matthews, Dale E. Brown (eds.), *The Parameters of War* (London and McLean, VA: Pergamon-Brasseys, 1987), pp. 243–56; De Fabribeckers, *La Campagne de L'Armée belge en 1940* (Brussels: Rossel, 1973).

100 See especially, John J. Mearsheimer, *Conventional Deterrence* (Ithaca, NY and London: Cornell University Press, 1983), pp. 67–133; Donald W. Alexander, 'Repercussions of the Breda Variant', *French Historical Studies* 8, No.3 (Spring 1974), 459–88.

101 Examples include Pierre Le Goyet and Jean Fussureau, *Calais: 1940* (Paris: Presses de la Cité, 1980); Brian Bond, *France and Belgium, 1939–1940* (London: Davis-Poynter,

1975; to be reprinted by Pergamon-Brasseys, 1990); Michael Glover, *The Fight for the Channel Ports, Calais to Brest 1940: A Study in Confusion* (London: Leo Cooper, 1985); Roy Macnab, *For Honour Alone: The cadets of Saumur in the defence of the Cavalry School, France 1940* (London: Hale, 1988); Paul Huard, *Le Colonel de Gaulle et ses blindés: Laon, 15–20 mai 1940* (Paris: Plon, 1980); General Sir David Fraser, *Alanbrooke* (London: Collins, 1982); Nigel Nicolson, *Alex: The life of Field-Marshal Earl Alexander of Tunis* (London: Weidenfeld & Nicolson, 1973); Nigel Hamilton, *Monty: The Making of a General, 1887–1942* (London: Hamish Hamilton, 1981); also the forthcoming biography of Field-Marshal Lord Ironside being written by Professor Wesley Wark of the University of Toronto.

102   Lt. Col. Charles de Cossé-Brissac, 'Combien de chars français contre combien de chars allemands le 10 mai 1940?', *RDN* (Juillet 1947), 75–89; R.H.S. Stolfi, 'Equipment for Victory in France in 1940' *History* 55 (Feb. 1970), 1–20.

103   Jeffery A. Gunsburg, 'L'Armée de L'Air versus the Luftwaffe, 1940', *Defence Update International* 45 (1984), 44–53; Herrick E. Chapman, 'Reshaping French Industrial Politics: Workers, Employers, State Officials and the struggle for control in the aircraft industry, 1928–1950' (unpublished Ph.D. dissertation, University of California, Berkeley, 1983; microform, edn., University Microfilms International, Ann Arbor, M1, 1984), pp. 345–63; Jean Truelle, 'La production aéronautique militaire française jusqu'en juin 1940', *Revue d'Histoire de la 2e Guerre Mondiale* 19e année, No.73 (Jan. 1969), 75–110; General Charles Christienne, 'L'industrie aéronautique française de septembre 1939 à juin 1940' in *Français et Britanniques*, pp. 389–410.

104   Gary D. Sheffield, 'Blitzkrieg and Attrition: Land Operations Europe, 1914–45', in Colin McInnes and G.D. Sheffield (eds.), *Warfare in The Twentieth Century: Theory and Practice* (London: Unwin Hyman, 1988), pp. 51–79 (quote from p. 69).

105   Some of these issues will doubtless be addressed in the forthcoming book on the battles for the Meuse crossings, 10–15 May 1940, by Colonel Robert A. Doughty, head of the military history department at the US Military Academy, West Point.

106   John Ferris, 'The British Army, Signals and Security in the Desert Campaign, 1940–1942' (revised typescript of a paper delivered at the Third US Army War College Conference on Intelligence and Military Operations, May 1988), 10–22; Robert A. Doughty, 'The French Armed Forces, 1918–40' in Williamson Murray, Allan R. Millett (eds.), *Military Effectiveness* (London: Unwin Hyman, 1988, 3 vols.) II, pp. 39–69; Anthony P. Adamthwaite, 'French Military Intelligence and the Coming of War, 1935–1939' in Christopher M. Andrew, Jeremy Noakes (eds.), *Intelligence and International Relations, 1900–1945* (Exeter: Exeter University Publications, 1987), pp. 191–208; Robert J. Young, 'French military intelligence and Nazi Germany, 1938–1939' in Ernest R. May (ed.), *Knowing One's Enemies: Intelligence Assessment before the Two World Wars* (Princeton, NJ: Princeton University Press, 1984), pp. 271–309;) Jean Stengers, 'Enigma, the French, the Poles and the British, 1931–1940' in Christopher M. Andrew, David Dilks (eds.), *The Missing Dimension: Governments and Intelligence Communities in the Twentieth Century* (London and Basingstoke: Macmillan, 1984), pp. 126–37; F.H. Hinsley (with E.E. Thomas, C.F.G. Ransom, R.C. Knight), *British Intelligence in the Second World War: Its Influence on Strategy and Operations* (London: HMSO, 1979–83, 3 vols.), I, pp. 89–158.

107   Minart, II, p. 103.

108   Pertinax, I, p. 92.

109   Minart, II, p. 79 (n. 3).

110   For example Fred Kupferman, *Laval* (Paris: Fayard, 1987); Serge Berstein, *Edouard Herriot ou la République en personne* (Paris: Fondation Nationale des Sciences Politiques,

1985); Marc Ferro, *Pétain* (Paris: Fayard, 1987); William D. Irvine, *French Conservatism in Crisis: The Republican Federation in the 1930s* (Baton Rouge, LA: Louisiana State University Press, 1979); Serge Berstein, *Histoire du Parti Radical* (Paris: Editions de la FNSP, 2 vols. 1980–82). See Thomas Ferenczi, 'Le retour du politique: La profession de foi d'une nouvelle génération d'historiens', *Le Monde* (18 Nov. 1988). A biography of Reynaud is currently being written by Julian Jackson of University College, Swansea.

111　See Maurice Matloff, 'Allied Strategy in Europe, 1939–1945' in Paret, pp. 677–702.

112　For the greater though still imperfect extent to which the changes and their consequences were grasped by Britain's leaders see David Reynolds, 'Churchill and the British "Decision" to Fight on in 1940: Right Policy, Wrong Reasons', in Langhorne, pp. 147–67; cf. Colville, *Fringes*, pp. 150–77; David Dilks, 'The Twilight War and the Fall of France: Chamberlain and Churchill in 1940' *Transactions of the Royal Historical Society*, 5th ser., 28 (1978), 61–86.

Chapter 2

Richard Overy

MOBILIZATION FOR TOTAL WAR IN GERMANY 1939–1941

I N JULY 1941 GENERAL THOMAS, head of the German armed forces economic staff, was invited to assess the chances of fulfilling the new aircraft programme which Goering and Milch had prepared for Hitler's approval. His views on the programme were pessimistic. The economy, he wrote, was completely overloaded with demands from the armed forces; all attempts to expand output much further by cutting back on civilian production would achieve very little; the economy was already close to full mobilization, further conversion 'will not bring anything more worthwhile for the armaments industry'.[1] Thomas calculated that 68 per cent of industrial labour worked on direct war contracts, and much of the rest was active in mining, transport and energy supply which was vital for wartime industry. He found it impossible to see where the extra capacity was going to come from.

It is difficult to reconcile this picture with the view that the German economy made only a limited commitment to war before 1942 at the earliest. Total mobilization in Germany, so the argument goes, was only phased in gradually, but deliberately, after the failure to defeat Russia; it became a full-scale commitment only with Goebbels' 'Total War' speech in 1943, and was not fully realised, according to a recent history of Germany's war economy, until 1944.[2] Was Thomas so ignorant of the government's intentions or so remote from economic reality to have misjudged altogether the nature of the German economy in the Summer of 1941? It is not very likely. Thomas was on the staff of Hitler's high command and was in constant touch with the heart of the war machine. He was also head of an elaborate network of inspectorates throughout Germany which gave him better access to what was happening in the factories and the workshops than anyone else in the administrative apparatus. His memorandum demonstrates that it had been the intention since the beginning of the war to convert the economy as fully as possible to military needs, and that by mid-1941 this ambition was close to fulfilment. It is the purpose of this paper to examine the origins and development of this strategy between 1939 and 1941; and to suggest a different way of explaining the large increases in armaments production during the later years of war.

The roots of a strategy of full economic mobilization can be found well before 1939. One of the most important lessons of the First World War for the German armed forces was the need to prepare thoroughly for the next. Germany, it was argued, should not be caught unprepared for war again, critically short of vital raw materials and war capacity, making up its wartime economic administration as it went along. The onset of rearmament after 1933 was accompanied by the building up of an armed forces economic organization designed to smother Germany with economic controls in the event of a major war and to prepare the economy in such a way that the transfer from peace to war would be a relatively smooth one. This required armament in depth, rather than width: in other words providing not just a stockpile of armaments, but the machinery, factory capacity, raw materials and labour which would be used to undertake large additional arms output once war had broken out.[3] All the evidence suggested that a future war between the major powers would be a long war of attrition again, with economic blockade and financial and industrial strength key factors in its prosecution. Hitler himself was haunted by the fear that Germany might fail the economic test as it had done in 1918.[4]

These considerations led Germany of necessity towards a strategy of total economic mobilization. The armed forces' policy of building a *Wehrwirtschaft* – a defence-based economy – was supported by the economic policies of the Nazi government. In 1935 Schacht was appointed Plenipotentiary for War Economy, coordinating civilian economic goals with those of the military where it was feasible to do so. After October 1936 this responsibility was taken over by Goering under the Second Four Year Plan. The Plan itself really makes no sense unless it is understood in terms of armament in depth, with its emphasis on raw materials, heavy industry and labour. Goering certainly thought that his responsibility was 'to prepare the German economy for total war,'[5] and to work out plans for the fullest use of civilian resources in wartime: 'the economy must be completely converted . . . No more place for printing presses, washing machines and the like, they must all make machine-tools'.[6] Before the outbreak of war the Four Year Plan authorized the Economics Ministry to begin a complete conversion plan for wartime, and established registers of labour so that in the event of war large numbers of female and less essential labour could be quickly converted to the war industries. In discussions throughout 1938 and 1939 full labour mobilization was seen as the key factor in Germany's economic mobilization: 'Female labour service in wartime is of decisive significance'.[7] The Plan also initiated new apprenticeship and retraining schemes, and undertook to place skilled labour, when it could, in vital industries. In March 1939 the army added its own voice by setting up a comprehensive study of labour questions in order to establish 'a unitary control over the supply of all labour capacity in peacetime and on mobilization'. The army's report stressed the necessity for better training, greater factory rationalization, 'and the fullest use of all labour resources to meet the prospective requirements of both the armed forces and the war economy.[8]

The object of the Four Year Plan was to set up a unified and centralized economic system which could provide through a heavy investment programme the necessary industrial base, or sub-structure, on which the superstructure of armaments output could be raised. In addition to material efforts, such a policy required preparing the population in peacetime for privations to come through cuts in living standards, and by cultivating 'the spiritual attitude of the people towards a *total war*'.[9] It also made it necessary to acquire, one way or another, the economic resources of central and eastern Europe to strengthen and deepen the German efforts at economic rearmament. As new areas were brought under German influence – Austria, the Sudetenland, Czechoslovakia – their economies were immediately brought under the Four Year Plan authority and co-ordinated with the military needs of the Reich.[10]

All of these policies were part of a long-war strategy designed, as has been argued elsewhere, to create a massive military machine for fighting the other major powers in the mid-1940s, after six or seven years of military build-up.[11] These plans were not the isolated aspirations of an anxious but ineffectual army staff, nor Goering's personal hobby horse. All the evidence on war preparations and military production plans confirms that the general expectation in Germany before 1939 was that any future war between the major powers (though not of course war against Poland alone), would be a total war from the start. The very nature of modern warfare made this imperative. War was now industrialized: tanks, aircraft, modern communications equipment, all required an industrial effort on a scale hitherto unknown. The German armed forces were obsessed with the need to be technically and materially advanced, professional to a fault.[12] By 1939 Thomas was able to compare Germany's rearmament effort with the levels of output achieved at the end of the First World War. To reach the higher levels of output required upon mobilization for war left no choice 'but to concentrate all economic resources on the strengthening of economic armament'.[13] It also needed time.

When war broke out in September 1939 the German economy was still in the transitional stage of building the economic sub-structure for major industrialized warfare. When it became clear that a general war had indeed arisen out of the Polish crisis the armed forces high command, on Hitler's instructions, announced a state of full mobilization on 3 September. The War Economy Decree was published the following day, enjoining 'every citizen to impose upon himself the necessary restrictions in living standards'.[14] On 9 September Goering published his first major policy statement on the economy, calling for 'the complete employment of the living and fighting power of the nation economically for the duration of the war';[15] a strategy to be carried out under the auspices of the Four Year Plan organization and its deputies and special commissioners, who constituted an economic 'cabinet'. During November and December Hitler, Goering and the military leaders discussed what form the war economy should take and the levels of mobilization necessary. The outcome was an unambiguous commitment expressed on 29 November in fresh guidelines 'for co-ordinating all efforts for increasing production for the armed forces'. 'The war', ran the decree, 'requires the greatest efforts in building up armaments. The High Command . . . recommends guidelines which have as their goal the strongest mobilization of all economic resources in the service of national defence'. All capacity and labour not concerned 'with goods essential for the war or for subsistence' was to be 'freed insofar as it can be put to work for strengthening armaments'.[16] When Thomas announced Goering's policy to a meeting of Reichsgruppe Industrie on the same day he called for maximum war output and sharp cutbacks in civilian production: 'today let the mistakes of the World War not be repeated . . .'.[17]

It is evident that Hitler himself was the inspiration behind the economic strategy worked out in the winter of 1939: 'The Führer has ordered that the conversion of the economy should be pursued with all energy', ran a report from the High Command in December. He argued that even if a quick victory could be achieved over France and Britain the economy should be converted on the assumption that a war of five or seven years' duration was likely.[18] Thomas reported Hitler's personal involvement in the plans for arms output in mid-November, calling for the fullest conversion of spare capacity, and in mid-December when Hitler, in the wake of the decree on 'Transition from Peace to War Economy', demanded 'a programme with the highest possible figures'.[19] Indeed it was in the detailed plans for increases in military output that clear evidence emerges on the direction the German economy was taking in 1939. Output of all classes of army weapons was planned to increase by 200–300 per cent in the first two years of war. Hitler in fact intervened in the establishment of the explosives plan to insist that the initial mobilization schedule (for 13,700 tons of high explosive a month by the end of 1940) should be increased to 63,000 tons per month. Though he was persuaded that such sums could not possibly be achieved in the short term, he still insisted, in a directive issued on 12 December, on a programme of 53,000 tons a month by October 1941.[20] Expenditure on infantry munitions, which was 590m RM in 1938–9 was scheduled to increase to 2.2 billion RM a year from 1940, an increase of almost 400 per cent. It was the same story for aircraft, planned at 20,000 a year in the first year of war, against peacetime production of 8,000 in 1939; and for submarine production, which increased from 15 in 1939 to 40 in 1940 and 196 in 1941, an increase of 1,300 per cent over two years.[21]

Demands for basic materials and machinery reflected the heavy demands for the output of armaments. Hitler personally intervened to order that all available iron ore and iron and steel production should be allocated to the manufacture of weapons. By January 1940 armed forces requirements were running at 620,000 tons a month, equal to the quantities at the end of the First World War; so high was the level of demand that armaments programmes throughout 1940 ran ahead of the capacity of the German economy to supply them. Once again Hitler was largely responsible for this situation. In January 1940 and again in April, Hitler expressed his desire to expand armaments output beyond the levels already scheduled.[22]

With the onset of a general European war in 1939, and with hints from Hitler that war with Russia could not be ruled out, the Nazi administration was forced to adjust its thinking very rapidly on how to achieve the large-scale economic mobilization that the arms programmes clearly required. The German economy was still far from ready in 1939 to cope with output on this scale. Between September 1939 and the following spring the economic authorities worked out a practical framework for achieving a phased transition to total war. This involved planning for wartime finances, for labour use, and the expansion of armaments capacity. Finance was of major importance, not only because of the high level of state and military expenditure required in wartime, but because it was a major instrument in regulating civilian consumption levels too. The Finance Ministry and the Four Year Plan Office were agreed on the need to restrict consumer spending and to divert money to saving and government loans: 'the excess purchasing power available through restrictions on consumption', wrote the Finance Minister, 'must be soaked up as quickly and thoroughly as possible'.[23] After some argument about the general merits of direct and indirect taxation, it was agreed to increase direct income tax and corporation tax and to tax luxury goods, increasing the total tax burden from 17.7 billion RM in 1938 to 32.3 billion by 1941. The main increase in the tax burden in Germany came between 1938 and 1941 as Table 2.1 shows. There was no substantial increase after 1941; and certainly not enough to suggest any major change of economic policy from the middle of the war. Indeed if price-rises are taken into account the *real* level of taxation in 1943 may well have been lower than it was in 1941. Further excess purchasing power was swallowed up through Reich war loans, 27 billion RM in the first year of war, 42 billion in the second. Military expenditures were covered in roughly equal proportions by government revenue and loans, taxation providing a slightly higher proportion in 1941 than in 1940.[24]

While the first two years of war showed the largest wartime increase in the tax burden, they also saw the highest rate of decrease in *per capita* consumption, which fell by 22 per cent between 1938 and 1941. The same pattern could be seen in levels of food consumption for the civilian population over the same period, with sharp increases in potato and vegetable consumption and sharp falls in the consumption of meat, fish, eggs, cheese, milk and fats.[25] Of course worse was to come as the war continued, though not much worse. The government was insistent that a basic minimum of food consumption should be available for all in order to reduce political risks. This required rationing, as it did in Britain. Strict rationing avoided the excesses of black marketeering that had occurred in the First World War. It ensured a fairer distribution of the sacrifices – 3.2 billion RM were set aside for soldiers' families in 1940 and 4.2 billion in 1941 – but it did not in any sense represent an effort to maintain or expand living standards after the outbreak of war, any more than it did in Britain. It should be remembered, when comparing wartime

Table 2.1 Taxation in Germany, 1938–1943 (tax years), in billion RM

Year	1938	1939	1940	1941	1942	1943
Income tax	8.19	12.23	14.79	19.20	21.81	21.95
Sales tax	3.36	3.73	3.93	4.15	4.16	4.18
Indirect tax*	2.83	4.43	5.60	6.20	6.20	5.94
Customs	1.82	1.70	1.41	1.12	0.83	0.64
Miscellaneous	1.52	1.49	1.51	1.66	1.71	1.66
Total	17.72	23.58	27.24	32.33	34.71	34.37
1938 = 100	100	133	154	182	196	194

Source: NA T178 Roll 15, frame 3671917, 'Statistische Übersichten zu den Reichshaushaltsrechnungen 1938 bis 1943', RFM Nov. 1944.
* includes tax on beer and cigarettes.

living standards, that consumption in Germany was already falling in 1938/9 and that German living standards were considerably lower than those of Britain and the United States. In 1939 average *per capita* incomes in Germany were two-thirds of average British incomes, and only 46 per cent of American. There was therefore much less room for cutting consumption and living standards in Germany than there was in the west, where both real wage rates and real weekly earnings rose to considerably higher levels between 1913 and 1938 than was the case for German workers. As it was, British civilian consumption fell by only 15 per cent in real terms between 1938 and 1941, a smaller fall than in Germany.[26]

The cut-back in consumption was evident everywhere. Goods rapidly disappeared from the shops, particularly consumer durables and clothes, as consumers rushed to buy up stocks in the autumn of 1939; the savings ratio increased; taxation and warloans steadily rose; and foreign trade shifted in favour of strategic imports. By the end of the first year of war there were shortages even of essential clothing for labourers – boots and overalls – and regular complaints of shortages of other essential civilian equipment, a great deal of which was diverted to meet the demands of Germany's very large armed forces.[27] Price controls were maintained to prevent rapid inflation, and excess demand was circumvented by simply withdrawing goods from the shops and encouraging greater saving through an energetic propaganda campaign. By 1941 the level of savings had increased 50 per cent above that of 1939.[28] As in Britain this was not done all at once, in the first weeks of war: there was a gradual but deliberate process of diverting resources away from civilian to war needs.

It was necessary, too, to divert labour and productive capacity to the same end. The government's policy was to demand the release of all labour and capacity not necessary for the war effort or for military production. On 28 September 1939 Goering published a general decree on skilled labour, requiring all firms to release workers for whom they had no need, or face the severest consequences. Armaments firms were instructed to keep their labour demands to what was really necessary, and all businesses and offices which needed new labour were ordered 'immediately with all energy to undertake the training of unskilled men and women'.[29] These efforts were made more difficult than had been intended because the register of labour begun in 1938 was not complete on the outbreak of war; and the job of allocating labour was shared uneasily by a number of different agencies, the Ministry of Labour, the Four Year Plan, the Labour Front, and the armed forces' own economic authorities under Thomas, so that no clear responsibility was established for control over labour by any of them. They each set in motion a series of 'combing-out operations', seeking out unemployed or inessential labour, or skilled labour drafted into the forces, and moving it to war work. In May the Four Year Plan produced a comprehensive set of guidelines on labour allocation for 'waging total war', so that the armed forces, industry and the administration would be clear about what kind of labour (age, skill etc.) they were entitled to. The Ministry of Labour also published regular checklists of labour shortages, again broken down into skills and trades, so that those carrying out the 'combing-out' knew what to look for.[30]

The labour strategy was linked closely with that on capacity. Additional industrial capacity was to be found from three main sources. First of all from the introduction of multiple shift-working, which was a central part of mobilization

Table 2.2 Statistics on investment in German industry, 1938–1944 (in billion RM)

Year	Buildings	Machinery	Machine tools*	Four Year Plan
1938	13.0	2.9	0.62	1.95
1939	12.8	3.5	0.69	2.10
1940	8.3	3.7	0.79	2.49
1941	6.9	4.1	0.86	2.49
1942	4.7	4.2	0.82	1.97
1943	4.0	3.7	0.79	n.a.
1944	3.7	2.6	0.65	n.a.

Source: R. Wagenführ, *Die deutsche Industrie im Kriege* (Berlin, 1963), pp. 160–3: D. Petzina, *Autarkiepolitik im Dritten Reich* (Stuttgart, 1968), p. 183.
* value of annual sales.

planning from 1936–7 onwards;[31] second, by investing in new plant and equipment; third, from converting existing plant to war work, both in Germany and in occupied Europe. This latter policy had been planned by Thomas's arms inspectorates and the Economics Ministry well before 1939, though once again the register of inessential capacity was not yet ready by September 1939, with mobilization plans available for about 60 per cent of Germany's industrial capacity. Goering and Hitler wanted war production 'decentralized' through the closing down *(Stillegung)* or limiting *(Verdrosselung)* of civilian production. The object was 'to concentrate important war production in certain, particularly suitable businesses, and to close down large parts of the productive economy, or to prepare this capacity for other war purposes *in a planned way* . . .'.[32] The Economics Ministry was instructed to carry out this policy across the winter of 1939–40. A decree of 21 February 1940 authorized compulsory closures, and by May the ministry reported that the process of conversion was almost over.[33] Aircraft and armaments firms found themselves moved into car factories, furniture works, breweries, electrical and household equipment factories etc.[34] Investment in new plant was higher in the capital-intensive sectors such as iron and steel, chemicals or synthetic oil, though investment in the arms sector was also important. Out of a total gross capital expenditure in industry of 36 billion RM between 1939 and 1941 some 11 billion went on weapons production.[35]

Investment as a whole in Germany reached a peak in 1938–9 and declined thereafter, largely due to the reduction in house construction. There was no major increase in investment after 1941, though there was a redirecting of investment away from basic industries to manufacture. Figures on gross investment are set out in Table 2.2. By 1941 approximately 50 per cent of building construction was earmarked for the armed forces directly (fortifications, airfields etc.), while the rest went to essential industry, transport and bomb repair.[36]

By the spring of 1940 the German economy was set on the path towards full mobilization. It was by no means a smooth transition, particularly as the German economy in 1939 had not been prepared for general war to break out so soon. Trade was immediately disrupted, which placed a great strain on domestic stocks of raw materials and industrial equipment, and led immediately to a comprehensive quota system for resources which proved difficult to enforce.[37] It was difficult, too, to get industry to take the mobilization plans seriously. The authorities found that industry 'hoped to keep its peacetime production, reckoning with a short war, so holding their labour back'.[38] The Labour Minister complained in November 1939 that 'the firms still believe that the war will soon be over, and hang onto their workforce, to prepare to carry on business after the war'.[39] Fear of unemployment also caused difficulties, for the government hoped to avoid any sudden increase in the number of unemployed during the transition period, which only encouraged firms to retain labour where they could. Much of the capacity that was released was left waiting for orders while the armed forces sorted out what production they wanted. The result was that many skilled workers were left underemployed during the winter, while large numbers of building workers and workers in civilian industry were thrown onto the job market or put on short time, all of which had just the effect on labour morale that the government had been trying to avoid.[40]

Industrialists blamed the problems on a lack of clear planning. 'Industry could manage much more', Kissel told Thomas, 'if clear tasks are given to them'.[41] Thomas blamed the problems on poor leadership by the civilian ministers, particularly Funk at the Economics Ministry, and on party officials who would comply only slowly with the demands for conversion, or who refused to abandon party or state projects on political as much as on economic grounds. The irony was that the military and state authorities, in their anxiety to convert the economy thoroughly and smoothly to war, while avoiding disruption on such a scale that it might evoke popular resentment, created instead a confused scramble, 'the war of all against all'.[42] The muddles were only slowly disentangled during the first half of 1940, though by no means completely so, helped by the greater centralization of decision-making under the Four Year Plan and by the appointment of Fritz Todt, first as Commissioner for Special Tasks, then as full Munitions Minister in February 1940. By the Battle of France the war economy was past its early teething troubles, though military output was still well below the levels ordered by Hitler during the winter.

The defeat of France, it has been claimed, brought this phase of the war economy to a halt; the pace of output slowed down, there was a revival of consumer production, the impact of war on the economy was reversed. In fact the picture in the so-called 'pause' in the summer of 1940 was the exact reverse. Of course there is no doubt that the easy victories of 1940 persuaded many Germans and many businessmen in particular that the war was effectively over, so that the armament effort in the summer months lacked the critical urgency of production in Britain. But it would be wrong to mistake this mood for a deliberate effort to slow down economic mobilization. Unlike the general public Hitler and his advisers knew that war with Britain was likely to be a long and costly affair, and that behind Britain's war effort lay the economic resources of the United States, whose own rearmament was under way in 1940. Moreover Hitler's views on the Russian question had now hardened into a decision to move against Russia too in the following year.[43] Under these circumstances it was necessary to maintain economic momentum and to continue to expand war output. It was out of the question, Goering wrote to the Economics Ministry in July 1940, to consider 'under present circumstances a revival of consumer industries'.[44]

Instead, the economy was presented in the summer of 1940 with even higher military demands, which required a further tightening up of mobilization procedures for the conversion and re-distribution of resources. In addition to the allocation of additional resources to the air force and navy, both of which had taken second place to the army during the land campaign, Hitler ordered the creation of an even larger army. In July he called for an army of 180 divisions, of which twenty should be armoured and a further ten motorized, an army as large as 'all enemy armies put together'.[45] This required, according to Thomas's calculations, some seven years of expansion at current levels of tank production, or three and a half years if tank output were doubled. Todt calculated increases in weapons production of eight or ten times existing output. Hitler's figure was even higher, an increase of stockpiles of munitions to reach a level twelve times greater than the peak level of munitions used during the French campaign.[46] The air force was to be doubled in size and aluminium output almost trebled to one million tons a year. Above all, new priority was given to naval production, essential in the face of British and American naval supremacy, with plans to produce twenty-five submarines a month, a level of output never actually reached throughout the war.[47] All of these plans amounted to an economic effort of enormous proportions, requiring in the summer of 1940 'considerable increases in war production, and with it additional materials, capacity and labour'.[48]

The answer was to squeeze the economy even more to achieve additional war-making capacity: 'a complete shutting down of all tasks not of the utmost urgency by both the armed forces and the civilian sector'.[49] Goering urged more combing-out of labour and shutting down of unwanted plant. Todt wanted absolute priority to go to those plants which produced most efficiently and to shut down less efficient plants, releasing additional labour and machinery for the others. The key problem was the question of labour. A shortage of 250,000 workers for the arms industries, mainly skilled metalworkers, had built up by February 1940. By the summer the situation was even worse. Thomas picked out labour supply as the major bottleneck in coping with 'the new decisions of the Führer'.[50] The combing-out operations in the civilian economy provided increasingly poor returns, though the authorities rightly suspected that labour hoarding was still going on. Hitler arrived at a stop-gap solution in September when he ordered the release of some 600,000 skilled men from the forces over the winter, to be recalled the following spring. The armed forces were unhappy about this decision because they argued that a professional, technically advanced service required a larger number of skilled workers for its own use, and it proved difficult to track down the right men and to allocate them in a co-ordinated way to the factories that needed them.[51] To prevent the army taking even more workers – and there were plenty of complaints from the firms that no sooner had they got the released soldiers back than the army came and took other workers away to replace them – a special priority rating was introduced (the so-called SS and S grades) for firms which were to be immune from conscription, protecting some 4.8 million workers by the spring of 1941. On 20 December Hitler followed up the earlier decision with the call for a special *Zeitplan*, a schedule which the armed forces and industry would work out together for allocating manpower resources between them on a long-term basis.[52]

The result of these fresh initiatives in the summer and autumn of 1940 was to bring the German economy by the following spring close to full mobilization. At a meeting of local armaments inspectors in February 1941 Thomas reported that of the 9.7 million working in German industry some 55 per cent were working directly on orders for the armed forces, against only 20 per cent in September 1939. Current demands for new labour from industry ran at 1.09 million, but were set to rise to 1.76 million by the summer, in addition to the extra 1.5 million that Hitler wanted for the armed forces. The combing out operations of the winter produced only another 100,000 men. There was little more, Thomas concluded, to be taken from the rest of the economy: 'on cutting back civilian production, on dispersal and closures there is nothing more to say'.[53]

It is worth looking at Thomas's claim in more depth, since labour mobilization was a major indicator of the level of economic mobilization as a whole. As might be expected, the pattern of labour distribution reflected the immediate needs of war. Heavy industry and metalworking expanded their labour supply, building and consumer industries contracted. What is perhaps of greater significance is the fact that the pattern of distribution actually changed very little between 1941 and 1943, showing no abrupt change in the middle of the war, as Professor Petzina has argued. Table 2.3 shows that the greatest changes again came between 1939 and early 1942. Indeed numbers in the 'consumer' industries actually went up again in 1943, reflecting how high a proportion of the workforce in these sectors was not working on

Table 2.3 Selected statistics on the German labour force, May 1939–May 1943 (millions)*

	May 1939	May 1940	May 1941	May 1942	May 1943
All industry	10.9	10.1	10.3	9.9	10.6
Iron and steel	0.35	0.33	0.36	0.36	0.41
Mining	0.59	0.58	0.61	0.62	0.69
Heavy manufacturing industry, including:	3.75	3.87	4.21	4.36	4.81
Chemicals	0.59	0.58	0.62	0.63	0.69
Engineering	1.97	2.08	2.31	2.44	2.67
Electrical industry	0.51	0.50	0.55	0.58	0.61
Metal goods	0.46	0.51	0.52	0.53	0.62
Building industry	0.91	0.71	0.72	0.51	0.44
Consumer industry, including:	3.58	2.94	2.84	2.54	2.59
Textiles	1.24	0.98	0.94	0.83	0.84
Clothing	0.34	0.28	0.28	0.26	0.27
Wood	0.30	0.25	0.24	0.23	0.28
Leather goods	0.25	0.18	0.18	0.17	0.19
Food	0.57	0.48	0.45	0.42	0.42

Source: Wagenführ, *op. cit.*, pp. 140–1.

* not all industries are included in the list, so column totals do not equal 'all industry' figures.

Table 2.4 German industrial labour force working on orders for the armed forces, 1939–1943 (per cent)

	1939	1940	1941	1942	1943
All industry, including:	21.9	50.2	54.5	56.1	61.0
Raw materials	21.0	58.2	63.2	59.9	67.9
Metal manufacture	28.6	62.3	68.8	70.4	72.1
Construction	30.2	57.5	52.2	45.2	46.7
Consumer goods	12.2	26.2	27.8	31.7	37.0
Index (1939 = 100)	100	229	248	256	278

Source: Wagenführ *op. cit.*, p. 159.

civilian orders at all, but on armed forces' orders for consumer products. In 1941 the services took 40 per cent of textiles output, 44 per cent of all clothing, 44 per cent of leather goods etc., which left much less capacity for civilian needs than the gross output figures would suggest.[54]

Nor do the global figures for other industries indicate how the workforce was distributed between civilian and military orders. It is these figures, set out in Table 2.4, which confirm that the main period of conversion to war was in 1939–41. In the metal manufacturing industries, which included most arms production, the increase in the numbers working on army orders was most marked, rising from 28 per cent in 1939 to 69 per cent by 1941 but only to 72 per cent by 1943. The increase in the proportion working on military orders in the consumer sector must also be set against the fall in the total numbers working in the consumer sectors, from 3.58 million in 1939 to 2.56 million by 1942.[55] There is no evidence here for any major change in economic policy in the middle of the war. All the figures show conclusively that the German economy had converted the great bulk of its labour and capacity to war work by the end of 1941.

These calculations still leave unresolved the question of the mobilization of Germany's female workforce. It is argued that Germany, unlike the other combatant powers, failed to mobilize women for the labour force. While it is certainly true that the number of German women employed between 1939 and 1945 hardly increased at all, it would be quite wrong to conclude from this that women were not mobilized for war work. The fact is that by 1939 women already constituted a very much larger part of the workforce than in other industrialized countries. If we compare Britain and Germany we find that the proportion of women in the German workforce in 1939 was already higher than the proportion of women in the British workforce at the very height of the British war effort in 1943. In 1939 women made up 25.7 per cent of the labour force in Britain, but 37.4 per cent in Germany. The corresponding figures for 1943 were 36.4 per cent in Britain and 48.8 per cent in Germany.[56] More women were brought into the workforce in Britain because there was a much larger pool of non-employed or unemployed women before 1939, as might be expected given the great difference in British and German unemployment levels. It would be reasonable to argue that there simply was not a much larger pool of women to be absorbed in the German war effort, that Germany was already close to a ceiling on female employment by the outbreak of war. The high 1939 figure reflects the large part played by female labour in the German countryside, which continued during the war as women were forced to cope with farming tasks usually carried out by conscripted men (one million from agriculture by mid-1941).[57] This suggests that women were forced to work harder and for longer hours during the war as well, to make up for the absent male workforce, a fact that the raw data on female employment fails to convey.

Not only were women already a large proportion of the workforce by 1939, but there was substantial *redistribution* of the female workforce, as might be expected, away from consumer sectors into war and war-related industries. Table 2.5 shows the extent of these movements between May 1939 and May 1943. Again, in the consumer sectors it should be recalled that in many of them some 40–45 per cent of the output was for the armed forces. The overall pattern is very similar to that of the other combatant powers – women moving rapidly in 1940–41 into heavy industries and manufactures serving the war effort, particularly metalwork, machinery and chemicals. Many of those women left in the consumer sectors were put on short time during the early years of the war until they moved to war work. The slight increase in employment in textiles, leather and ceramic industries in 1943 can be explained by the larger size of the armed forces (more cups, boots and uniforms) and by the demands of bombed-out families for essential replacement goods. It is clear that the 'failure' to mobilize women for war work in Germany

Table 2.5 Distribution of female workforce in Germany, May 1939–May 1943 (thousands)

	May 1939	May 1940	May 1941	May 1942	May 1943
Heavy industry					
Chemicals	184.5	197.4	204.7	215.8	255.9
Iron and steel	14.7	18.4	29.6	36.6	64.9
Metalworking, machinery	216.0	291.3	363.5	442.0	603.0
Electrical	173.5	185.4	208.1	226.3	264.7
Optical industry	32.2	37.2	47.6	55.6	67.2
Metal goods	39.1	171.3	172.0	192.2	259.5
Total	760.2	901.3	1,025.7	1,168.4	1,515.4
Consumer industry					
Printing	97.2	88.8	92.6	73.9	60.1
Paper goods	89.5	84.3	79.2.	71.9	73.1
Leather	103.6	78.7	85.0	81.8	95.6
Textiles	710.1	595.4	581.3	520.9	546.3
Clothing	254.7	226.5	225.3	212.8	228.9
Ceramic goods	45.3	41.4	39.5	37.1	42.8
Food	324.6	273.5	260.9	236.8	238.0
Total	1,625.3	1,388.7	1,364.0	1,235.4	1,284.5

Source: Wagenführ, op. cit., pp. 145–7.

is a statistical illusion. Women did move into war industry and became an important part of the rural economy during the war years. A higher proportion of German women were at work at every stage of the war than was the case in Britain. The bulk of the German workforce, both male and female, was mobilized for war work between 1939 and the beginning of 1942.

There is little doubt therefore that by summer 1941 the German government and armed forces were justified in assuming that they had created the framework for full economic mobilization. The paradox was that in spite of this large transfer of resources for war, the level of military output expanded very slowly between 1939 and 1941, particularly in aircraft production, which took almost 40 per cent of mobilized capacity. This situation was certainly not due to a lack of resources, which were never a serious long-term constraint on German war production. This judgement is borne out by the evidence on resources available for the German war economy both before and after 1941. The quantity of key resources available grew only slowly after 1941 and in some cases (notably machine tools and labour) actually declined from an earlier peak. Yet the output of weapons of all classes increased almost three-fold between 1941 and mid-1944.[58] The figures in Table 2.6 show that in most cases the German war economy was as well endowed with resources in 1940 and 1941 as it was later in the war. Moreover the evidence suggests that there was no major change in the distribution of these resources between civilian and military use during the later part of the war either, and certainly not on a scale sufficient to explain a three-fold increase in weapons output. The same proportion of iron and steel output – 52 per cent – went to direct military orders in early 1940 and in the first half of 1944. The military took some 82 per cent of aluminium in 1941 but only 78 per cent in the first quarter of 1943 and so on. The increase of labour working on war orders, as we have seen, was only 11 per cent between 1941 and 1943 but was 149 per cent between 1939 and 1941.[59]

The paradox can be illustrated another way. The largest German industry, aircraft production, had more labour, more machine tools and more aluminium than the British aircraft industry, but could only produce in 1940 about two-thirds of British output and in 1941 only half. By 1944 the German industry had approximately the same resource base, but turned out three times as many aircraft as it had

Table 2.6 Selected statistics on German industrial resources, 1939–1944

Year	Labour* supply (mill.)	Machine tools (000 tons)	Other machinery (000 tons)	Coal (mill. tons)	Basic chemicals (mill. tons)	Electricity supply (mill. kW)
1940	36.0	288	1,923	247.9	4.16	9.5
1941	36.1	315	1,979	248.3	4.44	10.4
1942	35.5	290	1,881	264.5	4.51	10.9
1943	36.6	273	1,500	268.9	4.54	11.9
1944	36.1	218	987	249.0	3.74	—

Source: Wagenführ, *op. cit.*, pp. 139, 163, 164, 170; USSBS, *The Effects of Strategic Bombing on the German War Economy*, pp. 90–105.
* includes foreign labour and POWs.

done at the beginning of the war.[60] The mounting evidence of this problem during the first half of 1941 prompted a major reassessment of German economic and military policy shortly after the invasion of Russia, when it became clear that eighteen months of economic mobilization had failed to provide the necessary weapons for a two-front war. Speer later commented that Hitler could have had twice the weapons in mid-1941 than he actually had if the converted resources had been more productively exploited.[61]

The crisis was sparked off by the air force. From the spring of 1941 there was growing evidence that aircraft production was grinding to a standstill. There were fewer aircraft available for the Russian campaign than for the French. Aircraft production was only fractionally higher in 1941 than 1940, and was only half the planned output for the first year of war. The Air Ministry began to put its own house in order and in the summer developed a new programme, designated the 'Goering Programme', intended to quadruple air force size.[62] The impact of these fresh demands on an already over-stretched economy was to bring the whole crisis out into the open.

General Thomas argued that the new programme could not possibly be fulfilled, for it would require a 50 per cent increase in raw material allocation for military purposes, and another 2.9 million workers. Industry already had current demands for 1.9 million additional workers, while new levels of conscription in the summer brought the total of productive workers taken by the armed forces to 6.6 million, including 827,000 metalworkers. Even on the most optimistic calculation Thomas could find only another 770,000 workers, and even this meant taking men back from the army and allocating half a million teenagers as trainee apprentices for the aircraft industry.[63] The Goering Programme exposed other problems too. There was evidence of serious bottlenecks and poor planning in the machine-tool industry. Transport was in serious difficulties, with shortages of locomotives and rolling stock and delays in repair; and energy supply (oil, coal and electricity) failed to match demand.[64] Finally the navy, hoping to improve its supply position after the Russian campaign, and impatient at the slow growth of submarine production, made strident demands for a new programme of its own. At the end of July the navy presented plans to build a large battle fleet for the proposed showdown with the west, consisting of 25 battleships, 8 aircraft carriers and 50 cruisers.[65]

The feeling at Hitler's headquarters was one of increasing desperation. Thomas minuted an urgent request for a Führer order to sort out the crisis of war production. On 14 July Hitler obliged with a comprehensive decree on the economy designed to bring to an end the long period of confused planning and poor co-ordination. The decree reiterated the government's commitment to total mobilization: 'all the available resources in Greater Germany [must be] mobilized as quickly and fully as possible'. Hitler chided the civilian economy for converting to war too slowly and incompletely since 1939 and ordered the civilian sectors to abandon 'even more than hitherto any production not vital for the war'. Hitler also turned to the contradiction between resources and output, ordering the armed forces and the economy to use their resources more productively. Rationalization was the core of the new economic strategy and after July it enjoyed Hitler's personal political backing.[66]

Over the next five months Hitler continued to intervene directly in economic policy. In August he instructed Field Marshal Keitel to publish new guidelines on contracting and distribution. He blamed the armed forces themselves for failing to match military demands and industrial capabilities, for lack of co-operation and wasteful duplication of industrial capacity: 'with the armed forces can and must come a simplification of equipment in a greater number of areas'.[67] Further instructions came from Hitler on introducing a full programme of rationalization, based around policies on labour use, better contracting arrangements and an end to wasteful construction projects in favour of more manufacturing capacity. He also reversed his previous decision on exploiting the resources of occupied Europe by ordering the output of military equipment there as well. All of these recommendations and orders evoked a flurry of activity in the rest of the war economic apparatus, although in some areas rationalization went back well before July 1941. Todt expanded and strengthened the system of production committees begun in 1940; Erhard Milch at the air ministry introduced a system of production circles for air force equipment which greatly simplified and streamlined the whole planning and control of production. And Goering, who by now realised that his personal power in the economy depended on following Hitler's lead, tried to install himself at the head of the whole rationalization drive. In November he announced formally a wide-ranging rationalization programme under the Four Year Plan and appointed his own special commissioner to carry it through.[68]

On 3 December Hitler published a further Führer decree to co-ordinate and define the rationalization strategy, satisfied on the basis of what had happened since July that this had been the core of the problem all along. The new decree, 'Simplification and Increased Efficiency of our Armaments Production' took as its starting point the assumption that Germany's labour and raw materials supplies were finite and that further increases in output could only be achieved through 'mass production' and 'the rationalization of our production methods'. Hitler had already formed the view that it was 'conveyor-belt production' that had saved the Russians since June and wanted the same methods in German industry. To achieve this sort of production, he argued, called for simplification in design of weapons and a greater priority for the technical needs of industry over those of the military: 'finally any *available weapon*, even if more modest and therefore of less efficient performance, is better than an *ideal solution* which cannot be produced because it makes demands that are too great for our limited raw material and labour position'.[69] The services were ordered to avoid duplication of effort, to avoid excessively technical products (which had led to a diversion of skilled labour to the armed forces to service them), and to make suitability for mass production a priority in designing future weapons.

By December improvements in the war economy were more urgent than ever with the failure to defeat Russia and the coming of war with the United States. New production programmes were worked out by Hitler's staff in December to cope with the changing war situation and were published in the Führer directive 'Armament 42' on 10 January. The directive also established the framework for raw material production, explosives and transport. This decree has sometimes been seen as the turning point of the economy, when Hitler ended the phase of economic *Blitzkrieg* and embarked on total war. In fact the decree merely confirmed the level

of mobilization established the previous July and reiterated the call for more efficient production.[70] The subsequent discussions surrounding the implementation of
'Armament 42' make it clear that the economy was not shifting from limited to
total war. The main problem was productivity: how to get more weapons out of
an economy already close to full mobilization. 'The task we have been given',
complained Thomas, 'is a great one, and becomes greater from day to day. The
resources meanwhile get less'.[71] At the conference of armaments inspectors in Berlin
on 21 January Colonel Neef reminded his audience of the policies laid down by
Hitler in the second half of 1941: 'to maintain and even here and there to increase
the old level of output with *less* labour, with *less* coal, and with *less* energy and with
fewer productive raw materials'.[72] The keynote was rationalization and efficiency:
'the greatest output is to be achieved with the smallest expenditure of resources'.[73]

This strategy left unresolved the question of who should take responsibility for
actually running the war economy on a day-to-day basis, which Hitler could clearly
not do himself. Up to the end of 1941 the economy was run by competing administrative empires, the one under the Four Year Plan, the other under the armed
forces. Hitler was critical of both, for he held them responsible for creating the
muddled, unrationalized economy in the first place. Hitler's answer was to bring
the economy more closely under his own general supervision and to give greater
responsibility for economic matters back to the industrialists and technical officials
who knew what they were talking about. This was the direct reverse of what
happened in the First World War when the civilian administration was forced to
give way to control by the armed forces. The opportunity for this political shift
came with Fritz Todt's accidental death in an air crash on 7 February 1942. Hitler's
architect, Albert Speer, who was passing through headquarters at the time, was
hastily appointed armaments overlord and given Hitler's direct personal authority
to rationalize and expand production.[74]

Having wrested control over armaments from Goering and the army, Hitler
then set about replacing military with civilian experts and party commissioners
whom he could trust. In a decree of 13 February Hitler noted how little economic
experts were involved in the war economy: 'in industry there stands ready an enormous amount of untapped expertise amongst designers and engineers'.[75] He gave a
personal address to industrialists enjoining them to take on more responsibility for
economic affairs through the principle of 'self-responsibility in industry'. The second
line of attack was on the excessive bureaucratization that had gone on since the
outbreak of war. During the first months of 1942 the armed forces, the administration and the party were ordered to rationalize their bureaucratic apparatus, to
close down unnecessary offices and to release extra manpower for the war effort.
There was to be no argument that 'further reductions are impossible' or 'it was
always thus'.[76] The failure to provide a clear political centre for the war economy
had allowed competitive bureaucratic machines to emerge side by side since 1939,
often doing exactly the same job but answerable to different leaders. Greater
centralization and a clear demarcation of responsibility made bureaucratic stream-
lining possible. This, together with industrial rationalization and the greater
participation of civilian experts, was the basis on which the great production achievements of 1942–4 were founded.

It is now necessary to return to the question of why there was such a disparity between the quantity of resources allocated to the war effort in 1939–41 and the actual levels of military output. There is certainly something in the argument that the outbreak of war in 1939, and Hitler's subsequent decision to go to war with Russia, came at a time when the economy was still only in the middle of transferring basic resources to war. The whole synthetic fuel programme for example, or the production of domestic iron ores, or the explosives plan, were vital elements in the military economy, which remained far from complete in 1939. Large quantities of investment and labour were devoted to the effort to complete this programme, denying these resources for the direct production of armaments until 1941 or 1942. Other very large construction projects competed directly with arms production during this period – the 1,000 bomber factories, the Nibelungenwerke and the Eisenwerke Oberdonau in Austria which turned out the bulk of German tanks in the last stages of the war, the Reichswerke iron and steel works at Salzgitter and Linz. Some of these projects were either never completed or only partly utilized during the war, so that their resources were largely wasted for the war effort.[77] By 1942 the building of the core industries for the war economy was more or less completed, with the result that more resources could be released immediately for direct arms manufacture. This redirecting of resources within the military economy was in itself an important explanation for the better productive performance during the rest of the war.

It could also be argued that the easy victories of the early years of war created an unfortunate psychological climate for the effort to mobilize economic resources fully for war. In the summer of 1940 and again in October 1941 the popular feeling was that the war was over, and all the propaganda effort before 1939 directed at preparing the population for sacrifices and privation seemed curiously inappropriate. While the authorities worked for total war the people stubbornly hoped for peace. It was this attitude that prevented, according to Colonel Neef of the High Command staff, 'a 100 per cent adjustment to war'.[78] It also explains the attention paid by the government to the question of propaganda, which it was hoped would supply a moral imperative for total mobilization. Yet it is impossible in the end to ignore widespread evidence of mismanagement of the war economy on a very large scale between 1939 and 1941, other circumstances notwithstanding. This position stemmed directly from the absence of any clear planning guidelines, or a coherent political structure with real authority in economic affairs, in striking contrast to the situation in Britain and later in the United States. Political conflicts openly intruded into economic affairs, particularly the contest between local and central authority, and between party and army. Hitler himself deliberately remained aloof from these arguments. He did not take a more direct interest in the economy until mid-1941, and only finally became part of the routine of war economic policy-making with the initiation of regular Führer conferences with Speer in 1942. Speer recognized at once that it was the failure to get direct backing from Hitler which had vitiated efforts to mobilize the economy before 1942.[79]

Conversion to war was also seriously affected by the attitude of industry. Left out of most decision-making about the war economy, industrialists did what the authorities told them to do but did not, either collectively or voluntarily, undertake to reduce what they saw as 'planlessness' or incompetence in the administration, both of which made the job of production so difficult. There was a general sense of demoralization about wartime planning which was only reversed when the participation of businessmen and economic experts in the war economy was openly invited with the reforms in production management and economic administration after 1941. A good example of the negative attitude of industry can be found in the question of shift-working. When Speer investigated the problem in 1942, some two years after it had been ordered as standard practice, he found that no major firm of the twenty he visited (including AEG, Siemens and Rheinmetall-Borsig) ran even a second shift. Instead larger military programmes were met by demands for more factories, many of which remained short of equipment, machinery and power-supply because of wartime shortages. The building of new factories absorbed 1.8 million construction workers at a time when the firms were only short of 500,000 to run a second shift.[80] This situation was made even worse by Goering's earlier directive that all strategically important production should be dispersed to at least three small plants rather than one large one, which raised the demand for new factory capacity still further, and made it harder to produce what was required on time because of delays in construction. Speer also found that the armed forces made very high stock allowances for their contractors, with quotas well in excess of what was needed. The most notorious example was the allocation of 16,000 pounds of aluminium for all aircraft types, ignoring the fact that completed fighter aircraft weighed only 4–5,000 pounds.[81] Stockpiles of aluminium lay unused or were used in products for which aluminium was not essential.

The real culprit in all this was the armed forces themselves. Not only were the forces unwilling to share responsibility for the war economy with civilians, since they had taken so much of the load of pre-war planning and preparation, but the individual services failed to co-ordinate their own production plans so that the same equipment was often produced by three different contractors for each of the three services. There was little interchangeability and rationalization in weapons production; modifications were required at every point in the production life of a weapon, making it impossible for the firms to plan proper long-term mass production. The armed forces' priorities – a high standard of finish, a flexible highly-trained workforce – encouraged excessive reliance on skilled labour and resistance to mass production. Some soldiers recognised this problem during the war: 'our economy has been orientated much more towards handworker methods with a particularly high quality of work rather than towards methods of mass production, and is still orientated substantially in that direction today'.[82]

Indeed the whole labour programme was disrupted by arguments over conscription and work methods between the armed forces and industry, since the forces both required skilled workers of their own and insisted on a high degree of skilled labour in armaments production. The forces wanted to make sure that the economy served military requirements on the military's terms. This meant putting military interests, both tactical and technical, first, at the expense of production. The armed forces were basically hostile to a productivist view of the war economy. The military planners, including Thomas, seem to have had little grasp of what could be achieved by the efficient use of existing resources and economies of scale. The Goering

Programme did not need the 50 per cent increase in raw materials nor the 2.9 million extra workers that Thomas predicted were necessary, but was in fact substantially exceeded in 1943 and 1944 with no significant increase in resources. Lacking experience of production, and excessively preoccupied with narrow technical detail, the armed forces tried to regiment the economy to an extent incompatible with a strategy of large-scale output.[83]

There was a second, more serious, problem here. The armed forces wanted after 1939 to avoid a repeat of the First World War. This meant ensuring that they started off where they had left off in 1918 under Hindenburg and Ludendorff, with extensive control over the economy, but this time exercised by professional armed forces with a high level of technical and engineering skills. There was to be no reliance again on industry responding to the challenge in its own way, because that took time. There was to be no excessive reliance on civilians either, who were deemed to know too little about military matters. Nor was there to be any indiscriminate mobilization of women and the unskilled into war work, as there had been in World War I, but instead a co-ordinated labour programme protecting the interests of skilled workers. Equipped with these priorities the armed forces built up a huge bureaucratic apparatus of their own, rivalling that of the government, the party and the economy. Labour diverted from civilian tasks was assigned to what were in practice unnecessary jobs designated as military necessities. The armed forces undertook to train unskilled labour as well, putting hundreds of thousands of young Germans through apprentice schools run by the army and air force, until Speer forced them to hand this job over to industry, where it could be done, as it was in Britain and America, in a matter of weeks instead of the two years assigned by the forces.

In 1942 the services finally lost their battle to dominate and run the productive side of the war economy. Labour was placed under Gauleiter Sauckel, armaments under Speer, aircraft under Milch (who was a civilian in uniform), and raw materials under Central Planning, and in effect under Speer. This did not mean an end to interference by the armed forces, nor to unnecessary duplication of effort, but it did avoid excessive interference with production in the factories, and led to a rationalization of the distribution of resources and better contracting procedures, all of which revolutionized output. The first long mass-production runs became possible in 1942 and 1943, only to be interrupted in 1944 by the bombing. Without bombing the output of weapons in Germany in the last years of war would have been even higher.

Of course it was also the case that some additional resources were made available during the 1942–4 period, particularly from occupied Europe, though Europe also absorbed German resources as well. The most important resource, foreign labour, was used to make up for losses to the armed forces and in combat, and was not a large net addition.[84] More investment was needed in 1943 and 1944 to cope with the bombing and the large underground construction and dispersal schemes, though this too was not a net addition but was substitute or replacement investment. But there was no great leap in resource allocation after 1942, and certainly not from the German civilian economy, to suggest a fundamental shift in strategy in early 1942 from limited to total war. There was instead a major improvement in productivity. Labour productivity in military production increased from an index figure of 100 in 1941 to 157 in 1942–3 and 234 by mid-1944, figures which are confirmed by the performance of individual firms.[85] That so much slack existed in the military economy was due to the ineffective rather than limited nature of mobilization before 1942. The great increases in output were brought about through redirecting and rationalizing resources within the military economy (from basic industries to armaments, from military bureaucracy to productive labour, from excessive stockpiles to more rational resource quotas etc.), through solving the political question about how the war economy should be run, and finally by the changing mood of the population as a whole as it began to realise how serious the struggle was, and the optimism of 1940 gave way to growing fear of defeat and bolshevization. It is perhaps this change in popular temper that has been mistaken for a change in strategy. The commitment to full mobilization was there from the start, but was, as Hitler later complained, 'mismanaged'.[86]

Notes

1   General Thomas to Field Marshal Keitel, 6.7.1941, Speer Collection, Imperial War Museum London, FD 5450/45.

2   E. R. Zilbert, *Albert Speer and the Nazi Ministry of Arms* (London, 1981), p. 116; L. Herbst, *Der Total Krieg und die Ordnung der Wirtschaft* (Stuttgart, 1982), pp. 118–26; A. S. Milward, 'The End of the Blitzkrieg', *Economic History Review*, 2nd ser., xvi (1963/4), 499–518; *idem*, 'Hitlers Konzept des Blitzkrieges' in A. Hillgruber (ed.), *Probleme des Zweiten Weltkrieges* (Cologne, 1967), pp. 19–40.

3   I[nternational] M[ilitary] T[ribunal], *Trial of the Major War Criminals* (Nuremberg, 1947–9), vol. 36, pp. 117–129, 'Vortrag gehalten vor Generalmajor Thomas, 24 Mai 1939'.

4   On the general background see W. Deist, *The Wehrmacht and German Rearmament* (London, 1981); B. Carroll, *Design for Total War: Arms and Economics in the Third Reich* (The Hague, 1968); W. M. Stern, 'Wehrwirtschaft: a German Contribution to Economics', *Economic History Review*, 2nd Ser, xvi (1963/4).

5   Conference with Field Marshal Göring at Carinhall, 16.7.1938, Bundesarchiv-Militärarchiv (BA-MA), Wi I F 5 412.

6   IMT vol. 27, p. 161, Conference with Göring, 14.10.1938, doc. 1301-PS.

7   IMT vol. 33, p. 151, second session of Reichsverteidigungsrat, 23.6.1939.

8   Heeres-Waffenamt, 'Die personelle Leistungsfähigkeit Deutschlands im Mob-Fall', March 1939, Imperial War Museum (IWM), Mi/14/478. The army was deeply concerned about the falling birth rate as well, which made it more necessary than ever to increase industrial efficiency in the 1940s in order to release enough men for the armed forces.

9   BA-MA, Göring conference, 16.7.1938, Wi I F 5.412, p. 2. Italics in the original.

10   R. J. Overy, 'Göring's "Multi-National" Empire' in A. Teichova and P. Cottrell (eds.), *International Business in Central Europe 1918–1939* (Leicester, 1983), pp. 269–93.

11   R. J. Overy, 'Hitler's War and the Germany Economy: a Reinterpretation', *Economic History Review* 2nd ser., xxxv (1982), 272–91.

12   M. Geyer, *Aufrüstung oder Sicherheit: die Reichswehr und der Krise der Machtpolitik 1924–36* (Wiesbaden, 1980), p. 505.

13   IMT, vol. 36, p. 129.

14   Circular from Oberkommando der Wehrmacht (OKW) 'X-Fall für die Wirtschaft', IWM Speer Collection, FD 1434/46 169: *Dokumente de deutschen Politik* (Berlin, 1940), vii. 403–09 'Kriegswirtschaftsverordnung, 4 September 1939'.

15   Speech by Economic Minister Funk, 14.10.1939: Foreign and Commonwealth Office Library, Case XI background documents, book 118-A, doc. 3324-PS.

16   OKW 'Kriegswirtschaftlicher Lagebericht no. 3,1.12.1939', IWM FD 5454 a/45: 'Richtlinien zur Zusammenfassung aller Kräfte zur Steigerung der Fertigung für die Wehrmacht', 29.11.1939, IWM FD 5445/45.

17   Speech by Thomas to Reichsgruppe Industrie, 29.11.1939, p. 5, IWM FD 5454 d/45.

18   OKW Kriegswirtschaftlicher Lagebericht, no. 3, 1.12.1939, IWM FD 5454d/45; conference on the Krauch explosives plan, 17.11.1939, BA-MA Wi I F 5.412; *Documents on German Foreign Policy* Ser. D, vol. viii (London, 1954), p. 193, memorandum of a conversation between the Führer and Count Ciano, 1.10.1939; *ibid.*, p. 141, memorandum of the conversation between the Führer and M. Dahlerus, 26.9.1933.

19   Minutes of meetings with General Thomas on 13.11.1939, pp. 1–2; minutes of a conference on 11.12.1939. BA-MA, Wi I F 5.412.

20   'Production and consumption of munitions by the armed forces', Speer Documents, FD 1434/46 169; Case XI, book 118a, doc. NI-7835, 'Development of the production plans for gunpowder and explosives, 15.7.1940'.

21   'Comparative review of the munitions programme 1939–1942', IWM, FD 1434/46 169; 'Review of the expansion of explosives production, 1939–1941' n.d., IWM, FD 1434/46 176; Nachschubzahlen für Luftfahrtgerät, 1.4.1938', N[ational] A[rchives], Washington D.C., T177 Roll 31, frame 3719681; United States Strategic Bombing Survey, Report 92, *German Submarine Industry Report*, Exhibit P.

22   OKW report 'Steigerung der Munitionsfertigung 19.1.1940'; OKW to Fritz Todt, 1.4.1940. IWM, MI 14/433 1.

23   Letter from Finance Minister von Krosigk to Funk, 21.11.1939, NA T178 Roll 15, frame 3671816. See too letter from Price Commissioner Wagner to von Krosigk, 21.12.1939, frame 3671852–3; and letter from Funk to von Krosigk, 19.1.1940, frame 3671873. 'The shutting off of excess purchasing power in favour of voluntary saving is to be promoted by every means'.

24   Letter from von Krosigk to Göring, 20.1.1940, NA T178 Roll 15, frames 3671896–7; RFM memorandum 'Die steuerlichen Massnahmen während des gegenwärtigen Krieg' n.d., *ibid.*, frames 3672285–92; Report from the Generalbüro of the RFM on war finances, 15.10.1943, *ibid.*, frames 3671758–78.

25   Deutsche Institut für Wirtschaftsforschung, 'Die deutsche Industrieproduktion im Kriege und ihre Messung' p. 9, IWM FD 5454b/45. On food consumption see United States Strategic Bombing Survey, Special Paper no. 4, *Food and Agriculture*, pp. 105–6, Exhibits D-F.

26   RFM 'Finanzieller Ueberblick über die vergangenen vier Kriegsjahre (1 Sept 1939–31 Aug 1943)', 14.10.1943. On German living standards see C. D. Long, *The Labor Force under Changing Income and Employment* (Princeton U.P., 1958), p. 369; F. Wunderlich, *Farm Labor in Germany 1810–1945* (Princeton U.P., 1961), pp. 235–68; T. Balogh, 'The Economic Background in Germany', *International Affairs*, March 1939, 237–40. On British consumption W. Hancock and M. M. Gowing, *British War Economy* (HMSO, 1949), p. 200.

27   Four Year Plan monthly reports, Sept. 1940, Oct. 1940, Feb. 1941, IWM FD 4809/45. H. Boberach (ed.), *Meldungen aus dem Reich: Auswahl aus den geheimen Lageberichten*

der Sicherheitsdienst der SS 1939–1944 (Berlin, 1965), reports no. 12, no. 29, no. 84, no. 143.

28   Letter from Funk to von Krosigk, 19.1.1940, NA T178 Roll 15, frames 3671869–73; RFM report on war finance, 15.10.1943, *ibid.*, frame 3671760.

29   Göring decree on skilled labour shortages, 28.9.1939, BA-MA Wi I F 5.3352.

30   Göring decree, 29.5.1940; Reich Labour Ministry 'Mangelberufsliste' IWM MI/14/478, 'Beitrag für die Rü-In Besprechung, 5.1.1940 betr. 'Auskämmaktionen' IWM FD 5078/45; 'Beitrag für Besprechung der deutschen Militärattachés, 26.8.1940' IWM FD 5078/45. On details of combing-out at local level see Sicherheitsdienst reports from Leipzig, especially 16.5.1940, pp. 12–16, BA NS 29 775.

31   See for example RLM report 2300, 6.10.1936, BA-MA RL3 84; Report from RLM to WiRüAmt, 6.9.1939, NA T177 Roll 3, frame 3684346.

32   Minutes of a conference in the RWM, 3.10.1939 p. 1, BA-MA Wi I F 5.412; Göring decree, 29.11.1939, IWM FD 5445/45. Italics in the original.

33   RWM decree 21.2.1940; FYP report 3.5.1940, IWM FD 4809/45.

34   Memorandum from head of Economic Group Aircraft Industry to all firms, 10.10.1939, NA T83 Roll 5 frames 3745418–9; Report of Göring conference, 9.2.1940 IWM Milch Documents vol. 65.

35   R. Wagenführ, *Die deutsche Industrie im Kriege* (Berlin, 1963), p. 160; speech by Albert Speer to Gau economic advisers, 17.4.1942, IWM FD 1434/46 no. 167.

36   IWM FD 5450/45, OKW minute, 26.8.1941.

37   H-E. Volkmann, 'NS-Aussenhandel im "geschlossenen" Kriegswirtschaftsraum' in F. Forstmeier and H-E. Volkmann (eds.), *Kriegswirtschaft und Rüstung 1939–1945* (Düsseldorf, 1977), pp. 92–130; W. Murray, *The Change in the European Balance of Power 1938–1939* (Princeton, 1984), pp. 326–32.

38   Conference with General Thomas, 13.11.1939, p. 3, BA-MA, Wi I F 5.412.

39   *Ibid.*, p. 7.

40   Todt to Düsseldorf Labour Office, 27.10.1939; Todt to Wirtschaftsgruppe Bauindustrie, 21.9.1939, Todt Correspondence, IWM AL 2564; Thomas to Syrup (Labour Ministry), 22.2.1940, 'skilled labour shortages for military production', IWM FD 5446/45; GBW 'Ubersicht über die Gesamtlage der Wirtschaft', 1.11.1939, pp. 1–3, BA-MA Wi I F 5.3352. On morale see Gestapo report 'Lohnmässige Schlechterstellung durch Dienstverpflichtung', 7.5.1940, IWM FD 5446/45.

41   Thomas speech to leading industrialists, 18.12.1939 p. 8, BA-MA Wi IF 5.412.

42   Auszüge aus Aktenvermerken über Besprechung bei Gen. Thomas, 23.10.1939, p. 4. BA-MA Wi I F 5.412.

43   A. Hillbruber, *Hitlers Strategie: Politik und Kriegführung 1940–1* (Frankfurt a M, 1965), pp. 157–91, 218–19.

44   Göring to Economics Ministry, 22.7.1940, BA-MA Wi I F 5.118, Teil 2.

45   Notiz über die Besprechung bei Chef Heeresrüstungsamt, 19.7.1940, IWM FD 5447/45.

46   Aktenvermark über die Tagung auf dem Plassenburg mit RM Todt, 5/6 Juli 1940, p. 1, IWM FD 5078/45; Aktenvermerk über eine Besprechung bei Gen. Thomas, 20.6.140, IWM MI 14/328; OKW to heads of armed forces, 9.7.1940, MI 14/433 (1).

47   Report from Tschersich (RLM) to Udet, 13.10.1940, BA-MA RL3 234; Admiral Raeder to Keitel, n.d., IWM FDS 5450/45; 'Aluminium Plan 1941' IWM FD 5450/45.

48   Thomas to Göring and Funk, 15.7.1940, p. 1, IWM FD 5447/45. See too circular from Göring on 'Dringlichkeit der Fertigungsprogramme, 18 July 1940' and

Hitler Directive for 20.8.1940 'Umsteuerung der Rüstung' in G. Thomas, *Geschichte der deutschen Wehr-und Rüstungswirtschaft 1918–1945* (Boppard a Rhein, 1966), pp. 413–15, 420.

49 WiRüAmt 'Steigerung der Rüstung' 25.9.1940, p. 2, IWM MI 14/433(1).

50 Aktenvermerk über Arbeitseinsatzlage, 15.2.1940, IWM FD 5446/45; Keitel memorandum, 11.5.1940, FD 5078/45; Beitrag für Besprechung der deutschen Militärattachés, 26.8.1940, FD 5078/45.

51 OKW Führerbefehl 28.9.1940, IWM MI 14/433 (1); Thomas conference with Todt, minutes of 10.1.1941, FD 5444/45; Conference with Keitel, 17.8.1940, pp. 4–6, FD 5447/45; Aktenvermerk über die Staatssekretärbesprechung, 24.6.1940, pp. 1–2, FD 5078/45.

52 OKW, Besprechung am 4.2.1941 mit den Wehrersatzinspekteuren, pp. 10–15, 23.

53 Protokoll über die Inspekteurbesprechung am 22.2.1941 bei OKW, 'Die Ersatzlage der Wehrmacht' pp. 34–67, IWM FD 5444/45.

54 D. Petzina, 'Die Mobilisierung deutscher Arbeitskräfte vor und während des Zweiten Weltkrieges', *Vierteljahreshefte für Zeitgeschichte* vol. xviii (1970), 452. For figures on consumer goods for military use see OKW conference 22.2.1941, p. 42. These figures were approximately the same in 1943: Wagenführ, *Deutsche Industrie*, p. 174.

55 Wagenführ, *Deutsche Industrie*, p. 159. Most of Wagenführ's figures are taken from the official records of the Reich Statistical Office.

56 On Britain see H. M. Parker, *Manpower* (HMSO, 1957), p. 481; on the alleged failure to mobilize women see Herbst, *Totaler Krieg*, pp. 118–19; S. Salter, 'Class Harmony or Class Conflict? The Industrial Working Class and the National Socialist Regime 1933–1945' in J. Noakes (ed.), *Government, Party and People in Nazi Germany* (Exeter, 1980), pp. 89–91; Petzina 'Mobilisierung', p. 455. None of these works compares the proportion of women working in the British and German workforces, but only the absolute increase/decrease. See J. Stephenson, *Women in Nazi Society*, (London, 1975), p. 101, for discussion of the high proportion of women in Germany in the workforce in 1939.

57 For conscription from agriculture see OKW 'Die Lage auf dem Arbeitseinsatzgebiet', 30.6.1941, IWM MI 14/433(2). The total recruited by 30.4.1941 was 1,114,986. See too Stephenson, *Women,* p. 82; Wunderlich, *Farm Labor, p.* 296, who shows that by 1939 there were 230,000 more women working in agriculture than in 1933, but 643,000 fewer men. The situation in the countryside perhaps explains the slow fall in the number of 'domestic servants' in the German workforce during the war. Many servants were living-in farm-workers, or helped with other small businesses run mainly by family helpers. See M. Thibert, 'The Economic Depression and the Employment of Women', Part I, *International Labour Review* vol. xxvii (1933), who points out that only a small proportion (44,000) of domestic servants were employed full-time in private houses, and the rest in family enterprises of one kind or another.

58 Wagenführ, *Deutsche Industrie*, pp. 178–9.

59 *Ibid.*, pp. 168–9: United States Strategic Bombing Survey, Report 20, *Light Metal Industry of Germany Part I*, p. 17a.

60 R. J. Overy, *Goering: the 'Iron Man'* (London, 1984), pp. 189–91.

61 A. Speer, *Spandau: the Secret Diaries* (London, 1976), p. 62: 'in the middle of 1941 Hitler could easily have had an army equipped twice as powerfully as it was. For the production of those fundamental industries that determine the volume of armaments was scarcely higher in 1941 than in 1944'.

62 Vortragsnotiz für Chef OKW 'Erweitertes Luftrüstungsprogramm', 6.7.1941; IWM FD 5450/45: Beitrag zum Vermerk über Steigerung der Luftwaffenfertigung,

27.6.1941, IWM MI 14/433(2); BA-MA RL3 146, Liefer-Plan 20/2 'Göring-Flugzeug-Lieferplan', 15.9.1941.

63   Vortragsnotiz für Chef OKW 'Die Lage auf dem Arbeitseinsatz', 30.6.1941; Vermerk über Steigerung der Luftwaffenfertigung, 27.6.1941, IWM MI 14/433(2).

64   OKW 'Lage auf dem Werkzeugmaschinengebiet', 30.6.1941, IWM LI 14/433(2); Wagenführ, *Deutsche Industrie*, pp. 98–103 on energy; file note of a discussion in the Reich Transport Ministry, 17.9.1941, IWM FD 5450/45.

65   G. Weinberg, *World in the Balance* (New England U. P., 1981), p. 89.

66   Thomas memorandum for Chef OKW, 29.6.1941, IWM M1 14/433(2); WiRüAmt 'Bericht über die Leistungen auf dem Gebiet der materiellen Wehrmachtrüstung' 10.7.1941, FD 5450/45; WiRüAmt. 'Umstellung der Rüstung' 17.7.1941, MI 14/433(2); Keitel (OKW) to Gen. Becker, 10.8.1941, *Ibid.*; 'Niederschrift über Besprechung Chef OKW mit den Wehrmachtteilen, 16.8.1941' in Thomas, *Geschichte*, pp. 458–67.

67   Keitel to Gen. Becker, 'Umstellung der Rüstung', 10.8.1940, IWM MI 14/433(2); OKW 'Niederschrift', p. 3, IWM FD 5450/45; Chef OKW Aktenvermerk betr. technische Ausstattung der Wehrmacht, 19.9.1941, *Ibid.*

68   Führerbefehl, 11.9.1941, IWM MI 14/433(2); Keitel (OKW) to heads of armed forces, 10.10.1941, *Ibid.*; NA Göring-Stabsamt, T84 Roll 8, frames 8005–6, Notiz betr. die Rede des Herrn RM am 20.5.1942.

69   Der Führer, 'Vereinfachung und Leistungssteigerung unserer Rüstungsproduktion', 3.12.1941, p. 3, IWM MI 14/433(2); Vermerk über Ausführungen des Reichmarschalls in der Sitzung am 7.11.1941, IMT vol. 27, pp. 65–6. Italics in the original.

70   'Umstellung der Rüstung' March 1942, pp. 4–7, IWM FD 1434/46 no. 170; OKW, betr. 'Rüstung 1942' 14.1.1942, MI 14/433(3).

71   Speech of Gen. Thomas to Rüstungsinspekteuren, 21.1.1942, p. 14, IWM MI 14/433(3).

72   Vortrag, Oberst Neef (WiRüAmt), 21.1.1942, p. 20, IWM MI 14/433(3). Italics in the original.

73   Führerbefehl, 21.3.1942, NA T83 Roll 76, frame 3447503.

74   Overy, *Goering*, pp. 208–11; M. Schmidt, *Albert Speer. Das Ende eines Mythos* (Munich, 1982), pp. 71–89. The shift in responsibility was made explicit in a Führer decree of 2.4.1942. See IWM FD 5454a/45.

75   Speech of Speer to Gauwirtschaftsberater, 17.4.1942, p. 22, IWM FD 1434/46 no. 167; see also Führerebefehl, 21.2.1942. NA T83 Roll 76, frames 3447503–4.

76   WiRüAmt, 'Rationalisierung des Menscheneinsatzes im zivilen Sektor', 27.1.1942, pp. 1–2, IWM FD 5444/45; Vortrage des Gen. Thomas über die militärische und wirtschaftliche Lage, 23.1.1942, *Ibid.*

77   WiRüAmt Bericht über die Leistungen auf dem Gebiet der materiellen Wehrmachtrüstung, 10.7.1941, pp. 6–7, IWM FD 5450/45.

78   Vortrag de Oberst Neef, 21.1.1941, p. 19, IWM M1 14/433(3).

79   A. Speer, *Inside the Third Reich* (London, 1970), pp. 201–7.

80   Speech of Speer to the Gauwirtschaftsberater, 17.4.1942, pp. 10–11, IWM FD 1434/46 no. 167.

81   *Ibid.*, pp. 16–17. United States Strategic Bombing Survey, Report 20, p. 13. D. Irving, *The Rise and Fall of the Luftwaffe* (London, 1973), p. 126. A fully equipped Me 109 weighed only 4,400 pounds.

82   Vortrag, Oberst Neef, 21.1.1942, p. 19.

83   Overy, *Goering*, pp. 158–62, 180–6.

84   N. Kaldor, 'The German War Economy', *Review of Economic Statistics*, vol. xiii (1946), 37.
85   Wagenführ, *Deutsche Industrie*, p. 125.
86   Speer, *Inside*, p. 202.

Chapter 3

Lawrence Freedman and Saki Dockrill

HIROSHIMA
A strategy of shock

N UCLEAR WEAPONS HAVE ONLY BEEN USED in anger twice since their explosive power was proved in July 1945. A few weeks after the New Mexico test two bombs were dropped on the Japanese cities of Hiroshima and Nagasaki. Hundreds more have been tested but none has been used since.

The unique nature of this event and its association with the conclusion of the Pacific War immediately sparked off a debate which may never be properly concluded. A widespread Japanese appreciation of the destruction of these two cities remains that this was a move that was more criminal than strategic, only loosely related to the preceding years of war. Thus the comprehensive study by the Committee for the Compilation of Materials on Damage Caused by the Atomic Bomb in Hiroshima and Nagasaki,[1] contains almost every scrap of information relating to the bombings, including an extensive discussion of the outrage prompted by the impact of Hiroshima and Nagasaki and the consequent protest movements, but only minimal reference to why the weapons were used. This discussion extends to two separate paragraphs. In one it is stated that:

> the A-Bomb attacks were needed not so much against Japan – already on the brink of surrender and no longer capable of mounting an effective counter-offensive – as to establish clearly America's postwar international position and strategic supremacy in the anticipated cold war setting. One tragedy of Hiroshima and Nagasaki is that this historically unprecedented devastation of human society stemmed from essentially experimental and political aims.[2]

In another paragraph this argument is repeated, citing as authorities two dated Western studies, one of which is by a communist,[3] and the other by Patrick Blackett who in 1948 was the first to assert that the atomic bombing was the first shot in the Cold War rather than the last in the Pacific War,[4] and a 1968 Japanese study. As the anniversary of the outbreak of the Pacific War approached, and the Japanese Diet moved to pass a motion apologising for initiating the war with the surprise attack on Pearl Harbor, there were suggestions that it would be appropriate if the United States reciprocated with an apology for Hiroshima and Nagasaki, a notion to which President Bush gave short shrift.

Those in Japan doubting the necessity of the atomic bombing have been able to cite in support a series of Western studies which have argued that (a) the war would have ended anyway without recourse to an invasion of Japan, (b) there were realistic alternatives to the actual use of the bomb against civilian targets, in particular a staged demonstration of its power, (c) all this was known to the Truman administration, yet (d) it still persevered because it wanted to strengthen its hand in its post-war dealings with the Soviet Union. This line of argument is now largely discredited among Western historians.[5]

With hindsight the likelihood of an early Japanese surrender is acknowledged (although *how* early remains moot), and the sensitivity of American policy-makers to their developing struggle with the Soviet Union is undoubted. Nonetheless, the weight of evidence supports the view that the primary motive for the atomic bombing remained the defeat of Japan and that a demonstration shot was discounted because there was no confidence that it would work.

It is not our intention in this chapter to rehearse once more this familiar debate. Rather we intend to look more closely at the question of the manner of the atomic bombing. Our contention is that it reflected a clear and coherent strategy of 'shock'. This was the only strategy that made much sense in the military circumstances of August 1945. It was reflected in the stress on the spectacle of a nuclear detonation and the consequent tactics of cryptic warning and inconspicuous delivery. For these reasons, and contrary to the hopes of at least some of those responsible, it also maximised the association of the bomb with mass destruction. We further argue that in practice it worked: the available evidence suggests that Japanese policy-makers were caught off guard by the news of Hiroshima and that, despite the best efforts of the hardliners, they never recovered their balance. Although the two developments remain hard to disentangle, the bombing may well have been more important in prompting the Japanese surrender than the entry of Russia into the war.

By the time that the United States began to consider seriously the employment of the first atomic bombs they were influenced by two critical factors: the limited number of weapons available and the limited number of targets left.

In April 1944 General Leslie Groves, in charge of the Manhattan Project, had informed General Marshall that several plutonium implosion bombs with a yield of between 0.7 and 1.5 kilotons might be available between March and June 1945. However, by the turn of the year Groves had been obliged to report that these hopes had been 'dissipated by scientific difficulties which we have not as yet been able to solve'.[6] By the Summer of 1945 it was clear that there were going to be very few weapons available.

It is important to note that prior to the New Mexico test of July 1945 this comparatively low-yield estimate remained the best judgement and influenced the first considerations of the weapon's employment.[7] With the uranium gun-type weapon, the type eventually used over Hiroshima, estimates were more confident at between five and 15 kilotons. It was only after it became apparent that the normal yield of the implosion bomb would exceed 0.5 kilotons that its use became 'subject to considerations of high-level policy'. At or below that level, it would simply have been handed over to the military for use without restriction.[8] By the Summer of 1945 the atom bombs were seen as single city-busters, but the confidence in this capability was quite recent.

There remained a lack of knowledge of the bomb's effects. This has been commented on in the literature as providing an experimental motive for the bomb. Certainly, this was one of Groves's criteria in deciding on a target. In practice it carried little weight. Most notoriously we have Groves favouring Kyoto as a target because, inter alia, it was large enough for the bomb damage to 'run out within the city' and so provide a 'firm understanding' of its destructive power, but this did not override Stimson's political sensitivity to the cultural importance of Kyoto. Equally, against the experimental criterion Nagasaki was a poor target. There was, as General Farrell, Groves's deputy, recalled, disagreement about it on the grounds that:

> the city was not a proper shape and dimension for the large bombs. It was long and narrow and was confined between two ranges of hills that would deflect the blast effect of the bombs. Also it had been very seriously bombed on several occasions before and it would be difficult to measure the effects of the atomic bomb in view of the previous damage.[9]

One of the first meetings to discuss the possible use of the bomb in 1943 considered as a possible target the Japanese fleet concentrated at Truk. This would have added attraction as a sort of retribution for Pearl Harbor. But by the time the bomb was ready the fleet did not exist.[10] Of course, at this time the priority targets would still have been German.

In 1944 there was some discussion of the possibility of tactical nuclear use. The weapons might be used as part of a force invading the Japanese mainland. General Marshall told David Lilienthal in 1947 that:

> We knew that the Japanese were determined and fanatical, like the Morros, and we thought we would have had to exterminate them, almost man for man. So we thought the bomb would be a wonderful weapon as a protection and preparation for landings.

Lilienthal records the number '12' in his diary, although in a later interview the number '9' was given by Marshall. The idea appears to have been to attack defences during the early stages of invasion with remaining bombs saved for Japanese reserves.[11] On the other hand Herbert Feis says there were no serious discussions of this in memos or directives.[12] This in itself may not be surprising as details would have been kept very close until senior commanders had to be told. However it had clearly not been taken very far because, as far as Lilienthal could tell, Marshall had not considered the effect of radioactivity on allied personnel. Marshall himself admitted that these plans were hatched when the real potential of the bomb was not known, and this was probably around the time when the invasion was first being seriously considered during the Summer of 1944, which was probably also the last point at which a stock of 9–12 bombs would at all have appeared feasible.

In a recent article, Barton Bernstein appears to confuse these thoughts of Marshall with some that occurred to him and a number of people concerned with planning for the November invasion of Kyushu, after the power of the bomb had become known as a result of its initial employment but before the Japanese surrender.[13] It does seem from Bernstein's work that at this point consideration did turn to 'tactical use'. For the purposes of this analysis, however, the key point is that this concept did not influence consideration of the initial use of the bomb.

By the Summer of 1945, absent the atomic bombs, the strategic question was whether the remorseless air campaign plus the blockade currently being conducted against Japan would bring about surrender or whether this would require a full-scale invasion, to which American policy-makers looked forward with deep foreboding. To hasten Japanese surrender the Truman leadership sought to commit the Soviet Union to the war (so as to tie down Japanese forces in China) and considered the possibility of hints to Tokyo that the Emperor's position might be respected in the event of an early surrender.

The awareness of the availability of a viable atomic bomb did not make a material difference to any element of this strategy, except possibly the bombing campaign. Planning for the invasion continued while the meeting of the 'big three' was under way at Potsdam, where Truman received news of the first successful test. Stalin was still urged to join the war and the possibility was again explored of conveying to Japanese war leaders the thought that not all honour would be lost through surrender.

Even with regard to the air war against Japan operations were only slightly affected, mainly in terms of preserving some serious civilian targets. General Curtis LeMay, who had been conducting the campaign, expected to run out of targets by October 'when there wouldn't really be much to work on except probably railroads or something of that sort'.[14]

The preoccupation of the historians' debate with the necessity of using the bomb has meant that it has been judged strategically against the prospective invasion rather than the actual air bombardment under way at the time and with which it was unavoidably linked in the minds of policy-makers. While the theorists of strategic bombardment had been left with a 'not proven' verdict following the air campaign against Germany, the raids against Japan were seen by those responsible as an opportunity to prove the independent worth of a strategic bombing force. In April LeMay wrote:

> I am influenced by the conviction that the present stage of development in the air war against Japan presents the AAF for the first time with the opportunity of proving the power of the strategic air arm. I consider that for the first time strategic air bombardment faces a situation in which its strength is proportionate to the magnitude of its task. I feel that the destruction of Japan's ability to wage war is within the capability of this command.[15]

The American distaste for area bombing had evaporated in the face of a set of Japanese targets marked by the complex intermingling of industry and society and fire-prone wooden structures. One only has to recall the most damaging single raid – the March 1945 attack on Tokyo which left nearly 80 000 dead and 300 000 buildings destroyed. Nobody involved in the decision on the atomic bombs could have seen themselves as setting new precedents for mass destruction in scale – only in efficiency. Indeed the appreciation of the bomb's potential should be seen in the light of a growing uneasiness among some senior policymakers over the conduct of the air war.

If the atomic bomb was to be seen simply as an extension of the air campaign then its necessity was doubtful. LeMay was of this view. He believed that the conventional campaign of strategic bombardment would bring about a Japanese surrender of its own accord and he saw no reason to see the atomic bombs as anything other than a supplement. We have already noted his view, which there is no reason to doubt, that the destruction of all Japanese targets was in reach. The conventional raids did not stop as a prelude to the introduction of the bomb: they continued up to the very moment of Japan's surrender. Indeed when discussion first began with regard to the choice of targets for the bomb, the 20th Air Force was noted to be

> operating primarily to laying waste all the main Japanese cities, and that they do not propose to save some important primary target for us if it interferes with the operation of the war from their point of view.

It was planning to increase its delivery of conventional bombs to 100 000 tons a month by the end of the year.[16]

At issue here was Japan's pain threshold, which by this stage in the war was judged to be high. General Arnold recorded in his memoirs his perception that there was nothing special about the atomic bombing other than the extra weight of destruction and thus his 'surprise' at Japan's 'abrupt surrender': 'We had figured we would probably have to drop four atomic bombs or increase the destructiveness of our Super Fortress missions by adding the heavy bombers from Europe.'[17] Military leaders not linked to the air campaign, who were also unconvinced by its value and discomforted by its ferocity, were unlikely to change their mind on being told of even more powerful bombs. Eisenhower's distaste for the atomic bomb has been regularly cited, although there is now doubt as to the extent of his actual opposition (and that of other military leaders). The point is largely that they showed no enthusiasm for the bomb.[18] General MacArthur, Supreme Commander in the Pacific, seems to have seen little need for its use.

Military leaders, however, played a limited role in the decision-making. Few of them were well informed on the bomb and they were not consulted by the key decision-makers. Far more influential in shaping decisions on the bomb's use were those responsible for its design and production. They did perhaps, as has often been suggested, have a special stake in their efforts being shown to bear fruit. For our purposes more relevant is their sense of the special quality of an atomic explosion and the awe which it might be expected to produce in all those who might witness it.

President Truman appears never either to have doubted that the bomb should be used if available or to have entered into any extended discussion of the strategic concept which might govern its use. In fact there was little debate anywhere over this matter. While it was probably discussed informally a number of times, the employment concept was actually forged in four meetings, apparently without great dissent, and only once reappraised under pressure from those scientists who argued that a demonstration shot was a feasible and much more desirable option.

The basic concept was that mentioned by Stimson in his 1947 memoir:

> I felt that to extract a genuine surrender from the Emperor and his military advisers, they must be administered a tremendous shock which would carry convincing proof of our power to destroy the Empire.

He described it as more than a weapon of terrible destruction; it was 'a psychological weapon'. Stimson also associated Marshall with this view. He was emphatic in his insistence on the shock value of the new weapon'.[19]

The idea of the atomic bomb, at least in its initial use, as a psychological weapon, seems to have come from Robert Oppenheimer. This is an inference from Oppenheimer's critical role at the key meetings convened to discuss the bomb's use in April and May 1945.

The first meeting, of which little is known, was at the Military Policy Committee (effectively the board of management of the Manhattan Project). The second meeting, at which General Groves transmitted the results of the first was of a Target Committee. This had been set up under Groves and met in April 1945 at the Pentagon. It consisted of two air force officers and five scientists and was chaired by Groves's Deputy, Thomas Farrell. The title of the Committee indicated its responsibility: to identify the most appropriate targets and the most effective form of attack. Groves brought with him criteria which presumably had been discussed at the Military Policy Committee:

> I had set as the governing factor that the targets chosen should be places the bombing of which would adversely affect the will of the Japanese people to continue the war. Beyond that, they should be military in nature, consisting either of important headquarters of troop concentrations, or centers of production of military equipment and supplies. To enable us to assess accurately the effects of the bomb, the targets should not have been previously damaged by air raids. It was also desirable that the first target be of such size that the damage would be confined within it, so that we could more definitely determine the power of the bomb.[20]

This ordering describes the eventual priority attached to these various criteria. Inevitably much of the speculation by historians relates to the way in which various cities found themselves earmarked for possible annihilation. Those on this Committee were not likely to reflect overmuch on the first criterion – 'adversely affecting the will of the Japanese people' as this was standard air force speak for area bombing, and there was no disputing that their task was to find a substantial civilian area, with some military role (which most in practice had) that had been left relatively unscathed. This required evaluating a number of cities against a variety of practical issues.

On 10 and 11 May this Committee met again at Los Alamos, with a formidable group of scientists present including Oppenheimer. It was Oppenheimer who set the agenda with a list of topics. The bulk of these were technical, concerning height of detonation, reports on weather, gadget jettisoning and moving on to questions of rehearsals and safety. More critical however were items E and F, 'Psychological Factors in Target Selection' and 'Use Against Military Objectives' respectively.[21] The main conclusion reached on the latter question was that the full impact of the weapon would be lost if only a discrete military target was attacked: 'it should be located in a much larger area subject to blast damage'. More thought was given to the former question concerning 'psychological factors'. The minutes identify two aspects of this:

> (1) obtaining the greatest psychological effect against Japan and (2) making the initial use sufficiently spectacular for the importance of the weapon to be internationally recognized when publicity on it is released.

The 'shock value' of this weapon thus had both short-term and long-term consequences and it was vital that both be maximised. When targets were discussed against these two criteria, shock might be derived from different features: thus Kyoto because the people there were 'more highly intelligent and hence better able to appreciate the significance of the weapon', Hiroshima because of the fraction of the city that would probably be destroyed, and the Emperor's Palace in Tokyo because of its status, although here there was a problem in that there could be no pretence that there was a military target close by.

The next critical meeting took place on Monday 31 May. This was the Interim Committee, set up to discuss the wider implications of the bomb which, almost by the way, addressed its actual employment. It included Secretary of War Henry Stimson and James Byrnes, soon to be Secretary of State. Also involved were a series of key luminaries of the scientific establishment who had been associated with the project since its inception, such as Vannevar Bush and James Conant. Robert Oppenheimer, General Groves and General Marshall were invited to attend.[22]

The Committee had one preliminary meeting before this fateful gathering.[23] At this second meeting the nature of the 'psychological factor' became more precise, again with Oppenheimer's prompting. After it had been noted that the effect of one bomb would not be different from 'any Air Corps strike of current dimensions', Oppenheimer interjected:

> the visual effect of an atomic bombing would be tremendous. It would be accompanied by a brilliant luminescence which would rise to a height of 10 000 to 20 000 feet.

It was on the basis of this spectacular quality that those considering the use of the bomb stressed its shock value. The report records how:

> After much discussion concerning various types of targets and effects to be produced, the Secretary expressed the conclusion, on which there was general agreement, that we could not give the Japanese any warning, that we could not concentrate on a civilian area, but that we should seek to make a profound psychological impression on as many Japanese as possible. At the suggestion of Dr Conant the Secretary agreed that the most desirable target would be a vital war plant employing a large number of workers and closely surrounded by workers' houses.

Note now how Groves's original criterion – 'to adversely affect the will of the Japanese people to continue the war' – had turned into making a 'profound psychological impression'. This formulation also reinforced the view that, in some way, the members of the committee had shifted discussion away from crude mass destruction. There is little record of the debate at the meeting, but we know that the President himself, Stimson and Marshall were all uneasy with regard to making civilians targets and had been thinking on how best to avoid this in the days before this meeting. On 29 May Marshall had told Stimson that he hoped the weapon 'might first be used against straight military objectives such as a large naval installation' and only later, if necessary, against 'large manufacturing areas', and only then after adequate warning.[24] We know too of Stimson's own conversations with his diary and with his President of his anxiety to spare civilians, and Truman's own conviction – sustained long after the bomb had been dropped – that it was directed at a large military target.

All this contradicted the logic of the target committee and the formulation agreed at the Interim Committee is best seen as a face-saving device. Stimson's only real influence on this matter exercised later was to spare Kyoto – whose people, it will be recalled, the Target Committee judged to be 'more intelligent and hence better able to appreciate the significance of the weapon'.

The tension in Stimson's position was adequately illustrated in his conversation with Truman a week after the Interim Committee's meeting. On the one hand he objected strenuously to continued area bombing. On the other:

> I was a little fearful that before we could get ready the Air Force might have Japan so thoroughly bombed out that the new weapon [the atomic bomb] would not have a chance to show its strength.

In practice, and despite the talk of military targets and psychological impact, the stress on the shock value of the weapon ensured that civilian casualties would be maximised. This is evident with regard to two issues also discussed by the Interim Committee. The first recorded in the minutes is of Oppenheimer's suggestion that the psychological impact be maximised by several strikes at the same time: Groves objected because this would require a rush job, the extra knowledge of the bomb's effects gained through successive blasts would be lost and 'the effect would not be sufficiently distinct from our regular Air Force bombing program'. Groves too understood now that this was not simply going to be an extension of the 20th Air Force's campaign.

The second issue was discussed over lunch and is not mentioned in the minutes. According to Arthur Compton he raised the possibility with Stimson of a 'non-military demonstration of the bomb's effects' and he broadened the discussion. The main obstacles to this course were soon identified: if prior warning were given there could be interference with the detonation; a failure following a great advertisement would be wholly counter-productive; a detonation on uninhabited territory might not impress those who most needed to be impressed. This discussion lasted ten minutes.

Despite the difficulty of devising a convincing demonstration, the scientific panel of the committee was asked to see if one could be found. Their efforts then merged with those of the Franck Committee of concerned scientists anxious to find any way of avoiding mass destruction.[25] As the Interim Committee observed at its next meeting after reviewing the issue: 'the difficulties of making a purely technical demonstration that would find its way into Japan's controlling councils were indeed great'.

Most important of all was the lack of warning. This was critical to the whole strategy. A general warning, already made credible enough by the air campaign, had been issued at Potsdam which threatened 'prompt and utter destruction' if there was no unconditional surrender. As Marshall observed: 'It's no good warning them. If you warn them there's no surprise. And the only way to produce shock is surprise.'[26] Groves made the same point. He claimed not to understand how 'anyone could ignore the importance of the effect on the Japanese people and their government of the overwhelming surprise of the bomb'.[27] A lack of specific warning also reduced the risk of the whole thing turning out to be a dud after being heralded as a spectacular instrument of destruction. Of the members of the Interim Committee only Ralph Bard, towards the end of June, became uneasy with regard to the lack of warning and suggested that this policy be reversed.[28]

The tactics of the attack involved distracting the attention of any Japanese air defences by carrying out other air raids on the same day and by using a single, unescorted plane on the assumption that the Japanese would take no notice of a lone plane flying at high altitude. If anything it would be taken to be a reconnaissance plane. Despite this assumption they still expected relatively moderate casualties on the basis of people taking shelter. Oppenheimer had estimated that 20 000 would die. This was one of his few calculations that was grossly in error.

Butow's classic study – *Japan's Decision to Surrender* – correctly points out that the dropping of the two atomic bombs on Japan, together with the Soviet entry into the war 'did not produce the decision' to end the war, but that they created an 'unusual atmosphere' in Tokyo, which facilitated Japan's hurried decision to accept the Potsdam declaration on 15 August 1945.[29]

Before the first atomic bomb was dropped on 6 August, most Japanese decision makers, including the Emperor, Prime Minister Admiral Suzuki Kantarō, Foreign Minister Tōgō Shigenori and many Japanese overseas diplomats, the Director of the Cabinet Board of Information, Shimomura Hiroshi (Kainan) and Navy Minister Yonai Mitsumasa agreed that Japan must end the war and thereby accept defeat.[30] Two interrelated problems remained unresolved: first, Japan's leaders were uneasy about what the price of a decision to surrender would be, since they did not want

Japan's termination of the war to bring about her complete downfall – in other words, the extermination of Japan as an entity, the so-called *Kokutai*. They feared that Japan might be eliminated as a nation-state as a result of its unconditional surrender. The *sine qua non* of the continued existence of Japan meant, for these leaders, the preservation of the Imperial system.

The second problem was how to achieve a consensus among the top decision-makers – the Prime Minister, the Foreign Minister, the Navy and War Ministers and the Naval and Army Chiefs of General Staff – for the surrender of Japan. Except for Yonai, the other military leaders, particularly in the army, believed that Japan should continue to fight on the mainland. If the Prime Minister overrode this military opinion, the Army Minister might resign from the Cabinet, and if the Army did not recommend a new Army Minister, the classic pattern of the dissolution of the Cabinet would be repeated. Similarly, those military leaders – although they were aware of Japan's appalling military weaknesses – still had to take account of the feelings of their middle-echelon officers, since, otherwise, there might be a repetition of the army revolts of the 1930s. Thus, the unity of the Japanese decision-making system depended upon a delicate balance between a powerful military hierarchy which was, at the same time, vulnerable to the actions of its subordinates.[31]

Consequently, before Japan decided to surrender, there were a number of uncertainties about the post-war future of the Imperial system under the Potsdam declaration and these tended to stiffen the attitudes of those who supported a final stand on the mainland. The Japanese leaders were unable to overcome the deadlock. Moreover, there remained the hope – albeit declining – that the Soviet Union, which had remained neutral in the Pacific War, might be persuaded to act as a mediator and enable Japan to extract more favourable terms than unconditional surrender from the Western Allies.[32] Thus, after the Potsdam declaration, Tokyo adopted a 'wait and see' policy, but this was complicated by the time factor. The situation in Japan was deteriorating rapidly in 1945, with shortages of food and other necessities (salt, sugar, soap, clothing, rice, etc.), an inability to produce aircraft and military equipment of all kinds and the scarcity of strategic materials, the declining morale of the Japanese people, especially as a result of American strategic bombings ('guests', as the regular bombing missions were called by the desperate Japanese public).[33] In the light of all this, it was clear that, as Louis Allen has pointed out, 'by any rational calculation . . . the time was months overdue for Japan to sue for peace'.[34] Certainly, some Japanese ministers and officials were increasingly pessimistic about the prospects for the maintenance of public order if the war continued until the Autumn of 1945 and beyond.

As the sequence of events leading to the decision to surrender on 15 August is well known, our focus is on the initial Japanese reaction to the first atomic bomb dropped on Hiroshima, and we will try to examine the importance of the impact of the American use of atomic bombs on the minds of the Japanese leaders at that time.

Lieutenant-Colonel Ōya of the General Staff was sent to Hiroshima at the end of June 1945 to re-organise the information/intelligence section dealing with Anglo-American affairs in the Headquarters of the Second General Army. Ōya originally intended to stay in Hiroshima for a short time, but he was asked to remain in the section until 15 August. On 6 August, the weather in the Hiroshima area was fine and warm, with a temperature of 26.7C. About seven in the morning, he heard an air-raid warning, but then recalled the all-clear sounding at about eight o'clock. According to Hattori, the warning was withdrawn about 7.30 am, but Japan's radio broadcast another warning at about eight that there were two B-29 bombers flying over Hiroshima which were probably on reconnaissance. Ōya was already working in the office and at 8.15 am he heard the noise of the B-29 bombers, and wondered why the air-raid warning had been withdrawn. He stood up and walked to the window behind his desk to look out. He saw two B-29 bombers flying due north-north-west, and he believed that they were flying away from Hiroshima city. He went back to his desk to continue his work, while other officers continued to watch the two aeroplanes, from the office windows. Then Ōya suddenly felt a tremendous shock and he sensed a terrific flash of light. He was blown out of his desk chair for a distance of about 2–3 metres and saw blood pouring from the bodies of the seven or so other officers. Of course he had no idea what was happening, but he remembered one of the officers, Captain Ishi, saying that 'this might be an atomic bomb'. Ōya knew that the Americans employed two methods of bombing: in the case of strategic bombing, they tended to use a large number of small incendiary shells, while for battlefield attacks, they used more powerful 'special new types of bombs'. However, he did not then believe that the weapons used at Hiroshima were atomic bombs.[35]

The Special Intelligence Section in the army General Headquarters, which had been established in July 1943 and was attached to the Chief of the General Staff of the Army, claimed that as early as May 1945 they were aware of some interesting American air activity, which might have been connected to the Hiroshima bombing.[36] Given their lack of radar, Special Intelligence had to rely on a radio direction-ranging apparatus (*Hōkō Tanchiki*) to follow up the movements of enemy planes through their radio signals. The special information section was unable to decode the contents of these signals, except for very simple communications, but they were able to identify roughly the number of enemy planes in a flight and the direction in which these planes were flying.[37] The Special Intelligence section noted in mid-May 1945 that one B-29 plane, flying from Hawaii to the Saipan area, despatched an unusually long telegraph to Washington. By mid-June, it became clear that this plane belonged to a small squadron of about 10–12 aircraft. From the end of June this plane, sometimes alone, sometimes with two to three others, flew over the sea near Tenian island in the Marianas and by mid-July, they were flying around the Japanese mainland before returning to an air base on Tenian island. The Special Intelligence Section assumed that this was 'some sort of training', but could not identify what it was for. Separate from the Special Intelligence Section, the 6th division of the Intelligence Department of the Army General Staff in charge of Anglo-American affairs was aware that 'there was a new experiment in New Mexico on 16 July', but they did not connect this with an atomic bomb explosion.[38]

About three in the morning of 6 August, the Special Intelligence Section intercepted a brief signal to Washington from an American aircraft. About one hour later, another signal from a group of 2–3 planes to an American base on Iwo island was monitored, which apparently stated that 'we are flying to our target'. This information did concern the intelligence officials, but no further radio messages were detected until 7.20 on the same morning, when both the Navy and Army intelligence intercepted a signal from a B-29 bomber, which was on its way to the Sea of Harima after flying to Hiroshima from the Bungo Channel, situated between Shikoku and Kyushu islands. This plane was not accompanied by other American planes, as was often the case with American weather reconnaissance squadrons, and this apparently solo flight puzzled the Japanese officials, who continued to monitor the Bungo Channel in the expectation that other American planes were following the first. Even more unusual, however, was that, at about 8.06, two B-29s appeared from the opposite side of the Bungo Channel, and flew towards Hiroshima. The Japanese Intelligence Community realised that they had been outmanoeuvred, but it was now too late to take any precautions against these enemy intruders.[39]

At 8.30 – about 15 minutes after the American bomb was dropped on Hiroshima – Kure navy depot in the Hiroshima prefecture reported to the Navy Ministry in Tokyo that the enemy had dropped an enormously destructive bomb.[40] Just after 10.00 on that morning, the War Ministry in Tokyo received a report from Hiroshima which stated that, given the information that the United States had been developing a new type of bomb, 'this must be it'. Neither of these sources, however, identified this 'new type of bomb' as an atomic device.[41]

During the afternoon of 7 August, an emergency meeting of key Japanese Cabinet ministers took place after President Harry Truman had publicly stated that the bomb which the United States had dropped on Hiroshima was an atomic weapon. However, War Minister Anami contended that, because the Army had not yet begun a thorough investigation into the circumstances at Hiroshima, they did not want to admit that Hiroshima had been subjected to an atomic attack. The Army General Staff was to send a group of investigators to Hiroshima, headed by Lieutenant-General Arisue.[42]

In the meantime, the Army persistently rejected any reference to the words 'atomic bomb' in Hiroshima in public announcements and there was a heated debate between the Army Headquarters and the Board of Information as to how the public were to be informed of the disaster that had taken place in the city. The information bureau argued that the public must be told the truth so that they could be psychologically prepared for a new phase of modern warfare, while the Army feared that such an announcement would destroy public morale.[43] Consequently, the radio merely announced at 15.30 on 7 August that a few B-29 bombers had dropped 'a new type of bomb' on Hiroshima and which had caused a fair amount of damage and many casualties.[44] The next day, the major newspapers, *Asahi*, *Yomiuri*, and *Mainichi*, reported on similar lines.[45]

Because of engine trouble in their plane, the despatch of the Arisue mission to Hiroshima was delayed by one day and the mission did not arrive in the city until about noon on 8 August, more than two days after the bombing had taken place.[46] In the early hours of 9 August, Chief Cabinet Secretary Sakomizu received the news about the Soviet entry into the war with Japan. Sakomizu felt as if 'the earth was shaking'. Tōgō urged the Prime Minister to end the war as soon as possible. The Emperor told Marquis Kido, the Lord Keeper of the Privy Seal, 'now that the Soviets have entered the war with Japan, there was urgent need to resolve the problem of a ceasefire' and Hirohito asked Kido to convey this Imperial message to Suzuki.[47]

The six members of the Supreme War Direction Council met at 10.30 am on 9 August 1945, followed by two Cabinet meetings from 14.30 till 22.00. During the Supreme War Direction Council meeting, the Japanese leaders were informed that a second atomic bomb had been dropped on Nagasaki. Except for the Navy Minister, the military leaders remained opposed to accepting the Potsdam declaration. The Army Minister insisted that Japan was still able to fight a victorious battle on the mainland. Given this division of opinion, Prime Minister Suzuki asked the Emperor to decide on the matter. The Imperial conference convened at 23.50 and Hirohito informed the leaders of his decision that Japan must accept the Potsdam declaration but on the understanding that its acceptance must not involve the elimination of the Imperial system.[48] As we know, it would require a second Imperial decision on 14 August before Japan finally surrendered, and this decision was broadcast to the Japanese people by the Emperor on 15 August 1945.

Because of the delay to Arisue's mission (his report was completed on 10 August and it identified the bomb dropped on Hiroshima as an atomic one)[49] and because of the subsequent Soviet entry into the war before the Japanese leadership had time to clarify their views on the effects of the dropping of the first bomb, it is difficult to separate the impact of the atomic bombs on Japan's final decision to make peace from the effect of the Soviet entry into the war on that decision. However, the following observations suggest that the impact of the atomic bombs was of crucial importance to, and in some respects possibly even decisive in, Japan's decision in favour of a ceasefire.

First, between the dropping of the first atomic bomb and the Soviet entry, the Emperor and his close advisers believed that Japan must now end the war. Prime Minister Admiral Suzuki, on learning of Truman's statement on 7 August that Hiroshima had been the target of an atomic bomb, was awed by the American achievement and he argued 'unequivocally' that Japan must sue for peace.[50] Prince Konoye also took the new development seriously and told Marquis Kido that the war should be ended immediately.[51] As soon as he heard the news Shimomura sent a message to the Prime Minister that it was imperative that Japan decided on peace.[52] When Foreign Minister Tōgō reported to the Emperor during the afternoon of 8 August that the bomb provided an overwhelming motive for Japan to end the war, Hirohito entirely agreed, telling the Foreign Minister that 'now that this kind of weapon had been used in the war, it was even more impossible for Japan to continue the war'. He continued:

> Japan could no longer afford to talk about the conditions of her surrender terms. She must aim for a speedy resolution of the war.[53]

Thus, before the Arisue mission's final report and before the Soviet Union declared war, the peace faction had resolved on a speedy ceasefire.

Secondly, while it was true that the Soviet entry into the war had shattered any lingering hope that the Soviet Union might mediate a negotiated peace between Japan and the Allies, many civilian leaders, who were shocked by the Soviet action, were already thinking of a ceasefire. Moreover, Foreign Minister Tōgō and his diplomats overseas had not placed much faith in the Soviet Union as a mediator.[54] Similarly, the Army was well aware that the Russians were preparing for war in the East and had been transferring troops from Europe to the Far East since February 1945. Moscow's declaration in April 1945 that it would not renew the neutrality pact with Japan, followed by Germany's unconditional surrender in May, seemed to prove the Soviet Union's ultimate intentions. The Soviet entry so soon after the dropping of the atomic bomb on Hiroshima added to the distress of the Japanese and also upset the Army's plan for the final battle on the mainland which involved transferring some 250 000 men and weapons from Manchuria to mainland Japan. Nonetheless, the imminent opening of hostilities by the USSR was not unexpected – indeed, the Army thought that it was merely 'a matter of time' before Moscow decided to enter the war against Japan.[55]

Thirdly, in comparison to the Soviet entry, the atomic bomb took Japan's leaders completely by surprise, since Army General Headquarters had concluded optimistically that the Americans would be unable to complete their research on atomic weapons before the end of the war.[56] A section of the Japanese Army had also been trying desperately, but without success, to develop atomic weapons.

As early as April 1940, Major General Yasuda Takeo, then director of the Institute of Aviation Technology in the Army, instructed his staff to work on the atomic bomb. His decision was partially influenced by German progress in this field. The Army's research was directed by Dr Nishina, head of the Institute of Physical and Chemical Research.[57] Three years later, in March 1943, Yasuda reported to General Tōjō that it might be possible for Japan to produce atomic weapons in the near future. General Tōjō, knowing that the Americans were also making progress with this weapon, believed that 'the atomic weapons might decide the outcome of the present war with the United States'.[58]

Accordingly, Tōjō ordered Yasuda to promote the research and development of atomic bombs vigorously and the Army's aviation centre, in collaboration with Dr Nishina's research office, took the first official step towards developing atomic weapons. The codename was 'Ni-gō' research – 'Ni' was derived from the first two letters of Dr Nishina's surname. This is why when Tōjō first learned of the Hiroshima bombing, he realised that this must be caused by the detonation of an atomic bomb.[59]

However, the Japanese scientists were unable to produce a chain reaction. Nor did Dr Nishina succeed in splitting the two uranium isotopes, 235 and 238. Uranium was in short supply and he asked the Army to obtain at least 2 tons for his research programme. The search for uranium only seriously began in 1943. As Japan produced so little, Captain Kawashima investigated gold mines near Seoul, Korea, but he discovered that the mines contained only a small quantity (one could obtain about a dozen uranium isotopes, each the size of the tip of the fifth finger, from 24 cubic square inches of ore).[60] The Army also hoped to obtain some from Germany, as Czechoslovakia, then under German occupation, was reputed to produce good quality uranium. After difficult negotiations, Nazi Germany agreed to give about two tons of uranium to Japan, which would be transported there by two submarines, despatched to Japan for this purpose. One never arrived in Japan, and the other was unable to sail after Germany surrendered in May 1945. Accordingly, the 'Ni-gō' research made slow progress, and finally, the Army had to abandon atomic research altogether in the Spring of 1945, when intensive air raids on Tokyo and Osaka destroyed a number of research centres working on atomic bombs.[61] The Navy, too, was involved in atomic research, but they soon realised that they could achieve little before the end of the war and switched their

efforts to the development of radio beams. This research also was never com
pleted.[62] Of course, given the secrecy attached to atomic weapons research, most
Japanese civilian leaders and military officials knew nothing about the project.
However, Army General Headquarters claimed that they had already suspected,
before the final Arisue report came, that an atomic bomb had been dropped on
Hiroshima.[63] Nevertheless, the Army leaders deliberately underestimated the
amount of damage caused by the bomb and were reluctant to give much information either to the civilian leaders or to the public (the latter did not know the full
truth about the atomic bomb until after Japan's surrender).[64]

The reality was that the military could do nothing to counter the threat of
atomic bombardment, except to suggest some defensive measures, which included
(1) a rapid evacuation of the populace into shelters if even one enemy plane was
sighted over Japan's air sphere; (2) to order the people to cover their bodies with
sufficient clothing, preferably with white outer clothes, and not to expose their skin
to radiation; (3) always to carry some ointment for burns; and (4) in the event of
evacuation, to make sure that fires were not started by carelessly discarding lighted
cigarettes, leaving on kitchen stoves, etc.[65]

While the Army contended that these measures would be sufficient to counter
the effects of atomic bombs, they soon shifted from an underestimation to an overestimation of the ability of the United States to produce these weapons. At the
Cabinet meeting on 9 August, War Minister Anami, who had obtained some
information from an American prisoner of war, told the Ministers that:

> One atomic bomb could destroy 6 square miles, which was equivalent
> to 2000 B-29s each with 300 conventional bombs of 500 pounds each
> . . . the Americans appeared to have one hundred atomic bombs . . .
> while they could drop three per day. The next target might well be
> Tokyo.[66]

Thus the Army's surprise at the American achievement in atomic technology in
contrast to Japan's inability to reach even the initial level of atomic research, their
consequent reluctance to use the words, 'atomic bomb' in any public announcements, (whereas the news of the Soviet Union's entry into the war was reported
in headlines of the major newspapers on 10 August), their ready acceptance that
the Americans possessed about 100 atomic bombs, all suggested the depth of the
shock of the atomic bomb on the minds of the military leaders.

Finally, and as the American leaders had anticipated, whatever the impact of
the Soviet invasion of Manchuria and Sakhalin may have been, it was *indirect*, whereas
the atomic bomb demonstrated *directly* to Japan's leaders that the United States
could totally devastate her mainland. The fact that one single bomb could kill and
injure 130 000 human beings instantly, as was initially reported, exposed the already
appalling military weakness of Japan to the entire leadership of the country.[67]

Of course, the impact of the atomic bomb cannot be discussed in isolation and
can be seen as the final phase of the cumulative damage already inflicted on mainland
Japan by the intensive American air raids which began during the Autumn of 1944.
Given that Manchuria and Japan's other occupied territories were still regarded as
'outside land' [*gaichi*], as opposed to Japan's mainland which was referred as 'inside

land' [*naichi*], the people of Japan were faced with the military reality of war for the first time when the United States began to bomb their homeland.

Prior to the dropping of the two atomic bombs, American strategic bombing had already killed some 665 000 people and destroyed 20 per cent of civilian housing in Japan.[68] After a massive air raid on 25 May 1945, the Army leaders were attacked by Cabinet ministers for their inability to find any measures to counter the American bombers. The Imperial Palace also caught fire and as a result War Minister Anami nearly resigned.[69] In May, an exhibition of weapons for the national volunteer army was held at the Prime Minister's office. Prime Minister Suzuki and other ministers were disgusted with the poor quality of the weapons on display. These included bamboo spears, bows and arrows, and pistols with only 50 per cent accuracy, which fired pieces of iron instead of bullets, which were by then hard to obtain.[70] The shortage and poor quality of these weapons were compounded by the untrained manpower available to deploy them – men who were either too young or too old to be in the regular forces.[71] Cabinet ministers feared that a tired and hungry populace might become defiant and that public disorder might result.[72]

Thus, the atomic bombs helped to bring home on a much larger scale to those of Japan's leaders who were already seeking a means to end the war, how potentially catastrophic Japan's situation was. At the same time, the military radicals, who could not conceive that Japan was on the verge of defeat, were angered by the growing official consensus about the need to accept the Potsdam declaration. However, the military leaders now had more power over their subordinates, since the Emperor, who was the Supreme Commander of the Japanese Armed Forces, had twice decided in favour of Japan's surrender at the Imperial Conference. War Minister Anami, the Chief of the General Staff Umezu and General Tōjō, the former Prime Minister, all refused to collaborate with plans for a *coup d'état* by the younger middle-echelon officers. On the night of 14 August, an attempted military coup by the radicals, designed to prevent any appeal for peace from the Imperial Palace and to steal the recording of the Emperor's announcement of Japan's acceptance of the Potsdam declaration, collapsed ignominiously.[73]

In conclusion, the atomic bombs succeeded in the American aim of shocking Japan into surrender. While it is difficult to separate the impact of the atomic bomb from the subsequent blow of the Soviet entry into the war, or to isolate completely the effects of the dropping of the atomic bombs from the cumulative effects of American strategic bombing, the events from 6 to 9 August 1945 helped to expedite the Japanese decision-making process, which was notoriously complicated and time-consuming, and finally led to Japan's decision to terminate the war. Japanese leaders were not only awed by the American ability to produce atomic bombs during the war, but were also taken by surprise when one was dropped on Hiroshima. The nature of shock was more direct than the news about the Soviet entry, which itself dramatically exposed Japan's appalling military weakness.

Indeed, Japan would probably have used the new weapons during the war if her atomic research had succeeded. Colonel Ogata, then a military aide-de-camp to His Majesty, believed, when he heard the news of Hiroshima, that 'if Japan had possessed atomic weapons, she could have attacked the United States, which might have changed the phase of the war in Japan's favour'. The view was, as Kojima has discussed, also echoed by some civilian leaders.[74] Those Japanese leaders who were desperate to avoid defeat or unconditional surrender would have taken any steps to avoid either alternative. Seen in this light, lingering Japanese criticisms about the American use of the atomic bomb (most of whose awful side effects were then unknown to United States leadership) are ill founded.[75] Conversely, the United States can claim that her use of the atomic bomb was in the end justifiable in that Japan also intended to use such weapons during the war if and when they became available.

Notes

1   The Committee for the Compilation of Materials on Damage caused by the Atomic Bomb in Hiroshima and Nagasaki, *Hiroshima and Nagasaki: The Physical, Medical, and Social Effects of the Atomic Bombings* (London: Hutchinson, 1981).

2   Ibid., p. 335.

3   J.S. Allen, *Atomic Imperialism: The State, Monopoly and the Bomb* (New York: International Publishers, 1952).

4   P.M.S. Blackett, *Military and Political Consequences of Atomic Energy* (London: Turnstile Press, 1948).

5   Gar Alperovitz, *Atomic Diplomacy: Hiroshima and Potsdam, The Use of the Atomic Bomb and the American Confrontation with Soviet Power* (New York: Vintage, 1985) still keeps the revisionist flag flying although his thesis is not taken very seriously now. For a spirited exchange involving a television producer who does, see Sheila Kerr, 'Alperovitz, Timewatch and the Bomb', *Intelligence and National Security* 5:3 (July 1990), and Robert Marshall, 'The Atomic Bomb and the Lag in the Historical Understanding', *Intelligence and National Security* 6:2 (April 1991), with rejoinders by S. Kerr, G. Warner and D. Cameron Watt. For the contrasting view, see the essays by Alperovitz and Warner in David Carlton and Herbert Levine (eds), *The Cold War Debated* (London: McGraw-Hill, 1988).

6   Richard G. Hewlett and Oscar Anderson, *The New World 1939–1946*, vol. 1 of a History of the USAEC (Pennsylvania: Pennsylvania State University Press, 1962) pp. 254, 322.

7   Letters to *Science* Magazine, 2 December 1959.

8   Arthur Compton, *Atomic Quest* (New York: Harper, 1950) p. 234.

9   See Leslie Groves, *Now It Can Be Told. The Story of the Manhattan Project* (New York: Harper & Row, 1962), pp. 272–3; L. Giovannitti and F. Freed, *The Decision to Drop the Bomb* (London: Methuen, 1967) pp. 247–8.

10   Hewlett and Anderson, *The New World*, p. 253.

11   The Journals of David E. Lilienthal, vol. 2, *The Atomic Energy Years, 1945–1950* (London: Harper & Row, 1964) pp. 198–9; John P. Sutherland, 'The Story General Marshall Told Me' *US News & World Report*, 2 November 1959, p. 53.

12   Herbert Feis, *The Atomic Bomb and the End of World War II* (Princeton: Princeton University Press, 1966) p. 10.

13   Barton Bernstein, 'Eclipsed by Hiroshima and Nagasaki: Early Thinking about Tactical Nuclear Weapons', *International Security* 15:4 (Spring 1991).

14   Giovannitti and Freed, *The Decision to Drop the Bomb*, p. 36.

15   Quoted in ibid., p. 35.

16   Views of Air Force Colonel on Target Committee, cited in Richard Rhodes, *The Making of the Atomic Bomb* (London: Simon & Schuster, 1986) p. 627.

17   General H. H. Arnold, *Global Mission* (London: Hutchinson, 1951) p. 260.

18   Barton J. Bernstein, 'Ike and Hiroshima: Did He Oppose It?', *The Journal of Strategic Studies* 10:3 (September 1987).

19   Henry Stimson and McGeorge Bundy, *On Active Service in Peace and War* (London: Hutchinson, 1948) pp. 364, 369–70, 373.

20   Groves, *Now It Can Be Told*, p. 267.

21   Rhodes, *The Making of the Atomic Bomb*, p. 631. The full document is reproduced in Michael B. Stoff, Jonathan F. Fanton and R. Hal Williams, *The Manhattan Project: A Documentary Introduction to the Atomic Age* (New York: McGraw Hill, 1991) pp. 97–103.

22   Other members were Ralph Bard, William Clayton, Karl Compton, George Harrison. Among those invited to attend were Enrico Fermi, Arthur Compton, E. O. Lawrence, Harvey Bundy and Arthur Page.

23   The minutes are found in Stoff, et al., The *Manhattan Project*, pp. 105–20.

24   Cited in Bernstein, 'Eclipsed by Hiroshima', p. 156.

25   Compton, *Atomic Quest*, pp. 236–44. This was the strategy, rather than the direct attack, that had been proposed with the clearest eye on the post-war world.

26   Giovannitti and Freed, *The Decision to Drop the Bomb*, p. 36.

27   Groves, *Now It Can Be Told*, p. 266.

28   On the question of warning, see McGeorge Bundy, *Danger and Survival. Choices about the Bomb in the First Fifty Years* (New York: Random House, 1988) pp. 172–7.

29   Robert Butow, *Japan's Decision to Surrender* (Stanford: Stanford University Press, 1954) p. 231. Despite the ever-growing literature on this subject, there have been relatively few articles from the Japanese perspective published in English. See Sadao Asada, 'Japanese Perceptions of the A-Bomb Decision, 1945–1980' Joe C. Dixon (ed.), *The American Military and the Far East – Proceedings of the Ninth Military History Symposium, United States Air Force Academy, 1–3 October 1980* (Washington DC: United States Air Force Academy and Office Air Force History Headquarters, 1980) pp. 200–19.

30   Tōgō Shigenori, *Jidai no Ichimen* (Memoirs) (Tokyo: Hara, 1989) pp. 330–42; Butow, *The Decision to Surrender*, pp. 104–111 ff; The Ministry of Foreign Affairs (ed.), *Dai'niji Sekai Taisen Shūsen Shiroku* (The historical record of the termination of the Second World War) vol. 2, (Tokyo: Yamate, 1990) pp. 448–66. (Hereafter cited as *Shiroku*).

31   S. Hayashi, *Taiheiyō Senso* (The Pacific War) (Tokyo: Chuokoron, 1980) pp. 438–52 ff; H. Suzuki (ed.) *Memoirs of Suzuki Kantarō* (Tokyo: Jiji, 1985) pp. 275–93; for Japanese civil-military relations, see S. Dockrill, 'Hirohito, the Emperor's Army and Pearl Harbor', *Review of International Studies* 18 (1992), pp. 319–33.

32   For instance, the subject was discussed at a meeting of the Supreme Council for the Direction of War on 11 May 1945, see *Shiroku*, pp. 448–64; Hayashi, *Taiheiyō Senso*, pp. 442–4.

33   Hayashi, *Taiheiyō Senso*, p. 406.

34   Louis Allen, 'Japan Surrenders: Reason and Unreason in August 1945', unpublished Conference paper presented at the Second Strategy Conference at the US Army War College, Carlisle Barracks, Pennsylvania, 7–10 February 1991.

35   For Ōya's oral history, on 11 Feb. 1976, see The Army Record: Hondo – Seibu-204. The Army Archives, The Institute for National Defence Studies, the Self-Defence Agency, Tokyo. We are grateful to the Japanese Self-Defence Agency, and especially Mr Ōya for allowing us to quote from Mr Ōya's oral history concerning his experiences in Hiroshima.

36   Eizo Hori, *Daihon'ei-Sanbo no Jōhō Senki* (The record of the war of Intelligence at the Army General Staff) (Tokyo: Bungei Shunju, 1989) pp. 208–14. For the recent study

on Japanese Intelligence, see Louis Allen, 'Japanese Intelligence Systems' *Journal of Contemporary History* 22:4 (October 1987), pp. 547–62; J. Chapman, 'Japanese Intelligence, 1918–1945: A Suitable Case for Treatment' in Christopher Andrew and Jeremy Noakes (eds), *Intelligence and International Relations 1900–1945*, Exeter Studies in History no. 15 (Exeter: University of Exeter, 1987) pp. 145–90; Edward Drea, 'Reading Each Other's Mail: Japanese Communication Intelligence 1920–1941', *The Journal of Military History* 55:2 (April 1991), pp. 185–96; H. Iwashima, *Jōhōsen ni Kanpai Shita Nihon: Rikugun Angō 'Shinwa' no Hakai* (Tokyo: Hara, 1984).

37   Hori, *Jōhō*, pp. 211–13.

38   Ibid, pp. 213–16; Ronald Spector, *Eagle against the Sun* (Harmondsworth and New York: Penguin, 1987) pp. 554–5.

39   Hori, *Jōhō*, pp. 216–19; William Craig, *The Fall of Japan* (Harmondsworth: Penguin, 1979) pp. 69–71.

40   K. Han'dō, *Seidan-Ten'nō to Suzuki Kantarō* (A· Sacred Decision: the Emperor and Suzuki) (Tokyo: Bungeishunjū, 1988) p. 330.

41   The Military History Section, The Self-Defence Agency (eds), *Sensi Sōsho* vol. 19 – *Hondo Bōkū Sakusen* (the Strategy for the air defence of mainland Japan) (Tokyo: Asagumo, 1968) p. 628. (Hereafter cited as *Sōsho*, vol. 19).

42   Ibid p. 635; Hayashi, *Taiheiyō Sensō*, pp. 456–7.

43   See Shimomura, *Shūsenki* (The Record of the Termination of the War) (Tokyo: Kamakura bunko, 1948) pp. 97–8; See also *Shiroku*, pp. 734–5; Yomiuri (ed.), *Shōwashi no Ten'nō* (The Emperor during the Showa era) vol. 7, (Tokyo: Yomiuri, 1972) p. 228.

44   The Military History Section the Self-Defence Agency (ed.), *Hondo Kessen Junbi (2)- Sensi Sōsho*, vol. 57 (Preparations for the decisive battle on the mainland) (Tokyo: Asagumo, 1972) p. 578. (Hereafter cited as *Sōsho*, vol. 57.)

45   See *Mainichi*, 8 August 1945; *Asahi*, 8 August 1945; *Yomiuri*, 8 August 1945; for the Soviet entry, see *Asahi*, 10 August 1945.

46   *Sōsho*, vol. 19, p. 635.

47   K. Kido, *Kido Diaries*, vol. 2 (Tokyo: Tokyo University Press, 1966) p. 1223; Hayashi, *Taiheiyō Sensō*, p. 458.

48   *Shiroku*, pp. 760–85; Kido, *Kido Diaries*, pp. 1223–4.

49   *Sōsho*, vol. 57, p. 579.

50   Suzuki (ed.), *Memoirs*, p. 294.

51   Kido, *Diaries*, p. 1222; Hayashi, *Taiheiyō Sensō*, pp. 456–7; T. Yabe (ed.), *Konoe Fumimaro* (Biography of Prince Konoe), vol. 2 (Tokyo: Konoe Furnimaro Denki Hensan Kanko-kai, 1952) p. 565.

52   *Showa no Ten'nō*, vol. 7, pp. 207–8.

53   Tōgō, *Memoirs*, pp. 355–6. Han'dō, *Seidan*, p. 335.

54   Tōgō, *Memoirs*, pp. 327–42ff; *Shiroku*, pp. 448–66ff; See also Sato, Ambassador to Moscow to the Ministry of Foreign Affairs, tels. 1143, 1328, 1416, 8 June, 12 July 1945, ibid., pp. 634–44; Butow, *Japan's Decision to Surrender*, pp. 104–11.

55   *Sōsho*, vol. 57, pp. 580–2; see also Mizumachi minute (undated), 'Japanese preparations as of February 1945 for a possible war with the Soviet Union', File 1003, Army Archives 56, the Institute for National Defense Studies, Tokyo.

56   *Shiroku*, pp. 731–2; Suzuki (ed.), *Memoirs*, p. 294.

57   *Sōsho*, vol. 19, p. 631.

58   *Sōsho*, vol. 19, p. 632; M. Hosaka, *Tōjō Hideki to Ten'nō no Jidai* (H. Tōjō and the Emperor's era), vol. 2 (Tokyo: Bunshun, 1988) pp. 102, 202.

59   For the outline of Japan's atomic research, see *Sōsho*, vol. 19, pp. 631–2.

60   *Sōsho*, vol. 19, p. 633.

61   Ibid., pp. 633–5.

62   *Shōwashi no Ten'nō*, vol. 7, p. 243; *Sōsho*, vol. 19, p. 635.

63   Ibid., pp. 635.

64   *Shōwashi no Ten'nō*, vol. 7, p. 228; *Shiroku*, pp. 727, 734–37; Shimomura, *Shūsenki* pp. 96–9; *Sōsho*, vol. 19, p. 635; *Sōsho*, vol. 57, p. 578.

65   See for instance, *Asahi*, 9 and 10 August 1945; *Sōsho*, vol.19, pp. 641–2.

66   *Shiroku*, p. 778.

67   Noboru Kojima, *Ten'nō*, vol. 5 (Tokyo: Bunshun, 1988) p. 278.

68   Hayashi, *Taiheiyō Sensō*, pp. 405–6.

69   Kojima, *Ten'nō* vol. 5, p. 214–18; Han'dō, *Seidan*, pp. 264–7; *Shōwa no Ten'nō*, vol. 7, pp. 158–60.

70   Ibid., p. 162; N. Kojima *Taiheiyō Sensō* (The Pacific War), vol. 2 (Tokyo: Chuko, 1988) pp. 334–5.

71   Akira Fujiwara, *Nihon Gunjishi* (Japanese Military History) vol. 1, (Tokyo Nihon Hyōronsha, 1987) pp. 237–61ff; Jun'ichiro Kisaka, *Taiheiyō Sensō* (Tokyo: Shoga'kan, 1989), p. 394.

72   *Shōwa no Ten'nō*, vol. 7, pp. 177–80; *Tōgō, Memoirs*, p. 342; *Shiroku*, pp. 730–1, 766–7.

73   *Tōgō, Memoirs*, p. 345; *Shiroku*, pp. 798–812; *Shōwa no Ten'nō*, vol. 7, pp. 177–8, 181–3, 228, 289; Hosaka, *Tōjō*, vol. 2, pp. 204–11; Shimomura, *Shusenki*, p. 50; Yuzuru Sanematsu, *Yonai Mitsumasa* (Tokyo: Yomiuri, 1990) pp. 365–401.

74   Kojima, *Ten'nō*, vol. 5, p. 279; Admiral Koshiro Oikawa, who served as Navy Minister between September 1941 and September 1942, also believed, in the aftermath of the battle of Okinawa, that Japan might have to use the new weapon. See the record of an interview with Itoh (undated, c. 1958), in 1-Shūsenshori (problems on the termination of the Pacific War)-4, Navy Archives, 10, the Institute of the National Defence Studies, Tokyo.

75   However, during the immediate period after Japan's surrender, the statistics showed that more people believed that the war was 'Japan's own fault' than those who blamed the Americans for their action at Hiroshima and Nagasaki. See Asada, '*Japanese Perceptions*' p. 202. More recently, a school of thought has suggested that while the Americans often say 'Remember Pearl Harbor', the Japanese do not equate the causes (Pearl Harbor) and the results (Hiroshima). See Shin Itonaga, 'Beikaigun no Tainichi Sensō Keikaku' (The US Navy's War Planning against Japan' in Ikuhiko Hata (ed.), *Shinjuwan wa Moeru* (Pearl Harbor Burning), vol. 1 (Tokyo: Hara, 1991) p. 102.

Chapter 4

Geoffrey Roberts[1]

IDEOLOGY, CALCULATION, AND IMPROVISATION
Spheres of influence and Soviet foreign policy 1939–1945

Introduction

FOR THE USSR THE SECOND WORLD WAR was an economic and human catastrophe of gigantic proportions. Politically and militarily, however, the war presented Moscow with a series of opportunities to achieve one of the main foreign goals of the Soviet state: the security of the socialist system. The chosen means to achieve this goal was the establishment of a sphere of influence in Eastern and Central Europe—a zone of Soviet strategic and political predominance unchallenged by any other great power. If there was one single underlying and persistent theme of Soviet foreign policy during the war it was to create a series of friendly regimes on the USSR's western flank. Initially this goal was sought in the context of an alliance with Nazi Germany. Following the Nazi attack on the USSR in June 1941, Moscow then attempted to conclude a broad-based, pan-European spheres of influence agreement with its new British ally. That most famed Soviet spheres of influence deal—the Churchill-Stalin 'percentages agreement' of October 1944—was more mythical than real, but in the middle years of the war Soviet officials did formulate grandiose plans for a postwar trilateral global condominium of Great Britain, the USSR and the United States. Nor was there anything imaginary about Soviet insistence at the end of the war on a military and political zone of Soviet security in Eastern Europe. In the event, however, this latter goal was achieved not through diplomacy, but by a combination of force of arms and local communist political mobilisation and manipulation. The culmination of this drive for security through spheres of influence was, ultimately, a Soviet-dominated and a communist-controlled Eastern Europe.

The expansion of Soviet influence and control in Eastern Europe has appeared to many historians as a purposeful and coherent pattern of territorial and political expansion. But there were a number of different phases of Soviet spheres of influence policy, each with a distinctive character and motivation. In the first phase (1939–40) the policy was one of a limited spheres of influence agreement with Nazi Germany designed to meet immediate and urgent security needs (mainly, staying out of the war and limiting German eastern expansion). In the second phase (1940–41) there was a Soviet striving for the negotiation and construction of a security bloc in the Balkans as a counter to German hegemony in Europe following the fall of France in June 1940. In the third phase (1941–42) the emphasis was on reaffirming the right to territory gained as a result of the Nazi-Soviet pact as well as arriving at postwar security arrangements with Britain (and the United States). In the fourth phase (1943–44)—what might be called the Grand Alliance phase—the construction of a sphere of influence across Eastern Europe became bound up with, and in some respects subordinated to, a much larger project of Soviet-British-American global trilateralism. The fifth and final phase, at the war's end, was characterised by the unilateral imposition of a Soviet sphere of influence in Eastern Europe. It was this development that precipitated the postwar denouement of Soviet spheres of influence policy—the outbreak of the Cold War and the division of Europe. But blocism, antagonistic coalitions and camps, and ideological, political and economic warfare with the West was never the desired outcome. The sphere of influence that Moscow initially wanted was designed to meet Soviet security requirements while being compatible with the construction of a co-operative, stable and peaceful postwar international order. It was certainly not the intention to provoke the counter-construction of an anti-Soviet western bloc.[2] Indeed, it is the great paradox of the Cold War that it came about not because of a communist threat to the West or the inevitability of inter-systemic conflict between the American and Soviet superpowers but because Moscow assumed that it would be possible to establish a sphere of influence in Eastern Europe and have good relations with Britain and the United States.

In the successive episodes of Soviet wartime spheres of influence policy the immediate motivaters of strategy and action were calculations of security, power and diplomacy combined with a large element of improvisation in the face of circumstances and the responses and actions of other players. Such a characterisation of the mainsprings of wartime Soviet diplomacy can now be buttressed by a considerable body of new evidence—published[3] and unpublished[4]—from the Russian archives; evidence which makes possible the telling of a more detailed and nuanced story of Moscow's foreign policy decision-making during the war.

At the same time, this new evidence can also help to clarify our understanding of the role of ideology in wartime Soviet foreign policy. As formulated by Walter Carlsnaes[5], the problem of ideology in foreign policy analysis is that of determining the impact of doctrine on belief (and hence action). In the Soviet case the question concerns the relationship between the doctrines of Marxism-Leninism (particularly those relating to views and analyses of international relations) and the perceptions, experiences, expectations and projections of Stalin, Molotov and other foreign policy decision-makers. The more evidence we have of internal deliberations on foreign policy the greater the indications of how and to what extent ideology figured in the processes of reasoning leading to decision and action. As we shall see in the narrative that follows, during the early part of the war ideology played a somewhat muted role in foreign policy decision-making. As the war progressed, however, ideology—aims, beliefs and discourses—assumed more and more prominence.

As many commentators have noted, there was in Soviet foreign policy a triple fusion of power, interests and ideology.[6] The maintenance of Soviet state security and power was defined as an ideological goal and its pursuit deemed to be in the long-term interests of socialism and communism. Equally, more strictly ideological goals could also define and shape the purposes of state power in the international arena. As we shall see, in the case of the spheres of influence policy what began as a calculated, pragmatic response to circumstances was ultimately transformed by ideology from a narrow power politics project into a design for the radical reshaping of the European political and international order. The goal became a people's democratic Europe. Although intended by Moscow as a counterpart to a peacetime grand alliance with Britain and the United States, it was perceived in the West as a policy of seeking 'ideological lebensraum' in Europe.[7] This mismatch between Soviet intentions and Western perceptions was, arguably, the critical factor in the origins of the Cold War.

The Nazi-Soviet pact: spheres of influence in the Baltic, 1939–40

Despite the persistence of the Soviet wartime pursuit of a sphere of influence the only explicit and formal agreement concluded by Moscow in this period was the Nazi-Soviet pact of August-September 1939. In a secret additional protocol attached to the German-Soviet non-aggression treaty of 23 August 1939 Poland was divided into German and Soviet spheres of influence and Finland, Estonia and Latvia allocated to a Soviet sphere of influence in the Baltic. Under the terms of the German-Soviet Boundary and Friendship Treaty of 28 September 1939 the German-Soviet demarcation line in Poland was adjusted and, in a further secret protocol, Lithuania was reallocated to the Soviet sphere of influence in the Baltic.[8]

The Soviet decision for a spheres of influence agreement with Nazi Germany was the result of three main factors. Firstly, the breakdown in mid-August 1939 of the Anglo-French-Soviet negotiations for a triple alliance against Germany.[9] Secondly, Moscow's preference for neutrality in the coming German–Western war over Poland. Thirdly, the security offered by the promise of German self-exclusion from the Baltic States and from Eastern Poland. It is also apparent from a detailed examination of the discussions and negotiations leading to the pact that this fundamental reorientation of Soviet foreign policy was the result of a somewhat hasty and *ad hoc* decision-making process. Uncertain of the consequences of Soviet participation in a less than satisfactory triple alliance with the Western powers, Stalin and Molotov opted at the last moment for what seemed to offer the best short-term security and defence advantages for the USSR.

The Soviet decision for a pact with Nazi Germany certainly had an ideological backdrop. Stalin and Molotov's intense suspicion of the Western powers was reinforced by doctrines concerning the capitalist-imperialist threat to the USSR.

The signing of the pact with the erstwhile enemy was indeed rationalised in ideological terms; for the Comintern, for example, it meant the abandonment of the
anti-fascist popular front politics of the 1930s (at least for a time). The decision
itself, however, was based on perceptions and calculations in which ideology played
only a marginal role. Moreover, in adopting this course of action Stalin and Molotov,
it seems, had no clear idea of its precise practical outcome. This only emerged in
the wake of Germany's rapid conquest of Poland in early September 1939. In
response Moscow decided to invade and occupy its sphere of influence in Poland
and subsequently to incorporate Western Byelorussia and Western Ukraine into the
USSR. Annexation and incorporation was also the ultimate fate of Estonia, Latvia
and Lithuania. But initially Moscow was content with mutual assistance treaties and
military bases and a friendly disposition on the part of the governments of the three
Baltic States. The total Soviet-Communist takeover of these states in Summer 1940
was fired by internal political upheavals in the region triggered by Moscow's decision to occupy them militarily and to demand the establishment of new, friendlier
and more manageable governments—itself a panicky response to Hitler's stunning
defeat of France.[10]

Finnish resistance to Moscow's demands for a mutual assistance treaty, territorial adjustments and military bases resulted in a Soviet attack on Finland at the
end of November 1939. The ensuing Soviet military campaign was conducted within
the ideological and political context of a radical programme of achieving a people's
democratic or socialist Finland. However, when it came to the peace treaty of March
1940 Soviet ambitions were limited to relatively moderate demands for territory
and military bases. Moscow's willingness to end the war on these terms was motivated by various political and strategic calculations: for example, the military cost
of a campaign of conquest and the danger of Anglo-French intervention on behalf
of the Finns. But important, too, was the dashing of ideological expectations
concerning the popular response in Finland to the outbreak of war. Ideological
conviction and rhetoric was constrained by political reality and strategic and other
priorities.[11] A similar process seems to have been at work at the end of the Second
World War when, in infinitely more favourable circumstances than in 1940, the
USSR chose neither to occupy Finland nor to pursue or encourage its internal soviet-
isation. Indeed, even Finland's incorporation into the postwar Soviet sphere of
influence was highly limited in character.[12]

The importance of the Nazi-Soviet pact for the future course and evolution of
Soviet spheres of influence policy cannot be over-emphasised. It initiated a practice
and tradition of such deals, including secret ones. It defined what became for the
Soviets the content of a sphere of influence agreement—basically, exclusive freedom
of political and diplomatic manoeuvre in a country or designated area. It also
provided the context and stepping stone for an ambitious attempt in 1940 to significantly expand the Soviet sphere of influence on the USSR's western borders.

Spheres of influence in the Balkans, 1940–41

For nearly a year after the Nazi-Soviet pact, Moscow's foreign policy goals focused
primarily on exploiting the advantages of the spheres of influence agreement with

Germany covering Poland and the Baltic States. That did not mean that other security concerns were entirely neglected. This period also saw important diplomatic initiatives in the Balkans. Activity focused on relations with two states: Bulgaria and Turkey. In the case of Bulgaria, Moscow attempted (unsuccessfully) to draw the country into the Soviet orbit by the proposed signature of a mutual assistance treaty. In the case of Turkey the main effort was directed at preventing the country's integration into an Anglo-French bloc in the Balkans and at enhancing Moscow's influence and control over the Dardanelles.

Although there was a degree of coordination with the Germans, Soviet policy in the Balkans during this period was generally unilateral in character. There was no suggestion of a spheres of influence policy in the sense of a desire for agreement with other players in the region on zones of interest and priority. A Soviet policy of spheres of influence in the Balkans only emerged after the Italian entry into the war in June 1940.

The possibility of negotiations with Italy about a common and agreed approach in the Balkans had been in the air for some time, but discussions had been stymied by the virtual breakdown of Soviet-Italian relations following the outbreak of the Winter War with Finland. However, the position began to change on the eve of Italian entry into the war. On 3 June Molotov asked Schulenburg, the German ambassador in Moscow, about a reported statement by von Mackensen, the German ambassador in Rome, that following Italy's imminent entry into the war there would be a peaceful resolution of Balkan issues between the USSR and the Axis powers.[13] On 6 June the Soviet military attaché in Bulgaria cabled that Germany and Italy were intent on excluding Soviet influence from the Balkans.[14] On 10 June Italy declared war on Britain and France. Three days later, on 13 June, Molotov had a positive and friendly discussion with Rosso, the Italian ambassador.[15] On 18 June Gorelkin, the Soviet ambassador in Rome, reported that Mussolini was said to be committed to the maximum improvement and development of Italian-Soviet relations.[16] On 20 June Rosso told Molotov that Rome remained committed to the 1933 Italian-Soviet pact of friendship, non-aggression and neutrality. He continued that while Italy was striving to improve its position in the Mediterranean it had no pretensions in relation to the Balkans, apart from trade and political friendship.[17] Shortly after that, on 23 June, Schulenburg confirmed to Molotov that the von Mackensen statement did represent the German view on the Balkans. Molotov pressed for clarification as to what this meant, but received none.[18]

In this uncertain situation—Italian entry into the war, the surrender of France, possible Turkish involvement in the conflict,[19] contradictory signs of German and Italian policy in the Balkans—Moscow did two things. Firstly, it delivered an ultimatum to Rumania demanding the return of Bessarabia and, for good measure, North Bukovina as well—a territory with a Ukrainian population, but one to which the Soviets had never laid claim before.[20] This was territory the Russians were not prepared to bargain about in the event of a general settlement with Italy and Germany in the Balkans. Secondly, on 25 June Moscow began to feel out the prospects for a spheres of influence agreement in the Balkans. In a formal statement to Rosso, Molotov offered recognition of Italian pre-eminence in the Mediterranean in return for recognition of Soviet predominance in the Black Sea. The statement also set out the Soviet position on the various territorial disputes in the Balkans, noted the positive character of Soviet-Bulgarian relations, and proposed a joint Soviet-Axis agreement in relation to Turkey. Presenting the proposal to Rosso, Molotov said that 'the statement was clear and definite and could provide a working basis for a durable agreement between Italy and the USSR. When in autumn 1939 the USSR and Germany began to speak in clear language they quickly agreed on cooperation'.[21]

Despite Molotov's gloss, this was all very vague, not so much a spheres of influence proposal as a possible prelude to one. The only really definite thing about the statement was its assertion that the Soviet Union had a view and role to play in relation to Balkan affairs. This was a point the Russians made to the Germans, too, in a leaked memorandum on Stalin's discussion with British ambassador Cripps on 1 July 1940. According to this memorandum Stalin had told Cripps that in his 'opinion no power had the right to an exclusive role in the consolidation and leadership of the Balkan countries. The Soviet Union did not claim such a mission either, although she was interested in Balkan affairs'.[22]

The emergence of a specific Soviet policy of spheres of influence in the Balkans was prompted by a developing crisis in relations with Germany in Summer 1940. Among Moscow's worries were, first, Rome and Berlin's silence about Soviet involvement in Balkan affairs; second, the USSR's exclusion from discussions leading to the Italo-German arbitration of territorial disputes between Rumania, Hungary and Bulgaria (the so-called 'Vienna Award' of 31 August 1940); and third by mounting evidence that German power and influence was growing across the board in Europe, even encroaching on the Soviet sphere of influence in the Baltic (i.e. Finland).[23] Moscow's response to all this was to attempt a new Nazi-Soviet pact centred on a spheres of influence agreement in the Balkans.

The catalyst and opportunity for an extension of Soviet-German spheres of influence arrangements to the Balkans was a letter from Ribbentrop to Stalin on 17 October inviting Molotov to discussions in Berlin about the USSR's relationship to the recently formed tripartite alliance between Germany, Japan and Italy.[24] Stalin replied on 21 October, accepting Ribbentrop's invitation on Molotov's behalf.

In a Stalin directive to Molotov dated 9 November Soviet aims in the forthcoming discussions were set out. First, to find out what German aims were in relation to the tripartite pact, especially regarding the project of a 'New Europe' and borders in Europe and Asia and the role of the USSR therein. Second, to explore the possibility of an agreement defining the spheres of interest of the USSR in Europe and the Near and Middle East, but not to conclude any such agreement until further talks with Ribbentrop in Moscow. Third, to make clear that Finland and Bulgaria ('the main question in the negotiations') were in the Soviet sphere of interest. Fourth, to establish that there would be no discussions or decisions about Turkey, Rumania, Hungary and Iran without Soviet participation. Fifth, to find out what the Axis intended in relation to Greece and Yugoslavia (Greece had been invaded by Italy on 28 October).[25]

Molotov arrived in Berlin on 12 November. He found himself faced not with negotiations about a new spheres of influence agreement but with the offer of a junior partnership in a German-dominated Axis alliance directed against the British empire. Instead of friendly discussions about spheres of influence there were blazing diplomatic rows between Molotov and Hitler and Ribbentrop.[26]

Back in Moscow, on 25 November Molotov delivered the Soviet response to the German proposals. The USSR was willing to join the tripartite pact providing that (1) Germany withdrew its military units from Finland; (2) the USSR concluded a mutual assistance pact with Bulgaria, including the establishment of military bases that would safeguard the security of the Dardanelles; (3) the area south of Batum and Baku in the general direction of the Persian Gulf was recognised as the centre of Soviet aspirations (as opposed to India and the Indian Ocean, proposed by the Germans); (4) an agreement was signed with Turkey that would provide for Soviet army and navy bases on the Bosporus and the Straits (as opposed to just a revision of the Montreux Convention which would close the Dardanelles to foreign warships); and (5) Japan renounced its rights to coal and oil concessions in North Sakhalin.[27]

On 25 November, too, the Soviets renewed their proposal to Sofia for a Soviet-Bulgarian pact of mutual assistance. That same day Stalin confided in the Bulgarian communist and Comintern leader Georgei Dimitrov, adding to the information about the Soviet offer to Bulgaria that 'our relations with the Germans are outwardly correct, but between us there are serious tensions'.[28] This turned out to be something of an understatement. There never was a German reply to the Soviet counter-proposal. On 18 December Hitler signed the directive authorising Operation Barbarossa. The Soviet project of a spheres of influence agreement in the Balkans collapsed in the face of a blatant and unilateral expansion of German power in the region that served as a prelude to 22 June 1941.

Soviet spheres of influence policy and Great Britain, 1941–42

During the period of the Nazi-Soviet pact Moscow (more precisely Stalin and Molotov) became accustomed to the idea of formulating, discussing and negotiating wide-ranging spheres of influence arrangements with other powers. That this practice retained a central place in diplomatic strategy and tactics after the German attack is apparent from the next episode in Soviet spheres of influence policy. In December 1941 British Foreign Secretary Anthony Eden travelled to Moscow to discuss an Anglo-Soviet treaty of alliance. On 18 December Eden met with Stalin who proposed that there should be two Anglo-Soviet agreements, one on mutual military aid and one on the settlement of postwar problems. To this second agreement, said Stalin, should be attached a secret protocol which would deal, in outline, with the question of the reorganisation of European borders after the war. Stalin then proceeded to make a series of detailed suggestions on postwar borders and other matters—suggestions embodied in a draft of an 'additional protocol' submitted to the British delegation.

First, the USSR's borders would be those extant in June 1941 (i.e. incorporating the Baltic States, Western Belorussia and Western Ukraine, Bessarabia and North Bukovina, and the territory ceded by Finland in March 1940). The Soviet-Polish frontier should run more or less along the 'Curzon Line' and Poland compensated for loss of prewar territories in the east by its expansion into German territory. Second, Czechoslovakia, Greece, Albania and Yugoslavia should be re-established as independent states within their prewar borders—in the latter case including gains at Italy's expense (e.g. Trieste). Third, in return for maintaining its neutrality Turkey should get the Dodecanese islands and some Bulgarian and, perhaps, some Syrian territory. Fourth, Germany should be weakened by various measures of disarmament and dismemberment. Fifth, Britain should have a military alliance with Belgium and Holland, including provision for British military bases in the Low countries (and, possibly, Norway and Denmark as well). (On the postwar future of France, Stalin deferred to British opinion.) Sixth, the USSR would have military alliances with Finland and Rumania and there would be provision for the establishment of Soviet military bases in those two countries. Seventh, overseeing postwar reconstruction and the maintenance of peace would be a military alliance of 'democratic states', headed by some kind of central council or other body.[29]

On the face of it this was a somewhat extraordinary proposal—an Anglo-Soviet settlement of the postwar order in Europe, only six months into the Soviet-German war and with the Wehrmacht still at the gates of Moscow and Leningrad! However, Eden's visit coincided with the development of the Red Army's counterstroke in front of Moscow into a general counter-offensive. Stalin, it seems, believed that victory over Germany was a matter of months, not years. The time was right for the settlement of a number of postwar issues.[30] Moreover, the Soviets had reason to believe that the British might be prepared to talk about the kind of deal proposed by Stalin.

Even before Soviet entry into the war the British had hinted at or proposed some kind of general settlement. For example, in October 1940 London had proposed an agreement that in return for the USSR's benevolent neutrality there would be consultations on the postwar settlement, *de facto* recognition of Russian territorial acquisitions in Eastern Europe and British economic assistance to Soviet defence preparations.[31] Perhaps more important, the genesis of the Eden visit to Moscow seemed to suggest to the Russians that the British Foreign Secretary was making the trip precisely in order to negotiate such a wide-ranging deal.[32] Moreover, from the Russian point of view, there was nothing particularly controversial about what they proposed. The maintenance of the 1941 Soviet borders was a given, which the British had hinted many times they were prepared to ultimately accept. Territorial transfers from Axis states was no big deal when hundreds of thousands of Russians were being killed. The proposed Soviet sphere of influence in Eastern Europe involved two countries, Finland and Rumania—both enemy states. And what could be more natural, in view of recent events, than British bases in Holland and Belgium? True, some of the proposals offended the principles of the Atlantic Charter, but both Britain and the USSR in endorsing Roosevelt's idealistic projections had entered caveats designed to ensure flexibility when it came to the protection of national security and national interest.[33]

Moscow's expectations and reasoning, however, were quickly dashed by Eden. Under no circumstances would the Foreign Secretary countenance such a deal without first consulting the War Cabinet, Washington, and the Dominions and without considering its implications for the principles of the Atlantic Charter. In response, Stalin and the Soviet side changed tack, placing the emphasis almost wholly on an agreement recognising the USSR's existing borders. But Eden would not concede even this. The discussions broke up in some disarray and on 22 December Eden returned to London.

In April 1942 the British finally responded formally to Stalin's proposals of the previous December. What they offered politically was a series of anodyne generalities about wartime and postwar cooperation which committed them to nothing and conceded none of the essential Soviet demands. On 22 April, Stalin wrote to Churchill that in view of the differences between the Soviet and British positions he proposed to send Molotov to London for negotiations.[34] Shortly after, Ambassador Maiskii informed Eden that Moscow insisted on, in effect, acceptance of the USSR's 1941 borders (including that with Poland) and some kind of secret agreement on postwar Soviet military alliances with Finland and Rumania. This was Molotov's theme, too, in his discussions with Eden and Churchill towards the end of May.[35] But the negotiations got nowhere and seemed set for deadlock. Then a curious thing happened. Molotov abandoned all his demands and agreed to sign a simple treaty of alliance on wartime cooperation and mutual assistance in the postwar period. Molotov had been instructed by Stalin to accept what the British were offering. The reversal in the Soviet position was clear. On 24 May Molotov had cabled Moscow that the proposed Anglo-Soviet treaty was 'unacceptable . . . an empty declaration which the USSR does not need'. Replying the same day, however, Stalin stated:

> We have received the draft treaty Eden handed you. We do not consider it an empty declaration but regard it as an important document. It lacks the question of the security of frontiers, but this is not bad, perhaps, for it gives us a free hand. The question of frontiers, or to be more exact, of guarantees for the security of our frontiers at one or another section of our country, will be decided by force.[36]

Stalin's turnabout on the Anglo-Soviet pact was prompted by military exigency. The war was going badly again on the Eastern Front and the opening of a Second Front in the West was now Moscow's priority. For the next two years a central theme of Moscow's diplomacy was the search for an agreement with Britain and the United States on the opening of a Second Front.[37] At the same time, in 1943–1944, a much more fundamental reorientation of Soviet foreign policy was in progress. In this period Moscow committed itself to achieving postwar security through a peacetime grand alliance with Britain and the United States. The project of security through spheres of influence was not so much abandoned as reconceptualised: a division of Europe and the world into American, British and Soviet spheres of influence would be the foundation stone of a postwar alliance between the USSR and the Western powers.

Spheres of influence and the Grand Alliance, 1943–44

A key event in the transition to the grand alliance phase of Soviet spheres of influence policy was the Moscow Conference of Foreign Ministers, October 1943.[38] The Moscow Conference was the first of the big wartime tripartite meetings convened to discuss allied policy and perspectives on the postwar world. Although it was conceived initially as just a preparatory meeting for the forthcoming Teheran

conference of the 'Big Three' it developed into a detailed and formal allied negotiating forum. Indeed, no allied conference of World War II had a more complex
and wide-ranging agenda. Among the decisions, declarations and discussions were
ones concerning the establishment of the United Nations, the setting up of inter-
allied negotiating mechanisms, the postwar treatment of Germany and Austria, the
occupation regime in Italy, policy on Persia and Turkey, and various aspects of
Soviet-East European relations. At its conclusion the conference was hailed, not
least in the Soviet press, as a major breakthrough in the development of allied cooperation, unity and friendship.[39] Privately, the Soviet foreign ministry lauded the
conference as 'a big event in the life of the People's Commissariat of Foreign Affairs'
which 'all PCFA workers must study in detail . . . and, if possible, make proposals
on the realisation of its decisions.'[40]

The Soviets had approached the Moscow Conference intent on highlighting
military priorities and issues within the allied coalition, particularly the question of
British and American commitment to the opening of a second front in western
Europe. In relation to the many political issues on the conference agenda (submitted
for discussion by London and Washington) the intention was to adopt a reactive
rather than a proactive role, to probe Anglo-American aims rather than to reveal
Moscow's own.[41] In responding to Western proposals, however, the Soviets were
forced to define and clarify their own aims and orientations.

Preparations for the conference also inspired an internal reorganisation of the
postwar planning machinery within the Soviet foreign ministry. As early as January
1942 the politburo had agreed to the establishment of a Commission for the
Preparation of Diplomatic Materials. Work had not progressed very far, however,
when in Summer 1943 this commission was superseded by two specialist commissions: an armistice terms commission headed by Voroshilov, the former defence
minister, and a commission on peace treaties and the postwar order headed by
Litvinov, Molotov's predecessor as foreign minister and ambassador to the US
before his recall to Moscow in 1943. It was in his capacity as head of this key
commission that Litvinov played a major role in Soviet preparations for the Moscow
Conference. After the conference a third commission was added: a commission on
reparations headed by Ivan Maiskii, erstwhile ambassador to Great Britain.[42]

The political-ideological framework for the work of these commissions was an
inter-allied one—the assumption that the peace and the postwar order would be
shaped jointly with the British and Americans. This can be illustrated by reference
to the central, defining issue of the commissions' planning for the peace: the postwar
treatment of Germany. The overarching goal of Soviet policy towards Germany was
the annihilation of German power and the elimination of the German threat to Soviet
security. This aim was to be achieved by the long-term occupation of Germany, by
its disarmament and denazification, by the dismemberment of the German state and
by the extraction of extensive reparations. Crucially, these policies were to be
implemented jointly with Great Britain and the United States. The desire to cooperate with the West on the containment of Germany lay at the heart of the Soviet
commitment to a postwar grand alliance.[43]

Where did the policy of spheres of influence fit into the grand alliance perspective embraced by Moscow from 1943 onwards? This was the question pondered
by Soviet planners working in the postwar preparations commissions. Perhaps the

earliest answer was that formulated by Litvinov in a lengthy report to Molotov on 9 October 1943. Litvinov posed the question: how should postwar security be safe-guarded—through collective security organised by a successor to the discredited League of Nations or on the basis of Great Power-controlled zones of security? Western, especially American, opinion favoured a new international organisation. But such an organisation, Litvinov argued, would not be able to function effectively as a security organ without the enforcement power of the Big Three and without a division of the world into American, British and Soviet zones of responsibility. Litvinov also thought that it might be possible to incorporate such a regional division into the formal structures of a new international organisation.[44]

Litvinov subsequently developed his line of thinking in a series of documents composed in his capacity as head of the postwar order commission. Other middle-ranking policymakers developed similar themes in their reports. The essence of this thinking about the postwar world was that spheres of influence were not just compatible with a peacetime grand alliance: they constituted its essential founda-tion. Spheres of influence would provide the means for each individual great power to safeguard its security while a trilateral division of the world would separate the interests and hence minimise the conflicts of the Big Three. But there would also be extensive allied co-operation within the United Nations and other inter-allied institutions, especially in relation to various 'neutral zones' which would be controlled by no single power. In sum, postwar allied political and military unity would keep Germany down, prevent the realignment of Europe into hostile and competing blocs, and provide the context for the settlement of inter-allied differences over security and other interests.

Informing this vision of the postwar world were a series of ideologically-influenced referents. First, that there was an objective, economic basis for the USSR's co-operation with Britain and the United States; second, that between Britain and the US there were inter-imperialist contradictions and rivalries that would keep the two states divided after the war; and thirdly, that out of the war was emerging a new, democratic Europe with a strong communist and left wing influence that would constitute a highly favourable political context for socialist-capitalist relations and co-operation over the long-term.[45]

This perspective of a peacetime grand alliance based on a benign spheres of influence deal was by no means universal in Soviet circles, however, particularly among officials rooted in the Comintern tradition. Deputy foreign minister A. Lozovsky (previously an official of the Comintern), for example, argued that intense social antagonisms between socialism and capitalism were inevitable after the war and that the main postwar aim of Soviet diplomacy should be the preven-tion of the formation of a British-American Western bloc ranged against the USSR.[46] Another example of this trend in Soviet thinking was the overturning in 1945 of the wartime decision by the Communist Party of the United States to liquidate the party into a more loosely organised 'Communist Political Association' that would support a continuation of allied cooperation into the postwar period. In Moscow the party's liquidation was viewed (at least by some) as being based on an exag-geration by CPUSA National Secretary Earl Browder of the prospects for postwar American-Soviet co-operation.[47]

Where did Stalin and Molotov stand in relation to these perspectives? Publicly and in diplomatic conversations they strongly endorsed the perspective of postwar unity and cooperation with the Western powers. Direct evidence of their private thinking remains scant but the indications are that while they went along with Litvinov's global trilateralism they also shared Lozovsky's traditional concerns, which pointed toward a more conflict-ridden postwar relationship with the West. Stalin and Molotov also faced the problem that it was far from clear how the grand bargain envisaged by Litvinov could be negotiated in practice, especially when the British and particularly the Americans were so implacably opposed to spheres of influence. Stalin and Molotov's resolution of this dilemma when the time came was what might be called a *de facto* spheres of influence scheme—the unilateral creation of a Soviet sphere of influence in Eastern Europe on the one hand, the implicit acceptance of an Anglo-American sphere of influence in the Mediterranean and Western Europe, on the other. Discussion of specific issues regarding activities within the respective spheres of influence was not precluded and neither was the possibility of negotiating a broad-based programme of postwar co-operation between Britain, the United States and the Soviet Union. But the bottom-line for Soviet security was a series of friendly regimes along the USSR's borders.

October 1944: spheres of influence as percentages?

Where does the so-called 'percentages agreement' of October 1944 fit into this unfolding scenario? Traditionally, it has been seen as the inception of the postwar division of Europe. However, close examination of that infamous encounter between Churchill and Stalin reveals that Moscow was not seriously interested in any spheres of influence agreement with the British alone, and certainly not one based on 'percentages'.

The story of the percentages agreement first came to light in the 1950s in Churchill's memoirs. Churchill recalls that at a meeting in Moscow on 9 October 1944 he said to Stalin:

> Let us settle about our affairs in the Balkans. Your armies are in Rumania and Bulgaria. We have interests, missions, and agents there. Don't let us get at cross-purposes in small ways. So far as Britain and Russia are concerned, how would it do for you to have ninety per cent predominance in Rumania, for us to have ninety per cent of the say in Greece, and go fifty-fifty about Yugoslavia?

Then came that famous piece of paper on which these percentages were written down, with the addition of a 50–50 split in Hungary and a 75–25 split in Russia's favour in Bulgaria. Stalin ticked this paper and then said Churchill 'might it not be thought rather cynical if it seemed we disposed of these issues, so fateful to millions of people, in such an off-hand manner? Let us burn the paper'. Stalin replied: 'no, you keep it'.[48]

It's a good story, but not necessarily true. Churchill's account and presentation of the meeting and of his conversation with Stalin has been questioned from a number of points of view. Both specialist studies[49] and recently published documentation[50] reveal that the October 1944 conference between Churchill and Stalin was far from being the occasion of a Soviet-British division of the Balkans. The Russians, for their part, had no need for such an agreement nor did they desire one.

Important to understanding what actually transpired in Moscow in October 1944 are three prior developments in inter-allied relations.

The first concerns the character of the allied control machinery and occupation regime established in Italy following its defeat in 1943. At first, the Soviet side, on the initiative of Stalin, proposed joint allied control of the Italian occupation. This, it seems, was in line with the then Soviet strategy of pan-European allied cooperation and control in all liberated states. In the event, however, the Soviets gave way to Anglo-American proposals that reduced their role in Italy to a purely advisory and consultative capacity.[51] Of interest as well is Stalin's intervention in Italian internal politics in early 1944. This was a period when the Moscow-based leadership of the Italian Communist Party was considering strategy and tactics in the new conditions in Italy. On Stalin's advice Togliatti agreed to participate in the post-fascist Badoglio government, to refrain from calling for the abolition of the Italian monarchy and to work for anti-fascist national unity. This was the origin of the PCI's famous 'Salerno turn' of March 1944. Stalin presented his policy advice in terms of the pressing needs of the anti-German struggle and the maintenance of the Grand Alliance—which lends itself to an interpretation of motive in terms of diplomacy, geopolitics, and, perhaps, spheres of influence. However, Stalin's intervention was also a matter of the communist politics of this period: the politics of national unity and popular fronts as a strategy for the achievement of people's democracy and then socialism in Europe. Stalin meted out similar advice to French communist leader Maurice Thorez in November 1944.[52] In this period, as in later times, detente with the West did not, for the Soviets, mean an end to internal processes of social and political change in the capitalist world.

The second development was the British effort in Summer 1944 to arrive at a military *spheres of action* agreement with Russia in the Balkans. Basically, the British wanted a free run for their operations in relation to Greece; in return, they offered a free hand to Moscow in relation to its impending operations against Rumania. Moscow deferred to the Americans on this proposal and only agreed to a 3 month trial period when Washington apparently assented, but then backed off in the face of further protests from the latter that it smacked of spheres of influence. In some ways the Churchill percentages proposal was an extension of this earlier, abortive initiative.[53] There had also been another important development and this was the surrender and Russian occupation in September 1944 of Bulgaria, Rumania and (imminently) Hungary.[54] The question arose as to the armistice terms for these three former Axis states and, more importantly, the character of the allied occupation regimes that would govern these countries after their surrender. What the admittedly confused and fuzzy haggling in Moscow over percentages was really about, was who would run the allied control commissions that would shortly emerge. This is clear from both the Soviet and British documents on the talks, including the famous Churchill–Stalin discussion of 9 October. What these documents also show is that for the Russians this was a minor issue. From Moscow's point of view the more important discussions concerned Poland, Germany and Turkey. Indeed, the

Soviets had no inkling that the issue of the allied control commissions was coming up[55] and when it did they were well aware of American objections to any kind of spheres of influence deal.[56] Most important, how the allied control machinery would work in Rumania, Bulgaria and (later) Hungary[57] was a foregone conclusion for the Russians: it would work the same way it did in Italy. The country or countries which occupied would control the occupation. If the British wanted to encapsulate this situation in percentage terms, Moscow, though bemused, had no objections. In the event, the outcome was a series of agreements establishing allied control commissions which the Soviets controlled—with no mention of percentages.

The fact that there was no Stalin–Churchill spheres of influence agreement does not mean that there was no Soviet spheres of influence policy in the Balkans in 1944–45. There was such a policy. A policy of securing in different ways and forms and in varying degrees the exclusion of Western influence from the region (and from the rest of Eastern Europe) and the establishment of friendly governments that would accept Moscow's leadership and meet Soviet security requirements. That strategy did not necessarily entail a policy of isolation and purely unilateral action to protect the Soviet security position. Far from it. When Churchill journeyed to Moscow the Soviets were still very much committed to a collaborative solution to the problem of peace and security in the postwar world (particularly in relation to Germany) and would remain so for some time to come. Nor did pursuit of a sphere of influence necessarily mean the communist subversion of Eastern Europe. As Stalin told Churchill at their meeting on 14 October: 'The Soviet Union had no intention of organising Bolshevik Revolution in Europe. He, Churchill could be certain of this in relation to Rumania, Bulgaria and Yugoslavia'.[58] Stalin's intentions, however, were not fixed and his were by no means the only intentions that mattered. What happened would depend on the outcome of the Soviet effort to harmonise a policy of spheres of influence with the maintenance of postwar allied unity.

Conclusion: towards the Cold War

The main lines of the story of the establishment of a Soviet sphere of influence in Eastern Europe at the end of the war are well known.[59] In the wake of the defeat of Germany and its allies in Eastern Europe there emerged a series of anti-fascist coalition governments in the region. Moscow used its military and political power to ensure, at a minimum, strong communist representation in these governments. The Soviet task in this respect was greatly facilitated by the rapid growth of the East European communist parties into a mass political force—with levels of popular support in the respective countries ranging from perhaps 20 per cent to 50 per cent of the electorate. It is also clear that the implementation of the Soviet spheres of influence policy was far from uniform. In some countries Moscow was determined to keep a firmer grip (Rumania, Bulgaria, Poland) than in others (Hungary and Czechoslovakia). In some countries (e.g. Yugoslavia) the local communists pursued more radical, socialistic policies than in others (e.g. Finland). It is also becoming increasingly clear that although the Soviets exercised (or attempted to exercise) close control over the political affairs of the East European states in the early postwar period,[60] the national communist leaderships also enjoyed much autonomy at the local level and themselves influenced Moscow's foreign policy to a considerable degree. The character of the Soviet sphere of influence in Eastern Europe was shaped from below as well as directed from above.[61]

In relation to the longstanding debate about the Soviet sphere of influence in Eastern Europe—whether or not the later full-scale communization of the region was intended from the very beginning—it seems clear from recent evidence that Moscow's initial aims were limited to the establishment of a series of friendly regimes that would protect Soviet security. However, that security goal of an East European buffer zone became linked to a more radical political-ideological project. This was the goal of a Europe of People's or New Democracies: a continent of progressive left-wing regimes in which the communists would play a leading role. Hence the Soviet sphere of influence in Eastern Europe was conceived as part of a wider political space of security in which Moscow's interests would be safeguarded by regimes of people's democracy.

How did Moscow expect to be able to harmonise the people's democracy project—which applied to Western as well as Eastern Europe—with the maintenance of the Grand Alliance after the war? First, people's democracy was conceived as a transitional form in which elements of the socialist future would coexist with the capitalist present—and would continue to do so for some time to come. People's democracy was a long-term strategy for socialism but not an immediate threat to the existence of capitalism. Second, the creation of people's democracy was seen as a function of internal socio-political developments in different countries. These internal developments were the terrain of a political struggle between the forces of democracy and social progress and the forces of reaction, including those in Britain and the US.[62] People's democracy was, moreover, a powerful social phenomenon that could not be held back or controlled by any international alliance. Third, the Soviets were prepared to defer to Western interests in areas deemed to be in the latter's sphere of influence. The classic example in this respect concerns Greece. As early as 1943 Moscow had begun to define Greece as falling within a British sphere of influence.[63] During the war the Soviets practised a policy of non-interference in the affairs of the country, except to encourage the communist-led partisans to seek a compromise with Royalist and right-wing forces. For their part Stalin and Molotov never tired of deflecting Anglo-American complaints about the exclusion of Western influence from Eastern Europe by pointing to Soviet forbearance in relation to Greece. After the war Moscow was very circumspect in its support for the communists in the Greek civil war, even after the start of the Cold War.[64]

A peacetime Grand Alliance, a people's democratic Europe, a demarcation of Soviet and Western interests—this was Moscow's alternative to the Cold War. But the political feasibility of the Soviet alternative depended on the Western perception and response to Moscow's foreign policy. And the problem was that the USSR's grand alliance partners saw Moscow's sphere of influence in Eastern Europe and the people's democratic project as threatening, as presaging Soviet expansionism and communist subversion on a continental scale. Consequently, there were various postwar Western counter-moves, which culminated in the Marshall Plan and the Truman Doctrine in 1947. These counter-moves were in turn viewed by Moscow as threatening to its vital security and political interests and only encouraged the application of a firmer grip on Eastern Europe and the pursuit of an ever-more radical communist strategy in the Soviet sphere of influence. The end-result of these mutually-interlocking threat perceptions was the abandonment of the people's democracy project, the outbreak of the Cold War and the full-scale communist takeover of Eastern Europe.[65]

For the next 40 years Eastern Europe was viewed by Moscow as a sort of 'geo-ideological'[66] space of Soviet security: the USSR's sphere of influence in Eastern Europe would be guaranteed by communist party control and ideological conformity with the Soviet model of socialism. Only with the advent of Gorbachev was this conception of Soviet security interests in Eastern Europe radically revised. Ironically, what Gorbachev sought was a version of the original postwar Soviet conception of people's democracy in Eastern Europe—a reformist communism that would harmonise with long-term coexistence and collaboration with the capitalist West.[67] As in the 1940s it was a project that proved to be stillborn.

Notes

1   The author would like to acknowledge the financial assistance of the Arts Faculty of University College Cork, which greatly facilitated the research and writing of this article.

2   See A. Resis, 'Spheres of Influence in Soviet Wartime Diplomacy', *Journal of Modern History*, September 1981.

3   Recently-published documentary evidence includes *Dokumenty Vneshnei Politiki*, 23 (1940–1941), Moscow, 1995 (book 1) and 1998 (book 2); *Komintern i Vtoraya Mirovaya Voina*, Moscow, 1994 (part 1) and 1998 (part 2); *SSSR i Germanskii Vopros*, 1 (1941–1945), Moscow, 1996; O. A. Rzheshevskii (ed.), *Voina i Diplomatiya: Dokumenty, Kommentarii (1941–1942)*, Moscow, 1997 (English Translation: O. A. Rzheshevskii (ed.), *War and Diplomacy: The Making of the Grand Alliance* (Harwood Academic Publishers, 1996); *Vostochnaya Evropa v Dokumentakh Rossiiskikh Arkhvov*, 1 (1944–1948), Moscow, 1997 and *Tri Vizita A. Ya. Vyshinskogo v Bukharest 1944–1946: Dokumenty Rossiiskikh Arkhivov*, Moscow, 1998.

4   Access to Russian archives remains restrictive and difficult but I have been able to consult a range of files on the war period in the foreign ministry archive (Arkhiv Vneshnei Politiki Rossiiskoi Federatsii-AVP RF), in the repository for pre-1952 communist party materials (Rossiiskii Tsentr Khraneniya i Izucheniya Dokumentov Noveishei Istorii-RTsKhIDNI), and in the government/state archives (Gosudarstvennyi Arkhiv Rossiiskoi Federatsii-GARF). These materials form the basis of a forthcoming study of 'The Soviet Union and the Grand Alliance, 1941–1947'.

5   W. Carlsnaes, *Ideology and Foreign Policy* (Oxford: Basil Blackwell, 1986).

6   See R. A. Jones, *The Soviet Concept of 'Limited Sovereignty' from Lenin to Gorbachev: The Brezhnev Doctrine* (London: Macmillan, 1990), ch. 6.

7   V. Rothwell, *Britain and the Cold War, 1941–1947* (London: Jonathan Cape, 1982), p. 145.

8   On the Nazi-Soviet pact: G. Roberts, *The Soviet Union and the Origins of the Second World War* (London: Macmillan, 1995). chs. 5–6.

9   See M. J. Copley, *1939: The Alliance That Never Was and the Coming of World War*, vol. 2 (Chicago, IL: Ivan R. Dee, 1999).

10 See G. Roberts, 'Soviet Policy and the Baltic States, 1939–1940: A Reappraisal', *Diplomacy and Statecraft*, November 1995.

11 Roberts, *The Soviet Union*, pp. 112–15; D. W. Spring, 'The Soviet Decision for War Against Finland, 30 November 1939', *Soviet Studies*, April 1986; T. Vihavainen, 'The Soviet Decision for War Against Finland, 30 November 1939: A Comment', *Soviet Studies*, April 1987; and M. I. Meltukhov, '"Narodny Front" dlya Finlyandiei? (K Voprosy o Tselyakh Sovetskogo Rukovodstva v Voine s Finlyandiei 1939–1940gg)', *Otechestvennaya Istoriya*, 3 (1993).

12 See J. Nevakivi, 'A Decisive Armistice 1944–1947: Why Was Finland Not Sovietized?', *Scandinavian Journal of History*, 19:2 (1994); M. Majander, 'The Limits of Sovereignty: Finland and the Question of the Marshall Plan in 1947', *Scandinavian Journal of History*, 19:3 (1994); and M. Korobochkin, 'Soviet Policy Towards Finland and Norway, 1947–1949', *Scandinavian Journal of History*, 20:3 (1995).

13 *Dokumenty Vneshnei Politiki*, 23 (hereafter DVP), doc. 178. Also: *Nazi–Soviet Relations, 1939–1941*, (New York: Didier, 1948 [hereafter: NSR]), p. 14.

14 *Izvestiya Tsk* KPSS, 3 (1990).

15 DVP, doc. 200.

16 Ibid., doc. 209.

17 Ibid., doc. 210.

18 Ibid., doc. 217.

19 On Soviet concerns about the possibility of Turkey entering the conflict following the Italian declaration of war see e.g. Molotov's discussion with the Turkish ambassador on 3/6/40 in DVP, doc. 176.

20 Ibid., docs. 217, 225, 229, 232, 236, and 238. NSR, pp. 155–63.

21 DVP, doc. 224. For an English translation of the Italian version of the formal statement see J. Degras (ed.), *Soviet Documents on Foreign Policy*, 3 (1933–1941), Oxford, 1953, pp. 457–8. See also Schulenburg's report on the Rosso-Molotov meeting in NSR, pp. 160–1.

22 NSR, p. 168. For the Soviet record of the Stalin–Cripps discussion, which contains no such statement by the Soviet leader, see DVP, doc. 240.

23 Ibid., docs. 288, 291, 348, 361, 366, 367, 373, 385 an 402; NSR, pp. 173 ff.

24 DVP, docs. 446, 458 and NSR, pp. 207–13, 216. Ribbentrop's letter was dated 13 October but was not delivered until the 17th. See also DVP, docs. 408 and 425.

25 'Direktivy I. V. Stalina V. M. Molotovu pered Poezdkoi v Berlin v Noyabre 1940g', *Novaya i Noveishaya Istoriya*, 4 (1995). Also published in DVP, doc. 491. On the nature and provenance of this document and an assessment of the Molotov visit to Berlin: L. A. Bezymenskii, 'Vizit V. M. Molotova v Berlin v Noyabre 1940g. v Svete Novykh Dokumentov', *Novaya i Noveishaya Istoriya*, 6 (1995).

26 The Soviet documents on the discussions, including the exchange of telegrams between Stalin and Molotov, are published in DVP, docs. 497, 498, 500, 502, 507, 510, 511, 512 and 515. For the German records: NSR, pp. 217–58.

27 NSR, pp. 258–9; DVP, doc. 548.

28 Diary entry of Dimitrov, cited by Bezymenskii, op. cit., p. 142. On Soviet policy in relation to Bulgaria see DVP, docs 532, 549 and 551 and *Komintern i Vtoraya Mirovaya Voina*, part 1, (Moscow 1994) docs. 127 and 132.

29 Soviet transcript of Stalin-Eden meeting of 16 December 1941 and Soviet draft of 'additional protocol', reproduced in O. A. Rzheshevskii, 'Vizit A. Idena v Moskvu v Dekabre 1941g. Peregovory s I. V. Stalinym i V.M. Molotovym', *Novaya i Noveishaya Istoriya*, 2–3 (1994), no. 2, pp. 90–100. For an English translation of this and other

documents on Soviet-British negotiations in 1941–1942 see Rzheshevsky, *War and Diplomacy*, (Amsterdam: Harwood Academic Publishers, 1996).

30   See J. Erickson, 'Stalin, Soviet Strategy and the Grand Alliance', in A. Lane and H. Temperley (eds.), *The Rise and Fall of the Grand Alliance, 1941–1945* (London: Macmillan, 1995), p. 143.

31   DVP, doc. 460. Also docs. 444, 447.

32   See Rzheshevskii, 3, pp. 110- 14 (diary report by Molotov of meeting with Cripps on 19/12/41).

33   W. LaFeber (ed.), *The Origins of the Cold War, 1941–1947* (New York: John Wiley, 1971), pp. 32–5.

34   *Stalin's Correspondence with Churchill, Atlee, Roosevelt and Truman, 1941–1945*, (London: Lawrence & Wishart, 1958), doc. 40.

35   The Soviet record of Molotov's talks in London in May 1942 are translated in Rzheshevsky *War and Diplomacy*.

36   Ibid., docs. 37–38.

37   L. V. Pozdeeva, 'The Soviet Union: Territorial Diplomacy', in D. Reynolds, W. F. Kimball and A. O. Chubarian (eds.), *Allies at War* (London: Macmillan, 1994), pp. 362–3; A. Filitov, 'The Soviet Union and the Grand Alliance: The Internal Dimension of Foreign Policy', in G. Gorodetsky (ed.), *Soviet Foreign Policy, 1917–1991* (London: Frank Cass, 1994), p. 98; *Sto Sorok Beced s Molotovym* (Moscow, 1991), pp. 69–70; Erickson, 'Stalin, Soviet Strategy and the Grand Alliance', p. 145; and I. V. Zemskov, *Diplomaticheskaya Istoriya Vtorogo Fronta v Evrope* (Moscow 1982).

38   The summary in this section is based on research on Soviet preparations for the Moscow Conference I conducted in the AVP RF. Compared to Teheran, Yalta and Potsdam the Moscow Conference has been neglected by historians, but see: K. Sainsbury, *The Turning Point* (Oxford University Press, 1986), ch. 4; V. Mastny, *Russia's Road to the Cold War* (New York, 1979), pp. 111–22; and idem., 'Soviet War Aims at the Moscow and Teheran Conferences of 1943', *Journal of Modern History*, September 1975.

39   The American records of the conference are in *Foreign Relations of the United States: 1943*, 1; the British records in F0371/37031; and the Soviet records in *Moskovskaya Konferentsiya Ministrov Inostrannykh Del SSSR, SSHa i Velikobritanii (19–30 Oktyabra 1943 g.)*, (Moscow, 1984)

40   AVP RF F.0511, Op. 1, D.1, L.72.

41   See, for example, the pre-conference briefing report prepared by deputy Foreign Affairs commissar Vladimir Dekanozov: 'K Predstoyashchemu Soveshchaniu v Moskve Trekh Ministrov', F. 6, Op. 5b, Pap. 39, D. 6, LL. 52–58. This document is also printed in *SSSR i Germanskii Vopros*, doc. 59.

42   'Zanyatsya Pogotovkoi Budushchego Mira', *Istochnik*, 17 (1994/5).

43   The internal processes of Soviet policy discussion and decision-making on the German question can be followed in detail in *SSSR i Germanskii Vopros, 1941–1949*.

44   'Vopros o Sovmestnoi Otvetstvennosti za Evropu v Protivopolozhnost Voprosu ob Otdelnykh Raionakh Otvetstvennosti', AVP RF F. 6, Op. 5b, Pap. 39, D. 5, LL. 36–50. This document is also printed in *SSSR i Germanskii Vopros*, doc. 62.

45   On Soviet thinking about the postwar world: V. O. Pechatnov, 'The Big Three after World War II: New Documents on Soviet Thinking about Post-War Relations with the United States and Great Britain', Working Paper 13, Cold War International History Project, July 1995; A. M. Filitov, 'Problems of Post-War Construction in Soviet Foreign Policy Conceptions during World War II' in F. Gori and S. Pons

(eds.), *The Soviet Union and Europe in the Cold War, 1943–1953* (London: Macmillan, 1996). A number of the relevant documents are printed in *SSSR i Germanskii Vopros*.

46   See T. Yu. Koyetkova, 'Voprosy Sozdaniya OON i Sovetskaya Diplomatiya', *Otechest-vennaya Istoriya*, 1 (1995), pp. 34–5. This reference was drawn to my attention by S. Pons, 'La Place de l'Italie dans la Politique Extérieure de l'URSS (1943–1944)', *Communisme*, 49/50 (1997).

47   The CPUSA's 1944 decision to change to a political association was reversed following the publication in April 1945 of a critical article in the French CP journal *Cahiers Du Communisme* by Jacques Duclos. The Duclos article was in fact largely a translation of an article that had already appeared in the CPSU central committee's confidential internal information bulletin on international affairs, *Voprosy Vneshnei Politiki* in January 1945. Even the translation from Russian to French was done in Moscow. See RTsKhIDNI, F. 17, Op. 128, D. 754, LL. 72–94.

48   W. Churchill, *The Second World War* (London: Cassell, 1962), pp. 196–7.

49   A. Resis, 'The Churchill-Stalin Secret "Percentages" Agreement on the Balkans, Moscow, October 1944', *American Historical Review*, April 1978; P. Tsakaloyannis, 'The Moscow Puzzle', *Journal of Contemporary History*, 21 (1986); P. G. H. Holdich, 'A Policy of Percentages? British Policy and the Balkans after the Moscow Conference of October 1944', *The International History Review*, February 1987; L. Woodward, *British Foreign Policy in the Second World War*, 3 (London: HMSO, 1971); G. Kolko, *The Politics of War*, (New York: Vintage Books, 1968), pp. 140–61; and Mastny, *Russia's Road*, pp. 207–12.

50   The Soviet record of the Stalin–Churchill meeting of 9/10/44 is reproduced in O. A. Rzheshevsky, 'Soviet Policy in Eastern Europe 1944–45: Liberation or Occupation?', in G. Bennett (ed.), *The End of the War in Europe, 1945* (London: HMSO, 1996). Russian transcripts of the meetings on 14/10/44 and 17/10/44 are reproduced in *Istochnik*, 1995/4 (17). Soviet reports of the Molotov-Eden meetings of 9/10/44 and 16/10/44 are in *Sovetsko-Angliiskiye Otnosheniya vo bremya Velikoi Otechestvennoi Voiny 1941–1945* (hereafter SAO), 2 (Moscow, 1983), docs. 140 and 147, which also contains an informational letter dated 21/10/44 from Vyshinskii to the Soviet ambassador in London on the discussions. For the British records of the various meetings see J. M. Siracusa, 'The Meaning of *Tolstoy*: Churchill, Stalin and the Balkans, Moscow, October 1944', *Diplomatic History*, Fall 1979.

51   Mastny, *Russia's Road*, pp. 105–8; Sainsbury, *The Turning Point*, pp. 69–80; and W. H. McNeill, *America, Britain and Russia: Their Co-operation and Conflict, 1941–1946* (Oxford University Press, 1953), pp. 306–10.

52   See M. M. Narinskii, 'Tolyatti, Stalin i "Povorot v Salerno"' in O. A. Rzeshevskii (ed.), *Vtoraya Mirovaya Voina*, Moscow, 1995 and *Istochnik*, 1995/4 (17) for the Stalin–Thorez conversation.

53   Woodward, *British Foreign Policy in the Second World War*, pp. 115–23.

54   On the military and political background to the Soviet investment of the Balkans, see J. Erickson, *The Road to Berlin* (London: Weidenfeld and Nicolson, 1983), ch. 6.

55   On 8 October Stalin messaged Roosevelt that he did not know why Churchill was coming to Moscow. At the Molotov-Eden meeting on 9/10 there was no hint of any percentages proposal (SAO, 2, doc. 140).

56   For example, on 13/10 Gromyko, ambassador in the United States, telegrammed that Hopkins had told him that Roosevelt was very unhappy about American exclusion from Soviet–British discussions on Balkans (*Sovetsko-Amerikanskiye Otnosheniya vo bremya Velikoi Otechestvennoi Voiny 1941–1945*, 2 (Moscow, 1984), doc. 135).

57   Inter-allied relations regarding Greece and Yugoslavia constitute distinct and separate stories.

58   The quote is from the *Istochnik* document cited in n. 50.

59   An old but good summary remains G. Lundestad's, 'The Soviet Union and Eastern Europe 1943–1947', in his *The American Non-Policy Towards Eastern Europe 1943–1947* (Oslo: Norwegian University Press, 1975).

60   In the case of Poland, Soviet control mechanisms are documented in *SSSR-Polsha Mekhanizmy Podchineniya 1944–1949gg* (Moscow, 1995). See also A. Polonsky and B. Drukier (eds.), *The Beginnings of Communist Rule in Poland*, (London: Routledge, 1980) and *NKVD i Polskoye Podpolye 1944–1945 (po 'Osobym Papkam' LI. V. Stalina)* (Moscow, 1994).

61   On Soviet relations with its East European communist allies in the early postwar period there are various essays in Gori and Pons, *The Soviet Union and Europe in the Cold War, 1943–1953;* N. Naimark and L. Gibianskii (eds.), *The Establishment of the Communist Regimes in Eastern Europe, 1944–1949* (Boulder, CO: Westview Press, 1997); M. M. Narinskii, *et al.* (eds.), *Kholodnaya Voina: Novye Podkhody, Novye Dokumenty* (Moscow, 1995); L. N. Nezhimskii (ed.), *Sovetskaya Vneshnyaya Politika v Gody 'Kholodnoi Voiny' (1945–1985)* (Moscow, 1995); and A. O. Chubaryan, *et al.* (eds.), *Stalin i Kholodnaya Voina* (Moscow, 1998).

62   This theme of progressive versus reactionary political forces dominates the reports on internal developments in various European countries published in the central committee's biweekly confidential bulletin on international affairs, *Voprosy Vneshnei Politiki*. The files of the bulletin for 1945–1946 are in RTsKhIDNI, F. 17, Op. 128, D. 49, 94.

63   AVP RF, F. 6, Op. 5b, Pap. 1, D. 1, LL. 89–93.

64   See A. A. Ulunian, 'The Soviet Union and the Greek Question, 1946–1953', in Gori and Pons, *The Soviet Union and Europe in the Cold War, 1943–1953*; I. D. Smirnova, 'Gretsiya v Politike SSha i SSSR 1945–1947 gg.', Novaya i Noveishaya Istoriya, no. 5, 1997; and M. Narinski, 'L'URSS et le problème de sphères d'influence et de frontières en Europe, 1939–1947, in C. Baechler and C. Fink (eds.), *The Establishment of European Frontiers after the Two World Wars* (London: Peter Long, 1995), p. 437.

65   I develop this argument further in G. Roberts, *The Soviet Union in World Politics: Coexistence, Revolution and Cold War, 1945–1991* (London: Routledge, 1998), ch. 2. On the transmutations of the people's democracy idea see also W. O. McCagg, *Stalin Embattled, 1943–1948* (Detroit: Wayne State University Press, 1978).

66   The phrase is from N. Gould-Davies, 'Ideology and International Relations', unpublished paper, BISA Annual Conference, University of Sussex, December 1998, p. 21.

67   On Gorbachev's yearning for a return to the era of people's democracy and the grand alliance, see A. D'Agostino, *Gorbachev's Revolution* (London: Macmillan, 1998).

Chapter 5

Jonathan Steinberg

THE THIRD REICH REFLECTED
German civil administration in the occupied Soviet Union, 1941–4

Il dramma d'un regime comincia quando non è più capace di trovare la verità: e finisce quando non ha più la voglia di cercarla.

[Giuseppe Bottai, *Diario, 1935–44*, ed. G. B. Gueri (Milan, 1982), 2 December, 1942]

IN 1957, ALEXANDER DALLIN published his *German Rule in Russia 1941–1945: A Study in Occupation Politics*, a work which in its scope and subtlety has still not been superseded. At the end of this vast book, Dallin reflected that beneath 'the failure of the German occupation . . . lay the political morality and the *Weltanschauung*, the nature of the Nazi system itself'.[1] Bernard Chiari, in a recent study of German civil administration in White Russia, likens the circumstances of German rule in Russia to 'laboratory conditions' for understanding the essential features of the Nazi state.[2] Nor is this surprising. The great spaces of Russia offered the Nazis a panorama worthy of their visions. Hitler had always looked east for the solution of the problem of *Lebensraum* or living space for his greater German Reich. In a speech in 1928, he explained his brand of spatial Malthusianism:

> When a people has too restricted a living space, that is, when a people lacks certain raw materials, when the land available for cultivation is too small, that leads to a certain crisis. Crisis, poverty, social sickness, finally bodily sickness, all these emerge from this imbalance.[3]

Again and again he hammered this message home. Germany must expand or die. As he explained to his generals on 10 February 1939, 'I have taken it upon myself to solve the German question, that is, to solve the question of space. You must take it as a fact that, as long as I live, this idea will rule my entire thinking'.[4]

Russia became the arena for his other grandiose schemes, for the final elimination of the poison of Jewish Bolshevism, for the colossal transfer of peoples that he envisaged, for the establishment of an empire which would make the Roman or British look feeble by comparison. In his prison notebooks, Speer used the term 'Rausch' (intoxication) to describe the effect Hitler's Russian visions had on him.[5] The German occupation of the Soviet Union cast into sharp relief central features of the Third Reich, in particular the administrative chaos that gave the regime a peculiarly Hobbesian character. The occupied Soviet Union became an arena in which every conceivable expert – agronomist, economist, racial and genealogical fanatic, technocrat, bureaucrat, student of Russian and Slavic cultures (the *Ostforscher*), colonizer and crank – attempted to mobilize some element of the great state apparatus to fulfil his visions. Most important of all, the SS was involved in the eastern enterprise from the planning stage to the final retreat. It followed the army just behind the front line in order to carry out the 'final solution of the Jewish question' in its own uniquely barbarous way.

Then there were thousands and thousands of job-seekers, unemployed party hacks, disgruntled Gauleiter looking for empires to build, bored city and county officials who saw themselves strutting a grander stage than domestic administration offered, ageing *Altkämpfer*, pioneers of the heady days of Nazi street brawls and Jew-baiting, who seized the chance to act out their sadistic urges. These people, the so-called 'Ostnieten' (the eastern nobodies), gave their own characteristic stamp to the conduct of civil administration and ethnic policy in the east. Many of them, as SS Obersturmbannführer Strauch contemptuously observed, were 'blockheads and ass-lickers, whose careers for the most part had depended on that of the Gauleiter'.[6] In front of this diabolical social frenzy stood the Wehrmacht, itself both spectator and participant in the conquest and then administration of the occupied Soviet lands. Everything that made up the Nazi regime played a part in the occupied Soviet Union between 1941 and 1944.

If the civil administration in the east offers us a laboratory for the study of the Nazi regime, the benches have not been crowded with working scientists. During the 1950s, there was a group of studies, such as Dallin's great book, and articles drawing on Nuremberg documents, especially in the *Vierteljahrshefte für Zeitgeschichte;* but during the 1960s and 1970s the interest shifted in line with the increasing preoccupation among historians of Germany with the enormities of the Holocaust. Those who studied the war in the east turned from looking at civil administration to study the role of the Wehrmacht in the execution of the final solution of the Jewish problem and the brutal treatment of Soviet prisoners of war. In the 1960s and 1970s, work by Hans-Adolf Jacobsen, Karl-Jürgen Müller, Manfred Messerschmidt and Christian Streit stripped the German army of its self-proclaimed innocence and led in the 1980s to an intense debate among historians about the character of the Wehrmacht. Had the old Prussian aristocratic army been brutalized by the war in the east and how much of that brutalization could be attributed to the acceptance of Nazi ideology among the younger officers and men?[7]

The process of studying Germany's activities during the Second World War did not, therefore, necessarily shift attention back from the front line to civil government. The team at the Militärgeschichtliches Forschungsamt in Freiburg im Breisgau under Messerschmidt and Wilhelm Deist began in 1979 to publish its great multi-volume history, *Das Deutsche Reich und der zweite Weltkrieg*, which covered everything from ideological and economic preparations to precise studies of the battles and tactics, but it has not yet published its research on civil government in the occupied Soviet Union. At the same time a team of East German historians published a series of documentary collections covering each state occupied by the Nazis during the Second World War with the title *Europa unterm Hakenkreuz*.[8] Yet, as Chiari pointed out in 1993, there is almost nothing which looks at German civilian government at the level where German occupation and native peoples met, although Theo Schulte's fascinating study of the army of occupation behind the front lines has a chapter on the army's relations with the civilian population.[9]

The following essay attempts to add some elements to the story by using documents drawn from Russian, Ukrainian and other east European archives, documents made available to me by the Special Investigations Unit of the Commonwealth of Australia when I acted as an expert witness in an Australian war crimes trial in 1992.[10] These documents were collected in central and local archives as evidence for particular charges levelled against named individuals but, because the defendants were relatively junior figures in the Nazi killing machine, the evidence reflects very sharply the local environments in which such crimes were committed. They put some new pieces into the complex mosaic of reconstructed reality which constitutes the history of the Nazi regime in occupied Russia between 1941 and 1944.

At the beginning of October 1944, Reichsleiter Alfred Rosenberg, the Minister for the Occupied Eastern Territories, set down his final thoughts on the great crusade in eastern Europe. A defeated man in the ruins of Hitler's defeated empire, he found the reason for the failure of German occupation policy in 'a boastful arrogance, which in wide circles, indeed sometimes even in public, proclaimed the inferiority of the subject peoples without the elementary political awareness that such an attitude must provoke hatred and resistance in any people'.[11] The next time, Rosenberg argued, the Germans must get it right. He presented a memorandum with a seven-point programme in which national, civil and religious rights would be guaranteed in all eastern territories; but, above all, he concluded, 'there must be one central, uncontested command which covers all areas of activity. This insight is the decisive conclusion of two and a half years of administration in the Occupied Eastern Territories.'[12]

Napoleonic administrators leaving the Kingdom of Westphalia or the Grand Duchy of Berg in 1814 would, I suspect, have recognized Rosenberg's feelings, but at least they left a legacy of achievement: civil codes, models of government and behaviour, ghettos abolished and careers open to talents. They bequeathed a type of rule and a way of life which flickered in the imaginations of many of the conquered for a generation afterwards. British and French governors and administrators in the twentieth century left political institutions, languages, cultural stereotypes, games and regimental silver when they abandoned their imperial outposts. Nazi civil government left literally nothing but scorched earth and loathing. The Germans entered territory which was not without certain possibilities for them. The Baltic republics had lost their independence in August 1940 and had suffered terribly under Stalinist rule. White Russia and the Ukraine had been ground down by the collectivization programme and the terror of the 1930s. There were national movements in all those states to encourage and allies to be won. None of that potential was realized.

Part of the failure of civil government in the occupied Soviet Union arose from the functioning of the regime itself. Hitler's Reich Commissars in the occupied eastern territories, like the prefects and consuls of the Napoleonic Empire, served rulers acknowledged to be geniuses. Napoleon and Hitler were beyond question or criticism. Yet by comparison with Napoleon, Hitler's rule seemed slack, chaotic and incoherent. Around Hitler, there raged, as General Thomas of the Waffenamt observed, 'A Hobbesian war of all against all'.[13] Rosenberg's Reich Ministry for the Occupied Eastern Territories had to fight Goebbels' propaganda ministry for control of the media, Ribbentrop's foreign ministry over policy, Göring's overlapping and conflicting economic ministries over resources, the high command of the armed forces for control over territory and personnel, and Himmler's police for control of law and order. Looking back on his military service in 1949, General Alexander Freiherr von Neubronn remarked: 'Since the numerous agencies at the dictatorial summit constantly fought one another, a chaos developed in government and the conduct of the war'.[14] This chaos has become familiar to historians as *Polykratie*, rule by many, and has even prompted some observers to see Hitler as a weak dictator. It certainly produced a struggle for control of policy in which little quarter was given.

In this battle of all against all Alfred Rosenberg had considerable assets. One of the very first Nazis, his *Myth of the Twentieth Century* had sold 250,000 copies by 1939.[15] If Hitler's *Mein Kampf* served as the Nazi gospel, Rosenberg provided the Pauline letters. Yet, as Joachim Fest tartly observes, 'It was Alfred Rosenberg's tragedy that he really believed in Nazism'.[16] Hitler claimed never to have read Rosenberg's great work and in any case not to have taken his ideas very seriously. 'We have picked our ideas from all the bushes along life's path', Hitler said in a flight of poetic fancy, 'and no longer know where they came from'.[17] The general opinion has come down to us that Rosenberg's *Myth of the Twentieth Century* is unreadable and, therefore, unread. That it is unread cannot be denied, but it is far from unreadable. It belongs to that genre of debased, sub-idealist German writing in which some great, indwelling *Ur-Sache* unfolds beyond the reach of man or the test of evidence. Whether it be the mysterious workings of the *Weltgeist* in its numerous post-Hegelian variations or Spengler's organicism, they all have the same mystifying surface glitter. Rosenberg's great truth, expressed in a suitably dialectical form, was the proposition that 'Seele . . . bedeutet Rasse von innen, und umgekehrt ist Rasse die Außenseite von Seele' [Soul expresses race from within and in return race is the external side of soul].[18]

Along with passages of high-toned philosophy come others which express the prejudices of the German petty bourgeoisie. The emancipation of women must lead, again by way of the racial dialectic, to the feminization of men: 'mincing men in patent-leather shoes with purple socks, festooned with bracelets, with delicate rings on their fingers, eyes shaded with blue, and red nostrils. Those are the types which in the future women's state [*Frauenstaat*] must become the general rule'.[19] What

Hitler made of Rosenberg is hard to assess. They were never close, and Rosenberg resented that distance bitterly. Just before he was hanged as a war criminal, he wrote:

> In the evenings the Führer often used to invite this man or that man for a long fireside discussion. Apart from the usual guests at his table, Goebbels, Ley and some others were favoured in this respect. I can say nothing on this subject, as I was not once invited.[20]

On 12 October 1944, Rosenberg wrote Hitler the following letter,

> I beg you, my Führer, to tell me whether you still require my service, since I have not been able to report to you orally, but the problems of the east are being brought to you and discussed with you by various parties; in view of this I must yield to the assumption that, perhaps, you no longer consider my activities necessary.

Hitler never even bothered to acknowledge his letter.[21]

It was a surprise to nobody except Rosenberg that in the period from the Nazi seizure of power to the invasion of Russia, Hitler had not given his court philosopher a ministry or post suited to his talents. He headed a party office dealing with foreign affairs, but was marginalized by Ribbentrop. He wrote further works and made speeches. After eight years of drifting Rosenberg's fortunes suddenly and quite unexpectedly changed. On 20 April 1941, as part of the preparation for the invasion of the Soviet Union, Hitler nominated Rosenberg 'Beauftragter des Führers für die zentrale Bearbeitung der Fragen des osteuropäischen Raumes' [Delegate of the Führer for the central treatment of questions of eastern European space]. Goebbels noted acidly in his diary that nothing would come of it, for 'Rosenberg can only theorize, not organize'.[22] Himmler was not pleased either. As he remarked to Bormann, 'dealing with Rosenberg is the single most difficult thing there is in the Nazi party'.[23]

Hitler knew that Rosenberg had special qualifications for his new post. A Baltic German born in Riga on 12 January 1893, Rosenberg had studied architecture in Moscow and knew Russia well. Over the years he had been the centre of a small but devoted group of eastern-orientated intellectuals, like the Ukrainian German, Dr Georg Leibbrandt, who had studied at Johns Hopkins in Baltimore, Arno Schickedanz, a Baltic German whom Rosenberg had first met in 1922 at Munich University, the chemical engineer Otto von Kursell and so on.[24] Rosenberg assembled his experts and began to explore his new role. On 17 July 1941, Rosenberg's office was elevated into the Reich Ministry for the Occupied Eastern Territories or 'OMi' in the bureaucracy's abbreviation. Goebbels noted on 29 June 1941 that Rosenberg was strutting about like 'the Czar of Russia; always the same thing: spheres of authority'.[25]

Because the establishment of a civil administration came late in the planning process for the war in the east, Rosenberg had trouble establishing his 'sphere of authority' not only against other agencies, but also within his own, hastily assembled, organization. Not all the senior administrators within the OMi shared the same objectives. This was part of the reason why the Ostministerium rapidly came to be known as the 'Cha-ostministerium'. There were those, like Consul-General Dr Otto Bräutigam, a career diplomat and deputy chief of the Political Department, for whom the war in the east gave the German Reich a unique opportunity to create an empire of loyal satellite states. As he argued in a memorandum written a week before the invasion in June 1941, the Germans must come as liberators not exploiters. For him, 'the war against the Soviet Union is a political campaign, not an economic predatory raid'.[26] Later Bräutigam argued for the establishment of a Vichy-style government in the Ukraine.[27] On the other hand, Dr Erhard Wetzel, who transferred into Bräutigam's section from the Nazi party's racial-political office, belonged to a group which we can call the 'colonizers'. These colonizers advocated massive transfers of peoples, huge clearances of racially inferior stock and their relocation in reservations in Siberia and other remote places. Once the racial dregs among the eastern peoples had been cleared away, German peasant settlements could be founded, rather like those set up by the Habsburgs in the eighteenth century on the so-called *Militärgrenze* in the Balkans. The 'colonizers' saw the east as a huge racial experiment and planned a kind of engineered, modern *Völkerwanderung*.

Wetzel himself was not untypical of the new employees in Rosenberg's OMi. Born in 1903 in Stettin, he studied law and became a legal civil servant, an Amtsgerichtsrat [counsel to the magistrates]. He joined the Nazi party rather late in the day, on 1 May 1933, and thus belonged to the so-called 'Mayflies', those who suddenly discovered they were Nazis once Hitler had seized power. Like many converts he made up in zeal what he lacked in seniority. While rising in the judiciary, he also rose in the NSDAP. He joined the race-political office of the party, and thus fused in his person party and state functions, while also maintaining 'rather murky secret relations to the Reichssicherheitshauptamt in the SS.[28] Helmut Heiber writes that 'Wetzel was as busy as a bee. Former superiors credited him with a weakness for extremely careful, detailed presentations and drafts'.[29] In 1941 he joined Rosenberg's Ostministerium and became its accredited racial specialist. Soon after taking up his new job he became an advocate of gassing Jews. In a letter of 25 October 1941, he wrote to the Reichskommissar for the Ostland, Heinrich Lohse, in the following terms:

> With reference to my letter of 18 October 1941 I write to inform you that Oberdienstleiter Brack [a central figure in the gassing of the mentally and physically handicapped] of the Chancellery of the Führer has declared himself ready to co-operate in the preparation of the necessary accommodation as well as the gassing apparatus. . . . In view of the present circumstances there are no objections if those Jews who are not capable of work are disposed of by the use of Brackian methods.[30]

Extermination of Jews was not for Wetzel an end in itself, as it was for some SS men. An enthusiastic 'colonizer', he saw attractive possibilities for the settlement of sturdy German peasants across the Russian steppes. On 4 February 1942, Wetzel took the minutes of a meeting in the OMi on the question of 'Eindeutschung': 'Germanizing' the Baltic lands. Here was the moment for those who thought in large sweeps. The representatives of the SS talked about evacuating all the 'racially unwanted' elements from the Baltic countries to western Siberia and the Germanizing of the rest. Wetzel's view was subtler:

> It was worth considering whether, through industrialization of the Baltic region, the racially undesirable elements of the population might not be more appropriately scrapped (*verschrottet*). If one gave them adequate pay and raised their cultural level, a fall in the birth rate was to be expected.[31]

The social engineering which Wetzel advocated required relatively humane treatment of the conquered peoples and a very long time to work, but this ran absolutely against the main thrust of Nazi attitudes. Industrialization was out of the question for eastern peoples. Hitler explained in one of his monologues in mid-September 1941 that 'we shall become the grain export land for all those in Europe dependent on grain. . . . We deliver to the Ukrainians kerchiefs, glass chains for jewelry and whatever such colonial peoples like'.[32] The view that the eastern peoples were primitive was widespread. Sixth Army Command reported in July 1941 that Ukrainian peasants were 'without initiative and needed to be directed'.[33] Such phrases recur at every level of civil administration as well. Documents from White Russia and the Ukraine repeatedly remarked on the people's good-natured docility, their 'kindisch zu nennende Unfähigkeit . . . sich klar und eindeutig auszudrücken' [childlike incapacity to express themselves clearly],[34] the 'erschwerte Auffassungsvmögen der Ukrainer' [retarded capacity of the Ukrainians to conceptualize],[35] and so on.

Hitler shared such views. Shortly after the invasion of Russia in July, 1941, he explained his radical ideas in this matter to Martin Bormann, head of the Nazi party organization and an increasingly close and influential associate:

> It is essential that we do not reveal our objectives to the world. . . . It must not be evident that a final regulation has begun. All necessary measures – shooting, transfer of residence, etc. – we must and can take in any event. We don't want to make any unnecessary enemies too early. We pretend that we are carrying out a mandate. We must be clear that we are never going to leave this territory. So what we do is
> 1. nothing that might block our way later but prepare the final settlements now;
> 2. assert that we are bringing freedom.
> As to detail: the Crimea must be cleared of all foreigners and settled by Germans; the old Austrian province of Galicia will become Reich territory. In principle the issue is to slice up the huge cake in such a way that we first control it, then administer it, then exploit it. The Russians have declared a partisan war against us behind the front. The partisan war has its positive aspect: it gives us the possibility to wipe out anybody in our way. . . . This huge territory must be pacified as quickly as possible. That will take place if we shoot anybody who even glares at us . . .[36]

Against this background, Himmler ordered the director of the Institute of Agronomy and Agricultural Policy of the University of Berlin, SS Standartenführer Professor Dr Konrad Meyer, to prepare a settlement and racial transfer plan, which he delivered on 28 May 1942, and which came to be known as the 'General Plan East'. Meyer reckoned that there would be a demand for 4,850,000 German or 'Germanized' settlers to be planted in the conquered territories.[37] Asked by the OMi to reply, Wetzel wrote a very long memorandum in which he reckoned that at the most there were some 850,000 people who could be 'resettled' and that

> German settlers are unlikely to stream into the settlement zones in the necessary masses. This becomes clear from my previous remarks. To what extent a certain force can be used on Germans in the Old Reich to accelerate the settlement of the east is another question.[38]

Even more embarrassing was the fact that the various racial theories on which these huge movements of peoples rested had no empirical foundation, even in the Nazis' own terms, since 'a racial analysis of the population has not taken place and our available evidence is so thin that we cannot even give a preliminary judgement in any way'.[39] Like Hitler, Himmler was impatient; indeed, he believed that impatience with obstacles of a practical kind showed him to be a man of iron will. As he observed to one of his subordinates, we must beat them 'with the whip of our words'.[40] He would hear no objection to the General Plan East and in June of 1942 wrote to Ulrich Greifelt of the Resettlement Office: 'In one point, I believe I have been misunderstood. In this twenty-year plan the total Germanization of Estonia and Latvia as well as the entire General-Government [of Poland] must be included. We must achieve that in twenty years. I am convinced that it can be done'.[41]

If the occupied eastern territories fascinated colonizers and social planners, they also attracted the attention of those responsible for securing the Reich's wartime food supplies. We can call this third group the 'economic exploiters'. The experience of privation and the threat of starvation during the First World War had left what Rolf-Dieter Müller has called a 'trauma' about Germany's capacity to feed itself during wartime. By 1939 experts reckoned that the Greater German Reich could meet not more than 83 per cent of its food needs from within its own borders.[42] As Götz Aly and Susanne Heim have shown, Göring's Four-Year Plan Ministry gave this problem the highest priority. By April 1941, as Otto Donner observed, the Four-Year Plan had become a 'Kommandostelle', dedicated to the ruthless exploitation of the resources of the conquered territories.[43] By the Spring of 1941, food rations had begun to run short in the Reich. Herbert Backe, State Secretary in the Ministry of Food and Agriculture, told Goebbels on 1 May 1941 that, unless things changed, meat rations for Germans in the Reich would have to be reduced to 100 grams on 1 June 1944.[44] On 2 May, Backe, Paul Körner and Erich Neumann, State Secretaries in the Four-Year Plan Office, Wehrmacht supply officers and representatives of other relevant ministries met in Berlin to consider the crisis. The protocol of the meeting began with two propositions:

> 1. The war can only be carried on if the entire Wehrmacht is fed during the third year of war from Russia;

2. As a result *n* millions will have to starve if what we need is extracted from the land.[45]

At the end of May 1941, the Four-Year Plan Office published its so-called 'Green Folder', a printed set of estimates and regulations for the exploitation of Russian wealth. The main object would be to restore Russian grain exports to the colossal levels last achieved in the prosperous years 1909–13 under the tsars. As a result of such considerations, Hitler gave Reichsmarschall Göring and his Four-Year Plan agency on 28 June 1941 'complete powers of decision with respect to all problems connected with the economy in the occupied Soviet territories'.[46] Rosenberg's Ostministerium had, in effect, lost a crucial battle even before it had begun to operate. He had to promise 'in no way to found an economic section in my administration. The economy would in substance and practice be administered by the Reichsmarschall and such personalities as he assigns to it'.[47] The consequences of this surrender soon made themselves felt in the occupied territories. In any conflict between Rosenberg's ministry and Göring's rapacity, the OMi always lost. When in 1942 Gauleiters, in what contemporary usage called the 'old Reich', began to report complaints from the German civil population about food shortages, Göring made the message absolutely clear to senior army and civil personnel serving in the occupied Soviet Union:

> You have not been sent here 'to serve the general good of those peoples entrusted to your tender care, but to extract what you can so that the German people can live'. . . . It is utterly indifferent to me if you tell me your people are falling over from hunger. Let them do so as long as no German faints from hunger.[48]

The aims of the 'exploiters' clashed with those of the 'colonizers' and the 'national liberators', but all three clashed with a fourth, yet more deadly agency: the SS. At the planning stage, the SS had been given the modest role that traditional police functions required. The place of the police in the chain of authority was taken from the established practices of the Prussian state. According to the formal organization of the Reich Ministry for the Occupied Eastern Territories, at each level of government an SS and Police Leader was directly subordinate to [*unmittelbar untersteht*] the relevant civil administrator. Thus there was a Higher SS and Police Leader [HSSPF] at Reich Commissariat level, an SSPF at General Commissariat level and a police commander at Kreis level.[49] In fact the Reich ministry never succeeded in gaining control of the police. Police power was the one branch of administration in which the usual Nazi chaos did not exist. From 17 June 1936, when Hitler issued a decree [*Erlaß*] establishing the position of Chief of the German Police in the Reich Ministry of the Interior, Heinrich Himmler had combined the post of head of a unified German police system and chief of the equally unified apparatus of party police. He could now style himself 'Reichsführer SS [party]' and 'Chef der Deutschen Polizei' [state].[50] This double designation was used in the occupied territories between 1941and 1944, the abbreviation SSPF – SS [party] and Polizeiführer [state] – reflecting the dual origin of the unified police apparatus. The final stage of this consolidation of police power was reached when Himmler issued the decree on

27 September 1939 establishing a Reich Security Main Office [Reichssicherheits-hauptamt], under SS Gruppenführer Reinhard Heydrich, which became in due course the world's most infamous terror and surveillance organization.[51] The extreme centralization of police power included everybody from the agents of the Gestapo to the rural constables. Police officers might be state or party employees; it was merely a question of which budget bore the salary costs.

In the 'old Reich', the SS competed with the traditions of a powerful and proud bureaucracy. Courts and law codes continued to exist, if diluted. In the occupied Soviet Union, there was an administrative vacuum. The German occupiers abolished the previous Bolshevik structures of rule and hastily tried to replace them with their own. The ramshackle authority of Rosenberg's civilian administration could not contain the dynamism and single-mindedness of the SS. Whereas the 'old Reich' was never entirely a police state, the Reich commissariats of the Ostland and the Ukraine were. The SS was hard to oppose, precisely because it had become more than just the police force of a tyrannical authority; in the east its members were the self-anointed agents of Nazi racial ideology in a war declared to fulfil that ideology. In that crusade, Rosenberg had contributed a classic text and hence shared its ends. As he wrote in his diary in November 1939, war would 'bring ideological issues to a new ferocity',[52] but not even he knew how far the SS had already gone. SS-Gruppenführer Reinhard Heydrich explained the policy in Poland to Admiral Canaris on 8 September, 1939: 'We want to leave the little people alone. The nobility, the priests and the Jews have to be done away with'.[53] If Heydrich's intentions were to be carried out, new structures of command would be needed. After uneasy and complicated negotiations between the SS and the Oberkommando des Heeres or OKH [the High Command of the Army], the latter issued its 'Geheime Kommandosache [secret command matter] Nr 324' dated 21 September 1939, which explained to the troops in the field that special *Einsatzgruppen* [Operational Groups] had been set up

> by order of and under instructions from the Führer to carry out certain 'volkspolitische Aufgaben' [ethno-political tasks] in the occupied territory. . . . The execution of these orders in each case shall be left to the commanding officers of the police *Einsatzgruppen* and lies outside the authority of the commanders-in-chief.[54]

Within weeks of the outbreak of war in 1939 the SS accomplished a first important breakthrough. Its killing operations would no longer be subjected to control by the armed forces nor restricted by military justice. Army discomfort at the sight of SS units murdering Polish and Jewish men, women and children led to friction and finally, in March 1940, to a meeting at which Himmler addressed the highest commanders in the Wehrmacht. According to Himmler's own notes, he told the commanders:

> *Executions* – the leading figures of the opposition movement – very hard but necessary – myself present at them – no wild excesses by subordinates – even less from me, know very precisely what is going on. In this meeting of the highest officers of the army I can speak openly: I do

nothing that the Führer does not know [*Ich tue nichts, was der Führer nicht weiß*].[55]

On 30 January 1941, the eighth anniversary of his coming to power, Hitler made a speech to the newly appointed Reichstag in which he said this:

> I shall today again be a prophet: if once again international Finance-Jewry in and out of Europe succeeds in pushing the peoples of Europe into a war, then the result will not be the Bolshevization of the earth and thus the victory of Jewry, but the destruction [*Vernichtung*] of the Jewish race in Europe.[56]

From the earliest stages of planning Operation Barbarossa, the code name for the Russian campaign, such intentions were overt. On 13 March 1941, the Oberkommando der Wehrmacht or OKW [the High Command of the Armed Forces] issued a set of 'Guidelines for Special Areas for Order No. 21 (Operation Barbarossa)'. The OKW made it explicit that

> the operational area of the army is to be kept as restricted in depth as possible. . . . In the operational area of the army the Reichsführer SS has received special tasks by order of the Führer to prepare the political administration, tasks which arise from the final struggle to be fought between two antagonistic political systems. Within the framework of these tasks the Reichsführer SS acts independently and on his own authority.[57]

The language used in this document may seem at first sight quite innocuous. The Reichsführer SS had received orders to carry out 'Sonderaufgaben' [special tasks], but in this coded language 'Sonderbehandlung' [special treatment], 'Umsiedlung' [resettlement], 'Aussiedlung' [transfer of residence], announcements of 'problems solved', or 'clarified', 'solutions' 'reached' and 'achieved', and all references to 'cleansing', 'clearing up' or 'purifying', were simply euphemisms for murder. Everybody involved knew that. The document itself offers an eloquent testimony to that fact. It is the only copy of the five originals of this top secret order to have survived the war and bears the date-stamp of the High Command of the Navy. Opposite the passage just cited, we can read the marginal note of an unidentified senior officer in the High Command of the Navy, who wrote: 'Das bedeutet einiges!' ['That really means something']. He apparently knew what 'Sonderaufgaben' meant.

The High Command of the Armed Forces issued its own full instructions to commanders on 19 May. Appendix 3, 'Guidelines for behaviour of the Troops in Russia', which was part of a general order of the OKW, states:

> Bolshevism is the mortal enemy of the National Socialist German people. Germany's fight is against this corrosive world-view and its bearers. This fight requires ruthless and energetic measures against Bolshevik agitators, partisans, saboteurs, Jews and ruthless elimination of active or passive resistance.[58]

The legal restrictions on killing civilians were being stripped away. SS units could take executive measures against civilians without interference. Soldiers could commit crimes without threat of prosecution, and certain categories of people could be killed even if resisting passively. The final step came with the 'Commissar Order' of 6 June 1941, so called because it directed both police and army authorities to execute without trial any political commissars of the Soviet Communist party found in uniform among Soviet prisoners of war. This step was justified in these terms:

> In the fight against Bolshevism it is not expected that the enemy will behave according to the principles of humanity or international law. In particular an odious, hate-filled, inhuman treatment of our prisoners of war is to be expected from political commissars of every sort, the true bearers of resistance. The troops must be aware that:
>
>   1. in this struggle mildness or international, legal considerations are a mistake in dealing with these elements. They are a danger to our own security and rapid pacification of the conquered territory;
>   2. the advocates of a barbaric, Asiatic form of war are the political commissars. Against them one must act at once and without further ado and with all severity. . . . After separation from other prisoners they are to be eliminated.[59]

Stated categories of people were guilty *per se* of crimes by virtue of their membership in that category. Against them the authorities are entitled to take what they called euphemistically 'vorbeugende Maßnahmen' [preventive measures]. All Bolshevik political commissars and all Jews belonged to this set of victims. Indeed, as Hitler had shown in *Mein Kampf*, the Bolshevik was indistinguishable from the Jew in any case, so the murder of Jews was doubly justified.

SS objectives – the destruction of Bolshevism and the extermination of Jews – clashed, as we shall see, with economic exploitation, with the objectives of some of the SS's own race and resettlement policies and, of course, with any idea that the war would liberate the peoples subject to Soviet rule. Against this unpropitious background Rosenberg had to construct his administration and define his 'sphere of authority'. Early in September 1941, he published his own set of administrative instructions and guidelines for his new ministry in the east under the title 'The Civil Administration of the Occupied Eastern territories', a document known as the 'Brown Folder' [*Braune Mappe*].[60] It offered a complete guide to the structures, competences and objectives of the administration. Hitler had agreed, when setting up a Reich Ministry for Occupied Eastern Territories, to establish four Reich Commissariats covering the whole territory of the Soviet Union to the Urals. A rump non-Bolshevik, Russian state would govern the Asian lands. Unexpected Russian resistance meant that of the four planned commissariats only two, one for the Ostland covering the territory of the three former Baltic republics and White Russia, and one for the Ukraine with headquarters in Rowno, were ever actually set up. In addition Hitler established a system of provincial and district administration on the Prussian model. The larger units were like old Prussian provinces and called 'Generalbezirke' [general regions]. They were in turn divided into smaller districts or 'Kreisgebiete'. The head of a Generalbezirk was a General Commissar; the head of the Kreis was the District Commissar [Gebietskommissar].[61] The scale of the operation was impressive. Within the four Reich Commissariats there were to be twenty-four general commissariats, in effect provinces, eighty main commissariats for the large towns and nine hundred district commissariats.[62]

In the introduction, the Brown Folder states that the districts administered are not to have 'a life of their own, but form part of the Greater German Living Space'.[63] The Hague Convention would not apply, because the Soviet Union had been dissolved. The occupied territories were to be governed according to ethnic principles which would involve 'differential treatment of the different peoples'.[64] Parts of the Folder deal with Rosenberg's peculiar interests in restoring ethnic German communities and respecting 'expressions of their folkhood', which include the avoidance of kitsch in cemeteries and the prohibition of Latinate words in their German. The Jewish problem was, of course, to be 'solved' and no obstacles were to be placed in the way of pogroms. Soviet Jews were to be 'excluded' and forbidden to practise professions or ritual slaughter.[65] Rosenberg set himself high goals. The Brown Folder claims that the new minister 'rules' in the name of the Führer and 'makes law'.[66] None of this had much to do with realities on the ground. There was, to begin with, the sheer scale of the task. Chiari offers some startling figures. In the District Commissariat of Glubokoye, an area about a third the size of Belgium with a population of 400,000, there were precisely 79 German administrators and of those 49 were in the section for food and agriculture.[67] No doubt the District Commissioners in the Sudan or the Punjab coped with similar numbers, but their ethnic prejudice did not preclude the use and training of native elites. In the crazy world of Nazi racism, Untermenschen had to remain just that.

Not only were civil administrators few and far between, but they were very randomly assorted and ill-prepared. Of those initially appointed to the notional 1,050 posts at District and City Commissariat level, 261 applicants came from the German Labour Front, 144 from the SA leadership (and hence were the object of almost automatic SS hostility and distrust) and 450 men from the Ministry of the Interior.[68] Few of them had Russian or any other native language, and many had equivocal pasts, like Gauleiter Wilhelm Kube, appointed General Commissar for 'White Ruthenia', as Nazi terminology described the area, who in 1936 had been removed from his office as Gauleiter for writing anonymous letters, signed 'a few Berlin Jews', accusing Bormann and others of having Jewish wives.[69] The behaviour of the civil administrators in post left much to be desired. In December 1941, Peter-Heinz Seraphim, an Oberkriegsverwaltungsrat [senior military administrative councillor] described the situation in the Ukraine. Professor Seraphim complained of the civil administration's totalitarian claims and its absurd pretences to 'lordship', with District Commissars 'drunk with power' [Im Machtrausch] going about their business with whips in their hands.[70] As another technical expert observed contemptuously, the new masters were 'Bürger without horizon or sophistication: the Spießer who likes to play Herr'.[71] Rosenberg dressed his satraps in an especially designed yellow-brown uniform, which soon earned them the pejorative title of Goldfasanen [gold pheasants] and the even more widely used nickname of Ostnieten.[72]

Throughout the occupation, the shortage of German personnel and the vastness of the task forced the German administration to rely on local help. Himmler had recognized as early as 25 July 1941 that 'since the tasks of the police in the occupied eastern territories cannot be executed with the manpower of the SS and police alone, it is therefore necessary to form as soon as possible auxiliary units out of those favourable ethnic groups in the occupied territories'.[73] On 31 July 1941, the chief of the Ordnungspolizei, Daluege, issued detailed instructions to carry out Himmler's orders. The new units were to be called Schutzmannschaften, known generally as 'Schuma', and were to be trained and officered by German police. In a *Dienstanweisung* [service instruction] for Schutzmannschaft in the occupied territory, the precise authority of the ethnic police auxiliaries with respect to German civilians is spelled out:

1. Through decree of the Commander of the Order Police 10/1 Sch. No. 1/41 of 6.11.41, Schutzmannschaften in the occupied eastern territories are auxiliary organs [*Hilfsorgane*] of the German police.

2. Schutzmannschaften employed on traffic duty have the right to issue directions to German vehicles in traffic-police matters but may not use coercion.

3. Members of the Schutzmannschaft are not entitled to arrest temporarily a Reich German or to carry out searches or seizures on him. If such measures are necessary, they are to be carried out by German police called for that purpose.

4. In case of emergency self-defence, or attacks on objects entrusted to their care or persons or objects under their guard, members of the Schutzmannschaft have the same rights and duties as the German police.[74]

In so far as German authority was visible on a local level, it took the form of the Gendarmerie posts manned by one or two elderly, green-uniformed, *Orgpo*, supported by squads of native auxiliaries with clubs and truncheons. Most of the other branches of the administration scarcely made a dent on village life in peasant communities which, in any case, often had more respect for, and contact with, Soviet partisans than their new German masters. The only other branch of German activity which made an impact at the local level was the agricultural service. Chiari has collected the biographies of the 360 agricultural service members for White Ruthenia of whom 201 were so-called Landwirtschaftsführer [agricultural leaders] responsible for the supervision and control of the farms. Practically all of these were men in their late thirties and forties, mostly peasants without any linguistic skills or technical preparation for their jobs.[75] They also found themselves caught in the struggle between the 'exploiters' and the 'liberators' on the question of the kolkhozy, the huge collective farms set up by the Soviet regime. Göring insisted on 27 July 1941 that 'to avoid, as far as possible, halts in production and interruptions in the delivery of agricultural products, the present kolkhoz system . . . will have to remain'.[76] Many observers believe that a great opportunity was missed in not privatizing and redistributing the land.[77]

The actual results of the ruthless exploitation of the occupied Soviet Union were disappointing. Not only, as Mulligan shows, did Germany extract more grain by peaceful trade with the Soviet Union between 1939 and 1941 than by forced extraction between 1941 and 1944, but, as a German economic survey of 1944 made abundantly clear, the idea of huge profits from the occupied east was imaginary. The Forschungsstelle für Wehrwirtschaft calculated that by the first quarter of 1944 the 'real value for Germany of the net profits extracted from the occupied territories amounted to (in milliards of Reichsmarks): occupied eastern territories RM 4.5; Belgium RM 9.3; the Netherlands RM 12,030; France RM 35,060'.[78] The Low Countries and France, under more civilized regimes, were many times more useful to the Reich than the 'predatory raid' on the Soviet Union: yet another example of the curious blindness of Nazi leaders to reality.

The extraction of labour posed another challenge to the viability of the eastern administration. From the establishment of Fritz Sauckel as special agent for labour, the Generalbevollmächtigter für den Arbeitseinsatz, on 21 March 1942, to the German withdrawal from Russia in 1944, the hunt for able-bodied young workers raged without limit. As Sauckel put it in his usual crude way, the German authorities were to abandon any 'humanitarian nonsense and, as in the old days in Shanghai, go out to catch people and to drug them with booze and promises in order to get them to Germany'.[79] The fact was that the Greater German Reich had run out of men. As the District Commissar in Kasatin wrote to his subordinates on 23 June 1943, 'according to the opinion of those in the highest positions, the provision of workers for the Reich is *the most important* [underlined in the original] task in the eastern territories'.[80] Round-ups began throughout the two Reich Commissariats. The 'increasingly ruthless *Aktionen*' led many young men and women to hide or desert to the partisans. Random seizures of family members of the Schutzmannschaften themselves also took place. As a result, the Commander of the Order Police in Zhitomir held a conference on 6 July to discuss the situation. As he explained,

> the Reich Führer SS lays great stress on a reliable and effective Schutzmannschaft, because in view of the extremely tight personnel situation in the Order Police we are going to have to rely on the 'Auxiliary Peoples' [*Hilfsvölker*] for the foreseeable future. . . . in general they must be promoted more often than in the past. They must not be seen as a tedious but necessary evil.[81]

Huge numbers of people from the occupied territories all over Europe were transported to Germany. Walter Naasner estimates that by August 1944 7.6 million foreign workers were employed in forced labour in the Reich, of whom 36 per cent came from the former Soviet Union.[82]

In addition to all his other problems, Rosenberg simply could not get his nominal subordinates to obey him. Gauleiters like Erich Koch, Heinrich Lohse and Wilhelm Kube went back a long way in Hitler's career, and he had a weakness for these brutal and outspoken *Altkämpfer*. Koch simply refused to obey any of Rosenberg's orders, and combined his post as Reichskommissar for the Ukraine with his previous position as Gauleiter of East Prussia. In battles with Rosenberg, he went directly to Hitler for confirmation of his actions and always got it. He closed schools when Rosenberg ordered them open, and made speeches rejecting any and all plans for even modest autonomy for the Ukrainians.[83] Others, like General Commissar Litzmann in Estonia or General Commissar Drechsler in Latvia, actively encouraged self-governing directorates to be formed against the explicit orders of their chief, Reichskommissar Lohse.[84]

The oddest case of disobedience is that of Kube, the General Commissar for White Ruthenia, who after a long career in the Nazi party suddenly developed scruples about exterminating certain Jews. On 16 December 1941, he wrote to Lohse, his superior in the Reich Commissariat Ostland, that the first consignment of German Jews had arrived for liquidation, but that he was having second thoughts: 'I am certainly hard and prepared to help with the solution of the Jewish question, but people from our cultural world are something entirely different from the local, degenerate hordes'.[85] At a meeting in Riga on 21 March 1942 with the other General Commissars under the chairmanship of Lohse, Kube pointed out that, because of the murder of the Jews, the White Ruthenian population had begun to hide their children, convinced that they were next on the list.[86] In another instance of his idiosyncratic attitude to official policy he tried to encourage the formation of a modified Ruthenian puppet government, for which the Obersturmbannführer Strauch accused him of conduct 'unworthy' of a German. Strauch reported at length to his superior von dem Bach-Zalewski that Kube insisted on maintaining German Jews in his headquarters as staff and even had the nerve to suggest that nobody would come to any harm if he listened to Jewish music, as long as it was from the nineteenth century. Strauch could hardly believe what he was hearing.

> I said that I could not understand how German men could disagree over a few Jews and . . . that because we had specialists remove gold fillings from the Jews as ordered, this was now an object of complaint. Kube replied that the way we proceeded was unworthy of a German man and of the Germany of Kant and Goethe. If Germany's reputation in the whole world went down that would be our fault.[87]

The establishment of civil administration in the occupied eastern territories took place against a background of mass murder. Hundreds of thousands of men, women and children were ruthlessly slaughtered by shooting them, generally in the back of the head, and then pushing them into pits. Not even Kube, with his direct access to Hitler, his early membership of the Nazi party, and his high office could prevent Strauch and his SS men simply marching into the General Commissariat office in July 1943, and rounding up the seventy Jews working there 'to take them for special treatment'.[88] The SS paid no attention to the outraged protest of a party functionary, no matter how exalted.

The brutality is terrifying enough, but much more mysterious and incomprehensible is the record-keeping. The SS kept exact records of its victims. One example must serve as illustration. On 1 December 1941, SS Standartenführer Karl Jäger, commander of Einsatzkommando 3 of Einsatzgruppe A, attached to Army Group North, compiled a complete list of the executions carried out under his orders in occupied Lithuania from 2 July 1941 to the end of November.[89] This document explicitly records day by day and place by place the murder of 133,346 Jewish men, women and children, murders carried out throughout the whole of Lithuania and listed with pedantic accuracy village by village. Children begin to appear in the bookkeeping about the middle of August. At Panevesys on 23 August 1941, 1,609

Jewish children died, along with 4,602 women and 1,312 men. With satisfaction Jäger could report that he had 'solved the Jewish problem in Lithuania. In Lithuania there are no more Jews except for work-Jews [*Arbeitsjuden*]'.[90] Jäger wanted to murder them too, but ran into the sharp opposition of the civilian administration, so he proposed instead compulsory sterilization of male 'work-Jews' to prevent reproduction. If a Jewish woman became pregnant, she could easily be shot anyway. He is equally frank about how his unit had committed its murders. It is all a question of organization:

> The Jews had to be assembled in one or several places. The march route from the assembly place to the pit normally amounted to four or five kilometres. The Jews were transported in groups of 500 to the execution place leaving gaps of about two kilometres.[91]

No very reliable figures exist for the number of Jews who died as a result of such crimes but, after a careful examination of the existing statistical evidence, Gert Robel concludes that in the Soviet Union, including the Baltic states, the number was just over two million.[92] Shmuel Spektor has made a recent study of the extermination of the Jews in the area known as Volhynia, a territory historically part of the Kingdom of Poland but ethnically largely Ukrainian, which became part of the Reich Commissariat of the Ukraine under the Nazis. Spektor reckons that in 1944 only 3,500 Jews were left in the entire territory, precisely 1.5 per cent of the prewar population.[93]

Against the background of this gigantic campaign of genocide, Rosenberg struggled to maintain some control over civil affairs. The Führer had, as we have seen, given to Himmler and the SS rights to carry out 'ethno-political tasks on the authority of the RFSS', and Rosenberg had to recognize that. Hence the Brown Folder explicitly excludes the civilian administration from control of summary executions.[94] Although the Higher SS and Police Leader was, according to the Brown Folder, directly subordinate to the Reich Commissars for the Ostland and Ukraine, as were the police commanders at lower levels to the equivalent General and District Commissars, in practice neither the Einsatz- and Sonderkommandos operating in the Reich Commissariats nor the Order Police, when dealing with 'ethno-political tasks', took the slightest notice of orders, decrees, regulations or entreaties of the civil administration. In an attempt to clarify the lines between civil and police authority, Himmler and Rosenberg issued a joint decree on 19 November 1941 in which the HSSPF and SSPF are, once again, asserted to be directly subordinate to the relevant civil authority except that they are charged with the management of all those matters in which the Reichsführer SS is the 'competent authority' in the Ministry of the Interior, in other words the very issues at stake between the two ministries:

> a) leadership and operations of all units of German police present in the Reich Commissariats;
> b) police administrative affairs (matters of substantive police and administrative law in so far as they are controlled by the Main Office of the Order Police and the Reich Security Main Office);

c) the direction of the native auxiliary police [Schutzmannschaften] in the Reich Commissariats and their tasks.[95]

On 16 January 1942 Himmler altered this decree unilaterally to give precedence to police and SS orders over those of District Commissars.[96] The result is vividly described in a complaint by Landrat Dr Knust of General District Zhitomir in a memorandum addressed to the Reich Commissar for the Ukraine on 9 March 1942:

> The administration of the police runs entirely independently alongside the ordinary administration . . . and thus my position as superior officer of the SS and Police Leader is near to illusory. . . . There is simply no question of a unified command structure from the centre down to the local agencies. In fact two Reich departments rule alongside one another quite independently, breaking the horizontal links which the Führer ordered.[97]

Such complaints were not unusual. In early December 1941, yet another independent agency, the Inspectorate of Armaments, sent a report dated 29 November 1941, prepared by Professor Seraphim, on the situation in the Ukraine.[98] He noted what had been happening to the Jews:

> The Jewish population were untouched by the direct effects of the military actions. First weeks and then months afterwards mass executions were carried out by special units of the Order Police. The actions went from east to west. They took place completely openly and involved Ukrainian militia, often unfortunately with the voluntary participation of men from the Wehrmacht itself. The way these actions which extended to men, the aged, women and children, were carried out was horrible [grauenhaft]. In the sheer scale of executions the action is so gigantic that it exceeds any similar measures taken in the Soviet Union. In total between 150,000 and 200,000 Jews have been executed in the area of the Ukraine assigned to the Reich Commissariat. Only in the last few executions have exceptions been made for a part of the Jewish population (artisans) who were not executed. Before that no account was taken at all of such considerations.[99]

Seraphim had another worry:

> We have to be absolutely clear about one thing, that in the Ukraine in the last analysis only Ukrainians can create economic assets. If we shoot dead all Jews, let the prisoners of war die, condemn citizens of the big cities to death by starvation and also in the coming year lose a part of the rural population through starvation, the question remains: who will produce economically valuable goods?[100]

To this question Rosenberg and his bureaucrats had no answer. Great areas of the occupied east were being denuded of all artisans. By June 1942 the General Commissioner for Zhitomir reported: 'The Jewish question in my General District has been largely clarified. That in the resettlements many valuable workers were eliminated is known'.[101] On 15 and 16 October 1942 the 'complete resettlement' of the Jews of Brest-Litovsk District was carried out, some 20,000 people. This 'resettlement' had an unsettling effect on the remaining locals, as Lieutenant Beuerlein, district gendarmerie commander in Brest-Litovsk, reported on 8 November 1942 to his commanding officer in Luck: 'A rumour is going round in the population that after the Jewish action first the Russians, then the Poles and then the Ukrainians will be shot. Whether the rumour was spread by fleeing Jews or by enemy propaganda could not be determined'.[102] Genocide provided a poor basis for civil administration. The Ministry for Occupied Eastern Territories was caught in the coils of its own ambivalence. The bureaucrats in Rosenberg's ministry clearly willed the end, the elimination of Jewry and the exploitation of Russian space and its resources – indeed their minister had been first to declare the great crusade – but the means being used made it impossible to govern. The SS was apparently winning Hobbes' war of all against all.

There was, however, an area to which Rosenberg's embattled bureaucrats could retreat: the bastion of the law. The extension of German rule to the occupied east had extended the network of Reich legislation to the new provinces, and in a grotesque, twisted way German bureaucrats still acted as if they were operating in a *Rechtsstaat*. The oddest example of this mentality was the battle between the Reich Ministry for Occupied Eastern Territories and the Reichssicherheitshauptamt over the 'Begriff Jude', the definition of a Jew. In following this strange affair, which incidentally sheds light on an aspect of the Wannsee Conference, the heart of Nazi darkness, the very essence of the regime, is revealed.

The two Reich Commissariats in occupied Soviet territory were, it must be remembered, integral parts of the Greater German Reich and subject, therefore, to German domestic legislation. Among the laws which Rosenberg's ministry assumed would operate in the new territories were the 'Nuremberg Laws' which defined the category Jew. Jewish policy would be guided by their distinctions, and hence clarity in their application in the east was required. The Erste Verordnung zum Reichsbürgergesetz [first decree with reference to the Reich Citizenship Law] of 14 November 1935, one of the so-called Nuremberg Laws, had made it clear in paragraph 5, section (i) that 'a Jew is somebody who by race has three full Jews as grandparents' or, as section (2) stated, two full Jews as grandparents if such person belonged to a Jewish religious community, was married to a Jew, or the child of such a marriage, etc. The other categories, 'Mischlinge ersten Grades' [half-breeds of the first degree] and 'Mischlinge zweiten Grades' [half-breeds of the second degree], were not immediately deprived of German citizenship or expelled from their posts.'[103] These categories rested, firstly, on the availability of statistics and of birth and death registers which stretched back for generations and, secondly, on the fact that 'half-breeds' carried not only noxious Jewish blood but also valuable Aryan blood. Neither premise existed in the eastern, occupied territories. How were the Nuremberg Laws to be enforced in the two Reich Commissariats in the occupied Soviet Union?

In October 1941, senior civil servants in the OMi turned their attention to this problem, and on 22 October a draft of new legislation began to circulate. The text rested firmly on that of the Nuremberg Laws and hence paragraphs 4 and 5 stated explicitly:

> 4) Legal and administrative provisions, which are decreed for Jews, apply to Jews of mixed blood only if this is explicitly stated.
> 5) Ordinances with regard to purity of blood which go beyond these regulations may only be issued with the agreement of the Reich Minister for the Occupied Eastern Territories.[104]

At the end of the month the three most involved civil servants in Hauptabteilung 1, the political department, took a look at the draft and decided unanimously that

> a regulation like that provided in the Nuremberg Laws is not feasible. The Nuremberg Laws rest their definition of the term Jew on descent from grandparents. Since in the Eastern Territories the documentary evidence required for such a determination, such as registry office records, church, baptismal, marriage and death registers is rarely available, the danger arises that, if the Nuremberg Laws are introduced, identity as a Jew will not be ascertainable. . . . The fact of circumcision is certainly a confession of Jewishness, but in districts where Mohammedans live the decision cannot rest on this fact alone.[105]

The issues under discussion involved life and death for tens of thousands of human beings. If there were no legal way to ascertain whether certain persons had the right to claim to be half-Jews or not, how could the exemption under the Nuremberg Laws for such persons be applied? In other words, put baldly, how would one know whom to murder? If one puts it in these terms, the sheer strangeness of the Nazi state emerges. Here are senior civil servants doing what such persons do in all modern governments, working through the implications of complex legislative problems. Yet in this case the object was murder.

In December 1941, Oberregierungsrat Labs from the Administrative Department of the OMi paid a visit to the Ministry of the Interior, where Regierungsrat Feldscher explained the likely development of the Jewish question:

> SS Obergruppenführer Heydrich had with the approval of the Führer received the task from the Reichsmarschall [Goering] of preparing arrangements to carry out immediately and uniformly a solution of the Jewish question in Europe after the end of the war. In pursuit of this objective Heydrich had called a meeting of State Secretaries of concerned ministries for the beginning of December, which then because of a meeting of the Reichstag had been postponed to January.[106]

Regierungsrat Feldscher went on to explain that this meeting, now world-famous as the Wannsee Conference of 20 January 1942, would have as its object a change in the Nuremberg Laws to extend the term 'Jew' to the mixed bloods of the first degree and a reduction in status of those of the second grade. Labs was shocked. He replied that the Nuremberg Laws were fundamental parts of the legislation of the Third Reich, solemnly adopted, and that there ought to be only one definition of the term 'Jew' for the whole of Europe.

Just before Christmas 1941 a group of civil servants in the OMi gathered in the office of Amtsgerichtsrat Wetzel, the specialist in racial questions whom we saw above as one of the keen 'colonizers', to discuss the situation. Wetzel pointed out that 'the Führer was unlikely to close his mind to a suggestion from the Reichssicherheitshauptamt', but for the time being it was agreed to do nothing until the Heydrich meeting.[107] A month later, on 20 January 1942, outside Berlin in a villa am Grossen Wannsee 56/58, that meeting on the final solution of the Jewish question took place. SS Obersturmbannführer Adolf Eichmann kept the minutes, and SS Obergruppenführer Reinhard Heydrich took the chair. Of thirty copies of the minutes, copy number 16 survived the war and is now in Bonn.[108] The OMi was represented by the deputy chief, Gauleiter Alfred Meyer, and Dr Georg Leibbrandt, Rosenberg's most trusted associate. All the other ministries were represented at equally senior level.

The Wannsee protocol is the single most famous piece of evidence in the entire history of the Holocaust, and its first pages are already familiar to historians. According to the protocol, Heydrich began by explaining his special responsibility for the 'final solution of the Jewish question', the leading role of the SS in that task and the history of the attempts to cleanse central Europe of Jews by emigration. He then made clear the exact scope of the operation. I quote from page 5, point three:

> In place of emigration another possible solution given the requisite approval by the Führer is the evacuation of the Jews to the east. These actions are to be considered as temporary possibilities, but here practical experience will be gathered which in view of the forthcoming final solution of the Jewish question will be of great importance.[109]

Heydrich then listed the Jewish populations in every country in Europe, amounting to some eleven million, and pointed to the difficulties in ascertaining who was Jewish in certain countries. He then outlined the plans for huge transports. In his words, Europe would be 'combed from west to east'. He expected the high death tolls involved and remarked on ways to deal with the 'Restbestand' [remaining stock]. As to the question which had been agitating the Reich Ministry for the Occupied Eastern Territories, Heydrich had a clear answer: 'Half-breeds of the first degree, in view of the final solution of the Jewish question, are to be treated in exactly the same way as full Jews'.[110] A few exceptions might be made, but such half-breeds in Germany were to be 'sterilized' as a condition of their exemption from deportation. The trickier problems occupied the rest of the meeting: mixed German-Jewish marriages, the exact status of half-breeds of the second degree, marriages between half-breeds of the first degree and persons of German blood, between half-breeds of first and second degree. The general view was that sterilization ought to be widely used and indeed made compulsory. Gauleiter Meyer of Rosenberg's ministry and State Secretary Bühler from the Generalgouvernement of occupied Poland agreed to begin preparatory work in their respective territories, but in such a way that any disquiet in the population would be avoided.[111]

One problem, however, the Wannsee Conference had not solved: there were now two different definitions of the 'Begriff Jude'. In the Old Reich half-Jews of the first degree were still exempt from the final solution, but in the occupied eastern territories they were not. The laws were no longer uniform in all German territories. New definitions and decrees would have to be issued to clarify the position. Leibbrandt of Rosenberg's ministry called a meeting for Thursday, 29 January 1942, at Rauchstrasse 17 in Berlin, to which representatives of the same ministries which had been present at Wannsee were invited to discuss an 'ordinance for the definition of the category Jew in the occupied eastern territories'.[112] It clearly distressed those present that two different definitions of half-breeds of the first degree now existed. The most serious friction was caused by the SS, who objected to the intervention of District and General Commissars in what had now been officially declared the province of the SS. Consul-General Bräutigam, the most passionate of the 'liberationists' in the OMi, gave in at once. When Oberreigierungsrat Labs chided him for conceding so easily, as it might set a precedent, Bräutigam replied that in the case of the Jewish question 'he did not regard it as undesirable to emphasize the jurisdiction of the SS and Police Leaders in such matters'.[113] There is no indication that he turned aside to wash his hands at that point.

It would have made no difference if Bräutigam had defended the civil administration, since, as Himmler made absolutely clear in an amendment to the Brown Folder dispatched on 29 January 1942,

> all measures with respect to the Jewish question in the eastern territories are to be carried out with a view to a general solution of the Jewish question in Europe. In consequence, in the eastern territories such measures which lead to the final solution of the Jewish question and thus the extermination of Jewry are in no way to be obstructed.[114]

In spite of Himmler's impatience, the bureaucratic negotiations continued. Meetings at state-secretary level took place in March and April.[115] Finally, in July, the OMi decided, 'in view of the different views on the solution of the question of the future treatment of Jewish half-breeds of the first degree . . . to ask for a decision of the Führer'.[116] The letter, dated 19 July and addressed to most of those who attended the Wannsee Conference, evoked a quick response from the Reichsführer SS. In exasperation, Himmler wrote to SS Obergruppenführer Gottlob Berger on 28 July 1942:

> I urgently request that no ordinance be issued about the concept of the Jew [*Begriff Jude*] with all these foolish definitions. We are only tying our hands. The occupied eastern territories will be cleared of Jews. The implementation of this very hard order has been placed on my shoulders by the Führer. No one can release me from this responsibility in any case, so I forbid interference.[117]

Within the occupation regime, German civil administration was simply swept aside. The murderous thoroughness of the SS defeated the Wehrmacht, the Reich Ministry for Occupied Eastern Territories, the diplomats, the economic agencies, everybody. The SS were doing what the regime acknowledged to be its primary object, but more thoroughly and much more ruthlessly.

The SS won the Hobbesian war of all against all inside Hitler's Reich because the other ministries knew whence Himmler's authority derived. As Amtsgerichtsrat Wetzel observed, Hitler was unlikely to close his mind to a suggestion from the Reichssicherheitshauptamt. The Nazi state may have been a chaos in many respects, but it was strikingly systematic in the execution of the final solution of the Jewish question. In this, as Heydrich told the participants at the Wannsee Conference, the Reichssicherheitshauptamt would be the managing agency – 'die Federführung'[118] – and it was. Civil government in the east rested on the same assumptions as those discussed at Wannsee. The Brown Folder of 1941 stated categorically: 'aus politischen Gründen ist ferner noch eine unterschiedliche Behandlung der verschiedenen Völker erforderlich' [for political reasons a differential treatment of the different peoples continues to be necessary].[119] Rosenberg's bureaucrats had to apply the principles of racial subordination to the subject peoples. No German, however low in rank, was required to obey any native policeman, however high. German drivers were even, as we have seen, exempt from coercion by native traffic police. No doubt the British in India and the French in Africa lived in the same way, but at least they offered the native policeman or bureaucrat some social advancement, some opening for cultural assimilation and some model to emulate. The German civil governors in the east could not create a hyphenated ruling-class, because by definition such inferior racial stocks were incapable of self-rule. In occupied Soviet territory no Vichy regimes were permitted.

Racialism so extreme ultimately makes civil administration impossible. Hitler's vast empire of slaves, graded like cattle in categories of worthiness, could never have survived, even in victory. Some accommodation with the humanity of the occupied would have been necessary. Fortunately for the human race, the experiment failed. Hitler was not kinder to the Germans. Four years before he took his own life amidst the rubble of his capital, he had remarked:

> I am ice-cold. If the German people is not strong and devoted enough
> to give its blood for its existence, so let it go and be destroyed by another
> stronger man. I shall not shed tears for the German people.[120]

On 19 March 1945 he ordered that 'all military, transport, communications, industrial and supply installations, as well as all material goods within the Reich territory, which might serve the enemy for the continuation of its fight, either at once or in the foreseeable future, are to be destroyed'.[121] This final paroxysm of hate and destructiveness was never triggered off, but it tells us something about the inhumanity, the coldness, the evil, at the heart of the Nazi regime. This was a regime, which, as General Helmut Stieff recognized in 1941, was dominated by a *Vernichtungswille*, a will to destroy, so complete that nothing could stand in its way.[122] On 18 May 1944, with the war already lost, the SS sent to their deaths a group of Dutch Jewish diamond cutters, who had been working in an SS-owned enterprise operating in the concentration camp in Hertogenbosch in Holland.

Murdering the diamond cutters not only ruined the SS's own business, but also ruined the non-Jewish industry in Amsterdam.[123] No regime, ruled by such dark impulses, could establish a civil government, either at home or abroad.

Hitler's will gave legitimacy to any enterprise in the Nazi state. In spite of his faithfulness to the racial doctrines of the regime and his long service, Rosenberg could never claim that he had secured the approval of that will. A brutal thug like Erich Koch, who neglected his duties and disobeyed his superiors, got away with any amount of impudence because Hitler liked and backed him. Himmler cited the Führer's will in his battle to exterminate all Jews. Nobody in the Nazi state doubted that he could evoke it, and by the end nobody dared to contest it. Yet Hitler's will, his style, his attitudes, were not unusual or remote from those he commanded. His tastes and prejudices were precisely the same as those of Koch and Kube, Lohse and Strauch. If the British Empire rested on the rigidities of the caste produced in the English public school, Hitler's new empire drew its inspiration from the brutalities and superstitions of the *Altkämpfer*, the SA men who came out of the murkier regions of the German *Kleinbürgertum*, aspirants from the lower reaches of the civil service, or marginalized men, like Rosenberg himself, expelled by the shifting borders after 1918 from German communities outside the Reich. Observers noticed that the *Ostniete* was the characteristic figure of civil government in the east, the little man on the make.

The German empire in the east bore Hitler's image – violent, brutal, pedantic, insecure, half-educated, and aggressively male in tone. Its behaviour patterns had been formed in the trenches and in clubs, racial cults, pubs, youth movements, leagues, circles and veterans' groups of the inter-war period. Its ideology rested, as Hitler's did, on the swill of debased, mystifying creeds which had been sloshing about the margins of German culture since the nineteenth century. These ideas and these men gave the civil administration of the east a peculiar energy but also ensured that it had no purchase on reality. Such ideas find their craziest formulation in the 'General Plan East', with its imaginary settlements of millions of mythical German peasants and the vast relocations of peoples according to indefinable racial categories.

There is another side to the Nazi empire in the occupied territories of the former Soviet Union. We have seen how the OMi discussed monstrous crimes against humanity in the categories of a modern bureaucracy. Much time was spent in the great offices of state on a proper legal definition of the 'Begriff Jude' and whether changes in the Nuremberg Laws should be by 'Verordnung' [ordinance] or 'Erlaß' [edict], when the object of the exercise was the murder of millions of people. What did Consul-General Bräutigam really think when he told Labs that the final solution of the Jewish question was best left to the SS? Did none of the participants at the inter-ministerial meetings and conferences ever see through the fog of pedantry, bureaucracy and euphemism to the consequences of their decisions, to the piles of bloody corpses in some Lithuanian or Ukrainian wood? And would they have acted differently if they had? Yet in spite of the bureaucratic procedures German civil administration in the occupied eastern territories does not conform to the model of modern bureaucracy developed by sociologists.[124] Whereas in the 'old Reich' the Nazi movement confronted a powerful bureaucratic state with a proud tradition of efficiency and a complex legal framework, in the east Nazi agencies created a clean slate. They abolished all pre-existing authority and declared the entire native leadership unfit by racial criteria to exercise authority. The invaders flattened the existing local institutions in the territories they invaded and retained only the kolkhoz, the least popular Bolshevik innovation.

This vacuum distinguished Nazi civil administration of conquered Soviet territory and at the same time released certain latent possibilities in National Socialism: the ferocious struggle among hybrid state/party agencies for control of policy, the bizarre combination of rationality and madness, of bloodshed and bureaucracy, of a modern police force turned into what Himmler himself called a monastic 'order', of meticulous planning and megalomaniac hybrids. By exterminating some and oppressing the rest of the inhabitants, the conquerors created a vast emptiness and then squabbled among themselves about how to fill it. The fits and starts of Nazi policy in the occupied east reflected the inconsistencies and self-delusions of the ideas and attitudes Nazism represented. The combination of chaos and single-mindedness which we have seen in the east expresses both the dynamism and uncertainty of a Nazism free of the constraining framework of the pre-Nazi state and at last able to unfold its full terrifying potential.

Acknowledgements

I should never have begun this research if I had not been appointed by the Director of Public Prosecutions of the Commonwealth of Australia to be an expert witness in the War Crimes Act prosecution of Nikolay Ivanovich Beresovsky in 1992. I am glad to be able to thank Sydney Tilmouth, QC, leading counsel in the case, Grant Nieman, Greg Nicholson and Sandra Pickham of the Adelaide Office of the D[irector of] P[ublic] P[rosecutions] and all their staff, and Graham Blewitt and Dr Martin Dean, then of the Special Investigations Unit of the Attorney General's Department for helping me to face the toughest test which can confront a professional historian: examination in a court of law. I want also to thank my old friend, Professor Sir John Elliott, Regius Professor of Modern History in the University of Oxford, and the Oxford Faculty of History for their invitation to deliver a Special Faculty Lecture in November, 1993, out of which this article has grown. The editor of the *English Historical Review*, Professor R. J. W. Evans, and his anonymous readers made me go back to look again at the existing literature in the field, for which I must thank them. Finally I am more grateful than I can say to my former pupil and colleague, Dr C. M. Clark of St Catharine's College, Cambridge, who read the typescript twice and whose sharp criticism forced me to think through my evidence again.

Notes

1   Alexander Dallin, *German Rule in Russia 1941–1945. A Study of Occupation Policies* (2nd edn., London, 1981), p. 665. Dallin's work rests on an exhaustive cull of the various war crimes documents. At that time the sheer volume of material led him to miss the importance of Reinhard Heydrich, the Wannsee Conference and other elements of the Nazi extermination of the Jews. The 1981 edition contains a postscript in which Dallin acknowledges later research, but the text has not been changed. Timothy

Patrick Mulligan published a fine study called *The Politics of Illusion and Empire. German Occupation Policy in the Soviet Union, 1942–43* (Westport, Conn./London, 1988), which should be used with Dallin. Neither Dallin nor Mulligan sees the significance of the Ordnungspolizei, the ordinary police and gendarmerie who were responsible for law and order at the base of the Nazi pyramid of power, and hence they fail to register the importance of the native police in the entire occupation. Mulligan (cf. p. 154, n. 5), faces more squarely than Dallin the issues of illusion/reality and rationality/irrationality in German policy.

2 Bernard Chiari, 'Deutsche Zivilverwaltung in Weißrußland, 1941–1944. Die lokale Perspektive der Besatzungsgeschichte', *Militärgeschichtliche Mitteilungen*, lii (1993), 70.

3 Hitler, speech, 18 Sept. 1928, quoted in Rainer Zitelmann, 'Zur Begründung des "Lebensraum" Motivs in Hitlers Weltanschauung', in *Der zweite Weltkrieg. Analyse, Grundzüge, Forschungsbilanz*, ed. Wolfgang Michalka (Munich, 1989), p. 555.

4 Ibid., p. 558.

5 Albert Speer, *Spandauer Tagebücher* (Frankfurt a. M., 1975), p. 609.

6 SS Obersturmbannführer Strauch to SS Obergruppenführer von dem Bach-Zalewski, 15 July 1943, in Helmut Heiber, 'Aus den Akten des Gauleiters Kube', *Vierteljahrsheft für Zeitgeschichte* [hereafter VZG], iv (1956), Heft I, Dok. 3, p. 82.

7 See Hans Buchheim, 'Zu Kleists "Auch Du warst dabei"', ibid. ii (1954), I. Heft, 177ff.; id., 'Ausgewählte Briefe von Generalmajor Helmuth Stieff', ibid., 3. Heft, 291ff.; Helmut Heiber, 'Der Generalplan Ost. Dokumentation', ibid. vi (1958), 3. Heft, 281ff.; Helmut Krausnick, 'Kommissarbefehl und "Gerichtsbarkeitserlaß Barbarossa" in neuer Sicht', ibid. xxv (1977), 4. Heft, 682ff.; Dan Diner, 'Rationalisierung und Methode. Zu einem neuen Erklärungsversuch der Endlösung', ibid. xl (1992), 3. Heft, 359ff.; Götz Aly, 'Erwiderung auf Dan Diner', ibid. xli (1993), 4. Heft, 621ff. In Theo Schulte, *The German Army and Nazi Policies in Occupied Russia* (Oxford/Providence, RI, 1989), pp. 1–27, there is an exceptionally thorough account of the debate on the role of the Wehrmacht in atrocities on the eastern front.

8 *Das Deutsche Reich und der Zweite Weltkrieg*, Bd. i, by Wilhelm Deist, Manfred Messerschmidt, Hans-Erich Volkmann, and Wolfram Wette (Stuttgart, 1979). Volume V, pt. I, treats aspects of occupation policy in various parts of Europe, but not the actual occupation in the east after the invasion. No volume has appeared in the series since Volume VI (1988), and doubts exist that the institute will continue at all, let alone finish the enterprise. The relevant East German undertaking is complete, and the volume on the occupied Soviet Union is *Europa unterm Hakenkreuz. Die Okkupationspolitik des deutschen Faschismus, 1938–1945. Die faschistische Okkupationspolitik in den zeitweilig besetzten Gebieten der Sowjetunion, 1941–44*, selected and introduced by Norbert Müller (Berlin, 1991). Cf. Omer Bartov, *Hitler's Army. Soldiers, Nazis and War in the Third Reich* (Oxford/New York, 1991).

9 Chiari, 'Deutsche Zivilverwaltung', 69. See Schulte, *German Army*, pp. 86ff., 134–5, and ch. 7; and, on relations with the civilian population, pp. 150ff.

10 References to such evidence will cite both the archive from which the document or documents come and, in brackets, the reference numbers used by the DPP, e.g. [KO 08]. The existence of other similar war crimes trials in Canada, England, Scotland and the USA has offered a small group of historians similar opportunities to mine, and in many cases involved extensive direct work in archives in the former Soviet Union and in the archives of Soviet allies. There is certain to be a wave of publications based on this material in the next few years.

11 *Europa unterm Hakenkreuz*, no. 265, p. 581.

12 Ibid., p. 583.

13 Alan S. Milward, *The German Economy at War* (London, 1965), p. 23.

14 Jonathan Steinberg, *All or Nothing: The Axis and the Holocaust, 1941–1943* (London, 1990), p. 199.

15 *Das politische Tagebuch Alfred Rosenbergs aus den Jahren 1934/35 und 1939/40*, ed. H.-G. Seraphim (Berlin/Frankfurt, 1956), p. 7.

16 Joachim Fest, 'Alfred Rosenberg: The Forgotten Disciple', in his *The Face of the Third Reich* (London, 1970), p. 163.

17 Ibid., p. 161.

18 Alfred Rosenberg, *Der Mythus des 20. Jahrhunderts. Eine Wertung der seelisch-geistigen Gestaltenkämpfe unserer Zeit* (29–30 printing, Munich, 1934), p. 2.

19 Ibid., pp. 506–7.

20 Fest, *Face of the Third Reich*, p. 171.

21 Seppo Kuusisto, *Alfred Rosenberg in der nationalsozialistischen Außenpolitik, 1933–1939* (Helsinki, 1984), p. 16.

22 *The Goebbels Diaries, 1939–41*, trans. and ed. Fred Taylor (London, 1982), 9 May 1941, p. 356.

23 Richard Breitman, *The Architect of Genocide. Himmler and the Final Solution* (London, 1991), p. 160.

24 Kuusisto, *Alfred Rosenberg*, pp. 168, 229.

25 *Goebbels Diaries*, 29 June 1941, p. 436.

26 Robert Gibbons, 'Allgemeine Richtlinien für die politische und wirtschaftliche Verwaltung der besetzten Ostgebiete', VZG, xxv (1977), 2. Heft, 255.

27 Bräutigam to Rosenberg, 25 Oct. 1942, in Mulligan, *Politics of Illusion*, p. 48.

28 Ibid., p. 12; Heiber, 'Generalplan Ost', 286.

29 Ibid. 286–7.

30 Wetzel to Lohse, cited in Hamid Moghareh-Abed, 'Rassenhygiene/Eugenik. Ideologisches Prädispositiv und Handlungsmotivation zum Genozid', in Michalka, *Der zweite Weltkrieg*, p. 808.

31 'Bericht über die Sitzung am 4.2.1942 bei Dr Kleist über die Fragen der Eindeutschung, insbesondere in den baltischen Ländern', Berlin, 7 Feb. 1942, Doc. no. 1: Heiber, 'Generalplan Ost', 295.

32 Götz Aly and Suzanne Helm, *Vordenker der Vernichtung. Auschwitz und die deutschen Pläne für eine neue europäische Ordnung* (Frankfurt. a.M., 1993), p. 378.

33 AOK 6 to Wirtschaftsstab Ost, 20 July 1941, National Archives, Washington [hereafter NA], T – 77, B. 1113, F. 303 [CB 23].

34 Ereignismeldung UdSSR 86, 17 Sept. 1941, p. 12, Bundesarchiv [hereafter BA] Koblenz, R 58/215–210 [KO 22 B].

35 Kommando der Ordnungspolizei, Zhitomir, 8 Oct. 1942, State Regional Archives, Zhitomir, Ukraine, 1536–1-1 [CB 228].

36 Gerd R. Ueberschär and Wolfram Wette, *Der deutsche Überfall auf die Sowjetunion. 'Unternehmen Barbarossa 1941'* (Frankfurt a.M., 1991), pp. 276–7.

37 Heiber, 'Generalplan Ost', 289–90.

38 Ibid. 319.

39 Ibid. 311.

40 Heinrich Himmler to Otto Pohl, 5 Mar. 1943, in Walter Naasner, *Neue Machtzentren in der deutschen Kriegswirtschaft,1942–1945. Die Wirtschaftsorganisation der SS, das Amt des General bevollmächtigten für den Arbeitseinsatz und das Reichsministerium für Bewaffnung und Munition/Reichsministerium für Rüstung und Kriegsproduktion im nationalsozialistischen Herrschaftssystem* (Boppard am Rhein, 1994), p. 472.

41   Heinrich Himmler to Ulrich Greifelt, 12 June 1942, Doc. no. 3, Heiber, 'General-plan Ost', 325.

42   Rolf-Dieter Müller, 'Die Konsequenzen der "Volksgemeinschaft". Ernährung, Ausbeutung, Vernichtung', in Michalka, *Der zweite Weltkrieg*, p. 241.

43   Aly and Helm, *Vordenker der Vernichtung*, p. 511.

44   *Goebbels Diaries*, 1 May 1941 p. 343.

45   Müller, 'Konsequenzen der "Volksgemeinschaft"', p. 240; Aly and Heim, *Vordenker der Vernichtung*, p. 372.

46   Gibbons, 'Allgemeine Richtlinien', 256.

47   *Europa unterm Hakenkreuz*, no. 13, 28 June 1941, p. 149.

48   'Stenographischer Bericht über die Besprechung am 6.8.1942', cited in Müller, 'Konsequenzen der "Volksgemeinschaft"', p. 248.

49   *Die Zivilverwaltung in den besetzten Ostgebieten (Braune Mappe). Pt. II: Reichskommissariat Ukraine*, Central State Archive, Moscow, [MO 04 A], p. 10.

50   'Erlaß über die Einsetzung eines Chefs der Deutschen Polizei im Reichsministerium des Innern vom 17. Juni 1936', in *Topographie des Terrors. Gestapo, SS und Reichs-sicherheitshauptamt auf dem 'Prinz-Albrecht-Gelände'. Eine Dokumentation*, ed. Reinhard Rürup (Berlin, 1987), Doc. 6, p. 61.

51   'Erlaß des Reichsführers-SS und Chefs der Deutschen Polizei vom 27. September 1939, die Errichtung des Reichssicherheitshauptamtes betreffend', ibid., Doc. 10, pp. 71–80.

52   Rosenberg, *Tagebuch*, 11 Nov. 1939, p. 87.

53   Helmut Krausnick and Hans-Heinrich Wilhelm, *Die Truppe des Weltanschauungskrieges. Die Einsatzgruppen der Sicherheitspolizei und des SD, 1938–1942* (Stuttgart, 1981), p. 63.

54   Heydrich to SIPO units in the east, 29 Sept. 1939, Nuremberg War Crimes Doc. No. 3363-PS [NA 02 B/KO 01 B].

55   Krausnick and Wilhelm, *Die Truppe*, p. 105.

56   Text in *Hitler. Reden und Proklamationen, 1932–1945*, ed. Max Domarus (4 vols., Munich, 1965), iii. 1058.

57   'Richtlinien auf Sondergebieten zur Weisung Nr 21 (Fall Barbarossa)', Ober-kommando der Wehrmacht, Geheirnsache! Nur durch Offiziere. 2. Ausfertigung, 13 Mar. 1941, Bundesarchiv-Militärarchiv [hereafter BA-MA], RM 7/95 [FR 02 A]. For the history of this and other similar documents in the planning of 'Barbarossa', see Krausnick, 'Kommissarbefehl und "Gerichtsbarkeitserlaß Barbarossa" in neuer Sicht', VZG, xxv (1977), 4. Heft, 682ff.

58   Ueberschär and Wette, *Der deutsche Überfall*, doc. no. 7, p. 258.

59   Ibid., pp. 259–60.

60   *Braune Mappe*, loc. cit.

61   'Erster Erlaß des Führer über die Einführung der Zivilverwaltung in den neu beseuten Ostgebieten', 17 July 1941, Zuschrift zu RK. 10714B, Reichminister Lammers an die obersten Reichsbehörden, Berlin, 18 July 1941, BA R 4311 [KO 08 B].

62   *Europa unterm Hakenkreuz*, loc. cit.

63   *Braune Mappe*, p. 25.

64   Ibid., p. 27.

65   Ibid., pp. 32, 35.

66   Ibid., p. 11.

67   Chiari, 'Deutsche Zivilverwaltung', 73.

68   Heiber, 'Generalplan Ost', 283, n.4.

69 Helmut Heiber, 'Aus den Akten des Gauleiters Wilhelm Kube', *VZG* iv (1956), 1. Heft, 68–9.

70 Oberkriegsverwaltungsrat Peter-Heinz Seraphim, 'Zur Lage im Reichskommissariat Ukraine', Rowno, 29 Nov. 1941, p. 6 [NA 07 B and FR 13 A]. Cf *infra*, p. 642, n.2.

71 Dallin, *German Rule in Russia*, p. 102; Mulligan, *Politics of Illusion*, pp. 22–3.

72 Dallin, *German Rule in Russia*, p. 103.

73 Reichsführer SS, Anweisung, 25 July 1945, BA RW 41/4 [FR 21 B].

74 Daluege, Dienstanweisung, BA RW 41/4 [FR 23 B].

75 Chiari, 'Deutsche Zivilverwaltung', 86–7.

76 Dallin, *German Rule in Russia*, p. 322.

77 John Barber and Mark Harrison, *The Soviet Home Front, 1941–45. A Social and Economic History of the USSR in World War II* (London, 1991), p. 103.

78 Mulligan, *Politics of Illusion*, Table 1, 'Soviet Foodstuffs Imported by Germany, 1939 – June 1941', p. 94, and Table 2, 'Production and Delivery of Agricultural Goods in the Occupied USSR, 1941–44', p. 102; Christoph Buchheim, 'Die besetzten Länder im Dienst der deutschen Kriegswirtschaft während des zweiten Weltkrieges. Ein Bericht der Forschungsstelle für Wehrwirtschaft'. *VZG*, xxxiv (1986), 1. Heft, 119, 123.

79 Naasner, *Neue Machtzentren*, p. 117.

80 District Commissar to SS and Police Leader, Kasatin, 23 June 1943, State Regional Archives, Zhitomir, Ukraine [ZH 26 B].

81 Kommandeur der Ordnungspolizei, Bezug: Besprechung der Schuma-Sachbearbeiter bei der BDO Kiew, Zhitomir, 19 July 1943, ibid. [ZH 23 B].

82 Naasner, *Neue Machtzentren*. p. 129.

83 Mulligan, *Politics of Illusion*, pp. 11, 15, and 61–75; Dallin, *German Rule in Russia*, pp. 125–6, 131–3, 458.

84 Mulligan, *Politics of Illusion*, pp. 81, 87, 108; Rosenberg to Lohse, 19 Nov. 1941, in which Rosenberg ordered the closing of all universities in the Baltic states: *Europa unterm Hakenkreuz*, p. 225.

85 Kube to Lohse, 16 Dec. 1941; Heiber, 'Aus den Akten des Gauleiters Kube', 75.

86 Ibid. 72.

87 Aktenvermerk, Minsk, 20 July 1943, ibid., doc. no. 2, p. 79.

88 Ibid.

89 'Gesamtaufstellung der im Bereich des E.K. 3 bis zum 1.12.1941 durchgeführten Exekutionen'. 1 Dec. 1941, Zentralstelle der Landesjustizverwaltungen, Ludwigsburg, O, no. 108 [SM 12 A/LU 05 A].

90 Ibid., p. 8.

91 Ibid., p. 7.

92 Gert Robel, 'Sowjetunion', in *Dimension des Völkermords. Die Zahl der jüdischen Opfer des Nationalsozialismus*, ed. Wolfgang Benz (Munich, 1991), pp. 501, 560.

93 Shmuel Spektor, *The Holocaust of the Volhynian Jews, 1941–44* (Yad Vashem, Jerusalem, 1990), p. 231.

94 *Braune Mappe*, p. 38.

95 'Zuständigkeit der Polizeistellen für die neu besetzten Ostgebiete', signed Himmler and Rosenberg, 19 Nov. 1941, BA Koblenz R 19/333, p. 15 [KO 75 B].

96 'Zuständigkeit der Polizeistellen in den neu besetzten Ostgebieten', signed Himmler, Heydrich and Daluege, 16 Jan. 1942, ibid. p. 50 [KO 76 B].

97 Der Generalkommissar, Shitomir an den Herrn Reichskommissar für die Ukraine, 9 Mar. 1942, pp. 4 and 5, Central State Archive, Riga, 83–117–2 [CB 59].

98   Seraphim, 'Zur Lage im Reichskommissariat Ukraine'. The document, a piece of evidence submitted to the Nuremberg Tribunal, is reproduced in *Europa unterm Hakenkreuz,* p. 48, and excerpts are quoted in Aly and Heim, *Vordenker der Vernichtung,* pp. 392–3, but leaving out Seraphim's graphic descriptions of the horrors of the massacres. This makes Seraphim look more brutal than he was. Seraphim belonged to that group of senior civil servants who made up what Aly and Heim (ibid., pp. 95 ff.) have called the 'pre-thinkers' [*Vordenker*] of the Holocaust.

99   Seraphim, 'Zur Lage im Reichskommissariat Ukraine', p. 6.

100 Ibid., p. 14.

101 'Lagebericht des Generalkommissars Shitomir für Monat Mai 1942', p. 6, BA Koblenz, R 6/310, p. 17 [KO 13A].

102 Gendarmerie Gebietsführer, Brest-Litowsk, 'Lagebericht für Monat Oktober 1942', 8 Nov. 1942, BA Koblenz, R 94/7 [KO 47 B].

103 'Erste Verordnung zum Reichsbürgergesetz vom 14. November 1935', BA Koblenz, R 6/74 [KO 07 B].

104 'Bestimmung des Begriffs Jude', Reichsministerium für die besetzten Ostgebiete, II.1.C, 22 Oct. 1941, BA Koblenz, R6/74, pp. 33 [KO 03 B].

105 Aktennotiz, Hauptabteilung 1, Dr Wtz/Fy, 31Oct. 1941, pp. 36–7, ibid.

106 Aktennotiz (undated), Jan. 1942, Ref. ORR Dr Labs, ibid., p. 54.

107 Ibid., p. 55.

108 Besprechungsprotokoll, Am Großen Wannsee, Nr. 56/58, 20 Jan. 1942, 'Uber die Endlösung der Judenfrage', P[olitical] A[rchive], Ministry of Foreign Affairs, Bonn, Inl. IIg 117 [BO 03 A].

109 Ibid., p. 5.

110 Ibid., p. 10.

111 Ibid., p. 15.

112 Reichsminister für die besetzten Ostgebiete, Schnellbrief, 'Betr.: Verordnung über die Bestimmung des Begriffs "Jude" in den besetzten Ostgebieten', 22 Jan. 1942, BA Koblenz, R6/74, pp. 62–3.

113 Besprechung am 29 Januar 1942, ibid., pp. 77–8.

114 Reichsführer SS Himmler to Amtsgerichtsrat Wetzel, BA Koblenz, R6/74, pp. 94–7.

115 Dr Georg Leibbrandt an die obersten Reichsbehörden, Berlin, 27 Apr. 1942, ibid., pp. 109–117 [KO 12 A].

116 Reichsminister für die besetzten Ostgebiete i.V. Gauleiter Alfred Meyer (Sachbearb. AGR Wetzel) an 1) Parteikanzlei (SS Oberführer Klopfer), 2) Reichsminister des Innern (Staatssekretär Dr Stuckart, 3) Chef der Sicherheitspolizei und des SD), 4) den Beauftragten für den Vierjahresplan (Herrn Staatssekretär Neumann), 5) das Auswärtige Amt (Herrn Unterstaatssekretär Luther), 6) das Rasseund Siedlungshauptamt beim Reichsführer-SS (SS-Obergruppenführer Hofmann), 18 July 1942, PA Bonn, Inl. IIg 177, fo. 95; also BA Koblenz, R6/74, pp. 158–9 [BO 04 A/KO 15 A].

117 Himmler to SS-Obergruppenführer Gottlob Berger, 28 July 1942, cited in R. Hilberg, *The Destruction of the European Jews* (rev. edn., 3 vols., London/New York, 1985), p. 368.

118 Wannsee Protokoll, p. 3.

119 *Braune Mappe,* p. 27.

120 Cited in Sebastian Haffner, *Anmerkungen zu Hitler* (Munich, 1983), p. 198.

121 Ibid., p. 197.

122 In a letter to his wife, dated 24 November 1941, Stieff described the army as 'ein Werkzeug eines despotischen Vernichtungswillens, der alle Regeln der Menschlich-

keit und des einfachsten Anstandes außer Acht läßt': doc. no. 10 in 'Ausgewählte Briefe von Generalmajor Helmuth Stieff', *VZG*, iv (1956), 1. Heft, 303.

123   Naasner, *Neue Machtzentren*, p. 367. Ulrich Herbert, looking at the same evidence in a recent article, arrived at the same conclusion. In the struggle between the demands of war and the imperatives of ideology, ideology always won. As he puts it: 'In the eyes of the Nazis, and in particular the advocates of systematic racism among them, the mass extermination of their ideological enemies was itself a "rational" political goal. . . . Racism was not a "mistaken belief" serving to conceal the true interests of the regime, which were essentially economic. It was the fixed point of the whole system': 'Labour and Extermination: Economic Rationality and the Primacy of *Weltanschauung* in National Socialism', *Past and Present*, cxxxvi (1993), p. 195.

124   Zygmunt Baumann, in his recent book, *Modernity and the Holocaust* (Cambridge/ Oxford, 1989), argues that Nazism embodies the negative aspect of modernity, that is, its capacity to apply bureaucratic rationality to destructive ends. The evidence from civil government in the occupied east suggests that Professor Baumann's hypothesis may not be very useful. He seems to me to confuse Nazism with the state framework in which it came to power. Where that framework was missing, Nazism as racial ideology can hardly be called bureaucratically rational. As Naasner and Herbert both argue (cf. previous note), no bureaucracy, modern or otherwise, would behave the way the Nazis did.

FURTHER READING

FOR ALLIANCE RELATIONS AMONG THE ALLIES (United Nations) generally, see the essays in D. Reynolds, W. F. Kimball and A. O. Chubarian (eds), *Allies at War* (London, 1994); and those in Ann Lane and Howard Temperley (eds), *The Rise and Fall of the Grand Alliance, 1941–1945* (London, 1995). Essential monographic studies are: David Reynolds, *The Creation of the Anglo-American Alliance 1937–41: a study in competitive co-operation* (London, 1982); K. Sainsbury, *The Turning Point: Roosevelt, Stalin and Chiang Kai-shek* (New York, 1986); Mark A. Stoler, *Allies and Adversaries: the Joint Chiefs of Staff, the Grand Alliance, and US strategy in World War II* (Chapel Hill NC, 2000); Martin J. Sherwin, *A World Destroyed: the atomic bomb and the Grand Alliance* (New York, 1975); and Jay Jakub, *Spies and saboteurs: Anglo-American collaboration and rivalry in human intelligence collection and special operations, 1940–45* (London, 1999). And see the essay by Maurice Matloff, "Allied Strategy in Europe, 1939–1945" in Peter Paret (ed.), *Makers of Modern Strategy from Machiavelli to the Nuclear Age* (Princeton NJ, 1986) pp. 677–702.

Much interest in the diplomacy of the Second World War has focussed on its connections with the origins of the Cold War: Vojtech Mastny, *Russia's Road to the Cold War* (New York, 1979); Victor Rothwell, *Britain and the Cold War, 1941–1947* (London, 1982); Walter LaFeber (ed.), *The Origins of the Cold War, 1941–1947* (New York, 1971) and Gabriel Kolko, *The Politics of War,* (New York, 1968). On Churchill and Roosevelt the literature is vast, but see in particular: Warren Kimball, *Forged in War: Churchill, Roosevelt and the Second World War* (London, 1998) and Robert Dallek, *Franklin D. Roosevelt and American Foreign Policy, 1932–1945* (New York, 1979). On neutrals, see the essays in Neville Wylie (ed.), *European Neutrals and Non-belligerents During the Second World War* (Cambridge, 2002).

On Stalin and Soviet diplomacy see: Geoffrey Roberts, *The Soviet Union and the Origins of the Second World War* (London, 1995); W. O. McCagg, *Stalin Embattled, 1943–1948* (Detroit MI, 1978); the articles by Alexei Filitov, "The Soviet Union and the Grand Alliance: the internal dimension of foreign policy," in G. Gorodetsky (ed.), *Soviet Foreign Policy, 1917–1991* (London, 1994) and "Problems of Post-War Construction in Soviet Foreign Policy Conceptions During World War II" in F. Gori and S. Pons (eds), *The Soviet Union and Europe in the Cold War, 1943–1953* (London, 1996); the articles by Albert Resis, "Spheres of Influence in Soviet Wartime Diplomacy," *Journal of Modern History*, 53 (September 1981) 417–39 and "The Churchill-Stalin Secret 'Percentages' Agreement on the Balkans, Moscow, October 1944," *American Historical Review*, 83 (April 1978) 368–87; and Geir Lundestad, "The Soviet Union and Eastern Europe 1943–1947," in G. Lundestad, *The American Non-Policy Towards Eastern Europe 1943–1947* (Oslo, 1975).

On diplomacy and grand strategy within the Axis see: Randall Schweller, *Deadly Imbalances: tripolarity and Hitler's strategy of world conquest* (New York, 1998); MacGregor Knox, *Hitler's Italian Allies: royal armed forces, fascist regime, and the war of 1940–43* (Cambridge, 2000); and Christian Leitz, *Nazi Germany and Neutral Europe During the Second World War* (Manchester, 2000); Rupert Matthews, *Hitler: Military Commander* (London, 2003); and Heinz Magenheimer, *Hitler's War: Germany's key strategic decisions 1940–1945* (London, 1999). No student of Nazi policy should overlook Jonathan Steinberg's *All or Nothing: the Axis and the Holocaust, 1941–1943* (London, 1990); Eleanor Hancock, *National Socialist Leadership and Total War 1941–5* (New York, 1991).

On the "imperial dimension" of diplomacy, strategy and high politics see: Martin Thomas, *The French empire at war, 1940–45* (Manchester, 1998); Christopher Somerville, *Our War: the British Commonwealth and the Second World War* (London, 1998); Martin Kolinsky, *Britain's War in the Middle East: strategy and diplomacy 1936–42* (Basingstoke, 1999); Suke Wolton, *Lord Hailey, the Colonial Office and the Politics of Race and Empire in the Second World War: the loss of white prestige* (Basingstoke, 2000).

The ability to produce armaments and mobilize the economy for total war was an important part of the strategic dimension. On this topic generally see: Alan Milward, *War, Economy and Society, 1939–1945* (Harmondsworth, 1987); Györky Ránki, *The Economics of the Second World War* (Vienna, 1993); and the essays in Mark Harrison (ed.) *The Economics of World War II: six great powers in international comparison* (Cambridge, 1998). For Germany and Japan in particular see E. R. Zilbert, *Albert Speer and the Nazi Ministry of Arms* (London, 1991); B. Carroll, *Design for Total War: arms and economics in the Third Reich* (The Hague, 1968); Erich Pauer (ed.) *Japan's War Economy* (London, 1999).

The most famous strategic innovation of the Second World War was that of "blitzkrieg": see Ronald Powaski, *Lightning War: blitzkrieg in the west, 1940* (Hoboken NJ, 2003); Alexander Rossino, *Hitler Strikes Poland: blitzkrieg, ideology and atrocity* (Lawrence KS, 2003); Adrian Gilbert, *Germany's Lightning War* (London, 2000); Gary D. Sheffield, "Blitzkrieg and Attrition: Land Operations Europe, 1914–45", in Colin McInnes and G. D. Sheffield (eds), *Warfare in The Twentieth Century: theory and practice* (London, 1988) 51–80.

For studies of the European fronts and campaigns see, for the eastern front: Alan Clark, *Barbarossa: the Russian–German conflict, 1941–1945* (London, 2000); John Erickson's classic, *The Road to Berlin* (London, 1983); and the short study by Bob Carruthers, *The Russian Front, 1941–1945* (London, 1999). For the war in the west generally see the short study by Charles Messenger, *The Second World War in the West* (London, 1999). On the war in Finland see Jukka Nevakivi, *The Appeal that was Never Made: The allies, Scandinavia and the Finnish Winter war, 1939–1940* (London, 1976).

On the war at sea: Jack Greene, *The Naval War in the Mediterranean 1940–1943* (London, 1998) and Correlli Barnett, *Engage the Enemy More Closely: the Royal Navy in the Second World War* (London, 1991).

On the war in Asia and the Pacific see: Ronald Spector, *Eagle Against the Sun: the American war with Japan* (New York, 1987); John Dower, *War Without Mercy: race and power in the Pacific War* (New York, 1986); Robert Butow, *Japan's Decision to Surrender* (Stanford CA, 1954); William Craig, *The Fall of Japan* (Harmondsworth, 1979); Richard Frank, *Downfall: the end of the Imperial Japanese Empire* (New York, 1999); Eric Bergerud, *Fire in the Sky: the air war in the South Pacific* (Boulder CO, 2000); Louis Allen, *Burma: the longest war 1941–1945* (London, 1984); and David Glantz, *The Soviet Strategic Offensive in Manchuria, 1945: "August storm"* (London, 2003).

Studies of intelligence have turned the subject into an industry of its own. Many of these are extremely detailed, but those that bear particularly on intelligence as a factor in the making of strategic decisions include the comprehensive and detailed three-volume official history on British intelligence edited by F. H. Hinsley, E. E. Thomas, C. F. G. Ransom and R. C. Knight: *British Intelligence in the Second World War: its influence on strategy and operations* (London, 1979–88). Several works by Bradley F. Smith focus on the United States and the sharing of intelligence: *The Shadow Warriors: OSS and the origins of the CIA* (New York, 1983); *Sharing Secrets with Stalin: how the allies traded intelligence, 1941–1945* (Lawrence KS, 1996); and *The Ultra-Magic Deals and the Most Secret Special Relationship 1940-1946* (Novato CA, 1993). On the Pacific, see Richard Aldrich, *Intelligence and the War Against Japan: Britain, America and the politics of secret service* (Cambridge, 2000). See also John Mendelsohn (ed.) *Covert Warfare: intelligence, counterintelligence and military deception during the World War II era,* vol. 1, *Ultra, Magic, and the Allies* (New York, 1989); John Bryden, *Best-Kept Secret: Canadian secret intelligence in the Second World War* (Toronto, 1993).

On codes and codebreaking in particular, see: David Alvarez (ed.) *Allied and Axis signals intelligence in World War II* (London, 1999); Stephen Budiansky, *Battle of Wits: the complete story of codebreaking in World War II* (London, 2000); Michael Smith, *The Emperor's Codes: Bletchley Park and the breaking of Japan's secret ciphers* (London, 2000); David Kahn, *Seizing the Enigma: the race to break the German U-Boat codes 1939–1943* (Boston, 1991).

On the scientific dimension there is Guy Hartcup, *The Effect of Science on the Second World War* (Basingstoke, 2000); the essays in Roy M. MacLeod (ed.) *Science and the Pacific War: science and survival in the Pacific, 1939–1945* (London, 1999); and Fredric Boyce and Douglas Everett, *SOE: the scientific secrets* (Stroud, 2003).

The periodical literature on intelligence is enormous, particularly in the pages of the journal *Intelligence and National Security*; in that journal see especially Richard J. Aldrich, "Imperial Rivalry: British and American Intelligence in Asia, 1942–1946," 3 (January 1988) 5–55; On the Soviets see Geoff Jukes, "The Soviets and Ultra" and "More on the Soviets and Ultra," 3 (April 1985) 233–47, and 4 (April 1989) 374–84. On Pearl Harbor see the arguments of John W. M. Chapman: "Pearl Harbor: The Anglo-Australian Dimension," *Intelligence and National Security* 4 (July 1989) 451–60, and "Signals Intelligence Among the Tripartite States on the Eve of Pearl Harbor," *Japan Forum* 3 (September 1991) 231–56. And also Jean Stengers, "Enigma, the French, the Poles and the British, 1931–1940" in Christopher M. Andrew and David Dilks (eds), *The Missing Dimension: governments and intelligence communities in the twentieth century* (London, 1984) 126–37.

Two subjects have attracted more attention than any others: the fall of France and the decision to drop the atomic bomb. On the collapse of France, useful places to begin are the essays in Joel Blatt (ed.), *The French Defeat of 1940: reassessments* (Providence RI, 1998), the short study by Andrew Shennan, *The Fall of France, 1940* (Harlow, 2000); and the synthesis by Ernest May, *Strange Victory* (New York, 2000). More detailed monographs are: Julian Jackson, *The Fall of France: the Nazi invasion of 1940* (New York, 2003); Jeffery A. Gunsburg, *Divided and Conquered: the French high command and the defeat of the west, 1940* (Westport CT, 1979); John Williams, *The Ides of May: the defeat of France, May–June 1940* (London, 1968); Philip M. H. Bell, *A Certain Eventuality: Britain and the Fall of France* (Farnborough, 1974); Alistair A. Horne, *To Lose a Battle: France 1940* (London, 1969); Guy Chapman, *Why France Collapsed* (London, 1968); William L. Shirer, *The Collapse of the Third Republic: An inquiry into the fall of France in 1940* (New York:, 1969); Brian Bond, *France and Belgium, 1939–1940* (London, 1975). On the atomic bomb see: Herbert Feis, *The Atomic Bomb and the End of World War II* (Princeton NJ, 1966); L. Giovannitti and F. Freed, *The Decision to Drop the Bomb* (London, 1967); Gar Alperovitz, *Atomic Diplomacy: Hiroshima and Potsdam, the use of the atomic bomb and the American confrontation with Soviet power* (New York, 1985) as well as his *The Decision to Use the Atomic Bomb and the Architecture of an American Myth* (New York, 1995).

PART TWO

Soldiers
Ideology, Race, and Gender

DECISIONS ABOUT GOING TO WAR are made by statesmen and politicians; decisions about how the war is to be fought are made by strategists. But
these decisions would be meaningless if there were no soldiers to mobilize, to deploy
and to fight. While this may seem to be stating the obvious, it may not be obvious
that who these soldiers are, what motivates them to risk their lives and kill others,
and what their leaders may assume about what they will and will not do is "historical" in the sense that these things change over time. On the surface, war may
appear to be a constant in human affairs, and certainly it has been with us
throughout recorded history, and no culture, no civilization appears to have
succeeded in avoiding organized conflict. Look beneath the surface, however, and
we shall discover that while organized killing may be part of the pattern of human
existence, its color, shape, and texture varies according to time and place. Soldiers
may be volunteers or conscripts; they may be dredged up from the dregs of society,
or they may be regarded as the best and the brightest; they may be mercenaries
or foreigners, paid a wage or offered booty; they may welcome the opportunity to
take up arms or they may be reluctant killers; they may be inspired by a belief in
religious or political ideals, or they may be prepared to engage in violence only in
defense of their families, their homes, and their villages. Thus, every war is the
same: it is about organized killing to achieve an objective; and every war is different:
it is conducted by people as varied as life itself.

The essays selected for this section of the *Reader* testify to some of the characteristics that made World War Two distinctive. Not unique, but distinctive. Since
the end of the war and the victory of the United Nations (the term insisted upon
by President Roosevelt as the name of the alliance) the war has been widely

perceived as a contest between "free" societies and "closed" ones, between "democracy" and "fascism". While this is certainly a vastly oversimplified version of complicated events, it is an important characterization that may assist in structuring a discussion of the soldiers' war. In democratic states without a tradition of large, conscripted, standing armies, men had to be persuaded either that it was their duty to step forward and volunteer to serve their country in its time of need, or that it was an unfortunate necessity forced on them by their enemies that the state had no choice but to compel them to serve through compulsory service. If the war was fought by democracies in order to preserve democracy, those who had to fight for it were defined as "citizen-soldiers" with both the values and the rights of citizens. So how could the state, which had enshrined the value of human life in its laws, convince its citizens that they could abandon such a deeply-felt belief? What was the role of training, education, indoctrination, and propaganda? – activities that took a very different shape in the different cultures at war with one another, and in ways that distinguished this war from previous ones. The soldiers' war is, therefore, about culture and values, about ideas and rights. Assumptions and attitudes concerning race, gender, and ideology were paramount in mobilizing men – and now women – to fight.

States have always used 'propaganda' to convince their people of the validity of their cause and of the necessity to fight for it. But, as Benjamin Alpers shows, this took a distinctive turn in the United States during World War Two. It may be difficult to believe from the vantage point of the early twenty-first century, but the United States was arguably, before the attack on Pearl Harbor, the most unmilitarized and antimilitaristic of the Great Powers. With a minuscule professional army, memories of a horrific civil war and a political culture that equated militarism with despotism, the government of the United States had to overcome profound misgivings among its people in order to fight the kind of war that it was necessary to fight in the middle of the twentieth century. Not surprisingly, the government enlisted Hollywood in this enterprise. Looking at film that ranged from *Sergeant York* to the "Snafu" films to the "Why We Fight" series, Alpers shows how propagandists strove to inculcate in the American people the belief that it was possible for a democracy to fight a modern war and remain democratic. In doing so they emphasized the differences between American soldiers and their enemies: while the armies of the Nazis and Fascists represented a regimented sameness, the US military was presented as enshrining the autonomy of the individual – men were shown to fight for their ideals, for their own conscience; multiethnic and multiregional combat groups were used to demonstrate how the differences that distinguished American society could be preserved while simultaneously encouraging teamwork in a common cause. Much of this was, of course, fictitious and ironic – but, ultimately, effective.

Less effective, as David French shows, were the efforts in Britain to inscribe a sense of hatred for the enemy among its soldiers. The dilemma confronting British officers was a variation on the theme of a "democratic military": how to "re-educate" civilians to overcome the powerful taboos against killing fellow human beings. How were clerks, miners, and teachers to be taught to stick a bayonet into the stomach of someone whose face they could see? By drill and discipline, by repetition of acts of violence and aggression, and by de-personalizing the enemy — persuading the civilian-soldier that the enemy was quite unlike himself and not quite human. But this attempted indoctrination seldom survived contact with the enemy, who was seen not as a faceless Nazi, but just another "poor bloke" much like oneself. And the efforts to persuade soldiers that they were fighting for democracy and tolerance never seemed to take hold of their imaginations: more effective was the realization that their homes and families were in danger — and, ultimately, self-preservation was the key ingredient in battle.

Edward Westermann reaches a very different conclusion concerning the effectiveness of "ideological training" in a different context: that of the German police battalions operating in the occupied zone of Soviet Russia. Those in charge of the police in Nazi Germany undertook a systematic campaign of Nazification before and during the war, with the result that 66 percent of all officers were party members, and 30 percent belonged to the SS. Moreover, they received systematic education in Nazi racial doctrines, effectively instilling in them the belief that it was both their duty and their destiny to destroy the racial and political enemies of the regime. It is important to note how important the details are. A detailed study of who volunteered to serve in the *Jäger* (hunter) platoons serves to illuminate the role of ideology — they represented those most highly committed to Nazi doctrines, and they were much more likely to engage in horrific atrocities and cold-blooded killing. In this case, looking into the face of the "enemy" did not convince that they were fundamentally the same: the enemy in this case was frequently a child, a peasant or an elderly woman — and the killing was often conducted by holding a pistol close to the head of the victim. These acts were not those of "ordinary men" seeking to protect themselves and their families, but of zealots, true believers in the Nazi war of annihilation.

Racial assumptions, stereotypes and doctrines were also essential elements of the war in the Pacific, as John Dower shows. In an interesting comparative analysis, he demonstrates how the assumptions operated on both sides — how propaganda in both Japan and the United States characterized the other in ways that elevated themselves while denigrating their enemies. While American caricatures of the enemies in Europe frequently included sketches of "good Germans" and "good Italians", there seemed to be no "good Japanese"; and while European enemies were often given the faces of Hitler or Mussolini, the Japanese were portrayed as homogeneous, with their round faces, buck-teeth and slanted (usually myopic) eyes. Conversely, Japanese propaganda portrayed Caucasians as degenerate and Anglo-Americans as too individualistic to withstand the challenge posed by the superior "Yamato" race, with its racial purity and selfless devotion to the group and the emperor. Did these racist ideas matter? It certainly seems so: the two most ferocious theatres of World War Two were the Pacific and in eastern Europe — where Nazi ideas of the enemy as *Untermenschen* were paramount.

Assumptions and stereotypes of a different kind were involved when it came to the role of women in the armed forces of the combatants in World War Two. On the one hand, mobilizing for "total war" inclined all of those responsible for the direction of the war to maximize their capacity by utilizing fully every resource at their disposal. The precedent for increasing the role of women during war had been established in World War One – but this had been limited almost entirely to replacing male workers with female in sectors of the economy previously closed to women, or to increasing the level of involvement in "traditional" capacities such as nursing. As D'Ann Campbell shows, by 1939–41 the need for women to serve, combined with their demands to do so, presented a series of puzzles to those who had to decide what their roles were to be. Should women be permitted to serve in the armed forces themselves? If so, should they be "auxiliaries" or "regulars"? Could they be conscripted, or should they be volunteers? If in uniform, should their roles be limited to clerical functions, or could they actually serve as soldiers? If they served as soldiers, could they be permitted to "man" the guns and fire the weapons – at men? Different societies answered these questions differently, and the answers also altered over time as the war, its devastations and demands, increased in ferocity. By looking comparatively at the role of women in the military in the United States, Britain, Germany and the Soviet Union, Campbell has been able to assess the ways in which cultural assumptions varied, and how social ideology either underscored or overrode these assumptions. In the US, for instance, a quiet experiment showed that women performed extremely well in anti-aircraft batteries – and General George Marshall was anxious that they should be deployed in this capacity overseas – but opposition to the idea of women serving in combat forced an end to the experiment, and their position in the military was limited largely to clerical roles. The British, facing the challenge of "the blitz" could not afford this luxury – and women deployed in anti-aircraft units soon demonstrated that they were at least equal to, and frequently superior to, men. Nevertheless, the British authorities could not take the next, logical step of permitting them to fire the weapons themselves: the cultural prejudices against permitting women to shoot at men were simply too great to overcome. In spite of the apparent difference in ideology and ideals, German women were treated in a manner remarkably similar to British: they replaced men in "traditional" non-combatant army roles as clerks, drivers, etc. and, once air attacks on Germany reached a significant level, were deployed in anti-aircraft units. Once again, however, there was an injunction against them firing weapons. Only in the last, desperate days of the war did Hitler approve the formation of female infantry battalions (and even this was more in the hope of shaming more men into doing their duty to the Reich). In the Soviet Union, with a generation of social revolution behind it, and facing the consequences of a near-triumphant invasion, the prohibition against women in combat was nonexistent and the intermediate stage of utilizing women as "auxiliaries" was bypassed altogether. Over 800,000 Soviet women served in the Red Army, and half of them in front-line units.

Chapter 6

Benjamin L. Alpers

THIS IS THE ARMY
Imagining a democratic military in World War II

O N J U L Y 2 , 1 9 4 1 , T H E F I L M *Sergeant York* premiered at the Astor Theatre in New York. Directed by Howard Hawks and starring Gary Cooper in the title role, *York* went on to become the top-grossing film of 1941. *Sergeant York* told the story of real-life World War I hero Alvin York, a tale spectacular enough that it needed relatively little fictional adornment. York, a poor farmer from Tennessee, had undergone a religious conversion before World War I and was a professed pacifist. Drafted into the army, York told his company commander, Maj. George E. Buxton, of his convictions. Unusually understanding, Buxton spent a long night discussing the Bible's teachings on war with York and eventually gave him ten days' leave to consider whether or not he wanted to fight; had York decided not to do so, Buxton would have given him a noncombat assignment. After much soul-searching, York decided to fight. In October 1918, acting virtually alone, York somehow managed to kill 25 German soldiers and take 132 prisoners, thus earning for himself, among other awards, a French Croix de Guerre and an American Congressional Medal of Honor. Although the film's subject was historical, its message was contemporary and clear. As the real-life York noted at the film's premiere, "millions of Americans, like myself, must be facing [today] the same questions, the same uncertainties, which we faced and I believe resolved for the right some twenty-four years ago." The film, understandably, buoyed interventionists and infuriated isolationists.[1]

Sergeant York was an odd piece of interventionist propaganda. Most of the many interventionist Hollywood films that appeared in the three years leading up to the attack on Pearl Harbor focused on the nature of the crisis in Europe and the threat that Nazism posed to the United States. Such films emphasized the politically strongest part of the interventionists' argument: well before Pearl Harbor, most

Americans felt that the Axis powers were unappealing and potentially dangerous. Although supporters of intervention liked to call attention to the Nazi sympathizers among their opponents, there were very few people in the United States who had anything good to say about Nazism by the end of the 1930s; by and large, interventionists and isolationists disagreed on what to do about the danger posed by the Axis powers, not whether that danger existed. *Sergeant York*, however, dealt with the most controversial part of the interventionist case: the need to send American boys overseas to fight in the war. And its action focused on a war that had retrospectively become extremely unpopular in the United States; during the 1930s even Alvin York had become critical of American participation in World War I. Yet *York* was by far the most successful of Hollywood's prewar interventionist tracts.[2]

York succeeded because it deftly suggested that military service, far from being a threat to normal American civilian life, could be an extension, or even fulfillment, of one's civilian existence. Alvin York, in real life as well as in the film, had been able to come to his own decision about participation in the war. Although the film preached duty to one's country, it suggested that even when the country had decided to go to war, each man would still be able to make the decision to fight or not to fight on his own. That was, of course, dramatically not the case for most American men of fighting age in 1917 and 1941. Alvin York's receiving from his commanding officer a few days' leave to think over whether to fight was highly unusual; most would-be conscientious objectors during World War I — especially those who, like York, belonged to relatively small and obscure sects rather than the larger and better-known pacifist churches — received harsh treatment from their draft boards, officers, and fellow draftees.[3] And by the time of the film's 1941 release, American men were already subject to the country's first peacetime draft. In addition to suggesting that each individual would be able to choose whether or not to fight, the film hinted that once one made the proper choice, experience in war, far from being utterly disruptive of one's civilian identity, could be a continuation of it. York's highly individual act of heroism suggested that modern warfare still allowed for autonomous, individuated achievement. Even the basis of that achievement could be found in civilian life: Cooper's York — and by some accounts the real-life York — succeeds on the battlefield by applying turkey-hunting skills learned in the mountains of his home state. Finally, the result of military success is civilian success: As a reward for his military success, the silver screen's Sergeant York — though not, apparently, the real Alvin York — receives a prize piece of bottom land, which allows York and his family to overcome the hardships, reminiscent of the depression, that they experience in the film's first reels.

In its representation of the military experience as a continuation and fulfillment of civilian life, York prefigured many of the American visions of military life that appeared in the war years. These visions played a crucial and often forgotten role in the political culture of the war years. Although there is a voluminous historical literature on the United States armed forces in World War II and an ever-growing body of work on the American home front, scholars have given little extended consideration to American ideas about the relationship between the military and democracy during the war.[4]

As war raged in Europe and the Pacific theater in the years leading up to Pearl Harbor, many Americans questioned the ability of a country to remain democratic while fighting a modern war.[5] This essay explores those fears and the responses to them by producers of American public culture, from social scientists to Hollywood moviemakers to military officers and politicians. These cultural producers attempted to imagine a democratic army. That imagining took place both in representations of the army — in film, radio plays, news reports, and other media — and in the military's own morale programs, personnel classification schemes, and the like. By discussing a wide variety of these visions of a democratic military, I hope to suggest that a major political-cultural concern of the war years was a lingering anxiety about the place of the military in a democracy and that a major, if ambivalent, political-cultural achievement of the period was the triumph of images of a democratic military. Ultimately, that triumph was more a result of the progress of the war than of the capacity of the visions to provide a solution to the problem of a military in a democracy. The concerns about the place of a military in a democracy were put to rest by the sheer fact of American victory: The United States helped win a modern war on the battlefields of Europe, Asia, and Africa, and — all but a few dissenting voices agreed — American democracy survived the feat. In fact, the images of a democratic military reveal more about how wartime American political culture envisioned democracy than about the sources of American victory.

The coming of war precipitated the need to imagine a democratic military; the fears, however, had a longer history. In the half decade before Pearl Harbor, as crisis and war enveloped Europe and Asia, American politicians, journalists, and academics faced the task of explaining the disturbing events taking place across the oceans. Not surprisingly, their explanations tended to center on the new, dictatorial regimes that had blossomed since World War I. Italian Fascism, German Nazism, and Soviet Communism had fascinated American observers from the start of these regimes and had aroused a wide array of responses in the United States. For a variety of reasons, over the course of the 1930s, American antifascists and anticommunists — as well as those who opposed dictatorships of both Right and Left — began to focus on the military in their explanations of these regimes and their differences from American democracy.

The military seemed important to the new dictatorships in two related but distinct ways. First, each seemed committed to the aggressive use of military power to resolve international disputes and expand the nation's power. The use of military force was clearest in the case of Italy and Germany. Following a huge military buildup, the former invaded Ethiopia in 1935. Germany also built up its military, occupied the Rhineland, and effected an *Anschluss* with Austria, all in open violation of the Treaty of Versailles. Later in the decade, both Germany and Italy provided arms and men to Gen. Francisco Franco's forces in the Spanish civil war. And Germany occupied much of Czechoslovakia in 1938 and 1939. Although Americans sympathetic to the Popular Front saw the Soviet Union as a bulwark against this fascist expansionism, many more Americans apparently saw its behavior as similar to that of the fascist powers. Many Americans were as suspicious of the Soviet-aided Loyalists in Spain as they were of the Italian- and German-aided rebels. The September 1939 invasions of Poland by Germany and Russia reinforced the sense of many in the United States that both systems were militaristic. The Soviet Union seemed especially cruel following its invasion of "little Finland" in the Winter of 1939–1940.[6]

The military also seemed to play a second, crucial role in each of these countries. American observers began to note that in Germany, Italy, Russia, and Japan, the military had begun to serve as a model for the larger organization of social life. "Regimentation" thus joined "militarism" as a principal way that Americans characterized these regimes. Once again, the regimes of the Right provided the clearest examples of this phenomenon. From the start, the most distinctive organizations of both Italian Fascism and German Nazism were militarized street fighters identified by their uniforms — Blackshirts in the case of Fascism, Brownshirts in the case of Nazism. Once in power, the Fascists and Nazis quickly extended regimentation beyond the organization of their most active supporters. One of the features of early Nazi policy in Germany that was most noted and criticized in the United States was Adolf Hitler's goal of *Gleichschaltung* — the policy of "coordination" of all political, economic, and social power.[7]

American anticommunists had long criticized the Soviet Union in similar ways. These criticisms, however, became more prominent over the course of the 1930s, especially as American observers began to lump Communism and fascism together as examples of a single phenomenon, the "totalitarian state" or, by the end of the decade, "totalitarianism." This equation of Communism and fascism under the term "totalitarianism" was given a major boost by the Nazi-Soviet Pact and the German and Russian invasions of Poland in the Summer and early Fall of 1939. In November 1939 in Philadelphia, the American Philosophical Society (APS) and the American Academy of Political and Social Science (AAPSS) hosted the first two academic conferences on the totalitarian state. Paper after paper at both the large APS gathering and the smaller AAPS meeting focused on militarism and regimentation as the most important aspects of totalitarian regimes and the telling similarity that linked the regime of the Soviet Union to the apparently ideologically different ones of Germany and Italy.[8]

There was a long history of Americans defining enemy nations in terms of their reliance on, and love of, military force and militarized models of society. Most recently, the official propaganda effort during World War I, led by the Committee on Public Information (CPI) under the leadership of the journalist George Creel, had largely built its case for the justness of that war on the evils of German militarism. The CPI suggested that such militarism was an essential cultural trait of the German nation. German *Kultur* (as American propaganda often called it) could threaten the United States either on the battlefield in Europe or through unassimilated elements in the United States itself. Either way, German militarism during World War I was essentially an external threat. Outside of some lonely dissenters such as Randolph Bourne, few suggested that war itself threatened to turn America into a country like Germany. Indeed, many Americans, particularly members of the older generation whose childhoods had been steeped in romantic tales of the Civil War and whose early adulthoods had witnessed the apparently quick and easy triumph of the United States in the Spanish-American War, positively celebrated martial virtues. Like the Germans during World War I, the Japanese during World War II were seen as an external threat. Even more explicitly racialized than the "Huns" had been in the first war, in American discourse during World War II, the Japanese were wholly "other," threatening the United States only from without. Despite the often irrational hatred and fear that the Japanese — and

Japanese Americans — aroused, nobody suggested that America could itself become like Japan.[9]

In the years leading up to World War II, Germany appeared to present a very different problem. Some American observers continued to view Nazism as an essentially foreign doctrine that could have no independent American parallel, only traitorous American sympathizers. But most American cultural producers suggested that what had happened politically in Germany might also happen in the United States. Nazism thus threatened the United States not only externally but also internally. The desperation of the Great Depression and the exigencies of war might turn Americans into fascists; Huey Long, Father Charles Coughlin, and even Franklin D. Roosevelt and Wendell Willkie were suggested by various opponents as possible American Hitlers. Fears about Nazi militarism, unlike most World War I-era concerns about German militarism, could thus easily dovetail with another old set of American fears: concerns about the ill effects of large standing armies on the functioning of democracy.[10]

During the late 1930s, in an effort to protect American democracy from these threats, interest in citizenship education, which had declined in part because of the restrictions placed on immigration in the 1920s, increased. Educating American citizens — even native-born ones — in the ways of democracy, many felt, was an important, nonmilitary response to the world crisis. In the late 1930s the National Education Association (NEA) inaugurated its Educational Policies Commission, a Washington-based group that devoted much of its time to pondering the role of education in democracy and the actions American educators could take to improve citizenship and save our democratic "way of life" from foreign and domestic foes. Following intense lobbying from educational groups, Congress passed a resolution declaring the third Sunday in May national I Am an American Day. During the late 1930s, these efforts at citizenship education often stressed the essentially peaceful and voluntary nature of American life, attributes that were exactly the opposite of the militarism and regimentation of the European dictatorships. Indeed, mere participation in a war threatened to turn a democracy into a totalitarian state. A decade of revisionist accounts of World War I and strong anti-interventionist sentiments during the late 1930s fueled this idea. A 1938 publication by the NEA's Educational Policies Commission put the case especially strongly:

> It has been wisely said that there will never be a war between a democracy and an autocracy because the moment war begins, the former will lose its democratic characteristics. Violence, whatever its forms, its agents, or its motives, makes for material destruction, intellectual regimentation, and spiritual and physical impoverishment.[11]

As Americans prepared for and eventually entered World War II, these understandings of the European dictatorships were a two-edged sword. On the one hand, long before Pearl Harbor, the American public had clear ideas about the difference between life in the Axis countries and life in the United States, ideas that could — and did — form the basis of important pieces of domestic propaganda and official statements of national purpose, such as the Atlantic Charter, the Four Freedoms, and the Declaration of the United Nations. Although convincing Americans that there were good reasons for their nation's participation in the war, the image of the enemy had already been well established before December 1941. The war that came did not pit democracy against totalitarianism, as the latter term was generally understood in the late 1930s. After the June 1941 German invasion of Russia, the Soviet Union became Nazi Germany's most powerful foe. The United Nations fighting against the Axis thus included one of the countries most often mentioned as an example of totalitarianism. Nevertheless, the dominant elements of the image of totalitarianism remained central to American understandings of the Axis powers: in his first fireside chat of 1942, the president declared that the United Nations were "committed to the destruction of the militarism of Japan and Germany."[12]

But this image of the enemy also presented enormous problems for the American war effort. For while it provided a clear and powerful understanding of the conflict ahead, it suggested that the very act of engaging in that conflict might be dangerous to America. Could a democracy go to war against autocracies and remain democratic? How could one organize a war effort and avoid the twin pitfalls of militarism and regimentation? This question was most pressing in regard to the military itself. The armed forces were both the most regimented institutions of any society and the ones most immediately responsible for militarism. How could a modern military be democratic?

The remainder of this essay explores answers, official and unofficial, given to this question during World War II. The simplest solutions — an appeal to American military history or the insistence that the United States fought only because it had been attacked — were frequently invoked, but they could not by themselves overcome more general fears about the place of a military in a democracy. In response to anxieties about militarism and regimentation, anxieties that existed within the military as well as in society at large, those writing for and about the troops developed more sophisticated ways of suggesting how the American military could be fit for a democracy. In training and morale materials for American soldiers and in representations of soldiers created primarily for civilian audiences, depictions of the military emphasized the continuing individuality and autonomy of each American serviceman. By describing the most regimented elements of military life as analogous to civilian life, by emphasizing the moral autonomy of men even in a military situation, by attempting to train Americans to fight for empirical, rational reasons, and by basing authority within the military on putatively objective data, American cultural producers attempted to construct, in word and action, a democratic army.

War had come to the nation many times before. Indeed, during this war, one of the standard modes of understanding the United States military was historical: World War II was represented on-screen and over the air as simply the latest in a long series of American struggles for freedom. Even the Civil War was frequently invoked, with both sides representing the fight for freedom. An old view that taking up arms itself was ennobling, expressive of the depths of society's willingness to sacrifice for democracy, and vital for forging masculinity found echoes in the World War II period, but it could never fully take hold. Even during World War I, romantic visions of war had belonged largely to an older generation. The concerns about militarism and regimentation made the celebration of warfare *per se* even more infrequent in America during World War II. A new, positive image of the military had to be forged that distinguished the military of the United States from those of its enemies.[13]

One simple way to do this was to insist that unlike Nazi Germany, the United States was an essentially peaceful, unregimented society that had been forced to defend itself. Pearl Harbor became a key element of this story; in many ways it remains so. Although it occurred over a year after the start of military conscription and months after the United States had begun to provide nations fighting the Axis with munitions and other material aid, although national polls from as far back as May 1940 showed most Americans expecting direct United States involvement in the war, the Japanese attack on December 7, 1941, almost immediately became the climax of a narrative in which a slumbering nation was suddenly awakened to the need to go to war.[14]

But the general cultural acceptance of the peaceful nature of the United States did not fully define the way a democracy might wage a modern war — a war against a system understood by many as grounded in militarism and regimentation — without becoming militaristic and regimented itself. Once the United States had entered World War II, fears about the antidemocratic effects of participation in the war usually concerned the postwar world. People disagreed about which aspects of the war effort would be deadly to democracy once the war was over. For many, peacetime military training most evoked fears. In late 1944 and early 1945, a national debate erupted over universal military training for men (with or without some equivalent for women) following the war, an idea supported by, among others, the American Legion, Eleanor Roosevelt, and Gen. George C. Marshall. Not surprisingly, many opponents of the scheme, who included representatives of labor, the churches, and education as well as political leaders, raised concerns that postwar conscription would make the United States like the very countries it was fighting. "The disciples of defeatism, the isolationists, and the crowd that wants to regiment Americans," Edwin C. Johnson, a Democratic United States senator from Colorado, declared in December 1944,

> are now whooping it up for compulsory military training. They would teach Americans to rattle sabers and to cook and to brush their teeth, and learn democracy from screwball masters; and they would launch a new worldwide armament race. That sounds like Adolph Hitler to me.

"Militarism breeds militarism," warned Sen. Claude Pepper in an article for the November 1944 issue of *Parents' Magazine* opposing military training. Dr. Charles A. Ellwood, a professor emeritus of sociology at Duke University, suggested in September 1944 that such training had laid the groundwork for the Bolshevik Revolution in Russia and was the surest way to bring about violent class warfare in the United States. "Military discipline provides excellent training for citizenship in a totalitarian society," argued the liberal *Christian Century* in an October 18, 1944, editorial. "Compulsory military training means militarism," Dr. John Haynes Holmes, pastor of the Community Church in New York, warned. "Militarism, sooner or later, means totalitarianism."[15]

Anxieties about the political effect of a nation's engaging in modern warfare extended into the military itself. On the eve of United States involvement in World

War II, the War Department began an unprecedented series of projects in military psychology. From developing "scientific" ways to screen out those most likely to become "psychiatric casualties" to investigating the morale of the troops, social scientists helped shape the American armed forces and the War Department's understanding of them. In May 1945, Lt. Col. Roy R. Grinker and Maj. John P. Spiegel, both psychiatrists in the Army Air Forces' Medical Corps, published *Men under Stress*, the most thorough study of the psychological effects of combat produced during the war. In a concluding chapter, "General Social Implications," Grinker and Spiegel considered what masses of returning combat veterans would mean for postwar America. Arguing that combat experience produced large numbers of "angry, regressed, anxiety ridden, dependent men," the authors suggested that veterans represented a potentially huge social problem:

> A far cry from the self-reliant American . . . [the combat veteran] offers little hope that his resocialization will be easy. To anticipate that in the normal process of events he will fit himself into his old routines, and not bother the nation with a new veteran problem, is indulging in naive and wistful optimism. Because he is so unhappy, so full of intense long-ings, so inadequate to satisfy himself through his own activity, he will be driven to seek a solution somewhere. Where will he find it?[16]

The answer, Grinker and Spiegel feared, might well be in a fascist organization. The authors described the mechanisms of group identification and transference of the "frustration of masculine independence and authority" to hatred of the group's enemy that "enable individuals belonging to fascist groups to function so effectively in peace or war, and [that] make them, after their defeat, such a severe problem to societies oriented toward more democratic policies." What made this threat most acute, according to Grinker and Spiegel, was that these mechanisms were quite familiar to their subjects:

> It comes with something of a shock to realize that these are also the mech-anisms which apply to the American combat soldier, both in psychologi-cal health and in the illness which overtakes him. In order to become an effective soldier, he must learn to adapt himself to a completely unde-mocratic group, which required of him submission and fixation in a depen-dent position. The fascist enemy, which is in essence a military group, cannot be dominated or held in check by a democratic society unless that society to some extent regresses to the level of the former. The first step in that regression is the formation of a large and effective military group. Whether or not this is also the last step in the regression, whether or not, after a victory, the remainder of the democratic world can proceed along its accustomed path and retain the personal dignity of the individual, cannot easily be foreseen at the present time.

Overly dependent, imperfectly masculine, and violently aggressive, the men des-cribed by Grinker and Spiegel bear a strong resemblance to the members of the regimented crowd that formed an essential component of prewar views of totali-tarianism.[17]

Grinker and Spiegel feared that the military experience could have profound, negative effects on postwar society. One way to hold such fears at bay was to interpret military life as fundamentally similar to normal, civilian life. As in *Sergeant York*, the war could be seen as but a change in circumstances, demanding a redirection of the skills and efforts of every American, but allowing even those men drafted into the armed forces to continue revised versions of their civilian lives. During World War II, the United States military classification system was designed, whenever possible, to place men in jobs similar to their civilian occupations. While the other two components used in classification, physical fitness and intellectual capacity, were measured using fairly rough scales — 4 physical classifications and 5 mental ones — the army had a list of 800 numbered Military Occupation Specialties. The system assumed that the more similar a man's military job was to his civilian job, the higher his morale would be. One result of this system, however, was that those who had no useful civilian trade, usually the young, less educated, or socially disadvantaged, were assigned to jobs with no civilian equivalents, which generally meant they became fighting men. This more or less built low morale into American fighting units.[18]

The army explained even those aspects of the military experience that draftees found most jarring as just like civilian life. In 1940 the army produced *The Soldier's Handbook*, a new, book-length manual designed to acquaint draftees with life in the army. "You are now a member of the Army of the United States," the *Handbook* begins. "That Army is made up of free citizens chosen from among a free people. . . . Making good as a soldier is no different from making good in civil life." Whenever an unusual aspect of army life is introduced, the *Handbook* likens it to an aspect of civilian life with which it might more readily be contrasted, an aspect that the military in totalitarian societies seemed to undo. The section "The Responsibilities of Group Life" provides a good example. It begins with two paragraphs about that least military of social groups — the family:

> 1. Before you joined the Army you were a member of a family of closely related individuals who had many things in common. The members of your family shared the same dining room, the same bathroom, and the same amusements around the house. All worked together, read the same newspaper, and were largely dependent upon each other for comforts, pleasures, and a living.
> 2. You learned that to get along with other members of your family you must have consideration for them, do your part of the work, and share things with the rest of the household. That was your golden rule and the primary law of family relationship and citizenship.

Only in the third and final paragraph of the section does the army enter the picture. Other than in scale, according to the *Handbook*, life in the army is exactly like life in the family: "You have the same obligations in the Army but instead of the small family group you are one of a much larger group." And far from creating an experience that potentially challenged civil life, group life in the army complemented life outside of it. "A soldier who has learned to respect the rights of his comrades," this section of the *Handbook* concluded, "has made a big step forward in his training as a soldier and as a citizen."[19]

Figure 6.1 Many propaganda posters such as this one of a soldier, a factory worker, and a sailor, published in 1941 by the Office of Emergency Management, stressed the continuity between civilian employment and the military. Courtesy Northwestern University Library, http://www.library.nwu.edu/govpub/collections/wwii-posters/

The *Handbook* described that aspect of military life that was most authoritarian — military discipline itself — in a whole series of home-front metaphors. "The average civilian or recruit coming into the Army," the section "Military Discipline" begins,

> often misunderstands the meaning of the words *military discipline*. He thinks of them as being connected with punishments or reprimands which may result from the violation of some military law or regulation. Actually, discipline should not be something new to you for you have been disciplined all of your life. You were disciplined at home and in your school when you were taught obedience to your parents and teachers, and respect for the rights of others. On your baseball or other athletic team you were disciplining yourself when you turned down the chance to be a star performer in order that the team might win; you were acquiring discipline in the shop, or other business, when your loyalty to your employer and your fellow employees was greater than your desire to secure your own advancement. All of this was merely the spirit of team play; that is, you were putting the interests of the "team" above your own in order that the "team" might win.

It is this final metaphor — the army as team — that dominates the rest of the section on military discipline in *The Soldier's Handbook*.[20]

Indeed, the idea of a team became one of the most significant ways in which American cultural producers assimilated the military experience to that of civilian life. "The American standard of discipline" General Marshall declared, "[is] cheerful and understanding subordination of the individual to the good of the team." "I'm not just a foot-slogger with a rifle in this new army," Infantry declares in Stephen Vincent Benét's radio script "Your Army" (written in 1942 and broadcast nationally during the first half of 1944). "I'm a member of a combat team, trained like a football squad and with plenty of razzle-dazzle stuff and the Rose Bowl stuff of modern war."[21]

The attractions of describing the army as a team are obvious. American team sports were themselves full of martial metaphors. Team sports, particularly football, were organized and regulated forms of violence. Perhaps the most important aspect of sports was the relation between team and individual success. Ultimately, the team's success was the measure of attainment in a team sport. Yet, each player had his own set of specialized tasks designed to fit both his skills and the needs of the team. And within his given role, each player could individually excel and receive notice for excelling.

The hope of preserving a space for individuality and individual attainment even on the front lines played a crucial role in the representation of the American military during World War II. The preservation of individual autonomy played a central role in pre-Pearl Harbor ideas about democracy and totalitarianism. The latter was the very antithesis of democracy in part because it eradicated the individual through regimentation. The ability of modern warfare similarly to reduce the individual to an expendable cog in a fighting machine was thus a particular concern. The scholar Paul Fussell notes that wartime journalists, conscious of the troops' experience of this tendency of modern warfare and their desire to maintain their prewar individual identities, frequently emphasized the names of — and minute biographical details about — the soldiers who appeared in their stories. However, Fussell fails to note the ideological dimension of such reportage. The primary audience for most reporting from the front was not the troops, but those who remained at home. For this latter group, assurance that their sons, brothers, and friends remained identifiable individuals, changed perhaps, but not fundamentally, from their prewar selves, was an important part of the image of the American war effort as democratic.[22]

Modern warfare allowed only limited opportunities for individual heroics. The advantage of metaphors such as the army as a team was that they acknowledged individuality while suggesting that individual attainment gained meaning only in relation to the group. The 1943 motion picture *This Is the Army* made the army into a male chorus. The film presents a fictionalized version of the creation of Irving Berlin's two military shows, the World War I-era *Yip Yip Yaphank* and the World War II-era *This Is the Army*, both performed on Broadway by actual soldiers. George Murphy plays a dancer drafted to serve in World War I. Wishing to use his talents to help win the war, he convinces skeptical officers that if the men put a show together, it will help morale both among the troops and on the home front. The show is assembled collectively, with different men contributing their own theatrical and musical skills. After a wildly successful Broadway run, an order arrives midperformance that the troops have to ship off to France. The Murphy character decides to end the finale (in which the troops sing of marching off to war) by marching the troops out of the theater and into waiting trucks rather than simply marching offstage; the audience immediately understands what is happening and roars with approval. In France, the company loses some of its soldiers and Murphy loses a leg; all, however, are glad they fought. As war approaches again in the 1930s, Murphy's son, played by Ronald Reagan, is drafted and assembles a similar show that provides the climax of the film. Once again, the troops march into the orchestra and off to battle. The World War II review itself features a huge chorus of uniformed men.

This Is the Army also made explicit something already implicit in the team metaphor and in World War II combat movies: All put the nonmilitary audience in the position of the fan. In *This Is the Army*, the existence of an on-screen audience emphasized the relationship. This may have played into Warner Brothers' decision to alter the musical's finale, "Dressed Up to Kill." Deeming that the piece was "not symbolic of the humane manner in which the United States has waged war," the studio altered the lyrics so that the soldier chorus, posing with lowered bayonets, sang instead that they were "Dressed Up to Win."[23] Warner Brothers' concern appears odd in retrospect because countless Hollywood films regularly showed the army killing "Japs" and, slightly less frequently, Nazis. Perhaps what was peculiarly troubling about "Dressed Up to Kill" was its expression of desire on the part of both the army and the audience for which that particular army had been assembled. It was more morally comforting to root for victory than for slaughter. Killing as an end in itself might have sounded suspiciously like the American conception of the enemy.

The collective star of *This Is the Army* was particularly pleasing to the Office of War Information (OWI), the principal federal propaganda agency during World War II. An OWI analyst praised the picture for

> the representation [it] gives of the American soldier, the unnamed soldier, of whom there are hundreds in the cast. This composite soldier is, against the competition of those of his comrades who do individual stunts, and against the competition of Hollywood actors in blazing technicolor, the star of the show. And that is how it should be.[24]

It is worth noting that even in praising the collective, the OWI spoke in the singular. The film's star is not the collectivity of the army but the "unnamed . . . composite soldier" for which the army is but a synecdoche. *This Is the Army* could nicely fit the left-liberal OWI's often self-contradictory attitude toward the American military and the movies' depiction of it. The armed chorus acknowledged the collective nature of modern war yet, in the words of the OWI, represented a form of democratic individualism.

But the mere structure of a metaphoric group, whether a team or (more infrequently) a chorus, could not by itself suggest that those who participated in a war fought by collectives would be able to retain their individuality. One of the most prevalent and important ways in which Americans figured individuality in the World

War II military was through the convention of the multiethnic and multiregional group. In films, books, and radio scripts, battalions and bomber crews inevitably featured a fellow with a Slavic name from the Midwest, a guy with an Italian or Jewish name from Brooklyn, a New England WASP, a southerner, and so forth. Although reaching its apogee during the war, the multiethnic combat group can be seen in some prewar movies. *The Fighting 69th* of 1940 and *Sergeant York* both feature such groupings, although their action takes place in World War I, when most American combat units were organized by home state and some were even organized by ethnic group. During World War II the multiethnic and multiregional unit became a central representation of the military.[25]

The multiethnic combat unit was such a powerful symbol because it represented the negation of American understandings of the enemy's military. The totalitarian military, like totalitarian society, demanded that its members be absolutely alike. In the case of Germany and Japan (and, to a lesser extent, Italy), this similarity was understood in the United States to be figured in terms of racial purity. The Soviet Union, the other country that United States public culture had widely understood to be totalitarian before mid-1941, notably did not figure its unity this way. The

Figure 6.2 This classic example of a Hollywood multiethnic combat unit from the movie *Bataan*, dir. Tay Garnett (MGM 1943), features a Mexican American, a Filipino, and an African American, along with an assortment of ethnically diverse white characters from different parts of the United States. From *The World War II Combat Film: Anatomy of a Genre*, by Jeanine Basinger. © Photofest Inc.

ability to accept and even celebrate ethnic diversity thus nicely distinguished between a wartime "us" that included the Soviet Union and a "them" that included the other European dictatorships and Japan. Marked by differences in mannerisms, accents, last names, and memories of home, the members of the multiethnic combat unit were in no danger of being reduced to identical automatons similar to the Nazi soldiers, goose-stepping through an occupied city or rallying at Nuremberg.

As an attribute of the troops viewed collectively, diversity was a crucial symbol. But the position of the multiethnic combat unit in World War II-era representations of the American military was possible only because what we would today call "ethnicity" mattered less as an individual attribute of white Americans than it had ever mattered before. Clearly, many Americans still harbored strong anti-Semitic, anti-Irish, anti-Polish, or anti-Italian feelings. But the long, slow process of ethnic whites becoming assimilated into once WASP-dominated American culture was well under way by Pearl Harbor. Two decades of immigration restriction meant that there were many fewer white, ethnic Americans whose linguistic and cultural differences clearly marked them as outside the cultural mainstream. The category of "race," once as easily applied in America to Jews as to blacks, had begun to fade as a way of differentiating among whites, perhaps in reaction against Nazi racial ideology. The Japanese provided an absolute racial other during the war years against which all Americans — with the notable exception of Japanese Americans — could be portrayed as standing united. Only after the war would novels, memoirs, and histories — perhaps first and most spectacularly Norman Mailer's *The Naked and the Dead* in 1948 — make clear to a larger American audience that some irresoluble interethnic tensions pervaded even the United States military.[26]

Much liberal opinion, including that of most social scientists, had come to see assimilation as crucial for American democracy, especially once the nonimportance of ethnic distinctions had become a central way of distinguishing the United States from its foes. Popular representations of the military always suggested that ethnic hostilities among Americans had no basis in fact and could lead only to division and defeat. Perhaps because they assumed that ethnicity and region of origin — the key differences between troops in Hollywood's multiethnic battalions — were, prima facie, attributes of no real consequence, the social scientists of the Research Branch of the United States Army's Information and Education Division, who surveyed Americans in uniform from the day after Pearl Harbor, for the duration of the war, shied away from analyzing the troops along ethnic or regional lines. The variable they studied most thoroughly was educational differences among troops. American social scientists, outside the military as well as in, were much more drawn to the issue of the color line than to questions of white ethnicity.[27]

When they did take up the issue of white interethnic conflict, American authors suggested that its central cause was the fallacious belief that any important difference at all existed between white Americans of different ethnic backgrounds. *Weapon of War* (1944), an animated short created for the *Army-Navy Screen Magazine*, the newsreel portion of military movie programs, warns its audience of soldiers and sailors about "the most ingenious weapon" created by the Nazis: "race hatred" and "religion hatred." In the cartoon, these appear as a bottle of poisoned liquid. The Nazis first try it on the German people in peacetime. The liquid from the bottle is poured onto a figure in a test tube: "if his right arm goes up, he was certified as a member of the great master race." The cartoon next shows the magic bottle conquering Europe. Small silhouettes run around confused as large ghostly figures intone, "This race. That race. This race. That race." Finally, the weapon of war is taken to the United States, a country, the cartoon points out, of 61 different nationalities and 259 different religious creeds. "Here, they thought, were jealousies and prejudices to play upon. [On screen, fragments on a map of the United States start flashing different shades.] Here was the perfect set up for their plan: divide and conquer." From atop a stage, a dark silhouette hawks the poisoned liquid packaged as a patent medicine, Dr. Hitler's Blood Tonic. "Is your system sluggish?" the salesman intones, "Try the world's most famous purge. Take home a bottle. Are you highstrung and irritable? Do you stay up at nights and worry about Armenians? Peruvians? Scandinavians? and Greeks? Try a bottle and you'll lick any feriner in town." The speaker goes on to mention Poles, Mexicans, Negroes, Chinese, Catholics, Presbyterians, Jews, Baptists, and other groups that might evoke his audience's anger. During this harangue, members of the on-screen audience look quizzical, but the audience watching the cartoon is assured of the illogic of the salesman's message because the stylized audience on screen, its members distinguished from each other only by being dressed as soldiers, sailors, or civilians, consists of absolutely identical white figures. When the spokesman for Dr. Hitler's Tonic suggests that "you and you and you are much better than you and you and you," all the figures he indicates are identical. The film ends with the tonic salesman's failure; his audience gives him an enormous Bronx cheer as "Columbia, the Gem of the Ocean" swells over the sound track.[28]

Ethnic markers thus provided a perfect way of representing the continued individuality of the men in an American combat unit and of suggesting that the national unity the United States had forged was pluralistic and thus fundamentally different from that created in Nazi Germany. This vision was, however, significantly clouded by the continued racial segregation of the American military. Hollywood films and other wartime representations of the military often attempted the basically impossible task of suggesting that African Americans were a full part of America's pluralistic armed forces while avoiding criticism of the military's own segregation and catering to an audience that included many people who were uncomfortable with the idea of integration of the military or American society at large. Some World War II combat films included a black enlisted man in their multiethnic battalions, but such characters invariably die, often more horribly than their white cohorts. *This Is the Army* neatly embodied the ambivalence toward the black troops in a different way. On the one hand, the film features a sequence celebrating black soldiers, the musical number "That's What the Well-Dressed Man in Harlem Will Wear," which includes heavyweight boxing champion Joe Louis, who upon enlisting in the army had instantly been made an icon of the "Negro soldier." On the other hand, "That's What the Well-Dressed Man in Harlem Will Wear" is a now-embarassing piece of latter-day minstrelsy, performed in front of a set featuring huge sambo figures. And *This Is the Army*, like the army itself, was wholly segregated: The black soldiers appear only in this one sequence, and with the exception of a short exchange between George Murphy and Joe Louis and an extremely brief shot of the black performers running offstage after their number, blacks and whites never appear on the screen at the same time. Race, unlike white ethnicity, was of great interest to the social scientists of the Research Branch, who devoted much effort to studying the color line in the American military. The Research Branch could, perhaps, assume interethnic peace in the ranks; no such assumption was possible across the color line.[29]

It was more difficult still to represent in a military setting what was perhaps the most crucial element of prewar and wartime notions of individual autonomy: voluntarism. If totalitarianism arose when members of a society gave up their free will and replaced it with blind obedience to a leader or a rigid system, democracy was possible only when people's political decisions were the result of rational, free choice. When in 1944 President Roosevelt suggested in his state of the union speech that the time had come for civilian conscription of war workers, the leading argument of the diverse and ultimately successful opposition to the plan was that such conscription would fundamentally violate democratic principles, the very principles for which the United States fought.[30]

The liberal Office of War Information (OWI) also made a point of emphasizing the voluntaristic aspects of the American war effort. In a 1942 addendum to its *Government Information Manual for the Motion Picture Industry*, the OWI's Bureau of Motion Pictures urged filmmakers to celebrate "the Children's Army" in an effort to "enlist America's youth in the war effort!" After describing how children can contribute to American prosecution of the war, the memo spent two of its eleven pages distinguishing the American youth effort from that of the Axis. Far from resembling the by-then-legendary efforts of the Nazis to indoctrinate German youth, the mobilization of children in the United States highlighted the differences between the two systems. "The contrast between our program of youth mobilization and the Axis system of regimentation and enslavement tells the story of what this war is about — of what we are fighting for and against!" The central difference was voluntarism: "The Axis makes use of children, too. Not on a voluntary basis, to be sure, for nothing in Axis countries is done on a voluntary basis." In fact, the forced mobilization of youth, either to work as slave labor or to be trained as slave masters, was the central way in which the Nazi system reproduces itself.[31]

But the military, even the United States military, would not seem to be a social space that allowed for much voluntarism. Men were, after all, drafted into the military and once there were assigned tasks. Movies such as *Sergeant York* could invent opportunities for characters to make the decision to fight totally voluntarily. Even within the army, voluntarism had an important rhetorical role to play. One of the most interesting examples of the rhetoric of voluntarism within the military comes from an unusual source: the Private Snafu films. These twenty-six cartoon shorts were specially produced for the Signal Corps by Warner Brothers' animation unit. Usually appearing as the final segment of the *Army-Navy Screen Magazine*, the Private Snafu films were quite popular with the troops. The cartoons were very high quality — other than being black-and-white, they were similar to other Warner Brothers cartoons in visual style — and well written. Indeed, the creator of Private Snafu and one of the chief writers for the series was Theodor Geisel, who later became better known to millions around the world as Dr. Seuss. The popularity of the series was certainly enhanced by the cartoons' mildly risqué quality: Private Snafu's very name was a piece of obscene army slang ("Situation Normal, All Fucked Up"), and the backgrounds of some frames featured seminude pinups posted on the walls of characters' barracks. Snafu films were light entertainment whose popularity probably derived both from their obvious quality as cartoons and from the opportunities for identification they offered their military audiences. Though only cartoons, Snafu films could pose as a step closer to the real, unsanitized army experience than most movies, which featured considerably more expurgated visions of raunchy, male army culture.[32]

But the more important aspect of the Snafu series is that each cartoon had a clear message; more than just entertainment, the Private Snafu cartoons were an important propaganda series. Private Snafu, as his name suggested, was constantly getting into trouble. In each cartoon, Snafu would make a different mistake — telling army secrets to civilians while on leave; writing army secrets to his girl friend; spreading rumors at his base; failing to take precautions against getting malaria — and in each instance, Snafu would regret his actions. First and foremost, the Snafu series was about military discipline and the consequences of not following it. But conspicuously absent from the films was the military disciplinary system itself. Snafu paid for his mistakes not by punishment but by risking, or more often losing, his life and the lives of his comrades at arms. Snafu's concluding regrets were sometimes issued from the afterlife.[33]

In *Censored* (1944), Snafu attempts to sneak a note revealing his unit's next mission to his girl friend, Sally Lou, back home. Twice, the army censor apprehends the note and redacts it. Finally, the "technical fairy," a tiny but coarse and hairy man dressed in a Tinkerbell outfit, appears and offers to deliver the note in code. The plan works; Sally Lou — shown, as are many women in the Snafu series, nearly nude — tells her mother over the phone that the unit is headed to Bingo Bango Island. The Japanese, naturally, are bugging her phone lines. Snafu and his unit arrive at Bingo Bango only to be blown to smithereens by awaiting Japanese forces. Luckily, the whole second half of the cartoon turns out to be a dream. Snafu gets his letter back from the technical fairy, who appears actually to exist, and rips it up. "Like I always said," concludes Snafu, "every man his own censor." *Censored* is typical of the series both in its celebration of army life — civilian life, and particularly women in civilian life, are hazardous — and in its voluntaristic notion of army discipline. Ultimately, the army's censor can be bypassed, but the result is death. The message of *Censored*, as Snafu himself indicates, is that each man in the army must individually accept the responsibilities of censorship.

In addition to their emphasis on voluntarism, the Snafu films also embodied another central theme in World War II-era representations of the United States military and that military's own self-understanding: the importance of knowledge of the truth. The plots of the Snafu films revolve around the use and misuse of key pieces of military information, some true and some false, from methods of malaria prevention to rumor-mongering. Even before the war, the public's ability to grasp the truth was a central component of some important American theories of democracy. The public opinion expert Hadley Cantril's 1940 analysis of Orson Welles's *War of the Worlds* broadcast concluded that those members of the audience who panicked had done so because they had failed to be skeptical of that which was obviously untrue. Democracy could be protected against the threat of such panics, and of many dangerous modern social movements, only by assuring that everyone in a society had sufficient material and emotional security to be able to distinguish between empirical truth and empirical falsehood. This faith in knowledge of the truth had its more pedestrian side as well: Hollywood films about Nazism often suggested that the ultimate barrier to its growth in the United States was that Americans knew nonsense when they saw it. Since America's enemies were largely defined by belief systems nearly universally seen in the United States as irrational and fanatical, the ability of individual soldiers and the military as a whole to marshal the empirical truth in the service of the war effort became a central way of representing the American military effort as democratic. This trope of empiricism took many different forms.[34]

In his first fireside chat of 1942, President Roosevelt began by asking his radio audience to "take out and spread before you a map of the whole earth, and to follow me in the references which I shall make to the world-encircling battle lines of this war." This was but one of many times that the American people would be asked to look at a map during the war. In newspapers, magazines, and films of the period, the map, illuminated by expert commentary, was a central way of presenting the facts of this global war. In fact, most of the geographic references in Roosevelt's speech were not to specific, obscure locales. Rather they occurred in Rabelaisian lists of places:

> Look at your map. Look at the vast area of China, with its millions of fighting men. Look at the vast area of Russia, with its powerful armies and proven military might. Look at the islands of Britain, Australia, New Zealand, the Dutch Indies, India, the Near East and the continent of Africa. . . . Look too at North America, Central America, and South America.

FDR's point was that, far from being removed by great oceans from the geographic center of conflict, the United States, along with the rest of the world, was at the heart of the action. But the president also made a more general point that evening, which would be echoed throughout the war:

> Your government has unmistakable confidence in your ability to hear the worst, without flinching or losing heart. You must, in turn, have complete confidence that your government is keeping nothing from you except information that will help the enemy in his attempt to destroy us. In a democracy there is always a solemn pact of truth between government and the people; but there must also always be a full use of discretion — and that word "discretion" applies to the critics of government as well.
>
> This is war. The American people want to know, and will be told, the general trend of how the war is going. But they do not wish to help the enemy any more than our fighting forces do; and they will pay little attention to the rumormongers and the poison-peddlers in our midst.[35]

This fireside chat explicitly dealt with one way in which truth became a central theme of wartime representations of American democracy, while implicitly acknowledging the other. On the one hand, the government's ability and duty to trust the public with the truth even in wartime was essential to democracy; on

THIS IS THE ARMY   163

the other hand, the possession and use of the part of the truth that was not public justified the seemingly undemocratic military hierarchy. The theme of acknowledging the truth was widely echoed. Describing the purpose of the government information program at the beginning of its *Manual for the Motion Picture Industry*, the OWI emphasized the importance of government truth telling:

> The Government of the United States has an unwavering faith in the sincerity of purpose and integrity of the American people. The American people, on the whole, are not susceptible to the Strategy of Lies. They prefer the truth as the vehicle of understanding. The government believes that truth in the end is the only medium to bring about the proper understanding of democracy, the one important ingredient that can help make democracy work. Axis propagandists have failed. They have not told the truth, and their peoples are now beginning to see through the sham. If we are to keep faith with the American people, we must not resort to any devious information tactics. We must meet lies with a frontal attack — with the weapon of truth.

The authors saw the chief obstacles to the truth much as Cantril had. Only "from the ignorant, the frustrated, and the poverty-stricken" could fascism marshal support.[36]

Needless to say, how much truth was the right amount was a topic of much government debate. Elmer Davis, head of the Office of War Information, pressed for more complete disclosure of American setbacks from early in the war effort. Davis tried in vain to allow newspapers to publish photographs of dead American service men. The White House and the Office of Censorship, however, resisted. Despite the nearly universal rhetoric of withholding information only in order to keep secrets from the enemy, opponents of greater openness often maintained censorship of evidence of United States defeats for a quite different reason: keeping up home front morale. Indeed, in the very fireside chat in which Roosevelt argued that the "government has unmistakable confidence in your ability to hear the worst, without flinching or losing heart," he knowingly underreported the amount of damage caused at Pearl Harbor.[37]

Government representatives also saw knowledge as essential to the morale of Americans troops. Troop morale had to be based on a knowledge of the facts if this was to be a war against fanatical belief systems. Thus, from very early in the forming of a military morale strategy, key figures stressed the importance to good morale of the troops' knowledge of the truth. Secretary of War Henry L. Stimson, addressing a conference of army public relations officers held in Washington, D.C., in March 1941, argued that:

> The success of the army depends upon its morale. . . . Nothing can undermine this morale . . . so rapidly as the [soldiers'] feeling that they are being deceived; that they are not being given the real facts about their progress and the progress of the cause which they are preparing to defend. This is true even in the case of the army of a free people. . . . Therefore, the army of such a country does not need to be bolstered up by false propaganda. What they want is to be sure of the fair truth; and,

Figure 6.3 The military's goal of morale through knowledge of the facts extended into army hospitals. This image, from *New Horizons* a 1944 pamphlet for recuperating soldiers, shows injured GIs attending an orientation meeting in front of a map of Europe. "A MAN DOES A BETTER JOB IF HE KNOWS WHY," the pamphlet confidently announced. From U.S. War Department, *New Horizons* (Washington, 1944).

if they feel they are getting that, they will carry through to the end. Therefore, it is vital that both the army and the people behind it must know the real basic facts, free from any false exaggerations either one way or the other.

A later memo from the War Department's Information and Education Division laying out the objectives of the morale program emphasized, among other goals, fostering both a "belief in the cause for which we fight" and a "resentment, based on knowledge of the facts, against our enemies who have made it necessary to fight."[38]

The earliest attempt to put a morale program into action was the Army Orientation Course, a series of lectures and pamphlets on the war presented to new troops. Begun in 1940, this original orientation effort proved a failure. The didactic lectures, which General Marshall felt were delivered extremely poorly, were precisely the wrong way to reach soldiers, particularly ones exhausted from the rigors of basic training. The pamphlets fared little better. By the Summer of 1941, Marshall began to consider alternatives to lectures and pamphlets.[39]

Frank McCarthy, a young aide to Marshall, brought to the general's attention two articles that had appeared in the *Atlantic* that spring: Stewart Alsop's "Wanted: A Faith to Fight For" and Cleveland Amory's response, "What We Fight For." Alsop, a self-described former "Marxist Liberal," called for the creation of a new American faith to rival those of Russia and Germany (at this point still allies against whom Alsop expected the nation to fight) and to replace (at least among what Alsop admitted was a small group of left liberals) liberal Marxism. Cleveland Amory, an army friend of Frank McCarthy's, dissented. America needs nothing more than it has, Amory argued. What it had was not a "faith," for "it cannot be expressed by any one word — least of all by any one word with an 'ism' on the end of it." Instead, America had "a very simple and undramatic idea . . . that plain, ordinary people, free people . . . can work out for themselves a better government than has ever been worked out for any people in any country." Inspired by these articles, McCarthy, who had worked in Hollywood as a technical adviser, suggested to Marshall that films made by someone from the entertainment industry could present ideas such as Amory's to the troops much more effectively than the lectures and pamphlets of the Army Orientation Course had. Marshall, a great fan of the movies himself, quickly warmed to the idea. From this germ was born the *Why We Fight* series.[40]

Shortly after Pearl Harbor, Frank Capra was named to head the Film Production Section of the Army Signal Corps's Special Services. In his autobiography, *The Name above the Title*, and in a famous 1984 television interview with Bill Moyers about *Why We Fight* Capra told a heroic story of his inspiration for his wartime films. Capra, suspicious of propaganda and unversed in documentary film making, was shown Leni Riefenstahl's *Triumph of the Will* in order to acquaint him with the opposition's propaganda skills. Capra was devastated by the film.

> I could see that the kids of Germany would go anyplace and die for this guy. The power of the film itself showed that they knew what they were doing. They understood propaganda, and they knew how to reach the

mind. So how do I tell the kid down the street — the American kid riding his bike — what he's got in front of him? How do I reach him? The thought hit me, "Well how did it reach me? *They* told me."[41]

So Capra decided to build his films around enemy propaganda images. After a heroic fight against Army Signal Corps brass, all of whom were against using the footage, little man Capra managed to bring his vision to the screen. Or so the story goes.

In fact, the idea of using enemy propaganda footage for Allied purposes did not originate with Capra. Long before Capra screened *Triumph of the Will* at the Museum of Modern Art, *The March of Time*, a monthly screen-magazine series, had concluded its feature-length *The Ramparts We Watch* (1940) with the German propaganda film *Feuertaufe* (Baptism by fire) in order to convince audiences of the brutality of the Nazi war machine. While Capra was planning the *Why We Fight* series, Samuel Spewack was assembling for the Office of War Information the documentary *A World at War* (1942), which also featured enemy footage. Even Capra's tale of viewing *Triumph of the Will* failed to mention that his reaction was shared by Edgar Peterson and Anatole Litvak, who had joined Capra's unit and watched *Triumph* and other German films with him.[42]

All of this is worth noting because the *Why We Fight* series should not be seen as the sole product of an *auteur* who imposed his vision over and against the desires of others. Instead, the series was typical of the War Department's morale effort and became that effort's centerpiece. As Joseph McBride argues in his biography of Capra, the seven *Why We Fight* films (*Prelude to War*, 1942; *The Nazis Strike*, 1943; *Divide and Conquer*, 1943; *The Battle of Britain*, 1943; *The Battle of Russia*, 1943; *The Battle of China*, 1944; and *War Comes to America*, 1945) along with the many other films produced by Capra's unit (including *The Negro Soldier*, 1944, and the infamous *Know Your Enemy — Japan*, 1945) were collaborative efforts. Capra did make his mark early in his unit's history by personally purging anyone he suspected of Communist sympathies. But far more accurate than his postwar assessments of his own personal importance was his statement during the war that "everybody from top to bottom deserves equal credit for anything we've done." Indeed, in addition to his film-making skills, Capra's most important personal contribution to his unit's success was the very vagueness of his own politics. Capra was more than willing to accept guidance from the War Department on the films' content. As the film historian Charles Maland has commented, "If we do discover some of Capra's social vision in the *Why We Fight* series it is probably because his vision coincided with and followed American policy and not vice versa."[43]

Although both *Prelude to War* and *The Battle of Russia* were released (unsuccessfully) to theatrical audiences, the intended audience for the *Why We Fight* series was United States servicemen. The films presupposed that factual knowledge about the war was the best basis for troop morale. As the authors of the War Department Research Division's book-length study of the effect of these films on the troops put it, the "two basic assumptions" of *Why We Fight* were:

1. That a sizable segment of the draftee population lacked knowledge concerning the national and international events that resulted in America's entry in the war.

2. That a knowledge of these events would in some measure lead men
to accept more willingly the transformation from civilian to Army life
and their duties as soldiers.[44]

The *Why We Fight* films use several means to emphasize that they are presenting
facts. Dates are flashed on screen and repeated by voice-over narration: "Remember
that date, September 18th, 1931," the narrator intones in *Prelude to War* as the date
graphically emerges from a map of Manchuria stabbed by an animated Japanese
bayonet, "as well as we remember December 7th 1941 for on that date in 1931 the
war we are now fighting began." Quotations from famous figures from Jesus to
Hitler are simultaneously spoken and printed on-screen, often with page references.
Events mentioned are graphically represented by actual newspaper headlines. At
other times, pictures of combat accompany the mention of particular battles.
Occasionally, as in the case of the German invasion of France in *Divide and Conquer*,
military experts appear on screen to explain strategy and tactics. Captured German,
Japanese, and, to a lesser extent, Italian footage is presented to indicate the true
nature of the enemy regimes by showing the Axis as the Axis nations presumably
wanted themselves represented. It was also, incidentally, a cost-cutting measure:
enemy newsreel footage was absolutely free. Film originally intended to produce
an emotive response from enemy audiences was thus presented in the *Why We Fight*
films as a factual representation of the enemy regime; the film still elicits an
emotional response, but it has become a response to fact. Much of *War Comes to
America* consists of animated renditions of public opinion polls and votes in Congress,
both presented as empirical representations of the general will. And always,
throughout the series, there are animated maps, complete with arrows to indicate
the directions of military movements and enemy ambitions.

Obviously any propaganda effort must convince its audience that it is presenting
the truth. But the insistence of the World War II United States military morale
effort — both within the texts it produced and outside those texts, in its public and
private self-presentations — that the morale of American troops had to be based
on factual knowledge had particular ideological significance. First, a strategy of facts
could be, and was, explicitly contrasted to the Nazis' by-then-famous strategy of
the "Big Lie." But beyond such a contrast, the notion that men could be motivated
to fight simply by a knowledge of the facts expressed a hope that this modern, total
war, a war caused by nations organized and motivated by isms, could be prosecuted
without planting the seeds of any dangerous ism in the minds of American troops.
Democracy demanded that the behavior of citizens, even citizen soldiers, be rationally informed and individually considered. By constructing *Why We Fight* around
the presentation of empirical fact, Marshall, Capra, and others involved in its
production embodied this principle.

But for all of its emphasis on knowledge of facts, *Why We Fight* was ultimately
more factitious than factual. Much of the footage was, quite simply, not what it
claimed to be. Following a cinematic tradition established long before by newsreels,
the *Why We Fight* series included footage from Hollywood features passed off as
actual battle footage, staged scenes of life in the Axis countries, and captured footage
taken entirely out of its original context. For Marshall, Capra, and other supporters
of the *Why We Fight* series, the films provided, in an exciting fashion, the empirical

foundation on which military audiences could rationally improve their morale. But others saw the films as positively dangerous. Lowell Mellett of the OWI's Bureau of Motion Pictures angrily denounced *Prelude to War* in a letter to FDR:

> I feel that it is a bad picture in some respects, possibly even a dangerous picture. . . . One of the most skillful jobs of moviemaking I ever have seen, the picture makes a terrific attack on the emotions. . . . Engendering nervous hysteria in the Army or in the civil population might help to win the war, although I doubt it. It won't help in the business of making a saner world after the armistice.[45]

Capra himself defended the film's style, while maintaining that it was simply the most effective way to package fact. In 1944 Brig. Gen. Frederick Osborn complained to Capra that *The Battle of China* incorporated many sequences that were "not actually pictures of historical events, but scenes taken from entertainment or other film to produce the desired effect." Capra responded by admitting that many of the films contained such footage but argued that the use of it was only a matter of style and was necessary to the job at hand.

> I know there are people in the War Department who claim we have put too much "emotion" in these films. They may be right. A dry recitation of facts might have been a "safer" way to present them. But my experiences with audiences has [sic] long ago taught me that if you want facts to stick, you must present them in an interesting manner. A teacher who can excite and stimulate the imagination will, in the long run, impart more lasting knowledge in his students.[46]

Both Capra and his critics, however, underestimated the films' audience. The Research Branch study of the *Why We Fight* series revealed that the men, by and large, had a very favorable response to the films. But many in the test audiences commented on the films' one-sidedness, repeated use of the same "fake" or "untrue" footage, "exaggeration," "unrealistic" presentation, and the very impossibility of obtaining some shots the films presented as authentic, particularly scenes of Hitler plotting with his inner circle and close-ups of combat. Most important, while the films did impart greater factual information about the war to their audiences, this factual information had little effect on "opinion items of a more general nature" and no effect whatsoever on morale or combat motivation. Indeed, the Research Branch concluded that *Prelude to War* might actually have decreased combat motivation. One of the more significant, if still rather small, general opinion changes that viewing *Prelude to War* seemed to produce was an increase in the troops' assessment of Axis military strength. The same study revealed a negative correlation between men's assessment of Axis strength and their own desire to fight.[47]

The Research Branch concluded that the central fault with the army's orientation strategy was the assumption that increasing factual knowledge about the war would produce changes in opinion that would then motivate the troops. Writing four years after the war, the Research Branch suggested that people might simply not be as rationally motivated as the orientation program assumed.

[I]t is possible that the lack of effects may be due simply to the fact that the attitudes and motivations investigated in these studies cannot be appreciably affected by an information program which relies upon "letting the facts speak for themselves." It may be that such a program will prove effective with only a small segment of the population whose attitudes are primarily determined by rational considerations. For most other individuals, motivations and attitudes may generally be acquired through nonrational channels and may be highly resistant to rational considerations.[48]

Such an assessment of the possibilities for popular rationality, which appeared in the third volume of the Research Branch's study without any dire warnings about the political consequences of such widespread irrationality, suggests a profoundly different sense of social psychology and its relation to democracy than that held by the architects of the army's information program, the authors of *Men under Stress*, and many others who considered the same issues during the war.

The experience of the war itself no doubt contributed to the difference. At the time of Pearl Harbor, the only group of Americans who had experienced battle recently enough that they might be subjects of a study on combat morale were those who had fought as volunteers in the Spanish civil war. John Dollard, a professor of anthropology at Yale and an important consultant to the Research Branch, completed a study of these men from the Abraham Lincoln Brigade for Yale University's Institute of Human Relations in 1943. Entitled *Fear in Battle*, Dollard's study concluded that the most important factor for high morale was "a belief in war aims." It was cited by 73 percent of the men surveyed as one of "the most important things that help a man overcome fear in battle" ("leadership," mentioned by 49 percent of the survey subjects, came in a distant second). The study concluded that knowledge of war aims could be something of a cure-all on the battlefield.

> War aims, say our informants, must be concrete, personal, intimate. The soldier must have the war aims within his skin, operating as personal motive to fight. It is not enough that statesmen know the cause is just. The soldier must know it and feel it. . . .
>
> Identification with cause is like a joker in a deck of cards. It can substitute for any other card. The man who has it can better bear inferior materiel, temporary defeat, weariness, or fear.

Among other important factors, hatred of the enemy could also help improve morale, but only if this hatred was properly directed at the enemy's cause, not his person. "Our informants are firm in the opinion that the long-term hatred excited by the symbols and agents of the Fascist cause is far more important" than the momentary anger felt toward the particular enemy soldiers who killed a comrade.[49]

But as Dollard himself noted, members of the Abraham Lincoln Brigade fought as volunteers for openly ideological reasons. This potentially made them quite different from conscripted soldiers fighting to defend their country following a military attack. Furthermore, Dollard argued, some causes "permit identification throughout society as a whole" more easily than others: America's Four Freedoms

Figure 6.4 This 1944 poster, published by the United States Treasury's War Finance Division, suggests that all that separates soldiers from other Americans is the special equipment produced by the generosity of civilians. Stripped of all his government issued equipment, GI Joe is just an average Joe. Courtesy Northwestern University Library, http://www.library.nwu.edu/govpub/collections/wwii-posters/

might have less immediate appeal than Japan's Asia for Asiatics. Despite these concerns, Dollard still drew the general conclusions that knowledge of one's own cause was the single biggest contributor to battlefield morale and that hatred of the enemy, while also important, must be directed toward the enemy's cause.[50]

Dollard's reservations were more on target than he may have hoped. Frontline reporters continually suggested that American troops were motivated more by local hatreds and loyalties than by hatred of a grand Axis cause or devotion to Allied war aims. "It makes the dogfaces sick to read articles by people who say, 'It isn't actually the Germans, it's the Nazis,'" commented the journalist and cartoonist Bill Mauldin. "Our army has seen few actual *Nazis*, except when they threw in special SS divisions. We have seen the Germans — the youth and the men and the husbands and the fathers of Germany, and we know them for a ruthless, cold, cruel, and powerful enemy" As far as knowledge of the Allied cause was concerned, Mauldin remarked that "friendship and spirit is a lot more genuine and sincere and valuable than all the 'war aims' and indoctrination in the world."[51]

The Research Branch's studies of American World War II troops similarly indicated a lack of "proper" orientation. Fewer than a tenth of the men surveyed in August 1942 had a "consistent, favorable, intellectual orientation to the war." During the Summer of 1943, the Research Branch surveyed troops' knowledge of the Four Freedoms. Partially incorporated into the Atlantic Charter and much repeated by President Roosevelt from early in 1942, the Four Freedoms — freedom of speech, freedom of religion, freedom from want, and freedom from fear — were often touted by government information campaigns as the essence of the Allies' war aims. Yet over a third of a three-thousand-man sample had never heard of the Four Freedoms and only 13 percent could name three or four of them. The Research Branch paradoxically concluded:

> The general picture in this volume of men preoccupied with minimizing their discomforts, acquiring higher rank or pay, securing safe jobs which would offer training useful in civilian life, displaying aggressions against the Army in many different ways, and in getting out of the Army as fast as possible does not suggest a particularly inspired work performance in the American Army. But Americans fought brilliantly and tenaciously when they had to, usually aided . . . by superior materiel.[52]

Despite the mounting negative assessments by its own Research Branch during the war, the army's Information and Education Division continued its orientation program. The notion that the wide dissemination of facts about the war could motivate troops to fight for rational reasons was powerful enough to last until the Allies achieved victory. But while the military and civilian information agencies suggested that the truthful presentation of most facts about the war was both evidence of the democratic nature of the United States and the foundation for preserving democracy in wartime, other facts were carefully withheld. Public pronouncements of openness would invariably include an exception for information that might be of use to the enemy, although the scope of such information was the source of much behind-the-scenes, interagency wrangling.

Restricted knowledge, as well as public knowledge, played a crucial role in the official effort to create and represent a democratic military. As we have seen, empirical truth was widely regarded as the safest — sometimes the only safe — basis for social solidarity in a democracy. By rationally arriving at the same conclusion based on thorough knowledge of important facts, the argument went, individuals in a democracy could engage in massive collective undertakings such as a modern war without falling victim to isms that threatened their very rationality and individuality. But empirical truth could also justify hierarchy in a democracy. As facts properly understood could yield objectively correct decisions, a greater knowledge of facts and of how to understand them could justify even the rigid command structure of an army as making democratic sense. And the idea that a particular set of empirical truths clearly indicated a single correct course of action could provide the state, which possessed a near monopoly of important facts in wartime, with apparently apolitical, almost scientific justification for the centralization of such command structures.

The organizational structure of the wartime military was built around an unusually rigid obedience to empirical facts. In addition to being designed to place men in jobs most similar to their civilian occupations, the highly articulated United States system of military manpower allocation — which specified eight hundred Military Occupation Specialties — was designed to centralize allocation decisions and to make those decisions on as "scientific" a basis as possible. In comparison with classifications used by the German military, American classifications were thus more specific, more reliant on quantifiable measures (as opposed to the professional opinion of examining physicians and psychologists), and, once made, much more difficult for field commanders actually in charge of the men to alter.[53]

Differences in officer evaluation procedures also reveal the greater importance of producing and analyzing empirical facts in the United States army's management procedures. German officers were evaluated once every two years by their superiors. Evaluating officers filled out a five-page-long form that required written answers. In contrast, the United States army required an Officer Evaluation Report to be filed every six months. This sixteen-page-long document contained eighty questions, answered, with an electrographic pencil, according to five different point systems. The form was then reviewed by the evaluating officer's superior officer, thus doubling the paperwork. Finally, the results were reduced to a single five-digit number. The United States Army insisted that officers fill out these forms in a timely fashion, even on the battlefield. One infantry officer recalled being awakened by a runner and requested to fill out an Officer Evaluation Report at midnight while sheltering in a shattered German bunker on the Siegfried Line in February 1945.[54]

Not only was the military organized by empirical knowledge, but the official field service regulations on military leadership sought to ground commanders' authority on such knowledge. Here the comparison with Germany is particularly instructive. Presumably because the official German manual on military leadership used during the war, *Truppenführung* (1936), was a lineal descendent of earlier German military manuals that were the foundation of modern military doctrine, the American manual, *Field Service Regulations* (1941), had long passages that were absolutely identical to the German regulations. In summarizing the differences between the two on the nature of leadership, the military historian Martin van Creveld notes that, unlike the German manual, the American regulations suggest that superior knowledge is the most important of the commander's attributes. The sections of the two manuals dealing with military decision making also differ. The German manual emphasizes creative, independent decision making, calling war a "free creative activity resting on scientific foundations," and warns that "it is impossible to exhaustively lay down the art of war in regulations"; the American manual puts much less emphasis on independent thought and goes into much greater detail on all points. In short, the United States Army's view of war put much more emphasis on doctrine and planning and less on individual initiative.[55]

There is a certain irony in the fact that the German military put more faith in creative individual decision making than did the American military. Van Creveld does not make much attempt to explain the American army's firmer insistence on knowledge and doctrine as the bases of leadership and command, but he suggests that it might have to do with "the fact that scientific management was first developed and widely applied in the United States."[56] But, by World War II, scientific management was widely known and, if anything, more widely used in the planned economics of Europe, including Nazi Germany. Apart from the military, the United States engaged in much less scientific management of human resources during World War II than did other countries fighting in the war.

The United States military's management style was based much more on contemporary democratic theory than on a general American predilection for scientific management. The home front could be, and was, managed in a more roundabout way: for instance, massive public spending to support the war effort created jobs; people voluntarily moved to where the jobs were. Unlike Great Britain, Canada, Australia, New Zealand, China, the Soviet Union, Germany, Italy, and Japan, the United States never attempted to organize home-front manpower through conscription, although the Roosevelt administration fought hard to persuade Congress to approve such a plan.[57] But a modern military necessarily requires a coordinated method of management, just as the military's fact-based orientation method attempted to create rational collective action, the United States military's scientistic, overquantified method of management attempted to rationalize command. Military leadership necessarily asks men to do what isms were said to demand of their believers: to be willing to kill and be killed for the cause. Like totalitarian states, the military necessarily regimented its men. The public commitment of the United States military to empiricism and rationality suggested that the military of a democracy might nevertheless differ from that of a totalitarian society.

The United States military during World War II attempted to ground its actions in rational, empirical decisions. From the classification of inductees to the orientation of troops, from the evaluation of officers to the method of making command decisions, military planners and publicists gave facts and their "scientific" analysis center stage. They did so, at least in part, because they saw empirical knowledge and rationality as the only acceptable reasons for collective action in a democracy and the only way to minimize the threat that such action might warp the psychologies of participants in the direction of totalitarianism.

The results of American attempts to envision a democratic military during World War II were deeply ambivalent. On the one hand, the images of a democratic army were a powerful balm for the concerns of the millions of Americans who feared that for a nation to involve itself in, let alone to win, a modern war it would have to become undemocratic. Like the pre-Pearl Harbor *Sergeant York*, a steady stream of films, stories from war correspondents, pictures from the front, radio plays, advertisements, and other texts suggested that American men were capable of fighting a modern war while remaining individuals, drawing creatively on their prewar civilian identities, and actually becoming better democratic citizens through the experience. The victory of the United States together with the apparent survival of its democratic system throughout the war suggested that the nation had succeeded in forging a military fit for a democracy.

On the other hand, the more practical efforts to make the American military democratic were, by and large, failures. The army's own studies and the work of scholars such as Paul Fussell suggest that the military's carefully crafted morale effort, unprecedented in its scope, ultimately contributed relatively little to American victory. The complicated military classification scheme disproportionately ended up putting those least educated and most socially disadvantaged on the front lines. Soldiers and sailors in the actual military were not remotely as united and ideologically clear in their aims as Hollywood's multiethnic battalions. Much more than in World War I, in which many who fought had at least begun the war with a sense of its meaning and a clarity of purpose, many soldiers in World War II were, from the start, determined but cynical.[58]

Even the successes of these wartime visions of a democratic military have left an ambivalent legacy. Unlike American wartime rhetoric of the World War I era, which quickly became as reviled after the war as it had been successful during it, the wartime vision of World War II as the "Good War" has had remarkable staying power. Although revisionist accounts of World War II have surfaced regularly since 1945, they have never dominated either scholarly discourse or public opinion. And the idea that a modern military can be truly democratic is now almost unchallenged in our public discourse, whether the notion takes the form of celebrations of the military as it is or of criticisms of the military's failure to offer a better reflection of democratic life. Fears that the military might be inherently undemocratic, that what is good for it might necessarily be bad for democratic life, have receded to the margins of American political life. Whether or not one ultimately sympathizes with such fears, they played a vital and useful function in American political culture before World War II. That they were so decisively defeated by Sergeant York, Private Snafu, and the countless other democratic fighting men of the imagination has proven to be a mixed blessing.

Acknowledgements

I would like to thank Daniel Rodgers, Gary Gerstle, Karen Merrill, Alan Brinkley, Norman L. Rosenberg, Jennifer Delton, and William C. Jordan for their valuable advice and criticism. I am also very grateful for the careful readings and insightful suggestions provided by my *Journal of American History* referees, Michael C. C. Adams, Michael Sherry, and the others who chose to remain anonymous. Finally, my heartfelt thanks go to David Nord, Susan Armeny, Lynn Pohl, Scott Stephan, Stew Warren, and the rest of the superb staff at the *JAH*.

Notes

1   James Robert Parish, *The Great Combat Pictures: Twentieth-Century Warfare on the Screen* (Metuchen, 1990), 354; David D. Lee, *Sergeant York: An American Hero* (Lexington, Ky., 1985), 110–11.

2   Interventionist films focusing on the dangers of Nazism include *The Mortal Storm*, dir. Frank Borzage (MGM, 1939); *Confessions of a Nazi Spy*, dir. Anatole Litvak (Warner Brothers, 1939); *The Man I Married*, dir. Irving Pichel (20th Century Fox, 1940); *Foreign Correspondent*, dir. Alfred Hitchcock (United Artists, 1940); *Arise My Love*, dir. Mitchell Leisen (Paramount, 1940); and *Man Hunt*, dir. Fritz Lang (20th Century Fox, 1940). For an anti-Nazi film that is less clearly interventionist, see *The Great Dictator*, dir. Charles Chaplin (United Artists, 1940). Poll after poll taken between the outbreak of hostilities in 1939 and the attack on Pearl Harbor showed the American public as generally hostile toward Germany, supportive of Britain and France, and worried about the world's future should Britain lose; Hadley Cantril and Mildred Strunk, eds., *Public Opinion, 1935–1946* (Princeton, 1951), 975, 1055, 1119. On Alvin York's criticism of American participation in World War I see Lee, *Sergeant York*, 100.

3   Lee, *Sergeant York*, 21.

4   For works on the war in American culture that have informed this essay but that I do not otherwise cite, see John Morton Blum, *V Was for Victory* (New York, 1976); William O'Neill, *A Democracy at War* (New York, 1993); Michael Sherry, *In the Shadow of War* (New Haven, 1995); and Michael Sherry, *The Rise of American Air Power* (New Haven, 1987).

5   For examples of the fear that participation in the war might destroy American democracy, see Benjamin L. Alpers, "Understanding Dictatorship and Defining Democracy in American Public Culture, 1930–1945" (Ph.D. diss., Princeton University, 1994), 210–54. A few stalwart anti-interventionists, most notably members of the anti-Stalinist Left such as Paul Goodman and Dwight Macdonald, suggested even after the bombing of Pearl Harbor that America's participation in the war would lead the country to totalitarianism. For a discussion of these thinkers, see Michael Wreszin, *A Rebel in Defense of Tradition: The Life and Politics of Dwight Macdonald* (New York, 1995), 105–13.

6   Between 1937 and 1939 seven national polls asked Americans which side they supported in the Spanish civil war. Two of those polls, conducted by the American Institute of Public Opinion on February 3 and December 16, 1938, showed three-quarters of the American public supporting the Loyalists and one-quarter supporting the rebels. However, neither poll recorded such answers as "No opinion" or "Neither side." The other six polls did. Among Americans willing to choose a side, public opinion ran three-to-one in favor of the Loyalists, but none of the polls showed more than 32% of the public supporting the Loyalists, strongly suggesting that a majority of Americans were ambivalent about the war. Every national poll on the Neutrality Act showed majority support for its continuation. Cantril and Strunk, *Public Opinion*, 807–8.

7   See Alpers, "Understanding Dictatorship and Defining Democracy in American Public Culture," 107–8; and Michael Zalampas, *Adolf Hitler and the Third Reich in American Magazines, 1923–1939* (Bowling Green, 1989), 34.

8   On the history of the term "totalitarianism" in the United States, see Alpers, "Understanding Dictatorship and Defining Democracy in American Public Culture," 96–126, 210–54; Thomas R. Maddux, "Red Fascism, Brown Bolshevism: The American Image of Totalitarianism in the 1930s," *Historian*, 40 (Nov. 1977), 85–103; Les K. Adler and Thomas G. Patterson, "Red Fascism: The Merger of Nazi Germany and Soviet Russia in the American Image of Totalitarianism, 1930's–1950's," *American Historical Review*, 75 (April 1970), 1046–64; Thomas E. Lifka, *The Concept "Totalitarianism" and American Foreign Policy* (New York, 1988); and Abbot Gleason, *Totalitarianism: The Inner History of the Cold War* (New York, 1995). For the papers from the two conferences in 1939, see "Symposium on the Totalitarian State from the Standpoints of History, Political Science, Economics, and Sociology," Proceedings of the American Philosophical Society, 82 (Feb. 1940), 1–102; and Robert M. MacIver, Moritz J. Bonn, and Ralph Barton Perry, *The Roots of Totalitarianism: Addresses Delivered at a Meeting of the American Academy of Political and Social Science, November 18, 1939* (Philadelphia, 1940).

9   On the romanticization of war during World War I, see David M. Kennedy, *Over Here: The First World War and American Society* (New York, 1980), 179–85. On American representations of the Japanese during World War II (and Japanese depictions of Americans), see John Dower, *War without Mercy: Race and Power in the Pacific War* (New York, 1986).

10 Dower and others underestimate the extent to which many people presented the Germans as cultural others during World War II; see Alpers, "Understanding

Dictatorship and Defining Democracy in American Political Culture," 305–54. On Huey Long and Father Charles Coughlin, see Alan Brinkley, *Voices of Protest* (New York, 1982). An example of opponents equating Franklin D. Roosevelt's political role with dictatorship is a 1940 anti-war button that reads: "Third International. Third Reich. Third Term!" Button collection (Fairbanks Museum, St Johnsbury, Vt). On similar fears about Wendell Willkie, see Peter Kurth, *American Cassandra: The Life of Dorothy Thompson* (Boston, 1990), 323–26.

11   Edgar B. Wesley, *NEA: The First Hundred Years* (New York, 1957), 307–9. On I Am an American Day, also called Citizens Day, see Joy Elmer Morgan, "The Significance of Citizenship Recognition Day," *Journal of the National Education Association*, 28 (Dec. 1939), 257; "Between Editor and Reader," *ibid.*, 29 (May 1940), A-87; Lemuel B. Schofield, "'I'm an American,'" *Christian Science Monitor Magazine*, May 5, 1941, p. 3; and Educational Policies Commission, *The Purposes of Education in American Democracy* (Washington, 1938), 29–30. On the incompatibility of democracy and modern war, see Educational Policies Commission, *The Education of Free Men in American Democracy* (Washington, 1940), 41–42.

12   "United Nations," rather than "Allies," was the term preferred by United States officials for the twenty-six countries fighting the Axis, although "Allies" appeared in informal contexts; Robert Dallek, *Franklin D. Roosevelt and American Foreign Policy, 1932–1945* (New York, 1979), 317–20. Franklin D. Roosevelt, *FDR's Fireside Chats*, ed. Russell D. Buhite and David W. Levy (New York, 1993), 214.

13   For the invocation of the Civil War in film, see *War Comes to America*, dir. Frank Capra (U.S. Army, Special Services Division, 1945); and *Ring of Steel*, dir. Garson Kanin (Office of Emergency Management Film Unit, 1942). For the invocation of the Civil War in a radio script, see Stephen Vincent Benét, "Dear Adolf: Letter from an American Soldier" (1942), in Stephen Vincent Benét, *We Stand United and Other Radio Scripts* (New York, 1945). 49ff.

14   Of Americans surveyed by the American Institute of Public Opinion on May 3, 1940, 51% believed that the United States would get involved in the war; Cantril and Strunk, *Public Opinion*, 969.

15   Statement by Edwin C. Johnson, in "Should the U.S. Adopt Peacetime Compulsory Military Training?," *Congressional Digest*, 24 (Jan. 1945), 13ff.; statement by Claude Pepper, *ibid.*, 15; statement by Charles A. Ellwood, *ibid.*, 21; editorial from *Christian Century*, *ibid.*, 27, 29; statement by John Haynes Holmes, *ibid.*, 31.

16   On psychiatric screening, see Allan Bérubé, *Coming Out under Fire: The History of Gay Men and Women in World War II* (New York, 1990), 8–33. On social science during the war, see Samuel A. Stouffer, "Social Science and the Soldier," in *American Society in Wartime*, ed. William Fielding Ogburn (Chicago, 1943), 105–17 . Roy R. Grinker and John P. Spiegel, *Men under Stress* (Philadelphia, 1945), 450. Although apparently not an official War Department study, *Men under Stress* was produced with the full support of military personnel; *ibid.*, ix–x. It was also frequently cited in the final study of the army's Research Branch: Samuel A. Stouffer et al., eds., *Studies in Social Psychology in World War II*, vol. II: *The American Soldier: Combat and Its Aftermath* (Princeton, 1949), 663.

17   Grinker and Spiegel, *Men under Stress*, 453–54; Alpers, "Understanding Dictatorship and Democracy in American Political Culture," 154–209.

18   Martin van Creveld, *Fighting Power: German and U.S. Army Performance, 1939–1945* (Westport, 1982), 69–71.

19   Infantry Journal, *The New Soldier's Handbook* (New York, 1942), v. 1–2. In 1942, Penguin produced this commercially available edition of the United States Army's

The Soldier's Handbook, reprinting the entire text of the manual with some additional material. For the original, see *The Soldier's Handbook* (Washington, 1940).

20   *New Soldier's Handbook*, 10; see also *ibid.*, vi, 5–6.

21   George C. Marshall quoted in "What Is Morale?," *What the Soldier Thinks* (Dec. 1943), 1; Stephen Vincent Benét, "Your Army," in Benét, *We Stand United and Other Radio Scripts*, 198.

22   Alpers, "Understanding Dictatorship and Defining Democracy in American Public Culture," 154–254; Paul Fussell, *Wartime: Understanding and Behavior in the Second World War* (New York, 1989), 73. FDR also emphasized the individuality of American soldiers. See Roosevelt, *FDR's Fireside Chats*, ed. Buhite and Levy, 229.

23   Thomas Doherty, *Projections of War: Hollywood, American Culture, and World War II* (New York, 1993), 123.

24   *Ibid.*, 123–24.

25   Today Americans tend to associate the multiethnic combat unit with film largely because the films of the World War II era are more widely disseminated than books, radio plays, and other cultural productions. For an example in a book, see Marion Hargrove, *See Here Private Hargrove* (New York, 1942); and Maxwell Anderson, introduction, *ibid.*, ix–xi. For a radio play, see Stephen Vincent Benét, "Dear Adolf." Jeanine Basinger, *The World War II Combat Film: The Anatomy of a Genre* (New York, 1986), 101; van Creveld, *Fighting Power*, 46; Kennedy, *Over Here*, 158.

26   For a different account of the significance of the multiethnic combat unit, see Lary May, "Making the American Consensus: The Narrative of Conversion and Subversion in World War II Films," *The War in American Culture: Society and Consciousness during World War II*, ed. Lewis Erenberg and Susan E. Hirsch (Chicago, 1996), 71–102. Many nonwhite groups were still largely understood through the category of "race"; see John Dower, *War without Mercy*. For a contemporary account critical of racialized views of Japanese Americans, see Robert Redfield, "The Japanese-Americans" in *American Society in Wartime*, ed. Ogburn, 143–64. For an image of a multiethnic America united against a racialized Japan, see the Oscar-winning *The House I Live In*, in which Frank Sinatra convinces a crowd of white children to stop harassing their Jewish schoolmate by telling them a heroic story of a multiethnic bomber crew taking revenge on "the Japs"; *The House I Live In*, dir. Mervyn LeRoy (RKO, 1945)

27   The work of the social scientists in the Research Branch was collected in the four-volume *Studies in Social Psychology in World War II*. In the first two six-hundred-page volumes, jointly titled *The American Soldier*, there is no attempt to break down the data on white soldiers by their ethnic backgrounds. There is one reference to attitudinal differences between Protestant and Catholic soldiers, and this is on the issue of military chaplains. Region of origin was a slightly more important issue, particularly in the area of race relations. The study mentions differences between northerners and southerners in general attitude, attitudes toward Negroes, health by climate, and job satisfaction; Samuel A. Stouffer et al., eds., *Studies in Social Psychology in World War II*, vol. 1: *The American Soldier: Adjustment during Army Life* (Princeton, 1949), 174–75. 349–50, 400; Stouffer et al., eds., *Studies in Social Psychology in World War II*, II, 618. For a study that shows the greater emphasis on the color line by civilian scholars, see Robert E. Park, "Racial Ideologies," in *American Society in Wartime*, ed. Ogburn, 165–84.

28   See also the army films *Don't Be a Sucker* (U.S. Army Signal Corps, 1945); and *War Comes to America*.

29   Basinger, *World War II Combat Film*, 74–75. For the work of the Research Branch on race, see the chapter on black soldiers in Stouffer et al., eds., *Studies in Social Psychology*

in *World War II*, I. It compares northerners and southerners (white and black) by educational level and considers attitudes toward the military police, willingness for combat, attitudes toward segregation, attitudes of whites toward blacks, and black attitudes toward northerners and southerners. See *ibid.*, 491, 560, 506, 512, 559, 580–82.

30   Opponents of the plan included Sen. Harry S. Truman's Special Committee to Investigate the National Defense Program, the American Federation of Labor (AFL), the Congress of Industrial Organizations (CIO), and the Chamber of Commerce of the United States. See "The Question of Civilian Conscription for War," *Congressional Digest*, 23 (April 1944), 101ff.

31   The Bureau of Motion Pictures (BMP), which had previously been part of the Office of Government Reports, was an important domestic branch of the Office of War Information (OWI). Under the direction of Lowell Mellett and Nelson Poynter, the BMP served as the federal government's point of contact with the motion picture industry. The BMP reviewed all Hollywood films, passed judgment on their war-related content, and attempted to elicit the voluntary cooperation of the Hollywood studios. On the BMP, see Clayton R. Koppes and Gregory D. Black. *Hollywood Goes to War* (Berkeley, 1987). United States Office of War Information, Bureau of Motion Pictures. "The Children's Army" (Fact Sheet No. 12, n.d.), in *Government Information Manual for the Motion Picture Industry* (Hollywood, 1942) (microfilm: NNGR 80.1161, reel 1), Records Concerning Newsreel Liaison, General File of Newsreel Liaison, Records of the Bureau of Motion Pictures, Records of the Office of War Information, RG 208 (National Archives, Washington, D.C.).

32   A number of other World War II-era films invent opportunities for their title characters first to evade the draft and then voluntarily to decide to fight. See *Lucky Jordan*, dir. Frank Tuttle (Paramount, 1942); *Mr Lucky*, dir. H. C. Potter (RKO, 1943); and May, "Making the American Consensus." On the popularity of the Private Snafu films, see "Measuring the Effectiveness of Informational Motion Pictures," *What the Soldier Thinks* (Aug. 1943), 100–101. On the Snafu films, see Eric Smooden, *Animating Culture: Hollywood Cartoons from the Sound Era* (New Brunswick, 1993), 70–95.

33   In *Spies*, Snafu's failure to keep a secret from Axis spies ends up with him literally blown to hell, where Hitler, in the form of the devil, reveals that Snafu was responsible for his own fate; *Spies* (Army Pictorial Service, 1944).

34   Hadley Cantril, *The Invasion from Mars: A Study in the Psychology of Panic* (Princeton, 1940), 114–18, 203–4. On Americans perceiving Nazism as nonsense, see *Weapon of War* (Army Pictorial Service, 1944); and the conclusion of *Confessions of a Nazi Spy*.

35   Roosevelt, *FDR's Fireside Chats*, ed. Buhite and Levy, 207–8, 213.

36   United States Office of War Information, Bureau of Motion Pictures, "The Framework of the Government Information Program," in *Government Information Manual for the Motion Picture Industry*. For another endorsement of wartime truth-telling, see Byron Price, "Censorship an Evil of War" (Oct. 28, 1942), in *Vital Speeches of the Day*, Dec. 15, 1942, p. 159.

37   On photographic censorship, see George H. Roeder Jr., *The Censored War: American Visual Experience during World War II* (New Haven, 1993). Roosevelt, *FDR's Fireside Chats*, ed. Buhite and Levy, 213–14, 214 n9.

38   Henry Stimson quoted in Thomas W. Bohn, *An Historical and Descriptive Analysis of the "Why We Fight" Series* (New York, 1977), 92–93. Memo quoted in Carl I. Hovland et al., eds., *Studies in Social Psychology in World War II*, vol. III: *Experiments on Mass Communication* (Princeton, 1949), 24.

39   Bohn, *Historical and Descriptive Analysis of the "Why We Fight" Series*, 95–96; Joseph McBride, *Frank Capra: The Catastrophe of Success* (New York, 1992), 455–56.

40   Stewart Alsop, "Wanted: A Faith to Fight For," *Atlantic Monthly*, 167 (May 1941), 594–97; Cleveland Amory, "What We Fight For," *ibid.* (June 1941), 687–89; McBride, *Frank Capra*, 455–56.

41   Bohn, *Historical and Descriptive Analysis of the "Why We Fight" Series*, 98; "WWII: The Propaganda Battle," prod. Corporation for Entertainment & Learning and Bill Moyers, dir. David Grubin (part of "Bill Moyers' Walk through the Twentieth Century") WNET New York and KQED San Francisco (PBS, 1982); McBride, *Frank Capra*, 466–67. The *Why We Fight* series has been re-released by a number of companies and is widely available.

42   McBride, *Frank Capra*, 466.

43   *Ibid.*, 453, 459–65, 470, 474.

44   Hovland et al., eds., *Studies in Social Psychology in World War II*, III, 22.

45   McBride, *Frank Capra*, 479–81; Lowell Mellett to Franklin D. Roosevelt, November 9, 1942, *ibid.*, 475.

46   Brig. General. Frederick Osborn to Frank Capra, *ibid.*, 482; Capra to Osborn, November 21, 1944, *ibid.*

47   Hovland et al., eds., *Studies in Social Psychology in World War II*, III, 56, 74–75, 85–86.

48   *Ibid.*, 255–56.

49   John Dollard, *Fear in Battle* (Washington, 1944), 40–42, 48; Stouffer et al., eds., *Studies in Social Psychology in World War II*, I, 26, 484n.

50   Dollard, *Fear in Battle*, 60, 63.

51   Bill Mauldin, *Up Front* (New York, 1945), 50, 60.

52   The Research Branch defined proper orientation as understanding the Four Freedoms, accepting the defensive nature of the war effort, and rejecting both "cynical" explanations of the war — such as blaming it on big business or British imperialism — and the "superficial theory" that the war was another example of the United States straightening out Europe's messes. Even without the Four Freedoms qualification, fewer than a fifth of the men surveyed measured up. Many of the troops apparently confused the Four Freedoms and the Bill of Rights. These men could correctly name two of the Four Freedoms: freedom of speech and freedom of religion. Stouffer et al., eds., *Studies in Social Psychology in World War II*, I, 423ff., 433, 485.

53   Van Creveld, *Fighting Power*, 65–70; Michael C. C. Adams, *The Best War Ever* (Baltimore, 1994), 81.

54   Van Creveld, *Fighting Power*, 64; Adams, *Best War Ever*, 81.

55   Van Creveld, *Fighting Power*, 32–33, 38–40, 131.

56   *Ibid.*, 37.

57   On the civilian conscription systems in these countries, see "Compulsory Service in Other Countries," *Congressional Digest*, 23 (April 1944), 107.

58   See Fussell, *Wartime*, 129–43.

Chapter 7

David French

'YOU CANNOT HATE THE BASTARD WHO IS TRYING TO KILL YOU . . .'[1]
Combat and ideology in the British army in the war against Germany, 1939–45

FOLLOWING THE ESTABLISHMENT of the General Service Corps in July 1942, all recruits were asked about their eagerness to enter combat. For the Army the results were disappointing. Of 710,000 recruits, only 5 per cent (36,000) were placed in the top category ('Markedly suited by disposition and personality to a combatant role') while 3 per cent (22,000) were marked as having a poor combatant temperament.[2] The remainder fell between these two extremes. This confirmed what senior officers already sensed. Shortly after the Battle of El Alamein, Montgomery wrote privately to the Chief of the Imperial General Staff (CIGS), Sir Alan Brooke, that 'The trouble with our British lads is that they are not killers by nature . . .'.[3] The military authorities faced a formidable task in transforming peace-loving civilians into men prepared to kill. This article will examine how they went about that and how front-line soldiers responded to the demand that they kill their German (and Italian) opposite numbers. And it will also try to determine the extent to which front-line soldiers retained a sense of common humanity that transcended the political divisions of the war, by analysing the ways in which they treated their enemies when they were completely at their mercy, either as prisoners of war or as civilians in occupied territory.

The Army set about its task using time-honoured methods. Just as in the German Army, British recruits were drilled and disciplined until obedience to orders became instinctive. However, unlike the German Army, the British made only a half-hearted and belated attempt to instruct their troops in the issues that were at stake in the war. After 1933, German soldiers were indoctrinated into the principles of the National Socialist State and imbibed a mixture of racism, anti-Semitism and anti-Bolshevism. Consequently, the Landser saw the war, particularly on the Eastern Front, as an ideological struggle against an enemy that threatened the validity of the Nazi State to which most of them were committed because they believed that it had redeemed the failures of World War One and had restored a sense of German identity that was uniquely valuable. Furthermore, German soldiers were brutalized by the disciplinary system of their own army to such an extent that they sought a vicarious release from a near-intolerable situation by brutalizing in turn those weaker than themselves. The upshot was that not only did the Landsers continue fighting despite casualty rates that quickly destroyed their primary groups, but they showed a barbarous disregard for the peoples whose countries they occupied and the prisoners they captured.[4]

Many British recruits enlisted with very little idea of why they were fighting. In the Spring of 1940, the commanding officer of an infantry training centre asked a group of recruits to answer three questions: with whom was Britain at war? Which countries were Britain's allies? Why was Britain at war? 'Some of the answers were rather astonishing and showed that the individuals concerned had few, if any, ideas on the subject'.[5] Two years later little had changed. Commanding officers of two primary training centres noted that 90 per cent of a recent intake of recruits 'lack enthusiasm and interest in the war and betray ignorance of the issues involved in it . . .'. Trained soldiers often showed a similar lack of interest in the progress of the war.[6] This partly reflected the confusion surrounding the way in which the British government and media presented the war. They pictured it as a conflict against the forces of darkness that threatened civilized society. Few people doubted that Hitler had to be stopped, but compared with the First World War there was little chauvinism and, except in the Summer of 1940, no rush of volunteers to enlist. The authorities tried to legitimize the war by appealing to commonly held beliefs in equality, democracy, justice, and the rule of law. They portrayed their citizens as ordinary, decent people who were fighting the war in defence of freedom. The Ministry of Information drew upon a Whiggish view of British history. Britain was a pioneer of the idea of justice and freedom in the face of foreign and domestic tyrants, and had developed along a path of balanced and gradual social improvement. Democracy was dead in Germany but it underpinned everything in Britain, from marriage and personal relationships to Women's Institutes, Parliament, and trades unions.[7] In the words of a Board of Education report written in December 1939, Britain's cultural roots 'are indeed bound up with conceptions of democracy, tolerance and kindliness'.[8]

Official British propaganda did not begin the war by systematically producing an image of ordinary Germans as sub-humans fit only for extinction. Before Dunkirk, the Ministry of Information made a clear distinction between the German people and the Nazis. They blamed the outbreak of the war on the fact that, twice in a generation, the German people had failed to prevent power in Germany from falling into the hands of a violent and ambitious minority. It was only in May 1940 that the Ministry tried to instil a sense of anger against all Germans. They were variously portrayed as Huns, Goths, and Vandals, innately aggressive and bent on world domination. Much emphasis was placed on Nazi brutality in occupied Europe and Hitler was labelled an arch-gangster and the embodiment of lust for power of the whole German people.[9]

These were the staple themes of official propaganda for the rest of war. But the Ministry's efforts had only a limited effect. It was not until the Luftwaffe began to bomb British cities in September 1940 that Home Intelligence began to report a real sense of bitterness against Germans. Soldiers like John Hillier, who were engaged in clearing bomb damage in Liverpool in late 1940, were angered by the destruction they saw 'and only thought of when we could give the Germans something back for all this loss of life and destruction'.[10] These sentiments peaked in the Winter and Spring of 1940–1 but they then subsided, to be replaced by grim satisfaction at the news of German cities being bombed.[11] Stereotyping the whole German people as innately aggressive smacked too much of the crude propaganda campaigns of the First World War. It had little appeal to a population that thought that it had been tricked into believing that it was fighting to create a land fit for heroes only to face the disillusion of the Slump. 'Reared on the cynicism following the First World War we would not allow ourselves any patriotic fervour', wrote one 8th Army veteran.[12] Asked by Gallup in January 1942 'What do you think our feelings should be towards Germany after the war', the largest group of respondents, 41 per cent, wanted to prevent Germany from ever making war again, 18 per cent wanted to shoot Nazis but to leave the rest of the German people in peace, 16 per cent wanted to punish the German people but not extract vengeance and 7 per cent wanted to 'invite the Germans to our democratic world'. Only 11 per cent wanted to exterminate them.[13]

The Army followed the lead set by the government but, compared with the Germans, its efforts to teach the troops about the political issues at stake were belated, half-hearted, and unsuccessful. Before 1939, the only indoctrination British soldiers regularly received concerned the history of their regiment. *King's Regulations* specifically forbade serving soldiers to take part in any political activities.[14] That ban remained in force throughout the war and soldiers who broke it were liable to face a court martial or to be administratively discharged. At Uniacke Barracks near Harrogate in late 1940, 'No one talked politics. The war was rarely mentioned'.[15] 'No reference was at any time made to the issues involved in the present war', noted one junior officer who had graduated from an Officer Cadet Training Unit in January 1941.[16] It was only in 1941 that the War Office realized that the morale of the German soldier was based to a large extent upon 'a set of convictions that have been seared into his mind by unscrupulous and skilful propaganda'. Unit commanders were, therefore, instructed to counterbalance this by lecturing to their men about why Britain was at war, the nature of German war aims, and what a German victory would mean for 'the man in the street in his standard of living, the security of his family, his freedom of action and thought . . .'.[17] And as part of Army Bureau Current Affairs (ABCA) training, they were ordered to set aside an hour each week so that their officers could conduct civics classes with their men.[18]

During the months and sometimes years they spent training some soldiers did think carefully about the political issues at stake. In the wake of the First World War and following press coverage of Nazism, a vague Germanophobia was commonplace in Britain even before 1939. Brought up in London's East End, Stephen Dyson remembered that 'From schooldays it [Germany] had been instilled in us as the land of the natural enemy, a view fuelled by constant media exposure of Hitler's Nazi domination and aggression since the early 1930s'.[19] In Peter Cochrane's family home, 'Hitler was looked on as unrelievedly evil by my parents'.

Some soldiers, like Major Bill Shebbeare, a former President of the Oxford Union and member of the Communist Party, already had a highly developed political consciousness before they enlisted. Shebbeare wrote on the eve of D-Day, 'Although I have been cut off from political life for four and a half years, I have maintained my socialist faith undimmed. My hatred of Nazism burns even more fiercely than it did in 1939, and my dearest wish is that I shall soon attack it—this time not from a platform in a market place, but from the turret of a tank'.[20] However, probably most soldiers, in default of more energetic official guidance, could not articulate what they were fighting for with any degree of fluency. Reflecting the fatalistic culture of so much of the British working class, they believed the '"Well we are all in this together for the duration, so let's make the best of it" attitude'.[21] Peter Roach found of the men with whom he trained in 1941: 'Almost without exception they were eager and ready to train and then to fight, not with any romantic fervour but because the job had to be finished before they could return to normal life, or so they thought'.[22] After listening to lectures and watching official films designed to clarify the causes for which they were fighting, one paratrooper thought that 'Getting the English worked up enough to defend democracy was an uphill task, as the average soldier appeared to have only three basic interests: football, beer and crumpet'.[23]

Richard Holmes has suggested that soldiers must go to war with an abstract image of the enemy in their mind, for without it 'and without the depersonalisation of the enemy during training, battle would become impossible to sustain'.[24] British soldiers under training were presented with a consistent picture of their German opponents as being brave, highly professional, and disciplined. Nevertheless, they also exhibited a sheep-like mental docility that made them too ready to swallow the lies of Nazi propagandists and ignore the rules of civilized warfare. A commonplace of training material was that the Germans would use 'any form of trickery, cunning, or treachery which may assist them in obtaining their object'.[25] Soldiers like R. L. Crimp went to the battlefield convinced that 'the Jerries' were

> The people with a congenital passion for playing at soldiers, who've touched off Europe twice within most of our lifetimes, and have just done their best to wipe out London and Coventry; who goosestep, applaud the Fuhrer's tirades in the Sportsplast with rapturous mass hysteria, chant the Horst Wessel song with self-conscious fervour, and obviously believe their cause as just as we do ours.[26]

One object of military training was to defuse powerful taboos against killing fellow human beings. Troops in training were taught that their function was not to use their weapons in self-defence, but to close with the enemy and kill them. 'The bull's eye and the bayonet sack must be represented as German soldiers, who will kill unless they are first killed'.[27] It was envisaged that this process would take place at very short ranges, for infantrymen were taught that rifle fire would seldom be accurate against individual enemy soldiers at ranges over 300 yards.[28] During bayonet training, troops were positively encouraged to be callous. According to an *Army Training Memorandum* issued in August 1940

The main object of [bayonet training] is to work upon the feelings of the squad by stories of German unfair methods and so get their blood up, and to inculcate real enthusiasm, fighting spirit and lust for the offensive.

What is aimed at in the instruction is 'blood, hate, fire and brimstone'. It is 'guts and gristle' instruction, with nothing peacetime or 'pansy' about it.[29]

I

However, the only brief systematic attempt to inculcate a hatred of the Germans was carried out in early 1942 at the GHQ Battle School, which had been established in December 1941. However, 'hate training' was soon abandoned when a psychiatrist attached to the school insisted that it would actually increase the rate of breakdowns amongst the troops.[30] One officer who subsequently led a platoon in action opined that

This artificial attempt to inculcate a fighting spirit, to imbue the soldier with an eagerness to get at the enemy and tear him to pieces, was a nonsense. A pugnacious disposition, natural or cultivated, was very little help in action, as anyone who came within a mile of an angry German or Japanese soon discovered. For the spirit of human aggression has a magical tendency to evaporate as soon as the shooting starts, and a man then responds to two influences only—the external discipline that binds him and the self-respect within him that drives him on.[31]

Some soldiers did internalize the ideas of government propagandists. In 1940, Denis Healey was trained by a captain who repeated the government's propaganda line, telling his men 'If you meet a German parachutist, don't offer him a cigarette. Kick him in the balls. Treat him as dirty as you know. Never forget, he's a Hun. The Hun knows no law. Shoot as many as you can . . . .'.[32] Men like that never forgot the political issues at stake in the war. John Hillier, an Anzio veteran, reflected in 1995 that nearly 3,000 of his comrades in 5th Division had died 'so we could live in Peace, with the freedom from fear, freedom of religion, freedom from want'.[33] In early 1944, Stephen Dyson and some friends visited a pub in the village of Chilam in Kent.

Somehow the warmth of the fire, the cosiness of the pub and the friendliness of the locals made our visit worthwhile. We sat there, drinking and chatting away on all sorts of topics, with some agreeing, some disagreeing. The scenario embodied the living proof of the freedoms we took for granted, and which the country was fighting to retain. The freedom of speech. The freedom to go anywhere, at any time. The freedom to choose our own way of life. The freedoms bestowed by democracy.[34]

But even he admitted that in June 1944 the dominant feeling in his unit was 'We felt it was a job that had to be done, and the sooner we got cracking the better'.[35]

The ideas that front-line soldiers took into battle were rarely more than a distant echo of the official propagandists. The historian of 3rd Division, one of the spearhead formations that landed in Normandy on D-Day and who had himself served in the division, believed that

> . . . The division was not fighting for some ideal, some hare-brained theory of racial supremacy, such as can inspire German divisions. The British are better at practice than theory, and the division fought well for no better reason than that the Germans had finally to be defeated at their own game of war: the alternative was to acknowledge them masters of Europe, if not of the world.[36]

For most men during battle, and in the intervals between battles, abstract notions of justice and democracy faded from the front of their minds. J. H. Finch went to France before Dunkirk believing that he was part of a crusade against Hitler. The evacuation from Dunkirk convinced him that victory would require more than courage and confidence in his cause; it also needed 'a harder, more professional outlook . . .'.[37] Landing in Normandy on 7 June 1944, Stan Whitehouse saw his first corpse. 'Stark reality hit me like a cold douche. So far I had regarded the cross-Channel invasion as a noble crusade, a grand adventure to recount later to my mates back home over a pint . . .'. Now his thoughts turned to how he would react when he was told 'to shoot a fellow human being'.[38] Most soldiers retained a generalized conviction in the righteousness of their cause and, as long as they did so, it helped to sustain their morale. But in March 1943, Neil McCallum believed that, 'It would be hard to find an infantryman who could define democracy', and that, 'It does not take long to learn that the causes we once held as valid reasons for fighting do not hold in front of the gun lines'.[39] Postal censorship reports collected in 1943–4 suggested that only a very small proportion of soldiers were concerned with the minutiae of postwar reconstruction but that there was an 'almost universal interest in the conditions of life by which that victory will be followed. The ordinary soldier is not pre-occupied with political theories, but he is intensely interested in "post-war planning" insofar as it affects his home, his job, and the prospects of his family'.[40] Some officers instinctively recognized the significance of this. On the eve of El Alamein a company commander in the 2nd Rifle Brigade motivated his men by reminding them that the sooner they won the battle the sooner they could return to their homes and families.[41]

In the front line concrete concerns took the place of abstract ideologies. Philip Fielden, a subaltern in an armoured car regiment in North Africa in July 1941, reminisced that when his squadron came out of the line 'he found it difficult to remember what was the background of the War at that time, and I don't think that any of us were very interested in it'.[42] The crucial questions for Fielden and his comrades were not the grand purposes for which the war was being fought, but the more mundane goals of how to secure a better armoured car or improved rations. Two years later, when W. A. Elliott joined the 2nd Scots Guards in North Africa, he was struck by the way in which officers of the battalion who had fought in the desert regarded the war as a species of sport.

Still fairly fresh from a Britain where we regarded each bomb dropped as an outrage and the Nazi aggressors as the slayers of innocent women and children, I still retained my civilian belief that we were engaged in a life and death struggle for democracy and the freedom of the world. Yet, here I found this struggle treated more as an incident in regimental history against a reasonably sporting opponent.

And so, day by day, this jocular but professional attitude to fighting (for they thought little of the war in general) had to be accepted as one sat in the officers' mess tent in the evenings . . . The talk of these fighting men had little to do with war aims or what we were supposed to be fighting for. Nor did it seem to pay particular attention to our 'glorious dead'.[43]

Religious faith helped to sustain some men. Douglas Walters had been a member of the Oxford Group before he was conscripted in 1940. After basic training he was posted as a driver to No. 1 Ambulance Car Company at Bradford where he realized that

I was completely dispossessed of all I had, in one sense.

Then the realisation came, not that I was without anything, but that everything, all England, the whole world was mine. I was responsible, and I was able to feel that I was fighting for them morally and spiritually, as well as physically.[44]

Only a few found in religion a motivating force to make them fight. Troops about to go into action were usually willing to attend a drumhead service and padres often chose hymns like 'Onward Christian Soldiers' and 'Fight the Good Fight' which sustained morale.[45] Some men brought their faith with them into the Army, like Joe Thomas, who joined the 4th Somerset Light Infantry in September 1944 and was 'Deeply religious with an open and simple faith, he said his prayers every night'.[46] But, as the senior chaplain of the 1st Division at Anzio reported in April 1944, there was no sign in the Army of a mass religious revival. There was no evidence of antagonism to Christianity, but there was a good deal of apathy and ignorance and 'Christianity is regarded much more as a source of comfort, rather than a way of life'.[47]

II

Senior officers recognized that they had constantly to reinforce the message that their troops had to kill their enemies. In September 1942 when X Corps was training for El Alamein, its commander, Lieutenant-General Herbert Lumsden, issued a training instruction that began with the injunction 'This war cannot end in our favour until we have killed sufficient Germans'.[48] However, because few soldiers actually fought in the teeth arms in the front line, only a comparatively small number of men were actually required to kill an enemy face to face. Front-line infantrymen on both sides were trained to practise concealment and many small unit actions took place in the dark when men shot at shadows and sounds.[49] Ambushed at night in southern Holland in October 1944 by a German patrol he could hear but not see, Stan Whitehouse reacted in blind self-defence. '. . . I felt I was about to be killed and there was nothing I could do about it. To combat my "bomb-happiness" I stood up and hosed another magazine down the road, this time finding relief by shouting "Come on you bastards, come on"'.[50] The reaction of those who did have the opportunity to fire at a visible enemy was varied. Sydney Jary, a platoon commander in north-west Europe in 1944–5 'had little stomach for sniping. More often than not, it was a cold and calculated way of killing which achieved no military advantage'.[51] However, others, like Private Tom Barker, a regular soldier who fought as a sniper with the Argyll and Sutherland Highlanders on Crete in April 1941, took a quiet professional pride in their skill.[52] Troops in combat rarely crossed bayonets, probably because the mere threat of hand-to-hand combat was sufficient to make one side or the other flee.[53] The attitude of a private in the London Scottish was typical of most soldiers contemplating the possibility that they might have to get to grips quite literally with an enemy. 'If I had a bloody bullet in my rifle there wouldn't be any bloody bayonet fighting. I'd fire the bugger before I got near enough to use the bayonet'.[54]

Most soldiers found it impossible to maintain a sustained hatred of the enemy.[55] The war was too large, impersonal, and prolonged to allow them to do so. Hatred of the enemy was an uncommon, but not unknown, emotion amongst front-line soldiers and front-line experience sometimes reinforced the propaganda picture of the German soldier. But in many more instances, the image of the enemy as an inhuman brute rarely survived first contact with him, especially if he was a prisoner. Norman Craig thought that the Afrika Corps prisoners he saw at El Alamein 'looked very different from the newspaper photographs of the victorious German Army in France'.[56] Similarly, Peter Cochrane soon discovered 'how formidable an enemy good Italian troops could be'.[57] A feeling of grudging respect was much more common. At Cassino in the Spring of 1944, J. M. Harvey Lee thought that the German paratroopers defending the Monastery were, 'the bravest and the best soldiers in the world . . .'.[58] As the war proceeded Robert Holding found that 'I, like many other infantrymen, felt closer to, and more in sympathy with our enemy counterparts than with our own politicians and so-called statesmen'.[59]

However, if many soldiers still had difficulty ignoring the taboo against killing in cold blood, they had less difficulty in doing so when they acted in hot blood. Revenge could be a powerful, albeit brief, force, impelling men to kill. In November 1941, R. L. Crimp met a sergeant just after the Battle of Sidi Rezegh who 'mentioning a pal of his, added bitterly: "Poor old Smudger got his lot. But I made sure of the sod that did him. Filled his guts with this bren, close range, the bastard"'.[60] Self-preservation was an equally powerful force impelling men to kill. During the Battle of Keren in 1941, an Italian machine-gunner pinned down Peter Cochrane's platoon. 'I was in a berserk state of rage at the machine-gunner he had frightened me so badly, and he was the first man I killed in the hand to hand scramble as we jumped over the breastwork'.[61] Cochrane seems to have felt no strong sense of remorse ('I was neither pleased nor ashamed at having killed a number of men, merely thankful that I had done so before they killed us'.[62]). Not so a corporal in the 1st Black Watch in late 1944 who shot an armed German soldier running directly at him. He examined the corpse and, finding a wallet of family photographs, broke down. He 'cursed at the system that had made him kill this family man . . .'.[63] Most front-line soldiers, therefore, seem to have regarded their enemies without sustained rancour and were often reluctant to kill them unless circumstances forced them to do so.

III

At the same time as soldiers were taught to kill, they were also taught that in certain circumstances they must exercise restraint.[64] A mixture of customary international law, the Hague Convention of 1864, and the Geneva Convention of 1929 governed the treatment of prisoners of war. They forbade various kinds of behaviour, including the killing or wounding of an enemy after his surrender had been accepted, ordering that no quarter be given, and the seizure or destruction of enemy property unless justified by the necessities of war. Prisoners were to be humanely treated, allowed to retain their personal property except arms, military equipment, and military documents, and given a receipt by an officer for any money taken from them. Prisoners were to receive the same rations, clothing, housing, and medical treatment as the troops who had captured them.[65] In addition, prisoners were also valued because they represented hostages for the good treatment of British prisoners in enemy hands and because they were a valuable source of intelligence.[66]

These agreements formed the basis of the British Army's standing orders for the treatment of POWs which were incorporated into its *Field Service Regulations*. Troops were instructed that as soon as prisoners had been captured they were to be disarmed, searched for any documents of military value, segregated by rank, and subjected to a brief preliminary interrogation to discover information of immediate tactical value while they were still suffering from the shock of being captured.[67] Orders for the disposal of POWs formed part of the administrative instructions issued before every battle. Their guiding principle was that fighting units were relieved of responsibility for the care of POWs at the earliest possible opportunity and that their evacuation from the front line must entail the smallest possible abstraction of strength from fighting units. Each division was expected to establish a divisional collecting post and units were ordered to send their prisoners to it as quickly as possible. Prisoners were to be treated firmly and warned that they would be shot if they tried to escape, but fairly and humanely. Troops were told to respect their private property 'with the same scrupulous care as is shown in dealing with those of our own casualties' and 'for reasons of humanity' arrangements were also made to issue prisoners with food and drink at divisional collecting posts.[68]

Senior commanders in the field usually tried to carry out the letter and the spirit of these instructions. Before departing for North Africa, Lieutenant-General Sir Kenneth Anderson, GOC 1st Army, issued elaborate standing orders which precisely repeated official strictures about the way in which POWs should be treated.[69] Before D-Day Lieutenant-Colonel J. N. Cheney, the Deputy Provost Marshal on the lines of communication of 21 Army Group, took pains to brief his subordinates about the correct treatment of POWs.[70] The medical standing orders of 49th Division insisted that wounded POWs 'will be treated in exactly the same way as our own wounded'[71] and battalion standing orders in the Division reflected official policy.[72] When British formations failed to meet their full obligations under international law it was usually due to inadequate planning or preparation, rather than deliberate malice. In December 1940, for example, 7th Armoured Division found that its arrangements to transfer Italian prisoners down their normal lines of communication quickly collapsed under the sheer weight of numbers and they had to use captured Italian lorries and drivers.[73] Some lessons were learnt from this and, in the expectation of taking over 170,000 POWs, towards the end of the Tunisian campaign 1st Army issued special orders to units to make preparations for the reception, feeding, and evacuation of large numbers of prisoners. Even so, the temporary cages which formations established just before the final Axis surrender were quickly swamped by the colossal numbers of men who were marched into them.[74]

However, there were some instances where senior officers did act in contravention of international law. In June 1942 4th Armoured Brigade, then operating in North Africa, issued an order that prisoners were not to be given any food or water until after they had been interrogated. A couple of months later the Germans captured an order issued to troops landing at Dieppe that German prisoners were to be bound to prevent them from escaping. The standing orders of the 1st Royal Irish Fusiliers in Tunisia in early 1943 stated that prisoners were not to be given food or water.[75] Neil McCallum remembered that in April 1943, when an Italian anti-tank gun had blown up one of his carriers and the gun crew had then promptly surrendered to the next carrier, his CO ordered that henceforth the battalion should not take any more Italian prisoners.[76] All of these orders were in contravention of the 1929 Geneva Convention.[77]

But brutal treatment of prisoners was more commonly a result of the chaos inherent in fighting which made it difficult for soldiers suddenly to switch from practising lethal aggression one moment to exhibiting humane restraint the next. As one company commander remarked after the end of the North African campaign,

> It is difficult to know what to do when Germans give themselves up during an attack. You'd sometimes find that half would go on firing and half would make signs of surrendering. You want to watch out that the ones who put up their hands and surrender don't pick up their rifles and fire at your back when you've gone past them.[78]

Some enemy soldiers were more likely to be taken prisoners than others. German or Italian soldiers who fired at their assailants until they were only a few yards away and then threw up their hands were unlikely to be shown any quarter. In March 1943, Peter Ross met a wounded New Zealand officer in North Africa who told him that

> The Ities were holding a pass with machine-guns. They killed my sergeant and three men, and wounded me and several others. When we got near they got windy and put their hands up. We went in and finished the job off with grenades.

No Prisoners?

Not bloody likely! They kill you from a safe position and when it get too hot they give themselves up. Too bloody easy.[79]

There were many instances of British soldiers being shot as they went forward to accept the surrender of enemy troops. Such episodes occurred either because of deliberate treachery, a misunderstanding, or because while part of an enemy force wanted to surrender, some of their comrades were determined to continue fighting.[80] When soldiers were fired upon as they tried to accept the surrender of enemy personnel, their habitual reaction was to retaliate in kind. On 30 July 1944 Lieutenant James Marshal-Cornwall (4th Grenadier Guards) was killed by a member of a party of Germans who were coming forward to surrender and, as his squadron commander laconically recorded 'This party was therefore liquidated.'[81] Even soldiers who had their surrender accepted were not necessarily immediately safe. An officer with 11th Armoured Division in Normandy noted that unless parties of German prisoners were escorted to the rear by British soldiers there was a risk 'of them falling foul of our follow up forces'.[82]

Some formations in north-west Europe, like the 51st Highland Division, developed a reputation for being reluctant to take prisoners. The origins of their attitude may have been rooted in an incident that took place on 11 June 1944, when a group of men from the 5th Black Watch were captured by the Germans and all but one were shot out of hand.[83] It seems to have persisted throughout the north-west European campaign. In February 1945 Stephen Dyson's tank battalion operated in support of a Black Watch battalion attacking a German position in the Reichswald forest. After the tanks had shelled the German defences the infantry attacked, losing their company commander, and Dyson was surprised at how few prisoners were taken. 'Were some of the Jocks overstepping the mark in their desire for retribution?'[84]

Enemy soldiers who offered little or no resistance had, on the other hand, a good chance of their surrender being accepted. Landing in Normandy on D-Day, Lieutenant E. Jones's platoon occupied a boarding house on the seafront only to discover a cellar full of German soldiers stunned by the barrage. They presented Jones with a dilemma because he had received no orders about how to deal with prisoners at such an early stage in the landing. He therefore adopted the common-sense solution of disarming them and locking them in the cellar.[85]

Martin Lindsay believed that most of his soldiers 'refer to the Germans half-affectionately as Jerry and are only too ready to give them a cup of tea as soon as they surrender'.[86] The military authorities frowned upon this kind of fraternization between front-line soldiers, concerned that it would make prisoners less willing to talk when they were formally interrogated. In February 1943, XI Corps in North Africa issued an order forbidding guards to give prisoners cigarettes or food promiscuously.[87] Nevertheless, these strictures could rarely undermine the deep fellow feeling, based upon common experiences and common suffering, which bound together the infantry of both sides and which helped to promote the humane treatment of prisoners. During fighting around Arnhem in September 1944, R. M. Wingfield's platoon took a group of German infantry prisoner and gave them food and cigarettes because, 'These blokes had been going through it just like us, only they'd had our Artillery thrown in as well. We knew what that meant. We'd had some. Regardless of race or uniform, we "flatties" were a people apart from, and superior to, other human beings. These Germans were men like us and they'd had a hell of a time since D-Day, shelled all day and denied sleep at night because they were retreating and being harried by the Allied Air Force'.[88] Unofficial truces to succour the wounded, like the one which took place near the village of Vassy-La Caverie on 7 August 1944, were not unknown. Major L. L. E. Morton of the 2nd Argyll and Sutherland Highlanders advanced alone carrying a Red Cross flag and arranged a thirty-minute truce with a German captain while each side evacuated its wounded.[89]

This fellow feeling was, however, not universal. Richard Eke's sapper platoon, angered by the way in which a group of German prisoners marched passed them whistling, threw lumps of mud at them in Italy in October 1944.[90] Nor was it extended very often to SS prisoners. The War Diarist of the 11th Royal Scots Fusiliers noted laconically that when two prisoners from the 2nd SS Division captured in July 1944 'Reported that they had not fed for five days—this report did not melt the heart of any Jock to the extent of sharing his rations'.[91] British troops did generally afford harsher treatment to SS prisoners than to other kinds of German or Italian POWs. In a letter written in September 1944, A. W. McLennan described them as 'loathsome savage creatures at the best of times . . . .'.[92] According to Stan Whitehouse the survivors of a battalion of the Tyneside Scottish who had encountered SS troops in Normandy and sustained very heavy casualties exhibited a 'hatred of the enemy [which] was more pronounced, more bitter than anything I had known'.[93] The probable cause of this rancour was the persistent belief that the SS were prone to kill their own prisoners. The first documented instance of this in connection with British prisoners occurred in May 1940 when soldiers of the SS Totenkopf Division murdered 100 British prisoners on the road to Dunkirk.[94] British troops encountered few if any SS soldiers again until they landed in France in June 1944 but soon the SS began to live down to their reputation. The military author-ities in Normandy were so worried that British troops might take reprisals against German prisoners that they deliberately censored reports of SS atrocities. In July, Charles Peake, the Foreign Office's political officer at Supreme Headquarters Allied Expeditionary Force (SHAEF), did his utmost to suppress newspaper reports of the shooting of thirteen Canadian prisoners by troops of the 12th SS Panzer Grenadier Division. He was afraid that if the news became widespread, the British would take reprisals against their own prisoners for 'when troops get really stirred up they are apt to go beyond the limits of the Geneva Convention, and it becomes difficult to restrict them to what is permitted by international law'.[95] Peake prob-ably had cause to be concerned. In August the men of 1/6th Queens were particularly reluctant to take SS prisoners following an incident in the French town of Livarot during which men from the SS 'Langemarck' Division were discovered shooting British wounded.[96]

The one aspect of the way in which the British treated their prisoners where they did regularly, if not systematically, depart from international law, concerned robbery. Many, but not all front-line soldiers, were willing to rob prisoners of their small valuables immediately after they had been captured. It is unlikely that their captors were motivated by the desire for personal gain, for the trinkets they appropriated—watches, rings, and fountain pens—were of such little worth that they hardly offered adequate compensation for the dangers and hardships they had undergone to acquire them. As disciplined soldiers, the Army required them to switch from behaving with the utmost aggression one moment to protecting and shepherding their captives from the scene of danger the next. Robbing prisoners provided them with an avenue to vent their frustration and displace the aggression that they had built up during combat and at the same time to maintain their combat discipline. Troops who stole from their captives justified their behaviour by saying that 'They're Hitler's mates, so what'.[97] Some men, however, retained moral scruples about such behaviour and either refused to take part in it, felt ashamed that they had done so, or in a few instances, returned property which had been stolen by their comrades.[98] Nevertheless, even those men who hesitated to rob ordinary Wehrmacht soldiers were happy to rob SS prisoners.[99]

Regimental officers often displayed a distinctly laissez-faire attitude towards robbing prisoners. Following the fall of le Havre in September 1944 the second-in-command of the 1st Gordons lined up a group of POWs in front of his men and said 'There you are, the Master Race. Help yourselves'.[100] He justified theft from German soldiers and, later in the war, looting from German civilians, on the grounds that the Germans had themselves plundered most of Europe and were only receiving a taste of their own medicine.[101] Other officers took a more stringent view. In July 1944 a company sergeant-major, two sergeants, six corporals, and two privates of 601 Company CMP were charged with stealing property worth £164.00 from prisoners they were guarding.[102]

IV

The proper attitude of soldiers to civilian property was carefully defined by British military law. It was an offence under the Army Act for any soldier, acting without orders, to wilfully damage or destroy private property on active service, to leave his unit to go in search of plunder, to break into a house in search of plunder, or to commit any offence against the person or property of any civilian. Men found guilty of any of these offences were liable to imprisonment if they were other ranks or cashiering if they were officers.[103] These strictures were transmitted to troops during their training. On the eve of D-Day, an infantry training conference held at the School of Infantry laid down the policy that every unit was expected to follow, namely that

> PROPERTY This unit does not loot. It does not admire it in other units and will not enter into competition.
> Watch officers—often the worst offenders. If petty pilfering etc, once starts wholesale looting will follow.[104]

In Tunisia, the Military Police erected signs warning looters that if they broke into abandoned houses and stole property they were liable to be sentenced to two years in prison.[105] However, in an emergency, and even when no officer was present, British military law also sanctioned requisitioning, i.e. the seizure of civilian goods by troops in return for a receipt that could be redeemed at a later date.[106] This provided a thin veil of legality for what was in reality looting. Periodically, senior officers in London and elsewhere were driven to issue strictures to commanders in the field about it.[107] At the beginning of August 1944 the Foreign Secretary, Sir Anthony Eden, having heard stories of British troops looting in Normandy and concerned that they might harm Anglo-French relations, asked Brooke to act. Montgomery's response, that with 1.5 million men in Normandy and a plethora of destroyed houses and villages 'it may well happen that cases of looting do occur', betrayed the attitude of most field commanders.[108] While the fighting was continuing they had far more important concerns to occupy them:

> During periods of active fighting the orders and regulations regarding looting are liable to be interpreted somewhat loosely, and in a very flexible manner, a good deal is overlooked, and it is only the obvious and flagrant cases that come to notice and are the subject of disciplinary action.[109]

Many of his senior subordinates shared his 'flexible' interpretation of what constituted looting. In April 1945, Sir Miles Dempsey, GOC 2nd Army, ignored evidence that the troops guarding his tactical HQ had been keeping looted chickens.[110] Horrocks told a funny story about an indignant German field cashier who had been robbed by a British soldier. When he was captured the field cashier 'complained very indignantly and said that the man in question could be identified as he held a signed receipt. He produced a grubby bit of paper on which was written: "This bastard had 11,000 Guilders. He hasn't got it now"'.[111] When the camp commandant of Montgomery's tactical HQ in Normandy accused some of the Field Marshall's personal staff of stealing a pig, Montgomery's Chief of Staff tried to persuade him that, compared with the widespread destruction occasioned by the war, the looting of one small pig was utterly insignificant.[112] It was only after the fighting stopped that Montgomery began to enforce a stricter policy. On 6 May 1945 he told his army commanders that henceforth all looting, whether by individuals or units, was strictly forbidden.[113]

In view of the lenient attitude of senior officers towards looting and their willingness to condone it provided it did not, in their opinion, threaten to get out of hand, it is hardly surprising that it took place on a large scale. The defeat of the Italian 10th Army in the Winter of 1940–1 by O'Connor's Western Desert Force gave its members considerable scope for looting and many of them took full advantage of it. An officer sent to Sidi Barani to recover captured Italian equipment reported that 'troops were showing definite signs of becoming "loot-minded" in their search for souvenirs'.[114] Within days of the fall of Sicily in August 1943 reports were reaching Alexander's HQ of widespread looting by British troops on the island.[115] When Bayeux fell to the 2nd Army in June 1944, the inhabitants soon began to complain of looting by the troops. However, the resources of the Corps of Military Police (CMP) were so stretched dealing with more important offences, that they paid comparatively little attention to looting. In Normandy in July 1944, for example, the CMP on the lines of communication investigated 327 cases of men who had gone AWOL but only two cases of looting.[116]

Soldiers did not loot indiscriminately. They developed an unwritten code concerning what it was and was not proper to loot and from whom it was proper to take it. In Italy the 2nd Rifle Brigade took freely from the well-to-do, assuming that they were fascist sympathizers, but they usually forbore from looting from the poor peasants on whom they were billeted, seeing them as much victims of fascism as they felt themselves to be.[117] Goods looted fell into several categories. They might take the form of souvenirs, or luxury goods such as mink coats or jewellery, which troops wanted as presents for their families, or goods for their own consumption, particularly food and alcohol.[118] In allied countries in areas of active operations empty houses and farms were fair game, but stealing from friendly allies was deprecated, although it sometimes happened.[119]

V

Most front-line soldiers in the British Army were reluctant killers. They usually treated their prisoners broadly in accordance with the international agreements that their government had signed. The only instances in which these agreements were commonly violated concerned the theft of private property from prisoners. Similarly, under some circumstances they were also ready to steal private property from civilians. But many soldiers also disobeyed their commanders' orders and fraternized with prisoners to the extent of sharing tea and cigarettes with them.

There are several reasons for this. Its senior field officers, who were, almost without exception, regular soldiers, set the tone of the Army. Many of them approached the war in a spirit of detached professionalism. Sir Brian Horrocks, who commanded a corps in North Africa and north-west Europe, admitted that, until his troops reached Belsen in 1945, 'I had been fighting this war without any particular hatred for the enemy . . . '.[120] Like Major-General David Belchem, another of Montgomery's senior protégés, Horrocks retained a considerable admiration for the professionalism of the German Army (although not the SS).[121] Senior officers encouraged their men to treat prisoners humanely because many of them regarded their enemies as fellow professionals whom it was not proper to hate. If harsh treatment was meted out to enemy prisoners, it would rebound on to the heads of British prisoners in their hands.[122]

More fundamentally, the British Army found it difficult to persuade its troops to kill in the cause of 'democracy, tolerance and kindliness'. Recruits brought with them into the Army attitudes that they had learned as civilians. They were the products of a civic culture that deprecated public violence. They were largely apolitical and they identified more strongly with their families and their homes than with any public institution or ideology.[123] Unlike their German counterparts, they were not subject to a brutal disciplinary regime that left them liable to be executed if they refused to fight. They therefore had less need to vent their own pent-up aggression on those weaker than themselves. The aim of most British soldiers engaged in front-line fighting was to defeat, not to exterminate, their enemies and then to return home to their families as soon as possible. Paradoxically, this could be a useful weapon in undermining German resistance. In March 1943, General von Arnim, GOC 5th Panzer Army in Tunisia, issued an order that troops spreading rumours about the fair way in which the British treated their prisoners would be punished.[124] In the opinion of one German regimental commander, 'As a prisoner the Englishman is arrogant, proud, cautious and is absolutely secure. When himself a prisoner he counts upon German justice and correctness, and usually behaves towards his own prisoners in a correct and fair manner. Experience to the contrary should perhaps be considered exceptions'.[125]

Acknowledgements

I am most grateful to the Trustees of the Imperial War Museum and the Liddell Hart Centre for Military Archives, King's College London, for allowing me access to manuscripts in their keeping and for permission to quote from them.

Notes

1   N. McCallum, *Journey with a Pistol* (London, 1959), 105.

2   Public Record Office [henceforth PRO], WO 277/19. Brigadier B. Ungerson, *Personnel Selection* (War Office, 1953),48; PRO WO 32/11519. DMT to all GOC-in-Cs Home Commands and C-in-C Home Forces, 22 April 1942.

3   Liddell Hart Centre for Military Archives [henceforth LHCMA], Alanbrooke mss 14/61/9. Montgomery to Alanbrooke, 27 November 1942.

4   S. G. Fritz, *Frontsoldaten. The German Soldier in World War Two* (Lexington, KY, 1995); S. G. Fritz, '"We are trying to change the face of the world"—ideology and motivation in the Wehrmacht on the Eastern Front: the view from below', *Journal of Military History*, 60 (1996), 683–710; O. Bartov, *Hitler's Army: Soldiers, Nazis and War in the Third Reich* (Oxford, 1991); O. Bartov, 'Daily life and motivation in war: the Wehrmacht in the Soviet Union', *Journal of Strategic Studies*, 12 (1989), 200–14; E. Shils and M. Janowitz, 'Cohesion and disintegration in the Wehrmacht', *Public Opinion Quarterly*, 12 (1948), 280–315; J. Förster, 'Motivation and indoctrination in the Wehrmacht', in P. Addison and A. Calder (eds), *Time to Kill: The Soldiers' Experience of War in the West, 1939–45* (London, 1997), 263–73; T. J. Schulte, 'The German soldier in occupied Russia', in Addison and Calder (eds), *Time to Kill*, 275–83; A. Steim, 'International law and Soviet prisoners of war', in B. Wegner (ed.), *From Peace to War. Germany, Soviet Russia and the World, 1939–41* (Providence, RI, 1997), 293–308. There are some excellent studies of the ideologies of British soldiers but they have focused on the Army at home and tell us comparatively little about what British soldiers thought they were fighting for when they were actually under fire. See S. P. Mackenzie, *Politics and Military Morale. Current Affairs and Citizenship Education in the British Army 1914–1950* (Oxford, 1992); J. A. Crang, 'Politics on parade. Army education and the 1945 general election', *History*, 81–262 (1997), 215–27; J. A. Crang, 'The British soldier on the Home Front: Army Morale Reports, 1940–45', in P. Addison and A. Calder (eds), *Time to Kill*, 60–74.

5   General Staff, *Army Training Memorandum No. 31* (War Office, 1940).

6   PRO WO 163/52/AC/G(43)10. War Office Committee on Morale in the Army Fourth Quarterly Report, November 1942-January 1943, 7 April 1943.

7   D. Morgan and M. Evans, *The Battle for Britain. Citizenship and Ideology in the Second World War* (London, 1993), 5, 18–23; I. McLaine, *Ministry of Morale. Home Front Morale and the Ministry of Information in World War II* (London, 1979), 150–2.

8   R. Weight, 'State, intelligentsia and the promotion of national culture in Britain, 1939–45', *Historical Research*, 69 (1996), 85.

9   A. Osley, *Persuading the People. Government Publicity in the Second World War* (London, 1995), 19–22.

10   J. Hillier, *The Long Road to Victory. War Diary of an Infantry Despatch Rider 1940–46* (Trowbridge, Wilts, 1995), 30.

11   McLaine, *Ministry of Morale*, 139–45.

12   P. Roach, *The 8.15 to War. The Memoirs of a Desert Rat* (London, 1982), 57.

13   G. H. Gallup (ed.), *The Gallup International Public Opinion Polls. Great Britain, 1937–1975* (New York, 1976), i, 53.

14   War Office, *The King's Regulations for the Army and the Army Reserve 1928* (War Office, 1928), 166.

15   D. Healey, *The Time of My Life* (London, 1990), 48.

16   PRO WO 216/61. Training of Officers. Report of a meeting called by the Secretary of State for War, on Wednesday 29th January 1941.

17   General Staff, *Army Training Memorandum No. 38* (War Office, 1941).

18   Mackenzie, *Politics and Military Morale*, 91–3.

19   S. Dyson, *Tank Twins. East End Brothers in Arms 1943–45* (London, 1994), 132.

20   General Sir C. Blacker, *Monkey Business. The Memoirs of General Sir Cyril Blacker* (London, 1993), 60.

21   Imperial War Museum [henceforth IWM] 89/13/1. G. H. C. Abrams ts. Memoirs. 'A male nurse in war and peace'; R. McKibbin, *Classes and Culture. England 1918–1951* (Oxford, 1998), 131.

22   Roach, *The 8.15 to War*, 26–7.

23   Sims, *Arnhem Spearhead. A Private Soldier's Story* (London, 1978), 22.

24   R. Holmes, *Firing Line* (London, 1987), 361.

25   General Staff, *Army Training Memorandum No. 41* (War Office, 1941); Army Bureau of Current Affairs, *War. No. 29. The British Soldier* (War Office, 1942); Army Bureau of Current Affairs, *War. No. 50. Mediterranean Journey* (War Office, 1943).

26   R. L. Crimp, *The Diary of a Desert Rat* (London, 1971), 16.

27   General Staff, *Army Training Memorandum No. 35* (War Office, 1940).

28   General Staff, *Small Arms Training. Vol. 1. Pamphlet No. 3. Rifle 1942* (War Office, 1942), 25.

29   General Staff, *Army Training Memorandum No. 35* (War Office, 1940).

30   PRO WO 199/799. Maj. A. I. M. Wilson to Lt.-Col. C. V. Britten, n.d. but *c.* 5 May 1942.

31   N. Craig, *The Broken Plume. A Platoon Commander's Story 1940–45* (London, 1982), 31.

32   Healey, *Time of My Life*, 48.

33   Hillier, *The Long Road*, 148.

34   Dyson, *Tank Twins*, 14.

35   Ibid.

36   N. Scarfe, *Assault Division. A History of the 3rd Division from the Invasion of Normandy to the Surrender of Germany* (London, 1947), 18.

37   IWM 90/6/1. J. H. Finch mss, 'The wanderings of a transport officer. Before Dunkirk—1939–40'.

38   S. Whitehouse and G. B. Bennett, *Fear is the Foe. A Footslogger from Normandy to the Rhine* (London, 1995), 13–14.

39   McCallum, *Journey with a Pistol*, 95, 107.

40   PRO WO 163/53/AC/G(44)22. War Office Committee on Morale. Eighth Quarterly Report, November 1943–January 1944.

41 Crimp, *Diary*, 138.

42 P. Fielden, *Swings and Roundabouts* (privately published, 1991), 31.

43 W. A. Elliott, *Esprit de Corps. A Scots Guards Officer on Active Service 1943–45* (Norwich, 1966), 12.

44 D. Walters, *Some Soldier. Adventures in the Desert War* (Yeovil, 1989), 18.

45 Crimp, *Diary*, 102; Dyson, *Tank Twins*, 86.

46 S. Jary, *Eighteen Platoon* (Surrey, 1987), 34.

47 LHCMA. Penney mss 7/21. Chaplain R. H. Butler to Maj.-Gen. W. R. Penney, 29 April 1944.

48 PRO WO 201/537. X Corps Training Instruction No. 1, 11 September 1942.

49 For a vivid description of a brief night action see R. Trevelyan, *The Fortress. Anzio 1944* (London, 1956), 24.

50 Whitehouse and Bennett, *Fear is the Foe*, 98.

51 Jary, *Eighteen Platoon*, 60.

52 T. Barker, '2982252, 1st Battalion Argyll and Sutherland Highlanders' (World Wide Web accessed on 14 June 1998 at stead@iinet.net.au).

53 PRO WO 201/527. Extracts from the report of a War Office observer in North Africa, May 1943.

54 J. M. Harvey Lee, *D-Day Dodger* (London, 1979), 45.

55 McCallum, *Journey with a Pistol*, 105–6; IWM 82/37/1. Sergeant E. P. Danger mss, ts. memoirs, 'Diary of a Guardsman', vol. 1.

56 Craig, *Broken Plume*, 59.

57 P. Cochrane, *Charlie Company. In Service with C Company 2nd Queen's Own Cameron Highlanders 1940–44* (London, 1979).

58 Harvey Lee, *D-Day Dodger*.

59 R. Holding, *Since I Bore Arms* (Cirencester, Glos., 1987), 90.

60 Crimp, *Diary*, 46.

61 Cochrane, *Charlie Company*, 55.

62 Cochrane, *Charlie Company*, 65.

63 Whitehouse and Bennett, *Fear is the Foe*, 120.

64 Holmes, *Firing Line*, 366.

65 W. M. Reisman and C. T. Antoniou, *The Laws of War. A Comprehensive Collection of Primary Documents on International Laws Governing Armed Conflict* (New York, 1994), 47, 150–1.

66 S. P. Mackenzie, 'The treatment of POWs in World War Two', *Journal of Modern History*, 66 (1994), 490; General Staff, War Office, *Field Service Pocket Book. Pamphlet No. 3. Intelligence-Information and Security* (War Office, 1939), 19–20; General Staff, *Army Training Memorandum No. 44* (War Office, 1942).

67 General Staff, *Army Training Memorandum No. 42* (War Office, 1941).

68 General Staff, War Office, *Field Service Regulations. Vol. 1. Organisation and Adminis-tration. 1930. Reprinted with Amendments (Numbers 1–11) 1939* (War Office, 1939), 209–212.

69 LHCMA, Brigadier E. J. Paton-Walsh mss 1/1/7. Lt.-Gen. K. A. Anderson, Standing Orders (Overseas) by Lt.-Gen. K. A. Anderson.

70 IWM. Brigadier J. N. Cheney mss 80/3/1. DMP's lecture, 13 May 1944.

71 PRO WO 177/399. Medical War Diary ADMS 49th Division, 28 May 1944.

72 PRO WO 171/1365. War Diary 11th Royal Scots Fusiliers. Battalion standing orders in the field, 10 May 1944.

73 M. Carver, *Out of Step. The Memoirs of Field Marshal Lord Carver* (London, 1989), 61, 67.

74 LHCMA. Brigadier E. J. Paton-Walsh mss 1/1/12. Brigadier A/Q, 1st Army, to Paton-Walsh, 11 April 1943; Paton-Walsh mss 1/1 /4. APM, 5th Corps, to Paton-Walsh, 24 May 1943.

75 PRO WO 32/10720. AFHQ to War Office, 28 February 1943.

76 McCallum, *Journey with a Pistol*, 113.

77 PRO WO 32/10720. Army Council to all GOC-in-C Home Commands, Middle East, India, 10 February 1943.

78 Army Bureau of Current Affairs, *War. No. 47. The Horse's Mouth* (War Office, 1943).

79 Peter Ross, *All Valiant Dust. An Irishman Abroad* (Dublin, 1992), 117.

80 See, for example, LHCMA. Sir Michael O'Moore Creagh mss. Points of general interest arising out of the operations December 9th to 15th 1940; M. Lindsay, *So Few Got Through* (London, 1946), 56.

81 LHCMA. Maj. Gen. G. L. Verney mss 1/1. Operation Bluecoat. Sunday July 30th. 6th Guards Tank Brigade. Narrative of events by Major C. M. F. Deakin, 4 Tanks Grenadier Guards.

82 PRO WO 232/21. Notes from Theatres of War. Normandy. Report by Captain L C. Coleman, AIF, 3 October 1944.

83 J. B. Salmond, *The History of the 51st Highland Division 1939–45* (Edinburgh, 1953), 141.

84 Dyson, *Tank Twins*, 139.

85 IWM. Lt.-Col. E. Jones mss 94/4/1. Ts. Memoirs.

86 Lindsay, *So Few Got Through*, 220.

87 PRO WO 32/10720. AFHQ to War Office, 28 February 1943.

88 R. M. Wingfield, *The Only Way Out. An Infantryman's Autobiography of the North-West Europe Campaign August 1944-February 1945* (London, 1955), 73.

89 PRO WO 171/1262. War Diary, 2nd Argyll and Sutherland Highlanders, 7 August 1944.

90 IWM 92/1/1. C. R. Eke mss, ts. memoirs, 'A Game of Soldiers'.

91 PRO WO 171/1365. War Diary, 11th Royal Scots Fusiliers, 1 July 1944.

92 A. W. McLennan, *Letters from a Soldier in Europe 1944 to 1946* (Gairloch Community Telecommunications Centre, 1992), 12.

93 Whitehouse and Bennett, *Fear is the Foe*, 88.

94 C. Sydnor, *Soldiers of Destruction. The SS Death's Head Division, 1933–45* (Princeton, NJ, 1977), 106–9.

95 PRO WO 32/10720. C. Peake to Sir A. Cadogan, 17 July 1944.

96 Wingfield, *The Only Way Out*, 31. It is worth noting that the divisional commander at the time, Maj.-Gen. C. L. Verney, gave a slightly different version of what happened in Livarot, insisting that just before the Queens had entered the town the Germans had shot six civilians. See Maj.-Gen. C. L. Verney, *The Desert Rats. The History of the 7th Armoured Division 1938 to 1945* (London, 1954), 225.

97 Hillier, *The Long Road*, 159.

98 Wingfield, *The Only Way Out*, 36; Dyson, *Tank Twins*, 49; IWM 85/6/1. P. G. Miners mss Miners to his mother, 14 September 1944.

99 Whitehouse and Bennett, *Fear is the Foe*, 58.

100 Lindsay, *So Few Got Through*, 84–5.

101 Lindsay, *So Few Got Through*, 85, 243.

102 IWM. Brigadier J. N. Cheney mss 80/3/1. Cheney to A Branch, HQ, Lines of Communication, 21 Army Group, 6 August 1944. Appendix. Monthly Report of 71 Special Investigation Section CMP for July 1944.

103   War Office, *Manual of Military Law 1929. Reprinted 1939* (London, 1943), 428–30.

104   PRO WO 204/1895. Infantry Training Conference No. 1. 20–24 April 1944.

105   IWM. Brigadier J. N. Cheney mss 80/3/1. DPM's lecture, 13 May 1944.

106   The Army's official attitude towards requisitioning was outlined in General Staff, *Field Service Regulations. Vol. 1. Organisation and Administration 1930. (Reprinted with Amendments 1–11) 1939* (War Office, 1939), 286–293.

107   PRO WO 214/62. Alexander to Montgomery, McCreery, and Robertson, 29 August 1943; Alexander to Leese, 17 September 1943.

108   LHCMA. Alanbrooke mss 14/29. Cadogan to Brooke, 4 August 1944; Montgomery to Brooke, 6 August 1944.

109   IWM. Viscount Montgomery mss BLM 121/50. Montgomery to Dempsey and Crerar, 6 May 1945.

110   Dyson, *Tank Twins*, 173.

111   Lindsay, *So Few Got Through*, 178–9.

112   Maj. Gen. E. de Guingand, *Generals At War* (London, 1964), 125–9.

113   Ibid.

114   PRO 201/352. Report on lessons of the operations in the Western Desert, December 1940, 31 December 1940.

115   PRO WO 214/62. Alexander to Montgomery, McCreery, and Robertson, 29 August 1943.

116   IWM. Brigadier J. N. Cheney mss 80/311. Cheney to A Branch, HQ Lines of Communication, 21 Army Group, 6 August 1944. Monthly charge sheet for July 1944; LHCMA (London, 1991). Col. F. Drake mss. Normandy 1944, from the angle of the Deputy Provost Marshal [n.d.].

117   Bowlby, *Recollections*, 209.

118   Dyson, *Tank Twins*, 162,179; Hillier, *The Long Road*, 159.

119   See, for example, the fate of the village of Lisogne in Belgium recounted in Lindsay, *So Few Got Through*, 163.

120   Sir B. Horrocks, *A Full Life* (London, 1960), 264.

121   Sir B. Horrocks, with E. Belfield and Maj.-Gen. H. Essame, *Corps Commander* (London, 1977), 234; Maj.-Gen. David Belchem, *All in a Day's March* (London, 1978), 210.

122   PRO WO 32/10720. Army Council to GOC-in-C Home Commands, Middle East and India, 10 February 1943.

123   McKibbin, *Classes*, passim.

124   IWM Maj.-Gen. R. Briggs mss 66/76/1. 1st British Armoured Division Intelligence Summary No. 112, 8 May 1943.

125   Australian War Memorial 3 DRL/6643/1/2Bii. Part 2. Appendix B to GSI, GHQ. Daily Intelligence Summary No 612, 22 January 1942. Report of 25 August, 1941. 104th Lorried Infantry Regiment (21st Panzer Division) in reply to Divisional Questionnaire. (I am grateful to Professor John Ferris for bringing this document to my attention.)

Chapter 8

Edward B. Westermann

"ORDINARY MEN" OR "IDEOLOGICAL SOLDIERS"?
Police Battalion 310 in Russia, 1942

> We police went by the phrase, "Whatever serves the state is right, what-ever harms the state is wrong." . . . it never ever entered my head that these orders could be wrong. Although I am aware that it is the duty of the police to protect the innocent I was however at that time convinced that the Jewish people were not innocent but guilty. I believed all the propaganda that Jews were criminals and subhuman. . . . The thought that one should oppose or evade the order to take part in the exter-mination of the Jews never entered my head either.[1]
>
> Policeman Kurt Möbius

THE ROLE AND IMPORTANCE of ideology in the Third Reich remains a central point of debate among contemporary historians. This debate achieved prominence in the late 1970s and 1980s with the increased emphasis on Holocaust research. Scholars studying the events and policies surrounding the destruction of European Jews and other "undesirable" groups sought to identify the well Spring of National Socialist racial policy. The macro-level ideological debate resulted in a division of academic positions denoted by the terms "intentionalism" and "functionalism/structuralism." The inherent difficulty in ascertaining the motivations of Adolf Hitler alone resulted in a heated and at times highly emotional debate. From the subtleties of this discourse emerged a graduated scale ranging from "strict intentionalists" to "moderate functionalists." The intentionalist and structuralist debate has receded from the frontlines of contemporary academic discourse; however, the issue of ideology continues to excite intense discussion as witnessed by the reaction to Daniel Goldhagen's provocative thesis in *Hitler's Willing Executioners*.[2]

By privileging ideology, the historian runs the risk of disregarding the diversity of individual motivations in an attempt to provide a universalized explanation. Metaphorically, the danger exists in focusing on the ideological forest at the expense of losing sight of the individual trees of human causation. Despite the risks associated with potential oversimplification, the historian cannot afford to ignore the role played by ideology when evaluating the actions of specific groups or individuals. Indeed, the motivation of the actors plays a crucial role in the historian's interpretation and evaluation of their actions. Recent historical research continues to uncover a litany of criminal actions and atrocities perpetrated by German civilians (medical personnel in the euthanasia program), public servants (police in Poland and Russia), and soldiers during the National Socialist dictatorship. What then was the role of racial ideology as a motivator for atrocity? This question does not lend itself to a facile answer at the macro-level of German society, despite Daniel Goldhagen's claim to contrary. In this respect, the actions of small groups appear to offer the most promising avenues for uncovering the expression of ideology among Germans during the period of the National Socialist dictatorship.

The use of micro-historical methodologies allows historians to examine the motives and actions of individuals, small groups, or organizations. Christopher Browning's study of a reserve police battalion and the actions of the unit's members in the mass murder of Polish Jews paints a convincing portrait of "ordinary men" largely motivated by mundane concerns for acceptance and conformity within a larger group.[3] Browning's detailed research and persuasive argumentation offer one possible interpretation concerning the actions of uniformed policemen. His "ordinary men" are not motivated by ideological hatred or fanatical adherence to National Socialism, but instead are guided by respect and deference to authority, concern for career advancement, and peer group pressure. The men in Browning's study, even more clearly than Adolf Eichmann, offer the perfect complement to Hannah Arendt's thesis on the "banality of evil." At the opposite end of this spectrum, Omer Bartov and Hannes Heer have catalyzed a heated discussion with their assertion that *Wehrmacht* forces on the Eastern Front embraced, or came to embrace, anti-Bolshevik/Slavic and anti-Semitic ideology before and during the Nazi war of annihilation in the East.[4] Wherein lies then the explanation for these seemingly contradictory models? Are these two models merely different sides of the same coin? Can they be reconciled with one another? Can the dichotomy between the two extremes be reduced to the general difference in the actions and motivations of overaged, civilian police reservists versus battle-hardened military professionals?

The actions of the members of Police Battalion 310 on the Eastern Front in the period between 1940 and 1943 provide an additional case study for evaluating the acceptance and support of National Socialist racial and ideological objectives at the small unit level. The repeated employment of the unit in military operations, anti-partisan actions, and acts of reprisal reflect the "success" of prewar efforts on the part of the Reich Leader of the SS and Chief of the German Police Heinrich Himmler and the Chief of the Uniformed Police Kurt Daluege to instill within the police "military discipline" and "unquestioning obedience."[5] In fact, a pronounced military influence existed throughout the entire history of the German police—a legacy that formed a crucial element in the systematic campaign by the National Socialist leadership to instill and strengthen a martial and ideological character within the uniformed police. The ultimate result of these efforts involved the evolution of the police from "protectors of the innocent"[6] to soldiers of the state, and, subsequently executioners.

I

The Weimar police ran the spectrum from a heavily armed *Landespolizei* (stationed in barracks), modeled along military lines and designed for employment in the event of large-scale civil disturbances to a *Gemeindepolizei* (community police) located in rural villages and responsible for finding lost cattle or children and enforcing work and noise restrictions on Sundays. The character of the average German precinct officer or *Schutzpolizist* balanced the extremes of the *Landespolizei* and the *Gemeindepolizei*. In many respects these men operated on a paternalistic model, rounding up married men from local bars on payday and escorting them home to their wives with their remaining money.[7] Weimar's "beat cops," especially those in large metropolitan areas such as Berlin, were, however, involved in an ever-increasing spiral of rightist and leftist political agitation.

In the final years of the Weimar Republic the police faced large-scale political demonstrations from the parties of the Left and the Right. These demonstrations often devolved into violent confrontations involving members from both groups as well as the police. Absent conclusive evidence, it still appears, however, that the police forces in Weimar displayed a preference for right-wing causes and movements versus those from the Left. George Browder, a historian of the Third Reich's Security Police apparatus, argues that "Anti-KPD [German Communist Party] indoctrination and physical confrontations with the KPD undermined police resistance to right-radical appeals." Browder continues, "Although lowered resistance would not necessarily make the police pro-Nazi, it enhanced NS [National Socialist] appeals for some."[8] The difficulty in gauging the resonance of the NSDAP within the police is compounded by the general prohibition on police membership in the party prior to the Summer of 1932. In fact, one estimate places the number of police in the NSDAP in early 1933 at a mere 700 uniformed policemen or 0.7 percent of the entire Reich police forces.[9] Ironically, it was Reich Chancellor Franz von Papen, and not Adolf Hitler, who created the precedent for the cooptation of the civil police apparatus in the pursuit of parochial political objectives.

On July 20, 1932, von Papen, under the pretext of the collapse of order in the federal state of Prussia, invoked a state of emergency under Article 48 of the Weimar constitution. Papen's justification for the intervention included the "failure" of the police to preserve law and order and the "lax" and "uncoordinated" leadership of the Prussian police.[10] The "Papen Putsch" resulted in the arrest and summary dismissal, of the Prussian Police President, Albert Grzesinski, his deputy, Dr. Bernhard Weiss, and the commander of the *Schutzpolizei*, Magnus Heimannsberg. All three were political appointees and decidedly opposed to the increasing political radicalism of the Right.[11] In the following two months, the Papen administration dismissed 94 of 588 Prussian political appointees including 22 Social Democratic

(SPD) Police Presidents and Police Directors.[12] Papen's action with respect to the Prussian police in many respects paved the way for subsequent actions during the National Socialist "seizure of power."[13] Indeed, Adolf Hitler and his party organization quickly grasped the potential of a system governed by fiat.

The appointment of Adolf Hitler as Reich Chancellor, on January 30, 1933, initiated the events leading to the National Socialist consolidation of power. In Prussia, Hermann Göring, Reich Minister without portfolio and Prussian Interior Minister, personally directed the "coordination" (*Gleichschaltung*) of Germany's largest police force. In a ministerial directive on February 28, 1933, Göring accelerated the process of coordination by privileging "National Socialist applicants . . . above all others for enlistment as police recruits in the Prussian Schutzpolizei."[14] He also "requested" that government offices responsible for the examination of police applications "make the most extensive use of the cooperation of National Socialist associations" including the *Gauleiter* and leaders of the SA, SS, and the *Stahlhelm*.[15]

The coordination of the Prussian police followed a dual strategy of subordinating the police executive to National Socialist political authority while replacing police officials deemed uncooperative or politically unreliable. Already on February 13, thirteen Prussian Police Presidents, including the two remaining SPD Police Presidents who had previously escaped dismissal during the Papen Putsch, were forced to retire.[16] In addition, 200 police officers or 7.3 percent of the Prussian police officer corps and 826 policemen from the ranks or 1.7 percent of the non-officer police corps were forced to retire.[17] Alone on March 25, SA and NSDAP leaders assumed the posts of Police President in Potsdam, Breslau, and Gladbach-Rheydt. In the following months, SS and SA leaders received appointments as Police Presidents in Koblenz, Kassel, Essen, and Erfurt.[18]

In March 1934, after negotiations with Göring, Heinrich Himmler received the post of Inspector of the Gestapo in Prussia while Kurt Daluege assumed command of all the Reich's uniformed police forces.[19] Daluege moved quickly in dictating the ideological direction within the uniformed police. On April 28, 1934, he issued a press release in which he stated that "veteran" and "proven" SS, SA, and *Stahlhelm* men would receive preference for entry into the entire Prussian police organization. Daluege described this measure "as a political necessity."[20] He further added "the politically schooled soldiers of the movement are the guarantors that the National Socialist ideology (*Ideenwelt*) will serve the general good of the Prussian police."[21]

In the National Socialist *Ideenwelt*, the police were charged with two primary tasks. First, the police "must execute the ideology of the state leadership and help create and maintain . . . order."[22] Second, the police "must safeguard the German people, as an 'organic, corporate entity.'"[23] In April 1937, Himmler published a circular that provided the guidelines for the "ideological training" (*weltanschauuliche Schulung*) of the police. The Race and Settlement Office received overall responsibility for the training. In addition, Himmler created the positions of training directors (*Schulungsleiter*) and special lecturers (*Schulungsredner*).[24] The selection standard stated the training directors "should have special training as teachers or lecturers, hold SS-leadership ranks [and] be especially competent in the areas of history and national politics."[25] The lecturers were to be drawn primarily from the ranks of the SS. Training included weekly meetings and a monthly propaganda lecture. The monthly propaganda lecture was the centerpiece of the indoctrination effort whose purpose was "the uniform political education of the whole Orpo in all basic ideological and political questions."[26] In June 1940, Himmler instituted "daily" indoctrination sessions (*Tagesschulung*) to be based on the examination of current events from the perspective of National Socialist ideology. The sessions were held at least three times during the week and lasted between fifteen and twenty minutes.[27] In addition to the indoctrination sessions, the publication of the biweekly *Political Information Service* (renamed the *Newsletter for the Ideological Training of the Uniformed Police* in May 1941) supplemented the classroom efforts. The purpose of this publication was to "instruct all members in especially important questions of [an] ideological, political, economic, and cultural nature."[28] The success of these initiatives is difficult to ascertain; however, they clearly indicate the value placed by Himmler and the uniformed police leadership on the ideological education of the police.

In conjunction with promoting ideological commitment, both Himmler and Daluege attempted to instill a "martial attitude" (*soldatisches Denken*) within the police during the prewar period.[29] The centralization of both the political and uniformed police under Himmler in June 1936 accelerated the process of the conversion of the police to state soldiers. The creation of a national police force ended the control of the German states (*Länder*) over their individual police organizations. Himmler used his position of authority to set the tone and direction of the unified Reichwide police force. One objective, the infusion of a military character into the uniformed police proceeded along dual lines incorporating military training and discipline as well as the gradual "merging" (*Verschmelzung*) of the SS and police corps. In September 1936, the desire to inculcate a stronger military character into the police resulted in an order for "the official basic and continued professional training" of the entire German police to be based on a "military foundation."[30] In line with the second objective of the Nazi conversion strategy, Daluege embraced the "merging" of the SS and police, and declared, "It can only be a question of time before the entire police coalesces with the SS corps into a permanent unit".[31]

By 1936, there was ample opportunity for SS, SA, and *Stahlhelm* members to enter the ranks of the uniformed police. At the end of 1935, the total strength of the uniformed police included 49,610 *Schupos*, 16,759 Gendarmerie, and 16,420 community policemen.[32] The reduction of the 1933 total strength of 126,000 men to the 1935 level of 83,000 men occurred due to the loss of the majority of the 50,000-man garrisoned *Landespolizei* to the *Wehrmacht* in March 1935.[33] The manpower shortage provided openings not only for members of the SS and SA within the police, but also for former members of the armed forces. In the Fall of 1936, *Wehrmacht* personnel released after completing between two and five years of military service received direct entry into the police at the rank of corporal (*Wachtmeister*).[34] The acceptance of separated soldiers introduced an immediate military character into the ranks of the police and provided a cadre for the future militarization of the uniformed police organization.

The public proclamations of the police leadership concerning the "merging" of the SS and police were not intended as empty platitudes. The National Socialist leadership initiated a series of actions designed to promote the linkage between the

SS and the police. These measures included the authorization for SS personnel serving in the uniformed police to wear the SS runes as well as the SS police sword.[35] In September 1937, Hitler awarded unit flags to the police in the "Blood Banner" (*Blutfahne*) ceremony. In this ceremony, Hitler grasped the unit colors of the police with one hand while holding the "Blood Banner" carried by the Nazis in the abortive beer hall putsch in the other hand. This ceremony was intended to demonstrate the blood bond between the party, the SS, and the police.[36]

The "Blood Banner" ceremony was largely symbolic. A more concrete example of the "merging" between the soldiers of the party (the SS) and the police occurred with the acceptance of commissioned graduates of SS officer candidate schools (SS-*Junkerschulen*) into the uniformed police. The number of graduates that entered the police ranks although small provides another indication of the importance placed by Himmler on the ideological conversion of the police.[37] By 1941 the success of Himmler's and Daluege's efforts was evident. Thirty percent of all *regular* uniformed police with officer rank belonged to the SS. Sixty-six percent of all *regular* uniformed police with officer rank held membership in the Nazi party with 20 percent of these recognized as "old fighters" (*alte Kämpfer*), members of the NSDAP prior to Hitler's appointment as Reich Chancellor.[38] In comparison, 7 percent of all *reserve* uniformed police with officer rank belonged to the SS and 67 percent of all *reserve* uniformed police with officer rank held membership in the NSDAP. By the opening of the campaign against the Soviet Union, the uniformed police was materially and psychologically prepared for the campaign of exploitation and annihilation to be waged in the East.

The membership of Police Battalion 310 and the unit's actions on the Eastern Front provide evidence in a case study for evaluating the success or failure of National Socialist ideological initiatives within the police. First, the nature of the unit's combat experiences offers one perspective for examining the forces shaping the battalion and an insight into the motivation of the battalion's members. Second, a demographic survey of the unit's members offers further evidence concerning their susceptibility to Nazi ideology. Finally, the actions and reports of the battalion provide an additional measure with which to evaluate their commitment to National Socialist racial policy.

II

The story of Police Battalion 310 is far different from that of Browning's Reserve Police Battalion 101. Police Battalion (P.B.) 101 participated in the initial invasion of Poland in September 1939 only to be withdrawn and returned to Hamburg on December 17, 1939. Approximately 100 of its career police officers received transfers to other units and were replaced by middle-aged reservists. Between May and November 1940, P.B. 101 participated in the "Germanization" or forced "resettlement" of the Polish population out of the annexed territory known as the Warthegau. At the end of November, P.B. 101 assumed responsibility for the guarding of the Lodz ghetto and was "practically dissolved" in May 1941 upon the battalion's return to Hamburg. From May 1941 until the battalion's transfer to Poland in June 1942 the unit underwent extensive training to prepare the police reservists for duty. In June 1942, less than 20 percent of the men remained from the unit's tour in the Warthegau. Police Battalion 101 had in fact become a "pure reserve battalion."[39]

A comparison between the unit histories of Reserve Police Battalion 101 and Police Battalion 310 reveals striking dissimilarities. Police Battalion 310 was one of twelve police battalions mobilized during August and September 1940 expressly for duty outside the Reich. Prior to its designation as P.B. 310, the battalion existed as a training unit in Berlin-Oranienburg. Upon its mobilization the unit consisted of a battalion staff, three regular companies, and one undersized company armed with "heavy" weapons (a heavy machinegun platoon and a mortar platoon). The battalion took its final shape with the addition of a company of recruits from the Training Battalion in Schneidemuhl on September 19, 1940.[40]

Police Battalion 310's first tour involved the replacement of Police Battalion 7 in the German occupied General Government on October 15, 1940. The district of Radom was the battalion's area of operations in the period between October 1940 and August 1941. On August 4, in the wake of the German invasion of the Soviet union, the Second and Third Companies received orders to move into Lwów (Lemberg) in the newly acquired district of Galicia, now added to the General Government.[41] The battalion remained in Lwów until its transfer to the Eastern Front south of Leningrad on February 21, 1942. The battalion was one of a number of police units sent to the front in a desperate attempt to halt the Soviet Winter offensive of 1941–42. Police Battalion 310 remained in position on the battlefront until its transfer to Daugavpils (Dunaburg) in Latvia in the middle of July 1942.

On July 9, 1942, Himmler ordered the creation of Police Regiment 15 consisting of Police Battalions 305, 306, and 310. Police Battalion 310 received the new designation III./15 (Third Battalion/Regiment 15). This numerical redesignation did not, however, result in a change in either the battalion's manning strength or personnel.[42] On August 21, 1942, the battalion arrived in the Belorussian city of Kobrin (Kobryn) and was primarily tasked with the conduct of antipartisan operations within the general district of Wolhynien-Podolien. At the end of November 1942, the battalion again moved to a position on the battlefront as the *Wehrmacht* once more mobilized all available forces in an attempt to repel the Soviet Winter offensive of 1942–43. In January 1943, the battalion was essentially annihilated after two months of fierce and continuous fighting. The catastrophic losses in the defense of the Don bulge resulted in the official deactivation of the unit and the removal of Police Regiment 15 from the German order of battle.[43]

Unlike Reserve Police Battalion 101, the history of Police Battalion 310 does not indicate the wholesale replacement or mass transfer of personnel prior to the unit's annihilation in January 1943. The battalion clearly remained a unit led by regular police officers despite its losses in the defense of Leningrad. This is all the more extraordinary when one considers that the battalion participated in two separate sustained periods of direct combat at the front as well as a period of extended antipartisan operations. More striking than the disparity between the unit histories of P.B. 310 and P.B. 101 is however, the dissimilarity in the professional background and organizational membership of the two battalions.

III

From its inception, P.B. 310 included a high percentage of NSDAP members within its ranks. The following table indicates the number and approximate percentage of NSDAP members in each of the battalion's companies in January 1941.[44] It is impossible to ascertain the exact number of men in each of the companies; however, each company (except the Fourth Company) consisted of three platoons and averaged between 137 and 146 men.[45] The Fourth Company consisted of two platoons with an estimated strength of 80 men and was officially disbanded in April 1941.[46] The total strength of the police battalion averaged 526 men (approximately 13 officers and 513 noncommissioned officers and troops).[47] In addition to the regular companies, the battalion consisted of a staff of 20 men, a signals unit of 13 to 19 men, and a transportation squadron of 70 to 73 men.[48]

JANUARY 1941

Staff	*1st*	*2nd*	*3rd*	*4th*	*Jagdzug*[49]	*Transpo.*	*Sqn*
#NSDAP	10	55	54	61	22	19	27
% NSDAP	50	39	38	43	28	45–54	38

(Based on 20 staff personnel, 142 men per company, and 35–42-man Jagdzug [Hunting Platoon])

A more detailed analysis of the fifty-five members of the NSDAP in the First Company for January 1941 provides the following information: 14 of 55 (25 percent) were *alte Kämpfer*; 18 of 55 (32 percent) entered the NSDAP in 1933; and 1 of 55 (2 percent) was a candidate member. From the fifty-five party members only two were born prior to 1902 and only two after 1913. The fact that forty-nine were born after 1907 indicates the relative "youth" among the company's party members. Berlin was most strongly represented with four NSDAP members while the rest came from areas throughout the Reich. The lower ranks, *Wachtmeister* and *Oberwachtmeister*, compromised thirty-five and three of the NSDAP members respectively or 69 percent. Additionally, one party member had served as a *Blockleiter* and four others as *Blockwalter*.[50]

A closer analysis of the party members of the Second Company for the same period yields the following results: 15 of 54 (28 percent) were *alte Kämpfer*, 8 of 55 (15 percent) entered the NSDAP in 1933 and 1 of 55 (2 percent) was a candidate member. From the fifty-four party members in the Second Company none were born prior to 1907 and five were born after 1912. Thirty-four party members or 63 percent were born between 1911 and 1912. Berlin was again most strongly represented with six and Potsdam with one NSDAP member. Eighty-five percent (46 of 54) were *Wachtmeister* and 9 percent (5 of 54) were *Oberwachtmeister*. Additionally, three party members had served as *Blockleiter*, two as *Blockwart*, three as *Zellenleiter*, and two as *politische Leiter*.[51]

The detailed information from the First and Second Companies reveals a high percentage of relatively young NSDAP members. The relative youth of the men in the battalion is important. For indeed, it was exactly the age cohort from the year groups between 1905 and 1912 that swelled the ranks of the NSDAP, and was significantly overrepresented in the party.[52] Additionally, the relative youth of the battalion is significant as most of the unit members came of age after World War I and fully experienced the political and economic turbulence associated with the failure of the Weimar Republic. The vast majority of the party members came from the lower police ranks, 89 of 109 (82 percent). In addition, 15 of 109 (14 percent) had served in NSDAP positions specifically created for the purpose of observing and reporting party attitudes among their neighbors and coworkers.[53] Finally, the geographical origins of the party members are essentially random and well distributed.

The example of the "hunting platoon" (Jagdzug) provides an apparent indication that party membership was by no means a "benign" indicator of ideological commitment. The number listed under the heading Jagdzug in the January 1941 report consists entirely of members of the hunting platoons. Daluege ordered the formation of the hunting platoons in July 1940 "for the conduct of *special tasks*" in the General Government.[54] In his letter, Daluege cautioned that "in consideration of the difficult tasks, which the police special detachments have to conduct . . . only Police *Wachtmeister* and Police *Wachtmeister* of the Reserves who are equal to the task are to be detailed."[55] The hunting platoons conducted small group (4 to 9 persons) antipartisan and anti-Jewish operations both in uniform and civilian clothing. Duty in the hunting platoons was largely voluntary, open to men in the entire battalion, and extremely dangerous. The hunting platoons operated independently and often engaged partisan units of greater strength. They also routinely executed captured partisans, "partisan helpers," communists, and Jews.[56]

The remarkable aspect of the January report involves the extremely high percentage of NSDAP members in a group that numbered between 35 and 42 men.[57] The high percentage of NSDAP members in the hunting platoons was not coincidental. The tedious and tiring hours spent searching for partisans in the forests and swamps of Poland and the Soviet Union were often punctuated by unexpected and fierce engagements. On the one hand, inducements for joining the hunting platoons included increased alcohol rations and additional home leave (*Urlaub*). Although the promise of alcohol and extra leave may have influenced the decisions of some men to join, it seems likely that the nature of the tasks and the high level of danger would quickly offset these benefits. On the other hand, it seems that the voluntary nature of the groups, their high percentage of party members, and their extensive participation in the conduct of atrocity offers compelling evidence of their commitment to National Socialist racial policy. The fact that in February of 1941 only one member of the hunting platoons belonged to the SS clearly indicates that the SS runes were not a necessary prerequisite for those choosing to serve as the cutting edge of the National Socialist racial sword.[58] The following table indicates the number of SS men in the battalion in February 1941.[59] The numbers indicate that by 1941 approximately one in ten of each company's members had gained entry into the Black Corps.

FEBRUARY 1941

	Staff	1st	2nd	3rd	4th	Jagdzug	Others
#SS	1	25	14	14	3	1	6
%SS	5	18	10	10	4	2	—

In June 1942, Himmler granted a "special exception" specifically targeting members of the police battalions with the rank of corporal (*Wachtmeister*) for membership in the General-SS. Himmler set the deadline of September 15 for completed applications. No data exists concerning the number of applications made by the men of the battalion; however, Himmler's offer is most interesting in that it targeted members of the police battalions who had "proved themselves in the field (*auswärtiger Einsatz*).[60] It was clear recognition by Himmler of the important "services" rendered by the men of the police battalions in the execution of Nazi racial policy. Another expression of Himmler's appreciation for the operations of the police battalions occurred on February 24, 1943. In special recognition "of [the] heroic and successful action" of the police, Himmler ordered the redesignation of all "Police Regiments" to "SS-Police Regiments."[61] The move toward a complete "merging" of the SS and police had advanced a step further.

An additional source for the statistical evaluation of the battalion is available from the records of a German federal criminal investigation involving the Second Company commander in 1966.[62] The investigation record lists the names of 202 persons who belonged to the Second Company between October 1940 and January 1943. The high number of entries, and the fact that the sample covers the entire three-year history of the unit provides a solid if partially incomplete cross-section for a statistical analysis. The entries for 183 of those listed included: birthdate, birthplace, current address, and status. Nineteen entries included only the names of the former company members without further information. A statistical examination of the 183 complete entries reveals the following:

Birth year:	after 1915	1910–1915	1905–1909	before 1905
Number	3	117	57	6
Percent	2	64	31	3

The above information indicates that at the beginning of 1940 66 percent of the members were younger than 30 years old, and only 3 percent were over 35 years old.[63] Michael Kater has shown that National Socialism held its "greatest attraction" for the generation born between 1905 and 1912.[64] This sample indicates that the overwhelming majority of the Second Company's men came from exactly this age cohort. In addition, the results of the earlier analysis of the age cohort for the battalion's NSDAP membership tends to confirm the representative nature of this sample.[65] The men in this age cohort were in fact highly susceptible to the influence of Nazi ideas and exhibited a marked predisposition for National Socialism. This clearly contrasts with the middle-aged police reservists of Reserve Police Battalion 101, with an *average* age of 39.[66] In addition, fifty former members (27 percent) of the Second Company, by far the largest group, were either born in Berlin or had taken residence in Berlin after the war. This again contrasts with P.B. 101, with the "vast majority" of its members coming from the area of Hamburg.[67]

The most startling, and, without a doubt, the most important statistic involves the casualty rate indicated in the sample. Sixty-six (36 percent) of the sample either died in the line of duty between 1940 and 1945 or were still listed as missing-in-action (MIA) in 1966. Forty-eight (26 percent) of the sample were already deceased or MIA by the end of February 1943. Additionally, six members (3 percent) were reported as prisoners of war.[68] The high losses experienced by the Second Company were to some extent directly influenced by the "annihilation" of the battalion in combat operations between November 1942 and February 1943. The loss of 26 percent of the sample is by no means, however, limited to the battalion's actions in the defense of the Don bulge. Additionally, this percentage does not take into account those who were severely wounded or injured between 1940 and 1943. The men of P.B. 310 were put into positions of great peril from the moment of their arrival on the outskirts of Leningrad in the Winter of 1941–42 to their fateful transfer to the battlefront again in November 1942. Indeed, the unit's assignment to Belorussia in August 1942 to conduct "pacification operations" in an area of significant partisan activity was itself a mission involving significant danger.

Police Battalion 310 faced their baptism by fire in the frontline near Leningrad in the Winter of 1941–42. In fact, the police battalions assigned to this sector suffered a casualty rate that averaged 24 percent for the period between December 1941 and March 1942.[69] In a speech to high-ranking police officials, Chief of the Uniformed Police Kurt Daluege described the sacrifice of the police battalions: "When these battalions despite the months long, difficult battle under relentless personal engagement fulfilled their duty in exemplary fashion, so is this fact a result of the fundamental National Socialist alignment [Grundausrichtung] of their leaders and men."[70] The police battalions' participation in frontline combat, however, took its psychic toll. Major General Ernst Rode expressed the consequences of the fighting: "They [the police battalions] too had to be released during the Winter for duty along the front, and were reassigned to the Chief of the German Police only about the middle of 1942, in an utterly exhausted condition."[71] In a later speech, Daluege warned the police leadership that the men of the SS and police stood in the foremost ranks at the front and that police involvement in combat would not decrease, but rather "increase dramatically" in the months ahead.[72] In contrast, the physical danger experienced by the reservists of P.B. 101 appears insignificant in comparison to that faced by the men of P.B. 310. Indeed, the members of P.B. 310 had undergone significant periods of severe deprivation in continuous and sustained combat with a determined enemy force.

A comparison between the experiences of the men of P.B. 310 and those of German soldiers on the Eastern Front reveals both similarities and distinctions. In *Hitler's Army*, Omer Bartov demonstrates the profound effects of the heavy manpower and materiel losses sustained by the *Wehrmacht* during initial operations in the Soviet Union. On the one hand, he maintains that these losses led to the "demodernization" of combat in the East as materiel shortages reduced the physical and psychological distance between German soldiers and their Russian adversaries. On the other, Bartov highlights the impact of high casualties in destroying the German Army's building blocks of unit cohesion, the "primary group." The destruction of the primary group and the process of demodernization, augmented by Draconian punishment and increased propaganda efforts, combined to induce a "distortion of reality" within the German army. Bartov states that this distortion of reality led to a "progressive dehumanization of the enemy and a parallel deification of the Führer."[73] He contends that as a result of these processes the German army experienced a type of ideological epiphany. In essence, the German army's baptism by fire catalyzed their conversion to "ideological soldiers." The men of P.B. 310

certainly experienced the "demodernization" of frontline combat and the destruc-tion of the "primary group." For P.B. 310, however, the unit's demographic makeup, the prewar ideological initiatives within the police, and frontline combat all combined to play a role in shaping the unit's behavior in the East.

The general youth of the unit members, their demonstrated predisposition to National Socialism as indicated by their organizational and party affiliations, and their extended participation in combat operations resulted in the creation of a unit that was from all outward appearances well suited for a war of annihilation on the Eastern Front. However, it would be the actions of the battalion's members that ultimately would provide the most profound evidence concerning their commit-ment to the National Socialist *Weltanschauung*.

IV

The actions of P.B. 310 (hereafter Third Battalion/Regiment 15) in the months of September and October 1942 demonstrate not only the inherent ruthlessness of the German antipartisan campaign in the Soviet Union, but also the willingness and vigor with which the unit undertook its duties. Exactly one month after their arrival in Kobrin, the unit participated in a large-scale pacification operation, codename "Operation Triangle" (*Unternehmen Dreieck*). On September 22, the Battalion Commander, Major of the Schutzpolizei Holling, issued an order for the employ-ment of the unit's three companies in the area northeast of Mokrany in the "bandit contaminated" villages of Borki, Borysowka, and Zabloice. The order called for the unit to "annihilate" (*vernichten*) the three villages. The Ninth Company (former First Company) supported by a motorized Gendarmerie platoon arrived in the village of Dywin on the evening of September 22. Meanwhile, the Tenth and Eleventh Companies (former Second and Third Companies) assembled in Mokrany at the battalion command post in preparation for the operation.[74]

The after action report[75] of the Tenth Company's second-in-command First Lieutenant Müller indicates not only the casual brutality of the operation, but also Müller's pride in the unit's efficiency and his indifference to the fate of the victims. The company along with one platoon from the Ninth Company departed Mokrany early on September 23. The drive to Borky "proceeded without a hitch." The forced requisition of panjewagons (two-wheeled, horse-drawn carts) was, however, complicated by several "unwilling farmers" who were not eager to relinquish their sole means of transportation. The company "took the necessary measures to ensure punishment" of the obstinate peasants.[76] Upon arrival at the village outskirts, Müller found that the map of the village did not indicate a number of outlying houses. In order to include these houses in the operation, Müller ordered the unit to conduct a "pincer movement" instead of the planned encirclement. "By this maneuver, I [Müller] achieved the complete seizure of all the village inhabitants and their successful movement to the collection point." The speed and surprise of the action proved a major advantage to the company as "the number of guards at the collec-tion point could be held to a minimum ensuring the availability of more personnel for the subsequent action (*Aktion*)." According to Müller, the purpose of the oper-ation was further disguised by the distribution of shovels among the work detail only after their arrival at the 700-meter distant execution site. The first indications of panic surfaced as the sound of shooting from the execution site reached the village. The attempted escape of two men at the collection point ended under a hail of bullets from an "unobtrusively placed" machine gun.[77]

The executions began at 0900 and ended in the early evening at 1800. From the 809 village inhabitants, only 104 could be classified as "politically reliable." The policemen executed the remaining 705 inhabitants including 203 men, 372 women, and 130 children. Müller wrote that the "execution proceeded smoothly and the procedure proved itself as entirely appropriate." Additionally, the company confiscated 45 horses, 250 cows, 65 calves, 450 pigs as well as a large amount of grain. Müller further reported that the unit expended 786 rounds of rifle machine gun ammunition and 2,496 rounds of pistol ammunition.[78]

Müller's remark concerning the expended pistol ammunition is significant in its implication that his men conducted the executions for the most part with pistols or machine pistols at close range. The average of three rounds per victim is indicative of both the inherent inefficiency of this method and the required close proximity of perpetrator to victim. In effect, the psychological distance of the shooters was almost zero. It does not, however, seem to have mattered as the executions extended over a nine-hour period. The killings conducted by the men of the Ninth and Tenth Companies cannot be compared with the actions of the inexperienced and naive police reservists of Reserve Police Battalion 101 and their execution of 1,500 Jews in Jozefow.[79] Unlike the men in Browning's study, the members of the Third Battalion were experienced and battle hardened. Their victims were not the "Jewish arch-enemy of the Third Reich," but rather simple peasants whose "political reliability" could not be guaranteed.

After two years in the East, the members of the battalion were capable of standing next to their victims despite the "mess" and relative inefficiency of this type of execution. The methodical execution of over seven hundred Soviet citizens was apparently far less demanding than the rigors of frontline combat. In fact, this was a unit that had experienced their "trauma" on the front lines at Leningrad. The execution of "political unreliables" was little more than one of many acts conducted by the battalion in the support of the National Socialist *Weltanschauung*.

The actions of the Ninth and Tenth Companies at Borki during Operation Triangle were not exceptional. In the after action report of the commander of the Eleventh Company, Hauptmann Helmuth Palm* (* indicates pseudonym), his enthusiasm and belief in the "rightness" of the measures taken is clearly apparent. Palm received the order to "destroy the village of Zablocie and to shoot its inhabitants."[80] The Eleventh Company, like the Tenth Company, was also supported by a platoon from the Ninth Company. The unit reached the outskirts of Zablocie at 0200 on the morning of September 23. By 0530 the village had been encircled and its inhabitants gathered together in the village school. After learning of a group of houses located seven kilometers from the village, Palm dispatched a detachment to bring the inhabitants to Zablocie. The arrival of several Security Service (SD) personnel and subsequent interrogations led to the release of five families. The remaining inhabitants were divided into three groups and taken to three separate execution sites prepared by work details consisting of the village men.[81] Palm wrote that the executions proceeded according to plan and without incident except for a single escape attempt. His words concerning the attitude of the condemned are, however, far more illuminating with respect to his own beliefs. Palm wrote, "The majority of the village inhabitants on account of their guilty consciences and not unaware of their own responsibility calmly met their *well-deserved* fate."[82] With this remark, Palm leaves little room for doubt that he agreed with both the spirit and principle of the operation. The murder of the 284 men, women, and children at the execution sites was followed by the summary execution of 5 persons found during a subsequent house search. The executions appear to bother Palm far less than the problems of transporting the village's confiscated livestock and grain supplies. In fact, the seizure of 30,000 kilograms of threshed and 50,000 kilograms of unthreshed grain in addition to 700 cows, 400 pigs, 400 sheep, and 70 horses stretched the capability of the 93 available panjewagons to the limit. Palm's suggestions for future operations included an increased number of men for perimeter duty, more panjewagons, and the availability of a threshing machine.[83]

Palm's concluding sentence in his report speaks volumes about his character; "The detail of qualified personnel is necessary for the care of the so to speak now ownerless (*sozusagen herrenlos gewordenen*) cows, in particular for the milk cows."[84] It appears initially incredible that the report concerning the execution of 289 men, women, and children should end with a joke about "so to speak now ownerless cows." It was, however, perfectly appropriate from Palm's perspective— for the executed Russian peasants in his philosophy and that of the Third Reich were indeed worth little if not less than the cattle in their possession. In fact, confiscated livestock constituted a valuable addition to the limited German resources within the occupied eastern territories, a fact reflected in a letter of July 26, 1941, from Himmler to the Higher SS and Police Leaders (HSSPF).[85] In this letter, Himmler prohibited the wholesale slaughter of captured livestock during "cleansing actions" and "clearing actions" (*Säuberungs- und Räumungsaktionen*). Instead, he ordered that all confiscated livestock be delivered to designated farms for breeding purposes.[86]

In addition to the actions in Borki and Zablocie, the Ninth Company (minus its two detailed platoons) in conjunction with a motorized Gendarmerie platoon conducted a similar pacification operation in the village of Borysowka and executed 169 men, women, and children.[87] In the wake of the operation a truly bizarre situation occurred which resulted in the company commander, Captain of the Schutzpolizei Kramer*, writing a special report (*Sonderbericht*) complaining of the behavior of an accompanying SD officer, SS-Hauptscharführer (Master Sergeant) Worms*. According to Kramer, Worms telephoned SS-Obersturmführer (First Lieutenant) Wagner* in Kobrin to complain about Kramer's planning for the operation. Kramer described Worms as being drunk and "completely undisciplined" and displaying an "unruly attitude." The apparent reason for Worms's "irrational" behavior involved his objection to the planned method of execution. In other words, a SD officer questioned the "humanity" of the execution method employed by the police.[88] Kramer in the final sentence of his report requested that Worms be forced to assume responsibility for his actions.

The Battalion Commander's (Major Holling) final report concerning the operation provides another glimpse into the mentality of the unit's leadership. Holling complained of poor maps and an inadequate number of men. He also reflected that the numerous outlying farmhouses that could not be included in the operation were exactly those most likely to house partisans. He did not, however, draw the reciprocal conclusion that in fact the vast majority of the executed villagers were then most probably not partisans and therefore innocent bystanders. Instead, like Palm, Holling complained most strongly about the inadequate preparations for the feeding of the confiscated cows and the late notification of the county officials responsible for arranging the subsequent transportation of the captured livestock. Once again the lives of the 1,470 captured cows counted far more than the deaths of 1,163 Russian men, women, and children.[89] In addition, no mention was made of captured weapons—an important point considering the alleged activities of the executed villagers.

The actions of Palm's company in the six-week period after the annihilation of Borki paint a chilling portrait of regularized atrocity. In reports detailing the unit's actions, Palm shows absolutely no remorse for the victims, but rather justifies the killings using standard phrases from the grotesque Nazi bureaucratese.

29.9.42: "around 0500 in the forest 2 kilometers from Wielkyorta 1 man and 3 women with contact to the Bandits were shot."

1.10.42: "a woman and 4 children (Ostmenschen) found wandering in the forest were arrested. . . . The persons taken into custody were executed on the same day in Zablocie."

2.10.42: "2 men, 5 women, and 3 children were taken into custody and executed in the forest."

The above is a sample of three days' activity by Palm's company.[90] The entry for October 1 demonstrates that in Palm's company, the fact that a woman and four children were "*Ostmenschen*" provided sufficient justification for their murder. Palm was in fact the prototypical National Socialist. Born in 1915, he joined the Hitler Youth in 1931, the SS in 1933, and the NSDAP in 1935. He was a graduate of the SS-*Junkerschule* in Braunschweig and had participated as a member of SS-*Verfügungstruppe* in a training course at Dachau.[91] His company's report for October 5 and 6 further demonstrate the unit's casual disregard for the lives of the Slavic "*Untermenschen*."[92]

5.10.42: "At 0300 25 men from the Second Platoon and 2 Officers and 18 men from the Third Platoon were sent to Kamienica-Zyrowiecka, Wolki, Kuraki, Zakije and Lazy. Here 11 men, 41 women, and 64 children (all Ostmenschen) were taken into custody. From these, 1 man, 11 women, and 15 children were executed on the same day in the forest 1-kilometer from Kamienica. The rest remained in custody in Kamienica."

6.10.42: "At 0530 hours in the forest 10 kilometers south of Podlesie the remaining Ostmenschen taken into custody during the previous day's action in Kamienica were executed. 10 men, 30 women, and 49 children were shot."

The most chilling aspect of the above entries is not only the clinical description of the cold-blooded murder of sixty-four children, but the fact that these types of operations were routine. Apparently, murder had become standard operating procedure in a war in which atrocity had been institutionalized at the highest levels. In fact, a Führer order of August 18, 1942, identified the increasing importance attached to antipartisan measures. In the order, Hitler remarked on the "unbearable scope" of the partisan activity, and he therefore authorized the "extermination" (*Ausrottung*) of the partisan forces through the combined use of the *Wehrmacht*, the SS, and the police.[93] Hitler's order was in fact a "blank check" offering institutional approval for the conduct of atrocity. On October 23, 1942, Himmler appointed Higher SS and Police Leader (HSSPF) Erich von dem Bach-Zelewski to coordinate all anti-partisan operations.[94] Hitler himself described von dem Bach as "one of the cleverest persons" and a man not afraid to take steps "not exactly in accordance with the regulations."[95] The men of the Third Battalion could only interpret these moves as an additional justification for the "correctness" of their own actions in regard to Soviet population. During the period between October 7 and 9, the men of the Eleventh Company murdered an additional 40 men, 47 women, and 28 children.[96] The term "*Ostmenschen*" appears four times in the report entries for the three-day period. The corrupting influence of National Socialist ideology resulted not only in murder based on racial grounds or partisan activity, but killing for revenge and reprisal as well.

The unit's operation on October 9 was a "reprisal action" (*Vergeltungsaktion*) directed against the villages of Lasowiece-Gora and Korostawka. One officer and twenty-five men from the First Platoon, two officers and eighteen men from the Second Platoon, and "all available men from the Third Platoon" (1 officer and 28 men) participated in the reprisal action. In other words approximately 53 percent of the company was involved in this single operation. The two villages were encircled at 0600 and all the inhabitants were forced to a collection point. A roll call was conducted using a listing of the village inhabitants (*Einwohnerliste*). Families missing any of their members were separated from the remaining village inhabitants. The assembled groups were then told that in the event of future actions directed against Germans "the most radical retribution measures" would be employed. Thereafter, members of the company executed 12 men, 11 women, and 14 children from the families missing relatives, siblings, or parents.[97] The company justified the executions based on the suspicion that the missing relatives from these families were most probably partisan members.

It is certainly true that atrocity and reprisal have been a part of warfare since time immemorial. However, it is important to distinguish between "hot-blooded" and "cold-blooded" atrocity. The former occurs during actions in which a unit comes under fire or experiences casualties. These "combat" situations have often spurred an orgy of blood lust involving the indefensible murder of civilians or the execution of prisoners. In contrast, the actions at Lasowiece-Gora and Korostawka are examples of cold-blooded atrocity. In this case, atrocity cannot be rationalized as a unit's primal reaction to the deaths of their comrades or the fear engendered by their own experience. The actions of the Eleventh Company clearly demonstrate the acceptance of reprisal and atrocity as a means of "signaling" the brutal consequences of actual or perceived support for the partisans. It was a practice that found repeated expression on the Eastern Front.

The actions of the Eleventh Company between October 11 and 12 further demonstrated their participation in the full spectrum of the National Socialist war of annihilation in the East. During this period members of the unit executed a man and a woman on the grounds that they were "Soviet citizens," 8 men and 9 women as "bandit helpers," 7 men and 9 women (*Ostmenschen*), and one Jew without identification papers. The report also indicates that "all available men from the company were detailed to a special action (*Sonderaktion*) in the city of Brest" on October 15. The report further states that the company returned from the "special mission" (*Sondereinsatz*) on October 16.[98] What the report fails to mention is that on October 15 and 16 police and auxiliary units summarily executed thousands of Jews in the Brest ghetto. Additionally, between 10,000 and 15,000 Jews were taken to the train station for transportation to execution sites in the area of Brona-Gora.[99] Clearly, the men of the Eleventh Company were "equal opportunity killers" ready to label their victims and cloak their actions in National Socialist euphemism, willing to murder in the name of a *Weltanschauung* that dehumanized those as "Soviet citizens," "Ostmenschen," or "Jews."

The actions and statements of one of the Eleventh Company's platoon sergeants, Hermann Schmidt*, provide additional evidence for determining the influence of ideology and the effect of war on the unit's members. Schmidt was born November 21, 1911, in Walsum am Rhein. He entered the SA and the NSDAP in 1933.[100] He was one of the police recruits from Schneidemühl who joined the battalion in September 1940. In testimony to the federal prosecutor's office in 1961, Fritz Lange* (Schmidt's former brother-in-law) recounted statements made by Schmidt while on leave from his unit during the war. After having had some drinks Schmidt told Lange that he had participated in the execution of Jews in Poland. Lange expressed disbelief, which then resulted in Schmidt's exclamation that "the Jews were not people but a danger to the German *Volk*."[101] Lange stated that Schmidt had told him of how mothers often pleaded for their children's lives. According to Lange, Schmidt described how he had first shot the child of one such mother so that she would see her child die. Schmidt told Lange, "We know no mercy."[102]

Lange was not the only person who provided testimony on Schmidt's activities in the East. After initially refusing to provide a statement, Schmidt's former wife subsequently agreed to speak with the prosecutor's office. She stated that her husband had told her of his "forced" participation in the execution of Jews. At one point during the war, she also overheard her husband saying that "earlier [before the war] he couldn't harm a fly, but now he could shoot a Jew in the head while eating a sandwich."[103] The former Frau Schmidt rationalized the actions of her husband as the product of the stresses of war. She stated, "My husband was okay earlier, I mean before the war, only after the war did I recognize he had become sadistic."[104] It is difficult to believe that the man who had boasted of his reputation as the "Terror of Lemberg" was an unwilling tool of racial policy.[105] Schmidt's conversion to an instrument of genocide whether "forced" or the result of the rigors of war was nonetheless complete.

Like Schmidt, Helmuth Palm also acted as an enforcer of National Socialist racial policy. The most telling example of Palm's absolute ideological conviction occurred during an antipartisan operation conducted by almost the entire Eleventh Company (3 officers and 104 men) and one platoon (1 officer and 23 men) from the Ninth Company. The members of the two companies under Palm's command initiated an "action" after receiving word from the SD office in Maloryta that "bandits" had been spotted in the vicinity of Chmielisce and Oltusz-Lesnia. The operation began at 0330, and by 0700 the units had encircled both villages. The inhabitants were gathered together and "those that could prove beyond a doubt that they had family members working in Germany" were separated from the remaining population. Palm then ordered the execution of all those without family members as forced laborers in Germany. The unit executed 28 men, 40 women, and 60 children. Palm's own ideological conviction was, however, apparent in a request on October 24. Palm questioned the policy of excluding from execution those villagers with family members working in Germany. He complained that "the worst bandits are numbered among them." He then wrote, "I therefore request permission to execute the remaining families in the villages of Chmielisce and Oltusz-Lesnia."[106] Palm truly demonstrated the enthusiasm of the true believer.

A report signed by Palm concerning the number of executions conducted by the company between November 8 and November 14 indicates the routinization of the killing process. In the seven-day period, members of the company executed 35 men and 44 women. Among the reasons given include the usual "bandit helper," Jew, "former communist official," and more interestingly an execution entry for November 14, entitled "vagabond."[107] It seems that by the middle of November the Eleventh Company had added the "asocial" to their list of victims.

The men of the Ninth and Tenth companies proved themselves equally willing and adept in the conduct of atrocity and "racial cleansing." On October 21, the Tenth Company conducted a mass execution of Jews in a work camp under the jurisdiction of the Todt Organization. The company shot 461 Jews at the work camp and two additional sites. On the following day an additional 43 Jews were executed at three sites. The platoon also seized and subsequently shot two "highwaymen" (*Wegelagerer*). The reason given for the execution of the alleged highway robbers was that they were "incapable of work" (*arbeitsunfähig*).[108] It appears that the execution of those incapable of work was by October 1942 standard operating procedure for the men of the Tenth Company. The killing of Jews was, without a doubt, by October 1942 standard procedure, and the company's "success" in accomplishing this task, between October 19 and 25, is best summarized by the remark that the Tenth Company's area of operation was "*judenfrei*."[109]

A report summarizing the actions of the Ninth Company, between October 26 and November 1, demonstrates that their area was still far from being "*judenfrei*." This situation could not, however, be attributed to a lack of effort on the part of the police. On October 30, three German police platoons operating in conjunction with 29 local auxiliaries conducted an operation involving the "killing of the Jews" (*Entjudung*) in the village of Samary. In addition to 74 Jewesses the unit also executed a Ukrainian family including one man, two women, and three children for "providing shelter to a Jewish woman." Hunting-platoon operations resulted in the execution of another 12 Jews in the reporting period.[110] The activities of a hunting platoon on October 20 provide a microcosm of the casual brutality demonstrated by the police forces operating in the East. A member of the platoon and a suspected partisan became involved in hand-to-hand combat as the result of a confrontation in a densely wooded forest. A second member of the platoon came to the assistance of his comrade and repeatedly struck the suspected partisan with blows from his rifle butt. The subsequent interrogation of the injured partisan elicited his name, birthdate, hometown, and an entire typed page of details concerning his past activities. The report concludes with the remark that the prisoner was shot after completion of the interrogation "on account of the severe head injuries he received."[111] In other words, a man capable of providing information filling more than one typed page had to be executed due to the "severity" of his head injuries.

V

The actions of P.B. 310 present a partial picture of police operations on the Eastern Front. In a speech to police leaders in January 1943, Daluege discussed the success achieved by uniformed police and auxiliary units operating in the East. He boasted that these forces had accounted for the capture of 4,000 prisoners and the deaths of 30,000 "bandits" and 3,000 "bandit helpers" and "saboteurs" in 1942. Police Battalion 310 was in fact only one of thirty-one police battalions operating on the Eastern Front during 1942.[112] The actions of other police battalions demonstrate that the men of P.B. 310 were not acting alone in the prosecution of a war of annihilation.

Reserve Police Battalion 133 was mobilized for duty on the Eastern Front in the Summer of 1942 from the battalion's home base at Nürnberg. In July 1942, the battalion received orders to proceed to Lwów (Lemberg). By the end of their first month in the East, the unit was clearly hard at work enforcing the racial policies of the Third Reich. In a report of the First Company's activities between July 25 and August 1, the company commander listed the unit's tally of victims.

> 1.) In the period from 25 July to 1 August 1942 the following were executed (*beseitigt*):[113]

a)	Bandits	—
b)	Partisan Supporters	9 (including 5 Jews)
c)	Beggars	27
d)	Thieves	7
e)	Vagrants	13
f)	Weapons Possession	1
g)	Mentally Ill	2
h)	Gypsies	24
i)	Jews	64

The unit's victims include the entire spectrum of racial, biological, political, and social "*Untermenschen*" reflected in Nazi ideology. However, the company's action with respect to the execution of the "gypsies" (Sinti and Roma) had apparently exceeded the scope of their authority. On August 13, 1942, the Commander of the Uniformed Police in the General Government, Lieutenant General of the Uniformed Police Becker sent a telegram to the district commanders of the uniformed police restating police policy with respect to Sinti and Roma. Becker wrote, "According to the opinion of the Reich Leader of the SS [Himmler], it is not for the police to take action against gypsies just because they are 'gypsies.'"[114] Becker did note, however, that this did not preclude "ruthless action" in instances where Sinti and Roma were involved in criminal activities or support of the partisans.[115]

The First Company apparently got the message that their job was enforcing and not dictating racial policy. The company's weekly report for the period from August 16 to August 22 stated that six "gypsies" were "arrested," with the final decision on their fate being referred to regimental headquarters.[116] By 1942, the involvement of uniformed police units in the execution of Sinti and Roma was neither a recent nor isolated phenomenon. Already in December 1941, uniformed police units operating in Estonia had executed 100 Sinti and Roma from the city of Libau.[117] In January 1942, Lieutenant General of the Police Jedicke (Commander of the Uniformed Police-*Ostland*) addressed the "Gypsy question" (*Zigeunerfrage*) in a letter to regional SS and Police Leaders (SSPF) and the regional commanders of the uniformed police. Jedicke wrote that at *his* suggestion Reich Commissar Hinrich Lohse had decided that Gypsies with "contagious diseases" and those Gypsies classified as "unreliable elements" were to be "handled exactly as the Jews." Jedicke closed his letter with the remark, "I request in any case that all necessary steps be taken [in support of this decision]."[118] Here again a police official was attempting to dictate the direction of racial policy by suggesting the use of a standard commensurate with the annihilation of the Jews.

VI

Police Battalion 310 was but one of many police units that served on the Eastern Front. Therefore, it is not possible to draw definitive conclusions with respect to all police battalions or their members. The case presented, although largely built upon circumstantial evidence, appears however to indicate *prima facie* the commitment of at least one battalion to the racial and ideological objectives of the Third Reich. Despite the absence of diaries, letters, or confessions of the battalion's individual members, it is still possible to identify agency and infer motivation. The attempt to attribute ideological motivations to the members of an organization is by its very nature both difficult and contentious.[119] It is, however, apparent that the men of Police Battalion 310 are not the same men portrayed by Browning in his study of Reserve Police Battalion 101. Can the historian explain the difference? Is it simply a difference between regular versus reserve police units? The attribution of ideological beliefs to groups or individuals may indeed be in many respects an indeterminable process. Motivation although often difficult to ascertain is not, however, therefore illusory. It can be found in the words and deeds of the battalion's members. It can be inferred from their membership and participation in party organizations and the susceptibility of their specific year groups to National Socialist ideas. Finally, it can be ascertained in their experiences on the Eastern Front, experiences that strengthened racial prejudices in a war of annihilation.

In a war of competing *Weltanschauungen* at least one general, a company commander, a platoon sergeant, and hundreds of the battalion's rank-and-file acted with the indifference or the conviction of the "true believer." Kurt Daluege captured the essence of this belief in a speech to the commanders of the uniformed police in January 1943. He stated, "The Führer is accomplishing an undertaking that will be the greatest in the history of the world. I know of nothing greater in one's life than to participate in this undertaking. What are the prophets of Christendom compared to this [undertaking] that we [the uniformed police] have to fulfill in support of the Führer's world view."[120] Like the crusaders of the Middle Ages, the men of the P.B. 310 believed that theirs was the task to "cleanse" the East of threatening "infidels" (*Ostmenschen*, Jews, Communists) in the name of their own "holy" ideology. The "*Kreuzzug im Osten*" was indeed a demodernizing if not an antimodern and atavistic campaign. The call for conquest did not come from a Pope and the Catholic Church, but rather from a "*Führer*" and the black-clad cardinals of a new racial order. The men of the SS and the police stood not before the walls of Jerusalem but rather before the gates of Moscow. The historical evidence indicates that many among Himmler's "knights," whether in the black of the SS or the green uniforms of the police, fit the description far better of "ideological soldiers" than that of "ordinary men." In fact, the nature of warfare on the Eastern Front left little room for either ordinary men or ordinary life.

Acknowledgements

The author would like to thank the Fulbright commission for funding the research leading to this manuscript. In addition, the friendly and expert assistance of Willi Dreßen and the staff of the German federal prosecutor's office in Ludwigsburg proved invaluable in the preparation of the manuscript. Special thanks are also due to Konrad H. Jarausch, Gerhard Weinberg, Chris Browning, Dennis Showalter, Omer Bartov, Michael Kater, Wolfgang Wippermann, Gerhard Baader, Dan Rogers, and the students of History 324 for their comments and suggestions.

Notes

1 Ernst Klee, Willi Dreßen, and Volker Rieß, eds., *"The Good Old Days." The Holocaust as Seen by its Perpetrators and Bystanders*, trans. Deborah Burnstone (New York: The Free Press, 1991), 220–21. Testimony given by Möbius in 1961.

2 Daniel J. Goldhagen, *Hitler's Willing Executioners. Ordinary Germans and the Holocaust* (New York: Alfred A. Knopf, 1996).

3 Christopher R. Browning, *Ordinary Men. Reserve Police Battalion 101 and the Final Solution in Poland* (New York: Harper Collins, 1992).

4 Omer Bartov, *Hitler's Army: Soldiers, Nazis, and War in the Third Reich* (New York: Oxford University Press, 1992) and Hannes Heer and Klaus Naumann, eds., *Vernichtungskrieg. Verbrechen der Wehrmacht 1941 bis 1944* (Hamburg: HIS Verlagsges., 1995).

5 From a speech by Heinrich Himmler to the German Gemeindetag concerning the community police. T-580, Captured German Documents Microfilmed at the Berlin Document Center (Collection of the National Archives), Roll 37. Speech of May 1939.

6 Klee, Dreßen, and Rieß, 220.

7 Dan Bar-On, *Legacy of Silence: Encounters with Children of The Third Reich* (Cambridge: Harvard University Press, 1989), 91.

8   George C. Browder, *Hitler's Enforcers: The Gestapo and the SS Security Service in the Nazi Revolution* (New York: Oxford University Press, 1996), 25. This anti-KPD inclination might in part explain the actions of some policemen in the Soviet Union after the German invasion.

9   Ibid., 28.

10 Hsi-huey Liang, *The Berlin Police Force in the Weimar Republic* (Berkeley: University of California Press, 1970), 154.

11 Ibid.

12 Peter Leßman, *Die preußische Schutzpolizei in der Weimarer Republik* (Düsseldorf: Droste Verlag, 1989), 371. In Prussia at this time, there were a total of 44 state police administrative districts with 44 Police Directors.

13 Karl Dietrich Bracher, Wolfgang Sauer, and Gerhard Schulz, *Die nationalsozialistische Machtergreifung* (Cologne: Westdeutscher Verlag, 1960), 709. The Prussian police force consisted of 54,712 men while the police forces of all the other German states combined, totaled 40,473 men.

14 "RdErl d. preußisches Minister des Innern von 28.2.1933-II b II 51b Nr.6/33," T-580, Roll 97.

15 Ibid.

16 Leßman, 386.

17 Ibid., 388. Of the 200 police officers, this included 22 of 32 police colonels.

18 Bracher, 435.

19 Heinz Höhne, *The Order of the Death's Head*, trans. Richard Barry (New York: Ballantine Books, 1966), 103. Although Daluege was named the overall head of the uniformed police forces, the individual German states still maintained control over their own police forces.

20 "Deutsches Nachrichtenbüro. Berlin, den 28. April 34." T-580, Roll 220, Ordner 61.

21 Ibid.

22 Karl-Heinz Heller, *The Reshaping and Political Conditioning of the German Ordnungspolizei, 1933–1945: A Study of Techniques Used in the Nazi State to Conform Local Police Units to National Socialist Theory and Practice.* (Ann Arbor: University Microfilms, 1971), 24.

23 Ibid., 24–25.

24 Ibid., 101–2. In 1938, Himmler transferred the responsibility for the ideological training of the police to the SS Training Office. In a speech on September 15, 1938, Daluege described this measure as "of fundamental significance for the ideological adjustment of the uniformed police corps." See T-580, Roll 216, Ordner 5.

25 Ibid., 111.

26 Ibid., 108–9, 115. These lectures were limited to one hour and were not to be scheduled after a "strenuous" duty period. In addition, the maximum size of each training group was limited to 90 men.

27 Ibid., 126–27. The sessions could be conducted separately or as part of the daily briefing.

28 Ibid., 162–64. The *Political Information Service* began publication in October 1940.

29 T-580, Roll 37. Speech by Himmler to the *Gemeindetag* in May 1939.

30 Gerd Rühle, *Das Dritte Reich: Dokumentarische Darstellung des Aufbaues der Nation, Das vierte Jahr* (Berlin: Hummelverlag, 1937), 272.

31 "Der Weg der Ordnungspolizei von SS-Gruppenführer, General der Polizei, Kurt Daluege," T-580, Roll 216, Ordner 5. Speech of September 15, 1938.

32 "Disposition zum Vortrag General Daluege., 'Die Ordnungspolizei.'," T-580 Roll 216, Ordner 5.

33 T-580, Roll 219, Ordner 57. The remainder of the *Landespolizei* forces were transferred to the *Wehrmacht* in March 1936.

34 Rühle, 272.

35 "Der Weg der Ordnungspolizei von SS-Gruppenführer, General der Polizei, Kurt Daluege," T-580, Roll 216, Ordner 5. Speech of September 15, 1938. Also "Der Führer, Berlin den 16. Januar 1937," T-580, Roll 219, Ordner 57.

36 Robert L. Koehl, *The Black Corps: The Structure and Power Struggles of the Nazi SS* (Madison: University of Wisconsin Press, 1983), 48.

37 Ibid., 331, and footnote 57 in Koehl.

38 "Zahlenmässige und statistische Unterlagen zur Besprechung der Befehlshaber und der Ord.-Polizei vom 1.-4 Februar, 1942," T-580, Roll 96. In contrast, approximately 9 percent of the entire German population had membership in the NSDAP. See Michael H. Kater, *The Nazi Party: A Social Profile of Members and Leaders, 1919–1945* (Cambridge: Harvard University Press, 1983).

39 Browning, 38–42.

40 Zentrale Stelle der Landesjustizverwaltungen (hereafter ZStL), II 204 AR-z 12/61, Bl. 389–391.

41 Ibid. The First Company reported to Lwów on October 22, 1941.

42 Ibid.

43 Tessin in Hans J. Neufeldt, Jürgen Huck, and Georg Tessin, *Zur Geschichre der Ordnungspolizei* (Koblenz: Schriften des Bundesarchivs, 1957), 31.

44 ZStL, Bestand UdSSR, Band 412, Bl. 715–16, 823, 953, 958–59.

45 R-20, Band 10, Seiten 3–4, 6–7, 14–17. These numbers are taken from the organizational strength charts for II./Police Regiment 14 (a sister battalion of the III./115) and are representative of battalion manning levels on the Eastern Front. *Bundesarchiv-Koblenz* (hereafter B.A.K.).

46 Tessin, 30.

47 R-20, Band 10, Seiten 3–4, 6–7, 14–17. B.A.K.

48 Ibid.

49 "Betr.: Aufstellung von Pol.-Jagdzügen zum Einsatz im General Gouvernement," T-580, Roll 97. This document is dated August 1, 1940.

50 ZStL, UdSSR, Bd. 412, Bl. 953.

51 Ibid., Bl. 958–59.

52 Kater, 139–48.

53 Friedemann Bedürftig, ed., *Das große Lexikon des Dritten Reiches* (Munich: Südwest Verlag, 1985), 78, 449–50.

54 "Der Reichsführer SS- und Chef der Deutschen Polizei im Reichsministerium des Innern," T-580, Roll 97. Letter is dated July 24, 1940 (emphasis added).

55 Ibid.

56 Edward B. Westermann, "'Friend and Helper': German Uniformed Police Operations in Poland and the General Government, 1939–1941." *The Journal of Military History* 58 (4): 658–59. See also Browning, 126–32.

57 "Betr.: Aufstellung von Pol.-Jagdzügen zum Einsatz im General Gouvernement," T-580/ Roll 97. This document is dated August 1, 1940.

58 ZStL, UdSSR, Bd. 412, Bl. 691–98 (Information for October 1940), 715–16 (Lists 19 SS members in January 1941). Also UdSSR Bd. 412, Bl. 748 (Lists SS membership for the hunting platoons as of February 1941).

59 ZStL, UdSSr, Bd. 412, Bl. 743–51.

60 Ibid., Bl. 793.

61 Tessin, 31.

62 ZStL, II 204 AR 32203/66.

63 Ibid., Bl. 398–99.4

64 Kater, 141.

65 The sample was compiled by questioning former members of the battalion as to the names of their fellow policemen. With incomplete statistical samples, there always exists the danger that the missing elements might fundamentally affect the nature of the results. However, the results obtained by this analysis are consistent with the history and demographics of the unit, especially with respect to the established age cohort within the battalion. The total number of missing entries for the company most probably lies between forty and seventy persons.

66 Browning, 48.

67 Ibid., 45.

68 ZStL, II 204 AR 3203/66, Bl. 398–99. It is also likely that a number of the members with incomplete information or missing from the sample perished in the East. This could in part explain some of the incomplete and missing entries.

69 "Rede des Chefs der Ordnungspolizei bei der SS-Führertagung des RFSS, Der Winterkampf der Ordnungspolizei im Osten," T-580, Roll 217, Ordner 6. Speech given sometime in early 1942. This percentage includes killed, wounded, and those who froze to death in their fighting positions. In comparison an American casualty rate of 17 percent at Tarawa was considered "something of a scandal." See Walter Millis, *Arms and Men. A Study in American Military History* (New Brunswick: Rutgers University Press, 1956), 125.

70 Ibid.

71 Donald S. Detwiler, ed., *World War II German Military Studies: A Collection of 213 Special Reports on the Second World War Prepared by Former Officers of the Wehrmacht for the United States Army*, vol. 6, *Command Structure* (New York: Garland Publishing, 1979), 8.

72 "Ansprache des Chefs der Ordnungspolizei SS-Oberstgruppenführer und Generaloberst der Polizei Daluege an die Befehlshaber und Inspekteure der Ordnungspolizei in Berlin, Januar 1943," T-580, Roll 220, Ordner 61.

73 Bartov, 178.

74 Paul Kohl, *Der Krieg der Wehrmacht und der deutschen Polizei 1941–1944* (Frankfurt/M: Fischer Taschenbuch, 1995), 230–31.

75 The formulaic nature of these reports makes analysis at times problematic. In these types of reports there is a tendency to emphasize the leadership qualities of the individual commander while excluding emotional reactions or personal observations. However, these reports still offer a valuable glimpse of motivations and beliefs.

76 Kohl, 233–34.

77 Ibid.

78 Ibid.

79 Browning, 74.

80 ZStL, UdSSR, Bd. 412, Bl. 836.

81 Ibid.

82 Ibid. (emphasis added).

83 Ibid., Bl. 836–37.

84 Ibid., Bl. 837 (emphasis added).

85 The Higher SS and Police Leaders exercised the highest level of police authority within designated areas in both the Reich and the occupied territories. They constituted the ultimate example of the merging of the SS and police functions. For the best discussion of the HSSPFs see Ruth Bettina Birn, *Die Höheren SS- und Polizeiführer. Himmlers Vertreter im Reich und in den besetzten Gebieten.* (Düsseldorf: Droste Verlag, 1986).

86   "Fernschreiben, Führer-Hauptquartier 26.7.1941," T-580, Roll 19, Ordner 59–60.

87   Kohl, 231–32.

88   ZStL, UdSSR, Bd. 412, Bl. 599–600. In the German text Kramer wrote that he was told by another SD official, "daß SS-Hauptscharf. Worms* die Exekutionsmethoden der Schutzpolizei hinsichtlich ihrer Humanität in Zweifeil gezogen habe."

89   Ibid., Bl. 597–98.

90   Ibid., Bl. 944–45 (emphasis added).

91   ZStL, II 204 AR-Z 12/6, Bl. 383.

92   ZStL, UdSSR, Bd. 412, Bl, 844–46 (emphasis added).

93   "Der Führer, OKW/WFst/Op. Nr. 00 281142g.K., F.H. Qu., den 18.8.42.," Bestand RW4 (*Oberkommando der Wehrmacht/Wehrmachtführungsstab*), Band 554, *Bundesarchiv-Militärarchiv*.

94   Tessin, 17.

95   Alexander Dallin, *German Rule in Russia 1941–1945: A Study of Occupation Policies*, rev. ed., (Boulder: Westview Press, 1981), 211.

96   Ibid.

97   ZStL, UdSSR, Bd. 412, Bl. 838.

98   ZStL, UdSSR, Bd. 412, "Lage-und Tätigkeitsbericht der 11. Pol. 15 für die Zeit vom 12. Bis 18.10.42."

99   Kohl, 276. See footnote 16.

100 ZStL, II 204 AR-Z 12/61. Bl. 1–289. The investigation started as a result of an anonymous letter written to the *Zentralrat der Juden in Deutschland*. The letter was forwarded to the prosecutor's office in Ludwigsburg in June 1960. During the investigation, the prosecutor learned that the letter had been written by Schmidt's daughter.

101 Ibid., Bl. 2–5. Lange's testimony cannot be dismissed as a case of familial retribution. He includes a number of specific details concerning the methods used in the executions and the procedures for disposing of the bodies. He had also told the story to an acquaintance prior to the start of the investigation.

102 Ibid.

103 Ibid., Bl. 29–30.

104 Ibid.

105 Ibid., Bl. 2–5.

106 ZStL, UdSSR, Bd. 412, Bl. 847–48.

107 Ibid., Bl. 843.

108 Ibid., Bl. 839–40.

109 Ibid. It is important to note that the battalion's area of responsibility included areas in which *Einsatzgruppe B* had conducted operations during the initial phases of the German invasion of the Soviet Union. See Helmut Krausnick, *Hitlers Einsatzgruppen. Die Truppen des Weltanschauungskrieges 1938–1942.* (Frankfurt/M: Fischer Taschenbuch a Verlag, 1981), 156–62.

110 ZStL, UdSSR, Bd. 412, Bl. 841–42.

111 Ibid., Bl. 107–9.

112 "Bericht des Chefs der Ordnungspolizei, SS-Oberst-Gruppenführer und General-oberst Daluege, über den Kräfte- und Kriegseinsatz der Ordnungspolizei im Kriegsjahre 1942." *Records of the Reichsführer SS and Chief of the German Police* (Collection of the National Archives). T-175, Roll 3, Frame 2503385.

113 ZStL, UdSSR, Bd. 410, Bl. 536.

114 ZStL, UdSSR, Bd. 410, Bl. 530.

115 Ibid.

116   ZStL, UdSSR, Bd. 410, Bl. 526.

117   ZStL, UdSSR, Bd. 245d, Bl. 9–10.

118   ZStL, UdSSR, Bd. 245d, Bl. 5. Letter dated January 12, 1942.

119   For an insightful discussion of the ambiguous nature of ideological conviction see Gerhard L. Weinberg, *Crossing the Line in Nazi Genocide: On Becoming and Being a Professional Killer* (Burlington, Vt.: The Center for Holocaust Studies, 1997). Paper given as the fifth Raul Hilberg Lecture.

120   "Ansprache des Chefs der Ordnungspolizei SS-Obergruppenführer und General-oberst der Polizei Daluege an die Befehlshaber und Inspekteure der Ordnungspolizei in Berlin, Januar 1943," T-580, Roll 220, Ordner 61.

Chapter 9

John Dower

RACE, LANGUAGE, AND WAR
IN TWO CULTURES
World War II in Asia

WORLD WAR II TRANSCENDS our imaginative capacities. It is simply impossible to grasp what it means to say that fifty-five million individuals, perhaps more, were killed in a prolonged frenzy of violence. It is even difficult for any single individual to imagine all the different wars subsumed by that oddly detached phrase, "World War II." Germany's early expansion in eastern Europe, Italy's in Ethiopia. The Berlin-Rome Axis versus the Anglo-Americans. The German invasion of the Soviet Union. The Nazi war against the Jews and other "*Untermenschen*." The antifascist partisan wars and resistance movements of the West. In Asia: the China War and Pacific War and what the Japanese called the "Greater East Asia War," embracing Southeast Asia. And also in Asia, the anticolonial war within the war. In both East and West, the war between the Axis and Allies enfolded a multilayered struggle between communists and anticommunists. For African Americans, World War II, under the rallying cry "Double Victory," was simultaneously the onset of an all-out domestic struggle for civil rights.

For most Americans, World War II always has involved selective consciousness. The hypocrisy of fighting with a segregated army and navy under the banner of freedom, democracy, and justice never was frankly acknowledged and now is all but forgotten. In Asia, Japan was castigated for subjugating the native peoples of the Dutch East Indies (Indonesia), British Hong Kong, Malaya, Burma, the American Philippines, and French Indochina—and neither then nor later did the anomaly of such condemnation sink in. Consciousness and memory have been deceptive in other ways as well. If one asks Americans today in what ways World War II was atrocious and racist, they will point overwhelmingly to the Nazi genocide of the Jews. When the war was being fought, however, the enemy Americans perceived as most atrocious was not the Germans but the Japanese; and the racial issues that provoked their greatest emotion were associated with the war in Asia.

With few exceptions, Americans were obsessed with the uniquely evil nature of the Japanese. Allan Nevins, who twice won the Pulitzer Prize in history, observed immediately after the war that "probably in all our history, no foe has been so detested as were the Japanese." Ernie Pyle, the most admired of American war correspondents, conveyed the same sentiment unapologetically. In February 1945, a few weeks after being posted to the Pacific following years of covering the war in Europe, Pyle told his millions of readers that "in Europe we felt that our enemies, horrible and deadly as they were, were still people. But out here I soon gathered that the Japanese were looked upon as something subhuman and repulsive, the way some people feel about cockroaches or mice." Pyle went on to describe his response on seeing Japanese prisoners for the first time. "They were wrestling and laughing and talking just like normal human beings," he wrote. "And yet they gave me the creeps, and I wanted a mental bath after looking at them." Sober magazines like *Science Digest* ran articles titled "Why Americans Hate Japs More Than Nazis." By incarcerating Japanese Americans, but not German Americans or Italian Americans, the United States government—eventually with Supreme Court backing—gave its official imprimatur to the designation of the Japanese as a racial enemy. It did so, of course, in the most formal and judicious language.

It is not really surprising that the Japanese, rather than the Germans and their decimation of the Jews, dominated American racial thinking. In the United States, as well as Britain and most of Europe, anti-Semitism was strong and—as David Wyman among others has documented so well—the Holocaust was wittingly neglected or a matter of indifference. Japan's aggression, on the other hand, stirred the deepest recesses of white supremacism and provoked a response bordering on the apocalyptic. As the Hearst papers took care to editorialize, the war in Europe, however terrible, was still a "family fight" that did not threaten the very essence of occidental civilization. One Hearst paper bluntly identified the war in the Pacific as "the War of Oriental Races against Occidental Races for the Domination of the World."

There was almost visceral agreement on this. Thus Hollywood formulaically introduced good Germans as well as Nazis but almost never showed a "good Japanese." In depicting the Axis triumvirate, political cartoonists routinely gave the German enemy Hitler's face and the Italian enemy Mussolini's, but they rendered the Japanese as plain, homogeneous "Japanese" caricatures: short, round-faced, bucktoothed, slant-eyed, frequently myopic behind horn-rimmed glasses. In a similar way, phrasemakers fell unreflectively into the idiom seen in the *Science Digest* headline: Nazis and Japs. Indeed, whereas the German enemy was conflated to bad Germans (Nazis), the Japanese enemy was inflated to a supra-Japanese foe—not just the Japanese militarists, not just all the Japanese people, not just ethnic Japanese everywhere, but the Japanese as Orientals. Tin Pan Alley, as so often, immediately placed its finger on the American pulse. One of the many popular songs inspired by Pearl Harbor was titled "There'll Be No Adolph Hitler nor Yellow Japs to Fear." Pearl Harbor and the stunning Japanese victories over the colonial powers that followed so quickly in Southeast Asia seemed to confirm the worst Yellow Peril nightmares.

World War II in Asia was, of course, not simply or even primarily a race war. Alliances cut across race on both the Allied and Axis sides, and fundamental issues of power and ideology were at stake. Where the Japanese and the Anglo-American antagonists were concerned, however, an almost Manichaean racial cast overlay these other issues of contention. This was true on both sides. The Japanese were racist too toward the white enemy, and in conspicuously different ways toward the other Asians who fell within their "Co-Prosperity Sphere." Thus the war in Asia offers an unusually vivid case study through which to examine the tangled skein of race, language, and violence from a comparative perspective—not only with the luxury of retrospect, moreover, but also at a time when United States–Japan relations are very different and yet still riven with racial tension.

Figure 9.1 As this popular song title reveals, Americans routinely regarded the German enemy as but one part of the German populace ("Hitler," "the Nazis"), while at the same time identifying the "Japs" as a whole with an even larger Yellow Peril.

The war exposed core patterns of racist perception in many forms: formulaic expressions, code words, everyday metaphors, visual stereotypes. Such ways of thinking, speaking, and seeing were often vulgar, but their crudeness was by no means peculiar to any social class, educational level, political ideology, or place or circumstance (such as the battlefield as opposed to the home front as opposed to the corridors of power and policymaking). On the other hand, in many instances the racist patterns of perception and expression were just the opposite: subtle, nuanced, garbed in the language of empiricism and intellectuality. This too was typical. Ostensibly objective observations often are laced with prejudice.

That racist perceptions shape behavior may seem obvious, but the war experience calls attention to how subtly this occurs, and at how many different levels. Myths, in this case race myths, almost always override conclusions drawn from sober, rational, empirical observation—until cataclysmic events occur to dispel or discredit them. It took Pearl Harbor and Singapore to destroy the myth cherished by Caucasians that the Japanese were poor navigators and inept pilots and unimaginative strategists, for example, and it required a long, murderous struggle to rid the Japanese of their conceit that the Anglo-Americans were too degenerate and individualistic to gird for a long battle against a faraway foe. We have become so mesmerized by the contemporary cult of military intelligence gathering that we often fail to recognize how extensively unadulterated prejudice colors intelligence estimates, causing both overestimation and underestimation of the other side. Beyond this, in its most extreme form racism sanctions extermination—the genocide of the Jews, of course, but also the plain but patterned rhetoric of exterminating beasts, vermin, or demons that unquestionably helped raise tolerance for slaughter in Asia.

* * *

Five categories subsume the racist perceptions of the Japanese that dominated Anglo-American thinking during World War II. The Japanese were subhuman. They were little men, inferior to white Westerners in every physical, moral, and intellectual way. They were collectively primitive, childish, and mad—overlapping concepts that could be crudely expressed but also received "empirical" endorsement from social scientists and old Japan hands. At the same time, the Japanese also were portrayed as supermen. This was particularly true in the aftermath of their stunning early victories, and it is characteristic of this thinking that the despised enemy could be little men and supermen simultaneously. Finally, the Japanese in World War II became the nightmare come true of the Yellow Peril. This apocalyptic image embraced all others and made unmistakably clear that race hates, and not merely war hates or responses to Japanese behavior alone, were at issue.

Dehumanization of the enemy is desirable among men in combat. It eliminates scruples and hesitation from killing, the reasoning goes, and this contributes to self-preservation; the enemy, after all, is simultaneously dehumanizing and trying to kill you. Among Allied fighting men in the Pacific, this attitude emerged naturally in the ubiquitous metaphor of the hunt. Fighting Japanese in the jungle was like going after "small game in the woods back home" or tracking down a predatory animal. Killing them was compared to shooting down running quail, picking

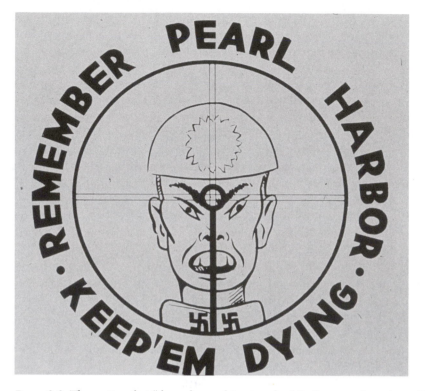

Figure 9.2 The notion that "the only good Jap is a dead Jap" was an American cliché during the entire course of the war. Undiluted rage at the surprise attack on Pearl Harbor greatly reinforced this sentiment, as seen in this graphic that appeared in a monthly magazine for marines early in 1942.

off rabbits, bringing a rabid and desperate beast to bay and finishing it off. The former sportsman was now simply "getting *bigger* game." One put the crosshairs on the crouching Jap, just as in deer hunting back home.

The kill did not remain confined to the combat zones, however, nor did the metaphors of dehumanization remain fixed at this general, almost, casual level. In the United States, signs appeared in store windows declaring "Open Season on Japs," and "Jap hunting licenses" were distributed amid the hysteria that accompanied the incarceration of Japanese Americans. The psychology of the hunt became indistinguishable from a broader psychology of extermination that came to mean not merely taking no prisoners on the battlefield, but also having no qualms about extending the kill to the civilian population in Japan. Here the more precise language and imagery of the race war became apparent. The Japanese were vermin. More pervasive yet, they were apes, monkeys, "jaundiced baboons." The war in Asia popularized these dehumanizing epithets to a degree that still can be shocking in retrospect, but the war did not spawn them. These were classic tropes of racist denigration, deeply embedded in European and American consciousness. War simply pried them loose.

Vermin was the archetypal metaphor Nazis attached to the Jews, and the appalling consequences of that dehumanization have obscured the currency of this imagery in the war in Asia. On Iwo Jima, the press found amusement in noting that some marines went into battle with "Rodent Exterminator" stenciled on their helmets. Incinerating Japanese in caves with flamethrowers was referred to as "clearing out a rat's nest." Soon after Pearl Harbor, the prospect of exterminating the Japanese vermin in their nest at home was widely applauded. The most popular float in a day-long victory parade in New York in mid-1942 was titled "Tokyo: We Are Coming," and depicted bombs falling on a frantic pack of yellow rats. A cartoon in the March 1945 issue of *Leatherneck,* the monthly magazine for marines, portrayed the insect "Louseous japanicas" and explained that though this epidemic of lice was being exterminated in the Pacific, "before a complete cure may be effected the origin of the plague, the breeding grounds around the Tokyo area, must be completely annihilated." "Louseous japanicas" appeared almost simultaneously with initiation of the policy of systematically firebombing Japanese cities and accurately reflected a detached tolerance for annihilationist and exterminationist rhetoric at all levels of United States society. As the British embassy in Washington noted in a weekly report, Americans perceived the Japanese as "a nameless mass of vermin."

Perception of the Japanese as apes and monkeys similarly was not confined to any particular group or place. Even before Pearl Harbor, Sir Alexander Cadogan, the permanent undersecretary of the British Foreign Office, routinely referred to the Japanese as "beastly little monkeys" and the like in his diary. Following Japan's capitulation, United States General Robert Eichelberger, alluding to the Japanese mission en route to the Philippines to arrange the surrender procedures, wrote to his wife that "first, monkeys will come to Manila." Among Western political cartoonists, the simian figure was surely the most popular caricature for the Japanese. David Low, the brilliant antifascist cartoonist working out of London, was fond of this. The *New York Times* routinely reproduced such graphics in its Sunday edition, at one point adding its own commentary that it might be more accurate to identify the Japanese as the "missing link." On the eve of the British debacle at Singapore, the British humor magazine *Punch* depicted Japanese soldiers in full-page splendor as chimpanzees with helmets and guns swinging from tree to tree. *Time* used the same image on its cover for 26 January 1942, contrasting the monkey invaders with the dignified Dutch military in Indonesia. The urbane *New Yorker* magazine also found the monkeymen in trees conceit witty. The *Washington Post* compared Japanese atrocities in the Philippines and German atrocities in Czechoslovakia in a 1942 cartoon pairing a gorilla labeled "Japs" and a Hitler figure labeled simply "Hitler." In well-received Hollywood combat films such as *Bataan* and *Guadalcanal Diary*, GIs routinely referred to the Japanese as monkeys.

The ubiquitous simian idiom of dehumanization came out of a rich tradition of bigoted Western iconography and graphically revealed the ease with which demeaning racist stereotypes could be floated from one target of prejudice to another. Only a short while before they put the Japanese in trees, for example, *Punch*'s artists had been rendering the Irish as apes. Generations of white cartoonists also had previously refined the simian caricature in their depictions of Negroes and various Central American and Caribbean peoples. The popular illustrators, in turn, were merely replicating a basic tenet in the pseudoscience of white supremacism—the argument that the "Mongoloid" and "Negroid" races (and for Englishmen, the Irish) represented a lower stage of evolution. Nineteenth-century Western scientists and social scientists had offered almost unanimous support to this thesis, and such ideas persisted into the mid-twentieth century. President Franklin D. Roosevelt, for example, was informed by a physical anthropologist at the Smithsonian Institution that Japanese skulls were "some 2,000 years less developed than ours."

In the world outside the monkey house, the Japanese commonly were referred to as "the little men." Their relatively short stature contributed to this, but again the phrase was essentially metaphorical. The Japanese, it was argued, were small in

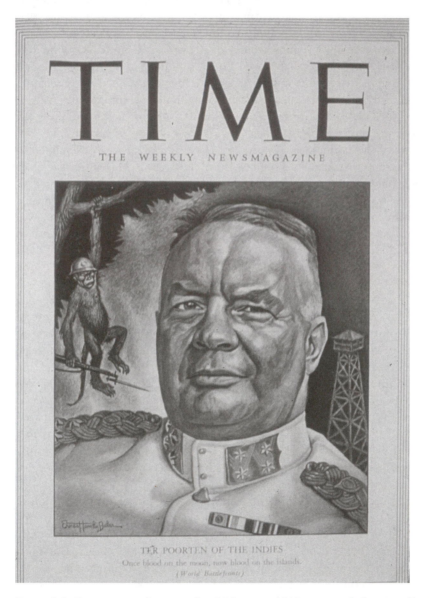

Figure 9.3 Time magazine's cover for 26 January 1942 conveyed the virtually ubiquitous Anglo-American perception of the war as a conflict between Japanese "monkeymen" and civilized Caucasians—in this instance, the Dutch commander of the Netherlands East Indies. © *1942 Time Inc.*

Figure 9.4 Dehumanizing the Japanese enemies made killing them easier. This cartoon from the *Chicago Tribune* typifies the prevailing American sense of a just war of retribution against a subhuman foe.

accomplishments compared with Westerners. No great "universal" achievements were to be found in their traditional civilization; they were latecomers to the modern challenges of science and technology, imitators rather than innovators, ritualists rather than rationalists. Again, the cartoonists provided a good gauge of this conceit. More often than not, in any ensemble of nationalities the Japanese figures were dwarfish.

Such contempt led, among other things, to a pervasive underestimation of Japanese intentions and capabilities by British and American observers at even the highest levels. Before Pearl Harbor, it was common wisdom among Westerners that the Japanese could not shoot, sail, or fly very well. Nor could they think imaginatively; as a British intelligence report carefully explained, this was because the enormous energy required to memorize the ideographic writing system dulled their brains and killed the spark of creativity. There can be few better examples of the

power of myth and stereotype over the weight of objective analysis than the unpreparedness of the Westerners when Japan attacked. Almost everything was a shock:
the audacity of the Pearl Harbor attack and the ability of the Japanese to bring it
off, the effectiveness of the Zero aircraft (which had been in operation in China for
over a year), the superb skills of the Japanese pilots, the esprit and discipline of the
Japanese ground forces, the lightning multipronged assault against the European
and American colonial enclaves. Equally shocking, of course, was the Western side
of the coin: the unpreparedness in Hawaii, the debacle at Singapore, the humiliation in the Philippines. In the long view, despite Japan's eventual defeat, the events
of 1941–42 exposed the dry rot of the old empires and irreparably shattered the
mystique of white superiority among the native peoples of Asia.

These Japanese victories—coupled with the spectacle of Japanese brutality and
atrocity—set whole new worlds of racial thinking in motion. The little men
suddenly became supermen; and at the same time, more elaborate versions of the
little-men thesis were developed. A remarkable intelligence report circulated by
psychological warfare experts within General Douglas MacArthur's command in
mid-1944, for example, masticated the old thesis with excruciating thoroughness:

> And yet in every sense of the word the Japanese are *little people*. Some
> observers claim there would have been no Pearl Harbor had the Japanese
> been three inches taller. The archipelago itself is a land of diminutive
> distances. Japanese houses are artistic but flimsy and cramped. The
> people, tiny in stature, seem to play at living. To a Westerner they
> and their country possess the strange charm of toyland. Centuries of
> isolation have accentuated the restrictive characteristics of their outlook
> on life.
>
> Being *little people*, the Japanese dreamed of power and glory, but
> lacked a realistic concept of the material requirements for a successful
> world war. Moreover, they were totally unable to envisage the massive
> scale of operations in which the United States is now able to indulge.[1]

At the same time, the little-men thesis also was elaborated on in ways that shed
harsh light on racist bias in the academic disciplines by revealing how Western social
sciences could be used to support popular prejudices. The war years witnessed the
emergence of anthropologists, sociologists, psychologists, and psychiatrists as the
new mandarins of theories of "national character," and on the whole they performed
a valuable service in repudiating the old theories of biological determinism. What
the social scientists did not dispel, however, were the racial stereotypes that had
been associated with biological determinism. On the contrary, they essentially
reaffirmed these stereotypes by offering new cultural or sociopsychological explanations for them.

This is seen most clearly in three of the most influential themes that American
and British social scientists introduced to explain Japanese behavior. The Japanese,
they argued, were still essentially a primitive or tribal people, governed by ritualistic
and particularistic values. The influence of cultural anthropologists was particularly
apparent here. Furthermore, it was emphasized that Japanese behavior could be
analyzed effectively using Western theories of child or adolescent behavior. Here

the Anglo-American intellectuals turned to Freudian-influenced theories concerning toilet training and psychic blockage at various stages of immaturity (the British social anthropologist Geoffrey Gorer was extremely influential on this theme) and also extolled the value of applying insights gained from American studies "of individual adolescent psychology and of the behavior of adolescents in gangs in our society, as a systematic approach to better understanding of the Japanese" (the quotation is from the minutes of a large 1944 symposium involving, among others, Margaret Mead and Talcott Parsons). Finally, in the third great preoccupation of the new intellectual mandarins, it was argued that the Japanese as a collectivity were mentally and emotionally unstable—neurotic, schizophrenic, psychotic, or simply hysterical.

In the final analysis, the "national character" studies amounted to a new way of explaining what the presumedly discredited biological determinists had concluded long ago: that the Japanese as a people displayed arrested development. Although this was not inherent in their genes, it was the inevitable consequence of their peculiar history and culture. All this was expressed with considerable erudition, and many of the insights of wartime social scientists concerning societal pressures and situational ethics remain influential today. For the proverbial man from Mars given access only to such wartime writings, however, it would be reasonable to conclude that imperialism, war, and atrocity had been invented in Asia during the twentieth century by developmentally retarded Japanese. They were unique, sui generis, and very peculiar indeed.

When all was said and done, however, these designations of Japanese peculiarity possessed a universal quality. They were formulaic and rested in considerable part on code words that transcended Japan and even transcended racial and cultural discourse in general. In suggestive ways, these code words also overlapped with vocabularies associated with discrimination based on gender and class. The central image of arrested growth, or "childishness," for example, was and remains one of the most basic constructs used by white Euro-Americans to characterize nonwhite peoples. This could be buttressed with pseudoscientific explanations (nonwhites being lower on the evolutionary scale, and thus biologically equivalent to children or adolescents vis-à-vis the "mature" Caucasian races) or meretricious social scientific equations (the "less developed" peoples of "less developed" nations, for example, or peoples alleged to be collectively blocked at a primitive or immature state psychologically by indigenous cultural practices or mores). In the milieu of war, the image of the Japanese as children conveyed utter contempt (as in *Newsweek*'s wartime reference to "the child mind of the Jap conscript"), but in less harsh circumstances it also was capable of evoking a condescending paternalism (as reflected in the depiction of Japanese after the surrender as "MacArthur's children" or as the beneficiaries of a student-teacher relationship with Americans). This same metaphor also is integral to the rationale of male domination and rule by elites. Thus, to describe women as childish or childlike is one of the most familiar ways men traditionally have signified both the inherent inferiority of women and their own obligation to protect or at least humor them. Similarly, dominant social and political classes commonly affirm their privileged status and inherent right to rule by dismissing the masses as irrational, irresponsible, and immature. In its softer guise, the elite sense of noblesse oblige masks class inequalities with a paradigm of parent-to-child obligations.

The resonances of this broader conceptual world also help clarify how Japan's attack on the West revitalized other fantasies. It is characteristic of the paranoia of self-designated master groups that even while dismissing others as inferior and "less developed," they attribute special powers to them. The lower classes may be immature to the elites, but they also are seen as possessing a fearsome potential for violence. Women may be irrational in male eyes, but they also are said to have special intuitive powers and the Jezebel potential of becoming castrators. Where Western perceptions of the Japanese and Asians in general are concerned, there is in fact a provocative congruence between the female and oriental mystiques as expressed by white male elites. Thus, even in the war years, the "femininity" of Japanese culture was indirectly if not directly emphasized. Traits attributed to the Japanese often were almost identical to those assigned to women in general: childishness, irrationality, emotional instability and "hysteria"—and also intuition, a sixth sense, and a talent for nondiscursive communication. It even was said that the Japanese, like women generally, possessed an exceptional capacity to endure suffering. Put negatively, these latter intuitive and emotional qualities could be equated with nonrationality and simply integrated into the argument of arrested development. Positively framed, they became suprarational powers—impossible to explain, but all the more alarming to contemplate.

Because nothing in the "rational" mind-set of Western leaders prepared them for either the audacity and skill of Japan's attack or the debacle of British, Dutch, and American capitulations to numerically inferior Japanese forces that followed in Southeast Asia, it was natural to look to nonrational explanations. Scapegoating helped obfuscate the situation—the United States commanders at Pearl Harbor were cashiered, and the West Coast Japanese Americans were locked up—but this was not enough. It also became useful to think of the Japanese as supermen. Graphic artists now drew the Japanese as giants on the horizon. Rhetorically, the new image usually emerged in a more serpentine or backhanded fashion. Thus the United States print media from 1941 to the end of the war featured a veritable "between the lines" subgenre debunking the new myth of the supermen. Battle A proved they could be beaten at sea, battle B that they could be beaten in the jungle, battle C that they were not unbeatable at night fighting, battle D that the myth of the "invincibility of the Zero" was finally being destroyed. The *New York Times Magazine* took it upon itself to address the issue head-on with a feature article titled "Japanese Superman: That Too Is a Fallacy." Admiral William Halsey, the most blatantly racist officer in the United States high command, later claimed that he deliberately belittled the Japanese as "monkeymen" and the like in order to discredit "the new myth of Japanese invincibility" and boost the morale of his men.

The myth of the superman was never completely dispelled. To the end of the war—even after most of the Japanese navy and merchant marine had been sunk; after Japanese soldiers in the field, cut off from support, had begun starving to death and were being killed by the tens and hundreds of thousands; after the urban centers of the home islands had come under regular bombardment—Allied planners continued to overestimate the will and capacity of the Japanese to keep fighting. There are surely many explanations for this, but prominent among them is a plainly racial consideration: the superman image was especially compelling because it meshed with the greatest of all the racist bogeys of the white men, the specter

Figure 9.5 Taking its caption from Rudyard Kipling's *Jungle Book*, this full-page illustration was published in *Punch* in mid-January 1942, as the Japanese were advancing down the Malay Peninsula toward Singapore.

of the Yellow Peril. Hatred toward the Japanese derived not simply from the reports of Japanese atrocities, but also from the deeper wellsprings of anti-Orientalism. *Time* magazine's coverage of the American response to Pearl Harbor, for example, opened on this very note. What did Americans say when they heard of the attack, *Time* asked rhetorically. And the answer it quoted approvingly as representative was, "Why, the yellow bastards!" *Time*'s cover portrait for 22 December 1941, depicting Admiral Yamamoto Isoroku, who planned the Pearl Harbor attack, was colored a single shade: bright yellow. At one time or another almost every mainstream newspaper and magazine fell into the color idiom, and yellow was by far the dominant color in anti-Japanese propaganda art. Among the music makers, we already have encountered Tin Pan Alley's revealing counterpoint of Hitler and the "Yellow Japs." Other song titles included "We're Gonna Find a Fellow Who Is Yellow and Beat Him Red, White, and Blue" and "Oh, You Little Son of an Oriental." In some American pronouncements, the Japanese were simply dismissed as "LYBs," a well-comprehended acronym for the double entendre "little yellow bellies."

Spokesmen for Asian Allies such as China were aghast at such insensitivity, and the war years as a whole became an agonizing revelation of the breadth and depth of anti-Asian prejudice in the United States. In the very midst of the war these revelations prompted a year-long congressional hearing to consider revision of the notorious "Oriental Exclusion Laws"—the capstone of formal discrimination against all people of Asian origin. What the Japanese attack brought to the surface, however, was something more elusive and interesting than the formal structures of discrimination: the concrete fears that underlay the perception of a menacing Orient.

Since the late nineteenth century, when the Yellow Peril idea was first expressed in the West, white people had been unnerved by a triple apprehension—recognition that the "hordes" of Asia outnumbered the population of the West, fear that these alien masses might gain possession of the science and technology that made Western domination possible, and the belief that Orientals possessed occult powers unfathomable to Western rationalists. By trumpeting the cause of Pan-Asianism and proclaiming the creation of a Greater East Asia Co-Prosperity Sphere, Japan raised the prospect that the Asian hordes might at last become united. With their Zero planes and big battleships and carriers, the Japanese gave notice that the technological and scientific gap had narrowed dramatically. And with the aura of invincibility that blossomed in the heat of the early victories, the Japanese "supermen" evoked the old fantasies of occult oriental powers. All this would be smashed in August 1945, when Japan capitulated. And it would all resurface three decades later when Japan burst on the scene as an economic superpower and other Asian countries began to emulate this "miracle."

*   *   *

Racism also shaped the Japanese perception of self and other—again in patterned ways, but patterns different from those of the West. History accounts for much of this difference. Over centuries, Japan had borrowed extensively from India, China, and more recently the West and had been greatly enriched thereby; and it acknowledged these debts. And over the course of the preceding century, the Japanese had felt the sting of Western condescension. Even when applauded by the Europeans and Americans for their accomplishments in industrializing and "Westernizing," the Japanese were painfully aware that they were still regarded as immature and unimaginative and unstable—good in the small things, as the saying went among the old Japan hands, and small in the great things.

Thus Japanese racial thinking was riven by an ambivalence that had no clear counterpart in white supremacist thinking. Like the white Westerners, they assumed a hierarchical world; but unlike the Westerners, they lacked the unambiguous power that would enable them to place themselves unequivocally at the top of the racial hierarchy. Toward Europeans and Americans, and the science and civilization they exemplified, the national response was one of admiration as well as fear, mistrust, and hatred. Toward all others—that is, toward nonwhites including Asians other than themselves, their attitude was less complicated. By the twentieth century Japan's success in resisting Western colonialism or neocolonialism and emerging as one of the so-called Great Powers had instilled among the Japanese an attitude toward weaker peoples and nations that was as arrogant and contemptuous as the racism of the Westerners. The Koreans and Chinese began to learn this in the 1890s and early 1900s; the peoples of Southeast Asia learned it quickly after 7 December 1941.

For Japan, the crisis of identity came to a head in the 1930s and early 1940s, taking several dramatic forms. Behind the joy and fury of the initial attacks in 1941–42, and indeed behind many of the atrocities against white men and women in Asia, was an unmistakable sense of racial revenge. At the same time, the Japanese began to emphasize their own destiny as a "leading race" (shidō minzoku). If one were to venture a single broad observation concerning the difference between the preoccupations of white supremacism and Japanese racism, it might be this: that whereas white racism devoted inordinate energy to the denigration of the other, Japanese racial thinking concentrated on elevating the self. In Japanese war films produced between 1937 and 1945, for example, the enemy was rarely depicted. Frequently it was not even made clear who the antagonist was. The films concentrated almost exclusively on the admirable "Japanese" qualities of the protagonists. The focus of the broader gamut of propaganda for domestic consumption was similar. In its language and imagery, Japanese prejudice thus appeared to be more benign than its white counterpart—by comparison, a soft racism—but this was misleading. The insularity of such introversion tended to depersonalize and, in its own peculiar way, dehumanize all non-Japanese "outsiders." In practice, such intense fixation on the self contributed to a wartime record of extremely callous and brutal behavior toward non-Japanese.

The central concept in this racial thinking was that most tantalizing of cultural fixations: the notion of purity. In Japan as elsewhere, this has a deep history not merely in religious ritual, but also in social practice and the delineation of insider and outsider (pure and impure) groups. By turning purity into a racial ideology for modern times, the Japanese were in effect nationalizing a concept traditionally associated with differentiation within their society. Purity was Japanized and made the signifier of homogeneity, of "one hundred million hearts beating as one," of a unique "Yamato soul" (Yamato damashii, from the ancient capital of the legendary first emperor). Non-Japanese became by definition impure. Whether powerful or relatively powerless, all were beyond the pale.

The ambiguity of the concept enhanced its effectiveness as a vehicle for promoting internal cohesion. At a superficial level, this fixation on the special purity or "sincerity" of the Japanese resembles the mystique of American "innocence." Whereas the latter is a subtheme in the American myth, however, the former was cultivated as the very essence of a powerful racial ideology. Like esoteric mantras, a variety of evocative (and often archaic) words and phrases were introduced to convey the special racial and moral qualities of the Japanese; and like esoteric mandalas, certain visual images (sun, sword, cherry blossom, snowcapped Mount Fuji, an abstract "brightness") and auspicious colors (white and red) were elevated as particularistic symbols of the purity of the Japanese spirit.

Where Westerners had turned eventually to pseudoscience and dubious social science to bolster theories of the inherent inferiority of nonwhite and non-Western peoples, the Japanese turned to mythohistory, where they found the origins of their superiority in the divine descent of their sovereign and the racial and cultural homogeneity of the sovereign's loyal subjects. Deity, monarch, and populace were made one, and no words captured this more effectively than the transcendent old phrase resurrected to supersede plain reference to "the Japanese": *Yamato minzoku*, the "Yamato race." "Yamato"—the name of the place where Jimmu, grandson of the grandson of the sun goddess, was alleged to have founded the imperial line in 660 B.C.—was redolent with the archaic mystique of celestial genetics that made Japan the divine land and the Japanese the chosen people. In *Yamato minzoku*, the association became explicitly racial and exclusionary. The race had no identity apart from the throne and the traditions that had grown up around it, and no outsider could hope to penetrate this community. This was blood nationalism of an exceptionally potent sort.

Many of these themes were elaborated in the ideological writings of the 1930s and early 1940s, and the cause of blood nationalism was elevated when 1940 became the occasion for massive ceremony and festivity in celebration of the 2,600 year anniversary of the "national foundation day." At the same time, the racial ideologues took care to emphasize that purity was not merely an original state, but also an ongoing process for each Japanese. Purity entailed virtues that needed to be cultivated, and preeminent among these were two moral ideals originally brought to Japan from China: loyalty and filial piety (*chūkō*). Why these became a higher expression of morality in Japan than elsewhere, higher even than in China, was explained by their ultimate focus in the divine sovereign. Purity lay in transcendence of ego and identification with a greater truth or cause; and in the crisis years of the 1930s and early 1940s this greater truth was equated with the militarized imperial state. War itself, with all the sacrifice it demanded, became an act of purification. And death in war, the ultimate expression of selflessness, became the supreme attainment of this innate Japanese purity. We know now that most Japanese fighting men who died slowly did not pass away with the emperor's name on their lips, as propaganda claimed they did. Most often they called (as GIs did also) for their mothers. Still, they fought and died with fervor and bravery, enveloped in the propaganda of being the divine soldiers of the divine land, and this contributed to the aura of a people possessed of special powers.

Both the Western myth of the superman and the bogey of the Yellow Peril had their analogue in this emphasis the Japanese themselves placed on their unique suprarational spiritual qualities. In Western eyes, however, this same spectacle of fanatical mass behavior also reinforced the image of the little men, of the Japanese as a homogeneous, undifferentiated mass. There is no small irony in this, for what we see here is the coalescence of Japanese indoctrination with the grossest anti-Japanese stereotypes of the Westerners. In the crudest of Anglo-American colloquialisms, it was argued that "a Jap is a Jap" (the famous quotation of General John DeWitt, who directed the incarceration of the Japanese Americans). In the 1945 propaganda film *Know Your Enemy—Japan*, produced by Frank Capra for the United States Army, the Japanese were similarly described as "photographic prints off the same negative"— a line now frequently cited as the classic expression of racist American contempt for the Japanese. Yet in essence this "seen one seen them all" attitude was not greatly different from the "one hundred million hearts beating as one" indoctrination that the Japanese leaders themselves promoted. Homogeneity and separateness *were* essential parts of what the Japanese ideologues said about themselves. In their idiom, this was integral to the superiority of the Yamato race. To non-Japanese, it was further cause for derision.

The rhetoric of the pure self also calls attention to the potency of implicit as opposed to explicit denigration. In proclaiming their own purity, the Japanese cast others as inferior because they did not, and could not, share in the grace of the divine land. Non-Japanese were, by the very logic of the ideology, impure, foul, polluted. Such sentiments usually flowed like an underground stream beneath the ornate paeans to the "pure and cloudless heart" of the Japanese, but occasionally they burst to the surface with extraordinary vehemence. Thus, in a book of war reportage titled *Bataan*, Hino Ashihei, one of the best-known Japanese wartime writers, described American POWs as "people whose arrogant nation once tried to unlawfully treat our motherland with contempt." "As I watch large numbers of the surrendered soldiers," he continued. "I feel like I am watching filthy water running from the sewage of a nation which derives from impure origins and has lost its pride of race. Japanese soldiers look particularly beautiful, and I feel exceedingly proud of being Japanese." These were the American prisoners, of course, whom Japanese soldiers brutalized in the Bataan death march. Hino's contempt for the "impure" American prisoners provides an almost perfect counterpoint to Ernie Pyle's revulsion on seeing his first "subhuman" Japanese POWs.

As a rule, however, the Japanese turned to one particular negative image when referring directly to the Anglo-American enemy: the demon or devil. "Devilish Anglo-Americans" (*kichiku Ei-Bei*) was the most familiar epithet for the white foe. In the graphic arts the most common depiction of Americans or British was a horned Roosevelt or Churchill, drawn exactly like the demons (*oni, akuma*) found in Japanese folklore and folk religion. As a metaphor of dehumanization, the demonic white man was the counterpart of the Japanese monkeyman in Western thinking, but the parallel was by no means exact. The demon was a more impressive and ambiguous figure than the ape, and certainly of a different category entirely from vermin. In Japanese folk renderings, the demon was immensely powerful; it was often intelligent, or at least exceedingly crafty; and it possessed talents and powers beyond those of ordinary Japanese. Not all demons had to be killed; some could be won over and turned from menaces into guardians. Indeed, Japanese soldiers killed in battle often were spoken of as having become "demons protecting the country" (*gokoku no oni*)—easy to imagine when one recalls the statues of ferocious deities that often guard Buddhist temples. Here again, like the flexible Western metaphor of the child, was an intriguingly malleable stereotype—one that would be turned about dramatically after the war, when the Americans became the military "protectors" of Japan.

During the war years, however, this more benign potential of the demonic other was buried. For the Japanese at war, the demon worked as a metaphor for the enemy in ways that plain subhuman or bestial images could not. It conveyed a sense of the adversary's great power and special abilities, and in this respect it captured some of the ambivalence that had always marked Japan's modern relationship with the West. At the same time, the demonic other played to deep feelings of insecurity by evoking the image of an ever-present outside threat. Unlike apes or vermin, the demon did not signify a random presence. In Japanese folklore, these figures always lurked just beyond the boundaries of the community or the borders of the country—in forests and mountains outside the village, on islands off the coast. In origin, they exemplified not a racial fear, but a far more basic fear of outsiders in general.

Contrary to the myth of being homogeneous, Japanese society was honeycombed with groups suspicious of one another, and the blue-eyed barbarians from across the seas became absorbed into patterns of thinking that had emerged centuries earlier as a response to these tense and threatening insider/outsider relationships. The Westerners who suddenly appeared on Japan's horizon in the mid-nineteenth century were the most formidable of all outsiders, and the response to them mobilized nationalist and racist sentiments in unprecedented ways. Symbolically the demonic other was already present to be racialized. There was, moreover, a further dimension to this complicated play of symbolic representation, for it was but a short step from the perception of an ever-present threat to the consciousness of being an eternal victim. This too is a sentiment that recurs frequently in the Japanese tradition, and in the modern world this "victim consciousness" (*higaisha ishiki*) became inextricably entangled with the perception of foreign threats. From this perspective, modern Japanese racism as exemplified in the demonic other reflected an abiding sense of being always the threatened, the victim, the aggrieved—and never the threat, the victimizer, the giver of grief.

Where images and actions came together most decisively, however, demon, ape, and vermin functioned similarly. All made killing easier by dehumanizing the enemy. The rhetoric of "kill the American demons and kill the British demons" became commonplace not only in combat, but also on the home front. A popular magazine published in late 1944 conveyed the fury of this rhetoric. Under the title "Devilish Americans and English," the magazine ran a two-page drawing of Roosevelt and Churchill as debauched ogres carousing with fellow demons in sight of Mount Fuji and urged all Japanese, "Beat and kill these animals that have lost their human nature! That is the great mission that Heaven has given to the Yamato race, for the eternal peace of the world!" Another magazine, reporting on the decisive battle in the Philippines, declared that the more American beasts and demons "are sent to hell, the cleaner the world will be." Iwo Jima, where United States marines called themselves "rodent exterminators," was described in official Japanese newsreels as "a suitable place to slaughter the American devils."

Figure 9.6 In the most common Japanese rendering, the Anglo-American enemy was demonized. This illustration, which appeared immediately after Pearl Harbor, accompanied a discussion of the road to war and depicts innocent Japan extending the hand of friendship while the United States and Britain (President Roosevelt and Prime Minister Churchill) feign amity and clandestinely extend their demonic claws (marked "conspiracy") to seize the Orient. From *Osaka Puck*, January 1942.

Demonization was by no means an essential precondition for killing, however. The most numerous victims of Japanese aggression and atrocity were other Asians, who were rarely depicted this way. Toward them the Japanese attitude was a mixture of "Pan-Asian" propaganda for public consumption, elaborate theories of racial hierarchy and Japanese hegemony at official and academic levels, and condescension and contempt in practice. Apart from a small number of idealistic military officers and civilian officials, few Japanese appear to have taken seriously the egalitarian rhetoric of Pan-Asian solidarity and genuine liberation of colonized Asian peoples. Never for a moment did the Japanese consider liberating their own Korean and Formosan colonies, and policy toward Southeast Asia—even when "independence" was granted—was always framed in terms that made Japan's preeminence as the "leading race" absolutely clear. The purity so integral to Japanese thinking was peculiar to the Japanese as a race and culture—not to "oriental" peoples in general—and consequently there emerged no real notion of "Asian supremacism" that could be regarded as a close counterpart to the white supremacism of the Anglo-Americans.

Figure 9.7 The Japanese counterpart to the Anglo-American exterminationist imagery of killing beasts entailed annihilating demons. In this poster from 1942, the bayonet of Japanese righteousness skewers the Anglo-American demons. The caption reads, "The death of these wretches will be the birthday of world peace." From *Osaka Puck*, February and December 1942.

Before the 1930s, the Japanese did not have a clearly articulated position toward other Asians. The rush of events thereafter, including the invasion of China and the decision to push south into Southeast Asia, forced military planners and their academic supporters to codify and clarify existing opinions on these matters. The result was a small outpouring of studies, reports, and pronouncements—many of a confidential nature—that explicitly addressed the characteristics of the various peoples of Asia and the appropriate policy toward them. That these were not casual undertakings was made amply clear in 1981, when a hitherto unknown secret study dating from 1943 was discovered in Tokyo. Prepared by a team of some forty researchers associated with the Population and Race Section of the Research Bureau of the Ministry of Health and Welfare, this work devoted over three thousand pages to analysis of race theory in general and the different races of Asia in particular. The title of the report gives an inkling of its contents: *An Investigation of Global Policy with the Yamato Race as Nucleus*.

The *Investigation* was a serious intelligence report, and its style was academic. In its way it was a counterpart to the "national character" writings of the Anglo-American social scientists who mobilized in support of the Allied war effort. The Japanese researchers called attention to Western theories of race and, while attentive to Nazi ideas, surveyed the gamut of racial thinking beginning with Plato and Aristotle. In the modern world, they noted, racism, nationalism, and capitalist imperialism had become inseparably intertwined. And though modern scholarship had repudiated the notion of biologically pure races, blood still mattered greatly in contributing to psychological unity. In this regard, as Karl Haushofer had observed, Japan was fortunate in having become a uniform racial state (Haushofer, the geopolitician whose writings influenced the Nazis, had done his doctoral work on Japan). At the same time, overseas expansion should be seen as essential not merely for the attainment of military and strategic security, but also for preserving and revitalizing racial consciousness and vigor. On this point the Japanese again quoted Western experts, including not merely the Germans but also the British. Looking ahead, it was predictable that the second and third generations of overseas Japanese might face problems of identity, and thus it was imperative to develop settlement policies that would thwart their assimilation and ensure that they "remain aware of the superiority of the Japanese people and proud of being a member of the leading race."

The focus of this massive report was on Asian rather than Western peoples, and its dry language provides insight into how racial inequality in Asia was rationalized. The central metaphor was the family. The critical phrase was "proper place"—a term that had roots in Confucian prescriptions for domestic relationships but was carefully extended to cover international relations beginning in the late 1930s. The family idiom is another example of the malleable social construct, for it suggests harmony and reciprocity on the one hand, but clear-cut hierarchy and division of authority and responsibility on the other; and it was the latter that really mattered to the Japanese. The authors of the *Investigation* were emphatic in condemning false consciousness concerning equality. "To view those who are in essence unequal as if they were equal is itself inequitable," they observed. And it followed from this that "to treat those who are unequal unequally is to realize equality." The family exemplified such equitable inequality, and the Japanese writers made clear that Japan was not merely the head of the family in Asia, but also destined to maintain that position "eternally." Whether the Yamato race also was destined to become the head of the global family of races and nations was left unanswered, although passing comments suggested that this was the ultimate goal. The opening pages of the study flatly declared that the war would continue "until Anglo-American imperialistic democracy has been completely vanquished and a new world order erected in its place." And as the *Investigation* made amply clear, the Japanese-led imperium in Asia would assume a leading role in this new world order.

Figure 9.8 "Destroy Anglo-American thought" published in *Osaka Puck* magazine in 1942.

Despite their Confucian overtones, the family metaphor and proper place philosophy bore close resemblance to Western thinking on issues of race and power. The Japanese took as much pleasure as any white Westerner in categorizing the weaker peoples of Asia as "children." In their private reports and directives, they made clear that "proper place" meant a division of labor in Asia in which the Yamato race would control the economic, financial, and strategic reins of power within an autarkic bloc and thereby "hold the key to the very existence of all the races of East Asia." A secret policy guideline issued in Singapore at the outset of the war was equally frank. "Japanese subjects shall be afforded opportunities for development everywhere," it stated, "and after establishing firm footholds they shall exalt their temperament as the leading race with the basic doctrine of planning the long-term expansion of the Yamato race." Despite their detailed country-by-country, race-by-race summaries, the Japanese were interested in other Asians only as subordinate members of the family who could be manipulated to play roles assigned by Japan. For other Asians the real meaning of Japan's racial rhetoric was obvious. "Leading race" meant master race, "proper place" meant inferior place, "family" meant patriarchal oppression.

* * *

Given the virulence of the race hate that permeated the Pacific war, at first it seems astonishing that Americans and Japanese were able to move so quickly toward cordial relations after Japan's surrender. Intimate face-to-face contact for purposes other than mutual slaughter enabled each side to rehumanize the other in the highly structured milieu of the Allied Occupation of Japan, which lasted from 1945 to 1952. Although the United States-dominated Occupation was ethnocentric and overbearing in many respects, it also was infused with goodwill and—in its early stages—a commitment to "demilitarization and democratization" that struck a responsive chord among most of the defeated Japanese. Contrary to the wartime stereotypes of propagandists in both the Allied and Japanese camps, most Japanese were sick of regimentation, indoctrination, and militarism. At the same time, the cold war facilitated a quick diversion of enmity, and anticommunism became a new crusade uniting the two former antagonists at the state level. Enemies changed, enmity did not.

On both sides, the abrupt metamorphosis from war to peace was cushioned by the malleability of racial, cultural, and ideological stereotypes. With only a small twist, patterns of perception that had abetted mass slaughter now proved conducive to paternalistic patronage on the American side—and to acquiescence to such paternalism by many Japanese. Racism did not disappear from the United States-Japan relationship, but it was softened and transmogrified. For the Americans, the vermin disappeared but the monkeymen lingered for a while as charming pets. The September 1945 cover of *Leatherneck*, for example—the first issue of the marine monthly to appear after Japan's capitulation—featured a cheery cartoon of a GI holding a vexed but thoroughly domesticated monkey wearing the cap, shirt, and leggings of the Imperial Army. *Newsweek*, in its feature article on what sort of people the Americans might expect to find in Japan when the Occupation commenced, ran "Curious Simians" as one subheading.

Other racist stereotypes traveled from war to peace in comparable ways. Although defeat temporarily extinguished the superman mystique, it reinforced the perception of the Japanese as little men or lesser men. Stated conversely, victory over Japan reinforced the conceit of inherent white and Western superiority. The more precise associations of Japan's "lesser" stature, however—the primitive social relations and attitudes, the childishness of the populace both psychologically and politically, the collective neurosis—all now provoked a paternalistic response. The American overseers of Occupied Japan thought in terms of a civilizing mission that would eliminate what was primitive, tribal, and ritualistic—an old but idealistic colonial attitude indeed. They would guide an immature people with backward institutions toward maturity. The Japanese "children" now became pupils in General MacArthur's school of democracy, learners and borrowers of advanced United States technology, followers of United States cold war policies. Where the Japanese psyche was tortured, the Americans would be healers.

These were not frivolous attitudes, any more than paternalism itself is necessarily frivolous. At the individual level, moreover, countless Japanese and Americans collaborated equitably in pursuit of common goals. Neither democratization and demilitarization nor—later—economic reconstruction and remilitarization were ethnocentric American goals forced on unwilling Japanese. The overall relationship, however, was inherently unequal and patronizing on the part of the Americans, and it is here that racist attitudes survived. United States policymakers at the highest level also were not above cynically manipulating Japanese racism to serve their own purposes. In 1951, when Japan's allegiance in the cold war was still not entirely certain, for example, John Foster Dulles recommended that the Americans and British take advantage of Japanese feelings of "superiority as against the Asiatic mainland masses" and play up the "social prestige" of being associated with the Western alliance. (In a fine example of a truly free-floating stereotype, Dulles and other American leaders also liked to emphasize that the Soviet menace could be better understood if one remembered that the Russians were an Asiatic people.)

On the Japanese side, defeat was bitter but peace was sweet, and certain attitudes associated with wartime racial thinking also proved adaptable to the postsurrender milieu. Proper-place thinking facilitated acceptance of a subordinate status vis-à-vis the victorious Allies, at least for the time being. In this regard it is helpful to recall that the "leading race" rhetoric of the war years was a relatively new ideology in Japan, and that for most of their modern history the Japanese had played a subordinate role in the world order. The militarism of the 1930s and early 1940s arose out of a desire to alter that insecure status, and it ended in disaster. To seek a new place in new ways after 1945 was in fact the continuation of a familiar quest.

In fascinating ways, the wartime fixation on purity and purification proved adaptable to this commitment to a new path of development. Individuals who had been exhorted to purge self and society of decadent Western influences before the surrender now found themselves exhorted to purge the society of militarism and feudalistic legacies. This sense of "cleansing" Japan of foul and reactionary influences was truly phenomenal in the early postwar years, and while this tapped popular aspirations for liberation, it also politicized the militarists' ideology of the pure self in undreamed-of ways. Universal "democratic" values now became the touchstone of purity. And the guardians at the gates, to cap these astounding transmogrifications, were the erstwhile American demons. The United States assumption of a military role as protector of postwar Japan was a hard-nosed, rational policy, but from the Japanese perspective it had a subtle, almost subconscious logic. The fearsome demons of Japanese folklore, after all, were often won over and put to use by the ostensibly weaker folk.

The transitional adaptations of proper place, purity, and the demon more or less deracialized the wartime fixations. They did not, however, eliminate racial tensions latent in the structure of institutionalized inequality that characterized postwar United States–Japan relations until recently. So long as Japan remained conspicuously inferior to the United States in power and influence, the structure and psychology of what is known in Japan as "subordinate independence" could be maintained. When relations of power and influence changed, neither side could be expected to rethink these fundamental relationships without trauma. The great change came in the 1970s, when it became apparent—abruptly and shockingly for almost everyone concerned—that Japan had become an economic superpower while America was in relative decline. In this situation, war talk became fashionable again: talk of trade wars; ruminations on who really won the Pacific war; doomsday warnings of a new yen bloc, a seriously rearmed Japan, a "financial Pearl Harbor." In American rhetoric, the simian subhumans were resurrected as "predatory economic animals," the old wartime supermen returned as menacing "miraclemen," garbed in Western business suits but practicing sumo capitalism. Japanese, in turn, often in high government positions, decried America's demonic "Japan bashing" and at the same time attributed their country's accomplishments to a "Yamato race" homogeneity and purity that "mongrelized" America could never hope to emulate.[3]

As times change, the malleable idioms of race and culture, power and status, change with them. They never completely disappear.

Acknowledgements

An earlier version of this essay, without the present illustrations, is included in *Japan in War and Peace* by John W. Dower, copyright 1993 by John W. Dower. Reprinted by permission of The New Press. This chapter summarizes some of the themes developed at length in my *War without Mercy: Race and Power in the Pacific War* (New York, 1986), where extensive annotations can be found. Here I have focused in particular on racial language in comparative perspective.

Notes

1   "Answer to Japan," 20. This report appears in several archival collections at the Hoover Institution, Stanford University. Cf. "Bonner Frank Fellers Collection," boxes 1 and 15; also "U.S. Army Forces in the Pacific, Psychological Warfare Branch," box 1.

2   From Hino's 1942 book *Bātān Hantō Kōjōki*, as quoted in Haruko Taya Cook, "Voices from the Front: Japanese War Literature, 1937–1945" (M.A. thesis in Asian Studies, University of California, Berkeley, 1984), 59–60.

3   I have addressed these themes in contemporary United States-Japan relations in greater detail in *Japan in War and Peace* (New York, 1993), 279–335.

Chapter 10

D'Ann Campbell

WOMEN IN COMBAT
The World War II experience in the United States, Great Britain, Germany, and the Soviet Union

WOMEN ARE THE INVISIBLE combatants of World War II.[1] The concern here is with regular combat soldiers in uniform, not resistance fighters or guerrillas. "Combat" means an organized lethal attack on an organized enemy (and does not include self-defense in emergency situations).[2] Hundreds of thousands of women engaged in combat. They served on both sides and on every front. German women soldiers helped inflict casualties on American and British forces, and in turn they were killed, wounded, or captured. Likewise, Soviet and British women fought bravely.

American women were not sent into combat. The question is why not—and what does that tell us about gender roles in America? Historians in recent years have been exploring the changes in gender roles during World War II. The general consensus is that on the home front women temporarily assumed new roles ("Rosie the Riveter") but that no permanent or radical transformation took place.[3] The question is more open regarding military roles: making women soldiers was the most dramatic government experiment in changing traditional sex roles ever attempted. Putting these women soldiers into combat constituted a radical inversion of the traditional roles of women as the passive sweetheart/wife/sex object whose ultimate mission was to wait for their virile menfolk to return from their masculine mission of fighting and dying for "apple pie and motherhood" (that is, for traditional social values.) The Pentagon was well aware of the performance of European women soldiers, and Army Chief of Staff George C. Marshall conducted a full-scale experiment to see how well American women could perform. There was never a question of an all-female unit; the issue at stake was whether mixed gender units could perform combat roles effectively. The experiment stunned the General Staff: mixed gender units performed better than all-male units. As the draft scraped further and further down the barrel, the availability of large numbers of potentially excellent unutilized soldiers became more and more an anomaly. The demands of military efficiency called for assigning women to combat.

The Luftwaffe lost the Battle of Britain in 1940 but remained a powerful force. It had to be defeated, and the ground soldiers' preferred solution was strong antiaircraft units (hereafter AA units).[4] In 1941 the British began using their women Auxiliary Territorial Service (ATS) soldiers in "protected" AA units; protected because these soldiers were immune from capture and their living conditions could be closely monitored. To help emphasize the importance of women serving in AA units to free more men to fight on the European continent, Winston Churchill's daughter Mary served in one such brigade. Marshall asked General Dwight Eisenhower to investigate the effectiveness of these mixed-gender AA units. When Eisenhower gave a positive report, Marshall decided to conduct his own experiment.[5] Security was tight—there were no leaks whatever until long after the war.[6]

Marshall wanted to recruit for his experiment women who had already volunteered for military service. He turned to the only official American women's organization at that time, the Women's Auxiliary Army Corps (WAAC) which in July of 1943 would become the Women's Army Corps. Waacs from the 150th and 151st WAAC Technical Companies and the 62nd WAAC Operations Company, a total of 21 officers and 374 enrollees, were selected for this experiment. From 15 December 1942 to 15 April 1943, they were trained in the Military District of Washington on two composite antiaircraft gun batteries and the nearby searchlight units. The Waacs served with the 36th Coast Artillery Brigade AA. Colonel Edward W. Timberlake, the immediate commander of these experimental units had nothing but praise for them. "The experiences . . . indicate that all WAAC personnel exhibited an outstanding devotion to duty, willingness and ability to absorb and grasp technical information concerning the problems, maintenance and tactical disposition to all types of equipment." Indeed the Waacs learned their duties much more quickly than the men, most of whom had been classified as "limited-duty service." Colonel Timberlake recommended that in the future the training periods for women recruits could be shortened. When evaluating the searchlight units, he reported, "the same willingness to learn and devotion to duty has been manifested in these units as in the gun batteries."[7]

In contradiction to generally existing stereotypes of women being physically too weak to perform combat jobs, Timberlake concluded that women met the physical, intellectual, and psychological standards for this mission. In an echo of a widespread belief at the time, he reported, "WAAC personnel were found to be superior in efficiency to men in all functions involving delicacy of manual dexterity." He specifically listed their operation at the director, height finder, radar, and searchlight stations, and concluded "their performance of repetitious routine duties is considered superior to that of men." Indeed he judged that WAAC personnel could be substituted for men in 60 percent of all AA positions. Because men and women were going to be working in close proximity, Timberlake was concerned about any possible scandals which might occur. Promiscuity, or even rumors of impropriety, could undermine the unit's combat effectiveness. He was relieved to find, "The relationship between the Army personnel and WAAC personnel, both enlisted and commissioned, has been highly satisfactory." No sexual harassment was noted;

instead he found, "A mutual understanding and appreciation appears to exist." Timberlake asked his superior, Major General John T. Lewis of the Military District of Washington, to judge the experiment for himself. Soon Lewis was as enthusiastic as Timberlake. Lewis wrote that Waacs could "efficiently perform many duties in the antiaircraft artillery unit." Their high morale and a paucity of disciplinary problems "increases materially the relative value of WAAC personnel in antiaircraft artillery in fixed positions." Lewis was so proud of his Waacs that in May 1943, he asked Marshall for authority to continue the experiment, increase the number of Waacs to 103 commissioned and 2,315 enrollees, and replace half the 3,630 men in his AA Defense Command with these more efficient soldiers.[8]

Marshall now had to make a choice. If he let Lewis have the women, the whole country would immediately hear that women were being sent into combat. What would that do to proposals to draft women? What would conservative Southern congressmen, who never liked the WAAC in the first place, do to Marshall's plans to expand the WAAC?[9] Would the general public approve? Would women stop volunteering? Would the male soldiers react favorably or not? If Marshall approved, he could no longer keep this experiment secret. The Judge Advocate General's Office said that Congress would have to change the existing legislation and it provided the wording for a suitable amendment: the new Section 20 would read, "Nothing in this act shall prevent any member of the Women's Army Auxiliary Corps from service with any combatant organization with her own consent."[10]

Marshall asked his staff for advice. They recommended that Marshall terminate the experiment immediately. General Miller White of the Personnel Division, General Staff, acknowledged that "The War Department believes the experiment . . . has demonstrated conclusively the practicability of using members of the Corps in this role." However, since the present strength of the WAAC was far below total requirements, he argued that the Waacs "can be more efficiently employed in many other positions for which requisitions are already in hand, and that their use in antiaircraft artillery to release limited service personnel is not justified under present circumstances."[11] In other words, the experiment was a success, but the Army needed these women for higher priority positions. Had Germany or Japan been able to pose a practical threat from the air to the continental United States then putting women in AA positions might have become a high priority. However, given the relative safety of both coasts by 1943, Waacs were most needed to serve in clerical and administrative positions. The AA units had been using men who could only be used for limited duty service and there were more than enough of these men to fill the current need for AA units. However, clerical and administrative positions which normally were filled by women in the civilian world were held by able-bodied men with football fingers who could be in combat instead.

In 1942, Marshall had discovered that some congressmen were so concerned about protecting the women sailors that they amended the law to forbid WAVES from serving overseas.[12] Marshall had been lobbying Congress to upgrade the WAAC from auxiliary status to full military status (the Women's Army Corps—WAC). He wanted the Waacs to serve overseas. The War Department withdrew the WAC bill entirely in April 1943, because of the "flak" over the Navy bill and resubmitted it in May. Finally Congress passed the WAC legislation on 28 June, with authority for overseas service.[13] Had Congress learned that Marshall wanted the Waacs to serve in combat units, then the WAC bill might have been lost forever or many new restrictions placed on the ability of the Army to utilize womanpower. General Russell Reynolds, Director of the Military Personnel Division, summarized the Army staff's consensus to eliminate the AA experiment before Congress got wind of it: "It is not believed that national policy or public opinion is yet ready to accept the use of women in field force units."[14]

Marshall made the decision. He terminated the experiment, reassigned the Waacs, ordered the results kept confidential, and never thought of using women in combat again.[15] America had drawn the gender line. If the decision had been made exclusively on the grounds of efficiency and performance, women would have been assigned to AA batteries. It was based rather on the current needs of the Army for female office workers, on the state of public opinion, and on the general hostility toward women in nontraditional gender roles in 1943.

To evaluate the full implications of Marshall's decision—to explore what might have happened—it is essential to study the model the United States was watching closely—the British experience. Before the war, in 1938, a prominent woman engineer, Caroline Haslett, was asked to visit the AA batteries at practice and advise the commanding officer, General Frederick Pile, if any of these jobs could be held by women. Except for the heavy work of loading ammunition, Haslett reported that women could perform all the other functions.[16] As the British military began reassigning the most able-bodied antiaircraft men to the field army, Pile decided to experiment with integrated or mixed batteries. The National Service Act of December 1941 drafted 125,000 women into the military over the next three years while 430,000 more volunteered. The largest of the women's units, Auxiliary Territorial Service (ATS), began as a woman's auxiliary to the military in 1938 and in 1941 was granted military status (with two-thirds pay of the men of equal rank).[17] Pile went to the ATS to find women soldiers to serve alongside his men who were battling the Luftwaffe bombers day and night. Sir James Grigg, Under-Secretary of State for War, declared Pile's proposal "breath-taking and revolutionary."[18] Prime Minister Winston Churchill was enthusiastic. He argued that any general who saved him 40,000 fighting men had gained the equivalent of a victory. By August 1941, women were operating the fire-control instruments, and men the actual guns in Richmond Park, near the headquarters of AA Command. By September 1943, over 56,000 women were working for AA Command, most in units close to London. The first mixed regiment to fire in action was the 132nd on 21 November 1941 and the first "kill" came in April 1942. As Pile observed, "Beyond a little natural excitement and a tendency to chatter when there was a lull, they behaved like a veteran party, and shot an enemy plane into the sea."[19]

The mixed batteries were commanded by men from the AA regiments. Women officers from ATS served as "gender commissars," whose only official function was to supervise the military bearing of the enlisted women.[20] ATS officers were given a brief course in the general principle of antiaircraft work, but the only women allowed to participate in the actual fighting were the ATS enlistees. The male chain of command handled all instruction and supervision of both men and women in the technical areas. In practice, the women officers soon took over some of the fire-control operations—a practice that was condoned by the AA Command and ATS leadership. As one woman explained, "When we arrived at our site we had all been

Figure 10.1 British women in the Auxiliary Territorial Service learn every aspect of this antiaircraft gun except to fire it, which was forbidden. *Courtesy of Imperial War Museum H-14274.*

trained for particular jobs, but since then we have learned to do every job in camp except fire the guns—and I bet we could do that too if we were allowed."[21] Soon women skilled in fire-control operations learned as well to set the range and bearing dials on the gun itself a few yards away and adjust the fuses on the shells. Indeed they could even take over the complete operation of a light 40-mm AA gun. But regulations strictly prohibited women from engaging the firing mechanism. They could not pull the trigger on a man, even if he was a Luftwaffe pilot.

ATS women were soon assigned to searchlight units.[22] These units were scattered around the gun complex and thus each searchlight was some distance from the next. Each unit had to be supplemented with a male soldier firing a tripod-mounted light machine gun to deter any raider who attacked down the beam; the women called him the "Lister Twister" since his other job was to crank the Lister generator providing the power for the light.[23] Some AA officers fretted about what the British public (or the Luftwaffe) might think about these one man/many women searchlight units.[24] The Germans never seem to have commented on the matter. Furthermore, the much-feared sex scandals never materialized in the searchlight or battery units.[25] At first middle-aged men (presumably more prudent) were sent to the mixed batteries. This policy was not a success because, "The girls regarded the older men as grandfathers, and they for their part found the girls a bit tiresome."[26] When younger men arrived, both sexes segregated themselves at work and were not encouraged to mix off duty. Soon, however, they developed close working relationships, a form of bonding which was vital when the batteries came under fire. As one British battery commander suggested, "Loyalty means loyalty in a mixed battery and 'devotion to duty' has a more definite meaning than it has had. Isn't a woman's devotion more sincere and lasting than a man's?"[27] The women developed bonds with fellow AA workers, male and female, which they did not share with former workers and friends. "After experiencing just a couple of months of communal life, I found that the girls (civilians) with whom I had worked before I enlisted were self-interested. . . . We no longer spoke the same language even and there seemed to be a barrier between us. It was even worse with the boys."[28] Pile observed, "The girls lived like men, fought their lights like men, and alas, some of them died like men."[29]

The first woman killed in action, Private J. Caveney (148th Regiment) was hit by a bomb splinter while working at the predictor—the device that predicted where the enemy plane would be when the shell finally arrived at the proper altitude. As had been practiced many times in the casualty drills, the woman spotter "stepped in so promptly that firing was not interrupted." In another attack, Privates Clements and Dunsmore stuck to their posts despite suffering injuries, caused "by being blown over by a stick of bombs dropped across the troop position." The total ATS battle casualties were 389 killed or wounded.[30]

Figure 10.2 ATS women were granted military status in 1941, and in August of that year they began operating the fire-control instruments in batteries while men operated the guns. The first "kill" came in April 1942. *Courtesy of Imperial War Museum H-5121.*

Figure 10.3 Prime Minister and Mrs. Winston Churchill inspect a mixed-sex anti-aircraft battery. *Courtesy of Imperial War Museum H-18484.*

Morale was high in the mixed batteries; soon the women were allowed to wear the AA Command formation sign on the sleeves and to be called Bombardiers and Gunners (only on duty).[31] As one recruit explained, "I don't know what it was about Ack girls but we always seemed to be smarter than the rest of the service" and they "acted accordingly."[32] In 1944, morale in the mixed batteries soared when news came that some were to serve throughout England (not just around London) and even on the continent. One woman volunteer described the command post situation at the Great Yarmouth Gun Defended Area during and just after a raid:

The atmosphere in the post was calm, almost subdued and little different from that which had prevailed during our many exercises in the past. This changed as soon as stand-down was given and, although we still had work to do, there was at least a buzz of excitement about the place and cigarettes were freely handed around. Somehow it seemed the thing to do for me to take one and light up as well—even though I didn't smoke, until then that is.[33]

The living conditions for both sexes were often primitive; the ATS women boasted how harsh it was out on the hilltops at night. Nervous uncles were appalled. Pressure soon mounted to provide better conditions for the women. Before such facilities could be built, one commander assembled the one thousand women of his brigade and offered to have any of them moved to another location within twenty-four hours. Only nine women asked for a change, and all of these were clerks who were not involved with the fire-control equipment.[34] One male leader of a mixed battery unit confessed that he initially hated the idea of commanding a mixed battery, "But now that I have joined this battery, raised it, watched it grow up and shared in its sorrows and joys, I can say I have never been happier than I am now."[35] After six months an AA corps commander told Pile that "It has been an unqualified success." He suggested that what immediately impressed observers was "the tremendous keenness and enthusiasm displayed by the ATS in assimilating their operational duties. They learn quickly, and once having mastered the subject very seldom make mistakes." He also remarked that, "Contrary once again to expectations, their voices carry well and can be clearly heard in the din of gunfire."[36] Not surprisingly, Pile concluded that "the experiment had exceeded even my more sanguine hopes."[37] The mixed unit had achieved a standard of drill and turn-out "better than in any male unit; for when the girls took to polishing their predictors, how could the men have dirty guns?"[38]

It is possible to ask how women compared with men doing identical jobs. British AA leaders concluded that women were inferior as spotters, comparable as predictors and superior as height finders. The British experience was more complete than the American four-month experiment, but there were no major differences in the findings. The women excelled in several areas, were comparable in others, and were inferior in a few. But phrasing the question in terms of men versus women is highly misleading. The British were not interested in setting up all-female units in order to promote feminism. Rather they set up mixed units so they could shoot down more enemy planes and buzz bombs, while making the most efficient use of the limited human resources available. The effectiveness of a military unit depends on the team performance; team members who are better at lugging heavy shells can be assigned to that task, while those who are better at reading the dials should be doing that. The effectiveness of a team is not the average of each person measured as a Jack/Jill of all trades. Rather it is a composite of how well each specialized task is performed, plus the synergy that comes from leadership, morale, and unit cohesion. The mixed units did very well indeed.

Britain had to balance public doubts and ingrained gender norms against pressing needs. When Pile and Churchill first assigned women to AA jobs they encountered resistance from public opinion. It was not so much that the women were in danger—every woman in every British city was in danger of death from German bombs, and tens of thousands did die. The public would not support a proposal to allow women to fire the AA guns. But the British were a practical people, especially when bombs were falling. They soon decided, "A successful air defence was an even stronger political imperative than the possible moral and physical dangers to the daughters of the nation."[39] The government did concede some details to public opinion by not formally classifying these AA jobs as combat and by symbolically prohibiting the women from pulling the lanyard. The mixed AA crews were as much combat teams as were the airplane crews they shot down.

One factor in whether nations employed women in combat roles was the urgency of the need for combat soldiers. The tail-to-teeth ratio was very high in the United States because Marshall felt only ninety combat divisions would be needed, and that the war would be largely won by the efficiency of the supply and support mechanism. Women were not needed in AA units (few men were actually needed), but they were urgently needed to handle clerical and administrative jobs. Marshall thought caution the better part of valor when he decided not to risk a confrontation with Congress and public opinion on the matter of gender roles. The British experience fits the next stage on this continuum. Men were urgently needed for front-line infantry units in North Africa at the same time the Luftwaffe threatened the homefront. British women were assigned to defensive missions to enable men to engage in offensive action. They were at risk of being killed, but there was little chance they could be captured. Living conditions, while difficult, protected them from unwanted sexual encounters. How did other European countries react to severe threats with their shrinking manpower assets? Did they employ maximum personpower?

Hitler had always insisted that women remain at home and be full-time wives and mothers; Nazi women were to guarantee the survival of the Aryan race in the labor room, not on the battlefield.[40] Even single women were not recruited for jobs in industry at the beginning of the war. By 1941 women were holding jobs in industry and serving in Female Auxiliary Units doing administrative work for the military. After the invasion of Russia, German women in Female Auxiliary Units increasingly began replacing men who were sent to the Eastern front. Berlin did monitor its Finnish ally, which successfully used "Lottas" as auxiliaries to the army.[41] But it was not until January 1943, when the war had clearly begun to turn sour and Albert Speer became the economic czar, that Germany began full mobilization of its human resources. Even so, measures to conscript women into industry were introduced "only with extreme reluctance, and were never efficiently implemented."[42] Not surprisingly, then, measures to draft women into the military— including Goebbels's 1944 Second Order for the Implementation of Total War —were even less well-enforced.[43]

German women, however, did serve in the military: in all, 450,000 joined the women's auxiliaries, in addition to the units of nurses.[44] By 1945 women were holding approximately 85 percent of the once all-male billets as clericals, accountants, interpreters, laboratory workers, and administrative workers, together with half of the clerical and junior administrative posts in high-level field headquarters.[45] These German women, in uniform and under military discipline, were not officially referred to as female soldiers. They were unofficially nicknamed "Blitzmadchen." While it may seem surprising that the Nazis ever allowed women to serve in the military in any capacity, to test our hypothesis we must examine the German model to see if women held more than combat support or combat service support positions.[46]

Antiaircraft units became increasingly central to Germany's war effort, so on 17 July 1943, Hitler, at the urging of Speer, decided to train women for searchlight and AA positions. Basic training was to take four weeks. These AA auxiliaries were placed as follows: three to operate the instrument to measure distances, seven to operate the radio measuring instrument, three to operate the command instrument, and occasionally one woman served as a telephone platoon leader. By the end of the war, between sixty-five thousand and one hundred thousand women were serving in AA units with the Luftwaffe.[47] Some searchlight units were eventually 90 percent female.[48] Similar to the British experience, German women who joined AA units were soon "proud to be serving as AA-Auxiliaries," and were "Burning soon to be trained well enough to be able flawlessly to stand our ground at the equipment."[49] In these units women developed the unit cohesion which had been evident in the British AA units. As one veteran recalled, "We have been raised with the same kind of spirit, we had the same ideals, and the most important was the good comradeship, the 'one for all.' "[50] Here again these AA-Auxiliaries emphasized their continued femininity. As Lotte Vogt explained:

> In spite of all the soldier's duties we had to do, we did not forget that we are girls. We did not want to adopt uncouth manners. We certainly were no rough warriors—always simply women.[51]

As in Britain, however, the German women serving with AA units learned all aspects of the guns, but were forbidden to fire them. Hitler and his advisers firmly believed that public opinion would never tolerate these auxiliaries firing weapons.[52] Indeed, German propaganda warned all women in the auxiliaries not to become "gun women" (flinten-weiber).[53] "Gun women" was the contemptuous German term for Soviet women who carried or fired weapons. Many Soviet women were without uniforms and thus considered de facto partisans. The Germans looked upon armed Soviet women as "unnatural" and consequently had no compunction about shooting such "vermin" as soon as they were captured. The verbal degradation of enemy females made it easier for German soldiers to overcome inhibitions about harming women.[54]

In November 1944, Hitler issued an official order that no woman was to be trained in the use of weapons. The only exception was for women in the remote areas of the Reich which could be easily overrun by the Soviets. In one such area, a twenty-two-year-old Pomeranian woman, "Erna," was awarded the Iron Cross (second class) when she, together with a male sergeant and private destroyed three tanks with bazookas. Indeed, the German propaganda suggested that the bazooka was the most feminine of weapons.[55] The Freikorps Adolf Hitler was formed in 1945 and trained in the use of bazookas, hand grenades, and automatic rifles. Lore Ley, daughter of a leading Nazi, once knocked out a Soviet armored scout car and took from its commander military documents and money.[56] In all, thirty-nine German women received the Iron Cross (second class) for their duty near the front. The majority of these women, however, were nurses.[57]

The true Nazis resisted weapons training for women auxiliaries serving with the Army or Luftwaffe until the final stages of the war. As Reichsleiter Martin Bormann sputtered to Reichsminister Dr. Josef Goebbels, as late as November 1944: "As long as there is still one single man employed at a work place in the Wehrmacht that could as well be occupied by a woman, the employment of armed women must be rejected."[58] More and more desperate every day, in February 1945 Hitler capitulated and created an experimental women's infantry battalion. Ironically, this unit's mission was in part to shame cowardly men who were evading their natural gender role of dying for their country (thousands of men were deserting in 1945). The cowards ought to stay with their units and fight like real men. The war ended before the women's battalion could be raised and trained.[59]

In contrast to the Germans, the Soviets mobilized their women early, bypassing the "auxiliary" stage entirely. About eight hundred thousand women served in the Red Army during World War II, and over half of these were in front-line duty units. Many were trained in all-female units. About a third of the total number of women serving were given additional instruction in mortars, light and heavy machine guns, or automatic rifles. Another three hundred thousand served in AA units and performed all functions in the batteries—including firing the guns.[60] When asked why she had volunteered for such dangerous and "unwomanly" work, AA gunner K. S. Tikhonovich explained, "'We' and 'Motherland' meant the same thing for us." Sergeant Valentina Pavlovna Chuayeva from Siberia wanted to settle the score and avenge the death of her father: "I wanted to fight, to take revenge, to shoot." Her request was denied with the explanation that telephone operator was the most vital work she could do. She retorted that telephone receivers did not shoot; finally a colonel gave her the chance to train for the AA. "At first my nose and ears bled and my stomach was completely upset. . . . It wasn't so terrible at night, but in the daytime it was simply awful." She recalled the terror of battle: "The planes seemed to be heading straight for you, right for your gun. In a second they would make mincemeat of you. . . . It was not really a young girl's job." Eventually she became commander of an AA gun crew. Private Nonna Alexandrovna Smirnova, AA gunner from the Georgian village of Obeha, did not like the training program in which men with little education, often mispronouncing words, served as their instructors. The uniforms they received were designed for men. Smirnova, the smallest person in her company, usually wore a size 34 shoe but was issued an American-made boot size 42. "They were so heavy that I shuffled instead of marching."[61] (In every nation the women's services had trouble with the quarter-master's notion of what a shoe should be.)

The noncombat-combat classification which preoccupied the Americans, British, and Germans proved an unaffordable luxury to the Soviets. In a nation totally controlled by the Kremlin, organized public opinion was hardly a factor. Implicit public opinion regarding the primacy of traditional gender roles was another matter, but the evidence available does not speak to that. (The Kremlin controlled the media and the historiography—and even the memories of World War II; perhaps someday *glasnost* will loosen some tongues.) Article 13 of the universal military duty law, ratified by the Fourth Session of the Supreme Soviet on 1 September 1939, enabled the military to accept women who had training in critical medical or technical areas. Women could also register as part of a training group and after they were trained they could be called up for active duty by the armed forces. Once war broke out, these Soviet women together with their fathers, brothers, and husbands went to the military commissariats, to party and Komsomol organizations to help fight. They served as partisans, snipers, and tank drivers.[62] After one woman's tanker husband died, she enlisted herself, served in a tank she named "Front-line Female Comrade" and perished in 1944.[63] Women constituted three regiments of pilots, one of fighter pilots (the 586th Fighter Regiment), one of bombers (the 587th), and the most famous, the 588th Night Bombers who proved so effective at hitting their targets that they were nicknamed by the Germans the night witches. According to one veteran German pilot, "I would rather fly ten times over the skies of Tobruk [over all-male British ack-ack] than to pass once through [Russia where] the fire of Russian flak [was] sent up by female gunners."[64] In all, Soviet women made up about 8 percent of all combatants. Between 100,000 and 150,000 of them were decorated during the war, including 91 women who received the Hero of the Soviet Union medal, the highest award for valor.[65]

The Soviets boasted that their women were in combat units, and even sent some abroad on publicity tours.[66] Combat roles were not publicized in Germany, Britain, or America, even as the generals realized that women soldiers in AA units had combat missions.[67] They were shooting at the enemy, and he (or she) was shooting back. The British discovered that Luftwaffe gunners fired at everyone around the search-lights or the guns and not just the men there. As Shelford Bidwell, the distinguished historian of artillery and of the ATS, concluded, "There is not much essential difference between manning a G.L. set or a predictor and firing a gun: both are means of destroying an enemy aircraft." He noted that, "The situation became more absurd when the advance of automation was such that the guns were fired by remote control when on target, from the command post." After June 1944, most of the targets were V-1 robots, but the women still could not shoot.[68] What stopped the British, Americans, and Germans from allowing the AA women to pull the trigger was their sense of gender roles—a sensibility that had not yet adjusted to necessity.

Understanding the reaction of the servicemen to women in combat involves study of the structure of gender roles in society at large and the military in particular, and calls out for a comparative framework. In the United States, most male soldiers were strongly opposed to the Women's Army Corps and urgently advised their sisters and friends not to join. Scurrilous rumors to the effect that Wacs were sexual extremists (either promiscuous or lesbian) chilled recruitment and froze the Corps far below its intended size. The rumors were generated almost entirely by word of mouth by servicemen. In point of fact, rumors were false because the servicewomen were much less sexually active than servicemen, and rather less active than comparable civilian women.[69] The rumors therefore reflected a strong hostility, but to what? Senior officers had mostly been opposed to the WAC, but almost unanimously reversed their position when they realized how effective the women were and how many men they could free for combat. Most of the senior officers had been trained as engineers (especially at the military academies) and perhaps were more sensitive to efficiency than to human sensibilities. Most women themselves probably opposed going into combat.[70] Some enlisted men with noncombat jobs were aghast at the idea (explicit in recruiting posters) that women who enlisted would send a man to the front. As one officer wrote from the South Pacific:[71]

> They [Wacs] are good workers and much more so than many of our regular men. You perhaps have heard many wild stories about them but I wouldn't believe everything that I hear. In comparison, our men are a lot worse. So many men talk about them and it seems they are the

ones who haven't seen a Wac, or doesn't know anything about them, or even is a little jealous. Then again some of the girls take over easy jobs that some of the men hold and they don't like it when they have to get out and work.

Young men furthermore saw military service as a validation of their own virility and as a certificate of manhood. If women could do it, then it was not very manly.[72] The exhilaration of combat could become an aphrodisiac, if not a sexual experience in its own right; perhaps like the "Tailhookers" of recent days they felt this should be forbidden territory to females.[73] The closure of territory to females was strongly enforced by every fifth word the men spoke—language deliberately offensive to women.[74] At a deeper level, can society allow women to shoot at men? (The "battered wife defense" is a case in point.)

The question of women in combat has generated a vast literature that draws from law, biology, and psychology, but seldom from history. The restrictions against women in combat that persisted for decades in the United States were not based on experimental research (quite the reverse), or from a consideration of the effectiveness of women in combat in other armies. The restrictions were primarily political decisions made in response to the public opinion of the day, and the climate of opinion in Congress. Still horrified by Belleau Wood, Okinawa, and Ia Drang, many Americans to this day visualize "combat" as vicious hand-to-hand knife fighting.[75] Major Everett S. Hughes displayed a keen insight into the issue of women in combat in a report to the General Staff:

> We have handicapped ourselves by numerous man-made technical definitions of such things as Combat Zone. . . . Some of us conclude that women have no place in the Theater of Operations, others that women have no place in the combat zone. We fail to consider that the next war is never the last one. We forget, for example, that what was the Combat Zone during the World War may be something else during the next war. We use technical terms that are susceptible to individual interpretation, and that change with the art of war, to express the idea that women should not participate here, there, or yonder. We are further handicapped by man-made barriers of custom, prejudice and politics, and fail to appreciate how rapidly and thoroughly these barriers are being demolished.[76]

Hughes's report was made in 1928, and was not rediscovered until after the war. It was not feminism but fear of the lack of sufficient "manpower" to fight World War II, which served as the catalyst for Marshall's experiment, Pile's mixed batteries, and the Soviet Night Witches. Necessity, once it was dire enough, could overcome culture. "If the need for women's service be great enough they may go any place, live anywhere, under any conditions," concluded Major Hughes. Success in combat was a matter of skill, intelligence, coordination, training, morale, and teamwork. The military is a product of history and is bound by the lessons it has "learned" from history.[77] The problem is that the history everyone has learned about the greatest and best-known war of all times has airbrushed out the combat roles of women.

Notes

1 Research support was provided in part by a grant from the National Endowment for the Humanities, Division of Research, RO-20660–84. I especially appreciated the comments of Col. Robert Doughty, Col. Kenneth Hamburger, Col. Paul Miles, Lt. Col. Judith Luckett, Capt. Richard Hooker, Connie Devilbiss, Nancy Loring Harrison, Richard Jensen, Dennis Showalter, and Judith Stiehm. Archivists, librarians, and historians were especially helpful at Indiana University; the U.S. Military Academy; the National Archives (NA); the Dwight Eisenhower Presidential Library; the WAC Museum at Ft McClellan; Maxwell Air Force Base Library; the Navy History Center, Washington; the Franklin D. Roosevelt Presidential Library; the George C. Marshall Library (ML); the U.S. Air Force Academy; the Imperial War Museum (IWM), London; the Public Record Office, London; the Canadian Archives, Ottawa; the Militargeschichtliches Forschungsamt (MF) Freiburg, Germany; Moscow State University; the Georgian State Museum, Tbilisi; the Royal Dutch Military History Museum; and the Austrian Federal Military Historical Service (MSH), Vienna. The Russian archives proved impossible to use. However, there is in Moscow a Soviet Women's Center which helped arrange very useful interviews for me in 1986. Special thanks to Larry I. Bland (ML); Colonel (Dr.) Roland G. Foerster (MF); Dr. Erwin Schmidt (MSH); and Dr. V. S. Murmantseva. Invaluable were the excellent translations made for me by Shannon Jumper.

2 "Combat" is used as it was defined at the time, particularly by the U.S. Army's Judge Advocate General's Office, and also by British policy makers such as Winston Churchill and General Frederick Pile.

3 D'Ann Campbell, *Women at War with America; Private Lives in a Patriotic Era* (Cambridge, 1984); Leila M. Rupp, *Mobilizing Women for War: German and American Propaganda during World War II* (Princeton, 1979); Maureen Honey, *Creating Rosie the Riveter. Class, Gender, and Propaganda during World War II* (Amherst, 1984); Ruth Milkman, *Gender at Work: The Dynamics of Job Segregation by Sex During World War II* (Urbana, 1987); Susan M. Hartmann, *The Home Front and Beyond: American Women in the 1940s* (Boston, 1982). William Chafe has argued for radical changes: *The Paradox of Change* (New York, 1992).

4 Robert R. Palmer, Bell I. Wiley, and William R. Keast, *The Procurement and Training of Ground Combat Troops* (Washington, 1948), 120–21.

5 Report no. 1101, Eisenhower to General Marshall, 12 August 1942. Women's Army Corps, NNMCSA, 1942–43, 291.9; Reel 306, Item 4688. Original in NA, copy in ML. Marshall to Eisenhower, 6 August 1942, and Marshall Memorandum, 18 November 1942, in Larry I. Bland, ed. *The Papers of George Catlett Marshall* (Baltimore, 1981–), 3:288–89, 443–44, also 561; Alfred D. Chandler, ed., *The Papers of Dwight David Eisenhower* (Baltimore, 1970–), 1:450–51.

6 The first mention of the experiment came in the official history by Mattie Treadwell, *The Women's Army Corps* (Washington 1954), 301–2. Treadwell's work remains the best single source on the WAAC and WAC (and the best on any women's unit during the war).

7 U.S. War Department, Organization and Training Division, G-3. 291.9 WAAC 7 July 1943, RG 165, Entry 211, Box 199, 1–3. Copy in ML, Xerox 2782.

8 Ibid., 5–10; 15 June 1943 Memorandum for Asst. C/S G-3, /s/ Lewis, 291.9 WAAC 7 RG 165, Entry 212, Box 199, 1.

9 Representative Carl Vinson, the major Congressional voice on military affairs, opposed women in combat. Marilyn A. Gordon and Mary Jo Ludvigson, "A

Constitutional Analysis of the Combat Exclusion for Air Force Women," *Minerva* 9 (Summer 1991): 1–34.

10   ASF Director of Administration, 020 WAAC, 11–18–42, RG 160, Box 1. [JAG to CofS] Xerox 2000, ML. Also see *Marshall Papers*, 3: 454.

11   Brigadier General Ray E. Porter, Asst. C/S, G-3, Xerox 2788 ASF, Director of Personnel, Military Personnel Division, RG 160, Entry 484, Box 491. 14 July 1943. /s/ Col. R. W. Berry, Exec. for Asst. C/S, G-1, copy in ML.

12   Campbell, *Women at War with America*, 20.

13   Ibid. See also Treadwell, *Women's Army Corps*, 220.

14   ASF, Director of Personnel, Military Personnel Division, RG 160, Entry 485, Box 491.

15   General George C. Marshall to Major General Lewis, 13 August 1943, RG 160, Entry 489, Box 492, copy in ML.

16   General Sir Frederick Arthur Pile, *Ack-Ack* (London, 1949), 186; See also J.W.N., "'Mixed' Batteries," *Journal of the Royal Artillery* 69 (1942): 199–206.

17   Pile, *Ack-Ack*, 187. Patricia J. Thomas, "Women in the Military: America and the British Commonwealth," *Armed Forces and Society* 4 (August 1978): 629.

18   Pile, *Ack-Ack*, 188. See also Shelford Bidwell, *The Women's Royal Army Corps* (London, 1977), 118–19, on British public opinion.

19   Pile, *Ack-Ack*, 188, 191, 193; Bidwell, *Women's Royal Army Corps*, 121–22.

20   "The Second World War Memories of Miss G. Morgan," MSS PP/MCR/115, 1, housed at the Imperial War Museum, London; Two ATS AA Officers, "Life in a Mixed Anti-Aircraft Battery," *Army Quarterly* 47 (October, 1943): 82, also points out the excellent discipline in these units.

21   Ibid. Freud would have a field day analyzing possible reasons women were not allowed to fire a gun (a phallic symbol) targeted on males.

22   According to Lt. Col. M. S. F. Millington, "The formation of the 83 Searchlight Regiment, with the exception of the Commanding Officer, was composed entirely of ATS and was the only women's Searchlight Regiment in the world." Millington, "Gunners' Mates," *Lioness* 52 (1979): 36. The British apparently did not know about the all-female Soviet units.

23   Bidwell, *Women's Royal Army Corps*, 127; Pile, *Ack-Ack,* 227–28. See also "The Work of AA Searchlights During the Last War," *Journal of the Royal Artillery* 75 (1948): 241–52.

24   W. Boileau, "Searchlight-A.T.S.," *The Gunner* 30 (April 1948): 12, copy at IWM; Bidwell, *Women's Royal Army Corps*, 127.

25   While this was the official version and no scandal campaign embarrassed the mixed battery units, some mixing of the sexes took place. "One of the girls cheerfully admitted to having been a prostitute before she joined up. . . . There were nights when she returned to the hut with her tunic and shirt in disarray and her bra slung somewhere around her neck." "Memories of Miss G. Morgan," 1.

26   Pile, *Ack-Ack*, 189; Bidwell, *Women's Royal Army Corps*, 124. But there were others who insisted on the strict propriety of all involved. According to ATS volunteer Muriel I. D. Barker, "There was an absolutely monastic segregation when it came to living quarters." Muriel I. D. Barker papers, ATS/WAAC 1941–1955, 73/31/1, especially 24–47, housed at IWM, quote from 47. One mixed battery commander explained that, "When a couple of girls walk out of a hut in dressing gowns to go to the ablution huts for a bath, nobody takes the slightest notice. This matter of fact atmosphere is what strikes every first time visitor." J.W.N. "'Mixed' Batteries," 206.

27   Ibid., 206.

28   "Memories of Miss G. Morgan," 11.

29   Pile, *Ack-Ack*, 36–37; Bidwell, *Women's Royal Army Corps*, 130.

30   Bidwell, *Women's Royal Army Corps*, 130–32.

31   Ibid., 126. See also "Life in a Mixed Anti-Aircraft Battery," 80–83.

32   This excerpted account, entitled, "A Woman's View of Life in a Mixed AA Battery," based on conversations held with one ATS Private, compiled and presented by Ronald Hadley, p. 10, is part of the "Second World War Memoirs of Miss G. Morgan," 1, PP/MCR/115 collection at the IWM.

33   Ibid., 35–36.

34   Pile, *Ack-Ack*, 376–81; Bidwell, *Women's Royal Army Corps*, 132; women assigned to AA units often held several different assignments; one woman was sent back to AA Signals course, then moved to the RAF Plotting Room and eventually to several AA headquarters. See Doris Madill, "Forty Years in Retrospect," *Lioness* 52 (1979): 41–42.

35   "'Mixed' Batteries," 206.

36   Pile, *Ack-Ack*, 192.

37   Ibid., 194; "'Mixed' Batteries," 202–4.

38   Pile, *Ack-Ack*, 194.

39   Bidwell, *Women's Royal Army Corps*, 119, 123. Perhaps women's poor records as spotters were due to their previous lack of experience in distinguishing aircraft. Few women came to AA positions having memorized the British and German models. In a similar sense, women sailors often took longer to memorize the differences in ships than did men who may have grown up "playing" sailors or pilots as young boys. Also, women typically took longer to learn a military rank system and to "spot" a senior officer approaching whom they must salute.

40   For discussions on the German division of gender roles and its effect on the mobilization of German women during WWII, see Jill Stephenson, *The Nazi Organization of Women* (London, 1981); Claudia Koonz, *Mothers in the Fatherland* (New York, 1987); Rupp, *Mobilizing Women for War*; Rupp, "Women, Class, and Mobilization in Nazi Germany," *Science and Society* 43 (1979): 51–69; Rupp, "Mother of the Volk: The Image of Women in Nazi Ideology," *Signs* 3 (Winter 1977): 362–379; Louise Willmot, "Women in the Third Reich: The Auxiliary Military Service Law of 1944," *German History* 2 (1985): 10–20; Judith Grunfeld, "Mobilization of Women in Germany," *Social Research* 9 (1942): 476–94; Richard L. Johnson, "Nazi Feminists: A Contradiction in Terms," *Frontiers* 1 (1975): 55–62; Jost Hermand, "All Power to the Women: Nazi Concepts of Matriarchy," *Journal of Contemporary History* 19 (1984): 649–67; *International Labour Review* 50 (1944): 335–51; Linda Gordon, "Nazi Feminists?" *Feminist Review* 27 (September 1987): 97–105; T. W. Mason, "Women in Nazi Germany," *History Workshop* 1 (Spring 1976): 74–113, and 2 (Autumn 1976): 5–32.

41   Lottas, founded in 1918, were to take jobs in the rear to replace men who could then fight on the front. They were disbanded in 1944 as part of the conditions of the Armistice because of their Nazi ties. See Else Martensen Larsen, "Das dänische weibliche Fleigerkorps," *Wehrkunde* 14 (August 1965): 403; Document KA:NL Raus B/186/1-Thema 21: "Improvisationen als Mittel der Fuhrung," Code number 851: 26, example #16. Copy supplied by MHS, Austria. For an overview on the Finnish experience, see Charles Leonard Lundin, *Finland in the Second World War* (Bloomington, 1957).

42   Willmot, "Women in the Third Reich," 11.

43   Ibid., 13, 14, 16, 17.

44   Jeff M. Tuten, "Germany and the World Wars," in Nancy Loring Goldman, ed., *Female Combatants or Non-Combatants?* (Westport, 1982), 52–53; see also "A German Antiaircraft General Speaks," *Antiaircraft Journal* 92 (March 1979): 46; General G. L. Appleton, "Flak: Some Comments on the German Anti-Aircraft Defences 1939–1945," *Journal of Royal Artillery* 74 (1947): 85–89; Franz W. Seidler, *Frauen zu den Waffen-Marketenderinnen, Helferinnen, Soldatinnen* [Women to Arms: Sutlers, Volunteers, Female Soldiers] (Koblenz/Bonn, 1978), 47, 50, 51, 59, 64, 65. For some of these jobs Seidler says that women were to replace men at a ratio of 3:2 (women to men), sometimes 4:3. Even in traditional women's work the Germans thought that more women would be needed to do the jobs formerly held by male soldiers; the Allies discovered just the opposite was true.

45   Seidler, *Frauen*, 60, 74. "The Guidelines for Emergency Employment of Women" explained that special care must be given to employing women according to their mental and physical disposition since they would not be able to do all the work done by men. "No work is to be given to women that requires particular presence of mind, determination, and fast action." Richtlinien für die Beschäftigung von Frauen im Mobfall [Anlage der Reichsarbeitsminister, IIc 565–38g, 16 September 1938], as cited in Ursula von Gersdorff, *Frauen im Kriegsdienst, 1914–1945* [Women in War Service, 1914–1945] (Stuttgart, 1969), 286; see also Tuten, "Germany and the World Wars," 56; Gersdorff, "Frauen im Kriegsdienst. Probleme und Ergebnisse," *Wehrkunde* 11 (November 1965): 578; copy at Federal Ministry for Defense of the Country, MHS, Vienna, Austria.

46   Franz Seidler, *Blitzmädchen. Die Geschichte der Helferinen der deutschen Wehrmacht im Zweiten Weltkrieg* (Koblenz/Bonn, 1979); Leopold Banny, *Dröhnender Himmel Brennendes Land: Der Einsatz der Luftwaffenhelfer in Osterreich 1943–45* (Vienna, 1988), 195; copy at MHS, Austria; Seidler, *Frauen*, 29–34. For examples of female soldiers not corresponding to the National Socialist conception of womanhood; see Anlage, Oberkommando der Wehrmacht, 5 September 1944, AZ. 26/27 Nr. 1649/44. Cited in Gersdorff, *Frauen im Kriegsdienst*, 441.

47   Seidler, *Frauen*, 60, 65, 86, 87; Tuten, "Germany and the World Wars," 55. Details on AA basic training are found in Der Reichsarbeitsführer Az. D1 Nr. 680/43g. 8 August 1943. Betr.: "Aufstellung von RAD-Flakbatterien" (Bundesarchiv NS 6/vol. 345); copy supplied by MHS.

48   Center of Military History, "Military Improvisations During the Russian Campaign," U.S. Department of the Army, CMH Pamphlet 104–1, 1986, 80.

49   Jutta Rüdiger, ed. *Zur Problematik von Soldatinner: Der Kampfensatz von Flakwaffenhetferinnen in Zweiten Weltkrieg—Berichte und Dokumentationen* (Munich, 1987), 29, quoting Lotte Vogt.

50   Ibid., 91.

51   Ibid., 28.

52   Docky Manner, *Die Frau in den USA. Schriftenreihe der NSDAP* (Munich 1942), 44, as cited in Seidler, *Frauen*, 153. See also 60 and Gersdorff, *Frauen im Kriegsdienst*, 441.

53   In February 1944 one of the naval auxiliaries wrote to a friend who had been captured: "I've been sent to the Naval Auxiliary Service. I am now a soldier who replaces you in the country. The service is not difficult as we are not raised to be gun women. What is good about it is that one is also treated as a woman. Obviously we must conduct ourselves honorably as women otherwise [indecipherable] is completely lost. We are amongst sailors but we have nothing to do with them." Excerpted in "Studies

of Migration and Settlement," Administrative Series. Field reports 8–12, "Women in Nazi Germany," part E. "Morale," 27, in Franklin D. Roosevelt Library.

54   Seidler, *Frauen*, 60, 153, 170; Gersdorff, *Frauen im Kriegsdienst*, 441. Seidler also states that the National Socialist propaganda mocked the American Wacs who were considered traitors to their sex because they were performing functions in the Army under the pretence of emancipation. Seidler, Frauen, 153. On brutalization, see Omer Bartov, *Hitler's Army: Soldiers, Nazis, and War in the Third Reich* (New York, 1991), 66–72, 89, 94, 135.

55   March 1945 order from Bormann (Reichsleiter) Rundschreiben 119/45. 5 March 1945. Bundesarchiv NS 6/vorl. 349, as cited in Seidler, *Frauen*, 349. For handling of bazookas in special cases, see Anlage, OKW No. 1350/45, 23 March 1945, cited in Gersdorff, *Frauen im Kriegsdienst*, 531. Seidler dismissed both the description of bazookas as feminine and the heroics by Erna as propaganda, Seidler, *Frauen*, 155. Bazookas were light-weight and did not have the heavy recoil that only a large body could absorb.

56   Guenther W. Gellermann, *Die Armee Wenck-Hitlers letzte Hoffnung. Aufstellung, Einsatz und Ende der 12. Deutschen Armee im Fruehjahr 1945* (Koblenz: Bernard und Graefe Verlag, 1984), 43–44; copy housed in MHS, Austria.

57   Seidler, *Blitzmädchen*, 99. Hitler's test pilots Hanna Reitsch and Melitta Schilla-Stauffenberg were the only women to receive the Iron Cross (first class); see Karl Otto Hoffman, *Die Geschichte der Luftnachrichtentruppe*, vol. 2, part 1 (Neckargemünd, 1968), 182, cited in Seidler, *Frauen*, 158.

58   BA R43 11/666c, Reichsleiter M. Bormann to Herrn Reichsminister Dr. Goebbels, 16 November 1944, cited in Gersdorff, *Frauen im Kriegsdienst*, 465.

59   Seidler, *Frauen*, 155; Tuten, "Germany and the World Wars," 56; Wilmott, "Women in the Third Reich," 18–20.

60   Anne Eliot Griesse and Richard Stites, "Russia: Revolution and War," in Goldman, ed., *Female Soldiers-Combatants or Noncombatants?* 69, 73; see also K. Jean Cottam, ed., *The Golden-Tressed Soldier* (Manhattan, Kans., 1983); Cottam, "Soviet Women in Combat in World War II: The Rear Services, Resistance Behind Enemy Lines and Military Political Workers," *International Journal of Women's Studies* 5 (1982): 363–83. Shelley Saywell, *Women in War* (Toronto, 1985); V. S. Murmantseva, *Soviet Women in the Great Patriotic War*, 2d ed. (Moscow, 1979) (in Russian); Murmantseva, "The Military and Labor Achievement of Soviet Women," *Military-Historical Journal* 5 (1985): 3–96; L. I. Stishova, ed., *On the Home Front and on the War Front: Women Communists during the Great Patriotic War* (Moscow, 1984). During May 1986, this author met in Moscow with several Soviet women veterans of World War II who explained the multiple roles women played during the war. There is little material written on these women and what is available is written with a "Military-patriotic" purpose as Cottam describes it; see K. Jean Cottam, *Soviet Airwomen in Combat in World War II* (Manhattan, Kans., 1983), ix-xiv.

61   S. Alexiyevich, *War's Unwomanly Face* (Moscow, 1988), 9, 49, 83–86; translated from the Russian by Keith Hammond and Lyudmila Laxhneva.

62   Murmantseva, *Soviet Women in the Great Patriotic War*, Chapter II, especially 126.

63   Griesse and Stites, "Russia: Revolution and war," 70,

64   Ibid., 69. On Soviet pilots, see also Cottam, *Soviet Airwomen in Combat*; Bruce Myles, *Night Witches: The Untold Story of Soviet Women in Combat* (Novato, Calif., 1981); Cottam, ed. and translator, *In the Sky Above the Front: A Collection of Memoirs of Soviet Airwomen Participants in the Great Patriotic War* (Manhattan, Kans., 1984).

65   Griesse and Stites, "Russia: Revolution and War," 74.

66   When Junior Lieutenant Liudmila Pavlichenko met with reporters in Washington, she was dumbfounded to be asked about lingerie instead of how she had killed 309 Germans. *Time*, 28 September 1942, 60.

67   The German military provided the female AA-Auxiliaries with special identity cards as they were considered "combatants" but this was not broadcast to the German public. These women had to be at least twenty-one years old, volunteers, and have no children. "Dienstordnung für Luftwaffenhelferinnen" Heft 2, Flakwaffenhelferinnen (Service Regulations for Female AA-Auxiliaries) 15 December 1943, BA-MA, RL 6/16, 1–5; copy from BA-MA, Freiburg, supplied by Militärgeschichtliches Forschungsamt, Freiburg.

68   Bidwell, *Women's Royal Army Corps*, 126–27.

69   Treadwell, *Women's Army Corps*, 191–218; Diane Gertrude Forestell, "The Victorian Legacy: Historical Perspectives on the Canadian Women's Army Corps" (Ph.D. diss., York University, 1985).

70   At least WAC veterans in the 1980s did not support the notion of opening contemporary combat roles to women. D'Ann Campbell, "Servicewomen of World War II," *Armed Forces and Society* 16 (Winter 1990): 263–66.

71   Letter from Air Force quartermaster officer, excerpted in "Monthly Censorship Survey of Morale, Rumors, and Propaganda: August 1944," in Maxwell Air Force Base Library, code 704.7011, August 44.

72   Samuel Stouffer et al., *The American Soldier: Combat and Its Aftermath* (Princeton, 1949), 2: 131–34; John Costello, *Love, Sex and War: Changing Values, 1939–1945* (1985): 192; William Arkin and Lynne R. Dobrofsky, "Military Socialization and Masculinity," *Journal of Social Issues* 34 (1978): 151–68; Judith Hicks Stiehm, "The Protected, the Protector, the Defender," *Women's Studies International Forum* 5 (1982): 367–76, on the necessity of women being absent; George L. Mosse, *Fallen Soldiers: Reshaping the Memory of the World Wars* (New York, 1990), 60–61, 203–10 on manhood and German motivations. The proscription against homosexuality likewise involved a protection of the ideal of manliness. Allan Berube, *Coming Out Under Fire: The History of Gay Men and Women in World War Two* (New York, 1990), 176.

73   Costello, *Love, Sex and War*, 169. For a Persian Gulf reference, see Peter Copeland, *She Went To War: The Rhonda Cornum Story* (Novato, Calif., 1992).

74   J. Glenn Gray, *The Warriors: Reflections on Men in Battle* (1959); H. Elkin, "Aggressive and Erotic Tendencies in Army Life," *American Journal of Sociology* 51 (1946): 408–13; Wayne Eisenhart, "You Can't Hack It Little Girl: A Discussion of the Covert Psychological Agenda of Modern Combat Training," *Journal of Social Issues* 31 (1975): 13–23.

75   Women soldiers did in fact die in hand-to-hand combat on Okinawa. The Japanese drafted high school students, male and female, into militia units that were hurled into combat, and killed to the last person. The saga of the all-female "Lilly Brigade" is now part of Japanese folklore. Thomas R. H. Havens, *Valley of Darkness: The Japanese People and World War Two* (New York, 1978), 188–90. If MacArthur had invaded Kyushu, he probably would have encountered thousands of women infantry. Apart from cartoons, I have never seen an American reference to fighting enemy women. In 1945 Willie tipped his hat to a Blitzmädchen he was taking (at gunpoint) to a POW compound. She wore a helmet, a Luftwaffe jacket, and a civilian skirt; a hand grenade was still tucked in her belt because he was too much of a gentleman to search her. The cartoon succinctly captured the uncertainty of an unexpected sex role. *Bill Mauldin's Army* (Novato, Calif., 1983), 348.

76   21 September 1928 "Memorandum for the Assistant Chief of Staff, G-1. Subject: Participation of Women in War" (copy in ML, Xerox 612; original in WDWAC 314.7) by E. S. Hughes (Major, General Staff), approved by Brig. Gen. Campbell King (Asst. Chief of Staff).

77   Ibid. M. C. Devilbiss, *Women and Military Service: A History, Analysis, and Overview of Key Issues* (Maxwell Air Force Base, Ala., 1990), comes to a similar conclusion that necessity has been a driving factor for the military in dealing with gender issues.

FURTHER READING

ON THE GENERAL SUBJECT of soldiers and combat a good place to begin is Joanna Bourke, *An Intimate History of Killing : face-to-face killing in twentieth-century warfare* (London, 1999), and see the essays in P. Addison and A. Calder (eds), *Time to Kill: the soldiers' experience of war in the West, 1939–45* (London, 1997). Some good general studies are: Martin van Creveld, *Fighting Power: German and U.S. army performance, 1939–1945* (Westport CT, 1982).

The experience of German soldiers may be studied in: Omer Bartov, *Hitler's Army. Soldiers, Nazis and War in the Third Reich* (Oxford/New York, 1991); James Lucas, *Hitler's commanders: German bravery in the field, 1939–1945* (London, 2000); and S. G. Fritz, *Frontsoldaten. The German Soldier in World War Two* (Lexington KY, 1995). Particular units or organizations are discussed in: C. Sydnor, *Soldiers of Destruction. The SS Death's Head Division, 1933–45* (Princeton NJ, 1977); Heinz Höhne, *The Order of the Death's Head*, trans. Richard Barry (New York: Ballantine Books, 1966); Theo Schulte, *The German Army and Nazi Policies in Occupied Russia* (Oxford/Providence RI, 1989); Christopher R. Browning, *Ordinary Men. Reserve Police Battalion 101 and the Final Solution in Poland* (New York, 1992); George C. Browder, *Hitler's Enforcers: The Gestapo and the SS security service in the Revolution* (New York, 1996). And see the essays by S. G. Fritz, "'We Are Trying to Change the Face of the World'" — Ideology and Motivation in the Wehrmacht on the Eastern Front: the view from below", *Journal of Military History*, 60 (1996), 683–710; and T. J. Schulte, 'The German Soldier in Occupied Russia', in Addison and Calder (eds), *Time to Kill*, 275–83. For German sailors see Timothy Mulligan, *Neither Sharks Nor Wolves: the men of Nazi Germany's U-boat arm, 1939–1945* (London, 1999).

On the experience of American soldiers see: Gerald Linderman, *The World Within War: America's combat experience in World War II* (New York, 1997); Gerald Astor, *The Greatest War: Americans in combat, 1941–1945* (Novato CA, 1999); Stephen Ambrose, *Citizen soldiers: the U.S. Army from the Normandy beaches to the Bulge, to the surrender of Germany, June 7, 1944–May 7, 1945* (New York, 1997); Peter Schrijvers, *The crash of ruin: American combat soldiers in Europe during World War II* (Basingstoke, 1998); and Edwin Hoyt, *The GI's war : American soldiers in Europe during World War II* (New York, 1988). Studies that focus on race and ethinicity are: Graham Smith, *When Jim Crow met John Bull. Black American Soldiers in World War II Britain* (London, 1987); and Jeré Bishop Franco, *Crossing the Pond: the native American effort in World War II* (Denton TX, 1999).

On the experience of British and Commonwealth soldiers see: David French, *Raising Churchill's Army: the British army and the war against Germany, 1919–1945* (Oxford, 2000); Jeremy Crang, *The British Army and the People's War, 1939–1945* (Manchester, 2000); David Fraser, *And We Shall Shock Them: the British Army in the Second World War* (London, 1999).

Some other useful works on the combat experience may be found in: Philip Jowett and Stephen Andrew, *The Japanese Army, 1931–45* (2 vols, Oxford, 2002); Mark Johnston, *Fighting the Enemy: Australian soldiers and their adversaries in World War II* (Cambridge, 2000).

On the experience of women in the armed forces see especially the work of K. J. Cottam on women in the Soviet Union: *Women in War and Resistance: selected biographies of Soviet women soldiers* (Nepean ONT, 1998); and K. Jean Cottam, *Soviet Airwomen in Combat in World War II* (Manhattan, Kans., 1983); and also see Bruce Myles, *Night Witches: the untold story of Soviet Women in combat* (Novato CA, 1981); Mattie Treadwell, *The Women's Army Corps* (Washington DC, 1954); Shelford Bidwell, *The Women's Royal Army Corps* (London, 1977).

The experiences of prisoners of war merits separate consideration. For Allied prisoners see: R. P. W. Havers, *Reassessing the Japanese Prisoner of War Experience: the Changi POW camp, Singapore, 1942–5* (London, 2003); Philip Towle, Margaret Kosuge and Yoichi Kibata (eds), *Japanese Prisoners of War* (London, 2000); John Nichol and Tony Rennell, *The Last Escape: the untold story of allied prisoners of war in Germany, 1944–45* (London, 2002); Frances Cogan, *Captured: the Japanese internment of American civilians in the Philippines, 1941–1945* (Athens GA, 1999). For Axis prisoners see: Bob Moore and Kent Fedorowich, *The British Empire and its Italian Prisoners of War, 1940–1947* (Basingstoke, 2002); Robert Billinger, *Hitler's Soldiers in the Sunshine State: German POWs in Florida* (Gainesville FL, 2000).

The experience of the air war was quite different and may be examined in: Josef Kammhuber and David C. Isby (eds), *Fighting the Bombers: the Luftwaffe's struggle against the Allied bomber offensive* (London, 2003); Robin Neillands, *The Bomber War: Arthur Harris and the Allied bomber offensive, 1939–1945* (London, 2001); Roger A. Freeman, *The Fight for the Skies: allied fighter action in Europe and North Africa, 1939–1945* (London, 1998); and Martin Middlebrook, *The*

Berlin Raids: RAF Bomber Command Winter, 1943–44 (London, 2000). And for the war at sea: Philip Kaplan and Jack Currie, *Convoy: merchant sailors at war, 1939–1945* (London, 2000).

Some interesting studies on individual battles are: David Glantz, *The Battle of Kursk* (Shepperton, 1999); Simon Foster, *Okinawa 1945: assault on the empire* (London, 1994); Robin Neillands, *The Battle of Normandy, 1944* (London, 2002); Alan Warren, *Singapore, 1942: Britain's greatest defeat* (London, 2002); Paul Adair, *Hitler's Greatest Defeat : the collapse of Army Group Centre, June 1944* (London, 1994).

On generalship see (in addition to those described in the 'Who's Who' guide): General Sir David Fraser, *Alanbrooke* (London, 1982); Nigel Nicolson, *Alex: The life of Field-Marshal Earl Alexander of Tunis* (London, 1973); Nigel Hamilton, *Monty: The Making of a General, 1887–1942* (London, 1981); Philip C.F. Bankwitz, *Maxime Weygand and Civil-Military Relations in Modern France* (Cambridge MA, 1967); Kenneth Macksey, *Guderian: panzer general* (rev. edn, London, 2003); John R. Colville, *Man of Valour: the life of Field-Marshal the Viscount Gort* (London, 1972); John Keegan (ed.) *Churchill's generals* (London, 1991); Correlli Barnett, The Desert Generals, (2nd edn, London, 1999); and Dik Daso, *Hap Arnold and the Evolution of American Airpower* (Washington DC, 2000); Robin Brodhurst, *Churchill's Anchor: Admiral of the Fleet Sir Dudley Pound* (Barnsley, 2000).

PART THREE

Home Fronts
People, Places, and Politics

M ODERN WARS ARE FOUGHT not on the battlefield alone, but "at home", both literally and figuratively. Cities and towns, neighborhoods and shops, homes and schools may be bombed from the skies. Civilians who ignore the reality of war do so at their peril, and those who object — conscientiously or other- wise – will have difficulty convincing the bombers that they are not targets. And, if defences fail to hold the frontier, as they did in France, Belgium and the Netherlands, in the Soviet Union, Greece and Yugoslavia, in China, Malaya and the Philippines (and many other places as well) civilians will find themselves regulated, policed, employed or imprisoned – whether they regard themselves as "combatants" or not. There were precedents, of course: ancient and medieval warfare frequently involved townspeople and city-dwellers, who were besieged and starved, perhaps pillaged, looted and raped. But the trend of history (in Europe at least) for several centuries seemed to be moving away from such barbaric practices, and in the direc- tion of wars being fought by professionals on distant battlefields in the countryside. World War One suggested a reversal of this trend, most famously with the German occupation in Belgium and northern France, then with the bombing raids on London and Vienna. The long-distance shelling of Paris by "Big Bertha" suggested another precedent, that of the "guided missile."

With the example of the World War One fixed in their minds, strategists between the wars tried to think through the implications: how could the fears of civilians be used to destroy the enemy's will to fight? how could the will of their own people be sustained? Theorists of the new warfare, ranging from Guderian to De Gaulle, from Fuller to Patton, saw in tanks, armoured personnel carriers, fighter planes and bombers, the opportunity to penetrate defenses, ignore fortifications and armies in mass and to strike instead at the heart of the enemy – at their capitals, cathedrals, parliaments, and universities. There was a military conceit that lay at the bottom of this strategy, one which regarded civilians as weak and vulnerable to even the threat of death or destruction, unable to sustain themselves in the face of such dangers as those to which soldiers were trained to withstand. In one sense, then, World War Two was by nature of a great experiment: how would the techniques of modern warfare alter the very nature of armed conflict? Would civilians panic when the bombs fell down upon them? Would they demand an end to the fighting when their own lives were on the line? Thus, at the same time that some strategists were planning to frighten civilians into submission, others were preparing to mobilize opinion, bolster morale, and stiffen resistance.

Many of those who anticipated the advent of war assumed that the "new," "totalitarian" regimes represented by the Nazi, Fascist, or Soviet states would enjoy significant advantages over the "old," "parliamentary" regimes in Britain, France, the United States, in western Europe and the British Commonwealth. With their highly centralized sytems and their formalized leadership principles, they should be able to mobilize their people and their productive forces to an unprecedented extent. The capacity of these new regimes to regulate and regiment, to propagandize and persuade seemed superior to those regimes that enshrined values of freedom, the individual and the right of dissent. Thus, World War Two was also an experiment in political life: how far would the nature of the regime, its organization and ideology determine its outcome?

Jill Stephenson's study of Württemberg opens an interesting window into the nature of the Nazi regime at war. Most of our images of "civilians at war" come from the cities: the bombing of London and Coventry, of Dresden and Hamburg – and the astonishing courage the people of those cities showed in facing the onslaught from the air. Less emotionally evocative is the experience of people who lived in the smaller cities and towns, in the villages and countryside. But it is here that she finds an interesting testing-ground for ideology v. tradition, conformity v. resistance. Nazi rhetoric idealized the German peasant: those closest to the soil were closest to the true *Volk*, the rugged warriors of the Germanic past who had resisted the Romans and forced their way into lands to the south and east. The Nazi reality, especially during the war, was different. Their policies favored the cities and the proletariat; the countryside was treated as a gigantic, outdoor warehouse supplying men for the army and food to the cities. This caused resentment. Local people saw the Nazis as modernizers, as outsiders, and they "resisted" the incursions of the regime into their lives – not in the conventional sense of guerrilla activities or assassination attempts, but in their determination to maintain traditional patterns and activities of life that contradicted Nazi doctrine. Church-going thus became a political act, while bartering and hoarding were regarded as traditional rights of individuals and the local communities in opposition to the regime's centralized, autarkic policy. The best illustration of the difference came with the foreigners sent by the Nazis to replace German men on the farms: the farmers tended to treat them as they always had their hired hands – eating with them and incorporating them within family life; and, when they were co-religionists (as was the case with the

Polish Catholic laborers) treating them with compassion – as their church leaders encouraged them to do. Thus, Stephenson concludes, Nazism was no more than a veneer which overlay village life during the war; the traditions of the community were more fundamental and were sustained even against the apparent dominance of a "totalitarian" police state.

Questions of who "resisted", and how and why they did so have become of greater historical interest as the distance between ourselves and those we study has increased. In the immediate aftermath of the war stereotypical impressions were etched on the experience of the Resistance. Those who resisted their occupiers were heroes, those who collaborated with them were traitors; the motives of the resisters were noble and virtuous, those of the collaborators were wicked and corrupt. There is now a vast literature which has succeeded in complicating and contextualizing the experience of occupation, collaboration, and resistance. Paula Schwartz adopts an unusual angle of approach regarding the resistance in France. She is interested in the nature of gender roles in this phenomenon. The role of women in the resistance is particularly intriguing because it offered opportunities to break through the barriers of tradition and custom (in which the Nazis in Württemberg had failed): were women to be utilized, as usual, in subordinate activities, as faithful helpers to the warrior-male? or would they participate fully in the armed struggle themselves? The unstructured, untraditional, unpredictable nature of the resistance could have, should have, meant that traditions and customs would be reduced in importance. And, she argues, up to a point, this was the case.

Women participated in the resistance in unprecedented ways, living the lives of outlaws with the *maquis*, conspiring in the killing of German officers, carrying guns. Ironically, this usually resulted not in a redefinition of gender roles, but in the conferring of an honorary "male" status on the female involved – as evidenced by the use of "gender tags." Paradoxically, the resistance used a whole set of assumed ideas of gender, the place and role of women, as an intrinsic part of their strategy: women pushing prams were less suspicious-looking, and so were used to transport guns; women, because they were "invisible" could be used as lookouts during operations; and women could be used as camouflage for a man – single men wandering the streets in wartime would attract suspicion that they would not if they were strolling arm-in-arm with a woman. So new, radical or revolutionary roles could be performed by women pretending to be acting according to custom. The more relaxed and informal the resistance was, the more opportunities it offered women to break with tradition; the more organized and formal it became, the more likely it was to utilize women in their customary roles. And – perhaps the final irony – women themselves were, after the war, more and more reluctant to talk about their "warrior" experience, often preferring to describe their activities in ways that made them acceptable to traditional norms and values.

Thus, the manner in which these events were "remembered" may differ from other kinds of records that we have of them. Take, for example, the legend of World War Two in Britain as "The People's War." Both during the war and afterwards participants and historians presented a picture of the conflict as one that simultaneously brought people together in the glorious, common cause of defending their islands against an aggressor, and as one that was fought for the idealistic purpose of defeating fascism abroad while promoting social justice at home. This was quite different from the remembrance of the First World War and its aftermath which seemed to have been fought for no good purpose and to have dealt a devastating blow to British society, producing a country rife with ideological conflict, regional divisions and economic disparities. This time a new and improved modern Britain would be produced by the war: one in which the health, the education and the social security of ordinary citizens would be assured through the creation of a "welfare state". Jose Harris suggests that historians now recognize the extent to which the sources that have been used to paint a picture of the war as one of social consensus and solidarity were – at one and the same time – the propagandists who were engaged in creating it. Thus, the films, the radio broadcasts, the newsreels, the posters and the paintings were produced by those whose job it was to mobilize public support for the war, and they did so by insisting that "the people" as a whole supported it – regardless of their class, their politics, their region, their age or their gender.

The twin symbols of the "People's War" were the Blitz and the Beveridge Report. The heroic manner in which the people of Britain responded to the bombardment of their cities showed the extent to which ordinary folk were prepared to stand up and fight for one another and for their belief in what Britain represented. The widespread support for the recommendations made by William Beveridge in 1943 – that there should be universal access to social services such as education and health care – showed that the country was united in its determination that the war should this time result in a better Britain. Harris, in surveying the historical literature on the subject, presents (once again) a more complicated picture than this. Some of the important social measures taken during the war were not the result of idealism or political consensus, but wartime necessity: the evacuation of four million mothers and children from British cities forced the government to deal with housing, health, and education issues; shortages forced the government to ration food, to determine what was "essential" and what was "fair." Nor was wartime solidarity as solid as supposed: crime rates rose; strikes were frequent; rural and suburban families were appalled by the savage and unsanitary habits of the urban poor – and did their best to avoid taking in evacuees. In reality, the war was full of ironies and contradictions. The monarchy, that symbol of tradition and conservatism, which had been dealt severe blows during the scandals of the 1930s, not only survived, but recovered much of its prestige; 10 percent of the families in Britain continued to own 80 percent of its wealth; in spite of the increase in sexual liberty, the nuclear family emerged from the war stronger and more tightly-knit than ever; respondents to surveys indicated their support for the provision of universal social services at the same time that they objected to increasing the size and role of government in their affairs; and, finally, many of those who fought to save Britain did so in defence of "tradition": of the loose, pluralistic, atomistic nature of British society – which stood in contrast to the strong, intrusive and centralized governments of Germany, Italy, and Japan.

Like the People's War in Britain, World War Two in the United States has received a good press. In the popular imagination, it has come to be regarded as the "Good War" for two fundamental reasons: it was fought (successfully) in defense of freedom (or Americanism); and it was fought by all, for all, in a spirit of mutual sacrifice. Mark Leff, recognizing that the successful mobilization of the "home front" was essential, undertakes to understand how this co-operation was achieved, how an ethos of wartime sacrifice came to dominate political discourse in the United States. In order to do this, he examines two different aspects of the "politics of sacrifice": first, the attempt of President Roosevelt to "cap" wartime salaries – and thus to symbolize the equality of sacrifice; second, the role of the War Advertising Council in co-ordinating a vast private advertising campaign in support of the war effort. The fact that the advertising campaign succeeded where the president failed illuminates our understanding of cultural values in wartime. Roosevelt's efforts clashed with fundamental American values – and entrenched social interests; the Advertising Council's efforts carefully built upon these values and manipulated them to their advantage.

In April 1942, Roosevelt announced that, as part of a series of steps within the war economy which would include wage and price controls and rationing, he would institute a 100 percent "super-tax" on individual incomes over $25,000, over $50,000 for families. This was crafted in a way that was meant to suggest an equality of sacrifice: if workers were to have their wages capped, it was only fair that the wealthy should make a corresponding commitment. As Leff shows, the gesture was entirely symbolic: the regulation might have affected, at most, one person in 50,000 (and income from investments were deliberately excluded, thus omitting the single largest source of income for the wealthy). Nevertheless, even as a gesture it backfired. The proposal, in attempting to set limits upon the ethos of boundless individual achievement was denounced as "communistic" and rejected by Congress. Roosevelt failed to adjust, in even a minor way, the cultural notion of the American Dream. By contrast, Leff demonstrates how the advertising industry – rocked back on its heels by the depression of the 1930s, and the absence of consumer products available for consumption during the war – saw the war as a golden opportunity to save itself. Madison Avenue succeeded where the president had failed: they convinced business that advertising on behalf of the war effort was "good business" even though the demand for their products during the war far exceeded the supply; then the Treasury ruled that businesses could write off 80 percent of their advertising costs against their taxable incomes – so, in essence, the US taxpayer paid 80 percent of the bill for the advertising directed at them. Culturally, the advertising initiative succeeded in suggesting to Americans that the war was being fought in defence of the "American Way of Life," which consisted of individual liberty, individual achievement, and right to benefit from this by freely consuming the goods and services that society could offer the successful. Agreement on these fundamentals reinforced the vision of social harmony being achieved through individual effort, and rejected the notion that society consisted of social groups in competition with one another.

The role of advertising is utilized in quite a different way by Marilyn Lake in her consideration of "female desires" and the war. She suggests that most treatments of the role of women in the war and postwar have regarded the period as one of a significant advance quickly followed by a dispiriting retreat. By focussing attention on the place of women in the workplace, and particularly as workers earning a wage or salary, most feminists and historians alike have treated the return of women to home and family after the war as a step backward, as an opportunity missed. Lake argues instead for a reconceptualization of the meaning of feminism itself, and she utilizes materials drawn from advertising both to illustrate and to prove this point. The 1930s witnessed the emergence of a new understanding of femininity, one which revolved around sexuality, physical attractiveness and youthfulness. Before the war women – especially younger women – came to regard sexual pleasure as a right, and one that could be obtained by enhancing their "sex appeal" through the use of products such as lipstick, beauty creams, hair dyes, etc. Thus, when war offered them the opportunity to move into the workplace, they saw this as their chance not to erase gender distinctions, but to reaffirm sexual difference; "war work" presented possibilities of sexual encounters and romantic adventures with men rather than economic independence from them. In other words, their aims were not those of the traditional, early feminists, with their devotion to causes such as voting rights and equal pay.

The language of love and romance, Lake argues, resonates throughout the diaries, journals and letters of women during the war. And the conditions of warfare stimulated the trends established before the war: the presence of attractive young foreign men (mainly American), the loosening of traditional restraints and disciplines (especially on the young), and uncertainty of what the future would bring served to encourage women to seize the moment and enjoy what pleasure they could, and provided them with increased opportunities for acting upon their desires. Finally, there was no "retreat," no dispiriting return to tradition when war ended. The very meaning of marriage and family were altered forever in the eyes of women: marriage come to be redefined as romance, with sexual fulfilment as a woman's right – which in turn meant that the woman saw herself less and less as mother and more and more as part of a romantic couple, which in turn meant limiting the intrusions and distractions of children, and creating the conditions within the marriage and home that would be conducive to love and romance. Expectations had forever changed, and the experience of war "on the home front" had played a vital role in changing them.

Chapter 11

Jill Stephenson

NAZISM, MODERN WAR AND RURAL SOCIETY IN WÜRTTEMBERG, 1939–45

T HE EFFECTS OF MODERN WAR on a major industrialized power are normally measured in terms of casualties, armaments production, resources for that production — both human and material — the dislocation of civilian life, the destruction of plant and buildings, and the disruption of communications. Because the weapons of modern warfare are produced in industrial concerns, generally in an urban environment, and because the most terrifying aspect of recent wars, from the civilian point of view, has been aerial bombardment, particularly of these same industrial, urban areas, the effects of war on civilian society, in Germany as elsewhere, have generally been estimated and analysed from the point of view of urban civilians.[1] While the contribution made by the rural population to the waging of modern war — directly through being subject to conscription into the armed forces, and indirectly through food production for those who produce armaments, as well as for themselves — is regarded as vital, the effects of war on rural society can seem trivial in comparison with the suffering in bomb-damaged towns and cities. The conscription of rural civilians into armaments manufacture and away from the land, for example, is seen as a problem chiefly because of its at least potentially damaging effect on *urban* society: a drop in domestic food production together with an enemy blockade which prevents imports can, as was the case with Germany in the first world war, be disastrous in towns, with far-reaching political as well as social consequences.[2]

It was this disaster which, according to Tim Mason, made Hitler determined that, in any future war, Germany's food supply would be safeguarded, and (thereby) popular morale maintained, thus minimizing any risk of mass disaffection, far less rebellion. It was assumed as self-evident that any such threat would come from the *urban* population, especially members of the urban working class. There was no thought of a peasant revolt: modern, twentieth-century rebellions were likely, it was believed, to be Marxist-inspired, and therefore the preserve of the 'proletariat', with its political and trade union organizations.[3] Peasants (especially peasant propri-etors), were overwhelmingly anti-Marxist, and such peasant protest as there had been in Germany in recent years had been successfully mobilized *by* the National Socialists, during the agrarian crisis whose origins pre-dated the great depression of 1929–33. If the 'middle-class thesis' of support for the NSDAP has recently been challenged, it nevertheless remains the case that many of the earliest supporters of the party were to be found in rural areas, and that agrarian distress drew many to a party that demagogically promised to put the interests of rural Germany first.[4]

Yet this promise was not met, because, where the interests of rural and urban Germany conflicted — as they often did, especially in wartime — the interests of urban Germany were given priority. The NSDAP is normally characterized as being 'reactionary' and 'fascist', and therefore anti-working class; yet the party's leader-ship was above all concerned to maintain at least the quiescence (if not the acquiescence) of the 'proletariat', the group that would, by staffing essential heavy industries, play a key role in both rebuilding Germany's industrial strength after the depression and preparing Germany for war. This meant adopting policies which led many rural Germans to become profoundly disaffected with the régime, provoking them not only into withholding co-operation from its officers during the war but even into positively obstructing their efforts in a variety of areas. These included, crucially, the maintenance of an orderly food supply and fraternization with 'aliens', in the shape of foreign workers. Ultimately, it would mean a refusal to try desperately to block the western allies' inexorable advance through southern Germany in 1945. A culture of illicit activity and disobedience developed — and increased as the war dragged on — with the mounting difficulties and final crises of the war intensifying villagers' interdependence and strengthening community loyalties in ways that thwarted the centralizing pretensions of the National Socialist régime, to the frustration of its more diehard adherents.

There is nothing remarkable about individuals acting self-interestedly and self-ishly, particularly in time of hardship and shortage. In the second world war there probably was not a belligerent or occupied country which did not have a black market in scarce goods or 'under the counter' transactions which defied rationing restrictions. In Germany, however, after six peacetime years of nazi rule, while recovery from the depression and the quest for autarky had perhaps brought benefit to some urban workers, it was inflicting severe pressure on rural society. Further, it was clear to ordinary citizens, both urban and rural, that party officials, from the highest to the lowest, would loudly proclaim the primacy of 'the common good before self-interest', while simultaneously feathering their own nests. This bred widespread cynicism about the nazi régime,[5] and legitimized, in many people's minds, the violation of laws and norms decreed by it. As Rainer Lepsius has said, under a dictatorship, 'the individual loses not only his right to political freedom, but also criteria for making political judgments', with the result that 'moral indiffer-ence and instrumental opportunism' prevail.[6] This was true not only of 'Aryan', 'politically reliable', 'socially valuable' people's attitudes towards the outcasts from nazi society — Jews, the 'asocial', homosexuals, 'gypsies', the 'hereditarily diseased' — but also of these same people's attitudes towards each other. In the 'atomized society' of the Third Reich, it is hardly surprising if it was a case of everyone for him/herself.

Yet this desperate individualism was clearly more to be found in the towns than in the countryside. That is not to say that there was no selfishness, lawbreaking or cheating in rural areas: indeed there was. Rather, however, the interests of groups and communities were paramount, facilitated by the persistence in rural areas of traditional structures and relationships — of the kind of 'sectoral, socially homogenous milieu' which is deemed to have been breaking down in urban society by about 1930.[7] In southern rural areas, traditional familial and community networks and relationships continued to obtain, at least to some extent, through to the end of the second world war, with corresponding hostility to disruptive outsiders, whether they were government officials or evacuees from northern cities. This was generally a matter of ingrained habit being reinforced by the wartime struggle for survival, but in some respects it was also a manifestation of opposition to — or, at least, a rejection of — nazi norms, values and demands which threatened to undermine these networks and relationships. For many rural dwellers, the nazi system in peacetime had brought unexpected and unwelcome change, with inroads into traditional loyalties and practices and the establishment of networks of control to try to enforce observance of new normative requirements. The massive demands of modern warfare greatly intensified this development, and — in spite of some determined resistance by families and groups of individuals — disrupted at least some of the bonds of personal relationships and mutual interest which had traditionally underpinned rural society. In particular, the long lists of men killed, injured or taken prisoner contributed to a massive change, with unprecedented burdens of responsibility thrust upon women especially,[8] while many of the westward flood of refugees, who would never return to their eastern home, settled in villages whose identity their presence altered irrevocably. If only by these brutal means, the nazi era brought an element of modernization to rural outposts. While Hitler's war lasted, however, its exigencies reinforced their ties of mutual interdependence.

There has been much debate about whether the National Socialists were a modernizing or a reactionary force.[9] At the very least, it is clear that, while the NSDAP had been uncompromisingly opposed to the *symptoms* of 'progressive' modernization — especially socialism — it was itself perceived in rural areas as a modernizing force, one which threatened traditional village life and practices quite as much as did the growth of industry and towns. Certainly, the adoption of new and effective campaigning methods enabled the National Socialists to challenge, on equal terms, the representatives of the other newer, 'modern' forces in society — the urban classes spawned by industrialization. The political parties and trade unions, as well as the middle-class associations, were no match for the NSDAP in the political cockpit of depression-wracked Germany. Disarmed and demoralized workers and disillusioned or opportunistic bourgeois were an easy prey, less able to withstand nazification and to resist nazi demands than were 'backward' rural sections of society, who might be insecure in time of agricultural depression, but whose traditional community relationships were much more difficult to infiltrate or subvert. Attempts to 'integrate' rural communities 'into the new system', in a way that, according to David Schoenbaum, occurred throughout society with the creation of a *Volksgemeinschaft* (people's community),[10] or to force them to change their habits or recognize new allegiances, often met a kind of guerrilla warfare in which groups and whole communities persistently undermined *Reich* (national), *Land* (state) or party policies at the most local level.

But it was perhaps only in wartime that the *Volksgemeinschaft* ideal was genuinely put to the test, with issues like the requisitioning and distribution of scarce resources, the closing-down of some small businesses, labour conscription for women, the deployment and control of foreign workers, and the billeting of evacuees from areas threatened or actually damaged by bombing, clearly demonstrating the persistence of traditional class and community allegiances and prejudices, in the southern German state of Württemberg, at least. It would be mistaken to regard this as 'resistance' to nazism in any conventional political sense: rather it was, on the one hand, a defensive strategy, retreat into a familiar refuge; and, on the other hand, it was a gesture of contempt towards a system which was widely seen as hypocritical and corrupt. This reaction was not peculiar to opponents of the régime or disgruntled neutrals. A sense of disillusionment developed among some of the régime's own footsoldiers — especially when they had their roots in the community which they now informed on, ordered, or policed. In the towns, with their shifting populations, individual party or state officials might have no roots in the community in which they operated, so that their loyalty might well be unswervingly to the régime's leadership — give or take bribes and blandishments offered by individuals for favours. But in the countryside, where conflicts developed between the régime and the community, NSDAP and local government officials might find their loyalties divided: it was not so much a case of 'going native' as of *being* native.

The circumstances of a modern war — its effects reaching into the remotest areas of the country — produced a higher rate of (internal) conflict than there had been in the peacetime years, and some officials clearly found it more comfortable to accommodate the desires of sections of their community than to try to impose the will of the régime whose executors they were supposed to be. Living in their native village or small town, they might find themselves either being drawn into deals or syndicates which breached the increasing battery of wartime domestic legislation, or else turning a blind eye to others who violated it. The failure to enforce some decrees undoubtedly owed much to the increasing shortage of manpower in the police and the judicial system as ever more men were called up into the armed forces. But it also derived in part at least from the connivance, and even in some cases the actual participation, of officials who were embedded in a culture of interdependence and mutuality within their own community long before they joined the NSDAP.

This pattern can be observed in Württemberg, a predominantly agrarian *Land* where industrialization had developed only slowly and on a smaller scale than elsewhere in Germany, without the growth of large heavy industrial concerns. Accordingly, Württemberg suffered less from the direct effects of the world economic crisis around 1930 than almost any other area of Germany, with unemployment rates at about half of the national average. It was only with recovery from the depression in the mid-to-late 1930s that the flight from the land there became significant, as industrial centres revived. Before the 1930s, then, Württemberg hardly felt the stresses of rapid, large-scale industrialization and urbanization; modernization was less immediate, traumatic and complete, especially in remote

rural areas,[12] where communities were insulated from the worst of the 'patholo-
gies and seismic fractures within modernity itself'.[13] In the 1920s and 1930s,
Württemberg continued to consist largely of rural or small town communities which
maintained much of their traditional character, while assimilating some of the
features offered, or imposed, by modernization.

In 1939, over 40 per cent of Württemberg's 2.7 million inhabitants still lived
in communities of two thousand or fewer: only three towns, Stuttgart (420,000),
Heilbronn (69,000) and Ulm (62,000), had a population greater than 50,000. Of
the 34 new districts created by administrative reorganization in 1938, 15 were
classed as 'agricultural' and 13 as 'mixed'.[14] Württemberg had more than its share
of marginal small-holdings: around 1930, the average size of farms was a mere 4.6
hectares, compared with 7.2 for the Reich as a whole. Altogether 35 per cent of
Württemberg's agricultural land — twice as much as in the Reich as a whole —
was farmed in units of less than five hectares. The land was relatively poor and
unproductive, and Württemberg farmers had on average a lower income than their
south German neighbours in Baden and Bavaria, to say nothing of farmers further
north. Uneconomic agriculture bred the part-time farmer, whose main employment
was in local industry or trade; in 1925, 15.2 per cent of all workers in these
economic sectors in Württemberg ran a part-time farm, compared with 10.8 per
cent in the Reich. In addition, there were commuters who lived on their part-time
farms and went elsewhere to work. In 1939, they accounted for 14 per cent of the
employed population in Württemberg. If agriculture continued to be structured
largely on traditional, pre-modern lines in Württemberg during the interwar years,
this was reflected in the maintenance of the village community as the most important
basic unit of rural society.

It was the persistence of this substantial rural population, many of them living
in villages which were genuine communities with traditions of local hierarchy, interdependence and mutual self-help, and pursuing their livelihood often by traditional
means — for example, trading goods and services instead of buying them with, or
selling them for, money — which proved an impediment to National Socialist
demands of a modernizing nature. To that extent, Ralf Dahrendorf may be justified in aligning opponents of National Socialism with 'reaction'.[15] His 'social
revolution' may well have occurred in cities, towns and some rural satellite areas
near large conurbations. The industrial revival of the mid-1930s revitalized blighted
areas and gave renewed impetus to labour migration, mechanization, technological
innovation and bureaucratic control of these developments. In remoter rural areas,
by contrast, production continued much as before, but with the added irritants of,
on the one hand, a serious labour haemorrhage, resulting from the industrial revival
and, on the other, attempts at bureaucratic interference by Reich and Land governments and the Reichsnährstand (National Food Estate).[16] Thus the new wave of
modernization touched even distant rural areas, and met resentment and obstruc-
tion. What was at stake for farmers, rural artisans and tradesmen was a traditional
way of life and work, many of whose features had already been obliterated by the
transport revolution, the lure of the towns, mass production and the 'total war'
effects of the first world war. The new mass media, too, were seen as alien and
threatening: complaints were made 'that too many films are shown which bear no
relation to reality and only encourage the flight from the land', while

> . . . the rural population never stops criticizing the radio station in
> Stuttgart for broadcasting jazz music which they cannot begin to under-
> stand. They say that insufficient consideration is given to the enter-
> tainment of the farmer and farm labourer, who want to hear popular
> songs, popular music (Swabian [local]) and marches.[17]

For these people, co-operation in nazi policies would necessarily mean relinquishing
many of the remaining habits and traditional practices of rural communities — the
real traditions of everyday life, not the invented traditions which the nazi state
devised as a cosmetic while trying to force alien modern practices upon them.[18]

The rural population, then, can be identified as a backward-looking, reactionary
force, clinging to outdated production methods, preferences and relationships, by
the mid-twentieth century an irrelevant brake on Dahrendorf's 'social revolution'.
But it can also be argued that only traditional, deeply-rooted ties and loyalties could
have some success in withstanding National Socialist claims to authority. By the
1930s, *modern* German society, in and around towns and cities, was both atomized
and deeply divided, with the newer collective forms of industrial society dissolving
under pressure of economic crisis. *Gleichschaltung* (co-ordination) closed down those
that remained by 1933 and imposed nazi-led collective structures on a disarmed and
defenceless urban population. In addition, the nazi régime — especially in the
person of Labour Front leader Robert Ley — was at pains to conciliate the mass
of the urban working class, to detach them from their former (socialist or
communist) political leaders, and to integrate them into the nazi system, using what
Tim Mason has characterized as a combination of repression and social policy. Many
of them proved receptive: as Gunther Mai puts it, 'in the labour movement, too,
there were "March violets"'.[19] Opposition to nazi demands on ordinary people at
local level therefore devolved largely on to traditional communities whose structures and institutions — with the Christian churches prominent — had either stood
the test of pressure from modernization or had not yet had to confront it. These
structures were organic and broadly-based, involving virtually all members of the
community: in fact, they already served as a practical 'people's community', where
some had more exalted status than others, but where everyone had a place. Since
the 'anomie' of individuals in the great industrial centres was not normally a feature
of life in the countryside, the nazis' spurious but plausible image of a 'people's
community' had neither the significance nor the appeal there that it perhaps had for
some of the rootless and rejected in the towns.

It soon became clear that, while attacking the 'progressive' symptoms of
modernization, the nazi régime was intent on replacing them with a difference
merely of emphasis, not of substance. Thus, while the industrial recovery may have
brought Hitler's government grudging acceptance from some formerly neutral or
hostile urban workers, criticism was soon aired about the government's neglect of
the chronic problems facing agriculture. Both government and *Reichsnährstand* were
determined to exert central control over agricultural production and distribution
virtually from the start, with increasing state intervention, under the Four Year Plan
of 1936, to promote autarky and prepare Germany to withstand the domestic strains
of war. To farmers, this was both irksome and irrelevant: centralized control
resulted in increased government demands rather than much-needed aid for the

hard-pressed producer. Further, jurisdictional disputes between party and *Reichs-nährstand* officials — who 'are not co-operating as they really ought to be doing nowadays'[20] — only added to the sense of bureaucratic incompetence and oppressiveness. The Third Reich did not create a paradise for the small farmers who had been so exalted in nazi propaganda: only a few came, literally, into their inheritance with the *Erbhof* (hereditary farm) system.[21]

Before 1933, the nazis had won enough active or passive compliance among the rural population to achieve power because they appeared to 'look forward to a better past'. But if the smokescreen of their pro-peasant propaganda is penetrated, it is obvious that their radical designs in both domestic and foreign policy would make modernizing demands which threatened to disturb the rhythms of traditional rural life. The priority given to heavy industry, the 'modern' sector of the economy, was National Socialist policy, to promote National Socialist expansionist aims. Industry-oriented government policies and the *Reichsnährstand*'s fatuous schemes had the twin effects, firstly of ensuring that small farmers struggled to survive and, consequently, of alienating large sections of them from National Socialism and all its works. It was reported from Württemberg in Summer 1939 that 'the *Reichsnährstand* is having great difficulty in finding suitable men to act as its officials . . . because the kind of people who are suitable are simply refusing to take on these "thankless" posts'. Rural local authorities in Württemberg did not enjoy the post-depression upturn in tax receipts which accrued to the urban local authorities, and therefore they remained impoverished, unable to mitigate hardship in their area, and thus unable to win popular support for the nazi system.[22]

The problems which had dogged small-scale agriculture for decades were intensified in the abnormal circumstances of a second twentieth-century war. The sacrifices required of civilians were radical, including the conscription of several million soldiers (many of whom would suffer death or injury) and the direction of civilians into essential war-work in modern industries. In rural areas, there was particular resentment at both the requisitioning of farm horses (which were an indication of status, as well as of obvious practical value) and the drafting of male members of a farming family and paid male labour, leaving the physically weaker members of a family — women, elderly parents, adolescents — to cope with the heaviest work which had been traditionally performed by men. Compensation, in the form of foreign prisoners-of-war or forced labour, brought new pressures and problems.[23] Evacuees from industrial northern cities like Essen, Düsseldorf and Hamburg who were billeted on farming families, had no experience of farm work, and in most cases showed little inclination to help

> . . . our farm women, who have to slave away from early morning until late at night. . . . we can understand that they [the evacuees] are in a difficult position, but it's not unreasonable to expect that, just a few times during their stay, they might make the effort to be useful'[24]

Further, the need to conserve Germany's limited resources, in order to avoid a recurrence of the popular disaffection caused by food shortages in the 1914–18 war, had led to the development of systems for regulating and monitoring food production and distribution which were implemented from August 1939, and which farmers and traders regarded as oppressive. In addition to rationing, these included surveys of soil types and crops grown, with quotas detailing the delivery requirements of each commodity from each farm to the relevant state depot. There were also periodic animal censuses, and attempts to control and monitor the numbers of live and slaughtered farm animals in villages and on individual farms. In particular, there were stringent regulations to restrict the slaughter of livestock, so that only limited amounts of meat would come on to the market at a time, to prevent the possibility of an immediate superabundance being followed by a severe shortage.[25] These devices, together with the allowance paid to the wife of a serving soldier *who was not a farmer*, along with the state-financed evacuation of urban families to safer rural areas, were geared towards placating the industrial workers who were essential to a modern war-effort and among whom 'Marxism' was believed still to have a hold.[26] If what looked like more favourable treatment for urban dwellers, together with attempts to regiment farming in unpalatable and unfamiliar ways, antagonized the rural population, then that was the price to be paid for maintaining order in the towns, the environment deemed most likely to foster any serious challenge to nazi authority. The overriding preoccupation was with the maintenance and promotion of control by the 'reactionary, fascist' National Socialist leadership, but the effect was modernizing, with greater concern about urban opinion, greater state control, and the relegation of agriculture in practice to the status of handmaid to the industrial, modern state.[27] The result was a resort to strategies for undermining nazi authority in rural areas.

Most of the instances where individuals or small groups refused to accept and operate the new controls introduced by the government involved violations of the War Economy Regulations which covered, in minute detail, the production, distribution and purchase not only of foodstuffs but also of other essential goods, like coal, soap and clothing material. Part of the problem was that the regulations failed to take account of existing practice, and where there was a conflict between the two, there was extensive violation of them. Particularly because of the prevalence of part-time farmers in Württemberg, there was an ingrained tradition of bartering both goods and services. Butchers and fruiterers would exchange produce rather than sell them to the public for money.[28] Tobacconists could obtain their supplies from urban wholesalers only if they paid for them with ham, butter or eggs. Tobacco products, too, were at a premium, and a peasant might offer a tobacconist a goose (also a much-prized item) in order to obtain cigars and cigarettes. Urban workers and housewives joined in, travelling to buy wine or potatoes direct from the producer.[29] In Ulm, a housewife who boasted that she had 150 preserving jars at home, and intended to buy a further 150, was regarded by the *Sicherheitsdienst* (SD — Security Service) as a typical example of someone investing in goods so as to be able to barter with farming families for food. The farmers, who were too busy at harvest time to go shopping, gladly exchanged foodstuffs for items that were hard to obtain.[30] Hoarding and the increasing incidence of bartering in wartime were a source of anxiety and frustration to leaders in party and state, but the implication of some NSDAP members and officials in these, and other, illicit activities made enforcement of the new regulations even more difficult, providing cover for barterers and black marketeers.[31] It is clear that some rural local government or party officials either would not risk unpopularity by trying to enforce the law, or else were themselves still so enmeshed in their village community that they tended to put that community's interests and habits before their loyalty to the régime.

Possibly Württemberg's most flagrant instance of a community breaching the War Economy Regulations was the syndicate connected with a Roman Catholic convent, the *Kloster* Untermarchtal, which was closed by *Gauleiter* (NSDAP regional leader) Wilhelm Murr in 1941, in what has tended to be portrayed as simply an anti-clerical attack. Catholic opinion certainly viewed it as such.[32] But the ensuing court case revealed a network of connections — including NSDAP members and officials, of whom two were local *Bürgermeister* — which was flouting the state's authority. The convent's leaders had, among other things, consistently claimed ration cards for between 10 and 20 more residents than there actually were in each of 18 distribution periods between Autumn 1939 and Spring 1941. Further, the convent had failed to make obligatory deliveries of eggs to the state depot in more than a year, but then so had the producers who were their neighbours, who had illegally sold their surplus to the convent. There were also abuses concerning meat, milk and other foodstuffs. The chief culprit, as identified at the trial, was the Untermarchtal *Bürgermeister*, who had issued fraudulent ration cards and tolerated other abuses. It emerged that he had deliberately given the convent preferential treatment, and in return had received gifts from its inmates. Nor had any of the host of relevant officials of both party and state, including the *Kreisbauernführer* (district *Reichsnährstand* official), pursued the matter over the previous year and a half, suggesting 'that even the responsible authorities set little store by the conscientious fulfilment of delivery requirements'. Six of the 20 accused were acquitted, eight faced imprisonment — ranging from three years for the Untermarchtal *Bürgermeister* himself, downwards — and the rest were fined.[33]

This case was by no means exceptional. In November 1942, a special court passed sentence on members of a syndicate who had engaged in the illegal slaughtering of pigs in Rottweil, depriving the state depots of hundreds of kilos of meat. It was far from uncommon for farmers deliberately to underestimate the numbers of their livestock when a census was taking place, and then to feel free to slaughter animals when they pleased, in excess of their quota, as based on the census.[34] In the Rottweil case, leading members of the illicit slaughtering syndicate included the *Bürgermeister* and the local *Reichsnährstand* official. The former was the officer responsible for granting certificates giving permission to slaughter and registering the weight of the slaughtered animals, and he had evidently sought to cover his abuse of these powers by employing his inexperienced young son as a clerk. Dozens of pigs were slaughtered between Autumn 1939 and Spring 1942, and the carcasses weighed without the head and, sometimes, other parts as well — a common tactic used to evade the official controls. This enabled members of the syndicate to hold back meat, either for their own consumption or else to sell on the black market. In their judgment, the presiding judges sent the ringleaders to prison for periods ranging from ten months to two years, the latter sentence being imposed on the *Bürgermeister*. The judges added in mitigation, however, that

    . . . they were — in a small community in which everyone knew everyone else, and everyone was related to everyone else by ties of blood or marriage — obviously in a difficult position in trying to fulfil their official duties when there was a conflict of interests.[35]

In other cases, an official might intercede on behalf of a farmer or tradesman who had broken the law. In December 1939, an NSDAP *Kreisleiter* asked for a sentence for hoarding to be set aside, because the guilty party 'had not been hoarding in a selfish fashion'. A senior local government official, in petitioning the Württemberg Economics Minister, endorsed this plea for leniency.[36] In January 1940, the *Landrat* in Horb am Neckar protested to the Württemberg Milk and Fats Trade Association about a threat it had issued to producers in his area who had failed to deliver their required quotas of milk. He did not deny the charge, but he strongly objected to the severity and the tone of the warning which, he claimed, would lead to hostility to the authorities 'which, today more than ever, must be avoided'.[37] In May 1940, a café owner in Trossingen claimed that his local *Bürgermeister* sympathized with his attempts to sell off his stock — which involved him in breaking the law — because he had been called up into the army and would have to close down his business. Certainly, the *Bürgermeister* had taken no steps to prevent him from continuing to sell rationed goods without receiving tokens in return, although he had been informed that this was happening.[38] Other *Bürgermeister* had, contrary to the law, given permission for the slaughtering of animals for private use, or made unauthorized ration cards available to individuals in their area.[39] Some members of the SD might report complaints about these practices and the view that 'hoarders and illegal slaughterers who are caught red-handed should immediately be brought before a summary court and given exemplary sentences'.[40] But detecting abuses in scattered villages, with a network of people involved and with local officials conniving, was a labour-intensive activity, and during the war labour was the commodity in shortest supply. Sending the NSDAP's local branch or district leader round farms to make a spot check on numbers of livestock or the volume of milk obtained from a cow might reveal abuse in a few individual cases,[41] but it seems not to have acted as a deterrent to farmers who fundamentally resented the wartime controls.

These controls were viewed not in isolation but as part of a package of disagreeable interference in traditional village life by outsiders. For example, removing native farmers and labourers for military service and replacing them with foreign workers — often Poles — was a poor enough bargain, but one that many farming families tried to adjust to and make the best of. Over and above that, however, the state then decreed precisely how these foreigners should be treated, and punished both them and the relevant Germans — sometimes with a ferocity which shocked the community — for transgressing prescriptions which, in the context of everyday life on a farm, seemed unreasonable and impracticable. If a Polish worker contributed significantly to maintaining the farm, why should he not take part in the family's meal and live under the family's roof?[42] Beyond that, the issue of fraternization with foreign workers also impinged on another major area of conflict between rural areas and the National Socialist régime, namely the authority of the churches. In Catholic areas of Württemberg and elsewhere, the local priest, an influential figure in a village community, often gave a lead in welcoming foreign co-religionists to regular services — contrary to decrees requiring devotional apartheid — and urging both compassion and the provision of material aid for the 'poor Poles' in particular.[43] This issue exemplified the opportunities provided by the war for the enhancement of the churches' role and profile in the community, completely contrary to what the régime had wished and hoped. In general, there was increased attendance at church services, as the imminence of mortality (for oneself or for a loved one) became more immediate, and even some leaders in the Hitler Youth were said still to be regular churchgoers.[44] The funerals contingent on military casualties gave the churches a clear opportunity, and from several places it was reported that 'the activity of the priests has had the effect of successfully exploiting the sudden grief of the relatives of the slain, so that *Christian funeral services have been held even for loyal National Socialists*'. A ban on Christian burial services would, in the view of an SD observer, be very damaging to the government, especially in rural areas, where 'even party officials are of the view that the best solution is for the party to take part in the church's services, because it is now regarded as being impossible simply to ignore these church services'.[45]

Again, the affair of the *Kloster* Untermarchtal was seen by many as primarily an attack on the Catholic Church by the nominally Evangelical Württemberg *Gauleiter*, Wilhelm Murr. While there clearly was a legitimate criminal case against the convent's leaders and their secular confederates, Murr's action in closing down not only the convent but also its related houses in other districts, and confiscating all of the property 'for the benefit of the state of Württemberg',[46] seems excessively punitive, especially when the individual culprits were being punished under the prevailing law. This was at a time when there was increasing state and party pressure on both the Evangelical and Roman Catholic churches, with the closure of their educational institutions and the shutting-down of their press, on the pretext of the exigencies of war. Such restrictions were regarded as offensive in small rural communities where the church remained both influential and central to the social life of a village.[47] In Württemberg there was particular outrage at the requisitioning, from Summer 1941 — and in some cases the melting-down — of bronze church bells, some of which were centuries old. This was perceived as a direct attack on religion rather than as a desperate attempt to utilize all available materials, although by this time there had been extensive collections of metal, and items like metal door-handles would soon be requisitioned.[48] As a concession to popular sentiment, it was decreed in December 1941 that any bell of particular artistic or historic value should be spared, and that, in any event, every parish should be left with at least one. While ceremonies which had been planned to mark the bells' removal (which were to include recording the sound of the requisitioned bells) were banned, it was conceded that reference could be made to their removal in regular church services. As a local official pointed out, it was essential not to antagonize the population.[49] But the issue of the church bells struck a chord of atavistic resentment, and one of the items on the postwar questionnaire about 'the last days of the war' in Württemberg's communes asked whether and when bells had been removed. The replies suggest that no distinction was made between the Evangelical and Catholic churches in this matter.[50]

The surrender of church bells may seem to those not affected a trivial sacrifice to make in wartime. That rural civilians regarded it as a particular affront to their community may simply confirm the impression prevalent in the towns at the time that many agricultural areas in southern Germany had little to complain about, compared with the desperate position in urban areas by the latter stages of the second world war. Certainly, most villages were in a more favourable position than the towns, from two points of view in particular. First, they were mostly spared the increasingly devastating bombing raids which in Württemberg had, by Autumn 1944, destroyed more than half of Stuttgart and most of Heilbronn, as well as damaging other areas like Friedrichshafen.[51] Second, the rural population was incomparably better off in terms of food supply. In wartime, there were bound to be shortages in a country which before the war had partly depended on food imports, especially in 1944–45 when Germany's empire was lost and refugees were flooding in. Urban consumers were, give or take ad hoc allotments or 'war gardens', utterly dependent on the dwindling supplies of food from rural areas. In December 1943, one urban scientist wrote disparagingly of farmers' (deficient) 'morals' and 'selfishness' in bartering food, or selling it without receiving ration tokens, reporting that one farmer

> . . . told me that the peasants were stupid if they delivered more milk than was absolutely necessary [to official depots] because they didn't receive what they saw as a reasonable price, and they would rather give any extra milk to their labourers, even to Ukrainian farm workers.[52]

But while the food producers and their neighbours were not in danger of starving, there were serious threats to their livelihood in the later stages of the war. There had by this time been protracted shortages of artificial fertilizer, fodder, working farm animals and, above all, labour. Annual attempts to attract urban volunteers, for example from the NSDAP's women's or youth organizations, to help at harvest time had never evoked much response,[53] showing farmers how little consideration urban fellow citizens had for them. In addition, a small minority of farms sustained damage either from bombing or during the Allied invasion in March/April 1945. All of this, together with the destruction of transportation systems, disrupted supplies to the towns and encouraged many farmers to resort simply to subsistence agriculture.[54] Over and above the practical difficulties, however, there was a strong sense of grievance about the way in which farmers' lifestyle and working practices had been threatened, and to some extent altered, by the centralizing demands of the National Socialist régime and the war which it had inflicted on them.

For the rural population, their identity was defined by their local community, not by the state at *Reich* or even *Land* level, which they perceived as an alien construct designed to promote the interests of urban citizens at the expense of those of the rural population where they conflicted — as they inevitably did, in wartime especially. This contributed to a widespread feeling in rural areas that they owed both the régime and urban society nothing. That perhaps contributed to the widespread violation of the War Economy Regulations in rural areas, and undoubtedly partly accounted for the hostility manifested by villagers towards urban evacuees, who often seemed better off than their hosts, and certainly behaved as if they were used to a significantly higher standard of living than they encountered in the countryside.[55] In the last year of the war, increasing numbers of evacuees, from Stuttgart,

Ulm and Heilbronn as well as from outside Württemberg, arrived and, at the same time, the influx of refugees from Germany's rapidly diminishing eastern European empire began. They had to be housed in unscathed rural areas, because the bombed urban centres could not cope with their own homeless, let alone incomers. While most evacuees went home after the war — but some not until 1946 — the refugees, from both urban and rural eastern regions, who made their homes in the south, were mostly there to stay, changing the character of villages indelibly and permanently.[56]

Yet the villages retained a sense of identity up to and beyond the end of the war, perhaps reinforced by the experience of 'the last days of the war', when the entire community (sometimes including foreign workers and prisoners-of-war) pulled together to prevent the destruction of their village, usually under the leadership of their *Bürgermeister*. Whether he had been a loyal National Socialist or a silent sceptic, his ultimate priority was the preservation of his native village and the safety of its inhabitants, if necessary in the face of orders from *Führer*, *Gauleiter*, *Kreisleiter*, or SS or army officers to resist the enemy. Being an NSDAP member — in some cases merely a pragmatic choice rather than a real commitment — did not prevent him from choosing loyalty to his village over obedience to party or army authority, sometimes in the face of credible threats of violence or death.[57] This was not necessarily (and perhaps not normally) a matter of taking a high moral stand, but rather another reflection — like connivance at violations of the War Economy Regulations — of a native official's commitment to his own environment.[58] It suggests that, in some rural areas at least, National Socialism was a veneer which perhaps changed some aspects of the outward appearance of village life, but did not alter the fundamental nature of village relationships, whatever new structures had been imposed on them from above.

Acknowledgements

An earlier version of this article was discussed at the Rutgers Center for Historical Analysis in November 1994. I should like to thank Omer Bartov, John Chambers and Regina Gramer for their helpful comments. I am also grateful to the British Academy for a grant which made possible the necessary archival research.

Notes

1   E.g., Jeremy Noakes, 'Germany' in Jeremy Noakes (ed.), *The Civilian in War* (Exeter 1992), 34–61; Earl R. Beck, *Under the Bombs: The German Home Front 1942–45* (Kentucky 1986); Eleanor Hancock, *National Socialist Leadership and Total War 1941–5* (New York 1991); Martin Kitchen, *Nazi Germany at War* (London 1995).

2   Jürgen Kocka, *Facing Total War* (Leamington Spa 1984), 24–60; N.P. Howard, 'The Social and Political Consequences of the Allied Food Blockade of Germany, 1918–19', *German History*, 11, 2 (June 1993), 161–88; Ute Daniel, *Arbeiterfrauen in der Kriegsgesellschaft* (Göttingen 1989).

3   Tim Mason, *Social Policy in the Third Reich: The Working Classes and the 'National Community'* (Providence/Oxford 1993), chap. 1, 'The Legacy of 1918 for National Socialism', 19–40.

4   M.R. Lepsius, 'Extremer Nationalismus. Strukturbedingungen vor der national-sozialistischen Machtergreifung' (first pub. 1970), *Demokratie in Deutschland* (Göttingen 1993), 62–7; J.E. Farquharson, *The Plough and the Swastika: The NSDAP and Agriculture in Germany 1928–45* (London 1976), chaps 2 and 3; Ian Kershaw, *Popular Opinion and Political Dissent in the Third Reich: Bavaria 1933–1945* (Oxford 1983), 37–40; Zdenek Zofka, 'Between Bauernbund and National Socialism' in Thomas Childers (ed.), *The Formation of the Nazi Constituency 1919–1933* (London and Sydney 1986), 37–63; Regina Gramer, 'Die Machtergreifung und Gleichschaltung 1933 in Bissingen an der Enz', unpublished paper, January 1981, section 5.

5   Found in point 24 of the NSDAP Party Programme of 1920. See also Ian Kershaw, *The 'Hitler Myth': Image and Reality in the 'Third Reich'* (Oxford 1987), 84–7, 91–104, 180–9; Staatsarchiv Ludwigsburg (hereafter StAL), K110, Sicherheitsdienst RFSS, SD-Leitabschnitt Stuttgart, Bü48: 'Betr.: Allgemeine Stimmung und Lage, 1. September 1941', 3, 36, 38; 'Bezeichnende Ausführungen eines Aussenstellen-Mitarbeiters zur Lageberichterstattung', 5.

6   M.R. Lepsius, 'Einleitung', *Demokratie in Deutschland*, op. cit., 8.

7   Michael H. Kater, 'Conflict in Society and Culture: The Challenge of National Socialism', 291, referring to Jill Stephenson, '"Triangle": German Civilians, Foreign Workers and the Nazi Regime: War and Society in Württemberg, 1939–1945', 339–59, both in *German Studies Review*, XV, 2 (June 1992). Walter Rinderle and Bernard Norling, *The Nazi Impact on a German Village* (Lexington, KY 1993), 155, assert that 'since village society was already homogenous, *Gleichschaltung* led merely to the addition of the word "Nazi" to club names'. See also: M.R. Lepsius, 'Parteien-system und Sozialstruktur' (first pub. 1966), *Demokratie in Deutschland*, op. cit., 31–50; H.A. Winkler in Kolloquien des Instituts für Zeitgeschichte, *Alltagsgeschichte der NS-Zeit. Neue Perspektive oder Trivialisierung?* (Munich 1984), 32.

8   This is the theme of Jill Stephenson, '"Emancipation" and its Problems: War and Society in Württemberg, 1939–1945', *European History Quarterly*, vol. 17 (1987), especially 351–61. See also Rinderle and Norling, *Nazi Impact*, op. cit., 164, 166–7, 171; and 64–5 on the first world war.

9   See, e.g, Ralf Dahrendorf, *Society and Democracy in Germany* (London 1968); Detlev J.K. Peukert, trans. Richard Deveson, *Inside Nazi Germany: Conformity, Opposition and Racism in Everyday Life* (London 1987), especially 15–16, 243–9; Michael Prinz and Rainer Zitelmann (eds), *Nationalsozialismus und Modernisierung* (Darmstadt 1991). Also, Jeffrey Herf, *Reactionary Modernism. Technology, Culture and Politics in Weimar and the Third Reich* (Cambridge 1984).

10   David Schoenbaum, *Hitler's Social Revolution* (London 1967), 293.

11   Thomas Schnabel, *Württemberg zwischen Weimar und Bonn* 1928–1945/46 (Stuttgart 1986), 189: 'Three quarters of all mayors in Württemberg survived the *Gleichschaltung* process unscathed. . . . In the smaller towns and communes there was relatively a very much smaller change in [local government] personnel than in the larger towns', in and after 1933. Rinderle and Norling, *Nazi Impact*, op. cit., 155, report that, with two exceptions, 'the NSDAP merely selected current village leaders to serve as Party functionaries, mayor and local officials.' See also 112–13.

12   Thomas Schnabel, '"Warum geht es in Schwaben besser?" Württemberg in der Weltwirtschaftskrise 1928–1933' in Thomas Schnabel (ed.), *Die Machtergreifung in Südwestdeutschland* (Stuttgart 1982), 186–8, 324–5; Willi A. Boelcke, 'Wirtschaft und Sozialsituationen' in Otto Borst (ed.) *Das Dritte Reich in Baden und Württemberg* (Stuttgart 1988), 33–5; Schnabel, *Württemberg*, op. cit., 68–73; George D. Spindler

et al., *Burgbach. Urbanization and Identity in a German Village* (New York 1973), 14, 17. Cf. Gunter Golde, *Catholics and Protestants: Agricultural Modernization in Two German Villages* (New York 1975), 16ff, especially 18 referring to 'the industrial "backwardness" of . . . North Württemberg as a whole', and the five north-eastern counties of Württemberg, where 'as late as 1961, the number of persons engaged in the region's agriculture was as high as it had been in 1882'.

13   Peukert, *Inside Nazi Germany*, op. cit., 16. See also Peukert's contributions to *Alltagsgeschichte der NS-Zeit*, op. cit., 41, 46.

14   *Statistisches Jahrbuch für das Deutsche Reich* (Berlin 1938), 13, 19; Hauptstaatsarchiv Stuttgart (hereafter HstAS), E151a, Bü673, 'Die Leistungsfähigkeit der Land- und Stadtkreise', 3–5. The remainder of the information in this paragraph is based on Schnabel, 'Württemberg in der Weltwirtschaftskrise', op. cit., 189–191.

15   Dahrendorf, *Society and Democracy*, op. cit., 412–13.

16   StAL: Bü44, 'Lagebericht des 4. Vierteljahres 1938' (1 February 1939), 18–20; Bü45, 'Lagebericht des 1. Vierteljahres 1939' (1 April 1939), 43–5; Bü46, 'Lagebericht des 2. Vierteljahres 1939' (1 July 1939), 38.

17   StAL Bü44, 11; Bü45, 22.

18   For an example of local cultural traditions, see Spindler et al., *Burgbach*, op. cit., 53–69.

19   Mason, *Social Policy*, op. cit., especially chaps 5 and 6; Gunther Mai, 'Arbeiterschaft und Nationalsozialismus in der Phase der "Machtergreifung"' in Klaus Malettke (ed.), *Der Nationalsozialismus an der Macht* (Göttingen 1985), 98. The 'March violets' were converts to National Socialism following the election of 5 March 1933. See also Gunther Mai, 'Arbeiterschaft zwischen Sozialismus, Nationalismus und Nationalsozialismus. Wider gängige Stereotypen' in U. Backes, E. Jesse, R. Zitelmann (eds), *Die Schatten der Vergangenheit* (Frankfurt/Berlin 1990), 206–12.

20   StAL, Bü46.

21   Farquharson, *Plough and Swastika*, op. cit., chap. 8, 'The Erbhof Law', 107–23, and passim; Harald Focke and Uwe Reimer, *Alltag unterm Hakenkreuz. Wie die Nazis das Leben der Deutschen veränderten* (Hamburg 1979), 149–55; Kershaw, *Popular Opinion*, op. cit., 42–53; Marlis G. Steinert, *Hitler's War and the Germans* (ed. and trans. Thomas E.J. de Witt, Ohio 1977), 32–3.

22   StAL: Bü46; Bü44, 22–3.

23   On the conditions and treatment of foreign workers in wartime Germany, see especially: Ulrich Herbert, *Fremdarbeiter. Politik und Praxis des 'Ausländer-Einsatzes' in der Kriegswirtschaft des Dritten Reiches* (Berlin/Bonn 1985); Edward L. Homze, *Foreign Labor in Nazi Germany* (Princeton 1967); Marie-Luise Recker, *Nationalsozialistische Sozialpolitik im Zweiten Weltkrieg* (Munich 1985), 79–81, 155–76; Peukert, *Inside Nazi Germany*, op. cit., 125–44; Robert Gellately, *The Gestapo and German Society. Enforcing Racial Policy 1933–1945* (Oxford 1990), 215–52; Gerd Wysocki, *Arbeit für den Krieg. Herrschaftsmechanismen in der Rüstungsindustrie des 'Dritten Reiches'*(Limbach, Braunschweig 1992). See also Kitchen, *Nazi Germany*, op. cit., chap. 6, and, on Württemberg: Paul Sauer, *Württemberg in der Zeit des Nationalsozialismus* (Ulm 1975), 417–24; Schnabel, *Württemberg*, op. cit., 570–3; Stephenson, '"Triangle"', op. cit.

24   StAL, Bü48, 43–8; Stephenson, '"Emancipation"', op. cit., 358–9; Rinderle and Norling, *Nazi Impact*, op. cit., 180–1.

25   Ibid., 169–72; Farquharson, *Plough and Swastika*, op. cit., 221–3; Jill Stephenson, 'War and Society in Württemberg, 1939–1945: Beating the System', *German Studies Review*, VIII, 1 (February 1985), 92–3, 96, 98.

26   Mason, *Social Policy*, op. cit., chap. 1; Dörte Winkler, *Frauenarbeit im 'Dritten Reich'* (Hamburg 1977), 80. See also Michael Prinz, *Vom neuen Mittelstand zum Volksgenossen* (Munich 1986), 300, 307.

27   Rinderle and Norling, *Nazi Impact*, op. cit., 170, claim that 'despite much official praise of peasants . . . after 1938 the Nazi regime reduced them to a state close to serfdom'. See also J.H. Grill, *The Nazi Movement in Baden, 1920–1945* (Chapel Hill, NC 1983), 300–4.

28   Heinz Boberach (ed.), *Meldungen aus dem Reich* (Munich 1968), 362, 390, 394; Bundesarchiv (hereafter BA), R22/3387, *Generalstaatsanwalt* Stuttgart to the Reich Minister of Justice: 30 September 1941, 31 January 1942; Stephenson, 'Beating the System', op. cit., 97–9; StAL, Bü48, 41.

29   StAL, Bü48, 41–2; StAL, Bü40, 20 August 1941; HStAS, E397, Bü37, 'An das Württ. Wirtschaftsministerium, Betr.: Schwarzhandel auf dem Lande', 5 December 1943.

30   StAL, Bü47, 24.

31   StAL, Bü40; StAL, Bü48, 'Bezeichnende Ausführungen . . .', 2–3,6–7; Boberach, *Meldungen*, op. cit., 185; Farquharson, *Plough and Swastika*, op. cit., 229–30; Stephenson, 'Beating the System', op. cit., 94, 104–5.

32   BA, R22/3387, *Oberstaatsanwalt* Stuttgart to the Reich Minister of Justice, 5 September 1941. See also Sauer, *Württemberg*, op. cit., 457–8; Jörg Thierfelder, 'Die Kirchen' in Borst (ed.), *Das Dritte Reich*, op. cit., 92.

33   HStAS, E397, Bü5, letter from the *Landrat*, Ehingen, to the *Ernährungsamt Abt. B*, 23 May 1941; ibid., *Sondergericht für den Oberlandesgerichtsbezirk* Stuttgart, 6 July 1942, 1–56.

34   StAL, K110, Bü47, 'Betr.: Allgemeine Stimmung und Lage', 15 July 1941, 15–16; Stephenson, 'Beating the System', op. cit., 92–105, with references to '*Schwarzschlachtungen*' (illegal slaughtering) on 92, 98, 100, 103–5.

35   HStAS, E397, Bü37, SL.Nr523–526/42. I22. SJs. 1313–16/42, report of judgment in the special court in Stuttgart, 24 November 1942.

36   Ibid., OStrafl. Nr. 312/39, letter from the *Landrat*, Rottweil, to the Württemberg Economics Minister, 12 December 1939.

37   Ibid., the *Landrat*, Horb am Neckar, to the Milk and Fats Trade Association, Württemberg, 31 January 1940.

38   Ibid., 'SD-Leitabschnitt Stuttgart an die Staatl. Kriminalpolizei Stuttgart', 22 May 1940.

39   Ibid., 'Zusammenstellung einiger Strafsachen und Dienststrafsachen auf dem Gebiet der Kriegsernährungswirtschaft . . . nach dem Stand vom 1. January 1943. I. Dienststrafsachen'.

40   StAL, Bü48, 'Bezeichnende Ausführungen . . .', 3.

41   Rinderle and Norling, *Nazi Impact*, op. cit., 169.

42   Sauer, *Württemberg*, op. cit., 417–24; Schnabel, *Württemberg*, op. cit., 570–3; Stephenson, '"Triangle"', op. cit., 343–52; John E. Farquharson, *The Western Allies and the Politics of Food* (Leamington Spa 1985), 22.

43   Stephenson, '"Emancipation"', op. cit., 355; idem, '"Triangle"', op. cit., 345, 347–9; Kershaw, *Popular Opinion*, op. cit., 288; Sauer, *Württemberg*, op. cit., 417.

44   Beck, *Under the Bombs*, op. cit. 168, 181.; Schnabel, *Württemberg*, op. cit., 463; StAL, Bü37, 29 April 1940; Bü38, 31 August 1940.

45   Ibid., Bü48, 13–15 (italics in original).

46   BA, R22/3387, 1 August 1941; Sauer, *Württemberg*, op. cit., 457–8. Murr left the Evangelical church in February/March 1942 (Sauer, 455).

47 BA, R22/3387, 3 July 1941; StAL: Bü47, 3–5; Bü48, 4–9; Schnabel, *Württemberg*, op. cit., 459–67, 513–18; Sauer, *Württemberg*, op. cit., 448–59. Cf. Grill, *Baden*, op. cit., 342–5; Kershaw, *Popular Opinion*, op. cit., 332–4, 340–57. See also Golde, *Catholics and Protestants*, op. cit., 159–76.

48 HStAS, E151a, Bü3621: 29 March 1938, 23 February 1940, 20 March 1940, 9 April 1940, 4 May 1940, 29 May 1940, 31 July 1940, 25 October 1940, 8 August 1942, 17 August 1942, 27 April 1943, 4 May 1943, 21 May 1943, 21 October 1944.

49 Ibid.: 9 August 1941, 15 August 1941, 27 November 1941, 9 December 1941, 20 December 1941.

50 Ibid., J170, Bü8 (Heilbronn): Affaltrach commune, 22 November 1948, 2; Biberach commune, 9 November 1948, 2; Gundelsheim commune, 8 September 1948, 3. See also the description of a teacher's lesson (c. 1970) about 'the history of the four great bells in the tower of the [Evangelical] church in Schönhausen . . . when they were cast, when melted down for armaments, when and by whom recast, and what tones they produce', in Spindler et al., *Burgbach*, op. cit., 110.

51 BA, R22/3387, 3 October 1944; Roland Müller, *Stuttgart zur Zeit des Nationalsozialismus* (Stuttgart 1988), 464–79; Kurt Leipner (ed.), *Chronik der Stadt Stuttgart 1933–1945* (Stuttgart 1982), 975–85; Schnabel, *Württemberg*, op. cit., 584–7; HStAS, J170, Bü77 (Friedrichshafen), *Bürgermeisteramt* Friedrichshafen Nr. 5640, 'Statistisches Material über Kriegsschäden in Friedrichshafen', 10 February 1954; Benigna Schönhagen, *Tübingen unterm Hakenkreuz* (Stuttgart 1991), 359–63. On the bombing of Württemberg, Sauer, *Württemberg*, op. cit., 346–61; on the bombing of German cities in 1944–5, see Beck, *Under the Bombs*, op. cit., chaps 8 and 9, 151–97.

52 HStAS, E397, Bü37, 5 December 1943.

53 StAL, Bü36: 28 April 1939; 19 May 1939. Cf. Regina Gramer, 'Wehrhaft und Wehrlos. Die organisierte Jugend in Bietigheim 1939–1945', unpublished paper, February 1983, 46–53; Jill Stephenson, *The Nazi Organisation of Women* (London 1981), 184.

54 Farquharson, *Plough and Swastika*, op. cit., 230–9; idem, *Politics of Food*, op. cit., 16–25.

55 StAL, Bü48, 43–8; Stephenson, '"Emancipation"', op. cit., 358–9.

56 HStAS, J170: Bü1 (Aalen) communes: Dewangen, 30 November 1949, 2; Flochberg, 2 August 1949, 1; Goldburghausen, 7 January 1950, 1; Bü18 (Ulm) communes: Schnürpflingen, 20 October 1948, 1; Sonderbuch, 18 October 1948, 1; Bü8 (Heilbronn), Auenstein commune, 1 November 1948, 1; Spindler et al., *Burgbach*, op. cit., 17–21; Rinderle and Norling, *Nazi Impact*, op. cit., 180–1.

57 Jill Stephenson, '"Resistance" to "No Surrender": Popular Disobedience in Württemberg in 1945' in F.R. Nicosia and L.D. Stokes (eds), *Germans Against Nazism: Nonconformity, Opposition and Resistance in the Third Reich. Essays in Honour of Peter Hoffmann* (New York/Oxford 1990), 355–65.

58 Cf. the self-serving account given by one *Bürgermeister* in HStAS, J170, Bü8 (Heilbronn), Gronau commune, 1–8.

Chapter 12

Paula Schwartz

PARTISANES AND GENDER POLITICS IN VICHY FRANCE

Dora: . . . Donne-mois la bombe. . . . Oui, la prochaine fois. Je veux
la lancer. Je veux être la première à la lancer.
Annekov: Tu sais bien que nous ne voulons pas de femmes au premier
rang.
Dora, dans un cri: *Suis-je une femme, maintenant?*
—Camus, *Les Justes* (italics added)

DISCUSSIONS ABOUT WAR as a vehicle of social change have focused most recently on the issue of gender: how does social upheaval affect gender roles and relationships between men and women?[1] This new angle can renew our understanding of the history and culture of the French Resistance of the Second World War, a political movement in which women played a much remarked and significant role, the nature of which has yet to be fully explained. Prevailing interpretations assess the role of women in the Resistance as a whole; however, the movement was actually comprised of different groups and forms of participation, some gender-specific, others gender-integrated. On the basis of oral and written sources, it is now possible to be somewhat more nuanced about issues of resistance and gender. This article examines the role of women in armed combat, a specific case that illustrates both the flexibility and resilience of gender roles in an area where men and women worked together.

Since the closing days of the Second World War, two principal interpretations of women's role in the Resistance, different but not necessarily contradictory, began to gain currency. Many contemporaries claimed that women had participated in the movement on equal footing with men. According to them, women played an important role because they were like men: they led networks and groups, made life-and-death decisions, commanded others. To support this claim, a few exceptional women who held positions of leadership—Bertie Albrecht, Lucie Aubrac, Marie-Madeleine Fourcade—are cited as evidence.[2] Another interpretation originated by the French Communist party (PCF) and renewed in the 1970s in the context of the women's movement, emphasized the specificity of women's activism and the contribution of so-called "ordinary" women. Both portray women's role in the Resistance as a break from past practice but tend to understate the limits of that change. Viewing a polyvalent movement from a vertical perspective, from the top down as in the first version, or from the bottom up as in the second, does not adequately account for variations among different political groups or sectors of activity within the larger movement. While looking at the distribution of political work between men and women in this particular case does bring some questions into sharper focus, it also reveals how complex the gender issue really is.

Different tasks within the Resistance movement were performed by women, by men, or by both. At least in the beginning, the novelty of the movement was the creation of new forms of political participation devoid of "gender tags." New tasks which arose in response to the needs of the moment—clandestine propaganda, unusual forms of intelligence collection, courier services—were not predefined as belonging to men or to women. Consequently, women could fill these unrestricted new areas until gender tags were affixed. Some forms of participation (including organizing demonstrations for food and providing food, clothing, and shelter for fighters and others) became "women's work," because they tapped women's traditional roles as housewives and mothers and politicized them under new conditions. Where they existed, gender tags restricted resisters to their own prescribed gender area. However, as we shall see, resisters also learned to manipulate or exploit gender tags to their own advantage.

The ultimate and most important task, that which all others were designed to prepare and support, bore an unmistakable gender stamp, in peacetime as in war: combat. Traditionally, combat was for men, and for men only. Yet a number of women, rare examples though they are, managed to break through the gender barrier during the war by becoming members of combat groups and even fighting alongside men. Although these *partisanes* were exceptions to the general rule, looking at their experience as women in a male preserve and seeing how men and women made sense of this breach of an ancient social convention, reveal the point to which gender roles could be stretched and the point beyond which they could not go.

With rare exceptions, women in combat or combat-support positions were either affiliated with or members of organizations linked to the French Communist party.[3] There are two reasons for this phenomenon. First of all, the Communist party simply presented more opportunities for combat because of the many unconventional forms of fighting that were to become its trademark: for instance, sabotages and guerilla attacks on individuals or installations of strategic or even symbolic significance. Such tactics were practiced by Communists in urban centers of the occupied zone, especially Paris, as early as 1941, long before they were condoned or imitated by other resisters, if ever.[4] Additionally, Communists added a paramilitary component to some activities that were not primarily military in aim: armed *groupes de protection* were formed to cover demonstrators and the highly vulnerable leaders of public street protests. Second, when the party was outlawed in 1939, women quickly assumed a crucial role by becoming human links to the leadership which had been forced underground. These party activists were the first liaison agents, some of whom would later bear arms. As the Communist party gradually reconstituted, women entered new structures on the ground floor, before the gender specific structures typical of later Resistance organization came into being. Thus, women who were brought into the movement under the auspices of the French Communist party, and at an early stage, were more likely than others to become involved in paramilitary or guerilla actions.

Women and combat

Although the historical record appears to be different, women activists remember the Resistance as an experience of equality with men: they shared tasks, responsibilities, and risks. They deny any significant gender division of labor in their groups and claim to have been well received by their male colleagues. Overwhelmingly, however, they qualify these remarks with a single, obvious exception: "women did not bear arms"; "in general, women did not engage in combat (*faire le coup de feu*)."[5]

Full-time, gun-toting *partisanes* were rare, but they did in fact exist. The prestige accorded them derives not only from their exceptionalism, but also because combat has become the most highly regarded form of resistance. As a rule, they were single women in their late teens or early twenties, more likely to engage in urban than rural combat. A group of fighters from the Compagnie Saint-Just, a guerilla team in the twentieth arrondissement of Paris specializing in sabotage, train derailments, and attacks on German soldiers, was commanded by the nineteen-year-old Madeleine Riffaud.[6] All-women units of the non-Communist Armée sécrète reportedly existed in Limoges and Lyon.[7] In the Groupes-Francs of Marseille, Madeleine Baudoin executed commando raids with heavily male teams.[8] Her first and self-appointed mission, a rite of passage for actions which were to follow, was a test of planning, nerve, and skill. It consisted of disarming a German non-commissioned officer—without killing him to get his gun:

> It was very crowded in the tram. His revolver was in a thick leather holster—the leather was so thick that he couldn't feel the gun. I exerted pressure on his back with one hand—when there is pressure above, you don't pay attention to what is happening below. I swiped [the revolver] without his ever feeling a thing. . . . I put it in a plain bag, the kind you might use for vegetables. Afterward, I went to see my buddy [the leader of the group]: "So, you wanted a revolver?" and I showed it to him. "Where did you find that?" he asked me. When I told him, oh! was he surprised! It wasn't necessary, I could have gotten it in my village, you could buy arms from peasants, hunting rifles and such, but it was expensive and we weren't exactly loaded.[9]

She later used this gun or one like it to stage a raid on a local city hall, an operation she planned and directed, to obtain food tickets and other supplies, which in turn were channeled to the underground.[10]

Another *partisane* recounted her role in the assassination of a notorious member of the Gestapo, reputedly the torturer of arrested resisters. Wearing her only dress set off to its best advantage for the occasion by the addition of a glamorous ostrich feather hat, "Claude" entered the renowned Parisian restaurant, Maxim's. Here dined the wealthy and privileged, German officers in particular, at a time when food for the French population was scarce and rationed. By her own account, a male co-worker (*copain*) escorted her into the restaurant, pointed out a man in uniform, and said: "He's the one. He has killed many of our own." Her eyes met those of the officer in question in a mirror over the bar. Presently the Gestapo officer beckoned to her, inviting her to dine with him. After an elegant meal remembered vividly for its rarity in a time of restrictions, "Claude" maneuvered their exit at a pre-appointed time, leading her suitor to believe their evening was to have a grandiose finish. The taxi waiting at the curb, as arranged, was driven by a party *camarade*. Claude climbed in first. In the back seat, she met the eager advances of her future victim with a revolver, deftly pulled from her left side before his roving hand could discover it, and fired point blank. The shot took place on the rue de Rivoli near the Louvre, a stone's throw from the restaurant on the rue Royale. She then alighted from the taxi and left on foot, taking a long, circuitous path to her clandestine hideout on the outskirts of Paris, while cab and body sped away. Never did she know the identity of the officer or the driver, or even what became of the body; the compartmentalization of tasks and information served to protect each operator, who was supposed to be ignorant of details unrelated to his or her own role.[11]

Despite the participation of some women in dramatic operations like this one, most women affiliated with combat groups were liaison agents who performed a whole range of support tasks associated with direct action without ever pulling a trigger or planting a bomb.[12] The close collaboration of women at the very core of combat groups was not uncommon. Although groups themselves were gender-integrated, tasks within them were often gender-specific. Partisan women planned attacks and did reconnaissance, procured and transported arms, recruited other fighters, and transmitted messages and instructions. Olga Bancic, a Romanian political refugee and the only woman depicted on the "Affiche rouge," stocked arsenals and ran guns for the Main d'oeuvre immigrée.[13] Others, like Mélinée Manouchian, posed incognito at the scene of a guerilla attack to observe carefully the movements of each actor and note the results of the operation and the reaction of the public—elements she used in the drafting of her report.[14] Chemist France Bloch-Sérazin provided raw materials from her laboratory and manufactured explosives for partisan fighters.[15] Still others, like Fanny Dutet and Betty Jegouzo, carried guns in shopping bags from one side of Paris to the other, stood look-out, retrieved still-smoking weapons from partisans after use.[16] All of these women were liaison agents who handled weapons a great deal but seldom if ever put them to use.

Women performed dangerous missions in gender-integrated combat groups, short of combat itself, because it was commonly recognized that of all resisters, they had the best disguise: they were women! The activities that prepared and surrounded combat were systematically performed by women precisely because they were invisible political agents. Male leadership on left and right agreed that women made ideal links as couriers or transporters of arms, jobs which required great mobility and subjected them to considerable exposure, because women were less likely than men to draw suspicion from the enemy.[17]

Gender tags were thus exploited by men who used women as go-betweens and by women who used their private roles as mothers, wives, lovers to "cover" them as clandestine agents. Hence the countless examples of women dissimulating weapons in "pregnant" pouches on their person, in baby carriages, and even in baby diapers to ensure safe transport. On occasion, women did attract attention from men, but as women more so than as suspects; this was an element of a woman's natural "cover" that was sometimes exploited, sometimes downplayed. Literature and testimony brim with tales of women resisters flirting their way past security checks or encouraging the gallantry of German soldiers who unwittingly carried suitcases packed with arms safely past checkpoints. On the other hand, some women were obliged to attenuate striking physical features which drew attention to their persons.[18]

Thus the invisibility which was said to give women an edge over men as covert operators was real, but only relative. Although it afforded a degree of protection that men did not have, it by no means spared them from arrest, deportation, and death.[19] For this reason, the all-women team of liaison agents for the Francs-tireurs et partisans (FTP) leadership in Paris was strictly forbidden to carry guns for their personal use at any time.[20] Ironically, they were too vulnerable to the risk of searches and seizures by police to enjoy the luxury of self-protection. The discovery of a weapon on a resister, male or female, implicated that person as a "terrorist" beyond the shadow of a doubt, and punishments were merciless. Male partisans in cities also were forbidden to carry arms merely as a matter of routine. Female liaison agents carried all the arms to the site of a "coup" and retrieved them after use. This technique concentrated the risk on a single "invisible" (and more expendable?) individual.

Above all, women were considered to be the privileged 'conveyors' of resistance to the population in general, hence the special mission assigned to women's organizers by the Communist party leadership. Their job as women was to mobilize housewives and mothers around food and home issues in order to create a groundswell of anti-Vichy and, later, anti-German sentiment. The women's popular committees, the only intentionally gender-specific formation in this period, organized demonstrations, circulated petitions, and marched in delegations to city halls and prefects' offices: all forms of so-called "legal" protest intended to complement illegal or underground actions. In the countryside their support of maquis in hiding was critical, not only to the physical survival of the group, but also to the group's acceptance by the surrounding population.[21] By 1944, in preparation for the battles of the Liberation, women were being called upon, individually and in groups, to formalize existing support networks for partisan fighters. Through a sponsorship program called "*marrainage*" or godmothering, groups of women provided comfort and necessities for particular detachments or battalions. They also staffed health care services (*services sanitaires*) for fighters living in the bush. On a neighborhood, village, or shop-floor level, women came together to sew arm bands for underground soldiers without uniforms preparing to emerge from the shadows. In these traditional "womanly" ways, women in cities, farms, and towns supported partisan fighters and other resisters, informally at first, and later in more formal structures. Women thus participated at every level, from the inner core of a small partisan band to the outer periphery of people who provided the material infrastructure for the fighters.

Gender-scrambling

Women were considered invisible political agents to such an extent that sometimes men actually "borrowed" gender aliases as women for safety and protection. By adopting female names as Resistance *noms de guerre*, a practice which seems to have been as widespread as it was novel,[22] men were able to benefit from the relative invisibility that a woman's name could afford them, at least until the name was paired with the person. In the Corrèze, for example, a *maquisard* named Georges was known as "Agnès" and his male teammate, "Mary."[23] Writing about daily life in the maquis, an eminent Resistance authority shows "gender-swapping" of this nature to be a common practice. At the same time, he suggests the presence of women in rural combat units to be uncommon, and through his use of language, betrays his own prejudice as well: "'Léontine'. . . . This by no means signifies that the group harbors a member of the weaker sex in its midst. . . . Léonie, Alberte, Annick, Christine, Héléne. . . . For security reasons, feminine first names abound in the maquis, and users have an unlimited variety from which to choose."[24]

Women also took male *noms de guerre*, benefiting from their own natural invisibility as women, but confounding their physical appearance with a male name. For women working in predominantly male groups, the adoption of a male code name may also have been a form of integration. Of course, gender-swapping was a limited form of protection that ended the moment a resister was physically confronted with his or her alias. Upon discovering the sought-after "Yvon" to be in fact a woman, the police closed the gap between her person and her name by dubbing her "Yvonne."[25]

Thus evolved a system of protection based on the dissimulation of one's true gender: men borrowed the protection of a female persona, and women enhanced their own natural invisibility by taking a man's name. Gender-swapping offered double protection, not only in the anonymity of a coded identity but in the temporary adoption of another gender—a surer way still to throw hunters off the trail. The code names "Georgette" and "Alice" figure on membership rolls of a Burgundian maquis, but they are not deciphered on a companion document. Are they rare examples of women fighters, or merely men covering their tracks? Forty years after the war, their aliases remain intact![26]

Sometimes the practice extended beyond gender-swapping, where men and women merely traded names. At its cleverest and most subtle, gender-swapping became "gender-scrambling," the adoption by men and women of intentionally ambiguous first names as *noms de guerre*, French names such as Claude or Dominique, which refer indiscriminately to men or women, or other names such as Paul(e), André(e), Marcel(le), which sound the same despite masculine and feminine variations in written form. In the following passage, a woman resister describes her "baptism" (the term is authentic Resistance lingo):

"First of all, what do you want to be called? Choose a first name." I wracked my brains, but everything I proposed had already been taken. Finally I resorted to a pocket calendar pulled from my purse and consulted the list of feast days around December 13, that of my patron saint. Daniel was the favorite. "Oh," said [my superior], "that's perfect, you'll be Danielle, that suits you well, and on hearing it pronounced, no one will know whether it refers to a man or a woman, excellent!"[27]

Other forms of gender-swapping have also been reported. A Communist maquis commander moved about by night disguised as a woman,[28] and a wounded partisan escaped the surveillance of hospital guards thanks to the escort of a complicitous young man in woman's clothes.[29] Soviet partisans of the same period frequently dressed as women, according to German reports.[30] Cases of partisan women masquerading as men, as did the warrior Joan of Arc, are rare, probably because their clandestine roles were already disguised and assuming a man's appearance would only have made them more likely to be caught.

Resisters played on the expectations of the authorities by exploiting gender tags, but was there any reason for these expectations to be unique to the opposition? Indeed, the subterfuge was so effective that other resisters were also fooled. Two revelatory incidents reported by different women in nearly verbatim terms bear this out clearly. In each case, a woman was so well disguised by her real gender that even male co-workers failed to recognize the importance of her role or her level of involvement in the movement.

The first example is an exchange reported by Juliette Dubois Plissonnier, a regional *responsable* in the political section of the underground party whose job required frequent travel and brought her into contact with local activists who did not necessarily know who she was.[31] She remembers that men were sometimes taken aback to encounter a woman in a leadership role. Upon arriving for a meeting which she was to preside, a male activist expressed surprise at finding her present, exclaiming: "What?! A woman here?" This provoked the reply from one of the group members, "She's not a woman, she's the boss."[32]

What is particularly striking is that another witness, this time a *maquisarde*, told a similar story in almost the very same words. Anna Pouzache, nicknamed "la Commandante rouge," was the liaison agent of Georges Gingouin, the colorful and controversial maquis leader of the Limousin. She often camped in the woods with the men between missions. One day, she reported, a new arrival to the maquis entered the camp, and seeing a woman among the partisans, remarked: "What? A woman in the maquis?" Springing to her defense, a fellow *maquisard* explained, "It's not a woman, it's Anna."[33]

Once decoded, the language of these exchanges reveals a hidden message. In French, as we know, "femme" can signify either "woman" or "wife"; context usually tells us how to interpret it. For the men who voiced their amazement, "woman" was less a gender distinction (woman as opposed to man) than a reference to a social role: woman as wife, girlfriend, lover. They reacted in part to a perceived violation of security and social rules, suspecting one of the men of admitting his wife or girlfriend to a secret hideout, of bringing not only a nonmember, but a woman, into the sanctity of the group.

When women succeeded in breaking the gender barrier by assuming leadership roles or combat positions, they were not considered women as such, but were sometimes conferred a kind of extraordinary status as "honorary men." In such cases, the gender of the person did not redefine a "male" task; rather the gender tag of the task redefined the person. Tasks were not so much gender-integrated, or open to women, as they appear. Rather, the woman herself was considered a sort of "honorary man," at least for the duration. Although such women were divested of their sexuality by the men with or over whom they were working, this probably actually facilitated their tasks as political agents. Women who made incursions into male territory at other times and places also became "honorary men." Thus we find "la Pasionaria," Dolores Ibarruri, praised by an admiring deputy for her remarks before the Spanish parliament as being "the only man who has spoken before the Chamber this evening,"[34] or Rosa Luxembourg and Clara Zetkin, reportedly lauded by Auguste Bebel as "the only men in the [German Social-Democratic] Party.'[35] Calling a woman a man could be intended or received as a compliment; it meant that she possessed courage, tenacity, intellectual or strategic prowess, so-called "virile" qualities, in spite of herself. This is significant when we consider that the two witnesses quoted above used similar anecdotes to make very different points about their degree of integration in the movement. Pouzache used her story to support her claim that she was on equal footing with the men in her group. According to her interpretation, not being a "woman" in the eyes of her male colleagues was tantamount to being considered a full-fledged member, "one of the men." By contrast, Dubois Plissonnier told a similar story to illustrate the difficulties she experienced as a woman in a "male" role.

Not only were some women in exceptional roles considered "honorary men" by men, but they may even have assumed a male identity to fit their new roles. Speaking today about her experience as a *partisane*, "Claude" says: "I am a man. . . . If I smoke and drink today, it's because I picked it up in the Resistance. I worked side by side with men, so I had to be like them, too."[36] Officially, "Claude," like Anna Pouzache, was a liaison agent working in combat groups with men. She also participated in several armed attacks on German soldiers or officers; on at least one occasion, as we have seen, it was she who pulled the trigger. Yet in every instance, she also played a role that a man could not, serving as "bait" by attracting the future victim as a potential lover. Her collaboration in the action was complete; her role as a woman in a gender-integrated combat operation was different, and this difference does not emerge in the image she projects of herself today. This phenomenon of gender displacement may explain in part why women report that there was little or no distinction between men and women in the underground and that they were received as equals by their male counterparts.

Partisan lifestyles

The extent and form of women's participation in combat groups could be influenced by a range of factors: region of activity, stage of evolution of the organization, social milieu, and the disposition of individuals. Primarily, however, variations in practice from one group to another were conditioned by the different forms of clandestinity in urban and rural settings. Maquis, or rural combat groups, were set apart from the population and fighters lived together in camps hidden in mountains, forests, or caves, depending on local topography. These partisan camps, in protective isolation from the outside world, developed around a male culture that, whatever the attitudes of individual men may have been, excluded women. This becomes increasingly clear with the progressive militarization of maquis folkways and practices. The more a particular group came to resemble a unit of the regular army, the less likely it became that women would have a place among the soldiers.

For urban fighters, living in a collectivity was an inconceivable security risk. Instead, tiny groups dispersed, each fighter hoping to hide in the crowd. In principle, urban guerillas lived alone in a series of revolving *planques*, or hide-outs, regrouping only for the planning or execution of a "coup." In fact, however, many lived as couples, real or staged, in an effort to blend into the local population. Thus women could dwell among partisans at the very heart of the organization in the city, but their presence in a rural camp was thought to undermine the legitimacy of the group.

For women to be included as full-fledged members of maquis groups was rare because of assumptions men held about women's behavior and about men's behavior around women. In some circles, women were regarded with suspicion because they were said to gossip: "Beware of women, and especially old maids," warned a list of security regulations.[37] Access to strategic information—the exact location of the camp, the identity of individuals, and operational plans—was limited to a trusted few. More importantly, the presence of women in the maquis, where rural partisans ate, slept, and washed together, broke a social code. Although it was possible for women to perform "male" tasks under certain circumstances, it was more difficult for them to enter a male space. Their presence in the bush where maquisards kept camp could encourage the formation of affective and sexual bonds considered inappropriate in the partisan redoubt. Even social visits to the maquis from wives and girlfriends were often prohibited, and new recruits were warned that taking to the hills meant leaving women behind. Not only could the presence of women provoke jealousies and erode the cohesion of the group, for many it also detracted from the seriousness of the partisan enterprise. Affairs between men and women, suspected or real, threatened the legitimacy of the maquis in its own eyes and in the eyes of the neighboring population on which the group relied for moral and material support.

In some quarters, the maquis was reputed to be a site of shameless revelry, a brigands' den, and above all, no place for women. Even when the maquis enjoyed the esteem of the population, awe and respect could be mingled with fear. So-called acts of "banditism," like the requisitioning of food and supplies from peasants and villagers, often at gunpoint, proved extremely unpopular. No doubt too, the mysterious nature of a secret group hiding in the bush fueled popular notions of what transpired in the maquis camp. These images find colorful expression in a contemporary account of life in the maquis written by a young woman allegedly taken prisoner by FTP partisans in the south of France. Against a background of drunken exuberance, orgiastic feasts, brutality, and tenderness, there emerges the portrait of a world unto itself, a group of men living a marginal and precarious existence in defiance of every imaginable code of social convention.[38]

Concerns about how others might judge the propriety of a life style that required partisans of both sexes to live in close proximity emerge in the way men and women evoke their maquis experiences. Attempting to avert any doubts, a *maquisarde* who often stayed in the camp with the men between reconnaissance and liaison missions volunteered, "We slept side by side and nothing ever happened; . . . we were waging war, not making love."[39] The question of male-female relations in the maquis is also addressed by a non-Communist member of the FFI general staff in the Paris region. Speaking of the women liaison agents, secretaries, and nurses who worked among the men, he writes:

> Finally, in our clandestine life, the presence of these companions in misfortune lifted our spirits. We had broken all ties with our families, and they helped recreate a sort of family atmosphere.
>
> It should not be inferred that this life of adventure, this breaking of family ties, occasioned in our resisters a loosening of morals. . . . This atmosphere was edifying in the highest degree: we were haunted by death, and each of us wanted to remain at peace with his conscience.[40]

The presence of women in rural combat groups was considered a blatant contravention of prevailing social mores. For some women this was probably an obstacle to joining or to being accepted by the groups.

The presence of women in urban combat groups had none of the same implications, because living conditions were different. Where partisan fighters had constant contact with the outside world, the presence of women was more easily accommodated. A woman and man living together, or strolling arm in arm, did not break a social code; on the contrary, the arrangement was a classic camouflage for liaison agents and partisan fighters, precisely because it appeared innocent and even "respectable." Whereas a single, anonymous man living alone fit the imaginary profile of a terrorist, a couple projected the image of an ordinary household.[41] The Rol-Tanguys, a real married couple who worked together in the FTP and FFI throughout the war, moved around Paris and the suburbs from one lodging to another. Cécile Tanguy, liaison agent and administrative secretary for the FTP and FFI, managed their "front" by cultivating cordial, but not close, relations with inquisitive new neighbors and local shopkeepers. She thus served as a buffer for her husband who had responsibilities at the summit of the underground partisan organization in the Paris region. They maneuvered to be "seen" as a couple, but "unseen" as a team of clandestine operators.[42]

Relationships between men and women, though a private issue, retained the attention of the party leadership and often provoked their intervention. A male *responsable* raised the delicate question of private life with a young liaison agent when she entered the FTP in Paris:

> Your husband has been arrested, I know. He is my close friend, and it embarrasses me to have to ask you this, but it's important for our security. Are you involved with another man at the moment? Because we must be very careful about who is involved, one way or another, in our activities. It's a risk for the whole organization.[43]

Unlike maquis commanders in the countryside, partisan leaders in Paris admitted the fact of men and women living together: One party leader exclaimed, "You can't ask a man to live like a monk! You can't ask a woman to lead the life of a nun! But everyone had to be extremely careful. . . ."[44] Realistically speaking, some believed, it was necessary, even inevitable for people subjected to constant danger to seek comfort and support; consequently such affairs had to be made as safe as possible. Although coupling between members of the same group or organization doubled the risk in the event of arrest, some leaders considered this preferable to a resister seeking solace in the arms of an "unknown" who could betray him or her, knowingly or not, to the Gestapo or police.

The phasing-out process

Curiously enough, the question of women's suitability for combat based on biology or previous experience has been raised only peripherally in literature and participant testimony. Perhaps this is because the argument would be difficult to sustain where guerilla combat is concerned, which involves quick, rapid-fire moves as opposed to the brute strength of conventional fighting.[45] That combat was a "male" task was not seriously called into question at the time. But if women were less likely to attract suspicion, would they not have made excellent guerillas as well as ideal liaison agents or gun runners?

Although it is true that women had little or no experience with guns and bombs, the same might be said for their male counterparts, especially men from the cities. Many young men, prime recruits for the *groupes de protection* and the maquis, were too young even to have performed their military service and had not even rudimentary knowledge of guns and fighting, a fact constantly bemoaned by partisan commanders.[46] The amount of time devoted to firing instruction in some maquis and the spate of clandestine "how to" pamphlets for amateur saboteurs and street fighters testify to their inexperience.[47] Although some prominent partisans like Rol-Tanguy and Fabien received their "baptism of fire" during the Spanish Civil War, many partisan men did not know how to use a gun any more than most women, and like women, they had to learn. Madeleine Baudoin, who managed to handle a revolver after only a few perfunctory pointers, claims that "it was as easy as learning how to make coffee."[48]

Nonetheless the Communist party leadership saw women's best place exactly where most of them were: in the paramilitary branch of the party, in combat-support roles, or in the political branch as organizers of other women, performing tasks that men were thought not to be able to do, or do as easily. The clandestine party press had launched a campaign to mobilize women as early as January 1940. Underground women's newspapers urged women "to fight" mostly in traditional support ways as mothers, wives, and heads of households. By the end of 1942, the call to arms had moved in to a literal register. Rousing appeals invoking contemporary models like the Soviet *partisanes* and French antecedents Louise Michel and Joan of Arc became the leitmotif of the flourishing women's press: "The duty of the women and girls of France is to take their place side by side with the FTP in the struggle for national liberation. . . . for women in the land of Joan of Arc and

Jeanne Hachette are capable of fighting. . . ."[49] Women who had given up their sons to the underground partisan groups were now urged to send their daughters, too.[50] By the Summer of 1944, propaganda reached fever pitch, and women were exhorted to form fighting battalions and to take to the barricades as their forbears had done. Through the use of combative language and imagery, women were mobilized for armed struggle, only to be channelled into parallel support tasks such as the recruitment of fighters, procurement of food, social service work, medical assistance, and liaison work. Was this a "bait-and-switch" tactic, or merely an attempt to enlist the broadest participation possible "from each according to her abilities" at a time when "resistance" and even "fighting" had expanded to include different forms of involvement in a broadening national movement? In any event, grass roots initiatives were not always congruent with the policies and priorities of the national leadership, and many women who rallied to the battle cry "aux armes, citoyennes!" expected to bear those arms in the literal, not figurative, sense.

Not all women resisters, of course, desired combat roles. Lily Lévy Osbert, member of the MOI and collaborator of Gilbert Brustlein, was happy not to be called upon to use a weapon.[51] Others claim that physical combat did not appeal to them—pointing out, for the record, that their participation in the movement was equal or greater than that of some fighters.[52] Some women, however, greeted the prospect of fighting with enthusiasm and even tried to join combat groups, but in several reported cases, their efforts met with failure. Party activist Yvonne Zellner remembered her disappointment at not being admitted to the FTP.[53] Organizer Josette Dumeix also asked to be transferred to the armed partisan groups, but her request was denied on the basis that she was more urgently needed in the women's committees.[54] Later, even women trying to organize social services for male fighters at the front faced opposition from military commanders, a situation which they vehemently denounced, contesting the argument that women's place was not in the barracks.[55]

For the party leadership, the most efficient deployment of limited human resources was paramount. The interests of the organization as a whole were to take precedence over the desires of individual women who sought active combat roles. Were these objectives necessarily mutually exclusive? In the estimation of party leaders, the placement of women in fighting positions was simply not politically rational. National Military Commissioner of the FTP, Albert Ouzoulias acknowledged that women under his direction often asked to fight, but ultimately "observed party discipline." He cites the example of his own liaison agent, Cécile Ouzoulias Romagon, who was also his wife:

> Cécile would have preferred commanding a company to being a liaison agent! And she had a thousand reasons for wanting to fight: her father had been shot by a firing squad and her brother deported to a concentration camp. But that is a personal reaction. And a personal reaction is very rarely a political one.
>
> During the insurrection of Paris [the women] said, "Finally! We're going to bear arms?" And they were told, "No, it's out of the question, liaisons must be maintained. It's infinitely more important for a liaison

to be maintained than to have an extra fighter. Your role is infinitely more important than that of a simple soldier. Thanks to you, these units are [connected as] a real army." . . . That's much more important than having one more guy around to derail a train.[56]

The participation of women in paramilitary and military support areas intensified in the Winter and Spring of 1944. Yet as the need for fighters grew, it became increasingly rare for women to take an active role in combat, aside from occasional exploits or short-lived stints in the heat of action. Women, the party repeatedly asserted, had a crucial role to play in the armed uprising of the Liberation. But never was there any question of detailing women into fighting positions, despite pressure from the rank-and-file, which was sometimes yielded to by local, if not national leadership. On the contrary, women were directed more than ever to critical support areas, perhaps so that men could be freed for combat, but especially because they were thought to be more effective than men in these roles. Leaders of the FTP and FFI looked to the existing women's committees for experienced, dedicated female cadres to fill administrative and liaison positions on a national and interregional level. Women who had seniority in the movement or in the party, demonstrated capacities for clandestine work, and moral and physical endurance were promoted to the very top of the underground partisan organizations—but not to leading troops into battle.

The distribution of labor between men and women in this later period followed the model established by the early partisan groups, but as the movement expanded, separate tasks evolved into separate structures. Women's roles became progressively more circumscribed when partisan units were integrated into regular combat forces and once it became clear that these same units were to outlive the Resistance as the nucleus of the new French army. While liaison agents were organized under a national authority headed by Cécile Ouzoulias, the women's committees turned their efforts from public protest to social services for fighters in such groups as the Comités d'aide aux FTP and the Auxiliaires des FTP.

As propaganda and recruitment campaigns exhorting women to take up arms intensified, preparations were underway for the gradual elimination of women from fighting units. In late 1943, instructions were issued to phase women out of the maquis and even to replace female liaisons with men.[57] Whether in fact these directives were implemented at the time remains uncertain, but the small gender-integrated combat teams of the early period did not survive the war. The elimination of women from partisan ranks was part of a larger "normalization" process aimed at turning partisan fighters into "real" soldiers merged in a single organization, the FFI, and ultimately, the regular French army. Taming the maverick partisan troops and bringing them under the control of a national command proved a challenge for career officers and a painful abandonment of autonomous action, culture, and identity for the FTP.[58] For women it meant either total exclusion or segregation in separate, all-women structures such as the women's auxiliary. After the battles of the Summer of 1944, when the newly reconstituted army had moved on to the front in eastern France, women of the FFI protested their retirement from the ranks:

Today, women have the same patriotic fervor as their husbands and brothers and want, like them, to serve the *Patrie*. It would be unfair to refuse them, to dampen new spirits, to reject elements capable of rendering great service to the nation.

Women who have been fighting for three or four years do not understand why they should be thrown back into civilian life now that the illegal period has ended and lose the rights they earned as soldiers. Why shouldn't the FFI keep its female fighters? And why wouldn't these fighters, these able administrators, be as qualified to lead women into battle today as they were before?

New army, new methods.[59]

But the "new" army had more in common with the old one than with irregular partisan forces of the Resistance period. As these forces moved above ground, gender roles ceased to he mediated by the exigencies of clandestinity, and the demand for "invisible" operators tapered off. The very "invisibility" that had been women's stock in trade during the illegal period, now doomed them to obsolescence when underground fighters emerged into the light of day.

Meanwhile, the presence of women within the French army had been institutionalized in January 1944 with the creation of a separate women's auxiliary chartered by De Gaulle's provisional government in Algiers. The Auxiliaire féminin de l'armée de terre, or AFAT (renamed from the original Corps féminin, a *double entendre* for "woman's body" that reportedly drew untoward remarks) was inspired less by the precedent of partisan women than by the express desire to "free able-bodied men for combat" by assigning support functions to women.[60] The AFAT was essentially comprised of career military women from Gaullist milieus, and by and large it failed to appeal to Communist women of the partisan groups. For some, the passing of the illegal period cast combat and combat-support tasks in a wholly new light. Using a curious mix of military and domestic metaphor (and a dash of hindsight), a liaison agent in the FTP who was later detailed to the General Staff of the FFI in Paris voiced her reaction to the prospect of serving in the regular armed forces:

> At the end of 1944, I was surprised to be considered a member of the military. I was asked if I wanted to be trained to serve in the regular army. . . . And go on to fight colonial wars in the name of France? Never! . . . Yes. I fought in the war, but I only did what had to be done. What would you do if someone came into your house to steal your food and kill your children? You'd fight back! Well, the house was France and the children were her people.[61]

Drops of mercury

In his famous treatise on guerilla warfare, Charles Tillon, commander-in-chief of the FTP, told fighters that the best strategy in a war of unequals was to strike swiftly in small groups and disband. In this way, partisans would elude their trackers, slipping from grasp like "drops of mercury."[62] As a subject to study some forty years later, French partisans, and especially women, remain "*insaisissable*." This is due in part to the usual problems associated with studying the war period: the slim documentary record left by a clandestine movement, the inaccessibility of Vichy government and police records, the fragility of participant testimony, and finally, the challenge of interweaving oral and written sources. Yet the role of women in armed combat is a particularly complex issue. On the one hand, the images, metaphor, and language of resistance might lead us to assume that women played a greater role in the fighting than was actually the case. On the other, an intricate web of taboos makes it difficult to obtain oral testimony from women about their combat experiences, which leaves us wondering where all the fighters are. The resulting confusion has had paradoxical consequences on the way resistance by women has been remembered.

In official and popular memory, armed combat has enjoyed recognition often denied other forms of participation. Not only was fighting more tangible and more prestigious, it fit prevailing notions of what "war" was all about. Consequently, underground work most often performed by women, which was anonymous and invisible to the public, became eclipsed by more spectacular combat actions that have left a lasting imprint on the French collective memory.[63] To a large extent, women have shared in this valorization of combat, or men's roles, to their own exclusion because they are rarely inclined to write.

Representations of resistance in general often emphasize combat despite the many different forms of participation which comprised the movement. The rare *partisane* poised on the barricade with machine gun in tow inspired the popular cliché of the woman resister, immortalized in legend and even in song.[64] By the end of the war, even noncombat resisters were occasionally and erroneously designated as partisans or *maquisards*. The attribution of military rank by the state to some non-combatants contributed to this "combat inflation." As officials strove to name and quantify the contributions of resisters for national recognition, compensation, and pensions, they faced the difficult problem of categorizing unprecedented forms of wartime patriotism. Although the tasks performed by many women defied existing categories, some were given military titles after the war that did not necessarily correspond to their roles, which, in reality, had been more diverse and often not military at all. A woman who bears today the rank of lieutenant in the FTP or FFI, for example, was probably a liaison agent who never engaged in armed combat; she is more likely to have run messages, typed reports, or transported arms under the direction of a male partisan attributed the rank of colonel.[65] Hence the primacy of combat over other forms of resistance has led to a contradiction: not only has it obscured the actions of many, primarily women, who were involved in non-combat actions, it has also created the false impression that women bore arms as a matter of course.

Despite frequent allusions to women and fighting, it is difficult, on the basis of their oral testimony alone, to identify women who held combat roles. Not only were partisan women rare to begin with, those who have survived the war remain guarded in interviews. The taboos which inhibit discussion of sensitive and controversial operations are by no means gender-specific or unique to Communist women. However, because so few women have committed their experiences to written form, unlike male fighters of even modest stature, their oral testimony is all the more important.

Although executions, sabotages, raids, and bombings were proudly claimed by the Communist resistance as a whole, individuals find it difficult, even dangerous, to speak frankly about methods which involved the taking of human lives. As a rule, these actions failed to enlist the support of the non-Communist Resistance and of many French citizens as well; their perpetrators were sometimes blamed for bringing smoldering tensions between occupiers and occupied to a dreaded crescendo. They also posed moral problems of choice and responsibility that prove difficult to explain to an outsider in today's very different world. Witnesses are sensitive to the fact that they were known as freedom-fighters to some—but as "terrorists" to others. Despite their reluctance to broach delicate topics, when questioned directly, they remain unshakably convinced of the justness of their cause and the means employed to defend it: *C'était la guerre.*

Another inhibition derives from clandestine codes of conduct put into practice forty-five years ago. Naturally resisters were forbidden to discuss their activities with anyone outside their immediate group, even family or other party members. Innocent or boastful "chatter," the leadership warned time and again, could cost lives and compromise the movement. Although total discretion proved difficult to instill even at that time, traces survive in many Communists who honor that silence today where sensitive procedures and identities, including their own, are concerned.[66]

Beneath the seamless image of Resistance often projected for popular consumption lies a painful memory that some activists are loathe to stir. Many lived in a state of fear and privation, suffered relentless repression in prisons and camps, and lost families, companions and camarades in the struggle. For those involved in violent actions, there are other blocks as well. One respondent finally managed to override the party-imposed code of secrecy only to face another obstacle. With much effort and many tears she recalled her first partisan attack: the victim, an isolated German soldier on patrol, clutched at her as he slumped to the ground in a desperate attempt to stay his fall, splattering her blue polka-dot dress with blood.[67] She had been unprepared for the shocking reality of a partisan attack, and recounting it for the first time many years later was an ordeal. Not surprisingly, of the few *partisanes* who did exist, fewer still have brought themselves to overcome so many obstacles.

Thus, after the war and even now, the "invisibility" of partisan women has been perpetuated in the public record. Yet for all their invisibility—relative once again—these women pushed the gender barrier to its outermost limit by engaging in combat in both conventional and unconventional ways. When that barrier was crossed, adaptive behavior and blurred identities explained and excused the trespassing of women into male gender territory. Gender roles in the underground partisan groups were reshuffled and rearranged to suit short-term needs. Whether some very striking changes carried over into the postwar period, and in what form, remains to be demonstrated.

Notes

1   The Conference on Women and War, held at the Center for European Studies of Harvard University in January 1984, brought these questions into a forum. See Margaret Randolph Higonnet, Jane Jenson, Sonya Michel, and Margaret Weitz (eds.) *Behind the Lines: Gender and the Two World Wars* (New Haven, 1987).

2   For Albrecht, see the biography by her daughter, Mireille Albrecht, *Berty: La Grande Figure féminine de la Résistance* (Paris, 1986). Aubrac and Fourcade have written their memoirs of the war years. Lucie Aubrac, *Ils partiront dans l'ivresse* (Paris, 1984); and Marie-Madeleine Fourcade, *L'Arche de Noë* (Paris, 1965).

3   These paramilitary organizations include the Organisation spéciale (OS), precursor to the Francs-tireurs et partisans français (FTPF, or more commonly, FTP), formed in April 1942. The Bataillons de la jeunesse was the combat wing of the Jeunesses communistes, the French Communist party youth group. The Main d'oeuvre immigrée (MOI) grouped French and foreign-born Jews and political refugees in France and was particularly active in commando attacks and sabotages. Combat groups from the various Resistance formations, Communist and non-Communist, merged officially in February 1944 to form the Forces françaises de l'intérieur (FFI).

4   A précis of French Communist party shifts and policies forms the background for a case study of the Limousin by Sarah Farmer, "The Communist Resistance in the Haute-Vienne," *French Historical Studies* 1 (Spring 1985): 89–116. For the full-length, exhaustive study of the PCF during the war years, see Stéphane Courtois, *Le PCF dans la guerre* (Paris, 1980).

5   Testimony cited in this article comes from an oral history project on women and the PCF from 1939 to 1945 conducted as part of my doctoral field work in France. All interviews took place in Paris unless otherwise noted.

6   Testimony of Madeleine Riffaud, AN, série 72 A-J, 4 July 1946, and conversation with Madeleine Riffaud, 14 September 1988.

7   AN, série F^{1a}. "Note au sujet de l'Armée sécréte et les Groupes Vény," 26 August 1943. The formation of several groups of partisan women in response to pressures from the rank-and-file is announced by the PCF leadership in April 1944. BN, Rés G 1470 (411), *Vie du Parti*, April 1944.

8   Madeleine Baudoin, *Histoire des Groupes-Francs (MUR) des Bouches-du-Rhône de septembre 1943 à la Libération* (Paris, 1962).

9   Interview with Madeleine Baudoin, 9 March 1988. Baudoin mentions this operation briefly on page 68 of her book, but attributes it to an unnamed "liaison agent of the Groupes-Francs." When asked why she chose to conceal her identity, she adamantly denied implications of what she called "feminine modesty" or self-effacement, asserting that the identity of the individual in question was only a detail and that personal reminiscences had no place in a historical account which was also her doctoral thesis. Throughout the book she refers to herself in the third person by the use of her code name, "Marianne Bardini."

10   Baudoin, *Histoire des Groupes-Francs*, 96–99.

11   It would have been preferable to quote this passage directly rather than paraphrase it, but the extreme sensitivity of the mission, coupled with personal reservations on the part of the speaker, led her to refuse the tape recorder and ultimately, even the taking of notes. For this reason, she shall be known here as "Claude"—only the last in a long line of coded identities, a device which, sadly, perpetuates the anonymity of yet another unknown resister. This account was related to me in a series of interviews and conversations throughout 1987 and 1988.

12 It is significant that *agent de liaison* was originally a military term used to designate a courier who ran between the rearguard and the front lines bearing messages and orders of battle.

13 Among the numerous, if brief, profiles of Olga Bancic, see Union des femmes françaises (ed.), *Livre d'or*, fasc. 2 (Paris, 1946), 28–29.

14 Interviews with Mélinée Manouchian, 19, 24, and 26 November 1986 and 1 December 1986.

15 Testimony of her friend and co-worker, Marie-Elisa Cohen, 18 March 1985; Union des femmes françaises (ed.), *France Bloch-Sérazin* (Paris, 1947), reissued in 1969.

16 Interviews with Fanny Dutet, 4 June 1978, and with Betty Jegouzo, 25 September 1985. Christiane Borras, a liaison agent with the FTP, remembers a tragicomic aspect of arms transport: forcing herself to walk spritely and erect in an effort to dissimulate the enormous weight of the guns and ammunition in her suitcase. Interviews of 17 and 24 April 1986.

17 The notion that women had greater chances of passing undetected than men emerges often in written and oral testimony. Communist party leaders who have expressed this view include André Tollet, conversation of 10 May 1978; Roger Arnould, interview of 10 June 1986; Albert Ouzoulias, interview of 15 June 1988. For concurring testimony from the right see the memoir by a career officer and self-proclaimed anti-Communist who became a member of the FFI General staff in 1944: Colonel R. du Jonchay, *La Résistance et les communistes* (Paris, 1968), 122–23.

18 Some women were reluctant to participate in public protest actions with one respondent because she was considered too attractive to pass unnoticed and so placed the security of the entire group in jeopardy. Concerned, she took up the matter with her female supervisor who retorted, "So much the better! While they are looking at *you*, *we* can get to work!" Interview with Maté Houet, 8 July 1988.

19 Of the six women mentioned above, five were ultimately arrested: Bancic, Bloch, Dutet, Jegouzo and Borras. Dutet, Jegouzo and Borras, arrested as dangerous "politicals," were deported to Auschwitz. Bloch was decapitated in a Hamburg prison. Bancic was spared death by firing squad, the fate reserved for the men in her group, supposedly because the German authorities feared French public reaction to the execution of a woman, but she was executed separately in Germany. Finally, Manouchian went into hiding upon the arrest of her husband and group leader Missak Manouchian, where she learned of his execution months after the fact.

20 Cécile Ouzoulias Romagon, *J'étais agent de liaison des FTPF* (Paris, 1988), 189.

21 Roderick Kedward, "The Maquis and the Culture of the Outlaw" in *Vichy France and the Resistance: Culture and Ideology*, ed. R. Kedward and Roger Austin (London, 1985). The term "maquis," originally a form of scruffy underbrush native to Corsica, was employed in this period to refer to partisan groups living in the bush. The term became generalized in such expressions as "to take to the maquis," which means "to join a rural partisan group" or even more generally, "to go into hiding."

22 Underground activists, Communist and non-Communist alike, used pseudonyms or *noms de guerre* for security purposes.

23 Association nationale des anciens combattants de la Résistance (ed.), *La Maquis de Corrèze: 150 combattants et témoins* (Paris, 1975), 10–11, présentation de Jacques Duclos.

24 Henri Amoroux, *La Vie des Français sous l'Occupation* (Paris, 1961), 316.

25 "Yvon's" real name was Jeanne Le Bozed. She was a radio operator for the Gaullist intelligence network, Confrèrie Notre-Dame. Rémy, *Histoires d'Ile-de-France* (Paris, 1971), 299.

26   AN, série 72 AJ 114 (Côte-d'Or), document A III—1, "Liste des inscrits."

27   Rémy, *Histoires d'Ile-de-France*, 147.

28   *La Vie d'un maquis de 'Auxois* (n.p., [1969]), 29.

29   Interview with Houet.

30   "A favourite is the masquerading as innocent countrymen or women." Reported in a British military study of Soviet partisan organization and tactics, which draws on German sources. Brigadier C. Aubrey Dixon and Otto Heilbrunn, *Communist Guerilla Warfare* (London, 1954), 36.

31   In French Communist party organization, a *responsable* is a supervisor or group leader, ranging from the *responsable* of a three-member triangle at the base, to the *responsables* at the summit. Each activist at every level reported directly to his or her immediate *responsable*.

32   Interview with Juliette Dubois Plissonnier, 18 October 1984.

33   Interview with Anna Pouzache, Limoges, 14 October 1984.

34   Quoted by Marguerite Ballé, "Le Grand discours de Madame Ibarruri aux Cortès," *La Française*, 4 July 1936, dossier of Dolores Ibarruri, Bibliothèque Marguerite Durand.

35   Karl Radek, "Clara Zetkin," *Bulletin communiste* 31 (July 1921): 521. Karl Radek concurs with Bebel's characterization of Zetkin, which he cites in her honor on the occasion of her sixty-fifth birthday. Although there are examples of powerful women figures in left-wing parties, politics was probably less a factor in their being dubbed "honorary men" than their being women in male gender territory.

36   Interview with "Claude."

37   From an unsigned, undated document, "Conseils générales à suivre," composed by the departmental Resistance leader of a non-Communist organization. AN, série F[7] 15156. An internal Communist party bulletin also warns activists to be wary of traitors who pose as "women": "Be careful of women! . . . An FTP let himself be seduced by a 'pretty' girl who was an *agent provocateur*. The result was the arrest of his entire group." BN, Rés G 1470 (40), *Bulletin de la Commission centrale des cadres* 1 (May 1944).

38   Nicole Fontclaire, *Prisonnière au maquis* (Paris, 1946). Whether or not Fontclaire's account is the true-to-life memoir she claims it to be in her preface, her most outlandish descriptions of maquis life and practices find parallels in police and prefects' reports of the same period. I am indebted to Dominique Missika for this reference.

39   Interview with Pouzache.

40   Du Jonchay, *La Résistance et les Communistes*, 123.

41   Cécile Lesieur mentions that one of her functions as a liaison agent for the FTP was to "escort" male fighters by posing together as a couple. Interview with Cécile Lesieur, 13 April 1988.

42   Interview with Cécile Rol-Tanguy, 13 July 1988. Ironically, their most intimate collaborators did not know them to be married: she was known simply as "Lucie," he as "Colonel Rol." Their coded identities concealed the fact of their marriage to members of the movement, while for the general public, their real status as husband and wife was exploited as "cover." Cécile Rol-Tanguy served as secretary and liaison agent in the FTP and later the FFI. Colonel Henri Rol-Tanguy became commander-in-chief of the unified FFI in the Ile-de-France.

43   This citation is from an interview in which the respondent paraphrases her *responsable's* speech as she remembers it. To protect her privacy, her name will not be given.

44   Conversation with Roger Arnould, 26 July 1986.

45   For example, MOI leader Adam Rayski hypothesized that women were rarely assigned front line roles in commando actions because it was necessary for partisans to flee the scene of an attack with lightning speed, and it was believed that women could not run as quickly as men. Interview with Adam Rayski, 20 June 1988.

46 "When it came time for the first combat actions, the simple act of holding a revolver was for us [Spanish Civil War veterans] something familiar. On the other hand, we saw young people say, as soon as you gave them a pistol: 'What am I supposed to do?,' 'You have to pull the trigger?,' 'But I'll kill someone . . .'" Interview of Henri Rol-Tanguy by Roger Bourderon, "Des Brigades aux FFI," *Cahiers d'histoire de l'Institut de recherches marxistes* 29 (1987): 91.

47 See, for example, Jacques Canaud, *Les Maquis du Morvan (1943–1944)* Château-Chinon, (1981), 207.

48 Interview with Madeleine Baudoin.

49 Jeanne Hachette was a fifteenth-century heroine who helped defend the city of Beauvais by felling the banner of the attacking army with a small hatchet, hence her name. "Avec les Francs-tireurs et partisans," *L'Humanité* (August–September 1942) in Germaine Willard, ed., *L'Humanité clandestine* (Paris, 1975). An underground flyer proclaims: "Daughters of France, imitate . . . your Russian sisters, do not hesitate to take up a machine gun or a revolver. . . ." Archives du Musée de la Résistance, Ivry (hereafter cited as AMRI), Tracts, "Pas une femme de France au STO—Jeunes filles les de France, aux armes" [1943].

50 AMR1, Tracts. "Appel aux femmes de France," January 1944.

51 Interview with Lily Lévy Osbert, 3 November 1987.

52 Interview with Lise London Ricol, 11 August 1988.

53 Interview with Yvonne Zellner, Ivry, 6 April 1978.

54 Interview with Josette Dumeix, 27 August 1988. Madeleine Riffaud also states that when she first attempted to join the FTP, her request was denied. She was admitted only months later to fill a post left vacant by the untimely death of a male group leader. Conversation with Madeleine Riffaud.

55 "This argument applies to uncivilized armies and no longer holds true for France," wrote representatives of the Union des femmes françaises to the General Staff of the FFI in September 1944. "One might suppose the greatest obstacle [to the proposed project] to be a material one, but that is not the case at all. The major difficulty is the attitude of certain FFI leaders, who oppose innovation of all kinds." From a document entitled "L'Action des UFF auprès des FFI," September 1944, AMRI.

56 His use of language in the last sentence shows how the gender tag of the task, in this case sabotage, redefines the sex of the person who performs it. Thus a female *saboteur* translates as "guy." Interview with Albert Ouzoulias (Colonel André).

57 AMRI, "Ordre au personnel féminin d'évacuer les maquis," 10 November 1943.

58 On these points, see the proceedings of a colloquium sponsored by the Comité d'histoire de la deuxième guerre mondiale in October 1974, *La Libération de la France* (Paris, 1976), especially Roger Bourderon, "Intégration des FFI de la Région 3 dans la 1ère Armée," 687–694; and Lt.-Col. Roger Michalon, "L'Amalgame FFI-1ère Armée et 2ème Division Blindée," 593–666.

59 AMRI, "Les Femmes dans la lutte armée," October 1944.

60 AMRI, Archives FFI-Ministère de la Guerre, AFAT charter, article 2.

61 Interview with Houet.

62 Charles Tillon, *Les FTP* (Paris. 1962), 51. Contemporary usage of this formula is found throughout the underground press. See for example, BN, Rés G 1470 (79), *Les Communistes et la lutte armée* 2 (July 1944).

63 For a discussion of how definitions of resistance have obscured the participation of women in scholarship and memory, see Paula Schwartz, "Redefining Resistance: The Activism of Women in Wartime France," in *Behind the Lines*, 141–53.

64   The song "La Maquisard," composed "in honor of the heroine of liberty" by Rose Noël and Alex Clairmon, is a musical tribute to a so-called "mysterious regiment" of partisan women. AMRI, Chants, "La Marquisarde" (Paris, 1945).

65   Liaison agents Cécile Rol-Tanguy, Maté Houet, and Cécile Ouzoulias received retroactively the military rank of lieutenant for their services in the FTP and FFI.

66   Rather than sidestep a probing question as some witnesses might, Jacqueline Rigault voiced her reservations directly by saying that procedural aspects of party organization in the clandestine period are best left unspecified in the event that the PCF be forced underground in the future. Interview with Jacqueline Rigault, 15 October 1985.

67   Interview with "Claude."

Chapter 13

Jose Harris

WAR AND SOCIAL HISTORY
Britain and the home front during the Second World War

I

THE 'HOME FRONT' in the Second World War has come to occupy a unique position in modern British folk-lore. The war is widely regarded as perhaps the only period in the whole of British history during which the British people came together as a metaphysical entity: an entity which transcended the divisions of class, sect, self-interest and libertarian individualism that normally constitute the highly pluralistic and fragmented structure of British society. This transformation is perceived as having occurred on two levels, the practical and the moral. The circumstances of total war forced the British government out of its traditional penchant for market economics and administrative muddling-through and into adoption of planning, rationing and economic management. As a consequence, the British people were ultimately subject to a greater degree of state-regulation and compulsory mobilisation of physical resources, including both male and female labour, than any other combatant power except the Soviet Union. And, secondly, the sense of desperate unity forged by common danger – particularly after the retreat from Dunkirk – engendered among the population at large a widespread and unprecedented ethic of self-sacrifice, social levelling and community spirit. The phrase 'the Dunkirk spirit' has entered into the English language as a synonym for cheerful communal endeavour against hopeless odds (often used by young people who have only the haziest notions about what Dunkirk actually was). 'People were friendlier in those days' is the common refrain of all surveys of public opinion that refer back to the war, a sentiment that becomes ever more marked as British society in the 1980s and 1990s has moved dramatically away from the post-war collectivist consensus into an era of privatisation and free competition.

Popular recollection of the war was for a long time reflected in, and perhaps to a certain extent influenced by, contemporary academic and autobiographical accounts. Politicians and historians writing both during and after the war continually re-affirmed the image of the war as the cradle of the welfare state, as the launching-pad of Keynesianism, and as an epoch of unprecedented social and moral solidarity. Evacuation, rationing, conscription and aerial bombardment were credited with bringing people of all classes together and with opening the eyes of the privileged to the condition of the poor. There was much stress upon the link between the confraternity of the common man and the rise of new methods of social organisation. 'Immediately a nation is involved in a great crisis . . . it is bound to become collectivist,' wrote the trade unionist Minister of Labour, Ernest Bevin. 'Individualism is bound to give place to social action; competition and scramble to order, and the role of law has to be applied in the place of anarchy'.[1] A 'revolution' had taken place 'in the minds of the people', claimed another Labour minister, Emmanuel Shinwell; while Foreign Secretary Anthony Eden declared that 'the old world is dead; none of us can escape from revolutionary changes, even if we would'.[2] William Beveridge, author of the famous Beveridge Plan of 1942 that was later regarded as the blueprint for the British welfare state, constantly referred to his social security scheme as a 'British revolution'; a 'revolutionary moment in the world's history is a time for revolutions, not for patching'.[3] The wartime rationing system and food control system was judged by its official historian to have embodied 'a revolution in the attitude of the state to the feeding of its citizens'; while the financial historian R. S. Sayers portrayed the switch to a Keynesian-style budgetary programme, with its emphasis on compulsory saving and confiscatory taxation of higher incomes, as 'the manifestation in the financial sphere of the national change of heart that marked the Summer of 1940'.[4] Similarly Richard Titmuss – still perhaps the most influential and imaginatively compelling historian of the domestic and civilian theatre of war – portrayed the Second World War in general, and Dunkirk and the Blitz in particular, as bringing about a revolution in popular expectations about the role of the state. Government was seen no longer, Titmuss argued, as merely the guarantor of private freedom and the provider of last-resort public assistance to the very poor. 'Instead, it was increasingly regarded as a proper function or even obligation of Government to ward off distress and strain among not only the poor but almost all classes of society . . . the mood of the people changed, and in sympathetic response values changed as well.' The war had entailed a great and permanent 'extension of social discipline' – a discipline that was only tolerable in a democratic society because it was combined with the removal of deep social inequalities. Such a change, Titmuss implied, entailed not merely administrative and attitudinal change but an intellectual revolution in the fundamental tenets of social and political theory.[5]

In face of the near-unanimity of commentators writing during and shortly after the war, it must be a bold historian who attempts to challenge this view of the social history of the Second World War period. And one would be foolhardy as well as bold to ignore popular memory, which must always be a benchmark against which to measure changes both in popular sentiment and in social structure. If the British people in the 1940s *felt themselves to be* more equal and more united than ever before, then this in itself is an overwhelmingly significant fact that no amount of analysis of income and wealth distribution can gainsay. Over the past two decades, however, a combination of factors has led to increasing re-assessment of many aspects of the conventional wisdom. The opening-up of many of the official and private archives of the war period; the shift of ideological climate in Britain that has affected historians no less than anyone else; and the sheer fact of judgemental distance and perspective, as the war recedes inexorably into half-forgotten history: all these factors have led to an opening-up of debate and controversy about the social history of the war and its longer-term implications for the structure and character of British society. These debates centre on many issues that cannot be adequately dealt with in a short article; but the most crucial themes may be summarised as follows.

First, there has been increasing scepticism among historians of both right and left about the supposedly 'revolutionary' impact of the war upon British social structure and institutions. It has been suggested that in spite of high wartime taxation, the war made little permanent impact (and indeed surprisingly little short-term impact) upon the distribution of wealth; that the dramatic scientific breakthroughs induced by the war (in electronics, nuclear physics and bio-chemistry) were grafted onto an industrial base that remained ramshackle, underfunded, managerially inept and culturally hostile to advanced methods of production; that, in spite of the mass mobilisation of both men and women, the war reinforced rather than subverted traditional class and gender roles; and that the very fact of ultimate victory in the war helped to arrest rather than accelerate change, by buttressing and legitimising many obsolete and reactionary social, economic and governmental institutions.[6]

Secondly, there has been much criticism of the 'consensual' image of the war. Recent research on the origins of the welfare state and the planning of post-war reconstruction has emphasised not the benevolent unanimity but the diversity of goals and conflict of principle that prevailed in government and party circles, over such issues as provision of a national health service, full employment, universal secondary education and the nature and extent of 'postwar reconstruction'.[7] And similarly, at the level of popular attitudes, historians have pointed to such factors as the very high level of strikes that prevailed in many key industries, particularly in the last three years of the war; to evidence of widespread popular participation in the black market and resentment against government controls; and to the often expressed resentment of soldiers, and more particularly of soldiers' wives, against the high wages and 'cushy numbers' enjoyed by workers in 'reserved occupations' (popularly known as 'Civvy Street'). There has been some questioning, too, of the mythological and methodological basis of the accumulation of popular memory by which the picture of popular consensus has been built up. Historians have become much more sensitive to the fact that many of the 'sources' for the wartime consensus were themselves part of the consensus-creating process. Cinema, radio, war artists, Pathe News and Picture Post were not passive recording angels but active agencies for promoting a certain frame of citizen mind. Press reporting was inevitably slanted by the fact that expressions of 'alarm and despondency' were officially discouraged by a vigorous propaganda campaign, while regulation 39B issued under the Emergency Powers (Defence) Act made it a criminal offence to publish material 'likely to be prejudicial to the prosecution of the war or the defence of the realm'. And, from a rather different angle, the re-interviewing by Tom Harrisson of people whom he had interviewed for the wartime Mass Observation surveys showed that (not just occasionally but typically) personal memories of wartime episodes differed widely from on-the-spot impressions of a quarter of a century before.[8]

Thirdly, there has been widespread reaction, partly ideological, partly based simply on scrutiny of primary sources, against what Cannadine has called the 'welfare state triumphalism' of much post-Second World War British historiography. The ideological wing of this reaction – incapsulated *par excellence* in Correlli Barnett's *The Audit of War* (1986) – has questioned not the substance of the established view that the war precipitated the welfare state but its wider implications. Barnett takes direct issue with the Titmuss approach by suggesting that the atmosphere of sentimental and uncritical moral solidarity induced by the war gave rise to wholly unrealistic, utopian expectations of a post-war world (governed by deficit-finance, job security, comprehensive welfare and indifference to economic consequences) that led inexorably to Britain's post-war economic decline. And, less dramatically than Barnett, many other historians have analysed the archives of wartime social policy formation and have come to the conclusion that the process was a more complex one than earlier historians often implied: that the breach with the past was less abrupt, that the aura of consensus was weaker, and that the range of ideologies and interest groups which had a hand in shaping Britain's post-war welfare state system was both broader and less mutually harmonious than was often supposed.[9]

For the rest of this paper I propose to identify the main areas of wartime social change, and to review the significance of those changes in the light of the controversies outlined above. I shall then try to suggest some possible alternative approaches to the social history of the period and to identify certain themes that have been either ignored or relatively neglected.

II

Firstly, then, the impact of the war on Britain's traditional social and governing institutions. Did the war period bring fundamental changes in social structure and organisation in Britain, or was the semblance of change merely a reflex of the peculiar circumstances of wartime? And, insofar as such changes did occur, were they directly induced by the war, or were they part of a much longer-term process of societal change that was occurring anyway, and in which the war was merely a passing episode?

Evidence for far-reaching institutional changes directly linked to the war can be found at many levels – legal, political, social, administrative and intellectual. The passage of the Emergency Powers Act in August 1939 meant that throughout the war the civil liberties conventionally enjoyed by British citizens were curtailed or in abeyance; and between 1939 and 1945 thousands of aliens (many of them Jewish refugees from Nazism), hundreds of fascists, communists and Trotskyites, and a small handful of industrial militants were detained for shorter or longer periods without trial.[10] Even during the first nine months of war – generally treated by historians as the last ineffective whimper of the regime of Neville Chamberlain – government commitment to total war policies in the form of conscription, rationing, mass evacuation, requisitioning and excess profits tax came much more swiftly than in 1914. And after the fall of Norway and the invasion of France – events which precipitated the replacement of Chamberlain by Churchill and the entry of Labour into coalition – pressure for new men, new methods and new administrative machinery became much more powerful and comprehensive. The traditional arena of high politics was taken over by a nexus of new policy-making institutions: a small co-ordinating War Cabinet, a series of specialist cabinet committees to supervise key areas of non-military policy, and a cluster of new ministries responsible for Supply, Information, Aircraft Production, Economic Warfare and Reconstruction. From mid-1940 onwards Whitehall was buzzing with businessmen, academics and trade unionists, many of them brandishing new brooms with which they aimed to sweep away the last vestiges of orthodox economics and administrative laisser-faire. The appointment of Ernest Bevin as Minister of Labour and of Kingsley Wood as Chancellor of the Exchequer symbolised both a new relationship between government, big business and labour and a by-passing and downgrading of conventional party channels. It was Kingsley Wood who imported J. M. Keynes into the Treasury and in 1941 promoted the first 'Keynesian' budget: a budget that introduced centralised regulation of national levels of consumption and investment, via the mechanisms of low interest rates, high taxation, cost-of-living subsidies for those with low incomes and compulsory saving for the better-off. Financial controls were accompanied by a massive extension of physical controls over manpower and raw materials, state takeover of many factories and public utilities, and very close state regulation of the management of private industry.[11]

Changes in governmental structure and in economic policy were accompanied by cataclysmic disruption of social life and by an unprecedented degree of state intervention in the provision of social services. At the most basic level the events of total war transformed the physical and material realities of daily life for large numbers of the civilian population no less dramatically than for those serving in the armed forces. Over the six years of war 62,000 civilians were killed by bombing, and nearly a quarter of a million suffered major or minor injuries. A quarter of a million homes were destroyed and nearly four million damaged, out of a total housing stock of about ten million. Two and a quarter million people were made homeless by the worst period of aerial bombardment (August 1940 to June 1941), a fifth of the nation's schools and hospitals were put out of action, and large areas of the business and manufacturing districts of cities and ports were damaged or destroyed.[12]

Such events precipitated a massive pragmatic revolution in British social administration. As soon as war broke out in September 1939 the government began to implement pre-war contingency plans to allay popular panic and to protect the health and safety of the civilian population. One and a half million women and children were evacuated from the major cities during the first few months of war, compelling local authorities (reinforced by a wide range of voluntary agencies) to set up reception centres and food and clothing depots and to arrange foster-homes in provincial villages and towns. Many trickled back to London and other large cities during the 'phoney war' period; but the onset of the Luftwaffe bombardment in August 1940 drove many back to the countryside again. Over the whole war period more than four million mothers and children were evacuated, some to camps and hostels, a privileged few to North America, the vast majority to the homes of private

citizens in the rural counties. From the start of the war all the nations' hospitals –
elite voluntary institutions, local authority and Poor Law infirmaries, small cottage
hospitals and thousands of temporary Nissen huts – were requisitioned by a single,
national Emergency Medical Service; and many doctors and nurses who had worked
in the voluntary sector became aware for the first time of the appalling conditions
widely prevailing in many Poor Law institutions. Moreover, aerial bombardment
and medical concentration on acute injury cases soon precipitated an unexpected
crisis in the treatment of long-term illness; and in 1940 air-raid shelters in big cities
were becoming distressingly full of poor, chronically sick, homeless old people who
had nowhere else to go – a problem that forced central government for the first
time in British history to take direct financial responsibility for civilian medical care
and provision of hospital beds.[13]

Similarly, the gradually intensifying economic blockade forced government into
the bulk-purchase and rationing of nearly all essential materials. Plans for food
rationing had been laid as early as 1936, partly to prevent starvation and malnutri-
tion, but partly also (a lesson learnt from the First World War) as a buffer against
hoarding, profiteering and rampant inflation. Petrol was rationed from the start of
the war; butter, bacon, sugar, meat, tea and margarine in 1940, cheese and personal
clothing in 1941, soap, sweets and chocolate in 1942; though throughout the war
the government managed to avoid the symbolic blow to civilian morale that would
have been dealt by the rationing of bread. Special rations were allowed to children,
nursing mothers and workers in heavy industry; and food prices were kept down
by exchequer subsidies that amounted by 1945 to £200 million per annum (a policy
designed not merely to maintain standards of nutrition but to reconcile consumers
to high levels and low thresholds of direct personal taxation). Regulated production of rationed 'utility' clothing and furniture (the former uniformly hideous, the
latter sparsely elegant) gradually replaced production by competitive private enterprise. 'National restaurants' were set up in all urban areas to provide cheap,
nutritious meals for working people, and from 1941 onwards there was a great
expansion of school meals and works canteens.[14] Throughout the country allotments, railway embankments, suburban tennis courts and the back yards of the poor
sprang to life with the growing of vegetables and the keeping of poultry, thereby
helping both to maintain standards of nutrition and to fuel the invisible workings of
a widespread, localised exchange-and-barter economy. Conscription of men
between the ages of 18 and 45 into the armed forces led to the gradual absorption
into industry of the residue of the pre-war unemployed, and to massive voluntary
recruitment of women (leading in early 1941 to industrial conscription of childless
women between the ages of 20 and 30). And in many spheres the powers of local
authorities – the traditional backbone of British social welfare administration and
parish-pump democracy – were severely curtailed, their functions being taken over
by non-elected, Whitehall-appointed regional commissioners with wide emergency
and discretionary powers.[15]

All these changes in themselves generated massive upheaval in the lives and
assumptions of ordinary people in Britain – accustomed as they were to a somewhat ramshackle free market economy, to a very parochial and family-centred social
structure, and to government by remote control. From the start of the war,
however, there were articulate pressure groups in many parts of British society

arguing that the experiments of wartime should be seen not merely as transient emergency measures but as the launching-pad for permanent and fundamental structural change. Wartime developments in hospital and health care, social and community work, infant-feeding and provision for mothers and children were increasingly viewed as precedents for permanent social reform; and similarly, the government was urged to treat the war economy as a model for economic management in time of peace. As the sacrifices required of the British people intensified it was widely urged that a prospect of radical 'social reconstruction' was not merely desirable in itself but an essential means of 'giving the British people something worth fighting for' and of sustaining citizen morale. 'Reconstruction committees' were set up in all parties, and demands for a 'British New Deal' came from right across the political spectrum – from liberals like Keynes and Beveridge, from socialists like R. H. Tawney and Evan Durban and from Tory social reformers like Hugh Molson and Quintin Hogg.[16]

The reformist mood infected many civil servants, and from 1940 onwards plans were being laid in Whitehall for far-reaching extension of health, education, workmen's compensation and social insurance services. Public enquiries were commissioned into community control of land values and town and country planning, and a Ministry of Reconstruction was set up under Arthur Greenwood (later succeeded by Sir William Jowitt). Modest plans slowly maturing in the corridors of Whitehall were overtaken, however, by a dramatic event – in the form of the Beveridge Plan of 1942, which catapulted 'social reconstruction' into the arena of popular discussion and the mass media. Beveridge's report on Social Insurance and Allied Services called for far-reaching state action to maintain permanent full employment, to set up a national health service, and to secure the British people against poverty by means of family allowances and comprehensive subsistence-level social insurance. The political essence of Beveridge's scheme was that social services should no longer be confined to 'the poor' or the 'working-class' but should be available to all social groups, without regard to means or social status and without the stigma of dependence, principles that rapidly became the hallmark of the reconstruction movement. The plan received wide coverage in the press and was widely portrayed as a sort of social Magna Carta. Early in 1943 widespread popular pressure and a backbench revolt in parliament forced a somewhat reluctant government to commit itself to the eventual implementation of the Beveridge proposals and to detailed post-war planning.[17] This commitment resulted in a long series of white papers on education, full employment, social insurance, a national health service, family allowances and care of neglected children.[18] None of these later papers made quite the dramatic impact of Beveridge. But together they re-wrote the agenda of public debate in British domestic politics and defined the issues upon which all parties fought the general election of 1945. They formed the basis of the social legislation of 1944–8 that created the British welfare state.

There can, I think, be little doubt that these events of wartime affected both the lives of ordinary citizens and the structure and power of government in many ways. How far did they add up to the kind of underlying 'social revolution' that was claimed by many contemporaries? This question may be posed and answered at many levels. At the political and administrative level the war precipitated certain fundamental changes in the relationship of government and society that were to prove irreversible, not merely in the short term but throughout the post-war years. The staff of central government at the end of the war was nearly twice as large as it had been in 1939, local government was never again to recover the degree of autonomy that it had enjoyed in the pre-war era, the annual budget was never to lose its wartime role as the major instrument of macro-economic management, and government policies of all kinds impinged far more directly than in the 1930s on the structure of everyday life. Government after 1945 never recovered from the wartime expectation that it should continually 'do something' in all spheres, rather than merely buttressing, subsidising and policing autonomous local and private economic and social arrangements. The fact that the 1945 election resulted in the first-ever absolute majority for Labour was in itself indicative not necessarily of radical social change but certainly of radical departure from the coalition of politics of the 1930s.

On the other hand it has been shown that the war brought little radical change in the actual personnel and composition of government. Labour itself, at least in the House of Commons, was a much more middle-class party than it had been in 1929. The civil service in 1945 was only marginally less dominated by Oxbridge humanities graduates than in the 1930s, and there was no permanent penetration into the upper reaches of public administration by scientists, businessmen or representatives of the working class.[19] Other traditional governing institutions were in many respects positively strengthened by the war. Parliament, for example, which throughout the 1930s had been attacked from both left and right as hopelessly unsuited to the needs of modern industrial democracy, during the course of the war resumed its ancient role as one of the great representative symbols of liberty and the popular will (a somewhat paradoxical reversal of image, in view of the fact that parliamentary control over government during the war was weaker than it had been for several centuries).[20] The British monarchy, which had spent much of the 1930s in a state of squalid crisis, was by 1945 probably more universally popular than at any previous moment in its history of nearly a thousand years. Similar double-edged points may be made about many other aspects of social and institutional structure. The war undoubtedly brought some changes in the distribution of income. Average real pre-tax incomes rose slightly over the course of the war, women's wages rose more than men's, unskilled wages rose more than skilled wages, and wages generally rose more than salaries and profits.[21] This pattern was accentuated by the impact of steeply progressive taxation, including a 100 per cent tax on war profits, and many people on professional and rentier incomes were undoubtedly worse off in 1945 than they had been in 1939. The war virtually eliminated private domestic service, thereby obliterating one of the major traditional frontiers of status and class. On the other hand the structure of private wealth changed surprisingly little (in the late 1940s 80 per cent of private assets were still held by the richest 10 per cent of the population).[22] And, in spite of the economic gains made by employed women, female earnings in 1945 were still only 55 per cent of those of adult males. Moreover, women throughout the workforce continued to be largely confined to the most humdrum, repetitive and menial positions; and there was an almost universal expectation that women who were married would return to husbands, hearth and home as soon as the war was over.[23] Evacuation and mobilisation tore apart many families, sexual mores became marginally more permissive (particularly among younger women), illegitimate births increased by 25 per cent, and the annual rate of divorce rose from one to five per hundred. But despite these difficulties, Mass Observation surveys recorded 'the continued and amazing strength of family feelings, loyalties and economic bonds'; and a recent study of wartime family life concludes that the nuclear family emerged from the Second World War stronger, more tightly-knit and more home-centred than it had ever been before.[24]

Similarly the class structure was dented but by no means dismantled – and may indeed have been strengthened by the ladders of rapid upward mobility that certain sectors of war administration and the war economy gave to ambitious new men. Fashionable educational thought at the end of the war rejected the notion of an hereditary class hierarchy, but replaced it by a new one: a meritocracy of measurable intellectual talent. In spite of the equalising effects of war, access to social services of all kinds remained widely unequal – determined not just by class but by region and local tradition (Scotland, for example, enjoyed a ratio of medical services to population that was much more favourable than that of Britain as a whole, while that of Wales was much worse). Moreover, the wartime growth of some social services has to be set against the wartime collapse of others; many schools had to close for long periods, and there was widespread disruption of school health services, maternity clinics and all forms of non-acute medicine.

Finally, psychological attitudes to social change and to the adoption of new social roles were widely contradictory and ambiguous. The unpublished research of the Nuffield College Social Reconstruction survey in 1942–3 found a widespread popular desire for greater health care, income maintenance and job security, combined with an almost universal hostility to the prospect of increased official direction of private lives.[25] In spite of the popular euphoria surrounding the Beveridge report, government surveys of popular opinion in the later years of the war found widespread indifference or hostility to the idea of social reconstruction,[26] a fact that may partly account for the lack of commitment to social reformist issues shown by Churchill and his closest advisors. Moreover, many archival sources suggest that throughout society those most vocally pressing for structural change were often those least willing to contemplate changes that would affect their own interests. Doctors, for example, successfully campaigned for retention of private contracts within a new, centrally funded public health service. Trade unionists demanded permanent state maintenance of full employment, together with instant post-war dismantling of controls over deployment of labour; while many employers wanted cheap state loans or interest-free credit, but as little as possible of any other form of permanent government control.[27]

III

What of the evidence for a new national wartime consensus, based on a convergence of political beliefs, unity of goals and a heightened sense of national social solidarity? We know from many sources, from the memoirs of right-wing liberals like Lionel Robbins through to ex-communists like Stephen Spender, that many intellectuals felt the war suddenly descending upon them like a great moral blanket, smothering and screening out the gigantic battles over principles and ideology that had polarised the intellectual politics of the 1930s.[28] Faced with the menace of Hitler in the Low Countries, many convinced and card-carrying British communists simply ignored their orders from Moscow and volunteered for military service. The politics of appeasement, which only two years earlier had commanded widespread public support, now became the object of universal revilement. Throughout the war period, from the 'phoney war' to VE day, from Dunkirk to doodlebugs, surveys of public opinion suggested an extraordinary degree of unanimous and single-minded commitment to unqualified resistance to Hitler. Doubtless, like other aspects of consensual politics, that unanimity was to a certain extent cultivated by the organs of mass opinion. But anyone familiar with the private archives of the period cannot but be struck by how unusual it is (in striking contrast to the First World War) to find expressions of the view that the war was not worth fighting or that Britain should seek a negotiated peace.[29] (When there were hints of the latter in elite circles the popular response was one of widespread scorn and indignation.)

Unanimity in opposing Hitler was one thing, however: social solidarity and brotherly love towards one's fellow-citizens quite another. After a brief lull in 1939 and early 1940, crimes against property soared throughout the war. Criminologists who had previously ascribed anti-social behaviour to poverty and deprivation now switched their attention to affluence, high wages and the felonious opportunities offered by the black-out. Indictable offences known to the police rose from 305,114 in 1940 to 478,394 in 1945, while the proportion of the population over sixteen found guilty of such offences rose from 150 to 223 per thousand. Female criminal convictions nearly doubled, male juvenile delinquency increased by 60–70 per cent and female juvenile delinquency by 100–120 per cent between 1938 and 1944.[30] Days lost in strikes never reached the astronomical levels of the First World War but were still high enough to throw some doubt upon the image of national solidarity. The black market still awaits detailed historical investigation; but almost certainly its operations were more extensive than the relatively low levels of prosecution and conviction suggest.[31]

Historians who have emphasised the theme of social unity have concentrated in particular on four main areas of social life: mass evacuation, military and industrial conscription, the 'social reconstruction' movement, and the communal experience of aerial bombardment in the great industrial and commercial cities. So far as I know, no scrutineer of the archives has yet attempted to de-mythologise the heightened sense of common humanity and melting of class differences that was apparently induced throughout Britain by the Blitz (though even at the time the enforced merging of proletarians and plutocrats was portrayed with barbed irony as well as good humour).[32] In other spheres, however, recent historical writing has viewed the class unity theme with increasing qualification. It has been suggested that, far from generating social sympathy, the evacuation movement served to confirm preconceived rural and middle-class stereotypes about the savage and insanitary habits of the slum-dwelling urban poor. Many rural and suburban households (particularly middle-class ones) did their best to evade or get rid of evacuees, and where they were unavoidable often treated them with marked lack of sympathy and social imagination. Head lice, insanitary habits and above all bedwetting – the latter often induced by the trauma of enforced removal from parents – were widespread flashpoints of recurrent social tension.[33] Ministry of Health officials found that it was almost impossible to find billets for an unmarried mother with a new-born baby, and in the opinion of voluntary welfare workers some of these mothers would not have been suitable for billeting. They needed a period of convalescence and training before they were fit to be in charge of a baby.[34]

Similarly, it has been claimed that conscription and war production, far from acting as great levellers, were fraught with conflicts based on skill, status, sector, gender, wages and social class; a claim for which there is extensive contemporary support in both the published and unpublished records of Mass Observation. A Mass Observation survey of 1942 (published just before the Beveridge Report with its ecstatic vision of the unity of the British people) found that throughout industry there was widespread resentment of both management and government, widespread absenteeism and work-dissatisfaction, widespread fear of displacement by women and unskilled workers, and widespread anger among managers about the perceived breakdown of industrial discipline that had been brought about by war.

In some sections of industry the things one group says about another are more belligerent than the things either of them say [sic] about the enemy, Germany, Italy, Japan. . . . In the conflict between employers and men . . . one looked and listened in vain for any sign of a unity binding all parties in the fight against Germany. . . . Both sides claim to be concerned only with improving the situation to increase the strength of the struggle against Fascism, but nevertheless, the real war which is being fought here today is still pre-war, private and economic.[35]

Lack of consensus has also been a central theme of recent writing on the reconstruction movement. Two decades ago historians emphasised the dominant role of a widely diffused, largely non-partisan 'progressive ideology' of which Beveridge and Keynes were 'the patron saints'. By contrast, more recent historiography has stressed the extreme reluctance of the Coalition government to espouse social reform, the divisions within the government about reformist priorities, and the yawning gulf between the cautious pragmatism of Labour ministers and the far more radical and utopian aspirations both of Labour backbenchers and of Labour supporters in the country at large.[36] And, finally, the 1945 election result itself – following upon Labour's withdrawal from government and Churchill's insistence on calling an early poll – may be seen as evidence of both politicians and people turning their backs on the politics of consensus, after a prolonged interlude of coalition government that stretched back to 1931.

IV

Thirdly, there is the issue of 'welfare state triumphalism', and the recent questioning among historians of the link often made between the events of wartime and the shaping of post-war social policy. I shall not deal here with the claims of Correlli Barnett, whose arguments about the long-term decline of post-war Britain largely fall outside the scope of this paper.[37] But more must be said about the growing body of scholarly monographs that have delved into the wartime origins of the British welfare state. It is perhaps important to emphasise that welfare state history, even in the 1940s and 1950s, was never quite so 'triumphalist' as Cannadine and others have claimed. On the contrary, even Titmuss, who first made the connection between the high moral tone of wartime and the growth of 'the caring society', *also* emphasised the crucial role of competing interest groups in social policy formation, and the continuing prevalence in post-war British society of long-term structural inequalities.[38]

Titmuss did, however, construct a loose chronological model of welfare state history, followed by many other historians, in which the depressed and deprived society of the 1930s gave way to the universal social security of the 1940s and 1950s – the agent of change being central government intervention, and the catalyst of change being the social and moral revolution of the Second World War. This pattern of interpretation has been challenged over the last two decades on a number of fronts. Although the 'pessimist' view of the 1930s still has powerful adherents, many historians have questioned Titmuss's account of the state of the British social services in the 1930s. It has been shown that public social welfare expenditure during the 1930s in fact grew at a faster rate than in any other peacetime period before the late 1960s; and that far from being a time of stagnation and retrogression the interwar period was a time of experiment and innovation in many areas of social reform. In particular, the exponential growth rate of health services in the hands of local authorities and approved societies before 1939 was considerably higher than under central government after the Second World War; and although the war is still seen as a unique catalyst of centralisation, this in itself is no longer viewed as a self-evident litmus test of progressive social change.[39]

More specifically, studies of wartime social policy formation and of the reconstruction movement now present a more complex and ambivalent picture than that fashioned by the official war historians. The range of interests and ideologies involved in reconstruction now appears much broader than was suggested by Titmuss. The route from wartime 'reconstruction' to the post-war welfare state was much less direct and more contested than was often imagined (partly because of economic constraints; but partly also because much reconstruction thought was based upon the premise of the permanent continuance of many social, economic and industrial controls that rapidly proved unacceptable in peacetime).[40] And, in all quarters, the attachment not to 'brave new world' but to old-established methods and underlying principles was much stronger than was once supposed. Universal family allowances, for example, which Titmuss had portrayed as one of the direct practical outcomes of the Dunkirk spirit, proved on closer inspection to be the fruit of a series of administrative trade-offs in Whitehall: trade-offs inspired partly by militaristic pro-natalism, partly by the need to offset the social impact of high wartime taxation, and partly by a cautious desire to invest the new social insurance system with the old Poor Law safeguard of 'less-eligibility'.[41] And it has been argued recently that Beveridge's own conception of a universal 'subsistence minimum' was much more spartan and restrictive, much more limited by orthodox budgetary constraints than many historians of social policy (including myself) had allowed.[42] Research of this kind has tended to undermine the view that social policy in wartime constituted a fundamental break with tradition, and suggests on the contrary a high degree of gradually evolving continuity. In social policy, no less than in high strategy, war looks increasingly like mere politics by other means!

V

All these new emphases in historical research suggest not that the old 'home front' thesis is categorically wrong but that it needs modification and revision. Titmuss himself in his classic study of the social history of wartime Britain from time to time expressed misgiving about whether there really was an entity that could be referred to as the 'popular conscience' or the 'people's mind'; and his descriptions of life under bombardment did continually stress the rich diversity and unpredictability of human reactions to the strains of war. But this side of Titmuss's work was much less emphasised by Titmuss's disciples – and indeed much less emphasised by Titmuss himself in his later writings[43] – than the theme of wartime national social solidarity. This latter emphasis was a potentially misleading one on two different counts. First, it under-estimated the fact that it was precisely the defence of the untidy, atomistic, ramshackle pluralism of British social life that for many people seems to have made the war worth fighting. And, secondly, it under-estimated the degree of ambiguity and contradiction in the popular desire for post-war social change. Much has been written about the war's reinforcement of the global trend towards collectivism. By contrast, surprisingly little has been said about the opposite effect: its strengthening and legitimation of a highly privatised and unstructured psychological individualism – an individualism that was explicitly opposed to fascism, but that also presented definite boundaries to collectivisation of all kinds. After 1941 the Ministry of Information tactfully fostered a favourable presentation of life in the Soviet Union, and there was a surge of popular interest in and sympathy for all things Russian. But this co-existed with an almost universal mistrust of political authority and officialdom in the context of day-to-day life in Britain. The popular cherishing of privacy was well expressed by the diary of Stephen Spender, spokesman of numerous pre-war leftist causes, who suddenly found himself in the Autumn of 1939 at one with Neville Chamberlain.

> The fundamental reason is that I hate the idea of being regimented and losing my personal freedom of action. . . . I dread the idea of being ordered about and being made to do what I don't want to do in a cause that I hate. This fear has even forced me into a certain isolation, in which I find that the personalities of my fellow beings often impose a certain restraint and unwelcome sense of obligation on me.
>
> There you are, you analyse your hatred of Fascism and it comes to a desire to be left alone.[44]

Numerous humdrum descriptions, including diaries of day-to-day life, in the wartime period suggest that Spender's feelings were shared by the vast majority of the British people in all social settings – at home, at work, in love and at play.[45] Among the recipients of evacuees – even among those of an altruistic and hospitable disposition – several years of compulsory billeting left many with a deeply engrained desire never to have visitors again. Popular humour and popular culture throughout the war were not collectivist but anarchic, celebrating not the unity of mankind but its absurdity; not the righteousness of the national cause but the fallibility of all in authority, be they civil or military, English or German, American or Russian.[46] Official exhortations against spreading alarm and despondency were obeyed in public but treated with widespread private derision. Expressions of a more idealistic or portentous note came mainly from two sources: from the small minority who were ideologically committed to a more thorough-going, principled collectivism; and from the immediate experience of those subject to bombing and aerial bombardment.

This latter exception points towards a further weakness of the consensus approach – which is that it lumps together the six years of the war as a uniform chronological period and fails to distinguish adequately between the ebb and flow of popular opinion and behaviour in different contexts and at different times. After the fall of Dunkirk, and during periods of nightly and sometimes daily bombardment – such as occurred during the late Summer of 1940 – there is indeed evidence that fear, excitement, desperation and the random immediacy of death induced in many people an almost ecstatic sense of transcendence of self and immersion in a mystic whole. 'Living became a matter of the next meal, the next drink. The way in which people behaved to each other relaxed strangely. Barriers of class and circumstance disappeared. . . . For a few months we lived in the possibility of a different kind of history.'[47] Such attitudes affected not merely private lives but wider social and economic behaviour, as was shown in the upward surge of productivity that occurred in British factories during the Summer and Autumn of 1940. But at both the personal and the economic level such feelings were for most people fairly transient; and what historians have sometimes overlooked is the much longer and more dreary period of waiting for the opening of a 'second front' – a period whose tensions, aimlessness and low morale were minutely chronicled in diaries, fiction and private correspondence (the 'lightless middle of the tunnel' poignantly captured by Elizabeth Bowen's mid-war masterpiece, *The Heat of the Day*).[48]

A third aspect of the social history of the period to which perhaps too little attention has been given is the sheer diversity of the wartime experience of different individuals, different localities, different organisations and different social groups. Even detailed social histories of the war, such as those by Calder and Marwick, have been mainly concerned with identifying overall trends and the heroic march of nationwide social democracy. But in all periods of modern British history social life has been characterised by microscopic diversity as well as by broader social movements, and the Second World War is no exception. There were many individuals who undoubtedly 'had a good war', many others (quite apart from the dead and injured) who suffered excruciatingly from separation from home and loved ones. For many the war meant years of compulsory employment at work which they hated, whereas for others it brought rescue from futility and boredom (like the mediaeval scholar whose work-in-progress was destroyed in the Blitz: 'In a state of indescribable elation, I walked into a pub and ordered a triple whisky and soda. "Heil Hitler!" I almost shouted aloud, thankful to world's enemy No. 1 for having taken the load off my hands, mind and heart').[49] For some conscripted women the war brought excitement, travel, career opportunities and a general enhancement of status; but for many more it meant a daily struggle to cope with work, shopping, transport, housework, queues, child care and marital deprivation, often with minimal community support.[50] In many parts of the country habits of religious worship and church attendance were dramatically disrupted by war, in some cases permanently; yet the role of the war in accelerating the national slide into secularism must be set against evidence of widespread 'conversion' and 'revival' in certain specific and localised contexts.[51] If there is one common theme that constantly recurs in letters and diaries (and indeed in the poetry and creative writing) of the period, it is not the grandeur of great events but the passionate cherishing of small, private, domestic, idiosyncratic matters: matters that often seemed doubly important because the pressures of war rendered them fleeting and precarious. The very nature of such a unifying common theme merely serves to underline the element of infinite diversity. 'There is NO one mood', reported Mass Observation at the end of 1942. '. . . there is no one all-pervading plan, purpose and drive, *no one mood shared by workers, managers, directors and civil servants* . . . a complete sweep of the pre-war pattern might produce a drastic change in people's work rhythms, liquidate the distinction of days, roles and rights . . . But in war any country depends on the roots of its culture. . . .'[52]

The social historian of the Second World War needs therefore to look closely not merely at large-scale, communal, 'progressive' forces but at those minuscule roots of idiosyncratic private culture. The latter were not only a major feature of British social structure in the period, but – no less authentically than the desire for equality and welfare – they embodied a tacit expression of popular war aims. Neglect of such roots has continually led astray commentators who have viewed the domestic history of the war mainly in terms of utopian promises that were later unfulfilled. However, in stressing the importance of those roots I have no desire to swing the pendulum too far in the other direction. The oral and written evidence of witnesses to the Beveridge Social Insurance committee provides overwhelming evidence that the British public (or at least that sector of it that was organised into pressure groups and voluntary associations) endorsed Beveridge's vision of collective social security.[53] Revisionist accounts of the war that minimise consensus and national solidarity may run the risk of overlooking significant archival 'silences' – silences that indicate certain areas of common agreement that were simply too profound and too self-evident to generate explicit comment or debate. And the war undoubtedly generated many long- and short-term processes of social change, including some that I have had no time to deal with in this paper.

Key areas of long-term structural change that deserve further attention from historians may be identified and summarised as follows. It seems probable that the sheer fact of state control on such a massive scale permanently modified the character of British political culture and played an important part in the long-drawn-out transformation of Britain from one of the most localised and voluntaristic countries in Europe to one of the most centralised and bureaucratic. The liquidation of massive foreign assets and the partial shut-down of the City of London as a major international financial centre meant that throughout the war and for some years thereafter financial elites and interest groups played a much more limited role in British politics and society than had been common over the previous half-century (and was to become so again when the post-war epoch came to an end). In spite of the large-scale absorption of women into the workforce, it is arguable that the war at least temporarily strengthened rather than weakened traditional perceptions of masculine and feminine gender roles (since the organisation of society for war buttresses patriarchy far more imperatively than any form of purely economic relationship).[54] Changing class relationships merit further analysis: we have heard a great deal about the impact of slum-dwellers upon the conscience of the middle classes, far less about the impact of those same middle classes upon the political consciousness of the slums. For the first time the British people were exposed to the full blast of North American culture, initially through the suspension in 1942 of the pre-war official quota on foreign films, and later through the physical presence of two million American and half a million Canadian troops stationed on British soil. The British found the Americans individually unlovable but collectively irresistible, as they have been doing ever since. The American presence introduced many British people to their first encounter with black people, to whom they responded with their usual diversity – ranging from colour-blind hospitable bonhomie, through self-conscious high-minded liberalism, to unabashed racial hostility.[55] The war also brought to Britain a large contingent of European refugees and prisoners of war, of whom nearly a quarter of a million (many of them Polish) were allowed to acquire permanent British citizenship. The enduring impact upon British society and culture of this often highly enterprising and largely Roman Catholic group still awaits its historian. In terms of future cultural change perhaps the single most significant social occurrence of the war was the temporary migration into Britain of several thousand West Indian workers and servicemen, many of whom returned after the war as permanent settlers.[56] But there was no inkling in 1945, nor indeed for long afterwards, that Britain was on the brink of a major ethnic revolution.

A final point that should be stressed is that nearly all the structural changes that occurred in Britain during the Second World War were paralleled by comparable changes in all other Western European countries, both Allied and Axis, both combatant and neutral. Such comparisons can be over-stressed, and each country has had its own unique institutional and cultural history. But no country in Western Europe has escaped the impact of mass social welfare, advanced health care, ethnic migration, consumerism and fiscal management; and in many cases such trends have been far more extensive than in Britain.[57] The wider history of Europe provides an indispensible backcloth against which to weigh the extent, meaning and significance of social trends and developments in Britain between 1939 and 1945.

Acknowledgements

This paper is a preliminary part of my contribution to an Anglo-American-Russian project on the military, economic and social history of the Second World War, directed by Dr David Reynolds and Professor Warren Kimball. I am grateful to members of that project for helpful comment, and for permission to publish my paper in this form.

Notes

1   Ernest Bevin, *The Job to be Done* (1942), 10.
2   Quoted in Hamilton Fyfe, *Britain's Wartime Revolution* (1944), 5.
3   *Social Insurance and Allied Services*, Cmd. 6404, 1942, p. 6.
4   R. J. Hammond, *Food*, Vol. 1 (1951), 353–9, Vol. 2 (1956), 753–9; R. S. Sayers, '1941 – the First Keynesian Budget', in Charles Feinstein, ed., *The Managed Economy* (1983), 108.
5   Richard M. Titmuss, *Problems of Social Policy* (1950), 506–8. Thereafter Titmuss, *Social Policy;* and *idem, Essays on the Welfare State*, 91958, 2nd ed. (1963), 84–5.
6   J. S. Revell, 'Income and Wealth 1911–50', paper to the International Economic History Congress, 1970; Correlli Barnett, *The Audit of War* (1986). Thereafter Barnett, *Audit*; Penny Summerfield, *Women Workers in the Second World War. Production and Patriarchy in Conflict* (1984). Thereafter Summerfield, *Women Workers*; Anthony Howard, 'We are the Masters Now', in M. Sissons and P. French, *The Age of Austerity 1945–51* (1964).
7   Harold L. Smith ed., *War and Social Change. British Society in the Second World War* (1986). Thereafter Smith, *War and Social Change*; Rodney Lowe, 'The Second World War, Consensus, and the Foundations of the Welfare State', *Twentieth Century British History*, Vol. 1, no. 2 (1990), 152–82. Thereafter Lowe, 'Welfare State'.
8   J. S. Lawrie, 'The Impact of the Second World War on English Cultural Life', PhD thesis (Sydney University, 1988). Thereafter Lawrie, 'Impact'; Philip M. Taylor, ed., *Britain and the Cinema in the Second World War* (1988); Neil Stammers, *Civil Liberties in Britain during the Second World War. A Political Study* (1983). Thereafter Stammers, *Civil Liberties*; T. Harrisson, *Living Through the Blitz* (1976); Penny Summerfield, 'Mass Observation: Social History or Social Movement?', *Journal of Contemporary History*, Vol. 20, no. 3 (1985), 439–52.
9   Barnett, *Audit*; Harold Smith, *War and Social Change*; Kevin Jefferys, 'British Politics and Social Policy during the Second World War', *Historical Journal*, Vol. 30, no. 1 (1987), 123–44 thereafter *HJ*; *idem, The Churchill Coalition and Wartime Politics, 1940–45* (1991).
10   Stammers, *Civil Liberties*, 24–5, 34–62, 66, 69–70, 117–20; Bernard Wasserstein, *Britain and the Jews of Europe* (1979), 81–133.
11   Paul Addison, *The Road to 1945* (1975), chs 2–5; D. N. Chester, *Lessons of the British War Economy* (1951); Margaret Gowing, 'The Organisation of Manpower in Britain during the Second World War', *J. Cont. Hist.*, Vol. 7, nos. 1–2 (Jan.–Apr. 1972), 147–67; Alan S. Milward, *War, Economy and Society 1939–45* (1977), chs 4, 7, and 8.
12   Titmuss, *Social Policy*, 324–31, 462–3, 557–61.
13   *Ibid.*, 183–202, 442–505.
14   Hammond, *Food*, Vol. 2, *passim*; H. M. D. Parker, *Manpower. A Study of Wartime Policy and Administration* (1957), 416–23.
15   Titmuss, *Social Policy*, 17, 199, 275, 315–18; J. M. Lee, *Reviewing the Machinery of Government 1942–1952* (1977), 114–16, 129–36. Thereafter Lee, *Machinery*.
16   Jose Harris, *William Beveridge. A Biography* (1977), 380–1. Thereafter, Harris, *William Beveridge;* J. M. Keynes, *How to Pay for the War* (1940); R. H. Tawney, 'The Abolition of Economic Controls', *Economic History Review*, Vol. XIII, no. i (1943), 1–30; H. Kopsch, 'The Approach of the Conservative Party to Social Policy during World War Two', Ph.D thesis (London 1970); Stephen Brooke, 'Revisionists and Fundamentalists: The Labour Party and Economic Policy during the Second World War', *HJ*, Vol. 32, no. 1, 157–75.

17   Harris, *William Beveridge*, chs 16 and 17.

18   *Educational Reconstruction*, Cmd. 6458, 1943; *A National Health Service*, Cmd. 6527, 1944; *Social Insurance*, Cmd. 6650–1, 1944; *Report of the Care of Children Committee*, Cmd. 6922, 1946.

19   R. K. Kelsall, *Higher Civil Servants in Great Britain* (1955), 146–60; Roger Eatwell, *The 1945–51 Labour Governments* (1979), 45–8.

20   Lee, *Machinery*, 114, suggests that 'suspension of regular elections to both the House of Commons and local authorities for the duration of the war may . . . have surprisingly done something to strengthen loyalties to traditional constitutional practice'.

21   A. M. Carr-Saunders, D. Caradog Jones and C. A. Moser, *A Survey of Social Conditions in England and Wales* (1958), 136–53.

22   *Ibid.*, 173–82.

23   Summerfield, *Women Workers*, 185–91.

24   Sheila Ferguson and Hilde Fitzgerald, *Studies in the Social Services* (1954), 103–9. Thereafter Ferguson and Fitzgerald, *Studies*; J. M. Winter, 'The Demographic Consequences of the War', in Smith, *War and Social Change*, 176; FR 64, Weekly Intelligence Service, 29 Mar. 1940, 76, Mass Observation Archive, University of Sussex.

25   Jose Harris, 'Did British Workers Want the Welfare State? G. D. H. Cole's Survey of 1942', in J. M. Winter, ed., *The Working Class in Modern British History* (1983), 200–14. (The archives of the Reconstruction Survey are in the library of Nuffield College, Oxford.)

26   Lowe, 'Welfare State', 174–80.

27   Beveridge Papers, IXa, 15, Employment investigation, report of a meeting with the TUC, 9 Feb. 1944; Jose Harris, 'Some Aspects of Social Policy in Britain during the Second World War', in W. J. Mommsen, ed., *The Emergence of the Welfare State in Britain and Germany*, (1981), 247–60; Charles Webster, *The Health Services since the War*, Vol. I (1988), 107–20.

28   Lionel Robbins, *Autobiography of an Economist* (1971); Stephen Spender, 'September Journal', in *Journals 1939–83*, ed. John Goldsmith (1985).

29   E.g. FR 510, diaries for Dec. 1940, Mass Observation Archive. A notable exception was the diary of Naomi Mitchison, *Among You Taking Notes: The Wartime Diary of Naomi Mitchison*, ed. Dorothy Sheridan (1985), 62–3.

30   Hermann Mannheim, *Comparative Criminology*, vol. 11 (1965), 597–8; *idem, Social Aspects of Crime between the Wars* (1940), esp. pp. 105–22; *idem, War and Crime* (1941), 129–44.

31   Edward Smithies, *The Black Economy in England since 1914* (1984), 64–84.

32   As demonstrated by innumerable cartoons of the period. See Andrew Sinclair, *The War Decade. An Anthology of the 1940s* (1989), 21. Thereafter Sinclair, *War Decade*.

33   Travis Crosby, *The Impact of Civilian Evacuation in the Second World War* (1986), *passim*; John Macnicol, 'The Effect of the Evacuation of Schoolchildren on Official Attitudes to State Intervention', in Smith, *War and Social Change*, 3–31.

34   Ferguson and Fitzgerald, *Studies*, 104.

35   *People in Production. An Enquiry into British War Production. A Report by Mass Observation* (1942), 24–5.

36   Compare, for example, Paul Addison, *The Road to 1945* (1975), with Stephen Brooke, 'Revisionists and Fundamentalists: The Labour Party and Economic Policy during the Second World War', *HJ*, Vol. 32, no. 1, (1989), 157–75, and Kevin Jefferys, *The Churchill Coalition and Wartime Politics 1940–1945* (1991).

37   I have discussed Barnett's interpretation more fully in my 'Enterprise and Welfare

States. A Comparative Perspective', *Transactions of the Royal Historical Society*, 5th Scr. Vol. 40 (1990), 175–95.

38   See e.g. Richard Titmuss, *Income Distribution and Social Change* (1962), and Titmuss's contribution to Morris Ginsberg, ed.. *Law and Opinion in England in the Twentieth Century* (1959).

39   Roger Middleton, 'The Treasury and Public Investment: A Perspective on Interwar Economic Management', *Public Administration*, Vol. 61, no. 4 (Winter 1983), 352; Noelle Whiteside, 'Private Agencies for Public Purposes: Some New Perspectives on Policy-making in Health Insurance between the Wars', *Journal of Social Policy*, Vol. 12, no. 2 (1983), 165–83.

40   Harris, *William Beveridge* ch. 17; R. P. Chapman, 'The Development of Policy on Family Allowances and National Insurance in the United Kingdom 1942–1946', MPhil thesis (University of London, 1990).

41   John Macnicol, *The Movement for Family Allowances 1918–45* (1980), 156, 169, 183–6, 202.

42   John Veit-Wilson, 'Genesis of Confusion: The Beveridge Committee's Poverty Line for Social Security', paper for a seminar at the Suntory-Toyota International Centre for Economics and Related Disciplines, London School of Economics, 1 Nov. 1989. I am grateful to John Veit-Wilson for permission to cite his paper.

43   In, for example, the essay on war in *Essays on the Welfare State*, where Titmuss the subtle and finely nuanced social historian was less in evidence than Titmuss the didactic social theorist.

44   Cited in Sinclair, *War Decade*, 14.

45   Lawrie, 'Impact', *passim*; *People in Production*, parts C, D, and E; FR 1364, 'Reconstruction, People's Hopes and Expectations', July 1942, Mass Observation.

46   'A Review of Some Conclusions Arising out of a Year of Home Intelligence Reports' by Stephen Taylor, Oct. 1941 PRO, INF 1/292; People in Production, 63–7, and *passim*.

47   Julian Symons, *Notes from Another Country* (1972), cited in Sinclair, *War Decade*, 76.

48   *People in Production*, 54–5, in the Autumn of 1942 wrote about the 'Dunkirk spirit' nostalgically, as though it were an episode in a distant and irrecoverable past.

49   Cited in Sinclair, *War Decade*, 90–3.

50   Summerfield, *Women Workers, passim*.

51   Robert Currie, Alan Gilbert and Lee Horsley, *Churches and Churchgoers. Patterns of Church Growth in the British Isles since 1700* (1977), 27, 30, 35–7, 62, 114–15. Mass Observation recorded a decrease in church-going but a 'strengthening' of faith, particularly in 1942 (FR 1200, Mass Observation Archive).

52   *People in Production*, 178–9.

53   Minutes of the Social Insurance Committee, March-Aug. 1942, PRO, CAB 87/76–8.

54   'Certain things go inevitably with war and are war', commented an anonymous member of the Mass Observation team in April 1940. 'The main thing is fighting, winning, killing and being killed, being masculine and aggressive and abnormally vigorous, violent and physical.' FP, 89, 'Morale Now', 30 Apr. 1940, Mass Observation Archive.

55   Graham Smith, *When Jim Crow met John Bull. Black American Soldiers in World War II Britain* (1987).

56   Peter Fryer, *Staying Power. A History of Black People in Britain* (1984), 330–67.

57   Peter Flora, *State, Economy and Society in Western Europe 1815–1975*. Vol. I: *The Growth of Mass Democracies and Welfare States* (1983); and Peter Flora, ed., *Growth to Limits. The Western European Welfare States since Second World War*, Vols I, II and IV (1987–8).

Chapter 14

Mark H. Leff

THE POLITICS OF SACRIFICE ON THE AMERICAN HOME FRONT IN WORLD WAR II

WAR IS HELL. But for millions of Americans on the booming home front, World War II was also a hell of a war. Both then and today, the mystique of home front sacrifice suffused visions of that wartime experience. The politics set in motion by a peculiar blend of profits and patriotism, of sacrifice amid unprecedented prosperity, gave a distinctive cast to American wartime life.

In subsequent American civic mythology, the public-spirited wartime community of World War II holds a cherished place. It is nostalgically recalled as *our* "finest hour," when Americans freely sacrificed selfish desires, did without, went all out, and "pulled together" in common purpose and spirit with "only one thing on their minds — winning the war."[1] The allure of this golden age of home front sacrifice is not merely retrospective. During World War II, Americans gloried in the feeling that they were participating in a noble and successful cause by making "sacrifices." In common parlance sacrifice did not require the suffering of terrible loss. It instead comprehended a range of activities — running the gamut from donating waste paper to donating lives — in which narrow, immediate self-interest was subordinated to the needs of the war effort.

Despite, or even because of, its variegated usage, *sacrifice* decisively shaped the discourse of wartime politics. But polychromatic concepts can raise unsettling questions. Most Americans conceded that they had not made any *"real* sacrifices," a freighted expression largely reserved for our boys at the front. While it was more apparent in the war years than it is in retrospect that not everyone was going all out, the consecration of sacrifice inspired declarations of willingness to shoulder new burdens. Admittedly no specific additional sacrifice jumped readily to mind, but Americans in public opinion polls pledged their support — at least in principle — to an imposing list of wartime activities and restrictions, including wage and price freezes, no strike pledges, rationing, and higher taxes. Amid these affirmations of unstinting patriotism, one contemporary commentator on wartime morale explained that the war had "subordinated or shelved" the previous "aims and values of individual citizens and special groups," as Americans "generally respond wholeheartedly to a major demand made of them when its essential necessity to the winning of the war is made clear."[2]

The mystique of unconditional sacrifice, forged in the war itself and celebrated in collective memory, has not fared well as an interpretive guide to wartime politics and mobilization. Even at the time, staffers of American mobilization agencies commonly despaired of the difficulties of transforming "willingness into action" and cracking "the shell of public apathy," given "desultory, half-hearted" citizen involvement and "reluctance to forego the ordinary pleasures and comforts of 'life as usual.'" Americans, they noted, were often able to compartmentalize their advocacy of the principle of sacrifice, to excuse failures of civic responsibility by claiming that their sacrifices would not really have helped the war anyway, that someone else was receiving favored treatment, or that some blockheaded bureaucrat was bungling the whole thing. In the quest for alibis, standards of proof could be conveniently low. "Each of us," a top mobilization official conceded, "is likely to be slightly more eager to hold down the other fellow's prices, wages or profits, and to raise the other fellow's taxes. . . . each of us will be looking for the moat in the other fellow's eye." President Franklin D. Roosevelt himself, despite warnings from pollsters that his "scolding approach" toward the shortcomings of American sacrifice might only impede cooperation, voiced his disgust at "the whining demands of selfish pressure groups who seek to feather their nests while young Americans are dying."[3]

As recent historians who expand upon this indictment remind us, what Americans called sacrifice often involved limits on substantial gains rather than the horrific deprivations and destruction suffered by the citizens of other belligerents. Such reassessments can lead to a Manichaean dialogue as to whether Americans on the home front in World War II were saints or sinners — a singularly unpromising question in which assessments of virtue depend on the assessors' original inclinations and selectively applied standards. More productive challenges await: not to gauge the extent of American cooperation in the war effort, but to examine how that cooperation was achieved, to clarify the principles by which policy makers decided that certain groups would have to give up something or forgo gains for the good of the whole, and to understand how the ubiquitous ethos of wartime sacrifice set the terms of wartime political discourse, shaping the public actions and manipulatory strategies of potentially affected groups.[4]

What were the boundaries of sacrifice in a global war that disrupted customary patterns of limited government? What could be required and of whom? Sacrifice was clearly a subject for negotiation across a broad range of issues encompassing both public and private choices. In public forums — in the speeches and press conferences of political leaders, in the public opinion polls commissioned by government departments, in the internal correspondence of mobilization officials — concern centered on what might be termed the calculus of political obligation. This article examines the public choices made there, the politics.

The wartime recasting of political obligation touched many facets of American political life, but this article focuses on two case studies. The first treats a celebrated but surprisingly insubstantial and ultimately abortive effort: Franklin Roosevelt's executive order capping all wartime salaries. This startling assault on the ethos of boundless individual achievement demonstrates both the apparently open-ended possibility for renegotiating symbolic values (was the ethic of sacrifice powerful enough to neutralize the American Dream?) and, in its quick and crushing repeal by Congress, the actual limits to the wartime revaluation of values. Interwoven in the seeming challenge to traditional marketplace values was a politics in which the level of comparative sacrifice — the degree of sacrifice relative to other groups — became a standard of justice.

The second case study offers a marked contrast: the successful merchandising of sacrifice through the formation of the War Advertising Council to coordinate a vast private advertising campaign supporting wartime programs and propaganda themes. The unique and consequential American arrangement whereby privately donated advertising carried the brunt of the domestic propaganda effort not only shows the adaptability of the imagery of sacrifice; it also raises provocative questions about the interplay of political forces in the United States that allowed certain groups to domesticate and delimit the meaning of sacrifice — to define it in terms that reinforced the validity of their own political interests and claims. What ultimately stands out in the calculus of home front obligation in World War II is a political process in which claimed sacrifices and contributions could be parlayed into political advantage or into efforts to shift war burdens to others. That process, which I have labeled the politics of sacrifice, established a dynamic that mobilizers and interest groups alike took into account. Since the process stands out most clearly in a comparative framework, I conclude by considering the starkly different political context of sacrifice in Great Britain.

Though sounding radical by current standards, President Roosevelt's salary limitation proposal emerged in stages throughout 1942, rather prosaically, as part of a coordinated effort to control inflationary pressures. In April FDR announced that price stabilization could only be effective if pursued on all fronts; thus he supplemented proposals for across-the-board price ceilings, wage controls, and rationing with a proposed 100 percent "super-tax" that would-draw off any "excess" income over $25,000 ($50,000 for families) once the federal income tax had been paid. This income limitation proposal garnered popular approval as "a symbol of the idea of equality of sacrifice," but editorialists soon buried it as a "Rooseveltian pleasantry." Just as deadly was the congressional response: utter dismissal — one contemporary comparison was to "a burp in church, something to be overlooked and forgotten as quickly as possible!" But in October Roosevelt used a broadly phrased authorization for price stabilization that he had just forced through Congress as the pretext for an executive order clamping an after-tax limit of $25,000 (equivalent to $200,000 in 1990 dollars) on all salaries. The order did not apply to total incomes or profits, partly because no interpretation of existing law sanctioned such use of independent executive action.[5]

From today's vantage point, one can easily predict the ferocious response from some quarters to this apparently daring initiative. Labeling it a product of communistic philosophy and class hatred, attackers called it an un-American assault on free enterprise that threatened the production necessary for an effective war effort. When the 1942 elections the next month buoyed the congressional conservative bloc with substantial Republican gains, the salary ceiling was doomed, despite FDR's efforts to save it. In March 1943 most House Democrats joined the Republicans to repeal it by attaching a rider to a veto-proof debt limit bill; the bill then passed the Senate by a 74-to-3 vote. Less than six months after FDR released his executive order and before it had really gone into effect, salary limitation had been beaten back.[6]

Why did the administration open itself to damagingly reproachful defenses of private property and free enterprise? Did the logic of sacrifice extend so quickly to the core of capitalism? A number of less extreme answers come to mind. Scapegoating campaigns against the abuses of "economic royalists" had long been a staple of Rooseveltian politics. In part, they can be traced to the president's patrician distaste for ostentatious wealth. Before the war, lessons embedded in the political culture about profiteering "merchants of death" — the unresolved public resentment over issues of sacrifice in World War I — spurred Roosevelt to proclaim that the "burdens of possible war" should be equalized to prevent "war millionaires" from enriching themselves from the sufferings of others. Once World War II began, Roosevelt's acute awareness of the privileged position of the United States also made him indignant at what he saw as selfish bickering and maneuvering for partisan or monetary gain at home. His sense of equitable and active war participation as a paramount moral obligation also shaped such politically divergent Rooseveltian lost causes as his national war service "labor draft" proposal and his veto of a loophole-ridden tax bill as "not for the needy but for the greedy."[7]

This ideological component had a firm practical political base. In 1940 and 1941, Roosevelt repeatedly fretted that the economic concessions needed to entice businesses into war contracts could clash with the public's antiprofiteering sentiments. His fears were well founded. Despite the bad press and the congressional criticism that FDR's proposals received, commentaries on the $25,000 salary order commonly assumed that the public would be receptive to limiting incomes. Public opinion polls, including surveys solicited by the administration itself, bore out those assumptions, registering majorities of more than two to one — and well above that among farmers and industrial workers — for a $25,000 ceiling.[8]

The salary limitation proposal had one other attraction: its potential victims were few and far between. The proposed ceiling applied to after-tax salaries. Given unprecedentedly high wartime tax rates, a salary earner needed to receive at least $67,200 (well over half a million in 1990 dollars) to fall under its provisions — a fate confined to roughly one in fifty thousand Americans. It is no wonder that one congressman was unsure if the salary order applied to any of his constituents. Roosevelt must have been aware of the advantages of his order's delimited impact in narrowing the potential base of opposition and in sidestepping any truly systemic challenge to economics as usual. In 1941, when batting around the idea of applying a 99½ percent tax rate to income above $100,000, he jokingly dismissed doubts by asking, "Why not? None of us is ever going to make $100,000 a year. How many people report on that much income?"[9]

So why bother? The salary order would have had no significant direct effect either in slowing inflation or in narrowing the budget deficit. The key lies in the order's symbolic value, in the messages it was intended to send, particularly to the labor movement. As Nelson Lichtenstein reports in *Labor's War at Home*, leaders of the Congress of Industrial Organizations (CIO) and the CIO-affiliated United Automobile Workers (UAW) in 1942 urged a $25,000 income limit. In March 1942 CIO leaders capitulated to corporate and government demands to extend factory schedules and thus speed production by relinquishing a major union objective and achievement: "premium pay" for weekend and holiday work. To forestall a revolt and to show that its weekend pay concession should not be read as a sign that it had gone soft, the UAW executive board simultaneously publicized a broad "Victory through Equality of Sacrifice Program" that included a call for a $25,000 limit on incomes. The logic was clear: By prescribing "what other groups in the nation should give up to correspond to labor's sacrifice," UAW leaders sought to anticipate and quiet rank-and-file resentment about shouldering a disproportionate share of the war's burdens.[10]

FDR's ill-fated plan to impose a "super-tax" on individual incomes above $25,000 represented a direct response to the challenge from labor. In accounting for the income limitation proposal, the undersecretary of the treasury explained that it "clarified the whole situation as far as labor was concerned in the Detroit area." The secretary of the treasury himself, referring to the antiprofiteering proposals of other mobilization officials, put it less kindly: "These stupid asses . . . in order to satisfy labor . . . want to go after the rich people."[11]

The stupid asses had a point. Fighting a losing battle against inflation in the first three-quarters of 1942, they felt it necessary to clamp down hard on wage increases. One analyst after another recognized that wage earners could most readily be swayed, not by a simple appeal to patriotism, but by a politics of comparative sacrifice in which others too could be shown as "sacrificing" rather than gaining at the wage earners' expense.

War sharpens and reframes domestic internal conflict by disrupting customary standards of comparison. Peacetime inequalities are often taken for granted as "neutral" results of an impersonal market. But in wartime these same inequalities could rank — and rankle — as inequities, both because of a common code of modern wartime societies that delegitimized "profiteering" from a collective effort in which many would give their lives, and because a planned wartime economy lends an element of purpose to every economic exchange, making it easy to blame inequities on conscious government decisions or on lobbyists' maneuverings. It is not coincidental that the term "relative deprivation" was coined during World War II, for war forges a sense of common aspirations and responsibilities. That sense broadens the range of others that individuals and groups consider in gauging their position and demanding equal treatment. As John Kenneth Galbraith recollected, "no feature of World War II or more recent mobilization experience has been more striking than the scrutiny which each of the several economic groups brings to bear upon what the others are getting."[12]

The importance of this comparative framework did not escape the Roosevelt administration. As early as 1940, "labor trouble" was very much on the president's mind. It is "a damn sight simpler," he explained, "for all of us to appeal to [worker] patriotism if we say we are using exactly the same principle for the owners of industry as we are with the workers in industry." In a closed-door meeting with his Business Advisory Council, Roosevelt urged a measure of restraint: "I can hold labor to the present level if I can say to them, 'You [industry] won't profiteer.'"

The Treasury Department highlighted the strategy, noting that "if we are to expect all classes of society, including laborers and farmers, to accept the sacrifices of the emergency period and not to press for every possible dollar of advantage, they must be convinced that sacrifices are being distributed according to ability and that no one is making unreasonably large profits."[13]

Such statements betokened no special insight; they merely mirrored the conventional wisdom. In public speeches and internal memoranda, Roosevelt's advisers highlighted this notion of contingent sacrifice. Americans, they noted, not only worried that more might be asked of them than of other groups but also demanded proof that their sacrifices would further the war effort and not fatten someone else's wallet. Field reports by the Office of War Information isolated such concerns as the critical barrier to mobilization. "Each group," the reports explained, "thinks the others are using the emergency to win selfish advantage. At the same time, each fears that it, alone, will be slighted." Interest group leaders in particular, the reports warned, simultaneously insisted "that there must be no favored group" while expecting "special recognition for their own particular interests." Each jockeyed "for the best bargaining position" and "tended to claim unequal sacrifices" as an excuse for postponing "the program most directly affecting his group." The final report of FDR's interdepartmental anti-inflation committee in April 1942 thus endorsed an income ceiling as a way of "dramatizing the equality of sacrifice implicit in the proposed over-all [price stabilization] program." The chairman of the National War Labor Board, speaking of the difficulty of gaining labor acquiescence to concessions on overtime pay, graphically made this point:

> If you say to the boys, "Why don't you make a sacrifice for your country?" they are going to say, "That is fine. I am making a sacrifice for my country, but I am not going to make it to increase the profits of General Motors." Well, that profit thing comes in all the time.[14]

Union leaders made the most of such resentments, publishing the salaries of industry executives and punctuating their speeches with reminders that "if labor is going to make these sacrifices . . . then labor certainly ought to ask the industrialists . . . to make a contribution somewhat equivalent to that contribution that you and I as workers must make." Polls of union members showed that they shared this quid-pro-quo "fair share" mentality. As one survey of industrial workers concluded, they "are willing to work overtime, they are willing to give up the right to strike, they are ready to make sacrifices for the war effort — *if* the other fellow will do the same, *if* the bosses don't reap new profits out of all proportion." But if the government did not respond to "labor's discontent with what it feels is an inequality of sacrifice," an Office of War Information report cautioned in the Summer of 1942, union leaders would continue to experience "difficulty in managing the discontent of the rank file," and "restlessness may be expected to increase and to manifest itself as small slow-downs, delays and walk-outs."[15]

In a wartime economy, other groups besides labor manifested this mind-set. If the anti-inflation effort was to succeed, everyone had to shoulder new burdens: price ceilings for farmers, frustrating shortages and rationing for newly flush consumers, ballooning tax bills for the millions of Americans of average income

Figure 14.1 Cartoon published in *United Automobile Worker*, October 15, 1942, p. 5.

previously exempt from income tax. Getting each group to accept its burden was no easy trick; Roosevelt's budget director despaired of what he termed "you-go-first" arguments in which "each group tries to shift the sacrifices to others." Roosevelt himself openly recognized the politics of sacrifice. In a fireside chat he explained that some were perfectly willing to endorse his entire anti-inflation package "except the one point which steps on their individual toes," while others "seem very willing to approve self-denial — on the part of their neighbors." The Roosevelt administration thus sought some sensational demonstration to show each group that it did not face economically painful restrictions alone. A proposed ceiling on incomes was an attractive vehicle for this drama: The absolute limit demonstrated the urgency of the situation, but the targeting of a relatively small number of rich salaried corporate executives (rather than, say, profits) personalized the demanded sacrifices without really threatening production. It was, as the president of the National Farmers' Union reminded Roosevelt, "most important as a symbol and token."[16]

Many union leaders embraced the salary limitation effort as a way to take full advantage of the politics of comparative sacrifice. They challenged employers to "match us in corresponding sacrifices," explaining that workers were "sore" not "because they are being asked to sacrifice" but "because they are being asked to tighten their belts when other people are outgrowing theirs because they are too damned small to go around their fat bellies." The articles and cartoons in union newspapers and pamphlets were no less hard-hitting. "What sacrifices are these fat cats making?" the *American Federationist* asked. "Will someone tell us, please?" One much-reprinted CIO cartoon depicted a "War Sacrifice Blood Bank." Two donors — "labor" and "farmer" — were laid out on hospital beds with their arms hooked up to a container labeled "war sacrifice." In the foreground were two typical capitalist caricatures, complete with top hats and bulging vests upon which were emblazoned "corporate profits" and "big incomes." As they casually waved off the idea of donating their blood, a no-nonsense Dr. FDR, with tubing in hand, pointed insistently to the empty beds. The cartoon was entitled "Labor Should Help Put These Fellows to Bed."[17]

On this battleground of corporate salaries and profits, defenders of business were at a clear psychological disadvantage. Some gave it their best shot, however. The *New York World-Telegram* pulled its readers' heartstrings by reporting that a utility holding company magnate and his wife "closed four of their five homes, put eight cars in storage, reduced the number of their household servants from twenty-five to ten, and shut off all except two floors of the thirty-room pink colonial brick mansion at 1130 Fifth Avenue where they now live." "Millionaires," it concluded, "are on the skids!" The *Wall Street Journal* ran an eight-part series called "The New Poor" about the prospective plight of illustrious corporate executives under salary limitation. The forecast included dwindling country club memberships, imperiled vacation homes, and the forced dismissal of faithful servants. Other newspapers interviewed prominent society women about the prospective damage to their clothing budgets.[18]

Such articles were deliciously easy to parody (the National Farmers' Union sponsored a satirical essay contest on "How to Live on $25,000 a year") and only played to the strength of salary limitation supporters. The issue itself, after all, was fundamentally symbolic; not only was the ceiling pegged at a stratospheric level but the salary order also specifically exempted investment income, the most important source of great wealth. Yet, to win cooperation with mobilization efforts, precisely measured equivalency — real "equality of sacrifice" — was scarcely the point. Merely targeting luxurious "excess income" promised to soothe resentments over new burdens and perceived inequalities.[19]

The politics of sacrifice moved the explosive issue of salary limitation from the periphery to the center of political debate. Yet Congress overwhelmingly bucked public opinion polls to repeal Roosevelt's salary order in March 1943. One might be tempted to attribute the administration defeat to shady manipulations by the media or special interests, to the limited political clout of a divided union movement, or to the unrepresentativeness of Congress or the American party system. But the explanation for repeal proves more revealing of the peculiar dynamics of wartime politics. Of undeniable importance was public exasperation with war restrictions, shortages, government bureaucrats, and other tangible barriers to the much-deferred "good life" — an irritation intense enough to overwhelm pledges of allegiance to ever greater sacrifice. After the 1942 elections, this attitude fueled the rise to dominance of a congressional conservative coalition that pounced on salary limitation to attack executive power grabbing and the remnants of New Deal reform. But, just as critically, the public image of business sacrifice itself was changing by 1943, giving way to a vision of United States war aims that cued the removal of salary ceilings. When combined with public resentment at wartime government regulations, the rise of business in popular estimation signaled a growing privatization of aspirations as the war progressed.[20]

The second case study, the formation of the War Advertising Council, illuminates and verifies this transition. Under the tutelage of this private organization, corporate executive targets of the call to sacrifice broadcast that call. Defensive recitations of "the truth about advertising" and attacks on the New Deal gave way to the merchandising of the industry's contributions to the war effort. This new politics of sacrifice, adopted with uncanny precision at the moment of Pearl Harbor, proved a brilliant strategic political shift, as advertisers seized the rhetoric and imagery of sacrifice to validate prewar goals of self-defense and expansion.

On the face of it, the saga of the War Advertising Council seems quite straightforward. According to a radio propaganda show sponsored by Wrigley's chewing gum in November 1945, it was a standard story of selfless sacrifice in which businessmen wholeheartedly lent their skills and high reputation to the war:

> *Narrator*: There was advertising . . . winning a big place for itself in our national life . . . and there was American business . . . just as anxious as you were to use all its resources, all its knowledge and experience, to help win the war. . . .
> *Businessman*: Then, our place in the effort is clear. We, who have by our advertising earned the confidence of the public, can use that advertising as a vehicle for the messages of the government to the people.
> *Voices*: Right. That's the way to do it . . .
> *Businessman*: . . . Now — let's prove we are worthy of the faith and trust given us. I say — ask the government to tell us what is needed — and *we'll* take the information to the public — *in our own way!*
> *Narrator*: That's the way it happened, — that's how the War Advertising Council came into being.[21]

Truth has never been the essence of the propagandist's skill. In fact, in 1941 Madison Avenue was running scared. Mobilization demands were increasingly allowing manufacturers to sell effortlessly whatever they produced, removing the main rationale for big advertising budgets. Advertising representatives were also painfully aware that their reputation had taken a beating in the depression decade. They found it very easy to spook themselves by compiling long lists of "anti-advertising New Dealers" who had attacked "the accuracy and truth of advertising," branded it an economic waste, or warned of its contribution to inflation. A "pessimistic miasma" descended on much of Madison Avenue at the prospect of such figures making do-or-die decisions on the fate of the advertising industry. As the "growing alarm" indicated, the war itself posed special threats that advertising was "going to be throttled." Foremost among advertisers' concerns was the question of whether the government would consider advertising a legitimate business expense for the purpose of corporate taxes and war contracts.[22]

Figure 14.2 This War Advertising Council advertisement, sponsored by local firms listed at the bottom, offers a haunting example of the motivational uses of sacrifice. *Woonsocket Call*, June 30, 1944, p. 7.

On the eve of Pearl Harbor, advertising trade journals overflowed with evidence of a siege mentality. One warned that "advertising is threatened today as it has never been threatened before." Another concluded that "all of American industry is in a mental state like anticipating a trip to the dentist." Sounding the alarm on the "imminence of the danger to all," the president of the Association of National Advertisers called on the industry to create "a united front." Rallying to the call that "the common cause is survival" (the pervasive martial imagery is all the more striking since the issue was not the nation's survival, but the industry's), the nation's two main advertising associations summoned a joint meeting of 630 advertising, industry, and national media executives for November 1941. In that meeting one speaker after another stridently denounced the unfair and uninformed attacks on the industry. An influential group of "moderate" voices at this meeting talked of advertising's potential social contributions in wartime. Those moderates brought in government speakers who took the edge off the meeting's belligerent mood by announcing their desire to work with advertisers in furthering the war effort. Yet even the moderates compared advertisers to "His Majesty's Loyal Opposition" and urged a commitment to winning "the war of business" by defending free enterprise and preparing "the Case for Advertising."[23]

The result of the conference was thus mixed. A consensus supported the need for advertisers to present a common front and to defend the advertising industry and the virtues of free enterprise. Yet some advertising executives feared that "a concerted campaign to preach the gospel of advertising at this juncture would fall on deaf or unfriendly ears" and advised that one essential part of the case for advertising was to "actively cooperate in solving national problems." In the immediate aftermath of the conference, its key organizers began to plan a new "governing group of the new Advertising Council or whatever it is to be called" to make that case.[24]

Then came Pearl Harbor. From a strategic point of view, it was a godsend, a ticket to respectability for a battered industry. As one advertising executive later recalled, "we were losing" but "we were saved by the bell." "Now advertising has a chance to redeem itself . . . to prove it has a right to exist," a leading advertising journal rejoiced. The war provided "the greatest, the most golden, the most challenging opportunity ever to face American advertising," adman Walter Weir proclaimed. "If we make advertising fight today, we'll never again have to defend its place in our economy." Government mobilization officials encouraged advertisers' urge to serve, portraying it as a patriotic duty (though Donald Nelson, the "production czar," rather menacingly added in an off-the-record meeting that advertisers might ultimately need to choose between closing down — in which case "your future chances of coming back are something less than doubtful" — or converting to war-related advertising, which would preserve skills and facilities for postwar survival).[25]

Thus the advertising industry formed what became the War Advertising Council, a private organization — currently called the Ad Council — that has dominated American "public service" advertising ever since. Composed of volunteer representatives from major advertising agencies, large corporate advertisers, and the media, the War Advertising Council worked with such government agencies as the Office of War information to plot out public information campaigns. By the war's end, it had supervised well over a hundred campaigns, using donated space to push war bonds, blood drives, food conservation, labor recruitment, and other

...headline and smile make blood-giving sound almost like fun!

"To think I had to be coaxed!"

Then the ad starts off with a husky sell on the Blood Donor theme...

I've gone and done it!

Bill's letter, this morning, was the last nudge. He wrote: "Haven't you given that pint of blood yet? You ought to be spanked!"

So I squirmed, and trotted to the Blood Donor Center, wearing a little extra lipstick to help me feel brave.

Well – there wasn't a *thing* to be brave *about*! A pin-prick, and then they have you clench your fist a few times, and then you get a little bandage...easy as that!

Sure made me feel good in the Conscience Department. So darn good I decided to come home and sail right into those other things I've been putting off!

I'm starting with my linen closet. Going to check up on my lovely Cannon Percale Sheets again. Want to make sure I'm not missing any linen-closet tricks to make 'em last longer!

Oops! How'd these get here?

Miscellaneous medicine bottles in the linen closet – that's bad! They might tip or leak and stain my sheets!

...the copy slips easily into conservation...with a little product sell

Hmmm – circulation's okay!

I try to give all my sheets equal wear. Fresh-washed ones go on top of the pile – and I take off from the bottom.

Nope – no mildew!

Got to watch that – bad mildew's incurable! I always iron my sheets the same day I sprinkle 'em – and I always make sure they're thoroughly dry before I put them away.

...and winds up with a good strong product sales story

And how're YOU doing girls?

If you cross-your-heart must have sheets – can't "make do" – consider Cannon Percales! Feel how soft and smooth – yet they cost about the same as heavy-duty muslin! And being woven with 25% more threads than the best-grade muslin, Cannon Percale Sheets are bears for wear!

Course, you may run into this ...

These days, you may not always find just the sizes you want in Cannon Percale. Then just ask to see Cannon's economy Muslin Sheets – well-constructed and long-wearing. P.S. Don't forget that Cannon Towels grow on the same family tree!
Cannon Mills, Inc., New York 13, N. Y.

FOR VICTORY – BUY U.S. WAR BONDS AND STAMPS

Cannon Percale Sheets
Made by the Makers of Common Towels and Hosiery

The whole ad is more timely, a better goodwill builder for Cannon, a better ad all-around because of the addition of the war theme!

Figure 14.3 Advertisement for the Young & Rubicam ad agency, in *Advertising & Selling*, 38 (March 1945), 98. The agency superimposes script on its own earlier Cannon Mills ad to show that even the dubious connection between percale sheets and a blood drive can be used to sell both.

mobilization demands deemed worthy of advertising support — with a value in space and personnel estimated (by the advertisers themselves, admittedly no strangers to exaggeration) at over a billion dollars.[26]

One would be ill advised to dismiss those donations as mere artifice and calculation. In urging advertisers to sponsor public service messages under the company name or to inject official war messages into their product pitches, the War Advertising Council drew upon strong strains of patriotism. Win-the-war appeals anchored the council's efforts to gain industry cooperation.

Patriotic exhortation was of course paired with reminders that "public service advertising is shrewd business," since hook-ins to the war enhanced the ad and the firm's reputation. Shrewdness here was all-important; clients with no consumer goods to sell or no need to use advertising to sell their goods faced the "evaporation" of buyer and dealer loyalty. Advertising strategies shifted accordingly. One disarming solicitation for advertising explained, "Advertisers have but one thought in mind: post war 'prestige.' Not just 'prestige,' — but 'dollars and cents prestige,' the kind that will reflect itself in actual sales in the future." But how to maintain brand visibility without clashing with the wartime ethic of sacrifice and without creating unfulfillable product demands? Combining the company name with public service messages offered an answer, providing "momentum" to secure future sales and influence.[27]

In the advertising industry, as in other sectors of American life, patriotism and public relations, sacrifice and self-interest intertwined. As one board member of the War Advertising Council put it, "Not for one minute is it necessary to say to an advertiser that he should try to win the war with his copy for the sake of winning the war." Instead, the advertiser was urged "that he can best serve his own selfish interests" by sensitivity to public demands, including the demand for information on how to contribute to the war. The War Advertising Council, its leaders repeatedly boasted, had combined "sensible idealism with the profit motive" in a show of social responsibility "which brings rich returns to those who act on it." That promise was an enduring part of the ethos of the Ad Council. As its president explained in 1947, "True, you are casting your bread upon the waters — but it will return to you well buttered."[28]

With advertisers' show of sacrifice, the feared government barriers to the growth of the advertising industry crumbled. Soon advertisers could display an honor roll of glowing commendations, emanating from Franklin Roosevelt on down, of the inspiring example advertisers had set in their support of the war effort. In May 1942 the Treasury Department, reliant on the War Advertising Council and private donations to promote its war bond campaigns, granted Madison Avenue what one trade journal later called "advertising's Magna Charta under the tax laws." This ruling's generous interpretation of necessary and legitimate business expenses allowed full deduction of advertising costs from taxable incomes, even when firms had next to nothing to sell to ordinary consumers. With high excess-profits tax rates, that meant that the government was footing more than 80 percent of some companies' advertising bills. Especially at these cut rates, goodwill advertising directed toward postwar sales, the continued allegiance of distributors, employee productivity, or political aims became a highly attractive investment.[29]

Thus the predicted wartime freefall in advertising budgets never took place. Even in the face of vanished consumer markets and supply shortages, expenditures on advertising — especially advertising in nationwide media — rose substantially, much to the relief of the industry itself. Favorable government decisions allowing certain advertising expenses to be factored into war contract prices and protecting advertised brands by including advertising in regulators' calculation of maximum allowable prices only bolstered the industry's assurance that the once-feared government was "friendly," "cooperative," and "helpful." "The important thing," admen exulted, "is that people *do* give us credit for doing the job." The council predicted all along that its show of sacrifice would reverse the antiprofiteering and antiadvertising attitudes that the industry had faced before Pearl Harbor, and the war indeed sharply raised the prestige of advertisers in particular and business in general.[30]

One would be well advised to take with a grain of salt any inferences (some tastefully "planted" by the council in the trade and general press) of War Advertising Council credit for this shift. Broader economic and political trends virtually assured a rise in business prestige even as the war began. As a leading pollster who contributed to the wartime boom in industrial public relations proclaimed in February 1942, the "dramatic theme" of the American production miracle "calls forth the deepest and sincerest praise the people can bestow," so that "out of this war should and can come renewed faith in individual enterprise and a lasting acclaim of the men who run the economic machine." Given the extent to which the government actually underwrote this expansion, this arrogation of credit to business (so much in contrast to the declining public stock of union leaders, whose involvement in strikes allowed them to be cast in that most unforgivable of roles: subverters of war production) was a tribute to careful and effective wartime public relations. John Blum and others have pointed to the administration's failure to forge a clear sense of the public purposes for which Americans were fighting and sacrificing, which left a vacuum that would be filled by private desires and conservative trends. Advertisers, newly legitimized by their "sacrifices" and empowered by their role as the chief messengers bearing government propaganda messages to the public, could thus press their own vision of war aims. As Frank Fox vividly demonstrates in his study of war advertisers, their depiction of American war aims in terms of an "American Way of Life" that encompassed abundant consumption and an absence of labor conflict reinforced other factors that cemented the postwar reputation and influence of "free enterprise" and the advertisers who celebrated it.[31]

The contrast to the humiliation of Roosevelt's salary limitation order is instructive. In a political discourse in which the war came to be interpreted as a precursor of abundance and a protector of a harmonious "Americanism," associations with rampant New Deal reformism and a class-tinged rhetoric of conflict could be deadly. Charges that salary limitation undermined economic incentive or smacked of communism and a capitulation to unions thus hit home. Despite the popularity of Roosevelt's executive order, the ideological legitimacy of the arguments against it allowed congressmen to repeal a still-popular measure without fear of effective political retribution. The limited and discredited union influence on public opinion only clinched the defeat of salary limitation. Though workers might seek evidence that their sacrifices were matched by management's, their power to extract this equivalency through the political process had diminished.[32]

The importance of this broader context for the politics of sacrifice emerges clearly in the contrast between American developments and home front politics in

Great Britain. One could make a persuasive logical case that a country under fire, as Britain was then, does not have the luxury of the "you first" mentality or the political positioning associated with the politics of sacrifice in the United States. In terms of sacrifice, after all, Britons made a virtue out of a necessity, while Americans could afford to make a necessity out of a virtue. Though British casualties and disruptions of life as usual paled beside those of such combatants as the Soviet Union and Germany, the war's toll on Britain's home front — the Victory coffee made of ground acorns, the scarcity of everything from soap to saucepans, "the dull dismal drudgery" of everyday life, on top of the bombings that killed sixty-one thousand civilians, damaged one-third of the nation's homes, and forced mass evacuations of London — stands in emphatic contrast to American conditions. Throughout the war, many Britons defined their essential strength as a people by these mutual sacrifices; the mind-set was expressed in Prime Minister Winston S. Churchill's pronouncement that "I have nothing to offer but blood, toil, tears and sweat." The characteristic understatement and humor in British propaganda, which seemingly took for granted an indomitable British spirit of sacrifice amid menacing peril, differs markedly from the tone of American propaganda, full of bluster, high emotion, guilt over the greater sacrifices of soldiers, and other techniques appropriate to a country virtually compelled to fight the war "on imagination alone." Given the lesser sense of urgency in the United States (which was geographically, economically, and even psychologically an ocean away from the battlefront), it is no wonder — the argument could continue — that Americans found political maneuvering room to manipulate images of sacrifice and to bargain over mobilization demands.[33]

That line of reasoning is consistent, but it is wrong. A more careful comparison between Britain and the United States shatters the assumption that only the United States experienced political jockeying, while casting a revealing light on the contrasting balances of forces in the two countries. One fact critical to understanding the British home front is that Churchill felt compelled to make concessions to attach the minority Labour party — which, though few would have predicted its end-of-the-war landslide victory, was clearly on the rise — to his governing coalition. The implications of that situation for the politics of sacrifice were profound. Labour forces seized the initiative in the all-important battle that advertisers waged so well in the United States: sculpting the political agenda by defining the purposes for which people were sacrificing. While Americans fought for the "American way of life," the British spoke of a "people's war" for a postwar world offering expanded social programs, security, and equity.[34]

A significant effect of the British "people's war" mentality is that the phrase "equality of sacrifice," which was at the core of arguments for salary limitation in the United States, cropped up more commonly in British debates, particularly in the speeches of the Labour party members. The effective use of comparative sacrifice themes emerges clearly in the debate in late May and June 1940 over the new coalition government's imposition of a 100 percent tax rate on corporate excess profits.

As a pure economic proposition, confiscatory tax rates make little sense, since they minimize incentive to produce while maximizing the temptation to avoid tax. But as with Roosevelt's salary ceiling proposal, the law's rationale was political, rather than financial. Early in the war, alarming reports recorded "a feeling among certain sections of the public that 'everything is not fair and equal and that therefore

our sacrifices are not worth while'"; such sentiments placed a premium on drama
tizing the equitable distribution of wartime burdens. Commenting ruefully on public sensitivity to what even he considered "unseemly" business profiteering, a leading
Tory mobilization official worried that the public's willingness to "accept hardship,"
so essential to the successful prosecution of the war, would be undermined by the
"social grievance" that "the only reason of it is to line the pockets of some individual." Fearing low worker morale, many warned of an "outburst of industrial unrest"
if domestic problems were ignored. If people were compelled to "suffer these reductions in their standards of living, they must be convinced that they are doing it" with
a goal of economic democracy that could justify their sacrifices.[35]

These concerns reached a fever pitch in May 1940, on the eve of the Dunkirk
evacuation. Recognizing the desperate need for Labour party help in reallocating labor
to weapons production, the newly appointed prime minister Churchill had enlisted
Ernest Bevin, Britain's top union leader, as his minister of labor. Bevin almost immediately received an unprecedented parliamentary authorization to direct workers to
war employment. But he subordinated compulsion to a "grand design . . . to carry
the assent of 'labour.'" The excess-profits tax fit neatly into this strategy. By seeming
to confirm that "wealth as well as labour" was being placed "at the service of the
nation," the levy on all profits in excess of 6 percent of capital was deemed "a most
wholesome clearing of the air . . . to make labour throw itself heart and soul into the
war effort." It thus facilitated a political "compromise": Labour party legitimization of
sometimes unpalatable mobilization measures, paired with enhanced Labour influence
in guiding mobilization and shaping home front goals.[36]

The long-standing class consciousness of British workers posed a dual threat:
the social and economic threat of a work force inclined to define its interest as
separate from the government's and the focused political threat of the Labour party,
which could vent workers' grievances. This challenge helps explain the British
concern with social service schemes, such as the Beveridge report, that "in a sense,
sanctified the nation's wartime sacrifices" by catering to aspirations for a postwar
society in which a certain "equality of sacrifice" would continue. The "rhetoric of
association between war sacrifice and peace-time reward" bolstered efforts to stave
off class resentments and buck up public morale. Richard M. Titmuss went so far
as to generalize from this British experience that the demands of mass cooperation,
participation, and sacrifice in modern total wars necessitate social policy actions to
reduce inequalities.[37]

The pinched wartime and immediate postwar expansion of the American
welfare state presents an obvious exception to this "Titmuss thesis," an exception
that impels greater attention to differing levels of "sacrifice" and to the contrasting
political contexts of British and American war aims. Yet these differences should
not obscure intriguing parallels in the symbolic and strategic elements of the politics of sacrifice. These parallel strategic considerations emerge, for example, in the
report of a Labour party M.P. and former coal miners' union president on a June
1940 miners' conference. The miners' representatives had pledged themselves to
sacrifice for the war effort. But they demanded a 100 percent excess-profits tax as
an essential counterpart to that commitment to assure that their efforts would not
redound to the mineowners' profit. "In the interests of the nation we have asked
the miners to give everything for the nation, and they will do so," he declared, "but

if it goes out from this House that we are giving the mineowners more profits, that will undermine anything that we are doing."[38]

The close correspondence to American arguments for income limitation is unmistakable. There is one telling distinction, however: Such arguments won in Britain and lost in the United States. Members of Parliament fell over themselves in endorsing the principle of taxing away all excess profits and of subordinating profits to patriotism. Amendments to soften the effects of the 100 percent rate through administrative adjustments and postwar credits were challenged and temporarily withdrawn, for fear of compromising the intended message of universal sacrifice. (The adjustments and credits were reinserted in succeeding laws while leaving the "principle" of a 100 percent rate intact — underlining the tax's symbolic function.) The results shocked some American conservatives. The financial editor of the *New York Sun* found it "difficult for many Americans to understand how Britain can expect anyone to make the tremendous extra productive effort required by war without some stimulus other than the vague one that it is necessary to save the country."[39]

A similar difference in political context is apparent in British advertising. The British and American cases are not strictly comparable, partly because government restrictions and shortages of newsprint forced drastic cutbacks in advertising space in Britain. The government became Britain's largest advertiser, paying for its own ads; filtering government propaganda messages through private business sponsors seemed dubious indeed in the context of a "people's war" ("I shouldn't need to be told what I am fighting for . . . by a group of individuals who by so doing hope to line their pockets," one scandalized Briton observed in explaining why American advertising "would not succeed over here"). Much more than admen in the United States, British advertisers felt besieged. Their ranks depleted by the war's impact on this "most depressed of industries," British advertisers at times found themselves locked out of positions of government influence and reduced to the status of "social 'unfortunates'" for whom the mere mention of their occupation might "rais[e] a frown or arous[e] an exclamation of piteous surprise." Characterized as "vested interests" from a profit-obsessed "bad old world" and faced with pressure from Parliament and government offices to curb wasteful advertising, they looked longingly at the cozy relations with government secured by their prospering American counterparts. Feeling desperate, aggrieved, and unappreciated, British advertisers combined limited efforts to gain goodwill through public service campaigns with a dogged commitment to "carry on" with ads that maintained trade names and protected postwar markets. Yet such efforts betrayed a defensive, even apologetic, mind set. Advertising that exploited associations with the war without serving a clear war information function might well be "open to criticism" as "a public scandal." The trade journal of the British gas industry, for example, conceded that "advertising which has no higher motive than to raise the prestige of the industry it serves certainly cannot justify its existence in time of war," since this would constitute an "unwarranted waste of money, labour, and raw materials, all treasonable offences."[40]

American advertisers would have found such use of the term "treasonable" impolitic and unnecessary. They recognized the delicacy of the task of manipulating images of sacrifice and war contributions. They operated, however, in an environment where the "miracle" of production and promised consumption could take center stage, whereas in Britain the scene was set by special demands for coalitional concessions to Labour party forces and back-to-the-wall displays of solidarity to avert chaos and defeat. Hence, in the United States, the interest of the "free enterprise system" and the "American way of life" increasingly pushed aside demands for "equality of sacrifice" and a "people's war." American advertisers were in a better position to master the politics of sacrifice.

The mystique of home front sacrifice did indeed permeate American life and politics in World War II. But changes in the vocabulary of political obligation did not imply automatic or open-ended commitment to the exercise of civic responsibility. The central role of sacrifice in wartime political discourse might have threatened "free enterprise" values, as the push for "equality of sacrifice" through income limitation seemed to suggest. But in the struggle over the meaning of sacrifice, at least as judged from the foregoing case studies, ascendant political forces were positioned to curb its subversive potential and channel it in more established political directions, so that much of the political topography could survive in recognizable form. Sacrifice proved symbolically malleable. It could justify mobilization programs or policy positions, revitalize deep-rooted political and economic values, mask privileged status or shield it from political challenge, or project war aims that helped reshape the contours of American political culture. The long-term consequences of this manipulation of symbolic content were not negligible; the privatizing of the wartime propaganda apparatus and war aims through the advertising industry, for example, resonated in the postwar consumer culture long after the war's end.

Recognition of the politics of sacrifice penetrates the surface of American home front conflict. Further studies — both comparative and domestic in focus — are needed to trace the shifting and contested meanings of sacrifice over the course of the war and to pinpoint the specific appeals used to solicit citizen cooperation in such intrusive mobilization programs as rationing, the mass income tax, or wage and price freezes. Broader comprehension of the political meanings of home front sacrifice should sharpen the historical definition of the American sense of obligation to community and nation, and of the standards of equity required to activate that civic responsibility. But the course of American economic mobilization, and the allocation of its blessings and burdens, depended less on underlying conceptions of civic responsibility than on continuing negotiation and manipulation. On the home front as on the battlefront, victory came not only to the tactically sophisticated, but to those with power and vital positions that allowed them to determine the arena of conflict. In the home front war, the politics of sacrifice prevailed.

Acknowledgements

Acknowledging that various versions of this article have exacted their own inequalities of sacrifice, I wish to thank Susan Armeny, Walter Arnstein, James Barrett, Rowland Berthoff, Alan Brinkley, Richard Fox, Jacquelyn Dowd Hall, Susan Hartmann, Frederic Jaher, John Jeffries, Carol Skalnik Leff, Cristy Lenski, Nelson Lichtenstein, Robert McColley, and Robert Ubriaco for their shocked objections, lavish assistance, and astute criticisms.

Notes

1   Mark Jonathan Harris, Franklin D. Mitchell, and Steven J. Schecter, comps., *The Homefront: America during World War II* (New York, 1984), 240, 162; David Craig, "Back Home Everybody Was Gung Ho to inspire the GIs," *Life*, 8 (Spring–Summer 1985), 85.

2   Hadley Cantril, ed., *Public Opinion, 1935–1946* (Princeton, 1951), 1178, 112–13, 1003, 822, 729, 1172; Herbert Blumer, "Morale," in *American Society in Wartime*, ed. William F. Ogburn (Chicago, 1943), 229, 226.

3   Bureau of Motion Pictures, Office of War Information, Fact Sheet #13, Appendix to "Government Information Manual for the Motion Picture Industry," 1942, General File of the Chief of Newsreel Liaison, Records of the Office of War Information, RG 208 (National Archives, Suitland, Md.); Fred M. Vinson, "The Question of Inflation," in "An Appeal to Business from the Country's War Leaders," July 14, 1943, "War Advertising Council: Reports and Results of Campaigns, 1942–1944" folder, series 13/2/304, Advertising Council Papers (University of Illinois Archives, Urbana); Hadley Cantril, *The Human Dimension: Experiences in Policy Research* (New Brunswick, 1967), 58; Samuel I. Rosenman, comp., *The Public Papers and Addresses of Franklin D. Roosevelt* (13 vols., New York, 1938–1950), XIII, 42.

4   See, for example, John Morton Blum, *V Was for Victory: Politics and American Culture during World War II* (New York, 1976); David Brinkley, *Washington Goes to War* (New York, 1988); and Richard R. Lingeman, *Don't You Know There's a War On? The American Home Front, 1941–1945* (New York, 1970).

5   Bureau of Intelligence, Office of War Information, "Survey of Intelligence Materials No. 32," July 16, 1942, p. 8. "Office of War Information" folder, President's Secretary's File 173, Franklin D. Roosevelt Papers (Franklin D Roosevelt Library, Hyde Park, N.Y.); "Survey of Intelligence Materials No. 24," May 20, 1942, p. 6, *ibid*.; "FDR's Program Punched Full of Holes," *United Automobile Worker*, July 15, 1942, p. 1; Exec. Order No. 9,250, 3 C.F.R. 1214 (1938–1943).

6   Thomas R. Amlie, *Let's Look at the Record* (Madison, 1950), 56–57.

7   Rosenman, comp., *Public Papers and Addresses of Franklin D. Roosevelt*, VII, 67; Franklin D. Roosevelt, *Complete Presidential Press Conferences of Franklin D. Roosevelt* (25 vols., New York, 1972), XV, 356; James MacGregor Burns, *Roosevelt: The Soldier of Freedom* (New York, 1970), 437, 433–34.

8   "Memorandum of Conference at the White House," July 8, 1940, p. 2, "Excess Profits Tax" folder, Records of Assistant Secretary John L. Sullivan, Records of the Department of the Treasury, RG 56 (National Archives); Ferdinand Kuhn to Henry Morgenthau, Jr., Nov. 4, 1942, "The Secretary: Memos to and from" folder, box 196, *ibid*.; Cantril, ed., *Public Opinion*, (313; Office of War Information, Report No. 27, "War Time Labor Problems," July 7, 1942, table 46, appendix 1, in Office of War Information, "American Attitudes: World War II," vol. IX: "Labor and Industry, 1" (Widener Library, Harvard University, Cambridge, Mass.).

9   *Congressional Record*, 78 Cong., 1 sess., March 12, 1943, p. 1955; John Sullivan to Morgenthau, July 30, 1941, "Sullivan, Daily Record July 1, 1941-Aug. 30, 1941" folder, box 200, Records of Assistant Secretary Sullivan.

10   Nelson Lichtenstein, *Labor's War at Home: The CIO in World War II* (New York, 1982), 99; "Equality of Sacrifice Demanded by UAW-CIO." *United Automobile Worker*, April 15, 1942, p. 1.

11   Morgenthau Diaries, June 2, 1942, book 535, p. 131, Henry A. Morgenthau, Jr., Papers (Franklin D. Roosevelt Library); Morgenthau Diaries, April 10, 1942, book 515, p. 89, *ibid*.

12   The logic of comparative sacrifice is ably developed and applied in Paul Addison, *The Road to 1945: British Politics and the Second World War* (London. 1977), 131; and Mary Heaton Vorse, "And the Workers Say . . . ," *Public Opinion Quarterly*, 7 (Fall 1943), 443–45. W. G. Runciman, *Relative Deprivation and Social Justice: A Study of Attitudes to Social Inequality in Twentieth-Century England* (Berkeley, 1966), 10, 24; John Kenneth Galbraith, *A Theory of Price Control* (Cambridge, Mass., 1952), 44.

13   "Meeting with the Business Advisory Council," May 23, 1940, p. 24, "Subject File: Hopkins, Harry L." folder, President's Secretary's File 152, Roosevelt Papers; Roosevelt, *Complete Presidential Press Conferences of Franklin D. Roosevelt*, XV, 370; Morgenthau to Franklin D. Roosevelt, July 14, 1941. "Taxes" folder, President's Secretary's File 186, Roosevelt Papers.

14   Special Services Division, Bureau of Intelligence, Office of War Information, Special Services Report No. 21 (revised), "Attitudes Obstructing the War Effort," Sept. 1, 1942, box 1843, entry 41, Records of the Office of Government Reports, RG 44 (National Archives, Suitland, Md.); Special Services Division, Bureau of Intelligence, Office of War Information, "Inflation Control Program" July 31, 1942, "Sp. Serv. Rep. No. 22" folder, box 1843, entry 41, *ibid.*; Special Services Division, Bureau of Intelligence, Office of War Information, Special Services Report No. 22, "How Leaders of Organized Groups React to President's Anti-Inflation Program," Aug. 11, 1942, *ibid.*; Claude Wickard et al., "Memorandum for the President Urging an Anti-Inflation Program," April 18, 1942, p. 5, Official File 327, Roosevelt Papers. William Davis's comments can be found in Transcript of the Executive Session of National War Labor Board, Feb. 6. 1942, pp. 1–2, Records of National War Labor Board, RG 202 (National Archives).

15   George Addes, in United Automobile, Aircraft, and Agricultural Implement Workers of America, *Minutes of Proceedings of War Emergency Conference* (Detroit, 1942), 13; "The Fortune Survey," *Fortune*, 27 (Feb. 1943), 9; Special Services Division, Bureau of Intelligence, Office of War Information, Report No. 20, "Effect of Little Steel Case on Labor Morale," box 1843, entry 41, Records of the Office of Government Reports.

16   Harold D. Smith, "A Call for Action," *Vital Speeches*, Aug. 1, 1942, p. 639; Richard Polenberg, *War and Society: The United States, 1941–1945* (Philadelphia, 1972), 24; Rosenman, comp., *Public Papers and Addresses of Franklin D. Roosevelt*, XI, 232; James Patton to Roosevelt, Sept. 3, 1942, "Price Fixing Jan.-May 1942" folder, box 2, Official File 327, Roosevelt Papers.

17   R. J. Thomas to Roosevelt, April 9, 1942, in United Automobile, Aircraft, and Agricultural Implement Workers of America, *Minutes of Proceedings of War Emergency Conference*, 61; Walter Reuther in United Automobile, Aircraft, and Agricultural Implement Workers of America, *Proceedings of the Seventh Convention* (Chicago. 1942), 93; "Labor Highlights," *American Federationist*, 49 (July 1942), inside cover; *United Automobile Worker*, Oct. 15, 1942, p. 5.

18   "In the Wind," *Nation*, Oct. 31, 1942, p. 451; *Wall Street Journal*, Nov. 11, 1942, pp. 1, 7; *ibid.*, Nov. 14, 1942, p. i; *ibid.*, Nov. 16, 1942. p. 8; *ibid.*, Nov. 21, 1942, p. 1; "Upper Crust Will Carry On Despite $25,000 Limit on Income," *United Automobile Worker*, May 15, 1942, p. 2; "Weep for the New Poor," *Labor*, Nov. 24,1942, p. 4.

19   "Farmers Union Opens Contest to Help $25,000-Year Men," *United Automobile Worker*, Oct. 1, 1942, p. 3.

20   John W. Jeffries, *Testing the Roosevelt Coalition: Connecticut Society and Politics in the Era of World War II* (Knoxville, 1979), 138–39.

21   Wm. Wrigley Jr. Company, "The First Line," episode no. 191, Nov. 1, 1945, transcript, 5–6, "Radio — General, 1945" folder, box 5, series 13/2/305, Advertising Council Papers.

22   "The Impact of Defense on Advertising," *Advertising & Selling*, 34 (Dec. 1941), 24; American Newspaper Publishers Association, *Advertising Bulletin No. 13* (New York. 1941), 45–52, "Public Rel. Publications" folder, box 111, series 100MM, National Association of Manufacturers Papers (Eleutherian Mills Historical Library, Wilmington, Del.); "No Anti-Ad Plot," *Editor & Publisher*, May 30, 1942, p. 18; Paul West, memo. Aug. 28, 1941, quoted in Harold B. Thomas, "The Background and Beginning of the Advertising Council," April 1952, p. 3, "The Background and Beginning of the Advertising Council" folder, series 13/2/304, Advertising Council Papers. On this advertising crisis and Madison Avenue's sometimes hysterical response, see Frank W. Fox, *Madison Avenue Goes to War: The Strange Military Career of American Advertising, 1941–1945* (Provo, 1975), 17–41.

23   "Foes of Advertising Are Ganging Up," *Printer's Ink*, Oct. 3, 1941, p. 9; "Impact of Defense on Advertising," 26; Paul West, memo, Aug. 28, 1941, in Thomas, "Background and Beginning of the Advertising Council," 4; Maurice Mandell, "A History of the Advertising Council" (Doctor of Commercial Science dissertation, Indiana University, 1953), 47; J. A. R. Pimlott, "Public Service Advertising: The Advertising Council," *Public Opinion Quarterly*, 12 (Summer 1948), 210; Theodore S. Repplier, "Advertising and 'The Forces of Righteousness,'" in *The Promise of Advertising*, ed. C. H. Sandage (Homewood, 1961), 59; Leon Henderson, "Advertising's Crisis Is Everybody's Crisis," *Advertising & Selling*, 34 (Dec. 1941), 100; James Webb Young, *Pills for the Angels* (Coapa, 1952), in "James Webb Young Christmas Books" folder, J. Walter Thompson Company Archives (Manuscript Department, Duke University Library, Durham, N.C.).

24   Thomas, "Background and Beginning of the Advertising Council," 10, 13–14; "Should Advertising Defend Itself — or the U.S.?" *Advertising & Selling*, 34 (Dec. 1941), 36.

25   "Fred Smith Tells How Ads Routed Washington Foe," *Editor & Publisher*, June 2, 1945, p. 34; "The Impact of War on Advertising," *Advertising & Selling*, 35 (May 1942), 20; W. J. Weir, "Opportunity!" *Printer's Ink*, April 10, 1942, p. 14; "Minutes of Meeting of Advertising Council," Feb. 5, 1942, p. 4, "Minutes, Jan.–Feb. 1942" folder, box 1, series 13/2/201, Advertising Council Papers.

26   Robert Griffith, "The Selling of America: The Advertising Council and American Politics, 1942–1960," *Business History Review*, 57 (Autumn 1983), 411–12; [War Advertising Council], *News*, Sept. 4. 1945, in "War Advertising Council — News Releases, 1945" folder, box 6, series 13/2/305, Advertising Council Papers.

27   Theodore S. Repplier to Frank Braucher, Nov. 16. 1945, "War Advertising Council — Publicity, 1945" folder, box 6, series 13/2/305, Advertising Council Papers; R. M. Dobie, "How Agencies Influence Clients to continue Ads," *Editor & Publisher*, March 7, 1942. p. 9; Advertisement for *Long Island Daily Press* et al., "Who Is Going to Buy Your Refrigerator after This War Is Over?" *Sales Management*, Nov. 10, 1943, p. 70; "The Word Is Mightier than the Sword," 1944, "Institutional-Production" folder, box 4, series 13/2/305, Advertising Council Papers.

28   John C. Sterling, "What Happens When the Shooting Stops," Nov. 18, 1943, p. 5, Association of National Advertisers file, box 1, series 13/2/305, Advertising Council Papers; Theodore S. Repplier, "Advertising Dons Long Pants," *Public Opinion Quarterly*, 9 (Fall 1945), 276; Pimlott, "Public Service Advertising," 213.

29   U.S. Department of Commerce, *Advertising and Its Role in War and Peace* (Washington, 1943), 3, 5, 8; Stanley E. Cohen, "Review of Ad Status under War Conditions," *Advertising Age*, Sept. 4, 1950, p. 21.

30 Estimates of the increase vary, mainly in their appraisals of national radio advertising. Compare U.S. Department of Commerce, Bureau of the Census, *Historical Statistics of the United States* (Washington, 1975), 856, and "Total Advertising Volume Estimate —1867 through 1953 — with Basis of Estimates," *Printers Ink*, Oct. 29, 1954, pt. 2, pp. 58–59, to the record-setting wartime advertising figures in "U.S. Ad Volume Gains 700% in Past 30 Years," *Advertising Age*, April 16, 1945, p. 2, and Howard Henderson to W. L. Rubin, May 25, 1945, "Correspondence 1940, 1942–46" folder, box 9, General Reference: Inactive Account Files, J. Walter Thompson Company Archives. For advertisers' wartime assessment of government policy, see "Advertising As Government Sees It; An Interpretation," *Printer's Ink*, Oct. 9, 1942, pp. 13, 30; "Henderson on Advertising," *ibid.*, Sept. 11, 1942, p. 78; and James D. Scott, "Advertising When Consumers Cannot Buy," *Harvard Business Review*, 21 (Winter 1943), 207–29. "Fred Smith Tells How Ads Routed Washington Foe," 34; Howell John Harris, *The Right to Manage: Industrial Relations Policies of American Business in the 1940s* (Madison, 1982), 116–17; Griffith, "Selling of America," 391.

31 A. E. Winger to Harold Thomas, Aug. 1944, "Minutes July-Aug. 1944" folder, box 1, series 13/2/201, Advertising Council Papers; Opinion Research Corporation, "A Nation at War Looks at Auto Conversion," Feb. 1942, p. 2, box 100, series 100JJ, National Association of Manufacturers Papers; Blum, *V Was for Victory*, 8, 19–21; Fox, *Madison Avenue Goes to War*. But see also the more encompassing discussion of the limited prospects for American liberal reform in John W. Jeffries, "Franklin D. Roosevelt and the 'America of Tomorrow,'" in *Power and Responsibility: Case Studies in American Leadership*, ed. David M. Kennedy and Michael E. Parrish (New York, 1986), 29–66.

32 Gary Gerstle, *Working-Class Americanism: The Politics of Labor in a Textile City, 1914–1960* (New York 1989), 301.

33 Paul Fussell, *Wartime: Understanding and Behavior in the Second World War* (New York, 1989), 200–209; Alfred F. Havighurst, *Britain in Transition: The Twentieth Century* (Chicago, 1979), 365. For Winston Churchill's speech, see U.K., *Parliamentary Debates* (Commons), 5th ser., vol. 360 (1940), col. 1502; Blum, *V Was for Victory*, 45; David Koval, "The Proximity of the Enemy: American and British Propaganda Posters during World War II," May 1988 (in Mark H. Leff's possession).

34 Addison, *Road to 1945*, 17–18.

35 Ian McLaine, *Ministry of Morale: Home Front Morale and the Ministry of Information in World War II* (London, 1979), 176–78; R. S. Sayers, *Financial Policy, 1939–45* (London, 1956), 85–86; Rachel Maines, "Wartime Allocation of Textile and Apparel Resources: Emergency Policy in the Twentieth Century," *Public Historian*, 7 (Winter 1985), 36–37; U.K., *Parliamentary Debates* (Commons), 5th ser., vol. 352 (1939), cols. 1110–12; *ibid.*, vol. 355 (1939), col. 117; *ibid.*, vol. 367 (1940), col. 36.

36 Keith Middlemas, *Power, Competition, and the State: Britain in Search of Balance, 1940–61* (London, 1986), 20–21; Alan Bullock, *The Life and Times of Ernest Bevin* (3 vols., London, 1960–1983), II, 20–23; *London Times*, May 23, 1940, p. 7; "Wages and the Workers," *Economist*, June 15, 1940, p. 1035; *London Observer*, June 2, 1940, p. 6. On the Labour party's strategic position as a minority coalition partner, see Edwin Amenta and Theda Skocpol, "Redefining the New Deal: World War II and the Development of Social Provision in the United States," in *The Politics of Social Policy in the United States*, ed. Margaret Weir, Ann Shola Orloff, and Theda Skocpol (Princeton, 1988), 113–19.

37 McLaine, *Ministry of Morale*, 182; J. M. Lee, *The Churchill Coalition, 1940–1945* (Hamden, 1980), 118–19; Richard M. Titmuss, *Essays on "the Welfare State"* (London, 1963), 83–86.

38   William De Maria, "Combat and Concern: The Warfare-Welfare Nexus," *War & Society*, 7 (May 1989), 75–77, 79; David Brody, "The New Deal and World War II," in *The New Deal*, ed. John Braeman, Robert H. Bremner, and David Brody (2 vols., Columbus, 1975), I, 268–69; Amenta and Skocpol, "Redefining the New Deal," 99–100; U. K., *Parliamentary Debates* (Commons), 5th ser., vol. 362 (1940), cols. 179–81.

39   U.K., *Parliamentary Debates* (Commons), 5th ser., vol 362 (1940), cols. 197, 210–11. For the enactment in 1941 of a 20% postwar refund of the excess-profits tax, see Sayers, *Financial Policy*, 86–90. I. F. Stone, *Business As Usual: The First Year of Defense* (New York, 1941), 162.

40   James Playsted Wood, *The Story of Advertising* (New York, 1958), 445; Patrick Rivers, "Comparison of U. S. with British Advertising," *Advertiser's Weekly*, Jan. 25, 1945, p. 113; "Goebbels Knows Why Ad. Men Do Not Control Our Propaganda," *ibid.*, July 10, 1941, p. 19; "Advertising Is 'Insult to the National Prestige,' Says Former P.R.O.," *ibid.*, Aug. 27, 1942, p. 174; "Signs of the New Advertising," *ibid.*, Oct. 8, 1942, p. iii; "Govt. Department's, Threat to Reminder Advertising Increasing," *ibid.*, Sept. 18, 1941, p. 217; "U.S. Government Boosts Advertising," *ibid.*, Nov. 18, 1943, p. 150; Davis M. DeBard, "Utility Advertising in War Time," *Edison Electric Institute Bulletin*, 10 (July 1942), 269; U.K., *Parliamentary Debates* (Commons), 5th ser., vol. 377 (1942), col. 1047; "War-Time Publicity," *Gas World*, Nov. 28, 1942, p. 589.

Chapter 15

Marilyn Lake

FEMALE DESIRES
The meaning of World War II

'**I EXPRESSED A DESIRE**', confided a twenty year old teachers' college student to her diary in 1942, 'to silly Jack P. for a Yank boyfriend (Melb. & in fact all Austr. is swarming with them — since Xmas — & I felt I'd missed life, not having even met one — Else and I spoke to some one night in the dark of Swanston St. but didn't pick them up, as most girls do now'. A few weeks later she was pleased to record her own war victory: 'Anyway, I can tell my Grand-children at least that during those momentous days when Austr. was rapidly accumulating thousands upon thousands of Yanks, when Melb. went bad, & every girl discussed her "pick-ups" I too had a little experience'.[1] The meaning of Australian women's experience during and immediately following World War II has been the subject of much historical writing, but I wish to suggest that the approach adopted by historians so far, by ignoring female subjectivity, has obscured significant aspects of women's experience. Most importantly, historians of World War II have generally failed to grasp the changing structure of femininity itself, the interplay of cultural forms and self-definition, and the way that changes in discourse were secured by the specificity of wartime conditions.

In studying the effects of war on the position of women in Australian society, historians have tended to measure the impact in terms of women's entry into the world of paid work. Within this framework, the experiences of women on the Australian home front during World War II, and after, are usually represented as opportunities cruelly cancelled, doors closed, hopes and dreams dashed — one step forwards, two steps backwards. 'The expectations the war had nurtured', observed Penelope Johnson in her study of the equal pay campaign, 'had not been realised'.[2]

In her path-breaking exploration of gender ideology in the *Australian Women's Weekly* Andree Wright observed in 1973:

Although some women welcomed the post-war chance to return to the home, other women wished to consolidate on their gains, and some might have been persuaded to do so had a magazine such as the *Weekly* taken the lead. But after the war the magazine refocussed its attention on the traditional sphere of feminine interests, always following old trends, rather than innovating new ones.[3]

In her suggestion of a dichotomy between the old and the new, traditional femininity and modern gains, Wright expressed what would become a common understanding of women's position. Thus most women's experience of the postwar years is conceptualised as a retreat, a surrender, a return to old ways, familiar patterns, traditional roles. There is often an implied criticism of women's failure to consolidate their 'gains'. Instead, women went home. 'As the war was ending', wrote Anne Summers, 'old ideas about what was appropriate for women began to be reasserted'.[4] Or as Edna Ryan and Anne Conlon put it: 'After the war . . . many women surrendered their wartime jobs and returned to a domestic role'.[5] And in her study of plans for post-war housing Carolyn Allport reached the same conclusion: the end of the war saw 'the reassertion of the traditional role of women as mothers, housekeepers and child-minders'.[6]

The problem with these accounts of the reassertion of the 'traditional role' is that they fail to see the historically changing structure of femininity itself. I wish to argue that the equation of the 'feminine' with the 'traditional' in these accounts is highly misleading, in that it obscures the emergence, in the 1930s, of a new understanding of femininity, one which revolved around sexuality, sexual attractiveness and youthfulness. Furthermore, I would suggest that this reconceptualisation of femininity was reinforced by women's experience of World War II.[7]

Femininity (and masculinity) are, as many feminist historians and theorists have pointed out, historical constructions, the products of diverse practices across a variety of sites or social domains — the workplace, the legislature, the schoolroom, the media. There is no one discrete 'sex role' dispensed by a master dramaturge, but rather competing, often conflicting, definitions of femininity. The task of the historian of women is, then, two-fold: first, to identify the variety of discourses in force at any one time and second, to explain why particular groups of women, in particular historical circumstances, were more likely to respond to some representations of their identity and experience than others. I shall present my argument in four stages — first, a brief summary of the meaning of women's new work experiences during World War II; second, an exploration of the transformation of femininity in the 1930s and 1940s; third, a consideration of how the conduct of the war itself sexualised the Australian female population and finally, suggest how different groups of women understood their lives, and negotiated their experiences in terms of these developments. It is often argued that the main differentiation of women in these processes was class; I wish to point to the significance of age.

Australia's participation in World War II led to a widescale mobilisation of 'manpower', which meant concerted efforts to woo, and then conscript, women into industrial labour. Faced with conflicting arguments from employers and trade unions about the desirable level of the wages of women in 'men's jobs', the Curtin Labour government established the Women's Employment Board (WEB) in 1942 to regulate the wages and conditions of those women doing men's work, for the 'duration' only. Numerous women benefited from the new guidelines, often receiving double the income of women who remained, stuck, in traditional female jobs, for example, in the textile and clothing industry. With higher wages, doing men's work and with male relatives away fighting, a number of women enjoyed a new sense of independence, self-reliance and autonomy. Clarice McNamara writing in the *Labor Digest* in 1945 likened these women to 'the lion that tasted blood'.[8]

In doing men's jobs, women also demystified them and the operation of the wartime economy generated refreshing acknowledgment of female capability. As Judge Foster of WEB exclaimed:

> To all of us it was an amazing revelation to see women who were yesterday working in beauty salons or who had not previously worked outside their own homes or who had come from the counters of retail stores or a dozen other industries rendered superfluous by war, who now stood behind mighty machines operating them with a skill and mastery that was little short of marvellous![9]

But rather than resulting in a blurring of gender distinctions, these transgressions prompted strenuous reaffirmations of sexual difference: 'When doing our job on munitions we don't neglect our appearance — but still keep our feminine charm by always having our Escapade lipstick with us'.[10] And in the process, femininity itself was being redefined as a sexual condition. Thus, I would argue, women were not so much pressured to return to old, traditional 'roles', as historians have usually asserted: rather they were invited to step into an alluring, exciting future. In place of the adventure of economic independence, women were offered the adventure of sexual romance.

The meaning of sexual difference and thus of femininity had been undergoing significant transformations during the decades preceding the outbreak of World War II. One new, modern, pervasive and invasive cultural form that played a prominent part in the construction of femininity in these years was advertising. Another was, of course, the cinema. The secret of the success of advertising, and the accompanying rise in consumerism, was its promise to secure sexual fulfilment and identity. Advertising simultaneously incited sexual desire and promised its gratification. To men it promised potency or power; to women sexual attractiveness or desirability. The advertising message was that femininity and masculinity could be secured through the purchase of commodities.

A number of historians have alluded briefly to the changing structure of femininity in the middle years of twentieth-century Australia. Jill Matthews in *Good and Mad Women* has pointed to a shift away from an understanding of femininity shaped by a populationist ideology, entailing a conception of woman as 'mother of the race', towards a femininity linked to the culture of 'permissive consumerism' in the 1950s.[11] Her later work on the British physical culture movement has explored the modernising of the female body in the interwar years. Leslie Johnson in a study of 'The Teenage Girl' has also identified a change: by the mid 1950s 'femininity became a question of glamour and charm'.[12] Rosemary Pringle in her study of secretaries has linked the replacement of the refined office wife by the 'sexy secretary' as the ideal secretary type in the 1950s to the changing structure of femininity.[13] A study of magazine advertisements between 1920 and 1950 enables us to identify more closely the ingredients of that charm and glamour, so central to 1940s and 1950s femininity, and to locate these discursive changes in the decades preceding the 1950s.

By the 1940s femininity was increasingly defined in terms of (hetero)sexual attractiveness. One important dynamic in this process was the work of sexologists such as Sigmund Freud, Havelock Ellis, Marie Stopes and Norman Haire. While much of their writing seemed to have the effect of locking women ever more tightly into sexual relationships with men, of stigmatising the reluctant as 'frigid', as Sheila Jeffreys has suggested,[14] it also opened up a discursive space in which, as Ann Curthoys has argued with regard to Marion Piddington, women could argue for their own sexual rights, for their rights to sexual pleasure.[15] This 'sexualisation of women', then, was profoundly ambiguous in its implications for women. In a heterosexual context, 'sexual freedom' might simply give new form and lend greater intensity to women's dependence on men. And yet it was a necessary advance. As Jill Matthews has observed of the physical culture movement:

> Here was a new and in some ways shocking attitude, which emphasised the role of wife and sexual partner, not mother, as the pinnacle of female ambition. Moreover it was an attitude that valued youth, and insisted upon woman's responsibility for her own life to the point of self-trans-formation and renewal if not self-creation. The argument that a woman must be fit and beautiful both for herself and in order to catch and keep a husband, as well as or instead of to raise healthy children. presented itself as the modern way . . .[16]

It was advertising's role to identify for women the means of their modern self-creation.

The task of advertisements, as Judith Williamson has pointed out, is to persuade the consumer of the differences between products that are essentially alike.[17] Advertisements directed at women between 1920 and 1950 argued that their product could more effectively secure 'feminine charm'. But as the years passed, the components of that charm were transformed. Woman's special charm, observed Ada Holman in *Everylady's Journal* in 1916 was 'grace and refinement'.[18] Advertisers agreed. In 1920 the promoters of 'Odo-ro-no' deodorant declared 'the loveliest charm a woman can have is daintiness'.[19] But by the late 1930s the prize for female consumers was 'sex-appeal'.[20] Femininity as an attribute of class distinction (emphasising white hands, soft skin, refinement, daintiness and other ladylike qualities) was succeeded by a sexualised femininity, democratically available (indeed, like voting in Australia, compulsory) for all women. These changes were symbolised in the emergence of a new social ritual in these years: the beauty contest. Opposing versions of femininity (those revolving around 'the mother of the race', for example,) still jostled for attention, of course, but increasingly all femininities had to accommodate themselves to the modern emphasis on sexual allure. 'Wives should always be lovers too'. The capitulation to the new imperative is evident in the words of popular songs, but also in the words of women themselves as they struggled to

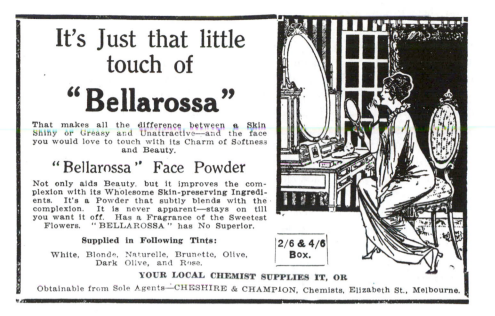

Figure 15.1 In the 1920s women sought confirmation of their 'loveliness' through the looking glass (*Everylady's Journal*, 6 December 1920). *Reproduced by permission of State Library of Victoria.*

negotiate competing demands. 'The husband of today wishes his wife to be a mother and a sweetheart and he is in his rights', commented a woman in the 1940s.[21] A husband 'wishes to come home to a woman who is smart in appearance . . . not a back number', said another.[22]

In the visual representation of modern, up-to-date femininity in the advertisements of the interwar years the impact of Hollywood is clear as the image of woman surveying herself in a mirror is replaced by woman scrutinised by men. The male gaze is made explicit within the frame with the men positioned as subjects offering their judgments of women in speech balloons. There is, of course, continuity as well as change in these representations. Throughout the period women are constituted as objects to be looked at, as sights. It is clear, as Margaret Betterton has argued, that the visual has long been central to definitions of feminity.[23] As the woman in the advertisement for Schumann's Salts says, 'I know how essential it is to have an appearance'.[24] Thus all personal products in these decades promise an outcome of beauty, relieving women of 'unsightly' blotches, freckles, flesh, roughness of skin, mousy hair or perspiration stains. Under this new regime the most unlikely products were found to have aesthetic dimensions, including tablets for period pain: Myzone tablets were called 'Beauty Tablets'. Betty Bright, modern business girl, kept her job with Myzone tablets, as her beauty was unspoiled by menstrual cramps.[25] Similarly, Siltex Sanitary Napkins were promoted as 'form-fitting, never betraying their presence even when worn with the closest clinging frocks and the lightest lingerie'.[26]

But the changes in the structure of femininity are perhaps more significant. By the 1930s it was essential not just to have an appearance, but to have a youthful

appearance. Femininity was the 'charm of youth'. It is striking, given later developments and assumptions, that the earliest ads for face creams and similar products
omitted considerations of age. Among the first to insist that beauty was youthful
was Helena Rubinstein in promotions for her Valaze range of products: 'Pretty
Women Die Twice. The rose dies in its fading, as well as its fall'.[27] In 1923
'Palmolive' was warning women to keep that 'schoolgirl complexion'.[28] By the
1930s, the promoters of Le Charme blackhead cream (for the removal of 'unsightly'
'disfigurements') could announce: 'Remember that Youthfulness is a Social
Necessity. Not a Luxury'.[29] And it was not sufficient to be young, one had to look
young. For the woman/object appearances were all important, as an ad for
Schumann's Salts in 1933 made clear:

> 'How old Isobel looks'. Yes, she had heard that stinging remark and the
> bitter truth was all she could bear. She was young — as young as her
> friends, yet time and again, people whispered things that hurt her
> terribly. At last some kind person told her about P.B.S. Poisoned Blood
> Stream.[30]

One of the most striking transformations in the advertisements over twenty
years is the change in visual codes from the woman gazing into mirrors of all shapes
and sizes to the woman explicitly scrutinised by men. In the 1920s, the text reinforced the significance of the mirror: 'Do you look your best? Are you worried
about your appearance? When you look in the mirror do you find your hair dull,
brittle . . .?'[31] The mirror renders woman an object of vision to herself. Men's entry
into the frame signifies an important shift as femininity is explicitly defined in terms
of heterosexual desirability. Women are incited to be attractive, alluring, exciting
— objects to men's positioning as subjects. Men look at women in the images and
speak to and about them; women either look into men's eyes (in surrender) or avert
their gaze. By the late 1930s women's bodies are being scrutinised, piece by piece,
and they are increasingly rendered as palpable and physical, rather than merely
aesthetic, objects: they become 'caressable', 'kissable' or offensively odorous. Their
bodies are invested with the prized new quality of 'sex-appeal', guaranteed to the
purchasers of the right product. The promoters of Sta-Blond Shampoo believed
this quality could be measured by scientists: 'Recent scientific tests show that light
fair-haired girls have 47 per cent more sex-appeal than the dark "Fairs"'.[32]
Sexual relations transgress the usual spatial barriers maintained by individuals. They
enable a close-up view: so skin needed to be 'flawless'; teeth 'dazzlingly white'.
But the proximity of bodies could offend senses other than sight. It was no longer
sufficient for women to look right; they had to please men's nostrils. An absence
of smell had to be purchased, as the promoters of Odo-Ro-No made clear in their
story of Marion:

> 'Just the girl that I've been waiting for!' men thought when they first
> saw Marion. They'd cluster around for introductions but they'd rarely
> dance more than one dance. For though Marion carefully bathed and
> dressed, she neglected the simple precaution — and trusted her bath
> alone to keep her safe from underarm odour. Fatal Error![33]

By the late 1930s, representations of femininity — the new discourses on femininity — were increasingly an incitement to sexual pleasure, which in turn was constructed as excitement, adventure and danger: 'Fair Girls Ought to be Doubly Careful'; 'Every Fair Girl Should Try Everything Once'.[34] Femininity was beginning to cast off its passivity as the logic of the incitement to pleasure took its course. Women take to the dance floor or embrace in passionate kisses. The bodies move. Lipstick brands proliferated in the 1930s and 1940s, promising lips that were 'seductive' and 'provokingly appealing'. A tension becomes apparent between women's positioning as sexual objects and their constitution as sexual subjects. The image of an active engagement in sexual pleasure (the strenuous kiss) is qualified by the caption that advises 'romance comes to the mouth that's kissable'. But the incitement to action becomes more insistent. Savage lipsticks offered 'new, more stirring lip colour . . . that stirs excitement for lips that wear it . . . all evening . . . until . . .!' Tattoo lipsticks had five South Sea Shades 'each aglow with reckless, red adventure'.[35] The background images of palm trees beckon women to try exotic, foreign pleasures.

That thousands of Australian women did try foreign pleasures in the 1940s in the form of sexual relationships with American servicemen was well recognised. Women's seemingly unrestrained sexual activity provoked responses as diverse as feminist campaigns, Vice Squad raids, Christian warnings, Albert Tucker's censorious series of paintings 'Images of Modern Evil', physical violence between Australian and American servicemen and the well-known 'Australian' joke that 'the trouble with the Yanks is that they are overpaid, oversexed and over here'.[36]

War, it is clear, is a gendering activity.[37] War restructures gender relations in ways that must be taken account of after the war. More specifically, I would argue that the stationing of foreign troops in a country has the effect of sexualising the local female population. Just as Australian servicemen rendered Egyptian, French and English women during World War I the objects of their desire, so too did the Americans based in Australian cities during World War II. Over one million American servicemen passed through Australia in those years, most arriving in 1942. And war conditions, as concerned contemporaries told each other, undermined traditional restraints and disciplines. Faced with an uncertain future, people lived for the day, seizing pleasure when and where they might find it. Thus the discursive construction of femininity as sexual, the incitement to pleasure and adventure, took place in circumstances increasingly conducive to sexual activity.

There is much evidence of young women's avid pursuit of sexual pleasure during wartime, in particular of their attraction to American servicemen. Though cautioned to 'discount the moonlight and the music and the war's urgency and the uniform', many young women had been prepared by Hollywood to see romantic heroes in the American visitors. 'The girls out here are just crazy about Hollywood', reported one American soldier.[38] Their constitution as sex objects — 'superbly tailored beige-pinks, olive-drabs and light khakis'— encouraged women to position themselves as subjects in the sexual drama.[39] The Americans were generous with gifts and compliments, but perhaps more important, many seemed to really enjoy the company of women. 'Americans have the gift of making the girls they escort feel like the finest ladies in the land' testified an Australian woman.[40] Australian women commented with surprise about these men who felt at ease with women, even liked women.

Witnesses to the wartime turmoil were alarmed and perplexed by women's and girls' active pursuit of sexual pleasure, by the prospect of girls, of all social classes, 'out of control'. Dr Cooper Booth, Director of Social Hygiene in Sydney, reporting the increase in venereal disease in young women between the ages of sixteen and twenty, told a meeting of the Housewives' Association: 'Don't get the idea that these girls are of one class only. Many of them come from the best homes and have a good education . . . The girls simply have a desire for sexual life'.[41] On another occasion, Dr Booth commended Newcastle on its superior moral standards: 'Newcastle to me seems a much saner place than Sydney. I didn't see anything like the number of corn-silk, peroxide-haired girls that I do in Sydney'.[42] Was Sta-Blond shampoo unobtainable, one wonders, in Newcastle?

The sexually active woman, neither prostitute nor married woman, defied old categories and could not easily be accommodated in prevailing discourses. A new name was coined: the 'amateur'. The army magazine *Salt* joined other authorities in warning soldiers against her:

> These amateurs represent all classes of the community, cannot gener-
> ally be classed as 'bad', and their only common traits are sex ignorance
> and promiscuity. Many of them genuinely like the man himself, as well
> as the act . . .[43]

In Sydney, it was reported that health and social workers estimated there were 7000 'amateurs' ('adventurous types of girls who seek no cash reward') in the metro-politan area.[44] Because women were deemed to be the source of venereal disease, the 'khaki-mad dabbler in sex', that is the sexually active woman, was declared by army authorities to be Public Enemy No. 1.[45] Col. Geoff Calway of the United States Army observed that girls in Melbourne were 'developed' at fifteen years and waited on street corners to catch Americans: 'They don't seem reluctant to play. Naturally a soldier on leave says to himself "Why shouldn't I. What have I got to lose."'[46]

Though impelled to categorise and name these women as a special type of womanhood — the 'amateur' — authorities were forced to recognise the diversity of women involved. On the one hand, there was abundant evidence of teenage 'underage' activity; on the other 'young married women whose husbands are away' were the major culprits.[47] On the one hand, they were 'vagrants' with no regular employment; on the other they were 'Jeckell and Hydes', shop and office workers by day and sexual adventurers by night.[48] Dr Lucy Gullett, addressing the United Associations of Women, preferred to cast men as the active (guilty) subjects, but allowed that 'many young girls' found it difficult to resist appeals from soldiers and resistance was further weakened by the amount of drink which was available.[49]

Official responses to the 'sexual epidemic' seemed as much motivated by a desire to punish women for their sexual assertiveness, their 'immorality', as by a desire to curb the spread of venereal disease.[50] Thus hundreds of women in Sydney found in the company of American soldiers and sailors were arrested and gaoled for vagrancy. But often the Vice Squad had to admit many of the women picked up in raids were not in fact vagrants, but women in employment.[51] The minority found on examination to have venereal disease were gaoled for treatment. The new

National Security Regulations of 1942 gave police unlimited powers to arrest suspected carriers of venereal disease, although, as a Federal Health department officer admitted, the new regulations impinged on women and girls more than men. When the National Health and Medical Research Council drew up recommendations to curb the spread of venereal disease it targeted young women:

> The Council urges that serious consideration be given by the appropriate authorities to severe restriction on the sale of alcohol for consumption by women, especially young girls and stricter control by public authorities of laxity of conduct, especially by young women in public places.[52]

Such were the observations of witnesses. An investigation of women's diaries and letters of this period provides some evidence of the terms in which young women themselves made sense of their experiences, of the ways they shaped their actions in terms of the available discourses. As Rosalind Coward has noted women (and men) must form their identities within available discourses, or, with difficulty, against them.[53] In women's diaries and letters we glimpse the ways in which the language of love and romance resonates in the minds of the targets of that discourse. One woman who committed her aspirations and anxieties to paper in 1942 was Patricia Jones, a twenty year old teachers' college student. Her diary self-consciously marks her pleasure at being young, recording the '1st flutterings of Youth'. She is grateful for the 'opportunities to be young' afforded her by student life (living away from home and mixing with both sexes), dreading 'the blind complacency of middle age' which must follow, and worse, 'cold old age'. She hopes that her life, as told in her diary, will constitute a 'nice romantic story' and all her energies seem to be directed to that end. She records her romantic outings (skating, the pictures, the Palais, the beach), her '1st real kiss' and 'falling in love'. She has a succession of boyfriends: one 'got to the stage of even saying "The Words"'. But she 'felt reckless', was looking for 'novelty' especially in the form of a 'Yank boyfriend', all the while competing with 'rivals', including 'attractive Ivy Baker' and Audrey Lang, 'an attractive little piece with all the necessary backchat'.[54]

Kissing is the significant sexual activity here — 'Stan got romantic and kissed me once'; 'Jack finally kissed me. I did enjoy it! More than Doug's technique — more experience I suppose'; 'I didn't quite understand what he meant by that kiss'. In July 1943, in the 'Letterettes' column of the *Daily Telegraph*, a debate erupted on the subject of the comparative talents of 'men' and 'girls' as 'kissers'. One correspondent opined that Australian girls were 'poor kissers', to which another countered that the problem was that they had too much practice and had become careless.[55] In this exchange the women's engagement was usually constructed in active terms (women were 'kissers') and it may be that, as Rosalind Coward suggests, for women kissing represents the 'consummation of sexual attraction and desire' and further, that 'kissing is a voracious activity, an act of mutual penetration'.[56] Recognising women's investment in kissing, some men knew how to frustrate women's desires. 'Marg. makes some excuse for me to accompany her to a store', wrote an American serviceman in his diary, 'I figure she wants me to kiss her. I do not comply with her desires . . . She apparently is angry'.[57]

Patricia Jones was preoccupied by the presence of American servicemen, but declines to 'pick-up' as many as her friends, Delma and Arlette, the 'Yank hunters' do. She is pleased, however, as has been noted, to record her one 'little experience' with an American soldier. She wonders why sexual relationships are so preoccupying and refers to psychology books she has read on the 'problem'. Marriage represents paradoxically both the culmination of youthful romance and its transcendence in 'maturity' — a much favoured term.

Another diarist, Marion Crawford, recorded her amorous adventures in similar terms.[58] 'Have got a pash on Eric Young. Only had 2 dances with him but boy he's a beaut dancer'. Returning from another dance with Jack: 'He insisted on bringing me home. Talk about funny. "Kiss me goodnight". I kissed him on the forehead'. After parting with Blue: 'Can't believe I've lost Blue but have a feeling he really kissed me for the last time'. As in the case of Patricia Jones, Marion Crawford divided her time between a variety of pleasurable activities: the pictures ('Jane Eyre', 'Fantasia', 'Irene', 'Rebecca', 'Sandy is a Lady', 'Dear Ruth', 'The Woman in the Window', 'The Valley of Indecision'), Luna Park, the Palais, swimming, dances and playing board and card games. She also pondered long and hard on whether she was really in love, an important matter to decide, for it meant marriage, a life-long commitment: 'I think maybe I'll marry Bill after all'. Romantic love was not only the basis for marriage in the 1940s, but for women it was meant to supply the meaning of life. Thus Marion Crawford wrote in April 1948: 'Something happened that I've been living my life through for — but didn't know it. If only I could believe it was true. Max kissed me!' But one week later everything was thrown in doubt: 'I know tonight that I don't love Max — I don't know what I feel really I'm too confused'.

In one entry in her diary, Marion Crawford wrote revealingly that she went to Myers and 'rode up and down on escalators — for my pleasure'. Hers was a generation of pleasure-seekers, intent on excitement and adventure. In their romantic adventures, they considered themselves the privileged beneficiaries of freedom and youth. They had a sense of themselves as the agents of their lives, 'picking-up' and discarding men at will. They were of course painfully aware that 'love' needed to be reciprocated and castigated themselves for 'imaginitis'. As the lucky inhabitants of the self-styled 'World of Youth', they were largely unresponsive to the cautionary voices of 'cold old age', voices that included those of feminists in organisations such as the National Council of Women, the Women's Christian Temperance Union and the United Associations of Women (UAW).

Feminists interpreted the world in different terms. In the young women's 'opportunities', feminists saw only danger and exploitation. The 'epidemic of sexuality' occasioned by the war, as Gail Reekie has shown for Western Australia, led to a widespread feminist mobilisation aimed at protecting women from male 'vice', from venereal disease, unwanted pregnancies, abortion and rape.[59] Reekie's primary interest is in the relationship of feminism to class. Arguing that middle-class feminist campaigns 'often translated politically into efforts to restrict working-class women's sexual activity', she is therefore surprised to find the extent of cross-class unity among feminists that is evident in the wartime campaigns around sexuality.[60] Unfortunately, her focus on class divisions obscures the emergence of an arguably more significant division between women — evident in the discourse on femininity

— a distinction based on age. It is not 'working class sexual values' of which these middle-aged feminists disapprove, but 'the moral standard of our young people', as the president of the Women's Justices Association made clear.[61]

Nor is it true to say that women's campaigns were 'unrelated to any cohesive theory of women's position in society'.[62] Indeed quite the reverse is true: the feminist concern about, and response to, the 'epidemic of sexuality' arose quite logically from established feminist positions. Jessie Street's intervention illustrates this well. In May 1943 fifty-four-year-old Street, as president of the UAW, wrote to the *Daily Telegraph* deploring the 'cesspool of vice' that was Sydney. She regretted that the authorities had opted to make 'sex indulgence' safe rather than preventing it and she called for the punishment of 'the seducers of young girls' instead of 'those seduced'. The 'debauchers', she said, should be removed from society.[63] For Street, the more sexualised women were, the more degraded. Economic independence would free women from their condition as creatures of sex.[64] Her vision of female emancipation could not include sexual freedom; chastity rather than 'sex indulgence' was the necessary pre-condition for women's 'advancement'. The double standard that punished women, while it let men go free, was thus the major target of feminist campaigns.

Street's analysis represented a development of the de-sexualisation strategy of nineteenth-century feminism.[65] Significantly, Street was a member of the British Association for Moral and Social Hygiene founded in 1870 by Josephine Butler, the crusader against contagious diseases legislation, and there is much evidence to suggest that Street's experiences of working with prostitutes in the United States in 1915 were formative for her feminism.[66] For Street, as for nineteenth-century feminists, prostitution was the paradigmatic female condition: women reduced to their sex.

Although feminism reached a high point during World War II — the Australian Women's Charter Conference, representing ninety women's organisations, was the largest feminist conference yet held in Australia — feminists, many in their forties and fifties by World War II, were ageing and losing touch with the aspirations of young women.[67] The feminist Charter for Equality, emphasising economic and political opportunity, could not accommodate female sexual desire. Street and others continued to speak of 'vice' and 'seduction'. There is evidence of indifference and resistance to feminist overtures among younger women. Organisers of the Women for Canberra movement, for example, despaired at young women's lack of interest: they 'were not seized with the seriousness of the matter'.[68]

Though differently motivated, feminists (concerned about the position of women) and Christian moralists (concerned to preserve Christian values) joined together in trying to curb the 'promiscuous' sexual activity of young women.[69] The Australian Women's Charter of 1943 advocated strict controls on the sale of liquor, the prohibition of 'literature calculated to stimulate crime and sexual laxity' and the provision of 'ample facilities for healthy recreation'. The Charter, like the churches and the Director of the Army Medical Corps, also called for the 'removal of obstacles to early marriage'.[70] While feminists sought to domesticate sexual pleasure, young women themselves embraced early marriage as a defiant expression of the freedom and sexual orientation of youth.[71] Some 12,000 Australian women married American servicemen. Marriage was seen as the gateway to sexual fulfilment, as a union of sweethearts.

These new understandings of marriage are present in women's diaries. They are also evident in the testimonies of Melbourne women who wrote to Dr V.H. Wallace in 1943 and 1944 about birth control, and of the 1,400 women who responded in 1944 to the invitation from the National Health and Medical Research Council (NHMRC) to Australian women to say why they were limiting their families. After analysing the letters from those who limited their families to two children, the NHMRC concluded: 'There are several important and quite genuine motives influencing this decision. Perhaps the two most important of these are the desire to retain the companionship of the husband and the happiness of married life, and the desire to see that the two children are properly equipped for their later life'.[72] 'I believe a happy marriage', a patient told Dr Wallace, 'is based on a happy sexual life between husband and wife'.[73] The women's letters to the NHMRC and to Dr Wallace in Melbourne spoke of the difficulty of reconciling motherhood with the new imperatives of femininity. 'Desiring a normal marital relationship with my husband', explained a Surrey Hills wife and mother to Dr Wallace. 'I had no wish to bear children indiscriminately or too frequently'.[74] Mothers, wrote one to the NHMRC, 'still have an urge for an evening entertainment or a much-earned holiday with only an attentive and loving husband'.[75] Another mother of two children suggested that the exhaustion consequent upon housework meant that it was difficult to be a sweetheart, too: 'washing up, wiping up, and a spot of darning, etc, then bed, feeling as if you could only fall into bed and sleep, but have to be a good wife to husband'.[76] Yet another considered that if she had the five or six children society apparently required 'I would have no time to spend with my husband, and to be a real companion to him'.[77] 'Women with too many children attend to the children (if they are real mothers) [and] neglect their husband [sic] then he goes elsewhere for companionship'.[78] 'Companion' was becoming code for sexual partner: '[The wife] ceases to be a companion to her husband in the later months of pregnancy and the early months after the baby arrives'.[79] One solution to the contradictions experienced by these women lay in the use of contraceptives. With the free availability of contraceptives, a woman might 'safely retain her husband's love without the fear of a dozen children'.[80] Contraceptives, all were agreed, offered 'freedom from fear'. They also offered unimagined pleasures. The combination of a new (second) husband and reliable contraceptives gave one woman 'more satisfaction and happiness than [she] ever thought possible'.[81] It seems clear from the testimonies of these women that by the 1940s the use of artificial contraceptives, in particular condoms, pessaries and diaphragms, was becoming widespread.[82] Many participants in the national survey expressed anxiety about the possibility of the NMRC recommending their prohibition. The majority of Dr Wallace's patients expressed satisfaction with his recommended pessary: 'it is a great pity that birth control cannot be taught free to the masses', proclaimed one happy beneficiary.[83]

In explaining their refusal to bear more children, many women also complained of the 'disfigurement' of pregnancy — the 'sacrifice' of woman's figure. 'This is the woman's point of view. She marries, she has a child, she loses her figure . . .'[84] 'Another reason for restricting families', wrote another, was the 'appearance' of the pregnant woman.[85] The Council's summary of the responses noted the regularity of references to the 'inconveniences, humiliations and physical distress of pregnancy': 'many women dwelt at length on this aspect'.[86] The incompatibility of motherhood with modern femininity was stressed by Dame Enid Lyons in a radio debate on the decline in the birth rate on the ABC in 1944: 'There is one other point of importance which I think women find to be a great deterrent to having many children. That is our standard today of feminine beauty . . . Who are those whose beauty today is extolled? Those who have kept the extreme slimness and suppleness of early youth'.[87] A similar point was made by Mrs J. Bowie to a women's meeting in Sydney when she suggested beauty contests were responsible for over-emphasising the bodily aspect of woman's personality.[88] Lyons regretted that sex had become an 'end in itself', while the child was regarded as of not very great importance.

The solution to the conflict was straightforward for one respondent to the national enquiry: 'glamorize motherhood'.[89] The National Health and Medical Research Council produced numerous recommendations for reforms to make mothering less expensive, less arduous and less alienating. But none of the recommendations really addressed the heart of the matter. As marriage came to be seen increasingly as an institution to secure sexual pleasure, for the gratification of hetero-sexual desire, for women as well as men, so the advent of children came to represent not the purpose of, but a direct threat to, marital happiness. 'The mental and physical adjustments [required by marriage] require time', wrote one respondent to Dr Wallace, 'and when a child is born too soon those adjustments are delayed, and possibly never made'.[90] Children intruded upon the 'privacy' of the married couple as they increasingly expected 'time together alone'.[91]

Rather than characterise the triumph of marriage and domesticity in the 1940s and 1950s as a conservative retreat, a return to old ways, we should rather understand these phenomena as the triumph of modern femininity, youthful adventurism and a path embarked on by women attempting to live as female sexual subjects and explore the possibilities of sexual pleasure. Women began to enter marriage with high expectations of personal pleasure and it is not surprising that the marriage boom of the 1940s produced a 'divorce boom' in the 1950s. Interestingly, in his chapter on 'Marriage Breakdown' for A.P. Elkin's book on *Marriage and the Family in Australia*, W.G. Coughlan attributed much marital instability in the 1950s to the high incidence of 'heavy petting' preceding marriage:

> Petting is taken for granted and expected from mid-adolescence, and is widespread among senior secondary school pupils, university students, apprentices and workers in every occupation. 'Heavy' petting and petting to climax figure in the case histories of most of the marriage counsellors' clients . . .[92]

Experienced in kissing and 'petting', the majority of young unmarried women were still, it would seem from surveys conducted by Dr Lotte Fink in the early 1950s, strangers to sexual intercourse: this was the novelty of marriage.[93]

Sexual satisfaction was now taken for granted as an adult right in the 'disease-free' 1950s and 1960s. Sexual relationships could be explored with relative impunity, though the costs were always greater for women. There could be no return to the old order at the end of the war. Indeed by the 1950s it was becoming clear that the tensions generated by the changing structure of femininity and by the concomitant wartime stimulation of female desire had created havoc with 'traditional roles'. A restlessness had been unleashed that could not be easily assuaged.

World War II saw both the triumph and demise of the old feminism.[94] The 1943 Charter Conference, the equal pay campaigns, the campaigns for the government provision of child care and the Women for Canberra movement together represent a peak of achievement; by the time of the second Charter Conference in 1946, however, feminism was on the defensive, branded anachronistic, prudish and divisive. Whereas the 1943 Charter included a separate section titled 'Woman as Mother and/or Home Maker', by 1946 this had been reduced to a sub-section of, subsumed under, 'The Family, the Home and the Community'. The mutuality of women's and men's interests and needs, emphasised by the dominant discourse on sexual partnership, came to be represented in the ascendant concept of 'the Family', a metaphor for woman's sphere that gradually and significantly eclipsed the earlier designation, the Home. But women's interest in, and right to, sexual pleasure had been established, so that when the new feminism — women's liberation — emerged in the late 1960s, sexual freedom and its assumed preconditions of abortion on demand and free contraception were key demands. Lesbianism, not chastity, was the choice of those eschewing sexual relations with men. Female desire was put on the political agenda.

Acknowledgements

Earlier versions of this paper were delivered to the 5th Annual Conference of the Stout Research Centre for the Study of New Zealand Society, History and Culture, 'A Warlike People? War in New Zealand Experience', 1–3 July 1988 and to the Melbourne Feminist History Conference, 28–29 May 1988.

Notes

1   Diary, original in author's possession. Entry, '"1942". Emergence into Full Youth'. I wish to express my thanks to Katie Holmes for sharing the two personal diaries, quoted in this article, with me. The names of the diarists have been changed to protect their anonymity.

2   P. Johnson, 'Gender, Class and Work: The Council of Action for Equal Pay and the equal pay campaign in Australia during World War II', *Labour History*, no. 50, May 1986, p. 146.

3   A. Wright, 'The *Women's Weekly*. Depression and War years Romance and Reality', *Refractory Girl*, 3, Winter 1973, p. 12.

4   A. Summers, *Damned Whores and God's Police*, Melbourne 1975. p. 149.

5   E. Ryan and A. Conlon, *Gentle Invaders. Australian Women at Work*, Melbourne 1989, p. 139.

6   C. Allport, 'The princess in the castle: women and the new order housing', in Third Women and Labour Conference Collective (eds), *All her Labours: Embroidering the Framework*, Sydney 1984, p. 149. See also K. Darian-Smith, 'A City in War: The Home Front in Melbourne 1939–1945'. Ph.D. thesis, University of Melbourne 1987,

p. 140; at the end of the war 'the past . . . reigns supreme' and Kay Saunders and Helen Taylor, 'To Combat the Plague: The Construction of Moral Alarm and State Intervention in Queensland during World War II, *Hecate*, vol. 14, no. 1, 1988 where (p. 26) the end of the war sees 'traditional' values 'ultimately reinforced'.

7   Aspects of this argument are anticipated in M. Lake, 'The War Over Women's Work' in V. Burgmann and J. Lee (eds), *A Most Valuable Acquisition*, Melbourne 1988.

8   C. McNamara, 'Must Women Return to the Kitchen?', *Labor Digest*, April 1945, p. 49.

9   Foster quoted in C. Larmour, 'Women's Wage and the WEB' in A. Curthoys, *et al.* (eds), *Women at Work*, Canberra 1975. pp. 50–1.

10 Quoted in Wright. *op. cit.*, p. 12.

11 J.J. Matthews, *Good and Mad Women. The historical construction of femininity in twentieth century Australia*, Sydney 1984, pp. 89–90; J.J. Matthews, 'Building the Body Beautiful: the Femininity of Modernity', *Australian Feminist Studies*, no. 5, Summer 1987.

12 L. Johnson, 'The Teenage Girl: the social definition of growing up for young Australian women 1950 to 1965', *History of Education Review*, 18, 1, 1989, p. 6.

13 R. Pringle, *Secretaries Talk Sexuality, Power and Work*, Sydney 1988, pp. 6–15, 193.

14 S. Jeffreys, *The Spinster and her Enemies: Feminism and Sexuality 1880–1930*, London 1985, ch. 9; also Stephen Heath, *The Sexual Fix*, London 1982. Judith Allen, *Sex and Secrets. Crimes Involving Australian Women Since 1880*, Melbourne 1990, points to the implications of sexological discourse for rape victims, pp. 152–3. Norman Haire, a leading sexologist in Britain and Australia, was prominent in Australia during World War II, expounding on the imperative of the 'sex urge' and advocating, like many sex reformers, eugenicist thinking.

15 Ann Curthoys, 'Eugenics, Feminism and Birth Control: The Case of Marion Piddington', *Hecate*, vol. 15, no. 1, 1989. See also Alison Mackinnon and Carol Bacchi, 'Sex, resistance and power: sex reform in South Australia *c.* 1905, *Australian Historical Studies*, vol. 23, no. 90, April 1988.

16 Jill Matthews, 'Building the Body Beautiful'.

17 Judith Williamson, 'Decoding Advertisements' in Rosemary Betterton (ed.), *Looking at Images of Femininity in the Visual Arts and Media*, London 1987, p. 49. See also Matthews *Good and Mad Women*, pp. 98–9, and Stuart Ewen, *Captains and Consciousness. Advertising and the Social Roots of the Consumer Culture*, New York 1976.

18 *Everylady's Journal*, 6 April 1916, p. 208.

19 *Ibid.*, 6 April, 6 August 1920; also the 'Oatine Face Cream' and 'Use it to be Dainty' advertisements, 6 July 1920.

20 See, for example, 'Sta-Blond' advertisement, *New Idea*, 24 March 1939.

21 National Health and Medical Research Council, *Reports on the Decline in the Birth Rate*, Analysis of the Contents of the Letters Received, 18th Session, Canberra, 22–24 November 1944, p. 73.

22 Dr V.H. Wallace Papers, 'Their Comments on Contraception'. Letter from Murrumbeena, 21 March 1944. University of Melbourne Archives.

23 Betterton, *op. cit.*, p. 7.

24 *Everylady's Journal*, 19 May 1926.

25 *New Idea*, 2 December 1932.

26 *Ibid.*, 29 July 1932.

27 *Everylady's Journal*, 6 May 1920.

28 *Ibid.*, 6 March, 5 May, 20 July 1923. See also ad. for Kilma Cream, 6 January 1923.

29   *New Idea*, 23 March 1934.

30   *Ibid.*, 8 September 1938.

31   *Everylady's Journal*, 20 August 1927.

32   *New Idea*, 24 March 1939.

33   *Ibid.*, 16 September 1938.

34   *Ibid.*, 24 March 1938.

35   *Ibid.*, 8 January, 24 March 1938.

36   Two recent studies of the relationships between Australian women and American servicemen in Queensland are R. Campbell's *Heroes and Lovers: A question of national identity*, Sydney 1989, which, as the subtitle suggests, is concerned with the impact of the relationships on the 'national identity'; and M. Sturma's article 'Loving the Alien: The Underside of Relations between American Servicemen and Australian Women in Queensland, 1942–1945' *Journal of Australian Studies*, 24 May 1989, which explores the 'darker side' of American relations with Australian women. Both studies position the Americans as the main subjects of their stories: women are the objects of *their* desires. Kay Saunders and Helen Taylor in 'To Combat the Plague' present women, especially working-class women, as victims of an aggrandising and punitive capitalist state. Women's general vulnerability to male violence in wartime is the theme of Judith Allen, *op. cit.*, pp. 218–25. It should be noted that the famous 'Australian' joke is also claimed as a New Zealand and British joke.

37   This is a point made in the Introduction to M.R. Higonnet *et al.* (ed.), *Behind the Lines: Gender and the Two World Wars*, New Haven 1987. p. 4, but it should be noted that Carmel Shute made the same point, in different language, in Australia as early as 1975. See C. Shute, 'Heroines and Heroes: Sexual Mythology in Australia 1914–1918', *Hecate*, vol. 1. no. 1, 1975.

38   Dymphna Cusack and Florence James, *Come in Spinner*, Sydney 1973 (first pub. 1951), p. 29. Cusack and James also wrote of the Americans' 'Hollywood love-making'.

39   E. Daniel Potts and Annette Potts, *Yanks Down Under 1941–45. The American Impact on Australia*, Melbourne 1985, pp. 330, 341.

40   *Ibid.*, pp. 342, 344–5.

41   *Daily Telegraph*, 10 April 1943.

42   *Ibid.*, 8 May 1943.

43   *Salt*, vol. 6. no. 7, 7 June 1943, quoted in Darian-Smith, *op. cit.*, p. 303. See also report of conference of United States and Australian Army medical officers. *Daily Telegraph*, 18 April 1943.

44   *Daily Telegraph*, 30 January 1943.

45   Darian-Smith, *op. cit.*, p. 303.

46   *Ibid.*, p. 305.

47   Dr Cooper Booth in *Daily Telegraph*, 29 June 1943.

48   *Ibid.*, 14 January 1943.

49   Women's News Column, *Sydney Morning Herald*, 23 April 1945.

50   See Sturma, *op. cit.*, p. 11; Saunders and Taylor, *op. cit.*; also K. Daniels and M. Murnane (eds), *Uphill All The Way: A Documentary History of Women in Australia*, St Lucia 1980, pp. 106–112.

51   *Daily Telegraph*, 15 July 1943.

52   *Sydney Morning Herald*, 31 May 1943.

53   Rosalind Coward, *Female Desire: Women's Sexuality Today*, London 1984.

54   This section of the diary is the record of the first part of 1942, entitled 'Emergence into Full Youth', written in May 1942. All quotes are from this record, which is not differentiated into daily entries.

55 *Daily Telegraph*, 3, 7, 8, 9 July 1943.

56 Coward, *op. cit.*, pp. 95–6.

57 Potts and Potts, *op. cit.*, p. 345.

58 Diary of Marion Crawford, entries from 1943 until 1948. Original in possession of diarist.

59 Gail Reekie, 'War, Sexuality and Feminism. Perth women's organisations 1938–1945', *Historical Studies*, vol. 21, no. 85, October 1985.

60 *Ibid.*, p. 576. Reekie's surprise at the cross-class unity of feminists ironically echoes the surprise of contemporaries confronted with the sexual activity of young women from all classes.

61 *Ibid.*, p. 580.

62 *Ibid.*, p. 577.

63 *Daily Telegraph*, 20 May 1943.

64 M. Lake, 'Jessie Street and "Feminist Chauvinism"' in Heather Radi (ed.), *Jessie Street*, Sydney 1990. See especially Street to *News Chronicle*, London, 27 October 1956, Jessie Street Papers, ANL, MS 2683/3/525.

65 See, for example, J. Walkowitz, 'Male Vice and Female Virtue: Feminism and the Politics of Prostitution in Nineteenth Century Britain' in A. Snitwo, *et al.* (eds), *Desire: The Politics of Sexuality*, London 1984; see also L. Gordon and E. Dubois, 'Seeking Ecstasy on the Battlefield: Danger and Pleasure in Nineteenth Century Feminist Sexual Thought' in *Feminist Review* (ed.), *Sexuality: A Reader*, London 1987.

66 Jessie Livingstone to Kenneth Street, 20 April 1915, Street Papers MS 2683/1/6; Jessie Street interview with Hazel de Berg, 18 March 1967, Tape 197, Oral History Collection, ANL.

67 For example, Jessie Street and Lucy Woodcock were fifty-four in 1943, Bessie Rischbieth was sixty, Millicent Preston Stanley was sixty, Muriel Heagney was fifty-eight.

68 *Sydney Morning Herald*, 9 February 1943.

69 *Ibid.* See, for example, 'The Pulpit' column, 18 January 1943, 8 March 1943; and Women's News Column, 24 February 1943, 26 February 1943.

70 *Australian Women's Charter*, November 1943, Sydney, pp. 14–15; see also report of Dr Lucy Gullett addressing the United Nations of Women on 'early marriage as a protection against venereal disease', *Sydney Morning Herald*, 23 April 1945 and Darian-Smith, *op. cit.*, p. 138.

71 Marriage rates climbed during World War II and continued to do so until 1955. See P. McDonald, *Marriage in Australia*, Canberra 1975, pp. 188, 192, and Gordon Carmichael, *With This Ring*, Canberra 1988, pp. 11, 14, 28–9.

72 *National Health and Medical Research Council Reports on the Decline in the Birth Rate. Analysis of the Contents of the Letters Received*, 18th Session, Canberra, 22–24 November 1944, p. 73.

73 Letter from Newport, 28 November 1943, Wallace letters.

74 Letter from Surrey Hills, 13 December 1943, *ibid*.

75 NHMRC, Letters Received, p. 72.

76 *Ibid.*

77 *Ibid.*, p. 82.

78 Letter from Finley, 13 October 1943, Wallace letters.

79 NHMRC, Letters Received, p. 83.

80 *Ibid.*, p. 81.

81 Letter from East Brunswick, 12 October 1943, Wallace letters.

82   See also Judith Allen, *op. cit.*, p. 224.

83   Letter from Carrum, 12 November 1943, Wallace letters.

84   *NHMRC*, Letters Received, pp. 72, 83, 91, 92, 93.

85   *Ibid.*, p. 81.

86   *Ibid.*, pp. 75, 84, 89.

87   *Ibid.*, p. 84.

88   *Daily Telegraph*, 14 March 1943.

89   Australian Broadcasting Commission, *The Nation's Forum of the Air*, 23 August 1944.

90   Letter from Brighton Beach, 17 December 1943, Wallace letters.

91   Letter from Parkdale, 16 October 1943, *ibid*.

92   W.G. Coughlan, 'Marriage Breakdown' in A.P. Elkin (ed.), *Marriage and the Family in Australia*, Sydney 1957, p. 133.

93   Lotte A. Fink, 'Premarital Sex Experience of Girls in Sydney', *International Journal of Sexology*, vol. 8, no. 1, August 1954, pp. 10–11.

94   This point is elaborated in Marilyn Lake, 'Jessie Street and "Feminist Chauvinism"', in Heather Radi, *op. cit.*

FURTHER READING

O N   T H E   " H O M E   F R O N T " in general, useful places to begin are: the essays in Jeremy Noakes (ed.), *The Civilian in War: The home front in Europe, Japan and the USA in World War II* (Exeter, 1992) and for the Soviet Union see John Barber and Mark Harrison, *The Soviet Home Front, 1941–45. A Social and Economic History of the USSR in World War II* (London, 1991). On Scandinavia the essays in Henrik S. Nissen, *Scandinavia During the Second World War* (Minneapolis, 1983) and Charles Leonard Lundin, *Finland in the Second World War* (Bloomington IN, 1957).

The literature on the home front in Britain is now enormous. The most import- ant works are: Angus Calder, *The People's War 1939–1945* (London, 1969) and his *The Myth of the Blitz* (London, 1991); the essays in Harold L. Smith (ed.), *War and Social Change. British Society in the Second World War* (London, 1986); Robert Mackay, *Half the Battle: civilian morale in Britain during the Second World War* (Manchester, 2003); James Chapman, *The British at war: cinema, state and propaganda, 1939–1945* (London, 1998); the essays in Nick Hayes and Jeff Hill (eds), *"Millions like us"?: British culture in the Second World War* (Liverpool, 1999); and Mark Rawlinson, *British Writing of the Second World War* (Oxford, 2000). On the politics of the war at home see: Paul Addison, *The Road to 1945: British politics and the Second World War* (London, 1975); Kevin Jefferys, *The Churchill Coalition and Wartime Politics, 1940–45* (Manchester, 1991); Neil Stammers, *Civil Liberties in Britain during the Second World War. A Political Study* (London, 1983) and D. Morgan and M. Evans, *The Battle for Britain. Citizenship and Ideology in the Second World War* (London, 1993). Finally, see: Tony Kushner, *The Persistence of Prejudice: anti-semitism in British society during the Second*

World War (Manchester and New York, 1989); Travis Crosby, *The Impact of Civilian Evacuation in the Second World War* (London, 1986) and Rodney Lowe, "The Second World War, Consensus, and the Foundations of the Welfare State", *Twentieth Century British History*, vol. 1, no. 2 (1990), 152–82.

The home front in the United States has also been the subject of considerable attention. See: David M. Kennedy, *Freedom from Fear: the American people in depression and war* (New York, 1999); William O'Neill, *A Democracy at War: America's fight at home and abroad in World War II* (New York, 1993); Richard Polenberg, *War and Society: The United States, 1941–1945* (Philadelphia PA, 1972); Richard R. Lingeman, *Don't You Know There's a War On? The American Home Front, 1941–1945* (New York, 1970); David Brinkley, *Washington Goes to War* (New York, 1988); John Morton Blum, *V Was for Victory: politics and American culture during World War II* (New York, 1976); Lewis Erenberg and Susan E. Hirsch (eds), *The War in American Culture: society and consciousness during World War II*, (Chicago IL, 1996); Steven Casey, *Cautious crusade: Franklin D. Roosevelt, American public opinion, and the war against Nazi Germany* (New York, 2002). More specialized studies include: Nelson Lichtenstein, *Labor's War at Home: The CIO in World War II* (New York, 1982); John W. Jeffries, *Testing the Roosevelt Coalition: Connecticut society and politics in the era of World War II* (Knoxville KY, 1979); Charles Chamberlain, *Victory at Home: manpower and race in the American South during World War II* (Athens GA, 2003); Daniel Kryder, *Divided Arsenal: race and the American state during World War II* (Cambridge MA, 2000); Frank A. Warren, *Noble Abstractions : American liberal intellectuals and World War II* (Columbus OH, 1999); Richard Steele; *Words Fraught with Death: World War II and the test of a free speech ideal* (Basingstoke, 1999).

On Germany many of the studies transcend the war years and encompass the entire Nazi regime. Those that seem particularly useful for students of the Second World War include: Earl R. Beck, *Under the Bombs: The German home front 1942–45* (Lexington KY, 1986); Marlis G. Steinert, *Hitler's War and the Germans* (Athens OH, 1977); Robert Gellately, *The Gestapo and German Society. Enforcing Racial Policy 1933–1945* (Oxford, 1990); Ian Kershaw, *The "Hitler Myth": Image and Reality in the "Third Reich"* (Oxford, 1987); J. Stephenson, *Women in Nazi Germany*, (Harlow, 2001); Edward L. Hornze, *Foreign Labor in Nazi Germany* (Princeton NJ, 1967). Works that focus on resistance to the Nazi regime within Germany include: Inge Scholl, *Students Against Tyranny: The Resistance of the White Rose: Munich 1942–43* (Middletown CT, 1983); Annette E. Dumbach and Jud Newborn, *Shattering the German Night: the story of the White Rose* (Boston, 1986); Klemens von Klemperer, *The German Resistance Against Hitler: the search for Allies abroad, 1938–1945* (Oxford, 1992); Francis R. Nicosia and Lawrence D. Stokes (eds), *Germans against Nazism: nonconformity, opposition and resist-ance in the Third Reich* (New York, 1990); Harold C. Deutsch, *The Conspiracy Against Hitler in the Twilight War* (Minneapolis MN, 1968).

On Italy see: Charles Delzell, *Mussolini's Enemies. The Italian Anti-Fascist Resistance* (Princeton NJ, 1961); Dante A. Puzzo, *The Partisans and the War in Italy* (New York, 1993); David W. Ellwood, *Italy 1943–1945* (Leicester, 1985);

Jane Slaughter, *Women and the Italian Resistance* (Denver CO, 1995); D. Ward, *Antifascisms: Cultural Politics in Italy 1943–1946* (London, 1996); and Roger Absolom, *A Strange Alliance: aspects of escape and survival in Italy* (Florence, 1991).

On Japan see: Thomas R. H. Havens, *Valley of Darkness: The Japanese People and World War Two* (New York, 1978); Haruko Taya Cook and Theodore F. Cook, *Japan at War: an oral history* (New York, 1992); and Peter High, *The Imperial Screen: a cultural history of Japanese cinema in the fifteen years war of 1931–1945* (Madison WI, 2003).

Elsewhere see: E. Daniel Potts and Annette Potts, *Yanks Down Under 1941–45. The American Impact on Australia* (Melbourne, 1985); James Holland, *Fortress Malta: an island under siege 1940–1943* (London, 2003); Tony Gray, *The Lost Years: the emergency in Ireland, 1939–45* (London, 1997); Ashley Jackson, *Botswana, 1939–1945: an African country at war* (Oxford, 1999); and M. Bunting, *The Model Occupation: the Channel Islands under German Rule* (London, 1995).

The phenomenon of military occupation and the resistance to it has created an enormous literature. Generally, see: Rab Bennett, *Under the Shadow of the Swastika: the moral dilemmas of resistance and collaboration in Hitler's Europe* (Basingstoke, 1999); Werner Rings, *Life With the Enemy. Collaboration and Resistance in Hitler's Europe 1939–1945* (London, 1982); Jacques Semelin, *Unarmed Against Hitler: Civilian Resistance in Europe, 1939–1943* (Westport CT, 1993); Stephen Hawes and Ralph White, *Resistance in Europe: 1939–1945* (Harmondsworth, 1976); Henri Michel, *The Shadow War: Resistance in Europe 1939–1945* (London, 1972); Jørgen Hæstrup, *European Resistance Movements (1939–1945): A Complete History* (Westport CT, Praeger, 1981); M. R. D. Foot, *Resistance: an analysis of European resistance to Nazism* (London, 1976); and Jonathan Steinberg *All or Nothing: The Axis and the Holocaust, 1941–1943* (London, 1990).

The German occupation of France, and the "Vichy experience" has been the focus of much attention. See Philippe Burrin, *Living with Defeat. France under the German Occupation 1940–1944* (London, 1996); John M. Sweets, *Choices in Vichy France: the French under German occupation* (Oxford, 1986); Robert O. Paxton, *Vichy France* (New York, 1972); Bertram M. Gordon, *Collaborationism in France During the Second World War* (Ithaca NY, 1980); Lynne Taylor, *Between Resistance and Collaboration: popular protest in Northern France, 1940–45* (Basingstoke, 2000); Miranda Pollard, *Reign of Virtue: mobilizing gender in Vichy France* (Chicago IL, 1998); and Sarah Fishman, *We Will Wait: wives of French prisoners of war 1940–1945* (New Haven CT, 1991).

On the German occupation of territories in the Soviet Union see Alexander Dallin, *German Rule in Russia 1941–1945. A Study of Occupation Policies* (2nd edn, London, 1981); Timothy Patrick Mulligan *The Politics of Illusion and Empire. German Occupation Policy in the Soviet Union, 1942–43* (Westport CT, 1988); and Martin Dean, *Collaboration in the Holocaust: crimes of the local police in Belorussia and Ukraine, 1941–44* (Basingstoke, 2000). On the occupation of Belgium: Werner Warmbrunn, *The German Occupation of Belgium 1940–1944*

(New York, 1993). On the occupation of the Netherlands see: Werner Warmbrunn, *The Dutch Under German Occupation, 1940–1945* (Stanford CA, 1963); Louis de Jong, *The Netherlands and Nazi Germany* (Cambridge MA, 1990); Bob Moore, *Victims and Survivors: the Nazi persecution of the Jews in the Netherlands 1940–1945* (London, 1997); Walter Maass, *The Netherlands at War 1940–1945* (London, 1970).

On resistance in the Low Countries and Scandinavia see: Olav Riste and Berit Nøkleby, *The Resistance Movement* (Oslo, 1986); M. R. D. Foot, *Holland at War Against Hitler: Anglo-Dutch Relations 1940–1945* (London, 1990); Jørgen Hæstrup, *Secret Alliance: a study of the Danish Resistance Movement 1940–1945*, 3 vols (Odense, 1976–77); Jeremy Bennett, *British Broadcasting and the Danish Resistance Movement 1940–1945: A Study of Wartime Broadcasts of the BBC Danish Service* (Cambridge, 1996).

On the French resistance see: H. R. Kedward, *Resistance in Vichy France: a study of ideas and motivation in the Southern Zone 1940–1942* (Oxford, 1978); John H. Sweets, *The Politics of Resistance in France (1940–1944): a history of the Mouvements Unis de la Résistance* (De Kalb IL, 1976); H. R. Kedward, *In Search of the Maquis: rural resistance in Southern France, 1941–1944* (Oxford, 1993); H.R. Kedward and Roger Austin (eds), *Vichy France and the Resistance: culture and ideology* (London, 1985); Frida Knight, *The French Resistance 1940–1944* (London: Lawrence and Wishart, 1975); Anny Latour, *The Jewish Resistance in France (1940–1944)* (New York, 1981); Jacques Adler, *The Jews of Paris and the Final Solution: communal response and internal conflicts, 1940–1944* (Oxford, 1985); Lucien Lazare, *Rescue as Resistance: how Jewish organisations fought the Holocaust in France* (New York, 1996); Margaret Rossiter, *Women in the Resistance* (New York, 1986) Margaret Collins Weitz, *Sisters in the Resistance: how women fought to free France, 1940–1945* (New York, 1995); Patrick Marnham, *The Death of Jean Moulin: biography of a ghost* (London, 2000); and Alan Clinton, *Jean Moulin, 1899–1943: the French resistance and the republic* (Basingstoke, 2002).

More specialized treatments of resistance are: David Stafford, *Britain and the European Resistance 1940–1945: a survey of the Special Operations Executive, with Documents* (Toronto, 1983); Arthur L. Funk, *Hidden Ally: the French Resistance, Special Operations and the landings in southern France* (Westport CT, 1992); and Leonid Grenkevich, *The Soviet Partisan Movement, 1941–1944: a critical historiographical analysis* (London, 1999).

On the subject of propaganda and publicity see generally: A. Osley, *Persuading the People. Government Publicity in the Second World War* (London, 1995); and I. McLaine, *Ministry of Morale. Home Front Morale and the Ministry of Information in World War II* (London, 1979). Much of the work on propaganda has focussed on film: Clayton R. Koppes and Gregory D. Black, *Hollywood Goes to War* (Berkeley CA, 1987); Philip M. Taylor (ed.), *Britain and the Cinema in the Second World War* (London, 1988); Thomas Doherty, *Projections of War: Hollywood, American culture, and World War II* (New York, 1993); Thomas W. Bohn, *An Historical and Descriptive Analysis of the "Why We Fight" Series* (New

York, 1977); H. Mark Glancy, *When Hollywood Loved Britain: the Hollywood "British" film 1939–1945* (Manchester, 1999); and Dana B. Polan, *Power and Paranoia: history, narrative and the American Cinema, 1940–1950* (New York, 1986). See also Frank W. Fox, *Madison Avenue Goes to War: the strange military career of American advertising, 1941–1943* (Provo UT, 1975) and George H. Roeder Jr, *The Censored War: American visual experience during World War II* (New Haven CT, 1993).

War as a "gendered experience" has increasingly become a focus of attention. In addition to the works concerning resistance referred to above (and in addition to those concerning women in the armed force), some of the more important works are: John Costello, *Love, Sex and War. Changing Values, 1939–1945* (London, 1985); Leila M. Rupp, *Mobilizing Women for War: German and American propaganda during World War II* (Princeton NJ, 1979); Hanna Diamond, *Women and the Second World War in France, 1939–1948: choices and constraints* (Harlow, 1999); D'Ann Campbell, *Women at War with America; Private Lives in a Patriotic Era* (Cambridge MA, 1984); Maureen Honey, *Creating Rosie the Riveter. Class, Gender, and Propaganda during World War II* (Amherst MA, 1984); Penny Summerfield and G. Braybon, *Out of the Cage: women in the Two World Wars* (London, 1987); Penny Summerfield, *Women Workers in the Second World War. Production and Patriarchy in Conflict* (London, 1984); Ruth Milkman, *Gender at Work: the dynamics of job segregation by sex during World War II* (Urbana IL, 1987); Susan M. Hartmann, *The Home Front and Beyond: American women in the 1940s* (Boston MA, 1982); and see the essays in Margaret Randolph Higonnet, Jane Jenson, Sonya Michel, and Margaret Weitz (eds) *Behind the Lines: gender and the Two World Wars* (New Haven CT, 1987). On some specialized topics see: Allan Bérubé, *Coming Out Under Fire: The history of gay men and women in World War II* (New York, 1990); Toshiyuki Tanaka, *Japan's Comfort Women: sexual slavery and prostitution during World War II and the US occupation* (London, 2002); Stephanie Carpenter, *On the Farm Front: the Women's Land Army in World War II* (DeKalb IL, 2003); Phyllis Lassner, *British women writers of World War II: battlegrounds of their own* (Basingstoke, 1998); and Maureen Honey (ed.), *Bitter Fruit: African American women in World War II* (Columbia MO, 1999).

PART FOUR

Memories
Victims, Heroes, and Controversies

MORE THAN HALF A CENTURY has now passed since World War Two ended, and fewer and fewer people are left who remember the events described by the authors in this collection. Surviving veterans of the military experience are in their eighties at least; even those who were children at the time are now likely to be senior citizens, retired and drawing a pension. And yet anyone reading this book may be said to have "memories" of this war, recollections of events in which they did not participate. Films have been made, novels written, exhibitions mounted, memorials constructed that have given us images and impressions of what the war was like, of who fought it, how and why. The heroic deeds of soldiers in battle, of Iwo Jima, of Stalingrad, of Normandy, of El Alamein has been "captured" on film, as has the heroism of the civilians who endured the Blitz, suffered through occupation, forced into labor or herded into camps. The memorialization of such people and events gives us the impression of having "been there," of having shared in their suffering and of participating in their triumphs. Images of Auschwitz, of bombed-out cities, of landings on beaches, of prison escapes, of mushroom clouds are indelibly etched on the minds of those who lived after the events, and take precedence over the academic understanding or intellectual knowledge offered in textbooks and classrooms.

The essays in this section testify to a growing interest on the part of historians in the construction of memory. Taken together, they show how politics and culture intersect, how organizations of veterans, survivors, political parties, movements and ideologies have worked to have their particular version — or memory — of the war etched into the consciousness of their political culture. Sometimes their efforts are idealistic, to enshrine forever the struggles and sufferings of those they represent —

"Lest We Forget" – but such efforts may be combined with realistic goals: pensions, health care and other compensations that no state would provide if its citizens were not reminded of the sacrifices that had been made on their behalf. They may, at the same time, be competing with others whose version of events, whose memory of them is quite different: heroes of the communist resistance in occupied France see the past differently than those of the Catholic right; the perspective of those who dropped bombs on cities is quite different from those who sought shelter from them – and we are seldom invited to explore the experience of war from more than one perspective at a time. We are encouraged (or manipulated) into identifying with heroes or victims, seldom with villains; the possibility that human beings can be many things simultaneously is rarely considered in evocations of war within popular culture.

But heroes and victims may also be engaged in a competition for attention, and our perceptions of both heroism and victimization may change over time. Pieter Lagrou begins by arguing that there has occurred a "reversal of memory" in remembrance of victims of Nazi persecution in Belgium, France, and the Netherlands. Today, Jews are most clearly "remembered" as the victims of Nazi persecution, along with homosexuals and gypsies to a lesser degree. In other words, today we remember as victims those who were victimized for who they were – not for what they did. This, he argues was not always the case: for twenty years after the war victims of the genocide were marginalized or forgotten, while martyrs of the national resistance were remembered and memorialized. To a certain extent, this was produced by the survivors themselves: those Jews who survived the Nazi death-camps were vastly outnumbered (approximately 20:1) by non-Jewish survivors, who quickly organized themselves into groups demanding recognition and compensation for their sufferings. But, he suggests, it was more complicated than this: there was also a lingering antisemitism in western Europe that wished to ignore the Jewish experience (and perhaps their own complicity in it); and, equally important, a need in these newly-restored regimes to create a "national" memory that valorized heroes of the resistance. Thus, the wish to create a "Belgian" a "French" and a "Dutch" identity were essential elements in the construction of memory, and in order to have a successful postwar political career, aspiring politicians were required to present their patriotic wartime credentials.

Thus, choices were made in each distinctive national context concerning who was to be memorialized, whose activities would be enshrined in cultural memory. The possibilities were, of course, wide-ranging: would communist guerrillas who fought not only their occupiers, but opposed the social and political system of their (capitalist) nation-state be treated as heroes, as representing the ideals of the nation? or those who had suffered the occupation in silence – perhaps overworked, malnourished and mistreated – but not actively engaged in "resistance"? The general trend in postwar western Europe was to make heroes of all "victims" regardless of whether they resisted the Nazi occupation overtly or not. But Lagrou's comparative perspective enables him to demonstrate how vital differing contexts were within this general pattern. The Belgian decision was to recognize as heroes those who had resisted (including different categories determined by the extent of the resistance) – which meant that Jewish survivors of concentration camps could be ignored, because they had not suffered as a result of their patriotic determination to resist, but simply because they were Jews. In France, De Gaulle attempted to construct a patriotic memory that distinguished the new France from Vichy, which separated the fighters of the Free French from the communist guerrillas, and in this the victims of the *déportation* were useful figures for glorification. In France, this discourse also identified the struggles of World War Two with those of World War One, in a continuing narrative of patriotic achievement. The Netherlands, neutral in World War One, and thus neither victor nor victim, responded differently again: the government declared "veteranism" un-Dutch and unpatriotic and refused to recognize resistance groups; instead, their position was that the nation as a whole had suffered, and that no groups should be singled out for their heroism or martyrdom. In conclusion, Lagrou shows how important a chronological perspective is in understanding memorialization: almost all of these postwar trends began to change in fundamentally significant ways in the 1960s as the Holocaust/Shoa captured the imagination and has dominated memories of the war ever since.

Different national contexts, and different mechanisms in the construction of memory, are presented in the essays by Lucy Noakes and John Bodnar. Noakes analyzes the nature and role of the "museum experience" in the central British myth of World War Two: that of the heroism of the British people during the Blitz. She suggests several reasons why it has come to occupy this central position (in spite of the fact that it was something actually experienced by only a minority of people): the horrors of aerial bombardment are easily imagined by observers after the fact – no specialized knowledge or study of events is necessary in order to appreciate its horrors. More importantly, it is part of the ethos of the Peoples' War: experience of the Blitz meant "everyone" was a soldier on the front lines of battle, and thus it represents a unity of experience denied to, say, the Battle of the Atlantic or the fall of Singapore. But her real interest is in the "museum experience" itself and the way it functions in the creation of community and identity. Here she shows how the Blitz was handled in two different museum evocations of it – at the Imperial War Museum in 1989 and at the Winston Churchill Museum in 1992.

In both cases, the museums succeeded (to varying degrees) in organizing their exhibits and the observers' experiences of them in such a way as to present the Blitz as a levelling, unifying adventure. In fact, she argues, national museums operated by the state have played an important role in representing the nation to itself, in stimulating a sense of community by making it "visible." Traditionally, they accomplished this through the preservation, arrangement and display of objects that represented the national heritage; but the new, "themed" experiences presented on the Blitz have moved beyond this, relocating the observer into participant, aiming to create the impression of "being there." In creating such an experience however, there are, almost inevitably, distortions. What the observer/participant is given is a sanitized version: gone from the shelters is the stench of urine, excrement and sweat; missing are the maimed and killed (or, if present, are marginalized on the periphery). And, given the aims of such an experience, gone is the sense of class antagonisms, uncertainties and despair – and in their place is the impression of a

nation united against a common, wicked enemy under the heroic leadership of
Churchill. "Memory," Noakes argues, is never fixed. It is open to reinterpretation
and reshaping according to the circumstances of the present and its preoccupations.
Thus, any understanding of such evocations as the "Blitz experience" must be
located in the circumstances in which they were constructed.

John Bodnar also examines the "re-creation" of the experience of war, but in
this case the medium is not the museum, but film. *Saving Private Ryan* was an
immensely popular "blockbuster" movie – and most critics and moviegoers were
particularly impressed and deeply affected by the re-creation of the American
landing at Omaha beach on the Normandy coast during the D-Day invasion. The
feeling of "being there" was achieved: the noise, the chaos, the terrors of battle
were evoked to an extent that was perhaps unprecedented in the history of film. But
Bodnar examines the sentiments and preoccupations that underlie the film and
argues that it too, may be located within the national psyche of the United States
at a particular time in its history. Although in some important ways *Ryan* harkened
back to the films and the sentiments of the 1950s, there are also intriguing differences that tell us something about the creation (and re-creation) of historical
"memories."

There is a point to the depiction of the brutality and horrors of battle, which
make it, in some ways, an anti-war film. Moviegoers were unlikely to leave the
movie theater with their romantic, heroic impressions of war entirely intact: war is
presented as a terrible, tragic event that destroys the lives of individual soldiers and
their families. Nevertheless, the narrative portrays the war as a necessary evil, one
in which virtuous, innocent, un-warlike American boys suffer in a necessary, noble
cause. And thus the American "nation" is imagined as a whole, as itself virtuous
and innocent, but united in its need to defeat evil. In this way, the individual,
common American is once again turned into a modernized version of the romantic
hero: war is inherently brutal, but the men fighting in this one were not – they
did not enjoy the killing, they were good men who wished only to return to their
families, but were prepared to sacrifice themselves for what they believed to be
right. Bodnar argues that while such sentiments were popular during and after the
war, there were many indications in the culture of the late 1940s and 1950s of a
more complicated response. Novels, stories, and films such as *The Naked and the
Dead*, *The Killers*, and *The Best Years of Our Lives* ask whether American society
itself was not in fact, inherently brutal and violent, whether those who fought really
did so for high-minded motives, and whether their wives and families at home were
really worth fighting for. Thus, the "memory" of the war became contested ground:
what was to be remembered, and what forgotten? who was to be memorialized and
who would disappear? *Ryan*, Bodnar argues, connects with the spirit of the times
in which it was created – contemporary American society is more inclined to
venerate the victim of tragic events than it is heroic generalship or leadership, more
inclined to focus attention on individual sufferings than the glory of patriotism. Like
Noakes, he concludes that memory is a work in progress, that it is not fixed and
static in the mind of the present.

Lisa Yoneyama asks whether, in fact, it is possible to construct a collective memory, or a public history, that the nation as a whole can agree upon. Dissecting the controversy that erupted when the National Aeronautics and Space Museum (operating within the Smithsonian Institution) planned to "commemorate" the atomic bombing of Hiroshima and Nagasaki in the "Enola Gay Exhibition" of 1995, she argues that the debate did not centre on historical "facts" – in spite of the efforts of both sides in the debate to marshal facts to their advantage – but rather on the issue of what was to be remembered, how. In this, she adopts a "postmodern" perspective (as evidenced by the terms she uses in her analysis: "facticity" "valorized" "cathected" "reify" "perspectival" "minoritized," and phrases like "amnesic hegemony" "subaltern historiography" and "antipodal appearance"), arguing that the division between "history" and "memory" is itself a false one, and that the contest over facts and language confirms the absence of a collective consciousness of the past (or the present). Reality is itself fractious, uncertain and fluid. Thus, conflicts over public commemorations are not really about "the past" but about what individuals, groups and perspectives can establish the authority to represent it within the present.

The controversy pitted those who considered themselves to be the guardians of the memory of US airmen against the curators who considered it their duty to represent the experience of all those involved in the event. Thus, the curators sought to display the suffering of the Japanese civilians in the cities – by presenting more than the usual aerial views from above – and to place the event within the broader context of the political and diplomatic environment – including the beginning of the nuclear age and the Cold War. The Air Force Association argued that this portrayal of the Japanese as victims was symptomatic of the moral relativism that was rampant in academies such as universities and museums in the late-twentieth century and that this represented something tantamount to treason to the patriotic memories of those who fought for the United States in the war. Thus, which photographs might be displayed, which documents could be presented were hotly contested. In the end, the exhibition took a very different shape than that which had been intended originally. Finally, Yoneyama intriguingly suggests ways in which modern reality is breaking down some of these binary national visions: because the debate became part of the public discourse in the United States, it transcended its boundaries and flowed over into Japan – with the result that elements and perspectives on each side of the Pacific intruded into the space of the other's national debate. In this way some peculiar, "modern" alliances took shape: between, for example American conservatives and Japanese liberals, both of whom believed that the imperialism, the militarism and the atrocities of Japan in China and the Pacific should be publicized and "remembered" as the most important features of World War Two. Perhaps, in the world of the twenty-first century, debates over history and memory can no longer be contained within the old, national boundaries.

Chapter 16

Pieter Lagrou

VICTIMS OF GENOCIDE AND NATIONAL MEMORY
Belgium, France and the Netherlands 1945–65

WHEN ASKED IN MAY 1995, precisely fifty years after the end of World War II in Europe, who the Nazis had deported to the concentration camps, 191 of 193 Belgian high-school students between fourteen and eighteen years of age, named the Jews as primary victims. The remaining two students named only Anne Frank. Homosexuals were the second most frequent category of victims to appear in the answers (98 students, or 50.7 per cent), followed by the handicapped (88 students, or 45.6 per cent), gypsies and political dissidents (both 75, or 38.9 per cent), arrested resistance fighters (62, or 32.1 per cent) and Communists (17, or 8.8 per cent). The high number of responses for homosexuals and the handicapped, and the low numbers for resistance fighters and Communists, is quite disproportionate to the actual share that these groups had in the total population of victims. Fourteen students (7.2 per cent) answered that the Nazis had sent non-European immigrants to the concentration camps, particularly blacks and Moroccans. Twelve students (6.2 per cent) included the elderly and the poor. These answers reflect the discourse which denunciates the intolerance and racism of the extreme right, rather than an insight into the historical reality with which it is identified. The image high-school students have of Nazi persecution, as manifested by this classification, is one of intolerance and exclusion, of a persecution of innocent civilians for what they were — Jews, homosexuals, handicapped, gypsies — and not primarily of the repression of opponents and rebels, who were persecuted for what they did.[1] The most obvious conclusion is that the Nazi persecution of European Jews has become part of the general knowledge of high-school students. If it is accepted that familiarity with the emblematic figure of Anne Frank supposes some knowledge of anti-Semitic persecution and genocide, then all of the students spontaneously thought of the persecution of Jews when asked about Nazi concentration camps. This article will place this conclusion in a historical perspective. Indeed, all the evidence available today suggests that the answers that a comparable group of students would have given in May 1945, or in any of the years thereafter during the 1940s and 1950s, would have ranked the groups very differently.

On 13 June 1945, the Gendarmerie Nationale noted in its general report for 15 March to 15 May:

> The announcement of the victory, the massive return of the prisoners and deportees, and the elections have been the three most striking facts of the period in question. The prisoners had known a prosperous and a fortunate France; they discover a poor country where everyone is assailed by the sorrows of the next day. The disenchantment is profound. As for the deportees, 'the best of the Nation', their clandestine struggle has enabled them to measure the depth of the chasm into which France has sunk; as a whole, the horrible experience they suffered has not blunted their abnegation and courage.

In the same report, some pages further on, an incident on 19 April in the fourth *arrondissement* of Paris is related: '250 to 300 people demonstrated, shouting "France to the French". A fight broke out with the Jews of the neighbourhood. The demonstration was occasioned by the expulsion of a person occupying the apartment of a Jew who had returned to Paris'.[2]

The researcher who investigates public opinion as regards the genocide and the return of the survivors of Nazi persecution from April to July 1945 discovers a picture that contradicts expectations. Repatriation was a major event that influenced the perception of the Second World War in occupied societies. Public opinion was shocked and sometimes obsessed by the images of the return: the arrival of the repatriation convoys in the railway stations and the welcoming parades organized in honour of the survivors. But the experience of the Jews and the discovery of the systematic killing of Jewish 'deportees' made far less impression than the 'concentration'; the ill-treatment and underfeeding of the other deportees not only resulted in relatively high death-rates, but also in the often shocking physical condition of the returning survivors.

A large proportion of the Jews deported from western Europe had transitted through the concentration camps on their way to extermination, and a small number of them survived the liberation. This fact contributed to their assimilation into the undifferentiated mass of 'deportees'. It seems that the awareness, the *prise de conscience* of the specificity of the Jewish experience, had not permeated contemporary public opinion and that in the reactions towards the survivors of genocide open hostility often prevailed. The hegemony with which arrested resisters dominated the received image of the populations of concentration camps immediately after the end of the Second World War, and particularly the marginal attention devoted to the Jewish victims of genocide, has been observed by several authors in different European countries.[3] Depending upon their own identification with a memory dominated by the experience of the Jewish victims or one dominated by that of arrested resistance fighters, the 'reversal' of the memory of Nazi persecution over the five decades since the end of the Second World War has stirred two very different reactions.

On the one hand, the marginal attention, the failure to perceive, or even — worded more strongly — the refusal to acknowledge the specificity of the treatment of Jews in the Nazi policies of persecution in the first two decades after the war nurtures the retroactive indignation of those writers who put genocide at the heart of the history of the period. The rediscovery of an interval much closer to the atrocities, during which governments, media and public opinion seemed untouched by the unprecedented tragedy of European Jews is seen as an extension of the injustice and discrimination Jews suffered during the war, and as a form of ongoing anti-Semitism. The place occupied by the Jewish experience in the respective national memories is, therefore, a matter of the national conscience and a denial of justice which must be remedied retrospectively. Revealing the 'de-Judaization' of the victims of genocide in post-war perceptions leads some commentators to an overall indictment of the prevalent ideologies of those years. The 'mythical amalgamation' of very different categories of victims is deemed to have been the result of a '*gauchissement*', a 'fabricated universality', or a very outdated form of 'Polish' anti-fascism.[4] Some British historians do not hesitate to blame contemporary British perceptions on Britain's 'exclusive national framework', 'assimilationism' and 'universalism', even though Britain was, by all accounts, rather peripheral to the continental genocide. All three of these terms are identified as devices for the imposition of a monocultural society: 'exclusivism' through the exclusion of people from other ethnic, cultural or religious backgrounds; 'assimilationism' through the absorption of these people into the society, thus eradicating their distinct identities; and 'universalism' through the axiomatic proclamation of the global validity of strictly West European, Enlightenment values. For one commentator, the failure to perceive the particularity of Jewish suffering even calls into question 'the liberal imagination' which lies at the source of the enumerated ills.[5] In a rather perplexing combination, both universalism and anti-Semitism, and assimilationism and exclusivism stand accused of 'de-Judaization'.

The 'reversal of memories' that has taken place in more recent decades is, on the other hand, a major source of frustration for the last surviving guardians of the patriotic memories of Nazi persecution. They resent their marginalization in the current interest into the Nazi period and cultivate a certain nostalgia for their post-war hegemony. It is, furthermore, a concern to some historians, who are alarmed by the one-sidedness of a historical consciousness of the period that is induced by a commemorative activism which isolates genocide from its context of 'ordinary' persecution.[6] They claim that a Judaeo-centric memory is, from the point of view of a historian, hardly preferable to a patriotic memory.

The present article is not concerned with the issues of justice and contemporary memory, but tries to approach the post-war national memories from a historical perspective. In order to do so, three goals will be pursued. First, a historical understanding of post-war memory supposes a change of focus from the experience of the war years to the perception of the post-war years. The survivors' self-understanding of their experiences, as expressed in eye-witness accounts, does not explain the receptivity of post-war society to such accounts. Secondly, the perspective of the historian requires a comparative approach, integrating different forms of persecution. The Nazi persecution of the Jews can, in retrospect, rightly or wrongly, be distinguished and isolated from, as well as compared and amalgamated with, the experience of other groups; yet the fact remains that the victims and survivors of the genocide were physically intermingled with victims and survivors of other forms of persecution, and that it is this mixture that conditioned contemporary perceptions. The fact that the genocide was not perceived in its specificity does not, in itself, provide an explanation. In order to understand the marginality of the memory of genocide, what is required is an investigation of what has hidden it from view and an analysis of the more urgent and obtrusive memories that mobilized post-war societies. Thirdly, an understanding of the processes at work in post-war memories benefits from a comparison of different national case studies. The way that each society has dealt with the traumatic memory of Nazi persecution is most often analysed through a prism of national traumas and policies. Vichy's particular responsibility for the extermination of Jews in France, and the extraordinary rate of Jewish extermination in the Netherlands — comparable only with that in Eastern European nations — engage both the moral and political responsibilities of those nations. Yet the general processes at work tend to be obscured by scrutiny of the national conscience and thus stand in the way of a historical understanding of the way that different national post-war societies dealt with the memory of similar events. In contrast to France and the Netherlands, in Belgium there is hardly a public debate on the national responsibility for the genocide. This absence of moral scrutiny is caused mainly by the current dismemberment of Belgium. No new nation is eager to inherit the moral debts of its predecessor, and the legacy of the genocide is one of the very few Belgian competencies none of the regions claim.

This article will survey some of the factors which explain the failure to perceive the singular experience of the tens of thousands of Jews deported from the national territories of Belgium, France and the Netherlands. It is not a study of the perception of the 'Holocaust' or the 'Shoah', which is the continental tragedy that took place mainly in central and eastern Europe, and in which one-third of world Jewry and two-thirds of European Jewry were murdered, destroying a centuries' old local Jewish culture. To attempt such a study for the two decades before 1965 would be anachronistic, since the very dimensions of the continental tragedy, as manifested in contemporary terminology, were very slow to emerge, even among professional historians.[7] As it is, the three countries that we are concerned with here failed to assess even the tragedy of their own Jewish populations, which made up — numerically — only a marginal part of the continental tragedy.

I From the social memory of the survivors to the historical memory of the dead

During the massive repatriation operations after the Second World War, the repatriates themselves were the most powerful vehicle for the memory of what had happened in German exile. The reports of the repatriation authorities and the police relate the tremendous impact of the arrival of the repatriation convoys in every town, even in the most remote villages. Welcoming committees and anxious families awaited the return of individuals, who, in the overwhelming majority of

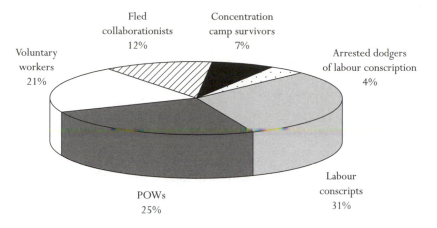

Figure 16.1 Repatriation to Belgium

cases, were workers and prisoners of war. Survivors of concentration camps were still less numerous than returning collaborationists, who had fled with the German army and were now obliged to endure a humiliating return. (Fig. 16.1)

Repatriates organized, and their associations immediately propagated, their partisan memories. The prisoners of war were successful in organizing and, not without difficulty, in having their conventional war experiences integrated into the national memory.[8] The deported workers, or STO as they are called nowadays in France, faced a bigger challenge.[9] Their social and national reintegration depended on the propagation of the memory of forced labour in Germany as both a form of national martyrdom and resistance. They were successful in Belgium; they were militant, but failed to get recognition in France; and in the Netherlands, they never even succeeded in overcoming the ostracism suffered by organizations of this kind.

Associations of the survivors of concentration camps were necessarily a distorted representation of the victims of the Nazi persecution. They included the inmates of national prisons and hostages or victims of torture who had never left national territory for German camps, but they did not comprise tens of thousands of victims who had disappeared in deportation. Most importantly, there were no survivors of the genocide strictly speaking. The only Jews who escaped the immediate annihilation that characterized the genocide and had a chance of survival were those who had been selected and registered to enter the concentration camps, or had ended up in concentration camps on their way to the centres of mass death. They were a very small minority of the survivors in repatriation convoys and associations.

In the mechanisms of social memory, the dead have no role to play. Only after a historical memory had emerged — that is, a memory integrating the dead — were the calculations different. If those who returned are counted, the Jewish deportees were outnumbered twenty to one by the non-Jewish deportees.[10] As regards deportation, they were five Jewish to one non-Jewish deportee in the Netherlands; in Belgium, they were five Jewish deportees to eight 'political prisoners' (a conglomerate of the Nazis' victims who were entitled to national recognition); in France, Jewish deportees and a comparable conglomerate made up of 'political deportees and internees' and 'deportees and internees of the resistance' stand almost one to one. (Figs 16.2, 16.3; and Table 1) These figures show the tragic proof of two very different realities: the genocide, on the one hand; and the concentration camp system for the Netherlands, and Nazi persecution in general in Belgium and France, on the other. Still, the question remains as to why both have been amalgamated in post-war memory.

II Anti-Semitism

As the aforementioned incident in Paris in April 1945 indicates, anti-Semitism is an inevitable context for the marginality of the memory of the genocide in post-war societies. Both blatant and latent anti-Semitism had been necessary pre-conditions for the massive deportations of Jews from the occupied societies, and it would be an underestimation of the inveteracy of anti-Semitism in western European societies to suppose that it suddenly disappeared with the discovery of the genocide in 1945.[11] First of all, there are manifestations of continuing anti-Semitism. Returning survivors were on several occasions registered as 'Jews' on official repatriation

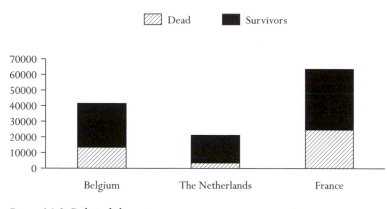

Figure 16.2 Political deportees

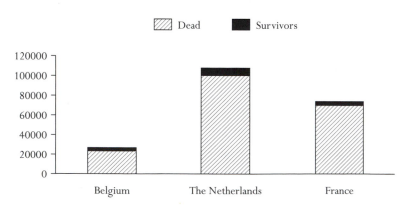

Figure 16.3 Jewish deportees

Table 16.1 Survivors of the concentration camps*

	Political deportees			Racial deportees		
	Deportees	Survivors		Deportees	Survivors	
Belgium	41,257	27,299	(66%)	25,475	1,335	(5%)
The Netherlands	22,200	17,915	(81%)	107,000	5,000	(5%)
France	65,000	38,000	(61%)	73,853	2,190	(2.7%)

*Sources: see n. 10

documents.[12] Contrary to what critics of the 'de-Judaization' of the survivors claim today, these repatriates very much resented being once again singled out as Jews, after having barely survived racial persecution.[13] The most shocking aberrations by repatriation officials were recorded by Dienke Hondius in the Netherlands. Stateless Jews, who had emigrated from Nazi Germany to the Netherlands in the 1930s and had been deported during the occupation, were arrested upon their return from Bergen-Belsen and imprisoned together with collaborationists as 'former German nationals'.[14] These repeated incidents caused indignant protests, but they indicate how weak the impact of the discovery of the genocide had been in wider circles, including those involved in administering the repatriation. In France, the Gendarmerie Nationale registered anti-Semitic graffiti in the first six months of 1945, such as that discovered in Courbevoie on 19 February: 'Down with the war, down with the denouncers, the firing squad for all Jews'.[15] The repatriation officials in Toulouse observed that 'the intrigues' of repatriated Jews risked 'to provoke or to foster a new crisis of anti-Semitism' and reported their efforts to halt the militancy of this group 'excessive both because of their small number and because of the fact that they are foreigners'.[16] Forced 'assimilationism' occurred when Christian churches — not the State — hid, educated and baptized Jewish children, and then refused to return them to their Jewish relatives or Zionist organizations.[17]

Secondly, anti-Semitism seemed in part to be strengthened by the genocide, taking up new themes, such as the lack of Jewish resistance and Jewish treason. A general tendency of thinking developed, which suggested that if the Jews attracted such unprecedented persecution, then they had to be guilty of something. Traditional Christian anti-Semitism was also reappropriated from the Nazis. In the Spring of 1945, a Dutch author living in liberated Belgium, at a time when the majority of the Netherlands was still occupied, took stock of the years of German occupation in both countries and of the challenges ahead. The book, which was published in May 1945 by a publisher situated close to the border, was distributed in the Netherlands immediately. In his chapter on the persecution of Jews by the Nazis, the author felt compelled to warn his readers not to credit Hitler for his accomplishments:

> Even if we accept that the power and influence of Jewry in our modern society are not imaginary, yes, if we even willingly admit that the right-eous resistance and fair measures against numerous Jewish practices

positively benefit Christian society, then still it remains no less true that no Christian of conviction can approve the phenomena that present themselves nowadays under the universal, as well as meaningless, name of anti-Semitism. If today we find a certain category of Christian (and it is not unimportant) who sympathizes with this persecution, we ought not to forget that if we Christians had in general shown more courage and conviction and faith in the first place, Jewish and liberal influences would never have permeated society to the degree that they did. The Jews were guilty of the murder of God's Son, but the Roman Pontius Pilate was no less guilty when he nailed an innocent to the cross out of cowardice . . . Of course, the Jewish problem is a burning question, but those who wish its solution out of hatred, and often out of anger and envy, have rejected Christian love and with it their Christianity . . . Christian love requires a different struggle, a different anti-Semitism. The mass murder of the Jewish people is the clearest proof that national socialism is not anti-Semitic, but anti-Christian. Of course, the Christian world will have to fight its war against Jewish hegemony, but a struggle according to its own principles and not according to the whispering of some evil spirit . . . The freedom we yearn for must not lead to licentiousness and anarchism, because they are the trump cards through which the liberal-Jewish hegemony can establish itself.[18]

An early awareness of 'the mass murder of the Jewish people' was not at all incompatible with a continuing, traditional, anti-Semitic discourse. Still, even if anti-Semitism was more widespread in 1945 and thereafter than an observer would expect today, it cannot account for the marginality of the memory of the genocide in society as a whole. Anti-Semitic attitudes are often concealed in the arguments of protagonists in the commemorative debate, yet they are not the only explanation.

III The construction of patriotic memories

Immediately after the liberation of the occupied countries of Europe, both in the East and the West, a patriotic memory of the Resistance emerged as a collective image of society during the war. Governments and political movements proceeded to 'nationalize' the resistance, reclaiming the merits of the minority of groups and individuals that had been active during the occupation. Even more explicitly, they modified the meaning of 'resistance' and expanded its scope to cover the whole of society. Various types of resistance were legally defined or proclaimed in polemical publications: civil resistance, moral resistance, spiritual resistance.[19] In France, former pro-Vichy circles distinguished '*resistancialisme*', from *la Résistance*, in which the whole nation had participated; and *resistantialisme*, from *les résistants*, who were no more than unruly elements, peripheral to the epic of the Nation. The shield-and-sword theory distributed the merit for the Resistance equally between Generals De Gaulle and Pétain.[20] Very similar discourses in the Netherlands and Belgium awarded this merit to the 'Dutch Union' or the Belgian secretary-generals. The former was a political movement during the first year of the occupation, that had defended loyalty towards the Nazis; the latter were the leading administrators who had stayed in office throughout the occupation under German orders.[21]

As a result, 'resistance' in the post-war debate no longer referred to a specific social group or type of actions, and because of the proliferation of definitions, it more often than not became a value judgement of attitudes held during the war. Therefore, it became the yardstick by which political legitimacy was measured. One had to prove patriotic merit during the war in order to qualify for a political role thereafter.

Resistance, as a collective self-image of the liberated societies, required an active denial of the actual experience of the occupation. Unprecedented military defeat, humiliating occupation, and liberation by other foreign armies, albeit friendly and allied, had been a triple demonstration of national impotence. The nation state, carefully constructed since the nineteenth century, was supposed to guarantee the protection of its civilians, the rule of law, national loyalty and international prestige. Defeat, collaboration, economic plunder, deportation of the work-force and unprecedented persecution threw it into a deep crisis of confidence. Active resistance had been the radical choice of a determined, and often, in political terms, a marginal minority. Heroism had not been the dominant collective experience of society, but rather economic hardship, individual suffering, humiliation and arbitrary persecution.

The liberated societies of Europe were traumatized and their now fragile national consciousnesses badly needed the kind of patriotic epic that only the Resistance could deliver. Persecution, as a more fundamental experience, was unspeakable and unacceptable in this context. Mourning without triumphalism would have undermined post-war national recovery. The threatening memory of impotence, humiliation and loss of meaning at best, and of complicity at worst, could only be commemorated through the prism of resistance and patriotism. Such a selective memory denied the distinctiveness of the Second World War when compared to previous conflicts, and particularly to the First World War.

The patriotic interpretation of the occupation had to come to terms with disruptive issues. There was no homogeneous and properly national *milieu de mémoire*, as the veterans of the First World War had been as conscripts of a national and regular army. The soldier-hero was replaced by much more controversial types of heroes, including terrorist guerrillas, who had often been primarily engaged in an ideological battle. Many were foreigners, and even more were Communists, who had fought for an ideal that was viewed as anti-national by traditional patriots. Could they be national heroes? The interpretative problem was even greater when dealing with the martyrs and necrologies: these were not fallen soldiers, but tens of thousands of civil victims of ideological persecution and genocide. Could they become national martyrs?

Martyrs die for a noble cause, which gives sense to their suffering. This sense could only be patriotic in the traumatized, liberated societies. This left commemorators with two alternative solutions. A government or political movement could decide to commemorate only victims of the Resistance, who had defied their fate and 'merited' or 'provoked' their suffering by heroism: this was the case in the post-war Netherlands. Yet the commemorative discourse could also include all the victims of persecution, no matter the reason for arrest or the category or context of the persecution. If not resister, then still patriot. Attempts at such a policy of memory were made with partial success in Belgium and France.

As the quotation from the gendarmerie report at the start of this article suggests, the 'nationalization' of the victims of Nazi persecution is an immediate assumption. All deportees are 'the best of the Nation', all have been engaged in underground struggle, all excel in abnegation and courage. Yet, this 'nationalization' of martyrdom was not just a spontaneous interpretation, but a political construct.

Belgium

In Belgium, the political debate as to the right attitude during the war was personified in the 'royal question'. The former Catholic party, re-baptized as the Christian Popular Party, supported the king and through him defended the various degrees of accommodation and 'tactical collaboration', including the policy of leniency as far as the purging of former members of collaborationist parties. Against the king and his supporters, liberals, socialists and Communists formed a left-wing, coalition government between August 1945 and March 1947. This self-proclaimed 'Government of the Resistance' prevented the king from reassuming the throne and launched a vast commemorative programme whose aim was to recognize and distinguish meritorious citizens from the rest.[22] The strong Catholic opposition in parliament often obliged them to make compromises, which led to a fragmented and overlapping legal patchwork, that recognized the 'patriotic merit' of various groups from various political backgrounds. Laws created procedures of recognition and benefits with which to award armed resisters, civil resisters, resisters of the underground press, intelligence agents, persons who hid in order to escape forced labour in Germany, workers who were victims of forced labour in Germany and — via the most prestigious act — 'political prisoners'.

The architect of the commemorative programme was a Communist minister, Jean Terfve. Terfve had been one of the leaders of the underground party, active in all the branches of the Resistance, including the partisans. His wife was repatriated from Ravensbrück in May 1945. Terfve's personal involvement granted him two important successes. First, the mediation of the ministry led to the creation of a single national association for all survivors of the German camps and prisons: the *Confédération National des Prisonniers Politiques et leurs Ayants-Droits*.[23] Secondly, Terfve obtained the support of this national association for his project to have an act passed for political prisoners that would create an honorary distinction and social aid programme for all victims. The project adopted the 'criterion of the suffering'.[24] The reason for arrest was irrelevant to the law, as there was a sufficient number of other laws recognizing all kinds of patriotic activism during the occupation. What really mattered was the dignity and courage with which the victims had endured their ordeal. It was this suffering, this sacrifice in the hands of the enemy, that elevated all victims to the rank of heroes of the Nation. However, in the everyday parlance and the legal dispositions, a notion dating from the First World War was also taken up: that of the 'political prisoner'. Already after 1918, the victims of the German repression of the *francs-tireurs* had been recognized and decorated with the same honour as those members of the regular army who had fallen in the trenches. This mixture of a traditional patriotic notion with the new situation of the post-Nazi era provoked immediate protest:

> When, after the war of 1914–18 one said of a person "he was a political prisoner", the public knew this person had committed an act of patriotism. There was no other meaning. Today things are no longer the same. When one says "political prisoner", public opinion — and our adversaries should have the courage to admit this — immediately asks the question "Communist? Jew? hostage? or resister?" It is not us who claim the distinguo, it is public opinion. Of course, there is no shame in belonging to one category rather than another. Yet it is normal that a prisoner is indignant if he is suspected of having acted during the German occupation from purely poltical motivation, when his acts were always inspired by the purest patriotism. You do not have to be anti-Semitic to be troubled if someone suspects you mistakenly of having been arrested as a Jew.[25]

Terfve's act was approved unanimously in the House of Representatives, after the intervention of the Catholic president of the Confederation. In the Senate, where the Catholic opposition was only one seat short of an absolute majority, the proposal was held up.[26] The opposition submitted an amendment which introduced a 'patriotic clause' into the act. The statute had considerable financial implications: the survivors would be entitled to free medical care, life-long indemnities, unlimited stipends for the schooling of their children and so on; however, the amendments were not concerned with the costs. Indeed, in the Belgian context no one could afford to exclude from the aid programme victims who had been arrested for reasons other than resistance. The subtlety of the Catholic proposal was that everyone would have equal rights to aid, but that only resisters would be entitled to the recognition of the nation and to the honorary clause of the statute: the title and the medal of political prisoner. The Catholic intervention also had another rationale. If, as public attention and respect indicated, the survivors of the camps — now called political prisoners — deserved national appreciation because of their sacrifices and patriotism, then they represented key symbolic and political capital. As a consequence, it was important that each party secured its share. In the total group of survivors, the Catholics were a small minority. Those who had been arrested preventatively and those who had been taken as hostages had been chosen for their pre-war antifascism and were mostly Freemasons and atheists. The racial deportees had been almost uniquely Jews. In short, only among the arrested resisters were there a fair number of Catholics to be found.

The unyielding attitude of the Catholic opposition forced the minister to search for a new compromise. The final text of the act stipulated that the honorary distinction was to be attributed to three groups: arrested resisters; all those arrested because of their political or philosophical convictions; and all those who could prove to have shown a truly heroic and patriotic attitude during their imprisonment.[27] Cleverly formulated, this compromise meant that the Jewish survivors of the camps were not entitled to this national appreciation. The Jews had not been deported for something they did or chose, but for being Jews. Today, it is precisely that which is seen as the ultimate transgression of Nazism, but this message was politically impotent in the immediate post-war years. Then the Jews were used as change in a political trade-off. Moreover, the statute only dealt with national merit. The Jews who were denied this merit, but still received aid, were a small minority. Only about 5 per cent of the Jews deported from Belgium during the occupation had Belgian nationality. For foreign political prisoners there was a second law.[28] According to this law only deported foreigners who fought in the Resistance could receive aid and naturalization.

Even though the governing majority denounced, incidentally, the 'anti-Semitism' of the Catholic manoeuvre, the Catholic boycott harvested little criticism and the compromise was welcomed with ecumenical satisfaction.[29] More decisive than the anti-Semitism had been the anti-Communism of the Christian Popular Party: the 'criterion of the suffering' was, in their eyes, no more than a trick to smuggle coverage into the statutes for those Communists who had been arrested on the night of the German invasion of the Soviet Union, after a year of anti-allied propaganda under the slogan 'ni Londres ni Berlin'. Forced to concede on the inclusion of the governing Communists, the Christian Popular Party settled for the peace offering which the Jewish survivors constituted.

The trauma of the concentration camps made a deep impact on the post-war years in Belgium and the special moral heritage of the survivors was universally respected. The quarrels concerning the statute ended in the 'national' compromise to exclude the Jews from the honorary distinction. The unity of the survivors was a unique accomplishment in post-war Belgium. The common experience of the camps and the solidarity that grew there enabled the survivors to surmount the deep divisions of Belgian post-war society. At the height of the royal question, the Confederation lent its moral prestige to a peaceful compromise between the parties, leading to the abdication of King Leopold and his succession by his eldest son.[30] The memory of the Nazi persecution was intimately intertwined in Belgian post-war politics. It was not only a social memory, it was political capital; and in this context, a historical memory had no chance.

France

Nowhere was patriotic legitimacy more crucial in post-war politics than in France. It was the only legitimacy General Charles De Gaulle had when he returned from exile and declared the constitutionally legitimate heir of the Third Republic, the Vichy regime, null and void.[31] The amalgamation of colonists and exiles that had made up his Free French forces was not a firm basis upon which to build a new regime. De Gaulle was thus forced to propagate a generous and collective vision of the French combat to liberate France: to silence the role of Vichy and the role of the allies, and to nationalize the contribution of the resistance movements on French territory. De Gaulle's commemorative policy — as provisional head of state between liberation and January 1946, from the opposition until 1958, and then as president of his self-styled fifth republic until 1969 — assimilated the Nation and the Resistance into a symbolic discourse that was at the same time heroic, emblematic, abstract and élitist. The national honour had been safeguarded throughout the ordeal of the war by the heroes who presided over its destiny, in exile or on French soil, as combatants or as martyrs. Gaullist speeches and rituals staged tributes to the army and the nation through exemplary models of patriotism and assimilated the ambiguous victory of the Second World War with the patriotic triumph of the First. Abstract commemoration and its consensual appeal suited De Gaulle better than the cult of veteranism. He opposed the re-establishment of a ministry of veterans after the liberation; he resented the organizations of prisoners of war and labour conscripts, both of which united hundreds of thousands of dubious heroes; and he certainly did not favour the proliferation of heroism over the many groups of veterans of the Resistance and victims of persecution.

The Communist memory has often been presented as the opposite resistance myth in all regards.[32] The national insurrection and partisan war of the internal Resistance took the place of the external Resistance and its classic military feats — the Maquis instead of Bir Hakeim. The war in the colonies and at the side of the western allies was replaced by the glorious victory of the Red Army. Instead of De Gaulle's abstract and ecumenical references to the Nation, the French Communist Party (PCF) identified strongly with concrete heroes and martyrs. It cultivated its martyrs — 'the party of the 75,000 executed militants' — and organized successfully a whole corona of veterans' associations of partisans, deported workers and victims of the Nazis. The immediate post-war period corresponds with the party's most expansive period. Communist ranks had been decimated by persecution and the party was actively canvassing for new members and voters, an operation that proved successful, partly because of the appeal of the aura of resistance. Instead of an exclusive memory, appropriating patriotic merit and stressing the distinction between the historically certified resisters and those who joined the myth *post factotum*, the PCF propagated a memory that was as open and inclusive as possible. The reference to the Nation, central to the Gaullist discourse, was replaced by the reference both to the working class, who were deemed to have embodied the resistance against a collaborating bourgeoisie and its reactionary ideology, and to anti-fascism. The paradigm of anti-fascism was the most inclusive. All political opponents of fascism, and even more all victims of fascism, could subscribe to it and become part of an anti-fascist family in which the Communist party played, presently and historically, a central role and where martyrdom and heroism, victims and veterans, intermingled and fraternally shared the heritage of victory.

The confrontation between Gaullist heroic and élitist patriotism, and Communist-inspired inclusive anti-fascism over the official recognition of the victims of Nazi occupation was parallel to the conflict between patriots and anti-fascists in Belgium. This debate did not end in a compromise though, but secured the dichotomy by two separate laws: one for the *déportés et internés de la résistance*, the other for the *déportés et internés politiques*, including the Jews; and through two separate associations: the *Fédération Nationale des Déportés et Internés de la Résistance*, which was exclusively for resisters, and the *Fédération Nationale des Déportés et Internés Résistants et Patriotes*, which was for all survivors, even if they had not been resisters.[33] The difference in vocabulary is revealing. In Belgium, the First World War term 'political prisoner' was taken up again, and through it the notion of resistance and patriotism crept into the debate. In France, a new notion was created, with an even stronger mythical appeal: *la Déportation*.[34]

Deportation as a mythical concept is crucial to the understanding of the trauma of the occupation for French society. Of all the occupied countries, France was the most humiliated, because of its pre-war standing and size, its unprecedented military defeat, and because of Vichy, the *collaboration d'Etat*. The captivity in Germany of 1.5 million French soldiers, later joined by half as many labour conscripts and 200,000 'deportees' of the Nazi persecution, was the most tangible and physical of all humiliations. Vichy, in spite of its extensive collaboration, had been incapable of preventing or reversing the stream of French citizens captured and taken to Germany. The paternalist Pétain, the soldier-hero of 1918 and the father of the troops, had been unable to bring his boys home. The *révolution nationale*, with its patronizing and corporatist discourse on the working class, had been unable to keep the workers in domestic occupations (*Travail*), with their families (*Famille*), or in their country (*Patrie*). Vichy had developed a moral and religious discourse of penance for prewar weaknesses and repentance in exile in preparation for renewal.

Similarly, De Gaulle had initiated, first in London and later in Algiers, an impressive propaganda campaign, which had been aimed at the Allies and the home front to convert the millions of young Frenchmen in German hands into the asset of a fifth column: a huge and organized secret army, ready for general insurrection at the first sign of invasion. Vichy and '*la France Libre*' competed in Germany for the allegiance of the displaced French citizens, through Petainist circles, Gaullist propaganda and a parcel post battle that sought to deliver as many Red Cross parcels as possible on each side. Repatriation became the first priority for De Gaulle and his minister, Henri Frénay. Frénay's dominant concern was to give a unanimous welcome to all victims of 'deportation' — captivity, forced labour and persecution — under the slogan: 'they are united, do not divide them'. This mythical unity had never existed in Germany, where French citizens had lived through very different experiences according to their fate. It did not survive their return either. The prisoners of war quickly went their own way, as did the deported workers and *déportés politiques*, and, as mentioned earlier, the latter split again between 'resisters' and 'political deportees', *sensu stricto*.

La Déportation became the stake in a bitter '*bataille de mémoire*'.[35] Charged with the myth of martyrdom and patriotism, the survivors of the concentration camps engaged in a battle to monopolize the term for their own use. In this campaign, resisters and 'politicals' united, in spite of the general meaning of the concept during the occupation and in the immediate years thereafter. The issue was magnified and redefined as 'the defence of the sacred title, symbol of the sufferings, endured for the liberation of the Fatherland'.[36] '*La Déportation*' became a founding myth of post-war France, together with '*La Résistance*', and was of equal strength. In 1956, Fernand Braudel, Lucien Févre, Albert Camus, Jules Romains, Vercors (Jean Bruller), Mgr Salièges and many others lent their prestige to a declaration against the use of the tide of *déporté* by deported workers:

> These *transplantés* are not Deportees. There is more at stake here than a simple question of semantics. The 'Deportation' did not enter history solely as displacement and forced labour: it implies torture, insane convoys, the gas chambers and the crematoria; the dehumanization and the extermination of millions of human beings. It is inseparable from an

ethic — that should be condemned for ever — by which the 'superior' being arrogates the right to degrade, before killing, those it judges inferior. It constitutes the greatest crime ever perpetrated against man, and its recurrence should be prevented at all cost. To diminish the horror by extending to others the *auréole* of the name of Deportee is committing at the same time a historical solecism, a denial of justice and an insult to the memory of all those who were also obliged into forced labour while waiting for an obligatory death. The draftees, victims of the Forced Labour Service [STO], do not benefit much by claiming the title of Deportee. But, through the confusion their demands create, they weaken our appreciation of the repercussions and enormity of the crime. Unconsciously, they render themselves accomplices to oblivion. They undermine the sacred cause of the defence of Man.[37]

Rejecting a possible amalgamation between forced labour and concentration camps, these French intellectuals, for all their prestige, subscribed to an amalgamation of a different kind. Deportation was a common and inevitable point of departure. Concentration — where death was very probable, but by no means 'obligatory' — and extermination — genocide, with gas chambers, mechanical devices for mass killing as opposed to crematoria, and mechanical devices to treat bodies — were very different destinations. A discourse of national martyrdom, with the concentration camp as the symbolic depository of national suffering, which excluded deported workers but included the victims of the genocide, created consciously or unconsciously a regrettable confusion and contributed to the oblivion of the singular treatment of the Jews by the Nazis.

The Netherlands

A very different policy of memory was pursued with astonishing coherence and consensus in the Netherlands. The Netherlands had remained neutral during World War I, so unlike Belgium and France there was no pre-established memory of the previous war to impose itself as a ready-made interpretation on the most recent war. The paradigm of the combatant and the social reality of veterans' movements, which were so pervasive in Belgian and French society, could not serve as references or devices by which to assimilate the disruptive memory of Nazi occupation with the heroic memory of the Great War.[38] After 1945, in Belgium and France, survivors of the camps had emulated these models in their commemorations, with symbols and rituals drawn from a military context, such as the use of banners or the laying of wreaths at the monument to the unknown soldier.

In addition to this difference, the peculiar chronology of the military operations that liberated western Europe set Dutch society apart from its southern neighbours. The failure of the assault on the Rhine at Arnhem in October 1944 condemned the largest piece of Dutch territory to a further nine months of occupation, until the Germans surrendered in May 1945. The harsh last Winter — the 'hunger Winter' — caused the whole population to suffer.[39] Whereas the suffering of specific groups — Communists, deported workers and Jews — had characterized the previous years of occupation, now famine, large-scale material destruction and massive

migrations of civilians to escape hunger, flooding and allied bombing caused indiscriminate suffering. At the time of the Dutch liberation, 1.5 million Dutch citizens
were displaced: one million refugees due to the military confrontation; tens of thousands because of hunger in the cities; 80,000 as prisoners of the Japanese army in
the former colony; and 350,000 workers in hiding. This greatly reduced the public's
capacity to commiserate with particular groups of martyrs — the *milieux de mémoire*
that had epitomized the experience of the nation in Belgium and France. Most
concentration camps had been liberated earlier than the Dutch heartland, and
displaced persons repatriated from Germany were greatly outnumbered by domestic
refugees. Extraordinary and extra-territorial suffering in German camps did not
come to public attention in the way that it did in Belgium and France, nor was the
return of the survivors anxiously awaited. The atmosphere of indifference towards
repatriates is illustrated, among many other reactions, by the Dutch historian
Hondius, who recorded the welcome one Jewish survivor received: 'Well, quite a
lot of your kind came back. Just be happy you were not here. How we suffered
from hunger!'[40]

This very different response was reinforced by a deliberate government policy.
The chaotic situation in the Netherlands in the Summer months of 1945 placed great
strain on the entire infrastructure of social and medical assistance, the distribution
and rationing of food, elementary household equipment and clothing, as well as on
the government budget. Faced with this widespread destitution, the government
decreed that 'an allotment of the landscape of war into categories of victims had to
be avoided at any price': 'Naming certain groups in any regulation in this matter
will inevitably cause new groups to claim their rights. As soon as the principle of
individual assistance is given up, a chain reaction of claims invoking the acquired
rights of others will cause an explosion of the budget'.[41] Social policy and national
recognition were therefore to be separated.

As a result, the government declared 'veteranism' to be a very un-Dutch and
unpatriotic activity that had shown its social uselessness in the pre-war years in
France, and particularly in Belgium. It ignored and boycotted all pressure groups,
including those of Resistance veterans. Any group claiming special merit or special
suffering not only threatened to be a burden on the national budget, but also endan-
gered the national consensus that heroism and martyrdom had been the collective
experience of the Dutch people, symbolized by that emblematic figure of national
affection, Queen Wilhelmina. This policy of forced consensus was even extended
to the regulation for war monuments, which had to honour the anonymous memory
of the Nation and carry an elevating message.[42] The inscription of the names of
those citizens who had fallen for the Fatherland and the erection of monuments
portraying identifiable heroes were not approved by the national commission which
was created to implement the regulation, and were consequently demolished.
According to the official line which guided government contact with the organizations of survivors of the Nazi camps, the objections to organizations of Resistance
veterans, who even if their activism disrupted the national consensus at least personified heroism and collective idealism, was all the more justified as far as 'political
prisoners' went (the Dutch having spontaneously integrated the Belgian vocabulary). The Nazis' amalgamation of victims from very different backgrounds in the
camps precluded any legitimate post-war activity on behalf of the survivors: 'Their

only goal can be claims for special benefits or political manipulation, since they are not in any way united by a common action or ideal'.[43]

The only organization that had the official endorsement of the government was the Foundation 1940–45.[44] It was a private charitable organization that took care of those victims persecuted for their participation in the Resistance, their widows and orphans. It was created by the Calvinist (Catholic in the south) clandestine relief organization. It opened its ranks to all resisters after the liberation, but activists from religious organizations continued to provide 90 per cent of its membership on local committees. From 1950 onwards, Communists were officially excluded. As a charitable foundation, it was not an organization of the victims of the Resistance, but an organization for them, in which their role was only passive, as recipients of aid. The financial resources of the Foundation came from private funding through local collection committees: house-to-house collections were a small part; the over-whelming majority of the funds came from donations from industry and commerce. In the Summer of 1947, the Dutch parliament passed a law establishing a special pension for victims of the Resistance, but it charged the private Foundation with the implementation of the law. Hence the Foundation was both judge and advocate in the distribution of remittances.

The founding statute of the Foundation defined its task as 'the care for the moral, spiritual and material needs of persons or groups of persons who during the occupation contributed to the internal resistance by deed or attitude, their families or next of kin'.[45] This definition marked the narrow national and Resistance posi-tion of the Foundation. Victims of German repression who had not committed acts of resistance were excluded: hostages, victims of retaliation, people who had been arrested because of their pre-war anti-fascist activities, and racial deportees. Yet, for the victims of the Resistance on national soil, the Foundation wanted the best treatment possible. The predominant influence of the Calvinist and Catholic volun-teers, the financial weight of the industrial and commercial élites, the patronizing structure of the assistance, the socially conservative distribution of available funds, the official role in the distribution of government pensions and the exclusively patri-otic selection all converged to turn Foundation 1940–45 into a respected national institution of charity and a custodian of a properly national memory of persecution.

The very limited target group of the Foundation left the overwhelming majority of war victims excluded. Compared with Belgium and France, the survivors of the concentration camps stand out. In both of these countries, the political prisoners and deportees formed the most active and respected *milieu de mémoire*. In the Netherlands, liberation and repatriation coincided, and in the midst of the chaos of the early Summer of 1945, when more than one-fifth of the population was displaced and large parts were underfed, public opinion remained relatively unimpressed and unmoved by the return of the inmates of the concentration camps. In this context, the experience of the survivors of the genocide went almost unnoticed. The only pressure group active in organizing survivors of the camps recruited the same target group of deported resisters, the Dutch Union of Former Political Prisoners (*Nederlandse Vereniging van Ex-Politieke Gevangenen*), or ExPoGe. Nationalist, and after 1949 fiercely anti-Communist, the organization never secured acceptance as the representative of the deported resisters. The government addressed itself exclu-sively to the Foundation and it did this upon the explicit demand of the Resistance élite. The anti-Communist zeal of the ExPoGe with its 'Combat Committee against the Concentration Camp System' (*Strijdcomite tegen het Concentratiekamp Systeem*) would lend it more respectability in the early 1950s and even lead to a rapprochement with the Foundation.

Survivors of the concentration camps who had not been part of the Resistance found refuge in the Communist organization, the United Resistance of the Netherlands, together with Communist and left-wing activists who had never been victims of Nazi persecution. From 1956 onwards, at the instigation of the *Fédération Internationale des Résistants*, the Communists created national committees of survivors of certain camps, the Auschwitz Committee being the most active and well known. From 1961 onwards, a government, anti-Communist Dachau committee, financed by donations from major Dutch private companies, counterbalanced the Communist influence mainly through anti-Soviet sensitization campaigns.

The severe crisis that hit the Dutch consensus model in the late 1960s also led to a crisis in the Dutch politics of memory. New types of associations for Resistance veterans and survivors of the camps emerged to claim national recognition and compensation. Both the claims and the subsequent legislation of 1972, which recognized the victims of Resistance and persecution, established the kind of national recognition that the same groups had legally obtained in France and Belgium immediately after the war. It was only the discourse that had changed: from the patriotism of the late 1940s to the welfare-state discourse of the late 1960s. Self-help associations and therapy groups united the 'damaged groups' that had been forgotten or silenced by the austere policy of national pride and collective and indiscriminate suffering.

IV The construction of Cold War memories

From 1947, the Cold War changed some of the basic features of the politics of memory in Belgium, France and the Netherlands. The Communist ministers left the government in Belgium, whereas the traditional, state, anti-Communism, which had never permitted Communists into government in the Netherlands, was invigorated. Only two years lay between the end of the Second World War and the start of this new 'war', which was fought in terms of propaganda and domestic politics. Inevitably, both camps developed a discourse concerning the memory of the Second World War, which was shaped in order to establish direct continuity between yesterday's and tomorrow's struggle, and particularly, between yesterday's enemy and today's enemy.[46]

The anti-fascist discourse denounced the aggressive fascism that had caused the war as the ultimate stage of capitalism. The extirpation of fascism, therefore, required the transformation of society and the socio-economic structures that had enabled its parasitic growth. During the occupation, the anti-fascist interpretation was widespread in left-wing Resistance circles, where it had been insistently claimed that the struggle was one of social liberation no less than of national liberation. However, after the division of Germany, this identification became much more concrete. Capitalist Germany, where the 'fascist trusts' which 'had supported Hitler' were still intact, and where the *Wehrmacht* was renamed the *Bundeswehr* and rearmed to restart its war against the Soviet Union, was the heir of the Third Reich. The German Democratic Republic, in this perspective, was the new Germany, truly de-Nazified. An alliance with the GDR was then high treason to the anti-fascist struggle.

The anti-Communists went one step further and bluntly equated Nazism and Communism through the concept of totalitarianism. Yesterday's enemy and today's enemy were basically two manifestations of the same regime: the first, brown totalitarianism; the next, red totalitarianism. The struggle for the 'Free World' or Christianity was continued without any fundamental alteration. The ultimate symbol of totalitarianism, the central cog of the wheels of the totalitarian state, was the concentration camp. In this way, the memory of Nazi persecution became the battle horse of anti-Communism. This continuity was not only a continuity of discourse. Accusations of the continued existence of concentration camps in the Soviet Gulag were first formulated in the context of the controversy over the administration of displaced persons left behind on German territory after the defeat of the Third Reich, and the repatriation of western citizens left behind in the Soviet occupation zone. Strictly applying the agreements made at Yalta, the Allies exchanged displaced citizens mutually. Anti-Communist activists spread rumours from the very first weeks of the repatriation onwards, that the western survivors of the Nazi camps were being directly transferred to Soviet camps. Repatriation authorities soon proved that these allegations were false. More importantly, for better relations with their Soviet partner, Soviet displaced persons were forcibly repatriated to the Soviet Union by the Americans, British and French alike, in spite of their protests, acts of insurgency and collective suicides.[47] Only in 1947 did forced repatriations cease and were Soviet displaced persons considered political refugees. The ensuing conflict with the Soviet authorities led in 1949 to the first official pronouncement by the American Department of State of the syllogism: Gulag = Concentration Camp $\Rightarrow$ Communism = Nazism.[48] Anti-Communists would hence use the concentration camp as a metaphor for the entire Soviet block: 'The barbed wire of the Iron Curtain encircles a gigantic concentration camp, where entire nations are imprisoned, who yearn to live in freedom'.[49]

In this confrontation, the survivors of the Nazi camps were mobilized as 'experts'. Their life experience in the camps during World War II charged them with the moral duty to prevent or combat the same happening again in the Soviet Union. An American Federation of Former Prisoners of Totalitarianism and substantial American funding soon created followers in France, drawing on the appeal of David Rousset. Similar initiatives soon sprang up in Belgium and in the Netherlands.[50] The impact on the associations of survivors of the camps was devastating: the Belgian Confederation scarcely survived a schism; Communists were expelled from the Dutch organization ExPoGe and had to seek refuge in an anti-fascist front organization; and the French *Fédération Nationale des Déportés et Internés Résistants et Patriotes* lost its anti-Communist members to the rival nationalist *Fédération Nationale des Déportés et Internés de la Résistance* (FNDIR), under the flag of the *Union Nationale des Associations de Déportés et Internés et Familles des Disparus* (UNADIF). Exclusive associations of former prisoners from the Resistance, fiercely nationalist and anti-Communist, took the lead in this campaign, to the detriment of inclusive organizations which were open to Jewish survivors, but were stigmatized for their Communist adherence.

This anti-Communist offensive provoked a predictable Communist reply, aimed at proving that the concentration camp, which was used as a central charge against Communism, was historical nonsense. On the contrary, the Nazi camps had been the destination of millions of anti-fascist militants from all over Europe, and as such, they should be commemorated as examples of what anti-Communism led to, and of what a re-militarized Germany that had not been purged of twelve years of Nazification would be capable of doing. To centralize this campaign, the Warsaw-based *Fédération Internationale des Prisonniers Politiques* was transformed into the *Fédération Internationale des Résistants*, open not only to resisters, but also to all the members of the former organization: victims of fascism, ergo anti-fascists, ergo resisters. International committees under Communist inspiration were created for each camp to organize the tenth anniversary of the liberation of the camps.[51] Buchenwald and Auschwitz were points of sombre gravity in this commemorative campaign and were respectively symbols of the martyrdom of anti-fascist Germany, the GDR and the anti-fascist and national Polish martyrdom.[52] The immediate propaganda aims of the campaign were paramount, and commemorations were occasions for speeches by politicians such as Walter Ulbricht and Erich Honecker denouncing the European Defence Community, German membership of NATO and western European integration.

The anti-Communists responded to this commemorative campaign on a tremendous scale, with pointed counter-offensives, particularly at Dachau, which was transformed into an anti-Communist monument by, among other actions, the construction of a Roman Catholic church, to be followed some years later by a Protestant church and a synagogue.[53] The ceremonies for the commemoration of the twentieth anniversary of the liberation of the camps constituted the apogee of the Cold War commemorations, with mass mobilization on both sides.

Despite being antagonists, both the anti-fascist and the anti-totalitarian commemorative discourses had one major feature in common: they systematically obscured the specificity of the genocide. The anti-fascist discourse assimilated all victims of fascism with anti-fascists. The genocide was not recognized as separate from the holistic, anti-fascist martyrdom. Nevertheless, this discourse was inclusive of all victims. It was not only a form of propaganda and a way of instrumentalizing memories, because it provided an interpretative scheme that ennobled the arbitrary and meaningless suffering of the anonymous victims and made it heroic. Many Jewish survivors internalized and identified with anti-fascism, refusing to interpret their experiences for what they had been: genocide and not anti-fascist persecution.[54] The anti-totalitarian discourse was more exclusive. Its freedom fighters had been mostly recruited from nationalist Resistance circles and fought inclusive organizations. Above all, the genocide was strictly incompatible with its aim. An assimilation of the Nazi persecution and the Gulag essentially required the omission of genocide.

V The emergence of a Jewish memory

The culmination of the Cold War commemoration on the occasion of the twentieth anniversary of the liberation in 1965 signalled, at the same time, the end of the hegemony of anti-Communist and anti-fascist memories. In the course of the 1960s, a Jewish memory emerged — that is, a memory of the systematic attempt to murder the Jewish population of Europe as an experience distinct from the amalgamations of 'freedom fighters' and 'anti-fascists'. The Dutch example is enlightening in this regard. Until 1966, the stern policy of national consensus and state anti-Communism had stifled official participation in any commemorative initiative concerning Auschwitz.[55] The secret services monitored the Dutch Auschwitz Committee closely, warning the government that the creation of this committee in 1956 was inspired by the 'pro-Communist' *Fédération Internationale de la Résistance* and that it was entirely manipulated by Dutch Communists, even if it admitted that 'the overwhelming majority of ordinary members are not Communists and belong to the Jewish part of the population'.[56] The Catholic prime ministers, J. E. de Quay and V. G. M. Marijnen, systematically instructed the members of their cabinets not to accept the annual invitations to the commemoration ceremonies of the liberation of Auschwitz, and the Dutch government refused to provide any subsidy for the construction of the international monument at Auschwitz. Although the official justification for this refusal was the standing policy not to subsidize any monument abroad, internal documents, most of which were drafted by the secret service, argued that as Auschwitz was situated in Poland, any subsidy for the monument would mean that the Dutch government would be financing Communist propaganda against its own foreign policy.

This line of conduct by the government of the western European country that had most Jewish dead to weep for in Auschwitz was increasingly embarrassing. Only Denmark, from where no Jewish citizens had been deported to Auschwitz, and the Greek dictatorship, had joined the Dutch refusal, while France, Norway and Belgium had made generous contributions.[57] The campaign for a Dutch contribution to the Auschwitz monument gathered increasing support. Intellectuals, university rectors and non-Communist politicians signed up to a patronage committee and the former socialist prime minister, Willem Drees, even called for a Dutch effort on public television. The reports of the secret services also registered increasing support from the official representatives of the Dutch Jewish community. Up until 1962, only the rabbi of the liberal Jewish community of Amsterdam had agreed to support the Auschwitz Committee, but in 1962, that is after the Eichmann trial in Jerusalem, the four main rabbis of the Netherlands adhered to the Committee and Jewish organizations participated in the distribution of invitations for the commemorative events organized by the Committee.[58] Even the Israeli consul participated in the commemorations, assisted only by his Polish and Soviet counterparts; moreover, the ambassador pressed the government to give more weight to the martyrdom of its Jewish citizens than to its anti-Communist reflexes.[59] In articles in the press, the repeated official refusal was criticized as 'heartless'.[60]

Meanwhile, the public notoriety of Auschwitz as a particular site of Jewish suffering received an enormous impetus with the great Auschwitz trial, where former Nazi camp officials were sentenced before a German court in Frankfurt in 1964. Public awareness of the Dutch part in the genocide of the Jews first broke through with the contemporary transmission on public television of the documentary series 'The Occupation', starring the national war historian Louis de Jong.

The first comprehensive history of the persecution and mass murder of Dutch Jews, by J. Presser, appeared in April 1965. Presser had initially worried whether the 10,000 printed copies would find buyers in the first two years after publication, as his publisher expected. The copies were sold out in two days, and before the end of the year more than 100,000 copies had been printed, including a pocket edition. Presser, overwhelmed by this completely unexpected public reaction, described it as 'an explosion' and 'a crushing experience'.[61] Only one year after the twentieth anniversary, the Dutch government finally decided to contribute to the monument at Auschwitz. The new Catholic prime minister, J. M. L. Th. Cals, abandoned the policy of his predecessors, arguing that 'the government is fully aware that Auschwitz is not the only place where an extermination camp was established, but the name of Auschwitz — and as such it occupies a very particular place — has grown into a symbol of the mass destruction of the opponents of the Nazi regime in the years 1933–1945.[62] The Auschwitz Committee continued its campaign in the following years, this time against the Dutch state's official neglect of Jewish survivors, as opposed to the victims of the Resistance, who had benefited from a special pension since 1947. A television documentary in February 1968 prompted interventions in parliament, which would finally, in 1972, produce a belated recognition by the Dutch state of its responsibility for the survivors of the genocide.

The conclusions from the Dutch example can not easily be generalized. The dimensions of the Jewish tragedy in the Netherlands were incommensurably greater, and while the exclusion of a Jewish memory during the first two post-war decades was more absolute, the emergence of a Jewish memory probably took place earlier in the Netherlands than in France and Belgium. One possible explanation for this could be the early official acceptance of the anti-fascist paradigm in the latter two countries. Jewish victims were, after all, not excluded from the national memory and from legal recognition, as had been the case in the Netherlands; and Jewish survivors were welcome in the French FNDIRP and the Belgian CNPPA. The peaceful co-existence of a Jewish memory and a pro-Communist commemorative activism would abruptly come to an end only with the Six Day War in 1967 and the anti-Semitic purges of 1968 in Poland. Survivors were, from then onwards, divided by the inescapable choice between their Communist and their Jewish allegiance. Auschwitz as a joint symbol of international Jewish and national Polish martyrdom became politically incompatible. Accusations from the Communist side that anti-Semitism was a West German monopoly would be replaced with anti-Communist accusations of anti-Semitic campaigns orchestrated in Cairo and Moscow. Henry Rousso points at the changing perceptions of the state of Israel in France, and the repercussions of De Gaulle's pro-Arab declarations, which prompted comparison of anti-Zionist policies with Vichy's anti-Semitism. Yet he situates the emergence of a Jewish memory only in the second half of the 1970s, with the 'affairs' involving Vichy officials implied in the deportation of Jews, the polemic on the transmission of the American television drama 'Holocaust' in 1979, and the emergence of 'negationist' militants on the hinge of the French historical profession denying the very existence of the genocide.[63] In Belgium, the absence of a public debate on the genocide seems to suggest that references to the particular experience of the Jews only really permeated the public discourse as they became instrumental in combatting the openly xenophobic extreme right as it entered parliament in the 1980s. The 'reversal of memories' referred to in the introduction was, in any case, a very gradual process, allowing for different chronologies in different countries, whereby the emergence of a Jewish memory did not signal the immediate and complete decay of patriotic and Cold War memories.

VI Conclusion

The occupied countries of Europe in the post-war years were in desperate need of patriotic memories. Defeat and occupation, and even liberation by allied foreign armies, constituted an unprecedented trauma for the national identities of France, Belgium and the Netherlands. A national memory glorifying the Resistance was a precondition for post-war recovery. The search for heroism comprised a patriotic commemoration of persecution. The concentration camp became the symbolic repository of national martyrdom. Yet the patriotic memory of the camps denied the heterogeneity of Nazi persecution, commemorating the heroic few at the expense of the majority of victims, particularly the Jews. The patriotic memory of the 'univers concentrationnaire' was a mythical amalgamation of very different realities, blurring the singular character of the genocide. A commemoration of the genocide as such had threatening implications and was thus incompatible with the reconstruction of national self-esteem. Guilt and shame were certainly equally responsible for the unspeakability of the memory of the genocide; however, the failure of post-war memories to recognize the 'otherness' of the genocide was only part of the national memories of the occupation as a whole. The absence of such a commemoration was caused by the limited ability of the traumatized post-war societies to commemorate something singular which was not part of the ordinary and recognizable context of persecution. Societies that were absorbed by their own crises of national confidence awarded a very low priority to remembering a tragedy that was, because of its extraordinary and extra-territorial character, peripheral to their national existence. The construction of a national epic had a pressing urgency. Since the memory of the genocide could not be instrumentalized and was not constructive for patriotic memories, its commemoration had the lowest possible urgency. It is revealing that the requirements for national memory in recovering nations are very similar to the requirements for national memory in an emerging nation. As the research of Idith Zertal and Tom Segev illustrates, the commemoration of the genocide was similarly incompatible with the combatant identity of the young state of Israel. The perceived passivity and defenceless victimization of diaspora Jews was rejected as the very opposite of Zionist activism and conquest. Until the capture and trial of Eichmann in 1960–61, Auschwitz was considered a shameful memory for international Jewry. Only the heroic memory of the uprising of the Warsaw ghetto could provide inspiration for the battles of the day. It was only afterwards that the 'Holocaust' was gradually integrated as a cornerstone of Israeli national identity.[64] De-Judaization — assimilationism in the case of inclusive anti-fascist memories, or exclusion and sometimes anti-Semitism in exclusive anti-Communist and patriotic memories — was a consequence of this and not its primary motivation.

From the late 1940s onwards, the construction of national memories was rein-forced by the construction of Cold War memories. The anti-Communists chose the concentration camp as the symbolic target of their campaigns. The equation of the Gulag with the Nazi camp, and the accompanying equation of Communism with Nazism in the doctrine of totalitarianism presupposed the active oblivion of the genocide. The Communist reply to this turned the Nazi camps into the symbols of antifascist martyrdom. Buchenwald and Sachsenhausen became symbols of a truly de-Nazified, popular-democratic Germany, whereas Auschwitz became the monu-ment to international Communist and national Polish martyrdom. Genocide did not meet the requirements of ideological mobilization on either side. Yet the commem-orative dynamic launched around the sites of these camps by pro-Communist groups, which created organizations, monuments, pilgrimages and rituals, would go on to contribute to the emergence of a Jewish memory in the Netherlands, France and Belgium during the 1960s and 1970s.

The commemoration of persecution during World War II as a strategy for mobilizing public opinion would prove self-defeating. From the social and ideolog-ical memory of the survivors' activism a historical memory of the dead would emerge — in other words, a predominantly Jewish memory. The memory of Nazi persecution, for patriots and Cold War activists alike, required the opposite profile to be worthy of commemoration (*commémorable*). When heroism, choice and ideology were the criteria, the victims of genocide did not stand out. Persecuted for something they had not chosen, for the simple reason of being born Jews, they were placed at the bottom of the hierarchy of martyrs. In a properly historical memory, the hero-victims, the examples of martyrs of national liberation or political opposition, are legion. They were commemorated because they could be integrated into a national epic and an ideological discourse. The victims of the genocide were not commemorated because they could not be integrated in this way and because their memory was inert to the chemistry of post-war commemoration. It is precisely this singular character that has taken more time to be recognized, but it has also proven less ephemeral in the long run.

Acknowledgements

This a much revised version of a paper presented at the conference 'Per una Memoria Europea dei Crimini Nazisti' in Arezzo in June 1994. The author wishes to thank Stuart Woolf and Eric Hobsbawm for encouraging him to submit this article for publication, Jean-Michel Chaumont and Cyril Adjei for their constructive crit-icism on earlier drafts.

Notes

1   This small survey is merely illustrative and cannot claim to be statistically represen-tative. The Nazi period is studied at the end of the last year of high school in Belgium and had not yet been dealt with in the history classes of those students participating in the survey. The author thanks Guy Putseys and the students of the Saint Albert College in Leuven for their co-operation. Prisoners of war were the seventh most

frequently named category (37 students or 19.1 per cent). For criticism of this discourse, see n. 6.

2 *Direction de la gendarmerie. Bureau technique. Paris, le 13 juin 1945. Synthèse pour la période du 15 avril au 15 mai 1945*. Section contemporaine des Archives Nationales, Paris, 72 AJ 384.

3 For France, see Annette Wieviorka, *Déportation et génocide: entre la mémoire et l'oubli* (Paris, 1992); Marie-Anne Matard-Bonucci and Eduard Lynch (eds.), *La Libération des camps et le retour des déportés* (Brussels, 1995); Richard C. Vinen, 'The End of an Ideology? Right-Wing Anti-Semitism in France, 1944–1970', *Historical Journal*, xxxvii (1994); Simone Veil, 'Réflexions d'un témoin', *Annales E.S.C.*, iii (1993); Béatrice Philippe, *Être juif dans la société française* (Paris, 1979), 369–72. For Belgium and the Netherlands, see Pieter Lagrou, 'Le Retour des survivants des camps de concentration aux Pays-Bas et en Belgique: de l'ostracisme à l'héroïsation', in Matard-Bonucci and Lynch (eds.), *La Libération des camps*. For the Netherlands, see Dienke Hondius, *Terugkeer: anti-semitisme in Nederland rond de bevrijding* (The Hague, 1990); Dienke Hondius, 'A Cold Reception: Holocaust Survivors in the Netherlands and their Return', *Patterns of Prejudice*, xxviii, 1 (1994); Connie Kristel, '"De moeizame terugkeer": de repatriëring van de Nederlandse overlevenden uit de Duitse concentratie-kampen', *Oorlogsdocumentatie '40-'45: Jaarboek van het Rijksinstituut voor Oorlogs-documentatie* (Amsterdam, 1989). For Poland, see David Engel, *Facing the Holocaust: The Polish Government in Exile and the Jews, 1943–1945* (Chapel Hill, 1993). For Poland and the former USSR, see Lucy Dawidowicz, *The Holocaust and the Historians* (Cambridge, Mass., 1981). For Great Britain, see Tony Kushner, *The Holocaust and the Liberal Imagination: A Social and Cultural History* (Oxford, 1994); David Cesarani, 'Le Crime contre l'Occident: les réactions britanniques à la "libération" des camps de concentration nazis en 1945', in Matard-Bonucci and Lynch (eds.), *La Libération des camps*.

4 Maxime Steinberg, Les Dérives Plurielles de la mémoire d'Auschwitz', *Centrale: périodique trimestriel de la vie communautaire juive*, cclix (1993), 6–9; cclx (1993), 11–14.

5 Kushner, *Holocaust and the Liberal Imagination*. The same theme is taken up by Cesarani, 'Le Crime contre l'Occident'; Tony Kushner, 'Different Worlds: British Perceptions of the Final Solution during the Second World War', in David Cesarani (ed.), *The Final Solution: Origins and Implementation* (London and New York, 1994); Tony Kushner, *The Persistence of Prejudice: Anti-Semitism in British Society during the Second World War* (Manchester and New York, 1989). In 1981, Lucy Dawidowicz pursued a similar line of thought in *Holocaust and the Historians*. Todd M. Endelman objects quite rightly to Kushner's and Cesarani's line of thought, arguing that 'hostility to Jewish particularism seems conceptually unrelated to any political creed, liberal, conservative, or socialist, no matter how broadly defined'; furthermore, he refers to Richard Bolchover, *British Jewry and the Holocaust* (Cambridge, 1993), who dismisses Anglo-Jewish fears about anti-Semitism as 'neurotic'. See Todd M. Endelman, 'Jews, Aliens and Other Outsiders in British History', *Hist. JL*, xxxvii (1994).

6 A balanced analysis can be found in Jean-Michel Chaumont, 'Connaissance ou reconnaissance? Les Enjeux du débat sur la singularité de la Shoah', *Le Débat*, lxxxii (1994). For France, the trial of Klaus Barbie and Paul Touvier on charges of 'crimes against humanity', and the ensuing legal debate as to which crimes could be prosecuted — genocide, or 'ordinary' assassinations of non-Jewish persons as well — amplified the debate. Very candid analyses are provided by Alain Finkielkraut, *La Mémoire vaine: du crime contre l'humanité* (Paris, 1989), 35–47; Eric Conan and Henry Rousso, *Vichy,*

un passé qui ne passe pas (Paris, 1994). The criticism by these four authors of a Judaeo-centric memory and of commemorative mobilization for the historical legacy of anti-racism — 'une bonne conscience morale à laquelle ne correspond aucun but' (Maurice Agulhon, as quoted *ibid.*, 281) — are much in line with recent criticisms from American scholars of the Holocaust. See Michael R. Marrus, 'The Use and Misuse of the Holocaust', in Peter Hayes (ed.), *Lessons and Legacies: The Meaning of the Holocaust in a Changing World* (Evanston, 1991); Peter Novick, 'Holocaust Memory in America', in James E. Young (ed.), *The Art of Memory: Holocaust Memorials in History* (Munich and New York, 1994).

7   Raul Hilberg remarks that when he was asked to contribute in 1968 to the *Encyclopedia Americana*, Auschwitz and Treblinka did not even exist as entries. On the slow comprehension of what had actually happened to European Jewry and its scale, see his 'Opening Remarks: The Discovery of the Holocaust', in Hayes (ed.), *Lessons and Legacies*.

8   The German policy regarding prisoners of war (POWs) had been deliberately divisive. In Belgium, Flemish POWs were liberated, but not all Walloons. In the Netherlands, all POWs were liberated in 1940, but later on very partially called back. In France, though the return of the POWs had been a major endeavour of the Vichy régime, 1 million of the 1.5 million soldiers initially captured lived through five years of captivity. In addition, the veterans of the 'army of the defeat' of 1940 had to challenge the commemorative hegemony of the veterans of the victorious army of 1918. See Christophe Lewin, *Le Retour des prisonniers de guerre français* (Paris, 1986). For the war years, see Yves Durand, *La Captivité: histoire des prisonniers de guerre français, 1939–1945* (Paris, 1980).

9   Pieter Lagrou, 'De Terugkeer van de weggevoerde arbeiders in België en Nederland, 1945–1955: mythen en taboes rond de verplichte tewerkstelling', in *De verplichte tewerkstelling in Duitsland, 1942–1945* (Brussels, 1993) (with French abstract). For France, see Michel Gratier de Saint-Louis, 'Histoire d'un retour: les STO du Rhône', *Cahiers d'histoire*, xxxiv, nos. 3–4 (1995); Conan and Rousso, *Vichy*, 179–82; Wieviorka, in Matard-Bonucci and Lynch (eds.), *La Libération des camps*, 236; François Cochet, *Les Exclus de la victoire: histoire des prisonniers de guerre, déportés et STO (1945–1985)* (Paris, 1992).

10   The comparative statistics for persecution by the Nazis in Belgium, France and the Netherlands present a major problem. On the one hand, German wartime sources and Belgian, French and Dutch post-war sources enable the compilation of accurate statistics for the deportation and return of Jewish victims. See Maxime Steinberg, 'Les Yeux du témoin et le regard du borgne: lecture critique d'un génocide au quotidien', *Cahiers du Centre de Recherches et d'Etudes Historiques de la Seconde Guerre Mondiale*, xii (1989); Maxime Steinberg, *Les Yeux du témoin et le regard du borgne: l'histoire face au révisionnisme* (Paris, 1990), 155–74; J. Presser, *Ondergang: de vervolging en Verdelging van het Nederlandse Jodendom, 1940–1945*, 2 vols. (The Hague, 1965), ii, 410–13; Louis de Jong, *Het Koninkrijk der Nederlanden in de Tweede Wereldoorlog*, 14 vols. (The Hague, 1978), viii, 887–90; Serge Klarsfeld, *Mémorial de la déportation des juifs de France* (Paris, 1978); Serge Klarsfeld and Maxime Steinberg, *Le Mémorial de la déportation des juifs de Belgique* (Brussels and New York, 1982). These statistics present scholars with baffling differences in the extermination rate of the Jewish population in the three countries, a question addressed by J. C. H. Blom, 'De Vervolging van joden in Nederland in internationaal vergelijkend perspectief', *De Gids*, cl (1987); Maxime Steinberg, 'Le Paradoxe français dans la solution finale à l'Ouest', *Annales E.*

S. C., iii (1993); Helen Fein, *Accounting for Genocide: National Responses and Jewish Victimisation during the Holocaust* (New York and London, 1979). On the other hand, the remaining category of non-Jewish victims presents manifold problems. The amalgamation of people persecuted for a variety of reasons — resisters, reprisal hostages, Communists, and black marketeers, for instance — greatly complicates the formulation of reliable statistics. Post-war national sources are established on the basis of legal and administrative criteria which are discussed further in this article. For Belgium, for example, they include the inmates of Belgian prisons who were detained for a minimum of thirty days, but exclude some categories of *concentrationnaires* of the Nazi camps. For France, national figures based on regional censuses are controversial: see Wieviorka, in Matard-Bonucci and Lynch (eds.), *La Libération des camps*, 234, 237. The juxtaposition of these figures with those provided for the Netherlands by historian Louis De Jong, should be interpreted with the utmost caution. The overall conclusions drawn by Maxime Steinberg as to the very different realities of genocide and 'Vernichtung durch Arbeit' cannot be doubted, but the provision of statistics of equal reliability for non Jewish victims would require an enormous amount of research, a task for which, as Steinberg himself mentions, the necessary sources are available, but not the necessary resources: Steinberg, *Les Yeux du témoin*, 165. Moreover, contrary to what Steinberg claims, figures of 'political prisoners' and Jewish victims should not be added up, since the former comprise a significant minority of the latter. The same reservation applies for the 'deportees and internees' in France.

11   Careful and Intelligent analyses of anti-Semitism in the Netherlands after 1945 are provided by Hondius, *Terugkeer* and 'Cold Reception'. Incidents of anti-Semitism in France are related in Eduard Lynch, 'Les Filtres successifs de l'information', in Matard-Bonucci and Lynch (eds.), *La Libération des camps*, 169. Though primarily concerned with the period after 1954, Richard C. Vinen's article 'Right-Wing Anti-Semitism in France', is also revealing for the earlier period. The most recent contributions, in spite of what their titles state, neglect the crucial period immediately after the end of the war: see, for example, Robert S. Wistrich, 'Anti-Semitism in Europe after 1945', in Wistrich (ed.), *Terms of Survival: The Jewish World since 1945* (London and New York, 1995); Frederick Weil, 'The Extent and Structure of Anti-Semitism in Western Populations since the Holocaust', in Helen Fein (ed.), *The Persisting Question: Sociological Perspectives and Social Contexts of Modern Anti-Semitism*, 3 vols. (Berlin and New York, 1987), i. At the other end of the spectrum, the piece by Philo Bregstein. 'Le Paradoxe Néderlandais', in Léon Poliakov (ed.), *Histoire de l'anti-semitisme*, 5 vols. (Paris, 1993), v, *1945–1993*, 416, seems to me an example of intellectual terrorism under the guise of the study of anti-Semitism. Bregstein accuses one of the foremost recent scholars of Nazi persecution in Belgium, Gie van den Berghe, of anti-Semitism in *De Uitbuiting van de Holocausat* (Antwerp and Baarn, 1990), for having criticized Israeli instrumentalization of the Holocaust in terms that were far more prudent than those of, among others, Tom Segev, Idith Zerthall, Amos Elon and Michael R. Marrus. One can only regret such abuses.

12   See, for example, the testimonies of Jo van Dam in Amsterdam, in Hondius, *Terugkeer*, 89, and of Fanny Segal in Paris, in Matard-Bonucci and Lynch (eds.), *La Libération des camps*, 122. Similar incidents occurred in Germany, where German civilians requisitioned by the Allies for the distribution of food-rationing cards marked the cards of Jewish survivors with the rubber stamp *Jude* from the Nazi administration: Wolfgang Jacobmeyer, *Vom Zwangarbeiter zum Heimatlosen Auslander: Die Displaced Persons in Westdeutschland, 1945–1951* (Göttingen, 1985), 44.

13   Wieviorka observes that the refusal by French repatriation officials to distinguish
      between Jewish and non-Jewish victims on official documents was a return to the
      republican tradition, and that any other line of conduct would have been vehemently
      rejected by Jewish organizations: Wieviorka, *Déportation et génocide*, 67. The official
      report on the Belgian repatriation effort prided itself on the refusal to distinguish
      between repatriates on the basis of 'race, religion or opinion': 'these principles are
      part of the spiritual heritage we have fought to defend and that has been safeguarded
      through victory' ('ces principes font partie du patrimoine spirituel pour la défense
      duquel nous nous sommes battus et que la victoire nous a préservé'). See *Rapport sur
      l'activité du Commissariat Belge au Rapatriement* (Brussels, July 1945), 8.

14   Hondius, *Terugkeer*, 79–85.

15   'A bas la guerre, à bas les dénonciateurs, les juifs au poteau', in *Synthése pour la période
      du 15 février au 15 mars 1945* (Paris, 12 Apr. 1945). The subsequent report, *Synthése
      pour la période du 15 mars au 15 avril 1945* (Paris, 22 May 1945), mentioned 'quelques
      graffitis prennent à part Juifs et communistes': Section Contemporaine des Archives
      Nationales, 72AJ 384.

16   'Jewish foreigners: Soon after the liberation, a certain number of Jews of foreign
      origin [nationality] engaged in excessive activity, both because of the small number
      of them and because of the fact that they were foreigners. The regional office has
      been assailed by requests for assistance, emanating from various Jewish associations
      who appear remarkably in accord with each other. Consequently, I have instructed
      my information service to do a survey of all the Jewish associations of Toulouse and
      the region . . . In order to put a stop to the schemes *[agissements]* of certain of these
      foreigners, which were likely to provoke a new crisis of anti-Semitism, I decided at
      the time of the creation of the local association for Political and Racial Deportees, to
      appeal for Jewish representatives — on the one hand to the Rabbi, and on the other
      to two members of very old and well-known Toulouse families — deeming that in
      this way the interests of a particularly oppressed group would be best served': *Ministère des Prisonniers de Guerre, Déportés et Refugiés: extrait du rapport de la Direction
      Régionale de Toulouse en date du 12 Février 1945* (Paris, 5 Mar. 1945), Section
      Contemporaine des Archives Nationales, F9 3172.

17   For the Netherlands, see Elma Verhey, *Om het joodso kind* (Amsterdam, 1991). For
      France, particularly the Finally affair, see Henry Rousso, *Le Syndrome de Vichy* (Paris,
      1987), 66–7; Vinen, 'End of an Ideology?', 372–3; Wieviorka, *Déportation et génocide*, 368–90.

18   Leo Hendrickx, *Gekneveld en Bevrijd* (Maaseik, 1945), 140–1.

19   Pieter Lagrou, 'Herdenken en Vergeten: de politieke verwerking van verzet en
      vervolging in Nederland en België na 1945', *Spiegel Historiael*, xxix (1994).

20   Rousso, *Le Syndrome de Vichy*, 42–55.

21   Peter Romijn, *Snel, Streng en Rechtvaardig: Politiek beleid inzake de bestraffing en
      reclassering van 'foute' Nederlanders, 1945–1955* (De Haan, 1989), 74–8; Lagrou, 'De
      Terugkeer', 218–20.

22   Pieter Lagrou, 'Verzet en naoorlogse politiek', in Luc Huyse and Kris Hoflack (eds.),
      De Demokratie Heruitgevonden: Oud en Nieu in politiek België, 1944–1950 (Leuven, 1995).

23   'Historique', *Bulletin officiel de la CNPPA* [i, 1946]; Brunfaut, 'interpellation',
      Parlementaire Handelingen Kamer (Brussels, 25 Oct. 1945), 1182.

24   G. Canivet, 'Autour du statut des prisonniers politiques', *Bulletin officiel de la CNPPA*
      (Nov. 1946), 1; G. Canivet, 'Het Statuut van den Politieken Gevangene', *Front*, ii
      (1946), 1, 3.

25   *L'Effort: union nationale des prisonniers politiques, 1940–1945* (Apr. 1946), 27. Though
       formally merged in the Confederation, schismatic organizations continued this oppo-
       sition on a very loosely structured basis, especially during the debate on the Act.

26   *Parlementaire Handelingen Kamer* (Brussels, 31 Oct. 1946), 4–14; *Dokumenten Kamer*
       (Brussels, 18 Sept. 1946), no. 187; *Parlementaire Handelingen Senaat* (Brussels, 14 Jan.
       1947), 368–85; (15 Jan. 1947), 389–94.

27   *Parlementaire Handelingen Senaat* (30 Jan. 1947), 499; for the vote (6 Feb. 1947),
       507–14, 516–17; *Parlementaire Handelingen Kamer* (Brussels, 13 Feb. 1947), 3–9, 16,
       passim; *Belgische Staatsblad* (16 Mar. 1947), 2703–8; René Fraikin, 'Allen rond één
       vlag', *Officieel Bulletijn van de NCPGR*, ii [Feb. 1947], 1.

28   *Belgische Staatsblad* (15 Feb. 1947), 1507.

29   'Ne donnez pas l'impression qu'une arrière-pensée vous anime: exclure du titre de
       prisonnier politique les juifs et les comunnistes arrêtés le 22 juin 1941': Brunfaut,
       Parlementaire Handelingen Kamer, 1183. Debates in the National Confederation of
       Political Prisoners (*Confédération Nationale des Prisonniers Politiques et leurs Ayant-Droits*,
       hereafter CNPPA) on the inclusion or exclusion of Jewish victims had been discon-
       certingly explicit. Catholic members opposed the inclusion of 'les juifs arrêtés
       simplement pour motif racial ou d'autres gens internés pour des motifs autres que
       patriotiques (p.ex. des traffiquants)', thus setting Jews and black marketeers on the
       same honourless footing. The macabre vocabulary of the 'solution of the Jewish
       problem' in post-war legislation did not provoke any reaction: 'A son avis il ne faut
       pas réintroduire la question du problème juif qui sera solutionée au sein des commis-
       sions d'agrégation'. Archives of the CNPPA, Brussels, 'Compte rendu de la réunion
       du Conseil National Elargi tenue à la CNPPA' (2 Feb. 1947), 4; (29 Jan. 1947), 5.

30   See Jules Gérard-Libois and José Gotovitch, *Léopold III: de l'an '40 à l'effacement*
       (Brussels, 1991), 287–302.

31   See Rousso, *Le Syndrome de Vichy*; Gérard Namer, *La Commémoration en France de 1945
       à nos jours*, (Paris, 1987); Pierre Nora, 'Gaullistes et communistes', in Pierre Nora
       (ed.), *Les Lieux de mémoire*, 3 tomes (7 vols.) (Paris, 1992), tome iii, *Les France: conflits
       et partages*, 3 vols., i, 360–71; Paul Thibaud, 'La République et ses héros: le gaullisme
       pendant et après la guerre', *Que reste-t-il de la résistance?* (special issue, *Esprit*, Jan.
       1994), 79–80.

32   See, in addition to the above, Marie-Claire Lavabre, *Le Fil rouge: sociologie de la mémoire
       communiste* (Paris, 1994), 190–219.

33   See Wieviorka, *Déportation et génocide*, 121–57.

34   See references to Wieviorka, Rousso, Finkielkraut, Lewin and Durand in nn. 3, 6,
       13, 14. Other historians continue to claim that post-war France was blind to the great
       and undifferentiated mass of all 'deportees'. François Cochet does so prominently,
       for all categories of repatriates, including POWs and workers, in the title of his book
       Les Exclus de la victoire. Bonnucci and Lynch do so for all survivors of the camps —
       Jews, resisters, hostages — in the very last sentence of their conclusion in *La Libération
       des camps*. They echo the commemorative activism of associations of different groups
       of repatriates, and thus deny the centrality of 'deportation' as a paradigm in French
       post-war society, as put forward by the previously cited authors and developed further
       in this article.

35   Paraphrasing Namer, *La Commémoration en France*, 7, 8, 11, *passim*.

36   *Le Déporté (UNADIF)* (May 1980).

37   'Mais ces transplantés ne sont pas des Déportés. Il ne s'agit pas d'une querelle
       de mots. La "Déportation" n'est pas entrée dans l'Histoire seulement comme un

déplacement et un travail forcés: elle implique les tortures, les convois démentiels, les chambres à gaz et les fours crématoires; la déhumanisations et l'extermination de millions d'êtres humains. Elle est inséparable d'une éthique — qu'il convient à jamais à condamner — par laquelle l'être "supérieur" s'arroge le droit d'avilir, avant de le tuer, celui qu'il estime inférieur. Elle constitue le plus grand crime qui ait jamais été commis contre l'homme, et dont il importe de prévenir le retour. Feindre d'en atténuer l'horreur, en étendant à d'autres le bénéfice de la triste auréole du nom de Déporté, c'est commettre à la fois un contresens historique, un déni de justice et une offense à la mémoire de tous ceux qui furent astreints, eux aussi, au travail forcé, mais en attente de la mort obligatoire. Les proscits, victimes du STO ne gagnent pas grande chose à exiger le titre de Déporté. Mais, per leur exigence, en créant une déplorable confusion, ils affaiblissent la compréhension, le retentiseement, le gigantisme due crime. Par là, ils se font inconsciemment les complices de l'oubli. Ils font perdre beaucoup à la cause sacrée de la défense de l'Homme': 'Déclaration publié par le Réseau du Souvenir', *Déportation et liberté*, x–xi (1956).

38   Pieter Lagrou, 'Patriotten en Regenten: het parochiale patriottisme van de na-oorlogse Nederlandse illegaliteit, 1945–1980', *Oorlogsdocumentatie '40-'45* (1995).

39   De Jong, Het Koninkrijk, x (b), 160–79; xii, 259–68, 298. For a critical assessment of the famine of 1945, see G. M. T. Trienekens, *Tussen ons volk en de honger: de voedselvoorziening, 1940–1945* (Utrecht, 1985), 398–407.

40   Rita Koopman, as quoted by Hondius, *Terugkeer*, 94; 'Cold Reception', 57. The translation by Hondius 'We were so hungry' does not render the suffering expressed in 'Wat hebben wij honger geleden'. Similar reactions occurred in France and even in Great Britain, but there they were rather exceptional, whereas they emerged in the Netherlands as the dominant response. Cf. 'Mon pauvre Charles, si tu savais comme on a eu faim ici'. Charles Baron, who was 19 years old, lost both parents in Auschwitz and was himself repatriated in April 1945: Charles Baron to Eduard Lynch, 15 Jan. 1995, in Matard-Bonucci and Lynch (eds.), *La Libération des camps*, 126. Gena Turgel, survivor of Auschwitz and Bergen-Belsen, heard the following upon arrival in England: 'We also had a hard time. We were bombed and had to live in shelters. We had to sleep in the Underground' (as quoted in Kushner, *Holocaust and the Liberal Imagination*, 238). See also a similar reaction by Ester Brunstein to David Cesarani, 21 Dec. 1994, in Matard-Bonucci and Lynch (eds.), *La Libération des camps*, 248.

41   Algemeen Rijksarchief, The Hague (Archive of the Cabinet of the Prime Minister, hereafter ACPM), box 127, 17 Jan. 1946, 'Notitie voor S. van V.' (memo to Prime Minister Schermerhorn by one of his advisers); 'map hulpverlening aan illegale werkers en nagelaten betrekkingen 1945–1952', nr. 355.358.361.

42   Lagrou, 'Herdenken en Vergeten'; D. H. Schram and C. Geljon (eds.), *Overal sporen: de verwerking van de Tweede Wereldoorlog in literatuur en kunst* (Amsterdam, 1990); Wim Rademaker and Ben van Bohemen, *Sta een ogenblik stil . . . Monumentenboek, 1940–1945* (Kampen, 1990).

43   H. W. Sandberg, secretary of the Advisory Commission of the Dutch Underground Movement (*Grote Adviescommissie der Illegaliteit*), to the local 'Plaatselijke Adviesraad der Illegaliteit te Dordrecht', Amsterdam, 13 Nov. 1945, concerning the association of former political prisoners: Archive of the *Grote Adviescommissie der Illegaliteit* (hereafter GAC), Netherlands State Institute for War Documentation, Amsterdam, 184, 4D.

44   See the surprisingly critical commemorative publication edited by the Foundation, *Woord Gehouden: Veertig jaar Stichting 1940–1945* (The Hague, 1985).

45 *Ibid.*, 22.

46 This theme is fully worked out in Pieter Lagrou, 'La Résistance et les conceptions de l'Europe, 1945–1965. Anciens résistants et victimes de la persécution face à la Guerre froide, au problème allemand et à l'intégration Européenne', *Cahiers d'Histoire du Temps Présent 2* (1997); reprint in: Robert Frank et Antoine Fleury (eds), *Le rôle des guerres dans la mémoire des Européens* (Berne, Peter Lang, 1997) 137–81.

47 See Jacobmeyer, *Vom Zwangarbeiter zum Heimatlosen Auslander*, 123–51, for the best treatment of the repatriation question. See also Mark Elliot, *Pawns of Yalta: Soviet Refugees and America's Role in their Repatriation* (Urbana, 1982); Nicholas Bethell, *The Last Secret: Forcible Repatriation to Russia, 1944–1947* (London, 1974). For the Netherlands, see M. A. P. van den Berg, 'De repatriantenkwestie na 1945: Terugkeer van Nederlanders uit de Soviet-Unie', in Roholl, Waegemans and Willemsen (eds.), *De Lage Landen en de Sovietunie: Beeldvorming en Betrekkingen* (Amsterdam, 1989).

48 See, for example, the article 'US asks UN Study on Slave Labor in Soviet Union', *Dept of State Bull.* (27 Feb. 1949), as quoted by Cathal J. Nolan, 'Americans in the Gulag: Detention of US Citizens by Russia and the Onset of the Cold War', *Jl Contemporary Hist.*, xxv (1990). In this article, Nolan makes an unfortunate connection between forced repatriation by the United States and a series of diplomatic conflicts over Soviet citizens claiming American citizenship, to arrive at the conclusion that the addition of these issues 'made it additionally difficult for officials in Washington to avoid seeing a parallel between the Soviet Union and Nazi Germany', thus paying a late tribute to Cold War propaganda.

49 Hubert Halin, 'Voyage d'étude de la Résistance en Allemagne de l'Est', *Les Deux Allemagnes* (special issue, *La Voix internationale de la Résistance*, 1960). Halin was one of the main proponents of anti-Communist agitation among European resistance veterans and survivors of the camps, defending NATO, European integration and *Wiedergutmachung*.

50 See Emile Copfermann, *David Rousset: une vie dans le siècle* (Paris, 1949), 113–42; Emile Copfermann, 'Les Occultations de la mémoire: le procès contre "Les Lettres Françaises et la Commission d'Enquête Internationale" sur les camps de concentration' (paper presented at the international congress, 'Histoire et mémoire des crimes et génocides nazis', organized by the Auschwitz Foundation, Brussels, Nov. 1992). Rousset's Dutch counterpart, Karel Van Staal's activities are thoroughly documented in ACPM, 355.358:343.819.5, 'Concentratiekampen' (hereafter ACPM, Con.).

51 Cf. Lagrou, 'La Résistance'; Hermann Langbein, 'Unterlagen zu meinem Diskussionsbeitrag "Internationale Organisationen der Uberlebenden der nationalsozialistischen Konzentrationslager ab 1954 bis heute — vor allem Auschwitz betreffend"' (paper presented at the international congress, 'Histoire et mémoire des crimes et génocides nazis', Brussels, Nov. 1992); Hermann Langbein, 'Entschädigung für KZ-Häftlinge? Ein Erfahrungsbericht', in Ludolf Herbst and Constantin Goschler (eds.), *Wiedergutmachung in der Bundesrepublik Deutschland: Sondernummer Schriftenreihe der Vierteljahrshefte für Zeitgeschichte* (Munich, 1989); Luc Sommerhausen, 'Buchenwald, Ravensbrück, Mauthausen, Auschwitz, Sachsenhausen: la mainmise de Moscou sur les comités internationaux des camps', *La Voix internationale de la Résistance*, xxxiii–xxxiv (1960), 2–3.

52 For Auschwitz, see, for example, Waclaw Dlugoborski, 'Auschwitz and Holocaust in the Memory of East-Central European Societies before and after 1989' (paper presented at 'Per una Memoria Europea dei Crimini Nazisti', Arezzo, June 1994). For a more general context, see the chapter on Poland in Dawidowicz, *Holocaust and*

the Historians, 88–124. For the East German sites, see, for example, Peter Sonnet, 'Gedenkstätten für Opfer der Nationalsozialismus in der DDR', in Ulrike Puvogel (ed.), Gedenkstätten für Opfer des Nationalsozialismus: Eine Documentation (Schriftenreihe der Bundeszentrale für politische Bildung, ccxlv, Bonn, 1987), 769–806; Eve Rosenhaft, 'The Uses of Remembrance: The Legacy of the Communist Resistance in the German Democratic Republic', in Francis R. Nicosia and Lawrence D. Stokes (eds.), Germans against Nazism: Nonconformity, Opposition and Resistance in the Third Reich (New York and Oxford, 1990); Claudia Koonz, 'Between Memory and Oblivion: Concentration Camps in German Memory', in John R. Gillis (ed.), Commemorations: The Politics of National Identity (Princeton, 1994). For the purge of Communist monuments since German reunification, see Zur Neuorientierung der Gedenkstätte Buchenwald: Die Empfehlungen der vom Minister für Wissenschaften und Kunst des Landes Thüringen berufenen Historikerkommission (Weimar-Buchenwald, 1992); Monika Zorn (ed.), Hitlers zweimal getötete Opfer: Westdeutsche Endlösung des Antifaschismus auf dem Gebiet der DDR (Reihe: Unerwünschte Bücher zum Faschismus, no. 6, Freiburg, 1994); Sarah Farmer, 'Symbols That Face Two Ways: Commemorating the Victims of Nazism and Stalinism at Buchenwald and Sachsenhausen', Representations, no. 49 (1995).

53   Harold Marcuse, 'Das ehemalige Konzentrationslager Dachau: Der Mühevolle Weg zur Gedenkstätte, 1945–1968', Dachauer Hefte, vi (1990); Barbara Distel, 'Orte der Erinnerung an die Opfer im Lande der Täter — Gedanken zur Arbeit und der Gedenkstätte des Ehemaligen, Konzentrationslagers Dachau', Bulletin de la Fondation Auschwitz, xl–xli (1994).

54   A very forceful testimony is given by Charles van West, 'Ce n'était pas encore une nécessité, mais maintenant c'est devenu une obsession', interview by Yannis Thanassekos and Jean-Michel Chaumont, Bulletin trimestriel de la Fondation Auschwitz, xxxii–xxxiii (1992).

55   See the correspondence on this matter from the international and the Dutch Auschwitz committees, the memoranda drafted for discussion in the cabinet meetings and the interventions by parliamentarians, particularly Goedhart and van der goes van Naters in ACPM, Con.

56   ACPM, Con., report 784.128, Binnenlandse Veligheidsdienst (24 May 1965). See also the reports: 10 May 1962; 10 Sept. 1964; 21 Jan., 22 Dec. 1965: 18, 28 Jan., and 18 Feb. 1966. The author wishes to thank the archivist of the Ministerie van Algemene Zaken, Fred van den Kieboom, for his assistance in obtaining the declassification of these reports in record time.

57   The cabinet systematically inquired through its embassies abroad which position other western European governments had adopted in this matter. Only the ambassador in Rome declined to inquire 'given the delicate character of this matter, concerning the Italian position during the war'. See ACPM, Con.

58   ACPM, Con., Binnenlandse Veiligheidsdienst (24 May 1965).

59   The cabinet had first contacted Willem Drees, who had recommended that the Israeli embassy be heard in this matter: ACPM, Con., Nota voor de Minister-President van Mej. de Jong (14 Sept. 1961); Nota voor de Minister-President (15 Feb. 1962).

60   Het Vrije Volk, 28 Jan. 1963. Earlier remarks in the Communist De Waarheid, 23 June 1961, and later in De Tijd/Maasbode, 1 May 1965, explicitly criticized the exaggerated anti-Communism that motivated the official refusal.

61   J. Presser, 'Een boek ziet het licht', Nederlands Auschwitz Comité: Herdenkingsnummer (Jan. 1966). In 'De jeugd en Auschwitz' in the same volume, Ch. Duyns mentioned that when sixty students between 14 and 18 years of age were asked 'what does the

name Auschwitz signify to you?', they all answered something to the effect of 'a concentration camp where the Germans have murdered many Jews'. None had heard of Auschwitz in school, just through reporting on the Frankfurt Process. Only three students spelled Auschwitz correctly, and one student confused it with Austerlitz. The diaries of the young Dutch girl, Anne Frank, recording her life in hiding in Amsterdam (not, of course, her deportation to Auschwitz and death in Bergen-Belsen), only became a commercial success in the Netherlands after the success of its translations abroad: 1,500 copies of the book were first published in the Netherlands in 1947; it was reprinted in small numbers until 1950, then disappeared from the book market until 1955; and only afterwards did sales very gradually reach the tens of thousands of copies. See Gerrold van der Stroom, *Rijksinstituut voor Oorlogs-documentatie: de Dagboeken van Anne Frank* (Amsterdam, 1990), 69–90; A. G. H. Anbeek van der Meijden, 'De Tweede Wereldoorlog in de Nederlandse roman', in [David Barnouw, Madelon de Keizer and Gerrold van der Stroom (eds.)], *1940–1945: Onverwerkt verleden?* (Utrecht, 1985), 73, 79.

62   The declaration did not mention the Jews by name and continued the amalgamation of Jewish victims and opponents of the regime, particularly by extending Auschwitz's symbolic importance to the start of the Nazi regime, that is, long before the invasion of Poland in 1939 and long before the opening of the camp and the commencement of the genocide in 1942: see ACPM, Con., *Rijksvoorlichtingsdienst*, 14 Sept. 1966.

63   Rousso, *Le Syndrome de Vichy*, 147–82.

64   Idith Zertal, 'Du Bon Usage du souvenir: les Israeliens et la Shoah', *Le Débat*, lviii (1990); Tom Segev, *The Seventh Million: The Israelis and the Holocaust* (New York, 1993), 593.

Chapter 17

Lucy Noakes

MAKING HISTORIES
Experiencing the Blitz in London's
museums in the 1990s

Presenting the past

> Look around you in this extraordinary country and contemplate the
> various Shows and Diversions of the People and then say whether their
> temper or Mind at various periods of our history may not be collected
> from them?[1]

THIS CHAPTER FOCUSES on the public production of the past. In the
drive to make the past 'come alive' which informs so many of today's *public*
histories – books, films, television programmes, theme parks and museums – the
Blitz is often privileged over other events of the war years. Two recent representations of the Second World War in London museums, the 'Blitz Experience'
in the Imperial War Museum, and the Winston Churchill Britain at War
Theme Museum near London Bridge, both focus on the Blitz in their histories of
the war.

Why is this? Both exhibitions attempt to represent the experience of the *people's*
war rather than information about diplomatic or political manoeuvring or military
tactics in wartime, yet the Blitz was by no means an experience common to all
British people in the way, for example, that rationing was. Air raids were concentrated on the large towns and cities, particularly sites of strategic importance such
as Portsmouth, Southampton, Coventry and London. The smaller 'tip-and-run'
attacks only occurred over the easily accessible coasts of southern and eastern
England.[2] Furthermore, the London Blitz was an experience peculiar to those living
in London in 1940–41, and the bulk of the bombing was concentrated on a few

boroughs, most notably those in the east of the city such as Stepney.[3] The Blitz, it would appear, is being moved from its position during the war as an important but by no means universal *experience* to the centre of public *memories* of the war.

There are several possible reasons for this. In part, it is because the Blitz is both exciting and easily accessible. One does not need a detailed knowledge of diplomatic missions or military tactics to appreciate the horror of being bombed. As large numbers of the visitors to both of these exhibitions are parties of schoolchildren, excitement and immediacy are an important part of their appeal. Moreover, the Blitz was an active, dramatic part of the war which affected women at least as much as men. As women were far more likely to remain in Britain, and in the home, than men, their chances of experiencing aerial bombardment were that much higher.[4] Thus perhaps women visitors to the exhibitions are able to identify with representations of the Blitz in a way which could be problematic if the experience focused on the armed services. The Blitz is likely to remain central to the personal memories of those who experienced it as a time of heightened emotions and personal and national importance. Its central position on the public stage reinforces its importance in these more private memories, and helps to position the personal experience as a part of public, national history. Representations of the Blitz are also, of course, representations of large-scale bombing of civilians, a key, defining, twentieth-century phenomenon with which we are all familiar, if not through experience, then through its many cultural manifestations such as Picasso's *Guernica*, films such as Boorman's *Hope and Glory* and Coppola's *Apocalypse Now*, and scenes on the television of Baghdad, Basra and Sarajevo. The Blitz is Britain's claim to inclusion in these events.

Perhaps more importantly though, the Blitz has become an important part of public memories of the war because public images and memories of it overwhelmingly present a unified picture of Britain at war; a time when 'we' were all soldiers in the front line. The common myth of the Blitz, as outlined in Angus Calder's book of the same name,[5] is that it was a time when the nation, led by Churchill and under bombardment from Hitler, overcame its internal divisions and aligned itself behind the values of 'freedom', 'democracy' and the 'rights of the individual'. If the Second World War can be seen as a key moment in our national identity and national history, then the Blitz is a key moment in the war. This chapter is an examination of how this particular history is reproduced in two London museums in the 1990s.

Both of the museum exhibitions mentioned above essentially tell this story: the Blitz was a levelling, egalitarian time when the nation, divided by the class conflict of the 1930s, became 'the people'; a time when everyone pulled together and 'we' were all in it together. This image of the Blitz is one which is given a particular legitimization by its inclusion and foregrounding in museum displays. Museums are powerful sites of cultural transmission and public education; they are an embodiment of knowledge and power, important hegemonic instruments. The state museum is an important site not only for the exhibition of objects, but also for the exhibition of national beliefs; it is a place where the 'imagined community' of the nation becomes visible.[6] The large national museums established in the eighteenth and nineteenth centuries were intended not only as display sites for the wealth and power of the imperial British nation, but also as authoritative sites of public education. The Museums Act of 1845 heralded an explosion in the creation of museums;

almost 300 were founded in Britain between 1850 and 1914, many of them in the urban, industrial centres of the North of England.[7] The same period saw a growth in the number of large state museums in London. As the British Museum's collections grew in size and scope they were divided: the National Gallery was founded in 1824, the National Portrait Gallery in 1856, the Science Museum in 1883, the Tate Gallery in 1896 and the Victoria and Albert Museum of Design and Manufacture in 1899.[8] This growth in the numbers of museums coincided with the growing economic, cultural and political power of the middle classes. Admission to the museums was free, and it was hoped that the urban working class, the site of so much bourgeois anxiety, would be 'improved' by entering the museums and looking at the exhibits. Like the municipal libraries which were also founded at this time, the museums were intended as sites of both entertainment and education for the working class; by actively displacing sites of culture and education which had been created by a politically radical working class, such as the Halls of Science, the museums and libraries of the nineteenth century came to dominate public cultural educational.[9] Museums became authoritative sites for the exhibition of the ideal nation.

The authority of museums was embodied in the form, as well as the content of these buildings. Their architectural form often deliberately recalled past ceremonial buildings such as palaces and temples, sites of authority, ceremony and worship. They were often sited in the middle of towns and cities, close to the town hall, the site of local civic power. London museums and galleries in particular were able to signify, through both their position in the capital and their physical appearance, close links with both the British state and with past institutions of power, knowledge and ceremony.[10] The museum or gallery, particularly the large, central state museum or gallery, was a place where ideas of the nation could be both legitimized and made visible.

The Imperial War Museum was founded in 1917, and formally established by an Act of Parliament in 1920,[11] with the specific aim of giving the British public an overview of the Great War of 1914–18. Whilst the museum was originally intended as a private enterprise, the War Cabinet and officials from both the armed services and the Ministry of Munitions soon had representatives on its Central Committee, and the official aim of the museum became 'to collect and preserve for British inspection objects illustrating the British share in the war'.[12] The museum was officially opened by King George V in 1920 at the Crystal Palace, moving from there to a temporary home at the South Kensington Imperial Institute, and in 1935 to its present home at the former Bethlam Hospital at Southwark.

From its inception, the Imperial War Museum was a consciously 'national' museum, with the aim of creating a sense of inclusion and membership of the nation amongst its members. As many members of the nation as possible were to be included in the museum's presentation of a nation at war, including munitions workers and Land Army girls. These goals were made explicit in the King's dedicatory speech at the official opening of the museum in 1920, when he explained that it stood 'not for a group of trophies won from a beaten army nor for a symbol of the pride of victory, but as an embodiment and lasting memorial of common effort and common sacrifice'.[13] The museum, despite its name, thus represented the First World War less as a great imperial victory for Britain, and more as a time of national unity, shared suffering and shared effort. The institution was surrounded from its inception by the imagery and language of common sacrifice and effort.[14]

This view of the war might perhaps have been the antithesis of the feelings and views of some of the museum's early visitors, who may well have been wondering just *what* they had fought and suffered for. The imagined visitors to the Imperial War Museum may have entered the building having only experienced *their* war, and perhaps carrying with them feelings of bitterness and anger, but, having viewed the exhibits, emerged with a picture of the *nation's* war, and a subsequent understanding and acceptance of the aims and values that they, along with the rest of the nation, had been fighting for. The ideal visitor to the museum would thus become the ideal citizen.

Of course, this ideal visitor, the passive 'subject' who absorbs the message of the museum or gallery without question rarely, if ever, exists. Our experience of museums, like our experience of everything else in life, is shaped by a variety of factors, gender, class, sexuality, religious and political beliefs being amongst them. If a museum is a text, then we all make our own readings of it, and an individual may also visit a museum and 'read' it differently at different points in his or her life. Nevertheless, the inclusion of an object from the past, or a representation of the past, in a museum is an important means of legitimizing it, of bestowing on it an aura of importance. When objects appear in museums, they become part of 'our' history.

The Imperial War Museum and the Winston Churchill Britain at War Theme Museum (hereafter referred to as the Winston Churchill Museum) are, in many ways, very different sorts of institutions. The Imperial War Museum is a national, state-sponsored museum, following in the traditions of the institutions discussed above and set up largely to educate its visitors in an inclusive sense of national history and identity. Until recently, admission to the museum was free, and its main purpose was to function as a site of officially informed education about British wars in the twentieth century. The Winston Churchill Museum, however, was conceived primarily as a commercial enterprise. Sited next door to the London Dungeon (a museum of crime and punishment featuring realistically gruesome waxwork models of murder victims), its aim seems to be to attract as many paying visitors as possible, and this is partly done by the emphasis in both its publicity material and displays on the most exciting and immediately accessible events of the war years.

However, what these institutions share is the special place of museums in the construction of a public sense of the past. Museums provide one of the principal means by which people can gain access to the past and a special historic legitimacy is conferred upon events and objects when they are included in museums. The past which is displayed in museums becomes known to the museum's visitors, and its place in a museum display ensures that it is embodied with a special significance, an importance which comes from its site within an institution which signifies knowledge and authority. When they become the subject of numerous or particularly important museum exhibitions and displays, aspects of the past can change their meaning. They cease to be just a part of *history* and instead have the potential to become a part of our shared, national, *heritage*.

It is important here to distinguish clearly between heritage and history. If 'history' can be seen as an attempt to represent the past, then 'heritage' is an attempt to take aspects of that past, and inscribe them as especially significant in the collective history of a group of people, be it a class, region or nation.[15] Heritage, then, is closely linked with our need for a sense of the past, a sense of continuity, belonging and identity. This is often represented through a commercialization of the past in 'heritage centres' and 'heritage experiences', the primary concern of which is to make money.[16] In the shift from history to heritage, certain aspects of the event, period or lifestyle being remembered will be prioritized over others, sometimes leading to a sanitized or romanticized view of the past. Of course, it is not just museums and heritage centres which have the power to create heritage; this happens when an aspect of history is foregrounded across a whole range of public sites of communication. However, the special role of museums, their place in our society as sites of authority and official knowledge, means that they have an ability to imbue the subjects of their exhibitions with a particular significance. It is this process which happens in the two representations of the Blitz discussed here.

Because of its inclusion in the Imperial War Museum's Second World War display, and especially because of the prominence it is given there, the Blitz is situated within the museum as an important part of the nation's heritage. However, like the main displays in the Winston Churchill Museum, the 'Blitz Experience' does not display a collection of objects from the past which have been designated as valuable and important enough to be preserved and displayed. Although both museums do display some artefacts from the Second World War, the Imperial War Museum more so than the Winston Churchill Museum, these objects are not a part of their 'Blitz Experiences'. Rather than build a display around historical objects, the curators have created a particular version of the past for people to visit and, importantly, to interact with. In this way, these displays differ fundamentally from more traditional museum displays, which rely upon the existence, discovery and acquisition of objects and artefacts in their presentation of the past.

The main objective of these displays is to present a theme, not to preserve and display a collection of objects. Yet paradoxically, the process of interpretation and recreation becomes less, rather than more, visible. In a 'traditional' museum display the objects on display are often in a glass case, chosen, classified and labelled by the visitors' knowledgeable intermediaries, the curators. In a display without artefacts, and without labels, this process of choice and interpretation becomes hidden. Because these themed museum 'experiences' or heritage displays begin with the choice of a period, event or lifestyle as particularly significant and worthy of commemoration rather than beginning with the discovery or acquisition of artefacts, they have the ability to tell us more about current preoccupations with the past than do the older, object-reliant, forms of museum display. Rather than *preserving* the past, they create it.

Within these themed displays, as within heritage centres, the past becomes a place which we can visit. We, the visitors to the past, are often guided through it by actors representing its inhabitants, telling us 'their' story. By making the historian or curator, the interpreter of the past, invisible, the themed display, or experience, gives a particular credence and legitimization to one particular version of events which cannot be achieved to the same extent in the more traditional museum display. The version of past events which they present can be one which sanitizes or omits contested or problematic aspects of the past. It is this process which can be seen in both the Imperial War Museum's 'Blitz Experience' and the Winston Churchill Museum.

Experiencing the Blitz

In 1989 the newly renovated Imperial War Museum welcomed the first visitors to the new 'Blitz Experience'. Publicized as an opportunity for the inhabitants of the late twentieth century to experience the sights, smells and sounds of the Blitz on London of 1940–1, the 'Blitz Experience' formed the new, interactive centrepiece of the museum's Second World War display.[17] Through the 'Blitz Experience', the Blitz is presented as a central part of the body of knowledge which the Second World War exhibition is meant to impart to its visitors. It is the highlight of the display.

The 'Blitz Experience' is situated near the exit from the Second World War display. Visitors are ushered into it by a guide, entering through a small, dark doorway to find themselves in a reconstruction of a London brick-built shelter. The visitors, or shelterers as they are now, are urged on into the shelter by the taped voice of 'George', a local air raid warden, and unmistakable as a working-class man from east London. As the shelter fills more voices appear on the tape, all with strong London accents. Some talk about their day whilst others complain of lack of sleep. As the bombs begin to fall George leads them in a hearty rendition of 'Roll Out the Barrel'. As the bombs get closer George's daughter Val becomes hysterical, her screams gradually drowning out the singing. A bomb drops uncomfortably close and the shelter reverberates. Everything goes quiet.

The shelterers are then helped outside by the museum guide, whose flashlight plays around the devastated street that they are now standing in. In front of them lies an upturned pram, its front wheel still spinning. Behind this are the ruins of a house. Before the new shelterers become too worried about the fates of the occupants of the pram and the house, the voices on the tape reassure each other that the owners of the house were 'bombed out' in the previous week, and so are no longer in residence. It is property which has been destroyed here, not lives. Next the flashlight picks out a bombed pub, and groans can be heard coming from beneath the rubble. This is Albert, the publican, whom, we are told, has always refused to come into the shelter, preferring to sleep behind his bar. The voices reassure Albert until, a few seconds later, the Heavy Rescue Squad appear to dig him out and carry him away on a stretcher, explaining to George's anxious wife Edith that he will be alright. None of this is seen, but is heard on tape. The background to this drama is a diorama of London on fire, dominated by the recurring symbol of London in the Blitz, St Paul's Cathedral. A gasworks in the distance of the diorama explodes and collapses, presumably killing a young warden George has been speaking to who was on his way there. As the shelterers are led through the remains of the street they see the front of a bomb-blasted shop, identified as George's, and hear his son, Harry, crying for his toys. An upper-class WVS woman is heard repeatedly offering tea to the now bombed-out family, and in a nice touch of class antagonism, Edith tells George that 'if she offers me a cup of tea once more I'm going to take that tea urn and ram it down 'er throat!' However, George goes on to tell the visiting

Figure 17.1 Photograph showing the Blitz Experience. *Courtesy of Imperial War Museum,* 1987-24-24.

shelterers that it was this WVS woman 'what sorted us out in the end with a place at a rest centre'. As the shelterers move towards the exit and the 1990s, George tells them that this was one of the worst nights of London's Blitz. He confides that what kept them going was the knowledge that 'we was all in it together.' As the shelterers leave blitzed London to become museum visitors once more, their last 'experience' of the Blitz is George's fading voice saying 'Don't forget us'.

In late 1992 this representation of London's Blitz was joined by the Winston Churchill Museum in Tooley Street. The publicity for the museum promises potential visitors that it 'makes World War Two come alive' and that visitors will 'experience the sights, sounds and smells of the London Blitz with amazing realistic effects'[18] Like the Blitz Experience, and like many other privately owned heritage centres, the Winston Churchill Museum does not set out to assemble and display a collection of objects from the past which have been designated as important enough, valuable enough, to be preserved and displayed. Although the museum does display some artefacts from the war, such as cigarette cards, clothes and toys, they are not the main reason for its existence. The display of these objects forms one of three main parts of the Museum, the other two being recreations of a London tube shelter, and of a blitzed street. Two-thirds of the museum are thus devoted to the interactive, themed, 'experience'.

There are two outstanding features of this museum which are particularly relevant to a study of public histories, public stories, about the Second World War. These are, once again, the foregrounding of the 1940–41 Blitz on London as a central, formative experience of the nation at war, and secondly, the emphasis placed, both within the museum's displays and in its title, on Winston Churchill's role as war leader; the intertwining of his personal biography with the history of 'the people' during the Second World War.

As with the 'Blitz Experience', the visitor is encouraged to understand the Blitz by 'experiencing' it, by interacting with it. The visitor is actively encouraged to share the experience of Britain at war, to 'see it . . . feel it . . . breathe it . . . be part of those momentous days'.[19] Descending in a rickety lift, the visitor emerges into a reconstruction of a Tube shelter, where she or he can sit on 'original bales of wartime blankets'[20] to watch a collage of wartime newsreels covering the period from the 'phoney war' of 1939 to the 1942 battle of El Alamein, often described as the turning point of the war for Britain, the British Army's first real victory against the Third Reich. Again, the set-piece shelter is a large communal shelter, although the highest estimate of the total Tube population on any one night was 177,000, less than 5 per cent of London's population.[21] Representations of the Blitz which focus on these large public shelters reinforce the idea that the Blitz was a time when the nation was unified by a common sense of purpose and experience. It is a sanitized version of a minority experience presented as a majority experience, and bears little resemblance to the Tube shelter recalled by a former shelterer in Calder's *The People's War*, who described a place where 'the stench was frightful, urine and excrement mixed with strong carbolic, sweat, and dirty, unwashed humanity'.[22] In contrast this shelter is fairly pleasant: there are chairs, bunk beds, a tea urn and even a well-stocked bookcase. The walls are covered with well-known posters from the war: 'Keep Mum, She's Not So Dumb', 'Careless Talk Costs Lives', and 'Dig for Victory'. All of these slogans would probably be recognized by a majority of adult British visitors to the museum. They act as powerful signifiers of a shared national past; a recognizable part of the dominant popular memory of the war.

Emerging from the Tube shelter, the visitor next walks along a corridor lined with photos of London during the Blitz and newspaper headlines of the time. At the end of this corridor the visitor can choose to enter an Anderson shelter, where she or he can listen to the recorded sounds of an air raid, look at an exhibition called 'The Home Front' which focuses entirely on women's experiences of the war, or pass straight on through 'The Rainbow Bar' (where dummies of a British woman and an American soldier are jitterbugging) to the centrepiece of the museum, the 'Blitz Experience'.

This exhibition differs significantly from the 'Blitz Experience' at the Imperial War Museum. There are no voice-overs and no taped narrative to guide the visitor; instead she or he is left to pick his or her own way through a devastated department store and street. The whole experience is far more disorientating than the Blitz Experience; the large room it is housed in is dark, the floor is uneven and the visitors make their way round the exhibition at their own pace, able to return for a second look at some things whilst bypassing others. There is no George here to guide the visitor, no reminder that 'We was all in it together'. However, like the other display, physical damage to people is minimal; the central figure in the display is a fireman carrying a girl to safety. What are perhaps first thought to be bodies turn out on closer inspection to be mannequins from the bombed shop. Again, the main damage is suffered by property, not people.

Winston Churchill is a central figure in the museum. The museum has chosen as its logo a line drawing of Churchill's famous 'V for Victory' salute and his presence is inescapable within the displays. Whilst the Imperial War Museum emphasizes 'the people's war', the Winston Churchill Museum makes explicit links between Churchill as the nation's leader and the nation as a whole. Illustrations of people during the London Blitz all have quotes from Churchill as their captions: 'Never has so much been owed by so many to so few', 'We shall defend our island whatever the cost may be', 'Give us the tools and we shall finish the job'. The majority of the photographs show people 'carrying on' during the Blitz; postmen picking their way over rubble, shopkeepers opening bombed out shops, people queuing up for tea from mobile WVS canteens. Churchill is linked with the war in a seamless narrative which has little space for hardship and suffering, and none at all for dissent or dissatisfaction.

Obviously these very public, official memories of the Blitz are partial recollections, foregrounding some images at the expense of others. The injury, death, fear and destruction which dominate some personal memories of the Blitz are overshadowed by images of togetherness and community. This 'writing-out' of problematic memories of the period is by no means unique to these displays, and is perhaps best illustrated by an examination of the problems that one group of people had when trying to find a public site for *their* memories.

On 3 March 1993, the East London Borough of Bethnal Green marked, for the first time, a wartime anniversary. A plaque was unveiled on the staircase of Bethnal Green Tube Station to commemorate the deaths of 173 people there during an air raid on 3 March 1943. The dead were not the direct victims of a bombing raid, but died of suffocation after a woman carrying a baby tripped near the bottom of the steps and fell in the darkness, causing those behind her to fall as well. People had rushed into the shelter after a salvo of new, unfamiliar anti-aircraft rockets from nearby Victoria Park had made them panic. The official Home Office statement said that 'There was built an immovable and interrelated mass of bodies, five, six or more deep'.[23] A local magistrate commented that 'the staircase was . . . converted from a corridor to a charnel house in from ten to fifteen seconds'.[24] The Home Secretary, Herbert Morrison, urged stoicism on the community, telling them that they were 'a people tested and hardened by the experience of the Blitz and as well able to bear loss bravely as any people in the world'.[25] The tragedy was not reported in the press for two days and when it did appear Bethnal Green was not named, and there was no mention of the possibility of panic amongst the shelterers. The disaster had no official commemoration, no real space in the public representations of the war, and so it became marginalized, a largely unwritten part of wartime history, and certainly not a part of 'our heritage', only really remembered by those whom it personally affected.

This marginalization of the Bethnal Green Tube tragedy made it ever more difficult for the survivors and bereaved to speak about it. Fifty years on, the unveiling of the commemorative plaque meant that some of them spoke for the first time in public about their memories. One woman remembered visiting the mortuary to find the body of her mother, whose hair had turned white overnight, and that of her two-year-old nephew who had died without a visible mark on him. Another told of trying to hold onto her best friend's hand in the crush, letting go only to find her the next day in the mortuary with her baby brother. Yet another woman said she had never used Bethnal Green station since; another how she ritually counted every one of the steps that people fell down when she used it.[26] There is no mention of this tragedy in either of the museum displays, just as there is no mention of the times when bombs fell on Balham Tube, injuring 600 people, at Bank, killing 100, or at Marble Arch, killing 20.[27] Memories like this, of death, tragedy and grief, have little space in the 'Blitz Experiences'. When they *are* present they are both marginalized and sanitized, surpassed by more positive images of the period.

When looking at the process of public remembering it is important to discover what has been forgotten, in order better to understand what has been remembered. Remembering, both public and private, is a process of sifting, as some events and images are discarded or put aside whilst others are carefully saved. However, the museum displays, like the wider public memories of the war, do not *entirely* forget memories such as these. If this was the case, they would not win such a wide audience; the absence of any suffering at all would mark them out as unrealistic representations of the period. Instead, problematic memories and images of the Blitz can be present, but tend to be sanitized and modified, overwhelmed by more positive images of the war. This process can be illustrated by the script for the Imperial War Museum's 'Blitz Experience'.

Whilst the 'Blitz Experience' privileges notions of community togetherness and national unity over images of fear and destruction, these more problematic images and memories are still present. Behind the singing of 'Roll Out the Barrel', the warden's daughter can be heard screaming hysterically. Houses are destroyed and people are injured. A young, unnamed warden of whom we hear once is killed when the gasworks explodes. George's shop is hit and he and his family have to move into temporary accommodation. He tells the visitors that 'some parts of London was prepared for the Blitz. Well, ours certainly wasn't . . . it was the most miserable Winter I've ever known'. However, these memories of fear, injury, death, discomfort and official incompetence are small in comparison to the more popular memories given prominence here: memories such as the community singing in the shelter, 'cockney' humour and the notion which is central to the 'Blitz Experience': 'We was all in it together'.

The fifth draft of the script for the 'Blitz Experience', the one which was being used for the display in 1993, illustrates the process by which problematic images and memories become marginalized and sometimes eventually disappear. The original script for the 'Blitz Experience' contained references to the physical destruction of *people* by bombs, the lack of sanitation, light and heat in the public shelters, and the fact that some shelters were built quickly without adequate cement, collapsing easily if a bomb fell nearby, and causing many casualties and deaths.[28] Gone is

George's original description of shelters with 'no lavatory – just a bucket. Cold, dark, damp'.[29] Gone too is Val's story about a shelter in which all the occupants died: 'They said it weren't built with any cement. Just collapsed it did. I saw them – bits of bodies everywhere'.[30] Missing as well is Val's description of the infamous Tilbury Shelter in the East End, where 'there's s'posed to be over 14,000 people living'.[31] In the eventual script, all these references were cut; they cannot be made to fit with a picture of the Blitz which privileges images of good-humoured cockneys, community spirit and national unity over and above the images of death, injury and destruction which feature in many individual memories of the period. There is very little space for these memories on the public stage.

There are many similarities in the processes of public and private remembering discussed here, both essentially being processes by which the past is shaped by the present; processes of selection, reordering and reconstruction. They are, of course, often interdependent on each other: the museum displays discussed here would not work if they were entirely unrepresentative of people's experiences and memories of the period; one of the reasons why people have felt it difficult to talk publicly about the Bethnal Green disaster is because of its lack of commemoration in the public sphere. Perhaps most importantly, memory is never fixed, but always open to further reinterpretation and reshaping according to present events and preoccupations. The conclusion will outline what these very public sites of memory can tell us about Britain in the 1990s.

Conclusions: remembering the Blitz

Ideas about the past are central to conceptions of British nationhood. Representations of the Second World War such as those discussed here work to remind us that 'We' can all 'pull together' if needs be; emphasizing notions of togetherness and community in the face of adversity. They present a picture of the nation in which 'the people' are central. Yet 'the people' of the 'Blitz Experience' and the Winston Churchill Museum are a people denuded of almost all class antagonism and of all revolutionary potential. In 1940, far from being an immediately unifying experience, the Blitz had the potential to increase the class divisions seen in the 1930s: one local Essex dignitary reacted to the influx of Londoners fleeing the bombs by declaring 'I won't have these people billeted on our people',[32] and the Communist Party organized an invasion of the Savoy Hotel's luxurious private shelter in protest at the lack of safe public shelters in the East End. This divisive aspect of the early days of the Blitz, when bombing was almost exclusively concentrated on the socially marginal working-class and immigrant areas of the East End, have all but disappeared from today's public representations of the Blitz. George in the 'Blitz Experience' tells visitors 'We was all in it together', whilst the display in the Winston Churchill Museum links quotes of Churchill with photographs of 'the people' to produce a seamless picture of a united Britain. Today's public memory of the war, the memory which dominates the museum displays discussed here, speaks to us of a nation unproblematically united in battle.

This public memory of the war is one which is specific to Britain in the 1980s and 1990s. It is a concept of the past which is central to ideas of British nationhood which have become closely associated with the New Right, and which was seen in particularly sharp relief during the Falklands/Malvinas War of 1982, during which links were drawn, both in political discourse and in much of the media, between the national aims of both wars, a national unity which overrode any internal divisions, and a Conservative leadership.[33] The democratizing, modernizing people's war, which led to the landslide electoral victory for a reforming Labour government in 1945, has been claimed and reshaped by the contemporary Right as a key moment in Britain's national past; the last time that Britain was still 'Great'.

The authoritative nature of museums, and the absence of visible interpreters of the past in the 'Blitz Experience' and the Winston Churchill Museum, makes them particularly powerful producers of a public past. The images of the Blitz seen here could be experienced by visitors as absolute and unquestionable; the aim being to produce an 'experience' which is as 'real' as possible. Oppositional or problematic images of the Blitz are overwhelmed by more positive images; images which serve to support the New Right's construction of British national identity as something natural and unchanging, untouched by 'modern' impositions such as the politics of gender, race or class.

In a nation which has experienced massive social economic and political changes over the past fifteen years the Blitz, a time of huge disruption and uncertainty, has come to act as a symbol of unity and continuity. It is this memory of the nation at war which is reinforced in these displays and passed on to visitors, including children and foreign tourists. The displays of the 'Blitz Experience' perhaps tell us more about our state of mind today then they do about Britain in the Second World War.

Notes

1   From the nineteenth-century scrapbook of a 'Mr W.A. of Peckham', cited in C. Sorenson, 'Theme parks and time machines', in P. Verso (ed.), *The New Museology*, (London: Reaktion) 1989, p. 61.

2   Remaining bombs were also often 'dumped' over coastal towns by German pilots returning to the Continent after bombing large towns and cities.

3   A. Calder, *The People's War 1939–1945* (London: Cape) 1969, p. 164.

4   Until 1943, more civilians than members of the armed forces were killed in the war. A total of 60,950 people died as a result of the bombing campaigns, of whom about half were women. P. Summerfield and G. Braybon, *Out of the Cage: Women in the Two World Wars* (London: Pandora) 1987, pp. 2–3.

5   A. Calder, *The Myth of the Blitz* (London: Cape) 1991.

6   The idea of imagined communities used here is drawn from B. Anderson, *Imagined Communities* (London: Verso) 1983.

7   R. Hewison, *The Heritage Industry. Britain in a Climate of Decline* (London: Methuen) 1987, pp. 86–7.

8   Ibid., p. 86.

9   E. Yeo and S. Yeo, 'On the uses of community from Owenism to the present', in S. Yeo (ed.), *New Views of Co-operation* (London: Routledge) 1988, p. 236.

10   C. Duncan and A. Wallach, 'The Universal Survey Museum', in *Art History*, vol. 3, no. 4 (1980) pp. 448–69.

11   D. Condell, 'The Imperial War Museum 1917–1920. A study of the institution and its presentation of the First World War', unpublished Mphil dissertation, 1985, Imperial War Museum, p. 34.

12   *The Times*, 26 March 1917, p. 20, cited in Condell 'Imperial War Museum', p. 23.

13   'The King's Dedicatory Speech, Crystal Palace, 9 June 1920', cited in Condell 'Imperial War Museum', p. 149.

14   Foster (1936), p. 215.

15   I recognize that this is a vastly simplified definition of history, practitioners of which of course choose to focus on particular areas and claim a special significance for their particular field of research. However, for the purposes of this chapter, it is necessary to define history in this way *specifically* in relation to heritage. History differs from heritage in the ways in which it is presented to and known by the public, and in the general significance given to particular aspects of the past. Consumption, perhaps, is the key difference between heritage and history.

16   N. Merriman, *Beyond the Glass Case: The Past, the Heritage and the Public in Britain* (Leicester: Leicester University Press) 1991, p. 8.

17   Publicity leaflet for the Imperial War Museum, subtitled 'Part of Your Family's History'.

18   Publicity leaflet for the Winston Churchill Britain at War Theme Museum, 1992.

19   Ibid.

20   Ibid.

21   Calder *People's War*, p. 157. These figures are given for 27 September 1940, near the beginning of the Blitz when the highest numbers of people were attempting to shelter from bombing.

22   Ibid., p. 183.

23   L. R. Dunne [Magistrate of the Police Courts of the Metropolis], *Home Office Enquiry into an Accident at the London Tube Station* (London: Home Office) 1943, p. 5.

24   Cited in *The Times*, 1 March 1993.

25   Ibid.

26   Ibid., and the *Independent*, 4 March 1993.

27   Calder *People's War*, pp. 338–9 and p. 183.

28   Ibid., p. 113.

29   'Blitz Experience Script' fifth draft, undated, Imperial War Museum, p. 3.

30   Ibid., p. 7.

31   Ibid., p. 11. This shelter, where thousands of people sheltered every night is vividly described by a Mass Observation team which visited it in September 1940:

> A dense block of people, nothing else. By 7.30 p.m. every bit of floor space taken up. Deckchairs, blankets, stools, seats, pillows . . . people lying every-where. The floor was awash with urine. Only two lavatories for 5,000 women, none for men . . . overcome by smell. People are sleeping on piles of rubbish . . . the passages are loaded with filth. Lights dim or non-existent . . . they sit, in darkness, head of one against feet of the next . . . there is no room to move and hardly any to stretch. Some horses are still stabled there, and their mess mingles with that of the humans.
>
> (cited in Calder, *People's War*, p. 117)

32   Calder *People's War*, p. 166.

33   For a detailed discussion of the memories of the Second World War dominant within political discourse in 1982, see A. Barnett, *Iron Britannia* (London: Allison & Busby) 1982.

Chapter 18

John Bodnar

SAVING PRIVATE RYAN AND POSTWAR MEMORY IN AMERICA

T H E   R E L E A S E   I N   1 9 9 8 of *Saving Private Ryan* by Hollywood director Steven Spielberg has revived again the debate over war and remembering. In this case, audiences have flocked to see a story of American troops, led by a dedicated captain, John Miller (Tom Hanks), attempt to rescue a young private from the field of battle just after the Allied invasion of Normandy in 1944. Some reviewers have stressed how Spielberg's film is the first to truly show the horror of battle, especially in its opening scenes, which depict the American landing on Omaha Beach, June 6, 1944. Modern technology has allowed the filmmaker to reproduce the frightening sound of German gunfire and the brutal reality of exploding body parts. American soldiers are shattered and maimed on the beachhead, and some fall apart emotionally from the stress of battle. As many reviewers have suggested, the movie counters images of heroic warriors by disclosing the real terror of combat and is in many ways an antiwar story.[1]

Ironically, while the Spielberg film reveals the brutality of war, it preserves the World War II image of American soldiers as inherently averse to bloodshed and cruelty. The war was savage; the average American GI who fought it was not. American men in this story are destroyed by war, and only a few actually enjoy killing Germans. At its rhetorical core, the story's argument would have seemed very familiar to audiences in the 1940s: the common American soldier was fundamentally a good man who loved his country and his family. He went to war out of a sense of duty to both, and he wanted to get it over with as quickly as possible. Rather than being a natural-born killer, he was a loving family man who abhorred the use of extreme force but could inflict it when necessary. This point is made well in the figure of John Miller. A high school teacher and part-time baseball coach from Pennsylvania, he disdains brutality and says that every time he kills another man he feels "farther from home." Traumatized himself at times by battle, this common man still has heroic potential and is always up to the task of taking on the German war machine. It is a model found in dozens of wartime films that depicted average guys from Brooklyn or Texas who loved their everyday life in America or the girl next door. Miller is ultimately a representation of the brand of common-man heroism that infused the culture of wartime America. Without a doubt, a platoon of men like him could save Private Ryan and win the war. Norman Corwin's famous radio broadcast of May 8, 1945, on the occasion of Germany's surrender, makes the case for the courageous possibilities of the ordinary person. "Take a bow, GI. Take a bow, little guy," Corwin told his listeners. "The superman of tomorrow lies at the feet of you common men this afternoon."[2]

Although anguish and bravery share narrative space in this film, they do not do so on an equal basis. The pain of the American combat soldier is revealed but is ultimately placed within a larger frame of patriotic valor. Some American soldiers in this story question the war effort and their superiors' decisions, but in the end the nation and its warriors are moral and honorable. The fact that combat was so frightening serves mainly to reinforce our admiration for these soldiers and their gallantry. The entire narrative, for that matter, is immensely "reverent" toward the nation and its warriors, attempting to uphold its patriotic architecture with opening and closing scenes at an American military cemetery in Europe. The very design of these sites of remembering was originally driven by the desire to proclaim the unity of the American nation, with their rows upon rows of white crosses, and to serve as "permanent reminders to other nations of the sacrifices made by the United States." If other nations were expected to recall their debt to America, Spielberg's film makes the additional claim that survivors of the war (like Ryan) and subsequent generations of Americans need to recognize their obligations to these brave combatants. Thus, at the film's end, Ryan can only look back over his life and the graves of the heroic dead and express the hope that he lived a life that merited the sacrifice his comrades made for him, one that consisted of devotion to family and country. In this veneration of patriotism and self-denial, the story takes us back to dominant political and moral values of the 1940s, which advocated collective goals over individual ones.[3]

But, as Spielberg remembers, he also forgets. Forties' calls to patriotic sacrifice were contingent on assurances of a more democratic society and world. Government leaders such as Franklin D. Roosevelt took pains to make democratic promises in pronouncements like "The Four Freedoms." And the Office of War Information (OWI) told Hollywood producers to make films that not only helped win the conflict but reminded audiences that it was "a people's war," which would bring about a future with more social justice and individual freedom. The democracy for which "the people" fought, in fact, was a cultural blend of several key ideas: tolerance, individualism, anti-totalitarianism, and economic justice. The representation of open-mindedness was aimed particularly at reducing ethnic tensions at home. American individualism was venerated in the call for personal freedoms and even in the rhetoric of military recruiters. They promised that army life would not destroy a man's self-interests but would preserve the same balance between individualism and teamwork that Americans experienced in their sporting endeavors. Frank Capra's series "Why We Fight" (1942–1945) was a vivid example of the use of anti-totalitarian images to encourage support for the war. And slogans like "Freedom from Want" acknowledged the popular desire for economic security after the 1930s.[4]

Spielberg's turn to the moral individual in heroism and in pain at the expense of the moral or democratic community, however, suggests just how much this film is a product of the late twentieth century and not of the 1940s. The attainment of democracy rested in the 1940s on a sense of reciprocity between individuals and the institutions that governed their lives. In a totalitarian state, government and institutions dominated individuals; in a democracy, a relationship of mutual respect existed between citizens and institutions. People served the nation because they believed the nation would serve their democratic interests in return. Narratives that endorsed this relationship, such as those found in many wartime films, effectively linked the fate of the individual with the fate of the nation. Today, however, narratives and images about the destiny of individuals command more cultural space than those about the fortunes of nations. As a result, both political speech and commemoration have more to say about victims or people who have met tragic fates. Spielberg's memory narrative of moral men represents very much the late twentieth century's concern with the singular person in the past, present, and future. Cohesive narratives that effectively link personal stories to collective desires for progress are harder to find. Those that exist are disrupted by images of victims. Heroism and patriotism remain, but they must fight for cultural space with the claims of those who have sorrowful tales from the past or those who insist on redress rather than self-denial. Many believe that, since Vietnam, it is harder to commemorate gallantry and victory or to suppress individual subjectivities at the expense of collective ones. Thus delineations of victims—from Vietnam, from the AIDS epidemic, from racism, from child abusers, from rapists, from drugs, even from World War II—now command more cultural space. Statements of what was lost now eclipse expressions of what was gained.[5]

This tension between the old patriotic narrative about the fate of the nation and the new expression of individual suffering and loss is expressed clearly on the Washington Mall, a central site of American cultural memory. In recent times, the process of nationalizing the representation of emotional shock and private pain appears arrested. The images of the old public history, dominated by powerful statesmen who were devoted to the nation have been substantially modified by the appearance of victims. Names (and possessions) of dead soldiers constitute the Vietnam Veterans Memorial, known simply as "The Wall." Statues of American troops reveal men moving cautiously through a battlefield scene from Korea (1995); they appear fearful that they could be killed or hurt at any moment. Figures standing in Depression-era bread lines or listening for words of hope command attention at the Franklin Delano Roosevelt Memorial (1997), and, nearby, thousands of images pertaining to Holocaust victims have been mounted for exhibit (1993). Explanations for this transformation remain elusive. Some attribute the change to the impact on American culture of the Vietnam War and traumatic events such as the AIDS epidemic. The overall effect of the Holocaust cannot be discounted. Certainly, the nation's ability to manage discourse about the past has withered as many more voices—including the mass media—have joined in the production of culture.[6]

Contests over public remembering were certainly not pervasive in most nations after World War II. Many countries were able to limit the representation of war trauma and homegrown victimization in their societies for a very long time after the war. In Japan, a long-term effort to conceal that nation's culpability for atrocities in China or for starting the war in the Pacific has fallen apart only in recent years. To some extent, this campaign was sustained by silences in Japanese history books and by memorials to the Japanese dead that tended to remember them as innocent victims, not brutal warriors. In postwar Germany, the Holocaust was substantially denied in public; in many instances, Germans referred to themselves as "victims" of Nazi aggressors, denying the realities of German-sponsored brutality toward others. In France, for some two decades after the war, citizens tended to recall the conflict in terms of a patriotic narrative: brave French Resistance fighters under Charles de Gaulle waged an unrelenting campaign to free their captured nation from the Germans. This version of the war had elements that were true, but it failed to acknowledge completely the role of some French citizens who collaborated with the Nazis in sending French Jews to death camps. In much of the Western world in fact, the contemporary memory of the Holocaust as an act of unparalleled barbarism did not emerge fully until the 1960s: publicity surrounding Adolf Eichmann's trial and the Arab–Israeli Six-Day War for a time recalled images of the death of Jews.[7]

In this essay, however, I want to argue that the narrative of heroism, patriotism, and democracy that permeated wartime America—the story that *Saving Private Ryan* seeks to restore only partially—began to decompose immediately in the aftermath of World War II. This would not be so apparent if one looked only at official commemorations and public monuments, such as the one dedicated in 1954 to the costly American victory at Iwo Jima. Mass culture, however, was more responsive to the range of personal emotions and recollections that resided in the hearts and minds of the people, and it frequently challenged "reverent" narratives by the late 1940s. Although limitations of space prevent a full discussion of the impact of mass culture on society, the central point must be made that mass cultural forms undermined disciplinary institutions (such as governments or churches) in their goal of managing the public expression of human wants. Films, for instance, thrived because they were able to broadcast the full range of human desires and emotions.

Long before *Saving Private Ryan* or even the Vietnam War, American mass culture was flooded with a torrential debate over the violence unleashed by war and, more importantly, over the turbulent nature of American society itself. Scholars have documented both political opposition to the American atomic build-up in the late 1940s and cultural expressions of anxiety over the possibility of world destruction by atomic weapons throughout the Cold War era. But this line of analysis is grounded too much in Cold War issues and fails to sufficiently appreciate the overall impact of World War II and the memory of violence and trauma that it generated. The war showed Americans that their fellow citizens were as capable of inflicting brutality as citizens of other nations, and it led them to search for the sources of such behavior within the home front itself. Public anxiety over victimization was as likely to be grounded in fears of dangerous impulses in the hearts and souls of fellow citizens as in fears about powerful weapons. The anxiety that linked popular nervousness over brute force in both wartime and peacetime America was articulated especially in the cinema and in literature. There, writers and directors challenged the sentimental views of the nation and the perspectives of the Office of War Information. In this oppositional view, American men and, for that matter, women were not inherently patriotic and loving but were domineering and ruthless. In its recognition of evil in the hearts and souls of "the people," this construction of the nation and its citizens worked against the hope of a more democratic and prosperous future. Once it was demonstrated that violence could be homegrown and did not reside only in the visions of dictators, it followed that America itself could produce victims as well as patriots, treachery as well as loyalty.[8]

From its inception in the eighteenth century, the nation-state has been haunted by visions of degeneration, chaos, and anarchy. Those potentially responsible for such destructiveness have been located both inside and outside national boundaries. Ideally, the nation was imagined as a united community that would protect its members, grant them rights, and foster their material progress. In the consciousness of nations, citizens entrusted powerful men with civic affairs and the defense of boundaries. Serving as statesmen, patriarchs, or dedicated warriors, these men merited the admiration and gratitude of females and others dependent on them. It was understood that leaders and warriors might sometimes need to suppress savages on the frontiers of the nation or even minorities within it. But hints that they themselves were bloodthirsty or cruel could not only weaken their elevated status but threaten the cultural stability of the nation itself.[9] Consequently war always involves cultural risks even if the nation wins. Omer Bartov has observed that modern warfare and the massive trauma it generated incited feelings of anxiety in all participants and prompted a wide search for enemies and victims.[10] This is what happened in much of the domestic politics of Cold War America and in the aftermath of Vietnam.

Even more central to my argument is the point that, after 1945, recognizing the war's incredible scale of brutality caused ordinary Americans and probably people elsewhere to connect the cruelty of warfare with other forms of malevolence in their lives and society. Once war exposed how savage men could be, it did not take much of a cultural leap to see that everyone was threatened by warlike behavior wherever manifested. This process had distinct implications for remembering the war. Dominick LaCapra suggests that extremely traumatic events often force the imagination to employ extravagant metaphors, invoking terms such as in one's "wildest dreams or most hellish nightmares." In a sense, both the mind and the culture must find ways to confront the "unimaginable magnitude" of what took place. Thus the search for extraordinary models of enemies and victims displaced the wartime representations of a democratic nation and common-man heroism, and it undermined future attempts to represent the national society in a positive manner.[11]

This argument moves away from standard paradigms regarding the relationship between trauma and memory. It accepts and notes that trauma can lead to a "lapse or rupture" in the memory of emotional shock but contends that this form of repression is incomplete. The psychoanalytic study of trauma has revealed that the painful event usually returns against the victim's will and only after an initial period of suppression or "absolute numbing"; the victim must first move away from the event before returning to it. This certainly appeared to happen to some extent in the public culture of the warring nations after 1945. But I will also offer evidence that a substantial amount of the trauma and anxiety, at least in the United States, was not restrained as much as it was displaced into the narratives of mass culture. One scholar has written that "the historical power of trauma is not just that the experience is repeated after its forgetting, but that it is only in and through its inherent forgetting that it is first experienced at all." I would amend this position by claiming that, to a considerable extent, both the personal anxieties and the collective concerns over the violence of war never really left American culture at all.[12]

Some observers who have studied the impact of the Holocaust on postwar culture are impressed by the fact that the cultural suppression of trauma involved in "acting out" the past in a nostalgic sense (something that suppresses the reality of pain) now appears to take place alongside the practice of working-through or confronting emotional disturbances. Nostalgia and mourning coexist. In looking at the films of postwar America and a modern feature like *Saving Private Ryan*, we clearly see what LaCapra calls "interaction, reinforcement, and conflict" between the need to forget and the desire to confront what happened.[13] In its opening scenes, *Saving Private Ryan* confronts the horror; in later scenes, when GIs go off on an adventure to save one individual, it often lapses into play acting and a desire to fight the war over again. The same sort of tension was noticeable in American films about the war in the decade after 1945, although the narrative resolution of contradictions was not always the same. In *Ryan*, patriotic sacrifice as a frame of remembrance stands above both trauma and democracy. But in the immediate postwar era, some films effectively contested patriotic ideals. They often displaced the representation of trauma from the combat zone to American society or to a distant past, but the discourse over the pain of war was real. Thus, between 1946 and 1949, hardly any *combat* films of the war were made. Many features, however, were issued about the devastating consequences of the war on Americans as well as the potential Americans had to inflict harm on others. Moreover, combat did not disappear completely but was often exiled into the genre of the Western. The most thoughtful of these latter films actually located savagery in the character of the American cavalrymen and not Native Americans.[14]

Wartime films were not without their own set of contradictions, to be sure, although patriotism, unity, and democracy dominated the stories. In tales about the war and gender relations, women were assigned crucial roles of support for the men they loved with devotion. This point was made clear in films such as *Since You Went Away* (1944) and *Pride of the Marines* (1945). Ethnic cooperation was fostered in numerous depictions of American platoons, such as *Bataan* (1943). Hatred for authoritarian regimes was certainly prevalent in movies such as *Sahara* (1943), and patriotic sacrifice was venerated in films such as *Wake Island* (1942), which evoked memories of American heroism at Valley Forge and the Alamo. The grim reality of war, the random and unheroic nature of much death, and the sometimes futile plight of the common soldier broke through in creative stories such as *A Walk in the Sun* (1945), but its cynicism was rare. More common was a film like *Air Force* (1943), which effectively merged personal interests and collective needs. In this film, men love their mothers and wives, naturally want to defend their nation, kill the treacherous Japanese, and fight bravely in the Pacific. A tailgunner who feels that he has not been treated fairly in the past eventually lets go of his anger as he joins the fight. The entire film is framed by a preamble from Abraham Lincoln's Gettysburg Address, suggesting that the military struggle is ultimately about "a new birth of freedom" and the need to preserve "government of the people, by the people, and for the people." *Saving Private Ryan*, by contrast, invokes the memory of Lincoln as an expression of the ideal of patriotic sacrifice, not as a call to work for more democracy.[15]

Postwar films moved away from wartime censorship and immediately into a discourse over how the violence unleashed by the war could wreak havoc with the American future. The suggestion that dangerous impulses resided in the souls of Americans themselves was at the core of *film noir* features of the later 1940s. In both mood and story, these films countered sentimental and optimistic assessments not only about the future but about Americans themselves. The 1946 film *The Killers* made evident the "ubiquity" of viciousness and victimization in everyday American life. The central character, played by actor Burt Lancaster, is drawn into a life of crime, betrayed by a woman, and gunned down in the symbolic space of American democracy—the small town. So much for the potential of stable gender relations. Dana Polan has argued that the war was a "disciplinary moment" in which diverse discourses came together to "empower a particular social reality." But it was increasingly clear in the immediate postwar period that critical images of America and Americans could no longer be domesticated and that, as Polan writes, "discourses of commonality" had reached the limits of their persuasiveness.[16]

The productions of *film noir* did not always connect despair directly to the event of World War II, but the popular classic by William Wyler, *The Best Years of Our Lives* (1946), certainly did. In this story, servicemen return home with deep emotional and physical scars. One is haunted not only by the memory of flying bomber runs over Germany but by the realization that his wife had been unfaithful while he was away. In other words, he was victimized by events both abroad and at home. Another veteran, who drinks excessively upon his return, manages to advance the cause of a just society; through his job at a bank, he makes it easier for ordinary veterans to get loans that will help them rebuild their lives. Trauma is acknowledged; the hope of a democratic future still persists.[17]

The most powerful cultural attack on the sentimentality and heroic quality of wartime culture came in Norman Mailer's 1948 novel *The Naked and the Dead*. Mailer was a veteran himself who had served in the Pacific and had seen firsthand some of the destruction caused by the atomic bomb in Japan. His narrative is one that centers not so much on the war as on the nature of American society and the patterns of male behavior it engendered. Stationed on a fictional island in the Pacific, Mailer's GIs are not particularly capable of patriotism or virtue. Rather, they are consumed by personal quests of power and destructiveness. A minor character on the island expresses the Roosevelt administration's view that the conflict is a "people's war" that will lead to a more democratic world for all mankind, a point that the OWI worked assiduously to inject into wartime films. However, General Edward Cummings, a major character in the story, envisions a postwar world dominated not by democracy but by the "Right" and the "Omnipotent Men" who will lead America. Clearly, Mailer saw an innate drive for power and dominion in American men that Spielberg does not. For Mailer, this drive was realized not only in the massive retaliation against the Japanese but in the lives of domineering men like Cummings, whose father had been sent him to military school to make him "think and act like a man."[18]

Cummings's perspective frames the novel's unflattering portrayal of American manhood, and Mailer contends that the male drive for dominance could be found in democracies as well as dictatorships. When someone suggests to Cummings that men would fight out of love for their country, he dismisses the notion as a "liberal historian's attitude." For Cummings, it is not democracy that motivates American men to fight. Instead, they learned to be aggressive from living in a society of unequals in which most men were trying to climb upward from humble origins.

Mailer's story is important not only because it represents a critique of the official views of why America fought and of the romantic images of the American fighting men but because it connects narratives of victimization from the 1930s with those of the 1940s. That is to say, he suggested that both experiences, economic conflict and war, can destroy lives. American culture in the postwar era still reverberated with the aftershocks of the Depression and with notions that revealed the pitfalls of capitalism. In fact, many conservatives had attacked the OWI during the war precisely because of its liberal orientation, which connected the idea of a "people's war" to the need to respect labor as much as business in narrative films. Numerous films continued to reveal the manner in which the nation's fundamental economic system destroyed as many individuals as it rewarded. In *All My Sons* (1948), an industrialist decides to place profits before patriotism, resulting in the production of planes with faulty parts. When American airmen lose their lives as the result of his decisions, the man is traumatized enough to take his own life. In *Champion* (1949), a man throws away relationships with people who care about him for a chance to become a boxing king. In this story, the boxing ring becomes a metaphor for the marketplace pursuit of wealth and fame.[19]

Remembering war as the progenitor of victims rather than heroes was central to a number of films in the late 1940s. In *Crossfire* (1947), soldiers bring their brutal ways back home. Some are described as capable of going "crazy" once there is no one around to give them orders. They engage in drunkenness and murder and even acts of anti-Semitism. In general, they do not seem to have the clear sense of purpose that soldiers in *Saving Private Ryan* exhibit regarding the desirability of resuming domestic arrangements or serving their country. Before *Crossfire* ends, one soldier even kills another.

Two years later, *Home of the Brave* (1949) connected the respective trauma-inducing abilities of war and society. In this tale, an African-American soldier, James Moss, suffers severe emotional distress due to the brutality of racism in the United States and the effects of combat. Moss undergoes treatment for what a military psychiatrist calls "traumatic shock." (In reality, the discovery of psychiatric stress during the war had a profound influence on the way the military treated this problem. Entering the war, the common assumption was that emotional breakdowns in battle were the result of a weak or less than manly character.) Moss is depicted as deeply disturbed by the insults he received in civilian life and from racist soldiers in the military. When he hears his good friend being tortured by the Japanese on a secret mission and is forced to leave his partner to die on an island in the Pacific, he breaks down and cries. The psychiatrist gives him a drug that allows him to relive and, therefore, to come to terms with his combat experience. He realizes that war trauma is shared equally by people of all races. As he goes back home to open a bar with a white friend, we get a hint that the success of a postwar future will depend not only on putting the trauma behind us but on resolving inequality and prejudice as well.

Even more traditional war films of the period were reluctant to temper the anguish of battle with simple images of bravery and valor. In *Battleground* (1949), the point of view of the ordinary fighting man was stressed. War for these "battered bastards" was confusing and painful. Some are looking for a "good clean flesh wound" that will get them out of battle and back to a field hospital and, perhaps, home. As Private Holley, actor Van Johnson claims that the PFC, or private first class, in his military rank stands only for the fact that he is "praying for civilian" status. In this film there is no cataclysmic battle or talk of democracy or patriotism, only an intent focus on fighting to stay alive or to take a small piece of ground. There is dogged determination on the part of American troops in this film against superior enemy forces and bitterly cold weather, but *Battleground* tries hard to say that the average GI was uninterested in putting any sort of political frame on an experience that he detested.

By 1950, a popular war film such as *The Sands of Iwo Jima* went a bit farther than the cynical commentary articulated in *Battleground* by mounting a direct attack on some of the men who won the war, even as it sustained heroic notions about them. John Wayne starred as a dedicated Marine sergeant capable of training soldiers and leading them into battle. This film was supported extensively by the Marine Corps, which supplied it with an array of military hardware, and it is often seen as a pivotal representation of the heroic American war myth. But there is considerable irony in this narrative. Shots of brave American fighting men attacking the Japanese on Tarawa and Iwo Jima are countered by expressions of regret over the fact that men like Wayne (Sergeant Stryker in the movie) ultimately elect the ideals of military life over those of domestic life. Unlike John Miller in *Saving Private Ryan*, Stryker is a zealous soldier who has little interest in maintaining close ties to his wife and family. War is brutal in this film, and men get killed, although 1950s film technology could not achieve the sense of fear that Spielberg's does. *The Sands of Iwo Jima* also made a much more determined attempt to work through the impact of war on men and to address the concern that military life exacerbated natural impulses toward violence, which would have devastating consequences for American society. Unlike the Spielberg film. *The Sands of Iwo Jima* made a specific plea to American men to put the violence of wartime behind them. Audiences watched as a young marine tells Stryker that he wants to raise his son to read Shakespeare, not the Marine manual. And they saw Stryker come to regret the way he mistreated his wife and son. Film historians astutely note that when Stryker is killed near the end, the heroic and violent warrior of World War II is symbolically destroyed. *Ryan* only asks us to honor these men and "earn" the freedom they have left us. Presumably, pacifistic pleas are unnecessary because in Spielberg's world these men are not inherently violent.

By the middle 1950s, it was clear that a far-reaching contest over how to recall and forget the war was under way. At the dedication of the Iwo Jima Memorial, citizens gathered to venerate victory and the men who earned it. This was by no means a suppression of popular sentiment. The memorial represented well the belief that ordinary men fought gallantly, that the war was worth the sacrifice. and that the trauma could be put behind us. The same point is made in the film *To Hell and Back* (1955), which depicts a brave and decorated soldier who is close to his family. But members of the wartime generation continue to represent some veterans as brutes who had no place in peacetime America in films such as *A Streetcar Named Desire* (1951), *Peyton Place* (1957), and *No Down Payment* (1957). During the war, women had already expressed fears that military experiences incited men to misogynistic behavior. In 1954, Harriet Arnow articulated another critique by writing a novel, *The Dollmaker*, of how the war (and capitalism) destroyed the independence of a woman.

For a time in the 1960s and 1970s, Cold War pressures reinvigorated heroic images of American men and quelled some of the cultural divisions that had marked the immediate postwar era. In 1962's *The Longest Day*, the prowess of the American military and men of all ranks was validated. This movie of epic proportions lavished attention on the planning that went into the Allied invasion of Europe in 1944 and the extent to which the "biggest armada the world has ever known" was firmly under American leadership. A small amount of space was turned over to the heroics of the British and the French resistance, but the "star" of the feature was the collective effort of the Americans. The Nazis in this feature were disorganized; the sons of democracy were eager and united in purpose. Heroism crowded out serious discussion here of personal trauma or the emotional and political longings of ordinary soldiers.

In 1970, the release of *Patton* again reaffirmed the brilliance of American military strategy and leadership, although this film also took an extended look at the psychological traits of a heroic leader as well. Neither *Patton* nor *The Longest Day* paid much attention to 1940s concerns about democracy or the potential for brutality of Americans themselves. For General George Patton, war was less an act to save democracy than it was an opportunity to realize his dream of becoming a brave combatant—a certain type of man. "All real Americans love the sting of battle," he reportedly told his men. He was famous for his intolerance of subordinates who were traumatized by battle, who failed to relish killing the enemy as he did, and who lacked the fighting spirit to be a brave warrior. That is why he loved so much leading the triumphal parades of victors into liberated towns in Europe. Cheering crowds reaffirmed his sense of what war and men were all about.

Catch-22 (1970) appeared at the same time *Patton* did, however, and it suggested that the cultural effort to laud the World War II experience of Americans was in deep trouble. Certainly, the impact of Vietnam was crucial here, but it should be recalled that the story was drawn from a novel authored by a World War II veteran (Joseph Heller), as was the film of *The Naked and the Dead* (1958). This cynical view of the American military in World War II Italy completely debunked not only the integrity of military leadership but any effort to look at the war in heroic or sentimental terms. In this story, American soldiers use their spare time looking for cash or sex and actually question orders to drop bombs on innocent civilians. One U.S. serviceman kills and rapes an Italian woman. The central premise of the narrative is an antiwar statement, pure and simple. Captain Yossarian, the central figure, wants doctors to declare that he is insane so he can get out of the war completely. The "catch" is that the wish to escape from war is a perfectly sane idea and, therefore, cannot be a basis for judging someone to be insane.

Today, stories of glorious rises and tragic falls dot the landscape of American cultural memory. The celebration of personal dreams is discussed more widely than collective destinies. Images of a proud nation are contested by those of a society capable of inflicting pain and suffering. In this culture of contradictions and silences, cultural memory is subjected, in the words of Griel Marcus, to "an anarchy of possibilities" and, in the terms of Pierre Nora, to a "series of initiatives with no central organizing principle."[20] But that "anarchy" is fiercely contested in the Spielberg film, not to restore the vision of a democratic nation but to rehabilitate traditions of good fathers, patriotic men, and self-sacrifice. Miller and Ryan do not challenge moral conventions, are not inherently violent, and are willing to relinquish personal dreams. They recognize that the fortunes of the nation take precedence over their own futures. The film *Saving Private Ryan* does not say that personal sacrifice is glorious as does *Patton* or that wars are free of death and trauma as does the Iwo Jima Memorial. Distinct boundaries between cultural categories, like the tropes of heroic soldiers and personal pain, have generally been difficult to maintain since 1945. But the film chooses to take sides in the modern culture of opposites by protecting a sentimental view of American men that was seriously disrupted by both World War II and Vietnam. In fact, it basically suppresses a critical view of American society as well, preferring to suggest that the American future will best be fashioned by moral individuals rather than by democratic reforms.

Postwar films tended to treat the American warrior and American society in a more evenhanded way. They shared with *Saving Private Ryan* a tendency to remember the turmoil and stress. This is not an invention of the 1990s. Postwar films and culture actually went further, however, in exploring the consequences of the war, which is exactly what Bartov argued when he claimed that the acknowledgment of victims impelled individuals to find reasons for the suffering.[21] Because the Spielberg film attempts to preserve the memory of patriotic sacrifice more than it desires to explore the causes of the trauma and violence, however, it is more about restoring a romantic version of common-man heroism in an age of moral ambivalence than about ending the problem of devastating wars.

The failure of *Saving Private Ryan* to evoke the memory of "a people's war," moreover, reveals the film's conservative politics. Past, present, and future are now contingent on standards of individual behavior rather than on democratic ideals such as the quest for equality, a just capitalism, or citizen participation in political life. Spielberg's film about trauma and patriotism suggests why the contemporary turn to memory, anguish, and the testimony of victims is about more than the demise of the cultural power of the nation. It also has a great deal to do with a sense of disenchantment with democratic politics and with turning political life over to "the people." Visions of a democratic community are feeble in this story, which remembers individuals in a more exemplary way than they were understood by their own generation.[22]

Notes

1   See Jeanine Basinger, "Translating War: The Combat Film Genre and *Saving Private Ryan*," *Perspectives* 36 (October 1998): 1, 43–47. Basinger suggests that Spielberg meant to speak to the "me" generation when Ryan asked his wife at the end of the film if he had earned the life that those who sacrificed themselves for him gave him. For Basinger, the film asks if one individual is worth the effort it took to save him (p. 47). See also Phil Landon, "Realism, Genre, and *Saving Private Ryan*," *Film and History* 28, nos. 3–4 (1998): 58–63. Landon calls the film a "morality play" because it raised the question of what obligations war survivors and subsequent generations have to the soldiers who gave their lives.

2   Norman Corwin, "On a Note of Triumph," audiocassette available from Lodes Tone, 611 Empire Mill RD. Bloomington, IN 47401.

3   The term "reverent" is taken from Stephen J. Dubner, "Steven the Good," *New York Times Magazine* (February 14, 1999): 38; *USA Today* (May 22, 1998): 7A. On the planned role for American military cemeteries in Europe, see G. Kurt Piehler, *Remembering War the American Way* (Washington, D.C., 1995), 129; see James Jones, "Phony War Films," *Saturday Evening Post*, March 30, 1963, for an argument that the depiction of war as a site for the realization or development of character is misleading.

4   Benjamin L. Alpers, "This Is the Army: Imagining a Democratic Military in World War II," *Journal of American History* 85 (June 1998): 129–63; Robert B. Westbrook, "I Want a Girl Just Like the Girl That Married Harry James: American Women and the Problem of Political Obligation in World War II," *American Quarterly* 42 (1990): 587–614.

5   On the declining cultural power of narratives of nationalism to efface realities of loss and tragedy, see Pierre Nora, ed., *Realms of Memory: Rethinking the French Past*, Arthur Goldhammer, trans., 3 vols. (New York, 1996–98), 1: xxiii, 5–7.

6   For an account of how the large loss of life from World War I challenged forms of heroic national memory in France, see Antoine Prost, "Monuments to the Dead," in Nora, *Realms of Memory*, 2: 307–30. On the popularity of the Roosevelt Memorial, see the *Baltimore Sun* (August 3 1997): 2F; Marita Sturken, *Tangled Memories: The Vietnam War, the AIDS Epidemic and the Politics of Remembering* (Berkeley, Calif., 1997), 8–9.

7   Haruko Taya Cook and Theodore F. Cook, *Japan at War: An Oral History* (New York, 1992); Henry Rousso, *The Vichy Syndrome: History and Memory in France since 1944*, Arthur Goldhammer, trans. (Cambridge, Mass., 1991); Omer Bartov, "Defining Enemies, Making Victims: Germans, Jews, and the Holocaust" *AHR* 103 (June 1998): 771–816; Peter Novick, "Holocaust Memory in America" in *The Art of Memory: Holocaust Memorials in History*, James E. Young, ed. (New York, 1994), 149–65; see also Sturken, *Tangled Memories*, 2–3. Julia A. Thomas, "Photography, National Identity, and the 'Cataract of Times': Wartime Images and the Case of Japan," *AHR* 103 (December 1998): 1475–83, suggests that Japan still has a difficult time in recalling certain traumatic aspects of the war. Claudio Fogu treats the managing of the memory of World War I in "Il Duce taumaturgo: Modernist Rhetorics in Fascist Representations of History," *Representations* 57 (Winter 1957): 24–29. For a discussion of how individual memory can challenge the goals of public forms of remembering "to tame the past," see Vera Schwarcz, *Bridge across Broken Time: Chinese and Jewish Cultural Memory* (New Haven, Conn., 1998), 92–93.

8   On Cold War anxieties, see Paul Boyer, *By the Bomb's Early Light: American Thought and Culture at the Dawn of the Atomic Age* (New York, 1985); and Margot A. Henriksen,

Dr. Strangelove's America: Society and Culture in the Atomic Age (Berkeley, Calif. 1997). See also Craig, Calhoun, "Introduction: Habermas and the Public Sphere," in Cahoun, ed., *Habermas and the Public Sphere* (Cambridge, Mass., 1992), 21–22. On the official ideology of World War II, see Clayton R. Koppes and Gregory D. Black, *Hollywood Goes to War: How Politics, Profits, and Propaganda Shaped World War II Movies* (1987; Berkeley, 1990), 168–9.

9   On the relationship between gender and the construction of the idea of a nation, see George L. Mosse, *Nationalism and Sexuality: Middle-Class Morality and Societal Norms in Modern Europe* (1985; rpt. edn., Madison, Wis., 1988); Richard Slotkin, *Gunfighter Nation: The Myth of the Frontier in Twentieth Century America* (New York, 1992), 10–13, 627–55; Robert B. Westbrook, "Fighting for the American Family: Private Interests and Political Obligation in World War II," in *The Power of Culture: Critical Essays in American History*, Richard Wightman Fox and T. J. Jackson Lears, eds. (Chicago, 1993), 199–201. On the debate over the proper behavior of women in the British nation during World War II, see Sonya Rose, "Sex, Citizenship, and the Nation in World War II Britain, *AHR* 103 (October 1998): 1161–64; on the tendency of women and other German citizens to displace accounts of German-inflicted violence from their stories of World War II, see Elizabeth Heineman, "The Hour of the Woman: Memories of Germany's 'Crisis Years' and West German National Identity," *AHR* 101 (April 1996): 354–60; on the rise of a dominant form of white male supremacy in the early American nationalism, see Dana D. Nelson, *National Manhood: Capitalist Citizenship and the Imagined Fraternity of White Men* (Durham, N.C., 1998), 2–7. The problem of representing and taking responsibility for violence is discussed in Jill Lepore, *The Name of War: King Philip's War and the Origins of American Identity* (New York. 1998), 13–14.

10   Bartov, "Defining Enemies, Making Victims." 771–816.

11   Dominick LaCapra, *History and Memory after Auschwitz* (Ithaca, N.Y., 1998), 180–81. Daniel J. Sherman, "Bodies and Names: The Emergence of Commemoration in Interwar France," *AHR* 103 (April 1998): 443–66, explores the tension since World War I in European commemoration between collective and personal history.

12   Cathy Caruth, "Introduction," in Caruth, ed., *Trauma: Explorations in Memory* (Baltimore, 1995), 4–8. LaCapra, *History, and Memory after Auschwitz*, 9–21, partially accepts the notion of repression but makes a more complex case for the idea that individual and collective memory exist within a dialogic framework, each testing and confronting the other. For insightful observations of how the scale of death in World War I and World War II prompted a search for an appropriate language of mourning, see Jay Winter, *Sites of Memory, Sites of Mourning: The Great War in European Cultural History* (Cambridge, 1995), 5–10.

13   LaCapra, *History and Memory after Auschwitz*, 10–46.

14   Jeanine Basinger, *The World War II Combat Film: Anatomy of a Genre* (New York, 1986), 153; Slotkin, *Gunfighter Nation*, 334.

15   Basinger, *World War II Combat Film*, 34–37; Thomas Doherty *Projections of War: Hollywood, American Culture, and World War II* (New York 1993), 122–48. *Saving Private Ryan* invokes a letter (traditionally ascribed to Lincoln) to a mother whose five sons "died gloriously on the field of battle."

16   Robert Jay Lifton and Greg Mitchell, *Hiroshima in America: Fifty Years of Denial* (New York, 1995), 238; Michael C. C. Adams, *The Best War Ever: America and World War II* (Baltimore, 1994), 12; Dana B. Polan, *Power and Paranoia: History, Narrative and the American Cinema, 1940–1950* (New York, 1986), 70–71.

17   See Kaja Silverman, *Male Subjectivity at the Margins* (New York, 1992), 77.

18   Norman Mailer, *The Naked and the Dead* (New York, 1981), 174.

19   See Koppes and Black, *Hollywood Goes to War*, on the OWI.

20   Griel Marcus, *Dead Elvis: A Chronicle of a Cultural Obsession* (New York, 1991), xvii; Pierre Nora, "The Era of Commemoration," in Nora, *Realms of Memory*, 3: 615; Antoine Prost, "Verdun," in *Realms of Memory*, 2: 377–401. Prost demonstrates how a "national memory" repressed a "veterans' memory" for a time after the bloody battle of Verdun in 1916. Ultimately, the pain and tragedy of the veterans, however, came to reassert itself in French culture.

21   Bartov, "Defining Enemies, Making Victims," 775.

22   Benedict Anderson, *Imagined Communities: Reflections on the Origins and Spread of Nationalism*, rev. edn. (London, 1991), 144. LaCapra, *History and Memory after Auschwitz*, 15, discusses the relationship between memory and a loss of faith in democratic politics.

Chapter 19

Lisa Yoneyama

FOR TRANSFORMATIVE KNOWLEDGE AND POSTNATIONALIST PUBLIC SPHERES
The Smithsonian *Enola Gay* controversy

There is no document of civilization which is not at the same time a document of barbarism. And just as such a document is not free of barbarism, barbarism taints also the manner in which it was transmitted from one owner to another.

—Walter Benjamin, *Illuminations*

THE EXHIBITION BY the Smithsonian National Air and Space Museum (NASM) of the *Enola Gay*, which commemorated the fiftieth anniversary of the end of the Second World War, set off a heated controversy concerning national ideologies, the collective memory of self-victimization, and contestations over historical knowledge. This essay explores the ways in which the Smithsonian debate was fought out primarily in the U.S. public media and in congressional hearings about history and memory. By examining some of the central narratives that constituted the debate, this essay investigates the following questions.

The first half of the essay focuses on the various predicaments in the attempts to produce a nation's public history and memory. What does it mean, and is it at all possible, to produce a single and definitive public history and memory shared commonly and objectively by a nation? Production of any overarching narratives about the past inevitably incites various contestations and struggles over historical truths. Inseparable from this process, therefore, is the question regarding the limits of a mode of argumentation that relies on the force of factual authenticity and objectivity. The essay cautions against the pitfalls of making too hasty a distinction, as was often the case during the controversy, between the commemorative desire that is thought to derive from one's personal experience and the claims for objective truths of historical knowledge.

The second half of this essay is devoted to illuminating what might be best described as the transnational warping of political positions in the Smithsonian debates. The Smithsonian controversy exhibited the tension common in any official memory making today, namely, the negotiations between the process by which various transnational and discordant factors participate in the generation of a nation-state's dominant historical consciousness and the process wherein such transnational movements in the production of collective memory have been constantly censored.[1] Even while reminding us of the tenacity of national imaginings and proving that nation-states can still lay powerful claim to a possessive relation with a single, uniform historical consciousness, the debates showed that disparities in historical awareness concerning the Asia-Pacific War and the two atom bombings do not necessarily originate in national differences. What appears to be a conflict limited to one national public sphere is in fact constituted by factors that cross the boundaries of a nation's official remembering. Through critiquing the problems of selective amnesia produced by a type of remembering that assumes an isomorphic relationship between a nation and a single coherent and consistent historical consciousness, this essay also proposes an alternative historiography, one that posits postnationalist public spheres in the production of historical knowledge.

The essay furthermore attempts to situate the Smithsonian debates within the larger context of the conditions of knowledge that circumscribe those of us who work in U.S. academic circles in the 1990s. It reflects on the claims made by House Speaker Newt Gingrich, talk-show host Rush Limbaugh, and others that the Smithsonian controversy ended with an American victory over "anti-American radicals" and cultural elites, who conspired to promote "political correctness."[2] How are we to locate such claims on our intellectual mapping of the U.S. academy? And what sorts of historical subjects do these claims attempt to interpellate?

Historical facts, commemoration, and critical knowledge

The Smithsonian *Enola Gay* controversy—or the "Smithsonian atom bomb exhibit debates," as the Japanese-language news media more precisely named it—concluded with a major departure from the comprehensive exhibit originally planned by the museum. During more than a year of negotiations between the public and the NASM curatorial staff, the scripts were rewritten a number of times, and in the end, all of the following were eliminated: the details of debates among U.S. political leaders, scholars, and military commanders over the decision to use the atom bombs; a great number of photographs and descriptions concerning Japan's military invasions and colonial atrocities committed in East Asia, Southeast Asia, and the Pacific Islands; photographs showing physical and human damage in Hiroshima and Nagasaki; and general observations about the subsequent development of the atomic age and nuclear weapons proliferation.[3]

Let us begin by examining two strikingly similar, yet contrasting, statements in the U.S. news media. A *Los Angeles Times* editorial titled "Wrong Place for Anti-Nuclear Message: Smithsonian Scotches *Enola Gay* Exhibit amid a Controversy That Shouldn't Have Happened" (February 1, 1995) indicated that the *Enola Gay* dispute was "one of those historical arguments in which the factual context is often obscured by ideological presuppositions." While admitting the significance of warning against the destructive force of the atomic bombs and questioning the subsequent nuclear arms race, it concluded that "a Smithsonian exhibit that rightfully should have been primarily dedicated to commemorating the end of World War II and honoring those who fought to defeat Nazism and Japanese militarism clearly was not that place." Contrast this remark with a *New York Times* editorial, "Hijacking History" (January 30, 1995). Cautioning against yielding to the political pressure of conservative Congress members and veterans, the editorial argued that "historians and museums of history need to be insulated from any attempt to make history conform to a narrow ideological or political interest."

These two statements remind us of the ways in which, as sociologist John B. Thompson puts it, the term *ideological* always precludes references to the self and is summoned only when used to condemn and discount others.[4] They also epitomize the way in which the notion of factual neutrality, despite the prominence of veterans' claims for experiential authority as witnesses, has served as the governing and most persuasive source for legitimacy across nearly the entire discursive terrain of the disputes between those who supported and those who attacked the exhibit plans prepared by the NASM curators. In their heated exchanges, both the historians and journalists who tried to save the comprehensive version of the exhibit and those who in the end succeeded in altering the exhibit so as to honor the plane's mission relied on the power of facticity to substantiate their credibility. Almost all who participated in the controversy emphasized that their positions were grounded in historical facts, thereby underscoring their objectivity and/or neutrality, while simultaneously denouncing their opponents as blinded by personal judgments, political bias, and emotional investment.

On the one hand, the so-called revisionist historians who defended the curators' plans sought to refute their opponents by emphasizing the academic authenticity of the prepared texts. For instance, Kai Bird, perhaps one of the most vocal and active historians to denounce the politicians' violation of curatorial and academic freedom, argued that the controversy stemmed from the "inaccurate but understandable belief of the veterans that the atomic bomb saved their lives from being sacrificed."[5] Still others defended the exhibit plan by differentiating the concepts "commemorative history" and "public history." Edward T. Linenthal, a professor of religion and American culture who served on the advisory committee for the original exhibit planning, promoted such a distinction in his efforts to counter the politicians' and veterans' interventions.[6]

In his testimony of 18 May 1995 at one of the public hearings that were convened before the U.S. Senate Committee on Rules and Administration to investigate the controversy over the Smithsonian's exhibition plans, Linenthal argued, "There is tension between the commemorative voice and the historical voice, which seeks to discern motives, understand actions, and discuss consequences that were impossible to analyze during the event itself. . . . It is a voice that to some can feel detached, even when those who speak out of this voice view their work as a way to deepen our understanding of an event."[7] When the newly appointed Smithsonian secretary I. Michael Heyman announced to the press the cancellation of the display of the ground-level effects of the bombs and the radical scaling down of the exhibit as a whole, he too signaled that the controversy originated in "a basic error in attempting to couple a historical treatment of the use of atomic weapons with the 50th anniversary commemoration of the end of the war" (my emphasis).[8] The Smithsonian staff's defenders, though of course in various ways, argued that the controversy stemmed from the clash between the academic attempt to produce a comprehensive and objective public history and the desire of those who witnessed the event to celebrate their—and, by imaginary extension, the nation's—honorable past.

Such characterizations, however, provoked vehement rebuttals from many veterans and conservative journalists and historians. Earlier, Martin Harwit, the director of the NASM who was eventually forced to resign as a result of the controversy, had portrayed the dispute as a conflict between a historical view that "appeals to our national self-image" and another historical perspective that is "more analytical, critical in its acceptance of facts and concerned with historical context."[9] A *Washington Post* editorial titled "Context and the *Enola Gay*" (August 14, 1994) reacted sharply to this depiction of the debate. The editorial criticized Harwit in no uncertain terms, charging that although he and others were quick to dismiss their critics' take on the *Enola Gay* exhibit as one that lacked "intellectual sophistication," the problem in fact lay in the "curatorial inability to perceive that political opinions are embedded in the exhibit or to identify them as such—opinions—rather than as universal, 'objective' assumptions all thinking people must necessarily share." The editorial also attributed the source of the problem to what the editors perceived as a growing postmodern relativism in the academy, an issue to which I will return. To counter the charges that they were simply being subjective and not academic, those who attacked the NASM curators tried to demonstrate the objective and analytical nature of their criticisms by listing the publications they relied on to construct their arguments.[10]

With respect to this endless exchange of facts, during the May 18, 1995 Senate committee hearing, Linenthal expressed the distress and frustration shared by many of the museum's staff. He pointed out that despite the immediate and substantial changes made to the exhibit plans in response to the criticisms of veterans and the historian of the Office of the Secretary of Defense (who at one point reportedly approved of the revised comprehensive version of the prepared text), the media's and the Air Force Association's attacks continued to intensify. At the same time, the museum staff was forced to negotiate with those who criticized the omission of photographs of the human devastation caused by nuclear weapons. Linenthal summarized the process as follows:

> As script after script deleted material about historical controversies regarding the decision to drop the bomb, added photographs of mushroom clouds and structural damage, and removed most photographs of dead Japanese, historians and peace activists met with museum officials to argue for what they believe should be restored or newly incorporated. The scripts were a kind of Rorschach test. People were concerned with different questions, paid attention to different "facts," and interpreted the same facts differently. In the end, everyone believed their history had been "stolen," resulting either in a "revisionist" exhibit or in one showing a disregard for the complexity and irony of history.[11]

Linenthal's observation that the two opposing camps were talking past each other and that both sides grounded their legitimacy on a selective use of historical facts and events unwittingly puts into relief a number of issues inherent in the politics of knowledge in general. Most important, his remark suggests that there are limits to a mode of argument that relies solely on positive factual accounts as a means of accessing the power to be represented in a public sphere. Accordingly, this problematizes the idea that habitually presupposes—as in Secretary Heyman's inaugural remark "Let the object speak for itself"[12]—that positive historical knowledge can automatically render a shared and unified history.

It is not my intention to undermine the work of professional historians who strive to identify through positivist methods multiple sets of competing, contingent, and often indeterminate factors that have worked to produce a single historical event such as President Truman's executive order to use the two atomic bombs. Throughout the entire course of rewriting the master historical narrative concerning the use of the atomic bombs, it has become increasingly evident that one cannot overemphasize the critical significance of uncovering and examining documents and records or the instrumental power that resides in the presentation of "facts." The findings of the so-called revisionist historians have played a pivotal role in putting the naturalized image of the past into critical perspective, however gradually.[13] In relativizing the ruling historical narrative by calling attention to particular "facts," historians have certainly disturbed our common sense, offering vital moments of suspicion about received knowledge. Moreover, as historian Barton Bernstein has emphasized, the very awareness of the fact that knowledge has been deliberately suppressed or withheld from the public further generates a critical consciousness of the government's censorship and the general ways in which the world is made known to us.[14]

What needs to be interrogated is not so much the historians' administering of facts as such, but rather the simplistic distinction between "history" and "memory," or "public history" and "commemorative desire." These binaries frequently figured in the discourses of both those who defended and those who attempted to sabotage the exhibit. Despite their instrumental value for rhetorical purposes, such oppositions cannot be posited a priori. History, like commemorative rituals, can always be mediated by the desire to speak in voices of and for the dead, to honor victims and martyrs, and to memorialize past events.

Furthermore, the clear distinction between a "commemorative exhibit" that is created out of empathy and the subjective judgment of those who hold shared communal ties to the remembered event, and a "public history" fashioned out of the analytical and detached examination of a historical incident assumes the possibility of attaining a transcendent and universal position from which a subject can observe the past. Such an understanding may also lead to the categorical dismissal of testimonial voices as personal, conjectural, and mystified, subordinating them too hastily to the knowledge produced by institutionalized expertise. The consequence of such a dismissal leads to a situation Dominick LaCapra observed in the German *Historikerstriet* over European memory and the history of Nazism. In his commentary on historians' texts on everyday life under the Nazi regime, LaCapra argues that the "overly simple oppositions between history and 'mythical memory' or between dry reconstruction of facts and ritualization" not only may serve as a psychological defense mechanism that disavows traumatic experiences but also may encourage the repressed to return, as a supplement, in a reified, uncritically valorized state. He proposes instead that we recognize, in addition to the scientific inquiry of historical accuracy, significance in identifying the ritualized aspects of psychological transference that shape any historical representation. For the ways in which the subject positions of scholars/rememberers are cathected to the objects of their inquiry/remembering determine the degree to which the processes of working through (*Durcharbeitung*) historical trauma can be attained or evaded.[15]

To draw an analogy in the Smithsonian debates, attempts to avert attacks by claiming that the opponents of the original plan were infatuated with their personal memories and that they lacked the intellectual authenticity of scientific history inadvertently prompted the return of what was repressed in such a counterfeit distinction between history and memory, reifying the originality and genuineness of the experiential truths advocated by many who witnessed the war. To be sure, in a given situation of amnesic hegemony, a singular witness account, as a reconstructed memory of a firsthand experience, can restore a heretofore suppressed past, although not in its originary form. It can thus initiate the demystification of officialized historical knowledge. There are countless examples of such workings in various kinds of subaltern historiography.

The Smithsonian debate was not really about facts, nor was it about which side represented the facts more accurately. Rather, it centered around questions about for whom, for what objectives, and for whose community the event needed to be remembered. The difference between the two camps did not reside in whether one side distorted the facts more than the other, although there were indeed a number of instances in which conservative politicians and veterans deliberately refused to acknowledge the existence of certain information and records, thus precluding a more comprehensive view of the event. On the one hand, many veterans, members of the Air Force Association, conservative politicians, and intellectuals desired to commemorate the important mission that led America to victory. They strove to memorialize the martyrs of their sacred war and to remember the atomic bombings through the mediation of the cold war paradigm, which justified the use of military power to achieve and maintain the doctrine of Pax Americana. On the other hand, those who planned the canceled exhibit aspired to remember the millions of victims of the war, including those who were killed before and by *Enola Gay*'s mission, those who have continued to suffer from radiation effects, and those who might in the future become victimized by yet another nuclear catastrophe.

It is imperative for us to reconsider in this particular light the significance of Harwit's choice of words when he described the curators' perspective as being "more analytical, critical in its acceptance of facts." The originally planned exhibit narrative was conditioned by a specifically "critical" perspective on our naturalized view of history, while it also warned of the present global condition in which we find ourselves thoroughly contaminated by nuclear weaponry. The prepared text was comprehensive and analytical, and thus objective at the level of cognitive knowledge, in its explication, for instance, of the processes that led to the decision to use the bombs. It was, however, no less perspectival than the opponents' narrative in that aesthetic and moral factors came into play in the construction of knowledge.[16]

In sum, the *Enola Gay* debate exhibited the predicament within the liberal under standing of the public sphere and its history, an understanding that uncritically presumes the possibility for plural yet harmonious commemoration.[17] It reminds us that, contrary to the ideal of a national public sphere that operates as an open forum in which plural voices freely enter into dialogues and negotiate with each other, certain voices that insist on representation are in reality capable of drawing disproportionate authority and power from the structural positions they occupy within existing social, economic, and political arrangements, and not only from experiential truths or factual authenticity. Likewise, we need to attend perhaps even more urgently to the controversy's unintended consequences. What is represented in a nation's public sphere in such places as the Smithsonian is rendered less susceptible to questioning as to whether it, too, might be partial. It becomes difficult to see that what is deemed to be the commonly shared historical truth is as factional and relatively constructed as what has not been represented in the public space. Given the reality in which their representation of history was in the end disallowed at the museum, there is a risk in even acknowledging that Harwit's and the other curators' position was grounded in critical perspectives.

This was especially true when conservative politicians and veterans repeatedly criticized the "presentism" and "historical relativism" of the prepared text. They argued that one cannot apply the Vietnam War generation's 1990s sensitivity to reconstruct the history of the 1940s.[18] Similarly, in a testimony that I discuss below in more detail, retired U.S. Air Force Major General Charles W. Sweeney, a member of the *Enola Gay*'s crew and the commander of the Nagasaki mission, alleged that the revisionists' intrusion into even this very patriotic site was caused by "the advancing erosion of our history, of our collective memory."[19] What is remarkable in this statement is that while it betrays the intimate association between a nation's history and the memory possessed by a specific collectivity, at the same time it authorizes the historicist position by grounding the speaker's perspective on experiential truths, thereby castigating the "presentist" view of history as an inauthentic construction. In their study on the production and consumption of colonial Williamsburg, Eric Gable, Richard Handler, and Anna Lawson succinctly summarize the danger I am describing here: "A relativizing rhetoric—in this case, an explicit recognition of historical 'presentism'—seems easier to apply to the cultures and histories of minorities than to those of the mainstream."[20]

Incidentally, there is yet another problematic aspect of Sweeney's evoking the term "memory" while simultaneously insinuating the subordination of his personal experience as a soldier and a witness to a formal and publicized "history." His statement reflects the perception that the position occupied by many veterans and political conservatives such as he is, as it were, being minoritized within present U.S. society, when in fact it was the veterans and conservatives and not the museum curators or revisionist historians who succeed in mobilizing the massive support of legislators.

The Smithsonian controversy thus eloquently demonstrates that one cannot effectively seek proper representation in a national public sphere solely by claiming to possess universal knowledge that is grounded on factual authenticity. To subscribe to the distinction between factual history and imaginary commemoration—an opposition enabled by simple trust in the power of facticity—is problematic precisely because it can prove debilitating when trying to prevail over those who adhere to diametrically opposed understandings of history. Moreover, as observed in the Smithsonian dispute, to rationalize the demand for representation in the public sphere by grounding one's legitimacy on factual authenticity alone may unwittingly help perpetuate the myth that the subaltern history is more partial, conjectural, and constructed than mainstream history. The recovery and accumulation of knowledge about the past—what Walter Benjamin called the "additive" method of universal history—do not themselves automatically produce new knowledge and perceptions. What matters is not how much we know about the past but rather through what structural access, and under what personal, social, and historical conditions, we come to an awareness of it.

There is still another important difference between the discursive strategies pursued by those who supported the prepared exhibit script and by those who disparaged it. In the following, I discuss the negotiations between, on the one hand, the desire to defend the imaginary border of one nation's memory and its boundary of empathy and, on the other hand, the endeavors to challenge the naturalized narratives of the past that were premised on the shared collectivity of remembering subjects and of the remembered.

Transnational warps and nationalist memories

The dissension centering on historical understandings about whether it was necessary and justifiable for the United States to use atom bombs against two Japanese cities has often been conflated, in both Japanese- and English-language contexts, with the national distinction between Japan and the United States. It is even typical for an individual researcher's opinion to be understood as emblematically representing an entire nation's viewpoint, or indicating what is often referred to as the "U.S.–Japan gap."[21] The tendency to regard disparities in perceptions of the destruction at Hiroshima and Nagasaki as corresponding isomorphically to national differences has governed the popular discourse on the Smithsonian controversy as well. For the offended veterans and others in the United States, to hold compassionate sentiments toward the ground-level suffering caused by the *Enola Gay*'s mission was often regarded as a position influenced by the "Japanese" viewpoint. Likewise, in the Japanese-language news reports, as the expression "[the differing] atom-bomb perceptions between the Japanese and American nations" (*nichibei ryōkokukan no genbakukan*) illustrates,[22] the clash of opinions in the Smithsonian controversy continued to be represented and understood within national frameworks.

Yet it is also true that the reporting of the Smithsonian debates simultaneously revealed that the national boundaries of collective memories have constantly been infiltrated.[23] Evidence of such transnational penetration and the national censoring of memory processes can be found in the language and activities of both those who supported the initial Smithsonian plans and those who opposed them. Several NASM staff members visited Hiroshima and Nagasaki at an early planning stage. By borrowing artifacts from the two cities, the curators sought to add a ground-level perspective to the pilot's-eye view of the atomic explosions. Such aerial images had thus far dominated national imaginings. The curators also hoped to complicate that historical moment so as to remember it not solely as the war's last act but simultaneously as the inaugural event in the subsequent nuclear age. However, for conservative politicians, journalists, intellectuals, veterans, and others who opposed the display of photographs depicting what they saw as "Japanese" victimization, the Smithsonian curators' contact with the former enemy was nothing less than a treacherous, "un-American" move. Herman G. Harrington, chairman of the American Legion's National Internal Affairs Commission, for instance, angrily denounced what he saw as the museum curators' willingness to "conform to the Japanese perspective" when they attempted to borrow artifacts from Hiroshima and Nagasaki.[24]

At the same time, while some tried to limit the Smithsonian debate to the U.S. national context,[25] those who opposed the exhibit frequently cited Japan to construct their argument. They attempted to justify their demands to eliminate artifacts and photographs that showed the effects of the atom bombs on humans by calling attention to present Japanese amnesia about the nation's past conduct, both before and during the war. They warned that unless one elaborated the "historical contexts" leading to the bombs' use, displays of the Hiroshima and Nagasaki destructions would only contribute to the historical understanding they saw as still prevalent in Japan, namely, that the Japanese were solely victims of the war and not the perpetrators of war atrocities and colonial aggression.

Major General Sweeney's testimony before the U.S. Senate Committee on Rules and Administration illustrates the case well. In identifying what he felt were problems with the prepared text by referring to the situation in Japan, Sweeney argued that knowing the "facts" and understanding the historical context allowed one to appreciate the necessity of President Truman's decision to drop the bombs. He recounted Japan's invasion of China and mainland Asia for the purpose of building the Greater East Asia Co-Prosperity Sphere and the numerous instances of plundering, torture, and massacres that took place throughout the area, beginning with Nanjing. He further noted the "sneak" attack on Pearl Harbor, together with the loss of American servicemen in Saipan, Iwo Jima, and Okinawa. Furthermore, he emphasized that Japan had not surrendered despite the commencement of air raids on Japan's major cities.

Continuing in his testimony, Sweeney asked why conflicts occurred concerning the bombs' necessity despite the unanimous view that the atomic bomb strategy had ended the war. He answered this question in the following way:

> Fifty years after their defeat, Japanese officials have the temerity to claim they were the victims. That Hiroshima and Nagasaki were the equivalent of the Holocaust.
>
> And believe it or not, there are actually some American academics who support this analogy, thus aiding and giving comfort to a 50-year attempt by the Japanese to rewrite their own history, and ours in the process.
>
> There is an entire generation of Japanese who do not know the full extent of their country's conduct during World war [sic] II.
>
> This explains why they do not comprehend why they must apologize.

He then cited such matters as the so-called comfort women issue and the medical experiments on Allied POWs as reasons for the Japanese refusal to apologize properly. He concluded, "In a perverse inversion, by forgetting our own history, we contribute to the Japanese amnesia, to the detriment of both our nations."[26] Sweeney thus tried to link American appreciation of the historical context for the atomic bombings to the lack of Japanese reflection on the past.

In this transnational citation of Japan's historical amnesia, Sweeney argued that remembering only Japanese victimization in Hiroshima and Nagasaki occludes the fact that the war's lasting almost fifteen years and Japan's colonial expansion that began at the turn of the century were acts of aggression. This statement is remarkable in that its reasoning employs the same arguments that many critics in Japan have routinely used in their efforts to contend with the cluster of deeply rooted issues that have contributed to Japan's historical amnesia. These include the Ministry of Education's textbook approval system, which had until recently censored overt criticisms of Japan's military aggression and colonial policies; the repeated refusal of politicians to fully acknowledge the magnitude of the destruction caused by Japan; and the insufficiency of the government's undertakings in dealing with its postwar and postcolonial responsibilities. In other words, there has been reflection among progressive citizens of Japan, including survivors in Hiroshima and Nagasaki, who recognize that remembering a historical event only in terms of unprecedented self-victimization may serve to mystify other national conditions in the past and present. The Japanese citizen's counteramnesic practices have been underpinned by the conviction that to secure the memories of Japan's prewar and wartime imperialism and military aggression in school textbooks and other public apparatuses that produce national history is inseparably linked to the pursuit of peace, human rights, and other democratic ideals of a civil society. Moreover, many construe the act of remembering Japan's military and colonial pasts as leading also to critically reflecting on Japan's postwar neocolonial economic dominance in the region.[27]

In the Japanese political and social context, those who have long questioned their country's insufficiency of remorse for its invasions and the suffering it inflicted on the people of Asia and the Pacific have until very recently identified primarily with the left or with progressives. They have also been challenging the historical view that for the past fifty years has supported the claims of members of the Japanese Association for the War Bereaved and conservative political leaders and intellectuals that colonial aggression and military expansion were justifiable. According to that understanding of history, establishing the Greater East Asia Co-Prosperity Sphere and waging the Greater East Asian War were acts of self-defense against and emancipation from the encroaching Western superpowers, and they did not have the invasion of neighboring Asian countries as their original objective. It is as if U.S. conservative interest groups, politicians, and intellectuals who attacked the Smithsonian staff took up the claims of progressives in Japan, "warping" the discourse to meet different political ends. The contradiction I am trying to identify here can be summarized as follows: As a result of its transference into a different national public sphere, the discourse has come to be used in support of a political position that was originally unintended or irrelevant. In other words, there appears to have been a binational warping of political positions.

This warping moreover, has a number of troubling effects. Above all, transferring a critical political position from one context to another for the purpose of justifying views guided by nationalist interests makes invisible various ongoing practices that try to critically intervene and challenge the present transnational and statist global ordering. (I will return to this point in conclusion.) At the same time, such warps obscure the fact that the questions of historical amnesia are not some other country's problem but very much our own and that they need to be addressed as questions common to many modern nation states and the formation of capitalism.

Indeed, despite its antipodal appearance, the selective amnesia that Sweeney identified in Japan in many respects parallels that found in the United States. This is evident in some of the presumptions concerning the U.S. role in Asia and the Pacific that are constitutive not only of Sweeney's own testimony but also of many other arguments deployed to attack the planned exhibit. For instance, although it interrogated Japan's colonial invasions, Sweeney's narrative totally omitted any mention of the United States' imperial expansion into the Asia Pacific region, its capitalist incentive for securing markets in China, and other related issues. It condemned the Japanese military's attack on Pearl Harbor but ignored the questions of how in the first place Hawaii had come to be a U.S. territory and why a U.S. naval base existed there. Those who opposed displays of atomic bomb victims tended to share an arbitrary and selective amnesia about their own country's history of colonial and military aggression.

Moreover, Sweeney's testimony summarizes the widely shared conviction that because we must properly tutor the Japanese to have a correct view of history, we as Americans ought to possess unadulterated historical knowledge. Sweeney's lengthy testimony further included a perspective on postbomb history that maintained that it was precisely because his country used the atomic weapons when it did that the Japanese people were enabled to receive various benefits in the postwar years. He alluded, for instance, to the view that the atomic bombings saved Japanese lives and rescued the Japanese people from the control of military fanatics; that they deterred a Soviet occupation and prevented Japan from becoming communist or experiencing territorial division; and that they created the conditions for Japan's subsequent democratic reforms and incredibly swift economic recovery. Furthermore, according to Sweeney's view of history, his own country's nuclear armament and military policy provided postwar Japan with a shield against the Soviet and Chinese threats while facilitating Japan's economic development. In short, such presumptions call on the Japanese to be grateful for the United States' "benevolent" and timely use of the atom bombs.[28]

It may also be worth noting that the paternalistic presumptions and understandings of history that inform Sweeney's and others' arguments are strikingly similar to those of Japanese conservatives who continue to insist that Japanese colonialism, despite—as they never fail to add—the "unfortunate" and regrettable outcome, contributed to the modernization and postwar economic development of Asian countries that had formerly been under Western colonial rule. Although it cannot be described fully in this limited space, there are also parallels in that Sweeney and the others, like their Japanese counterparts, characterize their compatriots unidimensionally as victims, thereby obscuring the history of U.S. imperialism and other acts of aggression against various parts of Asia and the Pacific.

The attacks on the NASM staff continued despite the fact that the curators, from a very early stage in the negotiations, agreed to incorporate what were often called the absent "historical contexts" into their exhibit narratives. The angry attacks by members of the American Legion, the Air Force Association, Congress, and a number of journalists and intellectuals concerning what they saw as the NASM curators' "un-American" and insulting attitude toward the glorious accomplishments of former political leaders and soldiers did not subside until all the displays of Japanese casualties were removed and Director Harwit was forced to resign. According to the August 14, 1994 *Washington Post* editorial cited earlier, the museum's critics charged that the planned exhibit would "build sympathy for the Japanese" by portraying the *Enola Gay* mission as causing "death, radiation sickness, despair and the beginning of nuclear terror."[29] Tom Crouch, the chairman of the NASM Aeronautics Department, who was central in designing the prepared exhibit, astutely observed that what continued to upset the critics was not so much how the story about the ground-level destruction was presented as the fact that the "whole story" was told.[30]

Let us briefly observe what happened at the other end of the binational warping. In the first draft of the plan for the Smithsonian exhibit, one phrase indicated that the United States fought the war in the Pacific in a way that was fundamentally different from the way it waged war against Germany and Italy. The draft stated that Americans had fought the war against the Japanese as a "war of vengeance. For most Japanese, it was a war to defend their unique culture against Western imperialism."[31] This phrase appeared in the script as an ironic summary of Japanese officials' gross justification for atrocities committed during the war, including the civilian massacre in Nanjing, the abuse against POWs, and the biological experiments on living human beings.[32] Again, curators revised the phrase at a very early stage of the negotiations. Yet critics continued to cite it out of context and to condemn the museum staff for suggesting that the United States was the victimizer and Japan the victim.

Historian Martin Sherwin was one of those who called for the need to contextualize this phrase, particularly for a Japanese-speaking audience.[33] Sherwin's intervention was an especially important one, for even while placing Japanese aggression within the broader historical context of the Western imperialist expansion into Asia and other parts of the world that preceded it, he also prevented this historicization from being appropriated by ultranationalists and conservatives in Japan, who continue to justify Japanese military and colonial aggression as acts of "self-defense." In other words, Sherwin's cautionary remarks to a Japanese audience sought to deter yet another warping of critical discourses by obstructing the dovetailing of the U.S. revisionist historians' progressive position with that of the Japanese conservatives.

The binational warping of political positions, in short, is an effect that results from the ways in which national framings of historical narratives deflect our analyses away from phenomena such as capitalist economic expansion, nationalism, and military domination that exist in common across national borders. The narrating of history premised on the self-contained unit of the nation-state is also a condition that allows the victimization of one segment of a society to stand for the victimiza-

tion of the entire national collectivity. Furthermore, insofar as such national assumptions remain unquestioned, it will not be possible to recognize that during most of
the twentieth century, the conservative elite in the United States (which has sought,
for instance, to obstruct "nonpatriotic" activities) and the conservative forces in
Japan (which continue to suppress critical activities, including opposition to the
emperor system) are in many respects complicit with each other in their capitalist
and nationalist desires.

Conclusion

The February 19, 1995 issue of the *San Diego Union Tribune* devoted an entire page
to introducing opposing perspectives on the *Enola Gay* controversy. An expansive
black-and-white aerial photograph of Hiroshima, taken approximately one month
after the bombing, occupies most of the page. The details of the city are vague.
Two rivers run dark, one at the bottom, another at the center of the photo, while
broad white avenues extend toward the hazy hills in the distance. Except for the
sparse remains of a few European-style buildings, the entire city appears to have
been burned down and is in ashes. Here again, as in the Smithsonian exhibit, the
damage suffered by civilians is obscured. Yet, precisely because one cannot see the
Asian faces or alien street scenes, the newspaper photograph serves to detempor-
alize and dislocate the image of the ruined city from any specific historical moment
and place. In other words, it could be argued that the photograph suggests the stark
reality of nuclear proliferation in this world, when such devastation can occur
anywhere and anytime beyond Hiroshima 1945.

   Yet how many people actually followed the concrete details of the controversy
in the newspapers and other media? Most likely, museum visitors were not fully
exposed to all of the debates surrounding the exhibits they saw. They may have
been indifferent to the discussions about the decision making that led to the use of
the two atomic bombs, or to the disputes about whether the museum's curatorial
freedom was violated by legislative intervention. Nor can we assume that those who
visited the NASM to view the commemorative exhibit were concerned about
nuclear issues in general. As one woman remarked in a CNN interview, what was
perhaps most attractive and thrilling about visiting the exhibit was the possibility of
access to a genuine historical artifact, that is, the ability to come close to the aura
of factual authenticity. This is precisely why it is highly regrettable that no objects
from the ground level—such as a mutilated lunch box, a photo of a disfigured horse,
a melted iron bar, a bloodstained school uniform, or a specimen of a deformed
fetus—were displayed. Perhaps even more than the exhibit's proponents, those who
opposed the plans for displays on Hiroshima and Nagasaki were fully aware of the
unsettling meanings that such artifacts could generate in viewers' minds.

   In closing, it should be emphasized that the museum curators' attempt to create
an exhibit that would encourage a rethinking of the nation's dominant understanding
of Hiroshima and Nagasaki, as well as of other nuclear-related issues, was inextricably linked to the ways that developments in the social and human sciences had
led to the interrogation of various accepted ideas and categories. The attack against
the curators' attitude—which Harwit had called "more analytical, critical in its

acceptance of facts"—must be understood in relation to various reactions against the increasing ambiguity of the post-cold war milieu and the accompanying broader reorganization of knowledge.

When war veterans and others, including Sweeney, vehemently criticized the curators, they were particularly disturbed by the script's suggestion that there were elements of U.S. aggression and imperialism even in what had been considered the most just and sacred of American wars. In the Senate testimony described above, Sweeney lashed out at his foes, saying that to remember the Japanese not just as villains but also as victims of the U.S. atom bombings was an "assault on our language and history by the elimination of accurate and descriptive words." It was, he said, equivalent to saying "Up is Down, Slavery is Freedom, Aggression is Peace." In contrast, fifty years ago, "the threat was clear, the enemy well defined."[34]

This disillusionment demonstrates that the conservatives' intervention in the Smithsonian's exhibit plans was not unrelated to the recent barrage of attacks against certain critical scholarship in the social and human sciences. This critical scholarship—which has included Marxism and critical theories, feminist theories, postcolonial and ethic studies, queer theories, and cultural studies, to name a few—has played a crucial role in the rethinking and complicating of reified concepts, routinized and institutionalized processes, the taken-for-granted, and essentialized categories. Critical scholarship has endeavored to question the transparency of accepted meanings. It asks, to take the concrete example of Sweeney, whether what we have assumed to be the progress of civilization (read "up") might instead connote a regression toward barbarism (read "down"), as critical theorists would argue; whether what has been uncritically acclaimed as increasing freedom from the old regime might in fact entail our enslavement to an oppressive society of self-surveillance and control (read "slavery is freedom"), as Michel Foucault would have it; or whether what has been unproblematically promoted as the means to achieve peace might be inseparable from tools of aggression (read "aggression is peace"), as the Smithsonian curators tried to show.

Newt Gingrich, in his gross debasement of the popular, announced "victory" in the Smithsonian controversy by arguing that "the *Enola Gay* fight was a fight, in effect, over the reassertion by most Americans that they're sick and tired of being told by some cultural elite that they ought to be ashamed of their history."[35] Yet this statement should not be taken literally as a simple celebration of the victory of patriotism. Rather, it may best be understood as an exulting over the successful defense of the stability of the language with which the nation's history is written against the infiltration of critical and reflexive knowledge. Perhaps this also explains why the conservative elites concluded that the controversy had ended in a victory over "political correctness."[36] In other words, the Smithsonian debate ended in the defeat of those who sought critical rethinking, as well as the defeat of those who questioned the self-evident, the natural, and the inevitable, and the victory of those who felt threatened by obfuscation of the contours of conventional knowledge. In this sense, the controversy centering on the Smithsonian ought to be understood as but one symptom of larger battles that are raging within the social and human sciences.

In closing, I would like to suggest an alternative to such conventional attitudes toward history and knowledge and to the warping of political positions. *In the Name of the Emperor*, a documentary on the Nanjing Massacre made by two Asian American directors, Christine Choy and Nancy Tong, offers us an important example of how historical memories can be made urgently relevant to the questioning of current global situations and may even render new alliances of critical discourses across nationality, ethnicity, class, and generation.

The documentary is composed primarily of historical film footage of and interviews concerning the Japanese Army's atrocities in Nanjing. The film manages both to reconstruct conditions at that historical moment and to interrogate the processes through which forgetfulness about the Nanjing Massacre has been produced in Japan. It questions, in particular, the fact that the film footage it contains was not used as evidence in the Tokyo War Crimes Trial and that this footage had been buried and deliberately forgotten for so long. It shows that the trial was inadequate because it failed to consider the emperor's war responsibility even though it had been the United States' and Japan's insistence on resolving the matter of the emperor system that had prolonged the war and resulted in the unnecessary and catastrophic loss of lives. Moreover, the film suggests that the trial was premised on a Eurocentric historical worldview and that it interrogated only Japan's crimes against the former Western colonial powers rather than the violence committed against the common people of Asia and the Pacific. In addition, the documentary touched on the recent apology demands of women formerly enslaved sexually by Japanese military. It furthermore implicates the United States by showing that its cold war policy led to the long-term postwar suppression of movements within Asian countries that had tried to expose the facts about war damages and colonial rule, including such movements in immediate postwar Japan.

While making each country and government absolutely accountable for its conduct, the directors at the same time refuse to represent the nation as a non-contradictory and undivided subject with containable boundaries. Concerning the crimes committed by the Japanese military on the Asian and Pacific peoples, the documentary relentlessly reminds its viewers that the conservative critics of Japan and the United States were in fact accomplices in promoting forgetfulness. By criticizing the transnational complicity between conservative and anticommunist elements in Japan and the United States, it produces a historical narrative that refuses to allow critical discourses to be subsumed by a single national position. Even as the documentary makes it absolutely clear that the Japanese Army committed atrocities against those identified as Chinese, it deploys one person's testimony to emphasize that the experiencing of the atrocities was at the same time inflected by class differences, for the wealthy had greater resources with which to escape the city. It thereby prevents the memories of the Nanjing Massacre from being subsumed under an imagined and singular national collectivity. While condemning the Japanese government's decades-long underemphasis of the massacre, the two directors do not fail to describe activism by which Japanese progressive historians have interrogated for many years the statist occlusion of Japan's wartime atrocities. The documentary also points out that concerning the issue of historical memory there has been a long accumulation of activism that involves feminists, labor activists, and other progressive critics in Korea, Japan, and Asian American communities. In this way, and contrary to the narratives exemplified by Sweeney's testimony Choy and Tong succeed in illuminating what the discursive warping I described above has made invisible—namely, the transnational alliances that are not compatible with the U.S. or other nationalist and corporate concerns.

The representation of history in Choy and Tong's documentary may be understood as an effective example of a postnationalist historiography, or what historian Miriam Silverberg has termed an "associative history" in her call for an examination of racial politics in prewar and wartime Japan.[37] To be sure, insofar as a nation-state exists as an institutional entity and its apparatuses of knowledge continue to produce their own distinct historical knowledge, its temporal and spatial specificities must be taken into account. Yet, it is also important not to confuse historically produced institutional distinctiveness with the ideological effects of corporate and other forms of nationalism. With regard to the histories of Hiroshima and Nagasaki, how one understands the two atom bombings is a question that concerns not only those who reside in Japan and the United States. Rather, it is a question that inevitably involves several tens of thousands of atom bomb victims who reside in North and South Korea; millions of people throughout Asia and the Pacific region who were victimized and affected by Japan's war of aggression, as well as by European, Japanese, U.S., and Chinese imperialist expansion, both before and after the war; and those who became diasporas as a result of colonial and military histories of violence, who now reside as the racially minoritized in Japan, the United States, and other parts of the world.

Perhaps one of the most valuable outcomes of the Smithsonian debates was that they generated a sense of urgency for the necessity of fashioning postnationalist public spheres in which diverse historical understandings can overlap in multiple ways and be shared coalitionally. The crafting of such spaces will at the same time help us establish a position from which it is possible to discern those crucial elements that have been excluded in the process of constituting a nation-state's dominant way of collective remembering. To secure a position critical of the paradigm that has long confined our memory work to the boundaries of nationality and nationhood will also keep us from reverting to patriotic appeals when trying to legitimate our arguments, as some historians involved in the Smithsonian debates inadvertently did in countering the accusation that their activities were "un-American."[38] Finally, such a coalescing of denationalized, discrepant historical memories will in turn broaden the scope of our historical inquiries and the questions we ask of our pasts and future.

Acknowledgements

This essay was originally prepared for the conference "The Politics of Remembering the Asia-Pacific War" at the East-West Center, Honolulu, September 7–9, 1995. An earlier, abridged version of the essay was published in Japanese as "Ekkyo suru sensō no kioku: Sumisonian genbakuten ronsō yomu," *Sekai*, no. 614 (October 1995): 173–83. A slightly different version appeared earlier in English as "Critical Warps: Facticity, Transformative Knowledge, and Postnationalist Criticism in the Smithsonian *Enola Gay* Controversy," *positions* 5, no. 3 (Winter 1997): 5–29. The research was supported by an Academic Senate Research Grant from the University of California, San Diego. Over the past years, I have had a number of occasions to present versions of this essay at different conferences and symposia. I wish to thank the many people who gave me useful feedback on these occasions. The essay especially benefited from comments by the following individuals: Chungmoo Choi, Tak Fujitani, Yoshiye Funahashi, Richard Handler, Yeong-hae Jung, Takeshiro Kurisu, Masao Miyoshi, Minoru Ōmuta, Michael Schudson, Takumi Usui, and Geoffrey White. I thank Eric Cazdyn, who worked as my research assistant, and Shun'ichi Matsubayashi, Kenji Ōhara, and Keisaburō Toyonaga for their generous efforts in collecting valuable and often difficult to acquire materials, including local newspaper, magazine, and journal articles, transcripts from TV news programs and interviews, and the first and final versions of the canceled Smithsonian script. I am especially thankful to Geoffrey White for sharing records of Senate committee hearings as well as other transcripts obtained through the Internet.

Notes

1   Geoffrey White has observed that the Smithsonian controversy was rooted in the inability to negotiate national and extranational ways of remembering what was in essence an international event: the war. He writes, "The particular difficulties for this exhibit in navigating between opposed calls for critical history and patriotic history stem from the fact that it was dealing with an intensely international subject in an intensely national site." See White, "Memory Wars: The Politics of Remembering the Asia/Pacific War," *AsiaPacific Issues*, no. 21 (July 1995): 1–8. White's earlier analysis of Guadalcanal's fiftieth-anniversary commemorative events alerted me to the transnational aspect of memory-making processes; see "Remembering Guadalcanal: National Identity and Transnational Memory-Making," *Public Culture* 7 (Spring 1995): 529–55.

2   See Mike Wallace, "The Battle of the *Enola Gay*," *Radical Historian Newsletter*, no. 72 (May 1995). 1–12, 22–32, for a succinct overview of the entire controversy and the quote from Rush Limbaugh.

3   Two important collaborative projects were produced in response to the legislators' censoring of national history. See "Remembering the Bomb: The Fiftieth Anniversary in the United States and Japan," special issue of *Bulletin of Concerned Asian Scholars* 27, no. 2 (April–June 1995), and the articles collected in "Hiroshima in History and Memory: A Symposium," special issue of *Diplomatic History* 19, no. 2 (Spring 1995). For readers of Japanese, historian Daizaburō Yui has succinctly summarized the entire course of events and the problems with the dominant historical understanding in the United States about the use of atom bombs. Yui's book also examines the U.S.–Japan gap in perceptions of the Pacific War, the Korean War, and the Vietnam War. See Daizaburō Yui, *Nichibei sensōkan no sōkoku: Masatsu no shinsō shinri* (Antagonisms in U.S.–Japan views on war: Deep psychology of conflicts) (Tokyo: Iwanami Shoten, 1995).

4   See John B. Thompson, *Studies in the Theory of Ideology* (Berkeley: University of California Press, 1984), 1.

5   Kai Bird, "A Humiliating Smithsonian Retreat from the Facts of Hiroshima," *International Herald Tribune*, October 12, 1994.

6   See Michael King, "Revisiting the *Enola Gay*," *Post-Crescent* (Appleton, WI), November 20, 1994.

7   U.S. Senate Committee on Rules and Administration, *Hearing: The Smithsonian Institution Management Guidelines for the Future*, 104th Cong., Ist sess., II and May 18, 1995, 48.

8   Quoted in Eugene L. Meyer and Jacqueline Trescott, "Smithsonian Scuttles Exhibit," *Washington Post*, January 31, 1995.

9   Martin Harwit, "The *Enola Gay*: A Nation's, and a Museum's, Dilemma," *Washington Post*, August 7, 1994.

10   See the statement of Herman G. Harrington in U.S. Senate, *Hearing: The Smithsonian Institution Management Guidelines*, 20–27.

11   U.S. Senate, *Hearing: The Smithsonian Institution Management Guidelines*, 49. The Rorschach test image also appears in Gaddis Smith, "Hiroshima: The Rorschach Test of the American Psyche," *Los Angeles Times*, July 30, 1995.

12   Quoted in "*Enola Gay* Exhibit Remains Unsettled," *San Diego Union Tribune*, March 12, 1995.

13   The most important of the earlier seminal works by revisionist historians include Gar Alperovitz, *Atomic Diplomacy: Hiroshima and Potsdam* (New York: Simon and Schuster, 1965); Martin J. Sherwin, *A World Destroyed: The Atomic Bomb and the Grand Alliance* (New York: Knopf, 1975); and Barton Bernstein, "Atomic Diplomacy and the Cold War," in *The Atomic Bomb: The Critical Issues*, ed. Barton Bernstein (Boston: Little, Brown, 1976), 129–35. The argument that Truman was aware in early July of Japan's likely surrender appeared in Gar Alperovitz, "*Enola Gay*: A New Consensus . . . ," *Washington Post*, February 4, 1995. In his more recent *Decision to Use the Atomic Bomb and the Architecture of an American Myth* (New York: Knopf, 1995), Alperovitz rearticulates the revisionist view and juxtaposes it, in great detail, to the ways the mainstream U.S. understanding about the bomb's use was manufactured. For the official manipulation of the estimated American casualties and deaths, see Barton Bernstein, "Understanding the Atomic Bomb and the Japanese Surrender: Missed Opportunities, Little-Known Near Disasters, and Modern Memory," *Diplomatic History* 19, no. 2 (Spring 1995): 227–73. For a summary of the historians' new consensus, see J. Samuel Walker, "History, Collective Memory, and the Decision to Use the Bomb," *Diplomatic History* 19, no. 2 (Spring 1995): 319–28.

14   This point was made by Bernstein in his remarks at the conference "Hoping for the Worst: The Planning, Experience, and Consequences of Mass Warfare, 1930–1950," University of California, Berkeley, November 1995.

15   Dominick LaCapra, "Representing the Holocaust: Reflections on the Historians' Debate," in *Probing the Limits of Representation: Nazism and the "Final Solution,"* ed. Saul Friedlander (Cambridge, MA: Harvard University Press, 1992), 108–27; see 122 for quote. For an earlier discussion of the difficulties and possibilities in the act of confronting the past, see Theodor W. Adorno, "What Does Coming to Terms with the Past Mean?" in *Bitburg in Moral and Political Perspective*, ed. Geoffrey H. Hartman (Bloomington: Indiana University Press, 1986), 114–29. See also Eric L. Santner, "History beyond the Pleasure Principle: Some Thoughts on the Representation of Trauma," in Friedlander, *Probing the Limits*, 143–54. Santner links LaCapra's discussion on "working through" to his conceptualization of the possibility of redemption through the proper form of "mourning" loss. Santner also points out that the German inability to mourn emerges as what he calls "narrative fetish," which serves as yet another repression of the repressed, in a manner similar to the "acting out" of historians that LaCapra observes. See also Eric L. Santner, *Stranded Objects: Mourning, Memory, and Film in Postwar Germany* (Ithaca, NY: Cornell University Press, 1990).

16   See Hayden White, "The Value of Narrativity in the Representation of Reality," and "Narrativization of Real Events," in *On Narrative*, ed. W. J. T. Mitchell (Chicago: University of Chicago Press, 1981), 1–23, 249–54. In understanding the hegemonic

tendency to misappropriate arguments that take into account the aesthetic and moral dimensions of the construction of knowledge, I find especially insightful Peter Novick's historical account of how the question of objectivity has been transfigured, primarily in the U.S. academic sphere since the beginning of the twentieth century. Novick writes that, given post-World War II conditions in which the empiricism/ objectivism of social science has been a vital source of ideological and intellectual legitimation in the U.S. academy, it is no surprise that critiques of constructionist arguments are still often articulated as attacks against "anti-American" ideals. See Novick, *That Noble Dream: The "Objectivity Question" and the American Historical Profession* (New York: Cambridge University Press, 1988).

17   Pin-hui Liao urges us to extend our rethinking of the Habermasian utopian presumption of a single, unitary public sphere to historical consciousness and memories. Following the critiques of Nancy Fraser and others, Liao underscores the significance of modifying the liberal public-sphere notion with respect to the postcolonial condition in Taiwan, when multiple layers of modern experiences and historical identities coexist. See Liao, "Rewriting Taiwanese National History: The February 28 Incident As Spectacle," *Public Culture* 5 (Winter 1993): 281–96.

18   Among numerous examples of this reasoning, see especially Edwin M. Yoder Jr., ". . . Or Hiroshima Cult?" *Washington Post*, February 4, 1995.

19   U.S. Senate Committee, *Hearing: The Smithsonian Institution Management Guidelines*, 11.

20   Eric Gable, Richard Handler, and Anna Lawson, "On the Uses of Relativism: Fact, Conjecture, and Black and White Histories at Colonial Williamsburg," *American Ethnologist* 19, no. 4 (1992): 792. I am especially thankful to Richard Handler for pushing me to think through the conflation of history and memory in Sweeney's testimony.

21   When a Harvard professor stated at the United Nations Hiroshima Disarmament Conference that he believed the use of the atom bombs helped hasten the war's end and saved both American and Japanese lives— which indeed is the dominant view shared by most people in the United States—*Asahi shinbun* reported the contention his statement elicited with the headline "'Nuclear Consciousness,' Japan–U.S. Gap" (December 11, 1992).

22   *Chugoku shinbun*, September 30, 1994.

23   In the Japanese-language media the controversy has offered opportunities for people in Japan to rethink such a simple nationalized perspective of history. Detailed reports on the controversy's background explained that the criticisms of the sympathetic portrayals of Japanese casualties in the prepared texts were not generated solely by World War II veterans but had been fostered by a series of recent conservative turns in U.S. society; including a patriotic reemphasis in history education, anti-immigrant sentiments exemplified by the passing of Proposition 187 in California, intensifying antiabortion terrorism, and attacks on affirmative action. Practically every major newspaper reported on the intense negotiations between the museum staff and their advisors on the one hand, and representatives of the American Legion, the Air Force Association, and conservative historians and journalists on the other. The newspapers and journals published their own interviews with individuals who protested publicly against Congress's intervention in curatorial research and intellectual engagements. Later in the year, when American University in Washington held a public symposium and opened its own exhibits on Hiroshima and Nagasaki, both the visual and print media very quickly introduced the exhibits' contents, along with accounts of the counterexhibit on the Rape of Nanjing that was organized by protesting Chinese

Americans. Unlike conventional arguments over nuclear matters, the fact that the various debates concerning the Smithsonian exhibit were publicized as a "controversy" *within* American society contributed to debunking the popular understanding that the United States upholds a single unified view about Hiroshima, Nagasaki, and related issues. See *Asahi shinbun*, June 15, 1995, for one of the most detailed articles that dealt with the overall social and political environment in the United States.

24   U.S. Senate Committee, *Hearing: The Smithsonian Institution Management Guidelines*, 24.

25   For instance, the spokesperson for the Air Force Association, Jack Giese, described the Smithsonian controversy as "an internal American debate with an American institution that wasn't doing their job." See Nigel Holloway, "Museum Peace: U.S. Curators Seek Truce over the Plane That Atom-Bombed Hiroshima," *Far Eastern Economic Review* (February 2, 1995): 32.

26   U.S. Senate Committee, *Hearing: The Smithsonian Institution Management Guidelines*, 11.

27   Elsewhere I have discussed at length the counteramnes(t)ic—namely, unforgetful and unforgiving—practices in postwar Hiroshima, as well as the intimate link present in Japan among the politics of representing the country's war of aggression, memories of colonialism, and the testimonial practices of the atom bomb survivors. See *Hiroshima Traces: Time, Space, and the Dialectics of Memory* (Berkeley: University of California Press, 1999).

28   For a statement that most succinctly reveals the understandings of history and U.S.–East Asia relations described here, see James R. Van de Velde, "*Enola Gay* Saved Lives, Period," *Washington Post*, February 10, 1995. The Smithsonian controversy also demonstrated that some of the cold war perceptions that justified the use of the atomic bombs and the subsequent nuclear buildup are still strongly upheld by many in the United States. See, for example, Thomas Sowell, "The Right to Infiltrate," *Forbes* (March 13, 1995): 74. It should be further noted that the view held by Sweeney, Van de Velde, and others need not necessarily be identified as a national (i.e., an American) one, for such a historical awareness is also widely found among citizens of Japan and other Asian nations. The irony, of course, is that such justifications for the bombs' use are premised on an argument that the prepared text's opponents have themselves been refuting. This cold war historical narrative in fact unwittingly appropriates the factual grounds used by so-called revisionist historians to argue that the atomic bombs were unnecessary from a strictly military point of view, that is, the argument that the decision to drop the bombs was necessary not for the purpose of bringing the war to a rapid close but rather for containing the Soviets in the postwar settlement.

29   "Context and the *Enola Gay*," *Washington Post*, August 14, 1994. See also Richard Serrano, "Smithsonian Says It Erred, Scraps Exhibit on A-Bomb," *Los Angeles Times*, January 31, 1995, for William M. Detweiler's comment in which he noted "the museum curators' attempt to depict the Japanese as victims and Americans as cold-hearted avengers."

30   Hugh Sidey, "War and Remembrance," *Time*, May 23, 1994. Crouch had been explaining to the public that survivors' testimonies and displays of articles that demonstrate the ground-level effects of the bombs made up the planned exhibit's "emotional center." It would have included photographs of mutilated women and children and audiovisual tapes of survivors' testimonies. Throughout the controversy, the museum curators' critics problematized the proposed exhibit for placing the emotional center on the destruction caused by the atomic bombing. See also James Risen, "War of Words," *Los Angeles Times*, December 19, 1994; and "War of Words: What Museum

Couldn't Say," *New York Times*, February 5, 1995. Journalists such as Air Force Magazine editor John Correll expressed their disgust at the fact that the museum curators' script would have included more photographs of Japanese casualties than of American soldiers. See "The Mission That Ended the War," *Washington Post*, August 14, 1994. That the number of Chinese killed by the Japanese military far exceeded either American or Japanese casualties was the least of their concerns.

31 Holloway, "Museum Peace," 32.

32 National Air and Space Museum, "The Crossroads: The End of World War II, the Atomic Bomb, and the Origins of the Cold War, First Script," National Air and Space Museum, Washington, D.C., 1994, mimeograph, 5.

33 Martin Sherwin, "Hiroshima gojūnen, rekishi to kioku no seijigaku" (Hiroshima fifty years, politics of history and memory), *Kokusai bunka kaikan kaihō* 6, no. 4 (October 1995): 8.

34 U.S. Senate Committee, *Hearing: The Smithsonian Institution Management Guidelines*, 12.

35 Gingrich's speech is quoted in Stephen Budiansky et al., "A Museum in Crisis: The Smithsonian Heads into Rough Times after the *Enola Gay* Debacle," *U.S. News and World Report* (February 13, 1995): 73–74.

36 For characterizations of the NASM curators' effort to include multiple dimensions of the two atom bombs' use as stemming from the sensitivities of "political correctness" and of the 1960s Vietnam War generation, see, above all, Sowell, "The Right to Infiltrate," 74; the testimony of Evan S. Baker, president of the Navy League of the United States, in U.S. Senate Committee, *Hearing: The Smithsonian Institution Management Guidelines*, May 11, 1995; and Risen, "War of Words." William M. Detweiler, who was one of the first to openly attack the NASM staff, drew a connection between the Smithsonian controversy and the National Standards for U.S. History, through which "students will learn more about the politically correct people, places and events." See "Assault on American Values," *Washington Post*, February 11, 1995.

37 Miriam Silverberg, "Remembering Pearl Harbor, Forgetting Charlie Chaplin, and the Case of the Disappearing Western Woman: A Picture Story," *positions* 1, no. 1 (Spring 1993): 24–76.

38 Kai Bird, for instance, argued that the Smithsonian script did not assault "the patriotism of World War II veterans. But neither should one question the patriotism of scholars who labor in the archives at the difficult task of peeling away layers of historical truth." See his "Humiliating Smithsonian Retreat." Martin Sherwin also responded to the press: "I'm appalled that Congress has come into this with an official history over the debate, leaving no room for informed debate. In my view, this cancellation undermines the democratic process for which these veterans fought in World War II" (quoted in Karen De Witt, "U.S. Exhibit on Bomber Is in Jeopardy," *New York Times*, January 28, 1995). It is unclear from this quote whether Sherwin himself is equating the democratic process with the particular U.S. constitutional process. But when read against the larger context of Detweiler's and others' accusation that the NASM staff and their supporters lack American patriotism, it produces precisely such an effect.

FURTHER READING

ON THE GENERAL SUBJECT of memorials and memorialization, a good place to begin is Jay Winter's work on the First World War, *Sites of Memory, Sites of Mourning: The Great War in European cultural history* (Cambridge, 1995) along with George L. Mosse, *Fallen Soldiers: reshaping the memory of the world wars* (New York, 1990). Interest in "memory" is particularly strong in French history, on which see: Henry Rousso, *The Vichy Syndrome: history and memory in France since 1944* (Cambridge MA, 1991); Claire Gorrara, *Women's Representations of the Occupation in Post-'68 France* (Basingstoke, 1998); and the essays in H. R. Kedward and Nancy Wood (eds), *The Liberation of France: image and event* (Oxford, 1995). Pieter Lagrou extends the subject to western Europe generally in *The legacy of Nazi Occupation in Western Europe: patriotic memory and national recovery* (Cambridge, 1999). On the United States, see G. Kurt Piehler, *Remembering War the American Way* (Washington DC, 1995). A stimulating short work on "remembering" the Battle of Britain is Richard Overy's *The Battle* (Harmondsworth, 2000) which explores the gap between memory and "history". Any reader interested in the subject would do well to read John Bodnar's *Remaking America: public memory, commemoration and patriotism in the twentieth century* (Princeton NJ, 1992),

Oral history as a documentary "record" that is inextricably interwoven with the subjectivity of memory may be approached in: Penny Summerfield, *Reconstructing Women's Wartime Lives: discourse and subjectivity in oral histories of the Second World War* (Manchester, 1998), which is focussed on the British experience; John Tateishi, *And Justice for All: an oral history of the Japanese American detention camps* (New York, 1984), and the essays in Robert Thobaben (ed.), *For Comrade and Country: oral histories of World War II veterans* (Jefferson NC, 2003), which is focussed on the American experience.

On film, literature and museums, see Jeanine Basinger, *The World War II Combat Film: the anatomy of a genre* (New York, 1986); Eric L. Santner, *Stranded Objects: mourning, memory, and film in postwar Germany* (Ithaca NY, 1990); Desmond Graham (ed.), *Poetry of the Second World War: an international anthology* (London, 1995); and Lucy Noakes, *War and the British: gender, memory and national identity* (London, 1998).

Some interesting essays on Hiroshima may be found in "Hiroshima in History and Memory: a symposium," special issue of *Diplomatic History* 19, no. 2 (Spring 1995), especially those by Barton Bernstein, "Understanding the Atomic Bomb and the Japanese Surrender: missed opportunities, little-known near disasters, and modern memory," 227–73 and J. Samuel Walker, "History, Collective Memory, and the Decision to Use the Bomb," 319–28. For further examples of Lisa Yoneyama's postmodern perspective, see "Critical Warps: facticity, transformative knowledge, and postnationalist criticism in the Smithsonian *Enola Gay* controversy," *positions* 5, no. 3 (Winter 1997): 5–29; "Remembering Guadalcanal: national identity and transnational memory-making," *Public Culture* 7 (Spring 1995): 529–55; and *Hiroshima Traces: Time, Space, and the Dialectics of Memory* (Berkeley CA, 1999). And also see the essay by Claudia Koonz, "Between Memory and Oblivion: concentration camps in German memory", in John R. Gillis (ed.), *Commemorations: the politics of national identity* (Princeton NJ, 1994).

GLOSSARY

Air Force Association: founded in 1946 in order to promote the idea of an independent air force in the United States (which was created in 1947). Now an independent veterans' organization advocating aerospace power and supporting the United States Air Force. In 1994 the association produced a special report on "The Smithsonian and the *Enola Gay*" exposing its "lack of balance" and securing a change in the exhibition. (See www.afa.org)

American Legion: founded in Paris in March 1919 by members of the American Expeditionary Force. Now the largest veterans' organization in the world, it has successfully lobbied for rights and benefits on behalf of veterans. In September 1994 it partnered with the Air and Space Museum to develop an exhibit for the *Enola Gay*; in January 1995 it agreed to a scaled-down version of the exhibit "without political commentary" which ended the Smithsonian controversy. (See www.legion.org)

Armée secrète: name given to underground resistance movements in both Belgium and France. The Belgian movement was royalist in inspiration and recognized as the official resistance organization by the government-in-exile in 1943. The French movement was formed in October 1941. A non-communist resistance organization, it merged into the National Council of Resistance organized by Jean Moulin in May 1943 and became its military wing.

Atlantic Charter: a joint declaration issued by Winston Churchill and Franklin Roosevelt on August 14, 1941 during their meeting off the coast of Newfoundland. Although the United States was not yet at war, the two heads of government unofficially renounced territorial aggrandizement, declared themselves in favor of self-determination, the restoration of sovereignty to states that had been invaded, disarmament of aggressor states, and various steps to protect the peace and freedom of peoples once Nazi tyranny had been brought to an end. The eight points of the declaration were constituted as the official war aims of the United Nations on January 1, 1942, following the US declaration of war.

Australian Women's Charter: The Charter Movement, launched in 1943, attempted to unite the diverse strands of the women's movement. The Charter outlined a series of postwar objectives acceptable to all, including equal citizenship rights, equal pay, anti sex-discrimination legislation, equal access to education, reform of divorce laws and a government-sponsored day-care system. It also advocated strict controls on the sale of liquor, the prohibition of "literature calculated to stimulate crime and sexual laxity" and the provision of "ample facilities for healthy recreation."

Auxiliaire féminin de l'armée de terre (AFAT): chartered by De Gaulle's provisional government in Algiers in January 1944, creating a separate women's auxiliary of the French army.

Bataillons de la jeunesse: the combat wing of the *Jeunesses communistes,* the French Communist party youth group, which played a significant role in the resistance.

Beveridge Report: submitted by William Beveridge (academic, journalist, and government adviser) and published by the British government in 1942, the report called for far-reaching state action to maintain permanent full employment, to set up a national health service, and to secure the British people against poverty by means of family allowances and comprehensive subsistence-level social insurance. It established the foundations of the "welfare state" following the war.

Blitzkrieg: literally, "lightning-war," this was a strategic conception that arose from the carnage and frustration of trench warfare on the western front in World War One. The strategy envisioned a quick war of movement through the combination of air (fighter planes and dive-bombers) and mobile ground forces (tanks and armored vehicles). The aim was to penetrate to the rear of the enemy, thus cutting off the essential communications and administration of the enemy, rather than defeating them with overwhelming manpower.

Cashiering: dismissal from military service – a punishment for an offence committed by a soldier, of lesser severity than imprisonment or court-martial.

Comité d'Histoire de la Deuxième Guerre Mondiale: the Committee for the History of the Second World War, it meets at least once every five years in conjunction with the International Congress of Historical Sciences.

Declaration of the United Nations: statement of war aims by the United States, United Kingdom, the USSR and 23 other states made on January 1, 1942. In addition to subscribing to the principles outlined in the Atlantic Charter, they pledged to cooperate with one another, not to sign a separate peace or armistice with their enemies.

Einsatzgruppen: literally "operational groups" special task forces created by Himmler within the SS under the leadership of Richard Heydrich following the invasion of Poland in September 1939. Their task was to create the conditions necessary for *lebensraum* in the east, specifically by eliminating the political enemies (mainly communists and socialists) of the Reich. They became mobile killing units and extended the range of operations to include the extermination of Jews and gypsies following the invasion of the Soviet Union in 1941.

Emergency Power (Defence) Act: during the Munich crisis of August 1938 the British prime minister, Neville Chamberlain, presented a series of sweeping measures to parliament to enable the government to mobilize the country for defense. Included were provisions for increasing volunteer services such as those connected with air raid warning and the Territorial Army.

ENIGMA: the electro-mechanical cypher machine used by the Germans during the war. It was invented during the 1920s and used for sending messages in code. Alan Turing and his colleagues at Bletchley Park (north of London, England) broke the code late in 1939 and by late 1940 were regularly decrypting German *Luftwaffe* messages; U-boat messages proved to be more difficult.

Enola Gay: the United States' B-29 "Superfortress" bomber that was used to drop the first atomic bomb on Hiroshima on August 6, 1945. When the National Air and Space Museum in Washington planned to exhibit the plane in 1994 it caused a controversy that led the museum's parent organization, the Smithsonian, to reconsider and revise the exhibition.

Fédération Internationale des Résistants: a postwar communist organisation founded in 1954 that emerged from the earlier Warsaw-based *Fédération Internationale des Prisonniers Politiques*. It was open not only to resisters, but to all "victims of fascism."

Fédération Nationale des Déportés et Internés Résistants et Patriotes [National Federation of Deportees, Internees, Resisters and Patriots]: one of the earliest postwar "resistance" organizations, established in France in October 1945, five months after the end of the war in Europe. It commemorates the memory of those who resisted through its support of publications and museums and engages in activities promoting peace and disarmament.

Four Freedoms: usually associated with the "state of the union" address given by Franklin Roosevelt to the 77th Congress on January 6, 1941. The aims for which the United States was fighting, he declared were freedom of speech and expression;

the freedom of every person to worship God in his own way; freedom from want; and freedom from fear "everywhere in the world". These aims were to be secured partly by economic understanding and reduction of armaments among the nations of the world which would create a "new moral order".

Francs-tireurs et partisans français: organization of guerrillas and partisans established by the French communist party as the military wing of its *Front National* in May 1941. It differed in aims and tactics with the *Armée Secrète* – preferring a campaign of harassment, sabotage, ambush of German soldiers and assassination of German officers rather than preparing for an Allied landing in France.

Forces françaises de l'intérieur [French Forces of the Interior]: combat groups from the various resistance organizations, communist and non-communist, merged officially in February 1944. The Germans refused to recognize them as combatants, thus depriving them of the rights of soldiers and treating them as criminals.

Gauleiter: literally, "Gaue leader" – political governors of one of the "*Gaue*" – major new territorial administrative units instituted by the Nazi regime in Germany. Gauleiter were appointed by Hitler himself and directly responsible to him, for the purpose of co-ordinating Nazi party activities in the region and for increasing the role of the party in the lives of the people. Their authority was expanded during the war, particularly over the economy of the region and preparations for defense.

Gemeindepolizei: literally, "community police" – local police forces established as part of the Nazi reorganization of police forces in June 1936.

General Service Corps: established by the British government in July 1942.

Geneva Convention of 1929: concerned the treatment of prisoners of war. It was signed by 47 countries (with the notable absence of the USSR and Japan) and provided for the neutral inspection of prison camps, the exchange of prisoners' names, and for correspondence with prisoners. Under the convention, prisoners could be compelled to give no more than their name and rank (i.e. no "personal" information) and were to receive adequate food and medical care. Enlisted men could be required to work (for pay, in non-military work) but officers could not. During the war, Sweden and Switzerland acted as the protecting powers.

Gestapo: short form for *Geheime Staatspolizei*, "secret state police" established in 1933 by the Nazi government in Germany in order to prohibit "all tendencies dangerous to the state." The organization was exempted from the laws of Germany, enabling it to act without restraint. Particularly infamous was the "protective custody" (*Schutzhaft*) it used to place suspected enemies of the regime in concentration camps without judicial proceedings.

Gleichschaltung: a term coined by the Nazi regime which is difficult to translate directly as "Gleich" means equal and "schaltung" means switch/switching. But it is usually translated into English as "coordination" as in practice what it meant was the Nazification of various associations and organizations in order to transform the party and the state into a single entity.

Greater East Asia Co-Prosperity Sphere: the foreign-policy objective outlined by the Japanese Minister of Foreign Affairs in a speech of June 1940 of remaking "Asia for Asians" in opposition to western colonialism. In practice, it meant that Japan was to be the industrial engine of Asia, with non-Japanese Asians supplying it with raw materials and then serving as the market for finished Japanese products.

Groupes-Francs: French resistance organization located in Marseilles.

Institut d'Histoire du Temps Présent [Institute for the History of Present Times]: founded in 1978, the Institution, located in Paris, opened in 1980 and is the location of the International Committee for the History of the Second World War. It maintains a library, a research staff, and publishes a bi-annual bulletin.

Japanese Association for the War Bereaved: an association of Japanese veterans, by 2003 it claimed to represent over one million families. Its leaders have frequently praised the spirit of the Japanese war dead, denied that Japan was guilty of a war of aggression and atrocities in Korea and China. Visits to shrines of the war dead have frequently provoked protests in Japan and East Asia.

Keynesianism: used to describe the philosophy of the English economist, John Maynard Keynes, who argued that the government could, through its monetary and fiscal policies, stimulate economic activity and employment.

Kokutai: the national polity of Japan, in which the Japanese people were encouraged to define themselves as part of the mystical body of the state, a national community headed by the emperor – as distinct from seeing themselves as independent, autonomous individuals.

Kreisleiter: local leaders within the new Nazi system of governance. They were responsible for leadership in the subdivision of the *Gaue* – there were approximately 400 *Gauleiter* within the system, and approximately 800 *Kreisleiter*.

Landespolizei: German police forces which were modeled along military lines and designed for employment in the event of large-scale civil disturbances.

Landser: an old German word for foot soldiers. Generally used to refer to common, or low-ranking soldiers.

Maginot Line: French line of defensive fortifications constructed between 1929 and 1940, named after the French Minister of War from 1928 to 1932, André Maginot. A vast network of mainly underground fortifications, it stretched from Switzerland to the Ardennes forest in the north, from the Alps to the Mediterranean in the south. It was particularly designed to protect the industries of Lorraine against a German attack. Because Belgium was a French ally, fortifications were not built along the Franco-Belgian frontier, enabling the Germans to launch an attack through the Ardennes in 1940. The "Maginot mentality" is used to indicate a cautious, defensive strategic policy.

Main d'oeuvre immigrée: a French resistance group which was comprised of French and foreign-born Jews and political refugees living in France. Particularly active in commando attacks and sabotage.

Manhattan Project: the code name given to the project to develop an atom bomb. Initiated by the US government in September 1942, the scientists involved succeeded in detonating an atomic device in New Mexico in July 1945.

maquis: originally a form of scruffy underbrush native to Corsica, during the war it was used to refer to French guerrilla bands living in the bush, members of which were referred to as *maquisards*.

Mass Observation: a social research project initiated in 1937 by three British social scientists who aimed to create "an anthropology of ourselves". They attempted to make the most detailed record possible of the daily lives of ordinary people. The project lasted into the 1950s, and is particularly valuable in studying the social history of wartime Britain. The archives of the project are housed at the University of Sussex.

Office of War Information: the propaganda agency established by the United States in June 1942. It consolidated a variety of previously overlapping authorities, including the Office of Facts and Figures, the Office of Government Reports and several others. Its activities included oversight of the release of war news, the creation of war posters, photographing American citizens engaged in the war effort (with inspiring captions for publicity purposes). It was abolished in 1945.

Phoney War: the term used to describe the period between Germany's defeat of Poland in October 1939 and the invasion of France in May 1942. During this time it seemed that the predictions of a devastating war on the scale of World War One might not come true, and that a negotiated peace was perhaps possible.

Reichsnährstand: the German organization that merged various farmers' groups as part of the Nazi *Gleichschaltung*. It was created in September 1933. It was also an integral element of the economic policy of autarky, and as such was responsible for wage and price controls within the agricultural sector, the import and exports of foodstuffs, distribution and rationing.

Schutzstaffel: "protection-squad," commonly known as the "blackshirts." It was an elite unit formed out of the *SA* by Hitler in 1925 in order to serve as his personal bodyguard. Heinrich Himmler was appointed head of the unit in 1929, when it had several hundred members; by 1933 it exceeded 200,000. When war broke out, the *Waffen-SS* was created, dividing the organization's activities into three categories: Hitler's bodyguard, elite troops serving alongside the *Wehrmacht*, and most notoriously, the Death's Head Units which administered the concentration camps.

Sicherheitsdienst: "security service," the intelligence unit within the Nazi *SS* created by Reinhard Heydrich in 1932. In 1938 it was given responsibility for intelligence operations on behalf of the state as well as the Nazi party. It was charged with detecting opponents of the regime and then neutralizing them. To accomplish this it utilized the services of hundreds of full-time agents and thousands of informants. Like the *Gestapo*, it reported to Heinrich Himmler, the Chief of Police.

Stahlhelm: literally "steel helmet" – the *Stahlhelm: Bund der Frondsoldaten* (Steel Helmet: League of Front Soldiers) was founded in 1918 as one of many nationalistic right-wing paramilitary (*Freikorps*) groups founded in opposition to the new republic in Germany ("Weimar"). By 1930 it had become the largest of such groups, with over one-half million members. In 1934 it was absorbed into the *SA* and was dissolved in 1935.

Sturmabteilung: literally "storm division," the assault troops first formed and utilized during the German Spring offensive of 1918. Hitler adopted the term when he formed the paramilitary SA unit or "brownshirts" in 1921 to protect him and the party leadership during public gatherings. It engaged in street combat with socialists and some of the most radical elements of the Nazi movement were found in its ranks. The leadership of the SA was devastated in 1934 in the "Night of the Long Knives" initiated when Hitler feared that its leaders were seeking to overthrow him. They were not disbanded, but it was reduced in importance and most of its members were absorbed into the *Wehrmacht* during the war.

Supreme War Council: based on their experience of coalition warfare in the First World War, Britain and France established this organization immediately after the outbreak of war in 1939. The first meeting was held at Abbeville, France on September 12, 1939. It was gradually expanded to include the United States, the USSR, and the other member-states of the United Nations. The term can be confusing because there were many other "Supreme War Councils" including those established by Chiang Kai-shek in China and by the Japanese.

Volksgemeinschaft: "people's community" – the Nazi ideal of a state based upon the purity of race, bringing the German people together in a sense of unity that would dissolve class, political, or regional differences.

War Advertising Council: initially established as the "Advertising Council" by the advertising industry in the United States in the month after the bombing of Pearl Harbor. It was renamed the War Advertising Council in 1943 with the purpose of supporting the war effort. Composed of volunteer representatives from major advertising agencies, large corporate advertisers, and the media, the WAC worked with various government agencies (such as the Office of War information) on "public information" campaigns. It was particularly active in using radio, magazine, and billboard advertising to promote the purchase of war bonds.

Wehrmacht: the German "defence force" established by the Nazi government in 1935 when it re-introduced conscription (replacing the *Reichswehr*). It included the three branches of armed forces: army, navy, and air force.

Wehrwirtschaft: the "defence-based economy" designed by Hjälmar Schacht, Minister of Economics in the new Nazi government in 1933. He believed that the German economy could recover by gearing it for war, and that the problem of unemployment could be largely solved through German rearmament. Schacht was replaced by Walter Funk as Minister in 1936, but Hermann Goering assumed the position of directing the economy through his "Four Year Plan", which continued to rely on the *Wehrwirtschaft* concept – including the virtual elimination of imported consumer goods, the implementation of wage and price controls, and the conscription of labor.

Weserübung: the German codename for the invasion of Denmark and Norway in April 1940. Germany invaded in order to prevent Allied plans to mine northern waters, which would have cut off the vital ore supplies coming from Scandinavia.

Women's Army Corps: because of the success of the WAAC, the US Army requested that it be transformed from an auxiliary organization into a full component of the army, which would enable it to meet the tremendous shortage of personnel. WAACS serving overseas were not entitled to the protection of regular soldiers if they were captured, or to benefits if they were wounded, so "regularizing" them would assist in recruitment. 75 percent of WAACS joined the WAC. The first battalion arrived in Europe in July 1943, and approximately 7,500 women were serving there by D-Day (5,500 served in the Pacific theatre) mainly as stenographers, clerks, typists, and in communications.

Women's Auxiliary Army Corps: there are two different organizations that share this designation. The first was established as a volunteer organization by the British government in January 1917, but was disbanded in 1921. The second was established by the US government in May 1942 as an auxiliary to the US Army – women thus served "with" the army, but were not in it; in July 1943 the corps was incorporated as a full component of the army and was renamed the *Women's Army Corps* (*WAC*).

Women's Auxiliary Territorial Service: created by the British government in September 1938, it was attached to the Territorial Army. The women, mainly telephonists, clerks, and cooks, were to receive two-thirds the pay of men. Three hundred women serving in the ATS were sent as part of the British Expeditionary Force to France in 1939. In 1940 women between the ages of 17 and 43 were permitted to serve, the roles they could perform were expanded, and by September 1941 its numbers had grown to 65,000.

Women's Employment Board: established by the Australian government in 1942 in order to regulate wages and conditions of those women doing men's work. The trade union movement had demanded that such women be paid 100 percent of the rate paid to men, but the government compromised, empowering the WEB to award 60-100 percent of the rate paid to men. This represented a radical transformation of previously arbitrated settlements of women's pay, which were based on the traditional "family pay" principle. Those who benefited most were women employed in munitions manufacturing, metal and aircraft production, who received approximately 90 percent of the male wage-rate.

Women's Volunteer Service: British organization formed in the summer of 1938 to amalgamate some 70 voluntary associations. They were particularly responsible for the relocation of children from the cities during the Battle of Britain. Recognizable in their distinctive — drab — grey-green overcoats, they were also active in the ambulance service and delivering meals and providing clothing to those who were bombed-out.

WHO'S WHO

The purpose of this guide is to provide readers with a brief biographical sketch of the principal characters mentioned in the essays. It is by no means a comprehensive guide to "Who was Who in World War Two". When there is a useful biography in English and/or an autobiography or memoir pertaining particularly to the World War Two, these are cited at the end of the entry (in cases where there is an abundance of biographical works available, only one is cited – with the preference being given to the most recent, scholarly, one-volume study).

Bevin, Ernest (1881–1951): a British trade union leader, he became general secretary of the large and powerful National Transport and General Workers' Union in 1921 and served in that capacity until elected as a Labour member of parliament in 1940. Churchill appointed him Minister of Labour in his coalition government in 1940, and he served in that capacity until the Labour government was formed in 1945, when he became Foreign Secretary, serving in that capacity until his death in 1951. See his *The Job To Be Done* (London, 1942), and the biography by Alan Bullock, *Ernest Bevin: a biography* (London, 2002).

Bloch, Marc (1866–1944): served in French army in World War One, taken prisoner by Germans. Appointed professor of medieval history at Strasbourg in 1919, then professor of economic history at the Sorbonne in 1936; one of the founders of the "Annales school" of history. Joined the army again on the outbreak of war, joined the French resistance in 1943, was captured and executed by the Germans. See Carole Fink, *Marc Bloch: a life in history* (Cambridge, 1989).

Bormann, Martin (1900–1945?): a World War One veteran, Bormann joined a right-wing *Freikorps* group afterwards and was imprisoned in 1924 for acting as an accomplice in a murder perpetrated by Rudolf Hess. After his release in 1925 he joined the NSDAP and moved up the party ranks to become a Reichsleiter in 1933. He served as Rudolf Hess's chief of cabinet in the office of the deputy führer from 1934 to 1941, replacing him after Hess's flight to Britain. He was an effective and outspoken adherent of the "Final Solution" and the war on the Christian churches. He disappeared in 1945 and was sentenced to death *in absentia* by the Nuremberg War Crimes Tribunal in 1946 and pronounced dead by a West German court in 1973. See Jochen von Lang, *Bormann: the man who manipulated Hitler* (London, 1979) – the American edition is entitled: *The Secretary: Bormann, the man who manipulated Hitler* (New York, 1979).

Chamberlain, Neville (1869–1940): a leading British politician, he served as mayor of Birmingham during World War One, was elected as Conservative member of parliament in 1919 and served continuously until his death. Twice Chancellor of the Exchequer, three times the Minister of Health, he became prime minister in 1937. He will forever be associated with the "appeasement" of Hitler during the Munich crisis of 1938. Resigned as prime minister in 1940 to make way for a coalition government under Winston Churchill. See David Dutton, *Neville Chamberlain* (London, 2002).

Churchill, Winston (1874–1965): son of the British Conservative politician, Randolph Churchill, and an American mother, Jenny, he was first elected to the House of Commons in 1900 as a Conservative, but switched allegiance to the Liberal Party in 1904. Joined the cabinet in 1908, and served as First Lord of the Admiralty before and during the World War One, resigning this position following the disastrous Gallipoli campaign in 1916. Returned to cabinet in the postwar Liberal governments, but switched allegiance back to the Conservatives in 1924 and immediately became Chancellor of the Exchequer. Out of office from 1929, he rejoined the cabinet as First Lord of the Admiralty when war broke out in 1939, and replaced Neville Chamberlain as prime minister in May 1940. Famously mobilized British public opinion in support of the war effort through his inspiring oratory, and successfully formed a close friendship with Franklin D. Roosevelt in support of the "special relationship" with the United States. The Conservative party were defeated in the postwar election of July 1945, but he returned as prime minister in 1951. See his *The Second World War* (London, 1997), Geoffrey Best, *Churchill: a study in greatness* (London, 2001) and Warren Kimball, *Forged in War: Roosevelt, Churchill and the Second World War* (London, 1997).

Daladier, Edouard (1884–1970): a Radical French politician before World War One, he served with distinction in the war, and became leader of the Radical Socialists in 1927. Served as Minister of War and Prime Minister briefly in 1933 and again in 1934. Appointed Minister for National Defence and War in the "Popular Front" government of Léon Blum from June 1936 to May 1940, supplanting Blum as prime

minister in April 1938. As prime minister he represented France at the Munich conference of September 1938 and has been associated with the "appeasement" of Hitler
ever since. He continued to serve as prime minister until March 1940, was arrested
by the Germans when France was defeated, whereupon he was interned until the end
of the war.

Daluege, Kurt (1897–1946): served in an assault division in the First World War,
leader of the Rossbach *Freikorps* afterwards. Joined the NSDAP in 1922, leader
of the SA in Berlin until 1928, when he moved to the SS. Chief of the Uniformed
Police after 1933 (*Ordnungspolizei*), appointed Reich Protector of Bohemia and
Moravia after the assassination of Reinhard Heydrich.

De Gaulle, Charles (1890–1970): an officer in the French army during World War
One, became a leading theorist/commentator on the strategy of mobile warfare afterwards. When France was defeated in June 1940 he fled to Britain and formed the
"Free French" forces to continue the fight against Germany. He entered Paris as
head of these forces in August 1944 and shortly afterwards became head of the
provisional government. Returned to politics as prime minister in 1958, serving
until 1969. See his *War Memoirs* (3 volumes, London, 1955–1960) and Charles
G. Cogan, *De Gaulle: a brief biography with documents* (London, 1997).

Duroselle, Jean Baptiste (1917–1994): a leading historian of modern France, the
author of *La Décadence* (1979) and *L'Abîme* (1983), unforgiving critiques of the
makers of French foreign and defense policy in most of the period from 1932 to
1945.

Eden, Anthony (1897–1977): British politician, he served as a junior army officer
in World War One. Elected to parliament as a Conservative in 1923, elevated to
cabinet in 1933, appointed Foreign Secretary in 1935. He resigned in 1938 as a
result of differences with Neville Chamberlain over "appeasement." Returned to
cabinet during the war under Winston Churchill, serving as Foreign Secretary from
1940 to 1945 (and again in this capacity from 1951 to 1955, when he became
prime minister, but soon resigned following the debacle of the Suez invasion in
1956). See his *Facing the Dictators* (London, 1960) and D. R. Thorpe, *Eden: the
life and times of Anthony Eden, first Earl of Avon 1897–1977* (London, 2003).

Eisenhower, Dwight D. (1890–1969): a junior US Army officer during World War
One, he rose to the position of assistant to General Douglas MacArthur, serving in
the Philippines from 1935 to 1939. Assumed command of allied forces involved
in the invasions of North Africa, Sicily and Italy in 1942–43, and on the strength
of these successes was appointed supreme commander of allied forces for the
D-Day invasion, and continued to serve in that capacity until the surrender of
Germany in May 1945. After the war he commanded US occupation forces
in Germany and served as chief of staff of the army until retiring in 1948. Elected
president in 1952, re-elected in 1956, serving until 1960. See his *Crusade in Europe*

(London, 1948) and Stephen E. Ambrose, *Eisenhower: soldier and president* (London, 1991).

Gamelin, General Maurice (1872–1958): a lieutenant-colonel in the French army during World War One. In 1935 became chief of staff and president of the Supreme War Council. Attempted to shift strategic policy from the defensive to the offensive during his tenure, building up mobile forces and planning to counter-attack Germany through Belgium and the Netherlands. When the army failed to withstand the German blitzkrieg of 1940, he was blamed and replaced by Weygand, after which he was tried and imprisoned from 1943 to 1945. See Martin Alexander, *The Republic in Danger: General Maurice Gamelin and the politics of French defence, 1933–1940* (London, 1992).

Goebbels, Josef (1897–1945): rejected for military service because of a physical disability in World War One, he joined the NSDAP in 1922 and became the party business manager in the Ruhr in 1925. Representing the "radical" social element within the party, he called for Hitler's expulsion for his "petty bourgeois" views in 1926, but became a supporter when this failed. In 1927 he launched a weekly news-paper, *Der Angriff* (The Attack) and its success led Hitler to appoint him the party's head of propaganda in 1929 where he was responsible for the creation of the "Führer myth." When the Nazis achieved power he became Reich Minister for Public Enlightenment and Propaganda (*Reichspropagandaleiter*), leading the *Gleichschaltung* of German culture. A gifted orator, his inflammatory speech ignited the *Kristallnacht* in 1938, and during World War Two he was instrumental in mobil-izing public support for the war effort and in promoting the Final Solution. See *The Goebbels Diaries, 1939–41* (Louis P. Lochner, trans. and ed.) (London, 1982) and Ralf G. Reuth, *Goebbels* (trans. by Krishna Winston, London, 1993).

Goering, Hermann (1893–1946): received the Iron Cross for his exploits as a fighter pilot in World War One, joined the NSDAP in 1922 and appointed head of the *Sturmabteilung* by Hitler. Had to flee Germany for four years following the failure of the "Beer Hall Putsch" in Munich in 1924, he was elected to the Reichstag as one of the first Nazi deputies in 1928 and was made its president in July 1933. As head of the *Gestapo* he was instrumental in establishing the concentration camps in the Nazi war on political opponents, and in destroying opposition within the party in the "Night of the Long Knives." In 1936 he was appointed head of the *Luftwaffe* and in 1937 he directed the Four-Year Plan, establishing a leadership role in the *Wehrwirtschaft*. In 1939 he was designated to be Hitler's successor, but his strate-gical failures in the Battle of Britain eroded his position within the party. Sentenced to death by hanging at Nuremberg. See R. J. Overy, *Goering: the "Iron Man"* (London, 1984).

Groves, Leslie (1896–1970): US Army officer, he graduated from West Point in 1918, entered the Corps of Engineers and was responsible for a succession of major construction projects before World War Two (including that of the Pentagon).

Assumed leadership of the "Manhattan Engineer District" (Manhattan Project) responsible for the development of the atomic bomb. See his *Now It Can Be Told: the story of the Manhattan Project* (New York, 1962) and William Lawren, *The General and the Bomb: a biography of General Leslie R. Groves, director of the Manhattan Project* (New York, 1988).

Halsey, William "Bull" (1882–1959): US Naval officer, he commanded destroyers during World War One and served as naval attaché in Europe afterwards. Promoted to rear admiral in 1938, vice-admiral in 1940. After Pearl Harbor he commanded US offensives in the Pacific, including the battle of Guadalcanal in 1942, after which he was promoted to the rank of admiral, in which position he worked closely with General Douglas MacArthur. Commander of the Third Fleet, 1944–1945 and fleet admiral in 1945. See E. B. Potter, *Bull Halsey* (Annapolis Md., 1985).

Heydrich, Reinhard (1904–1942): although he was too young to serve in World War One, he joined a *Freikorps* group when he was only 16. He joined the German navy as a junior officer in 1922 but was forced to resign for "conduct unbecoming an officer" in 1931, whereupon he joined the NSDAP. He was quickly appointed head of the new *Sicherheitsdienst* by Himmler and created a vast organization of spies and informers. He supplied Soviet agents in Germany with information against Red Army officers that led to Stalin's purges in 1937, fomented the unrest in Slovakia in 1939 that was used to justify the entry of the German army to "protect" Czechoslovakia in March, and faked the Polish attack on a German radio station on September 1, 1939 that was used to justify Germany's invasion of Poland. In Poland, Heydrich formed the *Einsatzgruppen* of the SS for the purpose of eliminating (mainly by murder) all opposition to Nazi rule, a pattern that was followed in the USSR after the invasion of 1941. Heydrich called together the conference at Wannsee in January 1942, where the mechanics of the Final Solution were agreed upon. Appointed Deputy Reich Protector of Bohemia and Moravia by Hitler, he was assassinated in Prague in May 1942. See Charles Whiting, *Heydrich: henchman of death* (Barnsley, 1999).

Himmler, Heinrich (1900–1945): an officer-cadet at the end of World War One, he became involved in paramilitary movements afterwards and participated in the abortive "Beer Hall" putsch in Munich in 1923. He served as head propagandist for the NSDAP from 1925 to 30, and was appointed head of the *Schutzstaffel*. Elected to the Reichstag as a Nazi deputy in 1930, he expanded the SS to a membership of 52,000 by 1933 and secured its independence from the SA in 1930. Combined this role with head of German police in June 1936 to become the leading force in putting the racist ideals of the regime into practice. In 1939 Hitler appointed him Reich Commissar for the Strengthening of Germandom, in which position he attempted to Germanize the east, served as Minister of the Interior from 1943 to 1945, when he committed suicide by poisoning. See Peter Padfield, *Himmler: Reichsführer-SS* (London, 1995).

Hitler, Adolf (1889–1945): born in Austria near the German border, he moved to Vienna in 1907, living on an orphan's pension, selling paintings and postcards, and absorbing the virulent antisemitism popular there. He volunteered for service in the German army when war broke out in 1914, attained the rank of corporal and received the Iron Cross First Class for bravery. After the war he joined the German Workers' Party and became its leader when it was reconstituted as the National Socialist German Workers' Party (NSDAP) in 1921. Led a failed "Beer Hall" *putsch* in Munich in 1923, for which he was sentenced to one year in prison, during which he dictated his ideas to Rudolf Hess, which were subsequently published as *Mein Kampf* (My Struggle). He led the party to an electoral breakthrough in the Reichstag elections of 1930, when they received 6.5 million votes and increased their representation from 12 to 107 seats. He placed second to the famous World War One hero, Field Marshal Paul von Hindenburg, in the presidential election of 1932, and in that year the party became the most popular in Germany, leading Hindenburg to appoint him Chancellor and to form the government in January 1933. After the death of Hindenburg he had himself made "Führer" – head of government, head of state, and commander-in-chief of the armed forces. He committed suicide in Berlin on April 30, 1945. See his *Mein Kampf* (trans. by Ralph Manheim, London, 1992), *Hitler's Table Talk, 1941–43* (trans. by Norman Cameron & R. H. Stevens, London, 2000) and Ian Kershaw, *Hitler* vol. 2, *1936–1945: Nemesis* (London, 2000).

Keynes, John Maynard (1883–1946): British economist, served as an adviser to the Treasury in both world wars. His *Treatise on Money* (1930) and *General Theory of Employment, Interest and Money* (1936) formed the basis of "Keynesianism" which was influential in the foundations of the welfare state in Britain and in the policies of the "New Deal" in the US See his *How to Pay for the War* (London, 1940) and Robert Skidelsky, *Keynes* (Oxford, 1996).

LeMay, Curtis (1906–1990): US aviator and Air Force officer, commanded the bomber force that conducted long-distance bombing of Japan during the last year of World War Two and was responsible for the planning of the atomic bomb attacks on Hiroshima and Nagasaki. After the war he rose to chief of staff of the Air Force, 1961–65. See his *Mission with Le May: my story* (with MacKinlay Kantor, New York, 1965).

Litvinov, Maxim (1876–1951): Russian politician and diplomat. He joined the Social Democratic Party in 1898, was exiled to Siberia but escaped. Active during the revolution of 1917, he was appointed by the new Bolshevik government to serve as ambassador in London, 1917–1918. Litvinov rose steadily in importance afterwards, becoming Deputy Commissar for Foreign Affairs in 1921, then Commissar from 1930 to 1939. Dismissed for his opposition to the Nazi–Soviet pact in 1939, he was appointed ambassador to the United States following the German invasion of the USSR, served in that capacity until 1943, when he was appointed Vice-Minister of Foreign Affairs, serving until 1946. See his *Notes for a Journal* (London, 1955) and Hugh D. Phillips, *Between the Revolution and the West: a political biography of Maxim M. Litvinov* (Boulder, Colo., 1992).

MacArthur, Douglas (1880–1964): US soldier, commanded a brigade in France during World War One. Appointed chief of staff of the army in 1930, he served as military adviser to the Philippine government from 1935 to 1941, when he was appointed commander of US forces in the Far East. Ordered to leave his men on the Bataan peninsula he famously declared "I shall return," established head-quarters in Australia as commander of the Southwest Pacific where he developed the island-hopping strategy that led to the successful return of US forces to the Philippines in October 1944. He was commander of allied forces when Japan surren-dered, after which he was appointed military governor of Japan from 1945 to 1950. See his *Reminiscences* (Greenwich, Conn., 1995) and Michael Green, *MacArthur in the Pacific: from the Philippines to the fall of Japan* (Osceola, 1996).

Marshall Jr, George C. (1880–1959): US soldier and statesman. He served in the Philippines during the insurrection of 1902–03 and as chief of operations with the US First Army in Europe during World War One. After the war he served as aide to General John Pershing (1919–1924), in China (1924–1927), rose to chief of the war plans division and deputy chief of staff (1938–1939) and finally to chief of staff of the US Army throughout World War Two. After the war he served as Secretary of State (1947–1949) during which time he initiated the "Marshall Plan" for European reconstruction. See *Dear General: Eisenhower's wartime letters to Marshall* (ed. by Joseph Hobbs, Baltimore, 1971) and Mark A. Stoler, *George C. Marshall: soldier-statesman of the American century* (Boston, 1989).

Molotov, Vyacheslav M. (1890–1986): Russian politician and statesman. Served as Prime Minister of the USSR from 1930 to 1941, Foreign Minister from 1939 to 1949 (and again from 1953 to 1956). Stalin's chief advisor at the Teheran and Yalta conferences. See *Molotov Remembers: inside Kremlin politics: conversations with Felix Chuev* (ed. by Albert Resis, Chicago, 1993) and Bernard Bromage, *Molotov: the story of an era* (London, 1956).

Montgomery, 1st Viscount [born Bernard Montgomery] (1887–1976): British soldier. Commanded the British 8th Army in North Africa, which defeated Rommel's forces at the battle of El Alamein in 1942. Instrumental in the planning for the invasions of Sicily and Italy in 1943, he was appointed commander-in-chief of ground forces in the Allied invasion of Normandy in 1944. Appointed Field-Marshal in 1944 and elevated to the peerage as Montgomery (of Alamein) in 1946. After the war he served as chief of the Imperial General Staff and deputy supreme comman-der of NATO in Europe. See his *From El Alamein to the River Sangro* (London, 1973) and Nigel Hamilton, *Monty: the man behind the legend* (London, 1987).

Mussolini, Benito (1883–1945): an Italian socialist before World War One, he edited the party newspaper *Avanti* from 1913 to 1914, resigning over the issue of

Italian entry into the war – which he supported in the newspaper that he then founded, *Popolo d'Italia*. During the war (in which he served in the military) he became an outspoken proponent of nationalism and militarism, founding a succession of short-lived "fascist" groups. In 1921 the National Fascist Party was formed with Mussolini as its "*duce*" (leader) and succeeded in capturing power after the "March on Rome" in October 1922. He launched a war of imperial aggression in Abyssinia in 1935, assisted the right-wing forces of Franco during the Spanish civil war, formed an alliance with Hitler before World War Two but did not enter the war until it became clear that Germany would defeat France in June, 1940. After a series of defeats he was forced to flee to northern Italy under the protection of German forces, where he was executed by partisans in April 1945. See his *The Fall of Mussolini: his own story* (trans. by Frances Frenaye, Westport, Conn., 1975) and Richard Bosworth, *Mussolini* (London, 2002).

Oppenheimer, J. Robert (1904–1967): American physicist, he began atomic research in the mid-1920s, which he continued while a professor at the California Institute of Technology and at the University of California at Berkeley from 1929 to 1942. In 1942 he joined the Manhattan Project's efforts to develop an atomic bomb before the Germans did so, and he became the scientific leader of the venture at Los Alamos, New Mexico. He resigned his position two months after the bombing of Hiroshima and Nagasaki, dismayed by the devastation it had caused. See *Robert Oppenheimer: letters and recollections* (ed. by Alice K. Smith and Charles Weiner, Stanford, Calif., 1995) and Peter Goodchild, *Oppenheimer: the father of the atom bomb* (London, 1983).

Pétain, Philippe (1856–1951): French soldier and statesman. Elevated to commander-in-chief of the French army in 1917, following his heroic leadership in the defence of Verdun, and made Marshal of France in 1918. Appointed deputy prime minister in May 1940, he negotiated the armistice with Germany following France's defeat in 1940 and became the head of state in the new government that was established at Vichy. His collaboration with Germany led to his trial for treason after the war, in which he was condemned to death – but this was commuted to life imprisonment; he died in prison. See Nicholas Atkin, *Pétain* (London, 1998).

Pile, General Frederick (1884–1976): British army officer; distinguished himself in World War One. He commanded Britain's anti-aircraft defences during World War Two and in this position was responsible for use of women in these units. Appointed Director-General, Minister of Works, in 1945. See his *Ack-ack: Britain's defence against air attack during the Second World War* (London, 1949).

Pyle, Ernie (1900–1945): American journalist and foreign correspondent. Famous for his reports on the personal lives of soldiers during the invasions of Sicily, Italy and Normandy. See his *Here Is Your War* (New York, 1943) and *Brave Men* (New York, 1944). He was killed during the US invasion of Okinawa in 1945. See James Tobin, *Ernie Pyle's War: America's eyewitness to World War II* (New York, 1977).

Reynaud, Paul (1878–1966): French politician, he succeeded Daladier as prime minister of France in March 1940. As prime minister during the fall of France he refused to sign an armistice with Germany and was imprisoned for the duration of the war.

Ribbentrop, Joachim von (1893–1946): joined the NSDAP in 1932, served as ambassador to Britain 1936–38. Appointed Foreign Minister in 1938, he was largely responsible for the Nazi–Soviet pact; served in this position until 1945, and was subsequently executed at Nuremberg in the following year. See his *Memoirs* (London, 1954) and Michael Bloch, *Ribbentrop* (London, 1992).

Rosenberg, Alfred (1893–1946): born in Russia, he emigrated to Germany after the revolution in 1917 and joined the NSDAP in 1919. In 1923 became editor of the party newspaper, the *Völkische Beobachter*. A leading Nazi propagandist and theoretician, author of *The Future Direction of German Foreign Policy* (1927), advocating the conquest of Poland and Russia, and *Myth of the Twentieth Century* (1934), which interpreted history on the basis of race. In April 1941, as part of the preparation for the invasion of the Soviet Union, Hitler nominated him "*Beauftragter des Führers für die zentrale Bearbeitung der Fragen des osteuropäischen Raumes*" (Delegate of the Führer for the central treatment of questions of eastern European space); in July 1941 elevated to Minister for the Occupied Eastern Territories. Found guilty of war crimes at Nuremberg and hanged in 1946. See Fritz Nova, *Alfred Rosenberg: Nazi theorist of the holocaust* (New York, 1986).

Schacht, Hjalmar (1877–1970): appointed president of the Reichsbank during the German economic crisis of 1923, he succeeded in stopping the dramatic increase in inflation. Minister of Economics in the Nazi regime, 1934–1937 and appointed Plenipotentiary for War Economy in 1935. He was dismissed from office in 1939 when he disagreed with Hitler over rearmament. He was interned throughout the war and acquitted of war crimes at Nuremberg. See John Weitz, *Hitler's Banker: Hjalmar Horace Greeley Schacht* (Boston, 1997).

Speer, Albert (1905–1981): joined the NSDAP in 1931 and was appointed "chief architect" by Hitler in 1934. Following death of Fritz Todt, he was appointed minister of armaments by Hitler in February 1942. Came out in opposition to Hitler late in the war, admitted to war crimes at Nuremberg and served a 20-year sentence at Spandau prison. See his *Inside the Third Reich* (trans. by Richard and Clara Winston, London, 1995) and Dan van der Vat, *The Good Nazi: the life and lies of Albert Speer* (London, 1997).

Stalin, Joseph (1879–1953): as a Russian revolutionary, he was twice exiled to Siberia before World War One and played an important part in the Bolshevik revolution of 1917. He was a member of the Communist Party Politburo when the Soviet regime was established and became General Secretary of the party's central committee in 1922 – a position he retained until 1953, and which he used to become virtual dictator of the USSR. During the 1930s he conducted a series of brutal purges of anyone he perceived of as enemies of the regime, including devastating purges of officers in the armed forces. In 1938 he signed a Non-Aggression Pact with Germany (the Nazi-Soviet Pact) but declared himself "generalissimo" after the invasion of the Soviet Union in 1941, and joined the Grand Alliance against Germany and Italy. See *Stalin's Correspondence with Churchill, Attlee, Roosevelt and Truman 1941–45* (London, 1958) and Edvard Radzinskii, *Stalin* (trans. by H. T. Willetts, London, 1996).

Stimson, Henry L. (1867–1950): American lawyer and politician. Served as Secretary of War 1911–1913 and Governor General of the Philippines, 1927–1929, Secretary of State 1929–1933. Refused to "recognize" the Japanese right to rule Manchuria after their successful invasion in 1932. Served as Secretary of War in Roosevelt's wartime cabinet, 1940–1945 in which capacity he was largely responsible for the mobilization of the American armed forces. Finally, as chief presidential advisor to Truman, he argued in favour of dropping atomic bombs on Japan in 1945. See his *On Active Service In Peace and War* (New York, 1948) and Godfrey Hodgson, *Colonel: the life and wars of Henry L. Stimson, 1867–1950* (New York, 1990).

Suzuki Kantarō (1868–1948): Japanese admiral who came out of retirement in April 1945 to become prime minister in April 1945 in the hope of negotiating a peace settlement through the mediation of Stalin. When this proved impossible, he agreed to the Potsdam Declaration on August 14, 1945 and resigned as prime minister the following day.

Todt, Fritz (1891–1942): appointed Inspector of Roads by Hitler in 1933, during which time he was responsible for the construction of the autobahnen and of the Siegfried Line of defensive fortifications. Appointed Commissioner for Special Tasks, then as full Munitions Minister in February 1940. Killed in an airplane crash in 1942.

Tōgō Shigenori (1882–1950): Japanese diplomat; appointed ambassador to Germany in 1937, to the Soviet Union in 1939. He was opposed to the formation of the Axis alliance. Joined the cabinet as Minister of Foreign Affairs in 1941, resigned in 1942 in opposition to the formation of the Greater East Asia Ministry. Rejoined the cabinet in 1945, where he favored an early, negotiated peace. He negotiated the Japanese surrender, after which he was sentenced to twenty years in prison for war crimes.

Truman, Harry S. (1884–1972): American politician, served in the artillery forces on the western front in World War One. Elected to the Senate as a Democrat in 1934 and reelected in 1940, when he chaired the Senate Committee to Investigate the National Defense Program. Chosen as the vice-presidential running mate of President Roosevelt in the election of 1944, he succeeded him as President when

Roosevelt died on April 12, 1945. Authorized the dropping of atomic bombs on Japan and the terms of the Japanese surrender. Elected as President in 1948. See David McCullough, *Truman* (New York, 1992).

Weygand, General Maxime (1867–1965): served as French chief of staff to General Ferdinand Foch in World War One and afterwards, then as head of the French army from 1931 to 1935. Gamelin's successor as head of the French general staff, from May 1940.

INDEX